VIOLENCE, ORDER, AND UNREST

A History of British North America, 1749–1876

Edited by Elizabeth Mancke, Jerry Bannister, Denis McKim, and Scott W. See

This edited collection offers a broad reinterpretation of the origins of Canada. Drawing on cutting-edge research in a number of fields, *Violence, Order, and Unrest* explores the development of British North America from the mid-eighteenth century through the aftermath of Confederation. The chapters cover an ambitious range of topics, from Indigenous culture to municipal politics, public executions to runaway slave advertisements. Cumulatively, this book examines the diversity of Indigenous and colonial experiences across northern North America and provides fresh perspectives on the crucial roles of violence and unrest in attempts to establish British authority in Indigenous territories. In the aftermath of Canada 150, *Violence, Order, and Unrest* offers a timely contribution to current debates over the nature of Canadian culture and history, demonstrating that we cannot understand Canada today without considering its origins as a colonial project.

ELIZABETH MANCKE is Canada Research Chair in Atlantic Canada Studies in the Department of History at the University of New Brunswick.

JERRY BANNISTER teaches History and Canadian Studies at Dalhousie University.

DENIS McKIM teaches in the History Department at Douglas College.

SCOTT W. SEE is Libra Professor Emeritus and former chair of the University of Maine's History Department.

Violence, Order, and Unrest

A History of British North America, 1749–1876

EDITED BY ELIZABETH MANCKE,
JERRY BANNISTER, DENIS McKIM, AND
SCOTT W. SEE

UNIVERSITY OF TORONTO PRESS
Toronto Buffalo London

Toronto Buffalo London
utorontopress.com

ISBN 978-1-4875-0511-0 (cloth) ISBN 978-1-4875-2370-1 (paper)

Library and Archives Canada Cataloguing in Publication

Title: Violence, order, and unrest : a history of British North America, 1749–1876 / edited by Elizabeth Mancke, Jerry Bannister, Denis McKim, and Scott W. See.
Names: Mancke, Elizabeth, 1954– editor. | Bannister, Jerry, 1968– editor. | McKim, Denis, editor. | See, Scott W., 1950– editor.
Description: Includes bibliographical references and index.
Identifiers: Canadiana 20190049006 | ISBN 9781487523701 (softcover) | ISBN 9781487505110 (hardcover)
Subjects: LCSH: Violence – Canada – History – 18th century – Case studies. | LCSH: Violence – Canada – History – 19th century – Case studies. | LCSH: Canada – Colonization – History – 18th century – Case studies. | LCSH: Canada – Colonization – History – 19th century – Case studies. | LCSH: Canada – Social conditions – 18th century – Case studies. | LCSH: Canada – Social conditions – 19th century – Case studies. | LCGFT: Case studies.
Classification: LCC HN103 .V56 2019 | DDC 303.6097109/033—dc23

The University of Maine's Canadian-American Center generously provided financial assistance for the publication of this book.

University of Toronto Press acknowledges the financial assistance to its publishing program of the Canada Council for the Arts and the Ontario Arts Council, an agency of the Government of Ontario.

Canada Council for the Arts Conseil des Arts du Canada

Funded by the Government of Canada Financé par le gouvernement du Canada

Contents

Section II: From Tory Imperialism to Liberal Settler Colonialism

Section III: Resisting Dispossession

Section IV: Legitimating and Contesting the Public Sphere

Illustrations

Preface

Violence, Order, and Unrest: A History of British North America, 1749–1876 is the result of a four-year collaborative project that involved nearly two dozen contributors and multiple academic institutions. Starting with the deliberately expansive title of "Unrest, Violence, and the Search for Social Order in British North America and Canada, 1749 to 1876," we solicited suggestions from colleagues on how best to examine these issues given the complexity of British North America, with its diverse Indigenous peoples and settler societies. We wanted to consider both governors and the governed, colonizers and the colonized, and how they envisaged social order, experienced threats or challenges to it, and imagined how tools of provincial and then federal states could be used to control disorder or achieve new political objectives. Our principal objective was a critical re-examination of pre-Confederation and early post-Confederation Canadian history, with an emphasis on sharpening our understanding of the deep and troubling consequences of the emergence of modernity as it played out in northern North America, particularly the contested idea that optimum social order could be imagined and then implemented, even if it entailed profound, if not violent, disruptions and transformations.

Across five thematic sections, this project explores three interrelated cycles of historical change: the imperial conflicts of the eighteenth and early nineteenth centuries; the expansion and entrenchment of settler colonialism in northern North America; and the responses of diverse Indigenous peoples and colonists to the first two cycles. Various contributors address the violence created by the dramatic expansion of British imperial power in the mid-eighteenth century, beginning with the founding of Halifax and the first large-scale incursion of British-sponsored Protestant settlers into the Indigenous territories that became the Dominion of Canada. The violence of this imperial expansion took a variety of forms – environmental, demographic, military – as northeastern

North America witnessed mass deportations and contested attempts to impose new conceptions of British imperial governance. These processes were geographically and ethnically uneven, initially affecting Indigenous and French peoples in the northeast before spreading across the continent to the Pacific. Our volume attempts to grapple with this diversity of experiences, as the impact of warfare and commercial and imperial expansion was felt across North America in a series of waves from the 1750s through the War of 1812.

Our project also seeks to understand the different ways colonial authorities sought to constitute social order in the territories claimed and retained by Britain. Like the impacts of structural and military violence, attempts to impose order were uneven and contested. While some stable settler-led polities emerged, most of northern North America remained Indigenous in culture and in sovereignty. One of the most contentious storylines of British North America turns on how long it took for the British to establish effective authority over lands where they claimed sovereignty but did not necessarily exercise it. This protracted, untidy projection of British sovereignty meant that colonial order developed in cycles, as the impact of settlers occurred in distinct stages, rather than consistently and uniformly across the continent.

Attempts to impose order carried with them outbreaks of unrest, as diverse peoples resisted efforts to introduce a bourgeois Protestant social order in North America. By exploring this third facet of the British North American project, our collection aims to capture the complicated, contentious ways in which authority was incessantly negotiated and often successfully resisted at the local level. Unrest, like violence, was an intrinsic part of the larger process of state formation. The making of British North America and the formation of Confederation were protracted and tangled processes, not a single, unambiguous event or even a discrete, definable series of events. Indeed, some would argue that they continue to influence modern-day affairs. In order to understand the forces that created Canada, we must grapple with the long-term factors that underpinned the development of British North America. Canada is, in other words, the byproduct of violence and unrest, order and disorder. Post-Confederation Canada cannot be properly understood without considering struggles over governance that occurred in previous centuries.

To address this broad agenda, we drew on the expertise of established scholars, as well as the contributions of their emerging counterparts whose research represents the ferment of new ideas. We started the collaborative group process by asking our contributors to submit provocative reflection papers, which were circulated in advance of a workshop at the University of New Brunswick in June 2015 and discussed during intensive plenary sessions – an approach designed for scholarly risk-taking and innovation. The following year, at Saint Mary's University, we convened again to discuss the more formal essays that were crafted in the light of the previous year's workshop. The chapters in this volume represent the revised and edited versions of those papers. Collectively they address the expansive range of themes we wanted to tackle, articulating important new ways of conceptualizing the pre-Confederation and early post-Confederation eras, but in no way purporting to be definitive. Rather they speak to the importance of these eras to the contested emergence of Canada and invite further scholarly reflection and engagement.

Our collection offers, then, a broad reinterpretation of Canada's origins. Drawing on cutting-edge research in numerous fields, it explores the development of British North America from the mid-eighteenth century through the aftermath of Confederation. The chapters cover an unapologetically ambitious range of topics, from Indigenous culture to municipal politics, public executions to runaway slave advertisements. Taken together, they examine the diversity of colonial experiences across northern North America. They provide fresh perspectives on the crucial roles of violence and unrest in attempts to establish British authority in Indigenous territories. In doing so, they present new analyses of how order was negotiated and contested in different social and political contexts. Drawing on specific case studies of law and state formation in both English and French Canada, they consider patterns of settler colonialism across the century before Confederation. The result is a collection that brings together innovative research in different fields to reconsider the ideology, governance, and political culture that underpinned British North America. In the aftermath of "Canada 150," and the geopolitical crises following the election of Donald Trump, our book offers a timely contribution to current debates over the nature of North American political culture and history. It demonstrates that we cannot understand Canada today without considering its colonial origins.

A host of institutions and individuals supported this initiative, and it is gratifying to be able to acknowledge their invaluable assistance here: the Atlantic Canada Studies Centre at the University of New Brunswick (UNB) and the Canada Research Chairs program provided the initial support; a Social Sciences and Humanities Research Council of Canada Partnership Development Grant funded the gatherings, with help from the Gorsebrook Research Institute at Saint Mary's University and the Canadian-American Center at the University of Maine, as well as the respective universities of all the contributors. The Atlantic Canada Studies Centre hosted the 2015 workshop, the Gorsebrook Research Institute sponsored the 2016 conference, and the Canadian-American Center at the University of Maine provided generous publication support. We are particularly grateful for the assistance of Dr Peter Twohig, executive director of the Gorsebrook Research Institute, and Dr Stephen Hornsby, director of the University of Maine's Canadian-American Center. Numerous people volunteered their time and energy to ensure that the workshop and conference ran smoothly, particularly Dr Sharon Weaver and Joe Blades at UNB, and Jackie Logan at Saint Mary's. Misty Sullivan expertly handled the finances for both gatherings.

The meetings from which these papers emerged were as enjoyable socially as they were edifying intellectually, and we thank the authors for their many stimulating contributions. Our dedicated session chairs – Gregory Kealey, Margaret Conrad, Linda Kealey, Gregory Kennedy, Michael Boudreau, Donald Wright, John Munro, Mark McLaughlin, and Corey Slumkoski – leavened the intellectual content of the panels and kept everyone focused. Jim Phillips was an energetic, insightful contributor to our meeting in Fredericton in 2015. We also recognize the contributions of our graduate student observer-participants (several of whom have moved on to greener pastures since our gatherings in 2015 and 2016), including Keith Grant, Annie Morrisette, Christine Harens, Hillary MacKinlay, Joseph Miller, Adam Nadeau, and Stephanie Pettigrew.

The editors drafted the introduction and section précis and began work on the epilogue during a fruitful gathering at the University of New Brunswick in 2017. In addition to contributing one of the essays, Colin Grittner provided yeoman service in helping to guide the collection into print. We appreciate the careful work of Barbara Tessman, our copy editor. Len Husband at University of Toronto Press has supported this project from its inception, and we are enormously thankful for his encouragement and suggestions for improvement.

We dedicate this collection to an incredible group – authors, observers, and session chairs – who have made this initiative such a fulfilling and collaborative endeavour. Their contributions have been assiduous, frank, thoughtful, and generous. We are abidingly grateful.

VIOLENCE, ORDER, AND UNREST

A History of British North America, 1749–1876

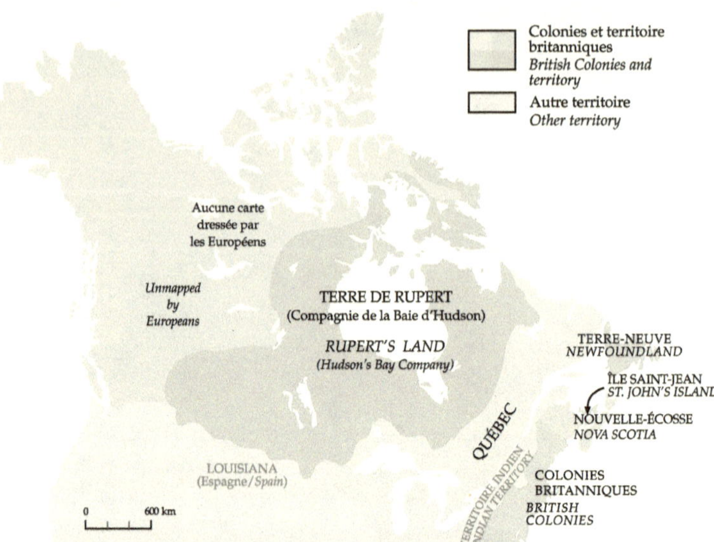

British North America, 1775. Source: Canadian Geographic.

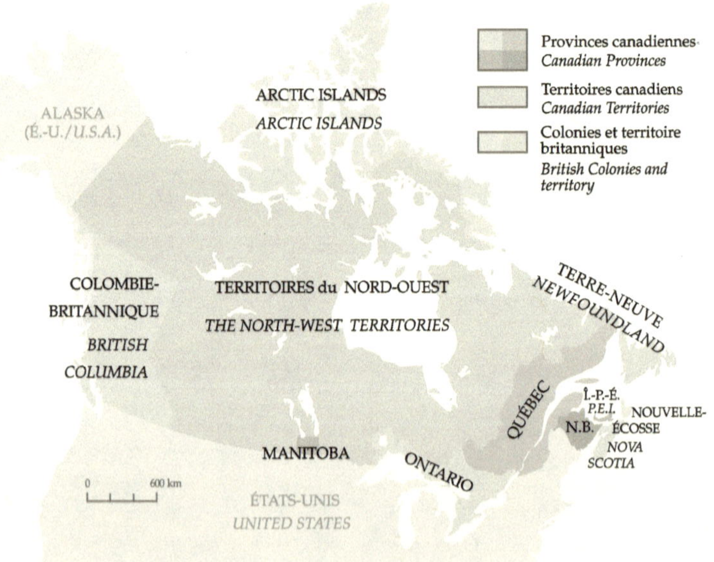

Canada, 1873. Source: Canadian Geographic.

Introduction

ELIZABETH MANCKE, JERRY BANNISTER, DENIS McKIM, AND SCOTT W. SEE

The world shares a historical myth that Canada does not have a defining legacy of violence.[1] Within Canada, there is a comparable, long-standing historical myth that the primary objective of British rule of the northern North American colonies before Confederation, and in the Canadian dominion after that event, was to achieve and maintain "peace, order, and good government." Like all stubbornly persistent myths, these perceptions have "one foot in the truth." Consequently, Canada has often been characterized by what it "lacks": a formal revolution, a catastrophic civil war, rampant "frontier" violence, and entire economies predicated on the brutality of slavery. This collection does not dispute the basic fact that, by international standards, Canada has had fewer large-scale episodes of bloody strife than other nations with which it is frequently compared, notably the United States.

Yet violence and disorder profoundly shaped Canadian history. From the intensification of British imperial influence in territories that eventually constituted part of the Canadian nation-state (as seen in the founding of Halifax in 1749) to the consolidation of a settler-dominated dominion (as reflected in the Indian Act of 1876), inhabitants of northern North America frequently encountered violent disputes, social upheaval, and systemic conflict: dispossession of Acadians and First Nations; destructive imperial wars from 1755 to 1815; cross-border disputes; fears of highly contagious diseases; nativist hostility towards influxes of immigrants; sectarian clashes and religious discord; workers' revolts; and anger over the political rights of Indigenous peoples and settlers in the West when Rupert's Land and British Columbia were incorporated into Canada. These developments, and others similar to them, played a crucial role in determining northern North America's institutional, cultural, and environmental trajectory. Depictions of the United States' northern neighbour as an unusually benign nation – a pervasive twenty-first-century expression captured by the cheerful slogan asserting that "the world needs more Canada" – therefore obscure, whether deliberately or not, the tumult and trauma that lie at the heart of the country's history.

Scholarly analyses of social disorder tend to rely on American or European analytical models in which violent and protracted struggles – the American and

French Revolutions, the European uprisings of 1848, the Civil War in the United States – were vehicles for social and political transformation.[2] Against these conceptual frameworks, disorder in early Canada – a topic that has traditionally been downplayed in favour of positivist accounts of Canada's comparatively placid evolution – scarcely merits mention.[3] Yet, to the extent that it was achieved, "peace, order, and good government" neither evolved naturally nor was achieved without widespread unrest, violence, and state coercion. This tension between blood-drenched American and Europeans approaches, on the one hand, and misleadingly tranquil Canadian ones, on the other, masks the pronounced extent to which violence is embedded in the institutional and ideological frameworks of the modern world. Myths notwithstanding, Canada is no exception.[4]

Our volume seeks to align studies of violence in Canadian history with a broader analysis of violence in the modern world. Scholars of the modern era, ca 1750 to the present, have approached violence from many socio-political angles. Imperialism, settler colonialism, labour exploitation, and state policing and regulation are major fields of scholarly inquiry worldwide, and historians of Canada actively work in each of them. Canadian history, however, is misaligned with scholarship on the Age of Revolutions, ca 1760–1850, an era often used as a synecdoche to mark the transition to modernity.[5] Canada's lack of a robust revolutionary tradition and its imperial ties can too easily carry the implication that it missed a critical step in the metanarrative of modernity, making the country more conservative, more deferential, and more risk averse than ones premised on revolutionary uprisings.

One of the flaws in this logic is that the forces that drove violent upheavals during the Age of Revolution were constitutional in substance, and British North Americans pursued them and their related causes, such as religious emancipation and the abolition of the slave trade and then slavery, vigorously. What all revolutions shared, and what made revolutionary action infectiously appealing, were contests over governmental power and how it should be distributed, shared, limited, and exercised, and by whom. Although northern North America did not experience revolutionary regime change, its peoples were by no means oblivious to this era's transformative developments. On the contrary, inhabitants of the British colonies that eventually became Canadian provinces grappled with many of the ideas, issues, and events that epitomized this remarkably dynamic, tumultuous age.[6] That this was so calls into question the notion – expressed in a resurgent American historiographical triumphalism – that revolutionary bloodshed was a sine qua non for attaining the benefits of democratic modernity.[7]

What characterizes the transition from the early modern to the modern era in world history is not violent upheaval so much as the contagion of constitutionalism: the spread of the idea that political systems did not have to be – indeed, *should not be* – authoritarian, and that political rights and privileges needed to extend far more deeply into society than they had under ancien régimes the world over. Thus, the epoch traditionally known as the Age of Revolution might profitably be recast as the Age of Constitutionalism, when claims to political rights burst the bounds of Anglo-Atlantic jurisdictions and became more universalized, laying the foundation for ever-more representative (though by no means perfectly democratic) political cultures.[8]

Although such developments could be liberating, they could also engender oppression. By the end of the Napoleonic Wars and the War of 1812, Britons, British North Americans, and US citizens increasingly worked in concert in responding to (and, often, neutralizing) revolutionary movements. In the British Isles, elites like Edmund Burke and ordinary subjects (notably members of "church and king mobs") alike lashed out at the perceived excesses of radical extremism, albeit in diverse ways. Such attitudes accompanied numerous Britons on their transatlantic journeys to settler colonies, influencing those colonies' political development in fundamental respects. For its part, the United States Constitution of 1787 instituted a powerful executive branch and a complex system of governmental checks and balances that were deliberately designed, in Alexander Hamilton's words, to counteract the "follies of democracy." Reactions against the flurry of radical uprisings that occurred around the beginning of the nineteenth century were not confined to the Anglo-American realm. The French Revolution had failed to establish and maintain a constitutional republic, lapsing back into an authoritarian regime, first Napoleon's and then with the return of the Bourbons. After failed invasions of the Rio de le Plata in 1806 and 1807, the British decided to support and assert influence over political changes in Spanish America through the advocacy of free trade, a new juxtaposition of avowed constitutional aspirations with commercial liberalization that would shape British imperial strategies through the nineteenth century and which the United States would follow, laying the groundwork for the emergence of an informal American empire.[9]

The dark underbelly of this post-1815 realignment of Anglo-Atlantic constitutionalism and ideas about global trade liberalization was the conceit that natural-born subjects of the British Empire and citizens of the United States acted as political vanguards in the spread of a peculiarly anglocentric vision of civilization that could embrace the British constitutional monarchy and a particular conception of American republicanism. This conceit justified them imposing their visions of constitutionalism and social order on others, often using forms of state-sanctioned coercion that their targets experienced as violent, such as the assimilative policies that anglophones imposed on French Canadians after the Lower Canadian Rebellion. It also heightened the sense that non-anglophone cultures, including Indigenous and francophone ones, were incapable of engaging effectively in progressive social change without anglophone tutelage and oversight, notwithstanding their own consensual forms of government. British North Americans still looked askance at the frequent resort to military violence in the United States – as evidenced by the removal of Indigenous peoples, the sabre-rattling over the Oregon Country, or the Mexican War – but they were not above coercing people in ways that did violence to their cultures, their families, and their long-term socio-economic welfare. Put another way, British North Americans consistently demonstrated a lower threshold or tolerance for overt violence than was the case with their southern neighbours, although this sensibility did not preclude subtler manifestations of violence and coercion.[10]

This volume represents a collaborative project that examines how British North Americans and Canadians, both governors and governed, envisaged social order and understood threats or challenges to it. It examines, in addition, diverse ways in which they imagined how tools of provincial and then federal states could be used to quell dissent and channel disruptive behaviour to achieve new political objectives. Ours is a major re-examination of pre-Confederation and early post-Confederation Canadian history – and by extension British imperial and North American history – and contributes to an understanding of the emergence of modernity and the disruptions and social and political transformations associated with it, about which more will be said.

Studies of violence often focus on two principal forms: on the one hand, interpersonal violence, particularly homicide; on the other, large-scale military conflicts ranging from revolutions to civil wars. Neither of these types of violence figures as prominently in Canadian history as they do in other countries, thus contributing to the Canadian "peaceable kingdom" myth.[11] British North Americans routinely reinforced this idea with rhetorical strategies that emphasized shared identities, public welfare, social stability, the rejection of tyranny, and a respect for authority. These popular perceptions were grounded in the particular imperial context of the British North American colonies that did not receive the same war-making powers as their seventeenth-century predecessors that constituted the future American states, where those powers had greater political and cultural currency.[12] The notion that Canada is a peaceable kingdom fortunately – perhaps providentially – free of the brutality and turmoil that mar other nations' pasts has traditionally been embraced by an astonishing array of observers, including Tories and Grits, easterners and westerners, imperialists and continentalists. Indeed, few themes in Canadian history – if any – can boast such an eclectic range of proponents. In recent decades, though, scholars have increasingly impugned the peaceable kingdom narrative, emphasizing instead the oppression, bigotry, and violence that have been integral to Canada's evolution. Yet many commentators – especially ones in the mainstream media from various countries referring to the sesquicentennial anniversary of Confederation, for example – continue to portray the United States' northern neighbour as a veritable oasis of peacefulness and stability in a distressingly violent, increasingly unstable world. Moreover, scholars who highlight the underappreciated salience of violence in Canada's past continue to acknowledge the peaceable kingdom myth, thereby testifying, however inadvertently, to its abiding potency as an explanatory mechanism.[13] For all its empirical shortcomings, then, the myth's cultural significance – both traditionally and in our own day – seems difficult to overstate.

This volume mainly explores the diverse range of violence between the two poles of interpersonal violence and warfare, although it does not deny the tremendous importance of such clashes as the Seven Years' War, the American Revolution, the War of 1812, and the Rebellions of 1837–8. In particular, it devotes substantial attention to the collective violence of riots, the legislated coercion of the state, and settler dispossession of Indigenous peoples. Our contributors consider both acts and perceptions of violence, including state-sanctioned policies that, for some peoples, had deleterious consequences.

We also recognize the ambiguity inherent in many kinds of violence. For instance, settlers welcomed treaties that opened up land for homesteading, while Indigenous peoples experienced the resultant upheaval as a coercive act of dispossession with violently disruptive consequences. Thus, the creation of peaceful, stable, prosperous circumstances for one segment of society – say, settlers – often entailed the acute mistreatment of another segment of society – say, Indigenous peoples. Rather than being incompatible, then, "peace, order, and good government" and various forms of violence were, ironically, linked. In British North America, one person's order was frequently the result of another person's disorder. Far from being unrelated, these divergent outcomes can be understood as opposite sides of the same colonial coin. To focus solely on benign developments is to deny the unmitigated injustice upon which many of those developments rested. If one were looking for a historical figure who embodied the paradoxically interrelated nature of order and violence in British North America, a promising candidate would be James Douglas, Chief Factor of the Hudson's Bay Company and mid-nineteenth-century governor of colonial Vancouver Island and British Columbia. Douglas has received praise for painstakingly negotiating treaties with Northwest Coast First Nations on Vancouver Island, an approach that contrasted sharply with the peremptory tactics employed by other colonial officials involved in land claims disputes in the region (notably Joseph Trutch), and with the "Indian Wars" waged in the later nineteenth century by the United States government against western Indigenous nations. However, Douglas also resorted to what he called "wholesome terror" – public executions, for instance – in attempting to neutralize perceived Indigenous threats to settlers' interests.[14]

Scholars have produced a substantial body of historical research on social order, anxieties about unrest, and responses to outbreaks of violence. Integrating their findings into mainstream historical narratives of Canada is difficult, however, because synthetic works have traditionally emphasized the orderly and evolutionary emergence of political institutions, such as democratic assemblies, and of social transformations, such as the expansion of the franchise or workers' rights. Regrettably, the emphasis on evolutionary development mutes the agency that ordinary northern North Americans had over social and political transformations by implying that they were largely quiescent, if not civically disengaged, notwithstanding the many people from diverse backgrounds who agitated with political skill and savvy. Likewise, such an approach tacitly downplays the efforts of colonial leaders who sought compromises, sometimes through mutual negotiations, at other times through vigorous challenges to imperial authorities.

Rather than rejecting the notion that Canadian history lacks the long list of sanguinary events that punctuate the histories of other nations, this volume contends that early Canada's social and political transformations were achieved through dynamic processes that were often contentious and, at times, acrimonious and coercive, and had a profound impact on all levels of society. For example, the concept of settler colonialism – a multifaceted phenomenon whereby newcomers to particular territories "carry their sovereignty with them" and impose it in diverse ways on Indigenous inhabitants – informs our understanding of violence in colonial contexts, with Canada serving as a prime example.[15] Until fairly recently, beneficiaries of British imperialism comforted themselves with the conceit that colonization was largely non-violent, in particular contrast to the comparatively cruel regimes instituted by rival empires, witness to which are favourable comparisons with the "Black Legend" of Spanish colonization in Latin America. Indigenous peoples, for their part, have persistently argued that dispossession from their lands and the removal of their rights of self-government have had negative – indeed, tragic – consequences. Only in the the most recent generation have popular non-Indigenous attitudes about settler colonialism started to change in the wake of continued challenges from Indigenous societies about their place in Canada and their historic mistreatment. Those dynamics are profoundly shaping the national agenda in the twenty-first century, most significantly with the 2015 report of the Truth and Reconciliation Commission exploring the devastating, multigenerational trauma of the residential schools catastrophe and putting forth its resonant ninety-four "calls to action."[16] One of the results has been the most fundamental rethinking of Canadian identity since the searching investigations launched several decades ago in consequence of the national unity crises precipitated by the rise of the Quebec sovereignty movement. This volume seeks to contribute to this root-and-branch reconceptualization of Canada's identity.

The tension between policies that some see as benign and others as malignant is central to modernist agendas, including the campaign to found Canada on principles of "peace, order, and good government." We are using the idea of modernism as it emerged from Enlightenment thought, with its confidence in the capacity of people and the states they constructed to foster progress rationally and to apply science and technology to mitigate suffering, all in the name of improving a universal human condition.[17] Such beliefs contributed to the willingness of many people to risk social disorder to achieve dramatic changes in the character of their communities' political and social fabric, as expressed in uprisings and revolutions in North America, France, and the Caribbean that endeavoured to achieve liberation. Yet such beliefs also engendered stark distinctions between "civilized" societies and those condescendingly deemed to be at lower stages of development. Confident that they were acting in accordance with laws of nature, agents of colonial regimes – including government officials and missionaries, entrepreneurs and educators – disseminated and imposed these beliefs with the objective of creating a benevolent social order.

Northern North Americans were not immune to the ferment Enlightenment ideals engendered, and we find their expression in the commercial lobbying in the 1750s for an assembly in Nova Scotia (first convened in 1758); in the efforts of Fleury Mesplet to circulate radical writings in Montreal in the era of the American Revolution; in the "Eddy Rebellion" in the Chignecto region in 1776; and in the agitation that resulted in the 1791 division of Quebec into two colonies – Lower and Upper Canada – each with an elected assembly. During the nineteenth century, the colonial provinces used a growing array of bureaucratic and scientific tools, such as censuses and public education, to monitor populations and shape them to specific ends, as historians of Lower Canada/Quebec have been particularly assiduous in analysing. The achievement of responsible government in the British North American provinces in the mid-nineteenth century and the federal design that was realized in Confederation in 1867 were profoundly moulded by the overarching assumption that governments and nations can be constructed in an orderly and non-violent manner.[18]

An ethos of constitutionalism undergirded this confidence in the Enlightenment ideals of modernity across the British world. For its proponents, Britain's unwritten constitution – an elaborate constellation of laws, institutions, and conventions – protected individual rights, limited state power, safeguarded property, facilitated commerce, and enabled participatory governments. Aspects of British constitutionalism were superimposed on and, by turns, adapted by the francophone population of the former New France after the Conquest that was formalized in 1763. They were reinforced by the arrival of the Loyalists in the wake of the American Revolutionary War in the late eighteenth century and by the waves of British immigrants who arrived in the aftermath of the Napoleonic Wars in the early nineteenth century. In principle, laws and jurisprudence encompassed all peoples residing in British North America. In practice, however, British justice was highly contested and variably applied. Diverse peoples invoked it both to impose and oppose policies emanating from Westminster. The benefits of constitutionalism were contingent on acceptance of British rule – in other words, liberty hinged on loyalty. British rights and protections were also predicated on a purportedly advanced level of agrarian social development. Communities with perceived deficiencies in terms of property ownership and agricultural improvement, such as many First Nations and residents of fishing outports, were denied the full array of constitutional rights and protections. Yet such communities were remarkably sophisticated, often circumventing colonial officials by petitioning the Crown for various forms of royally sanctioned equity or accommodation. Likewise, ordinary settlers who objected to imperial policies regarding such issues as land distributions, state-aided Christianity, banking ventures, and transportation schemes remonstrated against colonial and local elites when they felt they had been denied British justice.

This collection traverses the breadth of British North America from the planting of British settler communities to the consolidation of the Dominion of Canada. The essays are organized into five thematic sections. The first addresses the ideological constructs of loyalty, liberty, and constitutional order that informed British North Americans' visions of the societies they constructed. The second traces the contested transition from an imperial focus on accommodating multiple ethnic communities to prioritizing colonial aspirations at the expense of vulnerable peoples. That shift elicited considerable resistance from Indigenous peoples, blacks, and other minorities, a theme that is explored in the third section. The fourth section examines the convergence of diverse peoples in urban centres and the attendant struggles to control public spaces. Law, print culture, and voluntary societies, the focus of the last section, played central roles in the emergence of a dynamic colonial public sphere.

Our volume brings together topics and frameworks that are usually kept apart in North American studies. Over the past generation, Canadian history has become increasingly fragmented into specialties, such as legal history, that offer impressively deep yet tightly focused views of early Canada. Our contributors draw on a wide array of scholarly perspectives, such as borderlands, imperial history, public spheres, Indigenous studies, and intellectual history. Collectively, however, we are not bound by a single interpretive focus, which has arguably been a constraint in otherwise insightful studies discussing violence in Canadian history that examine a single phenomenon, such as political upheaval.[19] Rather, this approach fosters a creative conversation that links our varied understandings of the complex qualities of violence and institutional legitimacy in the modern era, and assesses – albeit in eclectic ways – their implications for British North America's social and political development. Our goal is to create a more expansive and creative conversation between and among specialist research, in order to gain a fuller understanding of the founding of Canada. Rather than attempting to construct a new synthesis, our hope is to offer fresh perspectives that move us beyond existing models, such as the liberal order framework. We believe that history works best when scholarship is based not on a single interpretive schema but, rather, on a dialogue among scholars who see Canada through different methodological lenses. Taken together, these lenses offer a complex yet ultimately coherent way of envisaging the making of British North America and then Canada, one that avoids the false choice of adhering to national narratives or rejecting national history altogether. Our volume demonstrates that it is indeed possible to avoid nationalism and to foster diversity while engaging with central questions – including considerations of the role of violence in northern North America's development – in Canadian history. The choice for historians today is not national versus transnational history but, rather, how best to promote discussion of the disparate factors that shaped the territories that became Canada.[20]

NOTES

1 By *violence*, we mean both physically harmful acts and other forms of aggressive or coercive behaviour that have traumatic ramifications. On the complexities inherent in the idea of violence, see Sophie Body-Gendrot and Pieter Spierenburg, eds, *Violence in Europe: Historical and Contemporary Perspectives* (New York: Springer, 2008); an older, enduringly insightful study is Hannah Arendt, *On Violence* (New York: Harcourt Brace, 1970).
2 For varieties of those scholarly approaches, see David Armitage and Sanjay Subrahmanyam, eds, *The Age of Revolution in Global Context, c. 1760–1840* (Houndmills, UK: Palgrave Macmillan, 2010); Crane Brinton, *The Anatomy of Revolution* (New York: Vintage, 1965); Bernard Bailyn, *The Ideological Origins of the American Revolution* (Cambridge, MA: Belknap Press of Harvard University Press, 1992); and Eric Hobsbawm, *The Age of Revolution, 1789–1848* (New York: Vintage Books, 1996).
3 Such accounts were especially pervasive, and influential, in the mid-twentieth century. See, for example, J.M.S. Careless, *Canada: A Story of Challenge* (Toronto: Macmillan,

1963); and A.R.M. Lower, *Colony to Nation: A History of Canada* (Toronto: Longmans, Green, 1946). Given their emphasis on the theme of peaceful evolution, such studies arguably had much in common with an older historiographical tradition that concentrated on Canada's constitutional development within the British Empire. See, for instance, Chester Martin, *Empire and Commonwealth: Studies in Governance and Self-Government in Canada* (Oxford: Oxford University Press, 1929).

4 For an overview of the historiography of violence in Canada and the United States, see Scott W. See, "Nineteenth-Century Collective Violence: Toward a North American Context," *Labour/Le travail* 39 (Spring 1997): 13–38.

5 In Armitage and Subrahmanyam, *The Age of Revolutions in Global Context*, the colonies that became Canada are referenced only in passing a handful of times.

6 Michel Ducharme, *The Idea of Liberty in Canada during the Age of Atlantic Revolutions, 1776–1838* (Montreal and Kingston: McGill-Queen's University Press, 2014).

7 Jonathan Israel, *The Expanding Blaze: How the American Revolution Ignited the World, 1775–1848* (Princeton, NJ: Princeton University Press, 2017). Israel's book, which positions the American republic at the forefront of a worldwide movement of liberation, can be read as an amplification of the controversial, patriotic thesis advanced in Gordon S. Wood, *The Radicalism of the American Revolution* (New York: Vintage, 1993).

8 M.C. Mirow, "The Age of Constitutions in the Americas," *Law and History Review* 32, no. 2 (May 2014): 229–35; and Linda Colley, "Empires of Writing: Britain, America and Constitutions, 1776–1848," *Law and History Review* 32, no. 2 (May 2014): 237–66.

9 Seth Cotlar, *Tom Paine's America: The Rise of Fall of Transatlantic Radicalism in the Early American Republic* (Charlottesville: University of Virginia Press, 2011); Boyd Hilton, *A Mad, Bad, and Dangerous People? England, 1783–1846* (Oxford: Clarendon Press, 2006); and Alan Knight, "Britain and Latin America," in *The Nineteenth Century*, ed. Andrew Porter and Alaine Low (Oxford: Oxford University Press, 1999), 126, 129–30.

10 Historian Richard Maxwell Brown argued that "American life has been characterized by continuous and often intense violence," which formed a "seamless web with some of the most positive events of U.S. history." See "Historical Patterns of Violence," in *Violence in America: Protest, Rebellion, Reform*, ed. Ted Robert Gurr (Newbury Park, CA: Sage Publications, 1989), 48.

11 For a discussion of the origin of the peaceable kingdom myth and the ways in which it persists – somewhat paradoxically – in modern scholarship, see Scott W. See, "The Intellectual Construction of Canada's 'Peaceable Kingdom' Ideal," *Journal of Canadian Studies* 52, no. 2 (Spring 2018): 510–37.

12 On the fundamental differences between the political culture of Britain's northern North American colonies and the Thirteen Colonies, see Elizabeth Mancke, "Early

Modern Imperial Governance and the Origins of Canadian Political Culture," *Canadian Journal of Political Science* 32, no. 1 (March 1999): 3–20.

13 See, for example, Dimitry Anastakis, *Death in the Peaceable Kingdom: Canadian History since 1867 through Murder, Execution, Assassination, and Suicide* (Toronto: University of Toronto Press, 2015).

14 J.R. Miller, *Skyscrapers Hide the Heavens: A History of Native-Newcomer Relations in Canada*, 4th ed. (Toronto: University of Toronto Press, 2018), 155; and Adele Perry, *Colonial Relations: The Douglas-Connolly Family and the Nineteenth-Century Imperial World* (Cambridge: Cambridge University Press, 2015), 188.

15 John G. Reid and Thomas Peace, "Colonies of Settlement and Settler Colonialism in Northeastern North America, 1450–1850," in *The Routledge Handbook of the History of Settler Colonialism*, ed. Edward Cavanagh and Lorenzo Veracini (New York: Routledge, 2017), 80. See also Laura Ishiguro, "Northwestern North America (Canadian West) to 1900," in *The Routledge Handbook of Settler Colonialism*, 125–38; Lorenzo Veracini, "'Settler Colonialism': Career of a Concept," *Journal of Imperial and Commonwealth History* 41, no. 2 (March 2013): 313–33; and the chapters in this volume by John G. Reid, Carolyn Podruchny and Émilie Pigeon, Thomas Peace, Elsbeth Heaman, and Max Hamon.

16 *Canada's Residential Schools: The Final Report of the Truth and Reconciliation Commission of Canada* (Montreal and Kingston: Published for the Truth and Reconciliation Commission of Canada by McGill-Queen's University Press, 2015).

17 C.A. Bayly, *The Birth of the Modern World, 1780–1914* (Malden, MA: Blackwell, 2004), 9–12; and Lauren Benton and Lisa Ford, *Rage for Order: The British Empire and the Origins of International Law, 1800–1850* (Cambridge, MA: Harvard University Press, 2016).

18 Works exploring issues discussed in this paragraph include Tina Loo, *Making Law, Order, and Authority in British Columbia, 1821–1871* (Toronto: University of Toronto Press, 1994); Allan Greer and Ian Radforth, eds, *Colonial Leviathan: State Formation in Mid-Nineteenth-Century Canada* (Toronto: University of Toronto Press, 1992); Phillip A. Buckner, *The Transition to Responsible Government: British Policy in British North America, 1815–1850* (Westport, CT: Greenwood Press, 1985); S.F. Wise, *God's Peculiar Peoples: Essays on Political Culture in Nineteenth-Century Canada* (Ottawa: Carleton University Press, 1993); and Bruce Curtis, *Ruling by Schooling Quebec: Conquest to Liberal Governmentality* (Toronto: University of Toronto Press, 2012).

19 Derek Pollard and Ged Martin, eds, *Canada 1849* (Edinburgh: University of Edinburgh, Centre of Canadian Studies, 2001).

20 On transnationalism and Canadian history, see Karen Dubinsky, Adele Perry, and Henry Yu, eds, *Within and without the Nation: Canadian History as Transnational History* (Toronto: University of Toronto Press, 2015).

SECTION I

Loyalty, Liberty, and Visions of Order

The chapters in this section examine, in various ways, the conceptions of social order that public figures – including prominent individuals from the worlds of politics and religion – envisaged and painstakingly strove to entrench in northern North America between the Conquest and Confederation. Although their visions were far from homogenous, they shared a commitment to the consolidation and perpetuation of British imperial influence – a multifaceted entity that elite observers routinely associated with the rule of law, private property, and constitutional monarchy, among other purportedly positive things – in territories that ultimately constituted part of the Dominion of Canada.

Such notions were often espoused by conservative figures in church and state who endeavoured to erect and sustain an elaborate hierarchy premised on complementary notions of noblesse oblige on the part of elites and deference on the part of the masses. However, other figures – for example, political reformers and Protestant Dissenters – also voiced support for the British regime, albeit in ways that diverged sharply from those of their conservative counterparts. Their expressions of loyalty were often couched in invocations of liberal aspects of the British tradition, including parliamentary democracy and toleration of religious minorities. The contrasting conceptions of "Britishness" articulated by conservative authorities and their liberal rivals attest to the contested nature of the enormously influential cultural phenomenon over which they struggled.

Bound up with many of these figures' support for the British regime in northern North America was a palpable sense of anxiety. Scott See's essay on "Aspirations and Limitations" analyses the elite's confidence in its ability to apply Enlightenment ideals of "peace, order, and good government" in British North America and the hardiness of those ideals, despite instances of deleterious failure. D.C. Bélanger explores how Quebec's Catholic elites used the British need for their support to craft an ideology of Catholic loyalty that in turn defended French Canadians against British attempts to convert them to one or another Protestant denomination. In this instance, Bélanger shows how social order in Quebec evolved through elite compromise and accommodation by both the British and Catholic Canadians. Similarly, as Denis McKim argues, Protestant Dissenters and Catholics in the Atlantic region and the Canadas crafted a "language of loyalty" that both undercut Anglican aspirations to offer the defining vision of an orderly British North America and established their importance in shaping civic culture and stability. In this section's final chapter, Jerry Bannister explores the tension between ideas and action, as well as the chasm that separated the dispassionate articulation of lofty ideals and the anxiety-inducing realities of nineteenth-century society. The management of emotions and the strategic deployment of sentiment were every bit as important as the dry logic of the utilitarian ends of Confederation.

These essays speak to how threats of republicanism and secularism prompted individuals from diverse walks of life to champion "Britishness" and its purportedly beneficial societal impact more vigorously than they might have done had such putatively pernicious phenomena not emerged as compelling concerns in the first place. For all their differences, British North American elites from varied ethnic and religious backgrounds contributed to the crystallization of a fundamentally British social order that could plausibly be seen as inherently contradictory. From the vantage point of its diverse supporters, this social order bolstered liberty, promoted prosperity, and ensured stability, and was therefore eminently worthy of celebration. By contrast, its critics, an equally eclectic group whose perspectives feature prominently in other sections of this volume, stressed the myriad injustices wrought by northern North America's prevailing social order – notably discrimination, dispossession, and subjugation – which they disdained as an unremittingly oppressive force foisted on disempowered groups. The tension between these diametrically opposed perspectives is one of this collection's principal themes.

1 Aspirations and Limitations: "Peace, Order, and Good Government" and the Language of Violence and Disorder in British North America

SCOTT W. SEE[1]

Rudyard Kipling, the iconic writer and champion of empire, would have made the architects of Confederation proud. In published letters from his travels across Canada in the early twentieth century, he reflected on the sturdy and no-nonsense qualities of the Canadians that he encountered. On the subject of the respect for justice, he observed: "The law in Canada exists and is administered ... as an integral part of the national character – no more to be forgotten or talked about than trousers. If you kill, you hang. If you steal, you go to jail. This has worked toward peace, self-respect, and I think the innate dignity of the people."[2] In a sweeping attempt to capture the essence of a nascent Canadian identity, Kipling observed the following:

> There is no mistaking the spirit of sane and realized nationality, which fills the land from end to end with precisely as the joyous hum of a big dynamo well settled to its load makes a back-ground to all the other shop noises ... The people, the schools, the churches, the Press in its degree, and, above all, the women, understand without manifestoes that their land must now as always abide under the Law in deed and in word and in thought. This is their caste-mark, the ark of their covenant, their reason for being what they are. In the big cities, with their village-like lists of police court offences; in the wide-open little Western towns where the present is as free as the lives and the future as safe as the property of their inhabitants; in the coast cities galled and humiliated as their one night's riot ("It's not our habit, Sir! It's not our habit!"); up among the mountains where the officers of the law track and carefully bring into justice the astounded malefactor; and behind the orderly prairies the barren grounds, as far as a single white man can walk, the relentless spirit of the breed follows up, and oversees, and controls.[3]

With limited personal experience in one of Her Majesty's dominions, Kipling managed to articulate an emerging national ethos: Canada as a nation of peace, order, and good government. The question of whether this dynamic was actual, imagined, or both undergirds many of the essays in this volume.

This chapter explores the language that contextualized and governed the political and social search for order in British North America from the late eighteenth century to the early Confederation era. Aspirational dynamics, as well as an essential paradox, shaped the elements of this study. British North American politicians, intellectuals, and social elites worked assiduously to convince themselves that they were establishing a haven, based on a liberal order framework with late eighteenth-century roots, in the British Empire and North America. The designers of British North America's provincial governments and legal codes, and later the authors of the grand design of Confederation, methodically sought to erect a formidable edifice of hierarchical order.[4] Yet even as they constructed and celebrated the ideal of peace, order, and good government, they struggled to provide a countervailing force for the troublesome realities of political, economic, ethnic, and religious divisions that were so much a part of the fabric of nineteenth-century British North American society.[5] They were quite concerned – even fearful – about rampant disorder, social violence, and the untidy and seemingly uncontrollable expression of popular will. Moreover, as numerous contributors to this volume compellingly demonstrate, while employing righteous oratory that touted the meritorious, measured, and logical elements of their efforts, they unfortunately fashioned institutions that repressed popular will and even facilitated disorder and violence, especially when directed against Indigenous peoples.[6]

Legislative documents and the published material of politicians, public figures, and intellectuals constitute the core evidence for this study.[7] The ideal of creating a nation-state that would prove to be a counterpoint to the United States was pervasive in this era, yet there was significant contemporary disagreement about the means to achieve such a lofty goal.[8] The language of disorder offers a good opportunity to concentrate on the ways in which government officials and elites characterized disorder, riots, tumult, and violence.

The origins of the search for order are located in the eighteenth century, where the code for order can be found in the ubiquitous use of words and phrases such as *public welfare, social stability, the rejection of tyranny,* and *respect for authority.*[9] A number of overlapping dimensions moulded this process: the loyalist agenda of the rejection of revolution and rebellions; the overarching and positive impact of the manifold connections to the British Empire and English civilization; the movement to Confederation as a confirmation of orderly development; a peaceful Western expansion in the late nineteenth century – under the firm yet judicious guidance of the North-West Mounted Police – as emblematic of Canada's superior design of national development; and the essentially negative model of an often violent, sometimes tyrannical, and increasingly imperialistic United States. These themes have been the subject of a great deal of scholarly attention, so there is no need to provide a comprehensive analysis of each in this chapter.[10] These ideas have infused the historiography and scholarship of Canada since the nineteenth century; they provide powerful clues to locating the seed bed for the emergence of the orderly and peaceable ideals.

Political leaders, business elites, and property holders were quite concerned about the frequency and intensity of political, labour, and social disorder in their times. They sought to tighten legal codes and buttress the constabulary in order to curtail popular demonstrations, contentious behaviour at the hustings, bruising confrontations between immigrants and more-established residents, discord between Protestants and Catholics, and disturbing clashes between Indigenous peoples and whites. The search for order and control emerged as a national ethos on a parallel path with the introduction of responsible government and the process of Confederation. The Canadian nation was to be, if nothing else, a paradigm of order. As contemporaries clearly understood, the pathway to nationhood evolved in a protracted and global atmosphere of revolutionary strife. Discussions among the country's creators were deeply influenced by the excesses of democratic zeal on the part of revolutionary peoples in Europe and by the horrific civil conflict that raged between the American states in the 1860s.[11] Violent clashes erupted between ethnic and religious groups on both sides of the Atlantic with disturbing regularity during the nineteenth century.

More directly, and with greater poignancy, the rebellions in Lower and Upper Canada, a generation before the Confederation debates, shaped the country's articulation of nationalism and its search for order. Although the Fathers of Confederation were reluctant to condone the events of 1837–8, several – including George-Étienne Cartier and Sir Étienne-Paschal Taché – had expressed sympathy for the rebels earlier in their careers.[12] The obvious affront, if not oxymoron, of embracing rebellion in a document that sought to preserve order created an ideological conundrum that necessitated the most skilful and nuanced of argumentation. Arthur M. Rankin of Canada's Legislative Assembly articulated that paradox: "No doubt there was much cause of complaint on the part of those who originated the agitation, which resulted in the rebellion of 1837. And speaking now in the light of the experience, many of us would probably be prepared to admit those gentlemen who took a prominent part in bringing about that rebellion, and whom we then considered it a duty to put down, were in reality true benefactors of the country."[13] Thus the creation of a Canadian federal apparatus in 1867 rested, in part, on the notion that the new country would provide an attractive alternative to a jaded Europe and a peaceful antidote to the violent spectacle of what many British North Americans believed to be the failed American experiment of republicanism. The ideal of the achievement of political and social order was a significant underpinning to Confederation.[14]

The phrase "peace, order, and good government" has performed yeoman service for over two centuries as political, social, and cultural benchmarks for Canadian identity.[15] It invoked, and arguably still does in many regards, aspirational dimensions.[16] The detailed instructions to General James Murray upon his appointment as governor of the Province of Quebec following the Royal Proclamation of 1763 included the following charge: "You are in the mean Time to make such Rules and Regulations ... as shall appear to be necessary for the Peace, Order, and good Government of Our said Province, taking care that nothing be passed or done that shall any Ways tend to affect the Life, Limb, or Liberty of the Subject."[17] A century later, the British North America Act, which anchored the organizing principles of the newly established Dominion of Canada, used the exact same sequence of words. Section 91, which defined the federal legislative responsibilities of the newly constituted Parliament, proclaimed, "It shall be lawful for the Queen, by and with the Advice and Consent of the Senate and House of Commons, to make Laws for the Peace, Order, and good Government of Canada, in relation to all Matters not coming with the Classes of Subjects by this Act assigned exclusively to the Legislatures of the Provinces."[18]

Although the thrust of its intent changed in important ways over time, the phrase became a versatile rationale for the reconstruction of existing colonies or the creation of new colonies in British North America between the Proclamation of 1763 and Confederation. For example, in 1784 the imperil instructions to John Parr, governor of Nova Scotia and the islands of St John and Cape Breton, borrowed the phrase from the proclamation almost verbatim.[19] A petition from Cape Breton inhabitants protesting the administrative annexation of their island to Nova Scotia reinforced that sentiment sixty years later. The petitioners suggested that the due diligence of peace, order, and good government would protect "the life, limb, or liberty, of the Subject."[20] Similarly, the phrase appeared repeatedly in the imperial documents that shaped the development of the colony of British Columbia in the mid-nineteenth century.[21] Thus, well before it became one of the most recognizable features of the British North America Act in 1867, "peace, order, and good government" played a role in setting the aspirational tenor of the administrative development of the colonies. Strikingly, it kept its utilitarian value in the late nineteenth century as the dominion extended its territorial expansion in the West. For example, the act that established the administration of the recently acquired Rupert's Land and the North-West Territories assigned powers to the lieutenant governor "to make provisions for the administration of Justice therein, and generally to make, ordain, and establish all such Laws, Institutions and Ordinances as may be necessary for the Peace, Order, and good Government of Her Majesty's subjects and others therein."[22]

Politicians and intellectuals were similarly mindful of the powerful relationship between the rule of law and the formation of a new nation-state. Although the Fathers of Confederation lacked a unified social vision of the nation they were constructing, they believed overwhelmingly in the strict adherence to legal principles and supported a governmental infrastructure that would assure the country's political survival.[23] The Quebec and provincial debates were laden with appeals to craft a nation on the bedrock of legal institutions. The subject had garnered special attention, which was not surprising given Lord Durham's mission, in the report that followed the Rebellions of 1837–8 in Lower Canada and Upper Canada. Durham exposed flaws in the provinces' legal and judicial apparatus in great detail, and in his report, true to the mixed reputation that it rapidly acquired in Canadian history, he was not shy in elaborating several ways in which the political elite should maintain law and order at the expense of a fickle and tempestuous popular will.[24]

Additional evidence of the concern for the rule of order can be found in the adaptation of codes from British jurisprudence that governed order and peace in public spaces and, in particular, sought to prevent riots.[25] From the late eighteenth century to Confederation, all of the British North American colonies adopted and refined laws that defined rout and riot, crafted guidance for the civil and military authorities to disperse crowds and defuse the possible outbreak of collective violence, and codified the penalties for engaging in riotous behaviour.[26] The language of public violence typically included terms such as *tumult*, *rout*, and *riot*. Emblematic of this process was a comprehensive act to amend and consolidate the criminal laws of the Canadas in 1850. The act defined a *rout* as "an unlawful assembly, moved or actuated by an intent not authorized by law, to do some act with tumult and violence, and tending to strike terror and alarm into others, make some motion, endeavour or advance towards doing the same, without doing or actually beginning to do the same." It further elaborated: "A Rout is such that if the act intended were done in the manner intended, it would be a riot."[27] The statute declared that in the eyes of the law, both routs and riots were unlawful assemblies. It borrowed a classic definition from British penal codes: "A Riot is where three or more being in unlawful assembly, shall without authority of law, join in doing or actually beginning to do an act with tumult and violence, and striking terror or alarm, or tending to strike terror and alarm, into others."[28] The codes that further addressed violence against order noted "menacing and turbulent language or gestures," the "show of offensive weapons," and using force to "demolish, pull down, or destroy" property.[29] Thus the codes for public violence addressed assaults against both persons and property.

Legislative assemblies implemented and refined numerous Riot Act statutes, which were often directly borrowed from British penal conventions, throughout the period under discussion. Most of these statutes used a threshold of three to twelve persons who were either threatening to engage or were engaging in physical harm or property destruction in the public sphere. The public reading of the Riot Act became a durable feature in the arsenal of civil authorities to avoid or curtail violence. The proclamation, which was to be delivered verbatim when public disturbances were deemed imminent or underway, read as follows: "The Queen commands all persons here assembled immediately to disperse themselves and peacefully to depart to their homes or lawful business, under the penalty of the law against unlawful assemblies. God save the Queen."[30] In British North America, the proclamation could be announced by "any Sheriff, or by the Mayor or other chief executive officer of any District, County or Municipality, or of any City, Town or Village, or by any Magistrate or Police Magistrate."[31] Punishments for rioting, which was characterized as a felony, varied throughout the provinces. Transgressors typically faced at least one year of hard labour or transportation for life to another British colony.[32] Legislators, following through on the constitutional mandate to fashion an overarching federal criminal code that would be employed in each of the provinces, passed a Riot Act bill and honed the legal language for quelling public disorder in the immediate wake of Confederation.[33]

The use of the military in confronting riots and public disorder was of tremendous concern for contemporaries in the nineteenth century. It is well beyond this chapter's scope to address the nuanced and oftentimes litigious boundaries between the military and civil authorities, especially in the context of public disorder and violence in urban locations.[34] Military officers routinely expressed concern about inserting their forces into contentious situations – for example, during public election polling and clashes between religious and ethnic groups. Similarly, civil authorities increasingly accepted the mantle of maintaining public order as an essential component of control, typically through the reinforcement of the constabulary and professional police forces. Published procedures and manuals addressed the thorny relationship between military and civil authorities in performing an active role in suppressing public disorders, especially riots. Customarily, military officers needed to be formally requisitioned by magistrates or sheriffs to assist civil forces in riotous situations. Although officers were within their rights to respond to threats in situations where civil authorities were not present, they were urged to be cautious in resorting to deadly force because of the potential to damage already tenuous relations between civilians and soldiers.[35] This question of the boundary between the military (or militia) and civil authorities in confronting public disorder continued to be addressed after Confederation.[36]

The political debates that transpired in Quebec City in October 1864 and thereafter in the respective provincial assemblies and conventions were often characterized as being the product of an essential order that was benevolently imposed and nurtured by Britain. John A. Macdonald, one of the central figures in the Confederation era, clearly enunciated that principle on more than one occasion. He delivered a succinct statement on that theme to the Canadian Legislative Assembly in February 1865:

> We should feel ... sincerely grateful to beneficent Providence that we have had the opportunity vouchsafed us of calmly considering this great constitutional change, this peaceful revolution – that we have not been hurried into it, like the United States, by the exigencies of war – that we have not had a violent revolutionary period forced on us, as in other nations, by hostile action from without, or by domestic dissentions within. Here we are in peace and prosperity, under the fostering government of Great Britain – a dependent people, with a government having only a limited and delegated authority, and yet allowed, without restriction, and without jealousy on the part of the Mother Country, to legislate for ourselves, and peacefully and deliberately to consider and determine the future of Canada and of British North America.[37]

During the Confederation debates, delegates and other interested parties paid close attention to the abundant examples of social conflict and discord that were shaped by ethnic, religious, and cultural identification in nineteenth-century British North America. George Brown, the acerbic editor of Toronto's *Globe*, spoke at length about the challenge of confronting "prejudices of race and language and religion."[38] Those heavily invested in crafting a nation certainly recognized the monumental difficulties in tempering passions along those fault lines, and some deemed the ideal of a true collaboration of races "utopian."[39] Nonetheless, Confederation advocates generally acknowledged the role that clearly defined federal and provincial legal and judicial institutions would have in ensuring that order would be a hallmark of the new dominion. The following extended address by Macdonald to the Legislative Assembly in Kingston in 1865 illustrates that point:

> The criminal law too – the determination of what is a crime and what is not and how crime should be punished – is left to the General Government. This is a matter almost of necessity. It is of great importance that we should have the same criminal law throughout these provinces – that what is a crime in one part of British America, should be a crime in every part – that there should be the same protection of life and property as in another ... Under our Constitution we shall have one body of criminal law ... I think this is one of the most marked instances in which we take advantage of the experience derived from our observations of the defects in the Constitution of the neighboring Republic.[40]

The national criminal code enshrined in the British North America Act indeed became one of the signal differences between the constitutions of the North American neighbours; moreover, it emphatically proclaimed the new nation's adherence to order and peaceful interaction.

Evidence that British North Americans thought of their colonies as a haven in North America, with an essentially non-violent tradition and mission, abounds. Lt. Col. George T. Denison, one of the founders of the Canada First movement in the late nineteenth century, grounded his arguments on the belief that the Loyalists deserved credit for establishing a law-abiding and orderly civilization in the wilderness of British North America. As he elaborated in a presidential address to the Royal Society of Canada, "It is a blessing to us that we all live in a country where the laws are honestly administered, where justice is not bought, where crimes are punished, where life and property are secure, and where we enjoy as much real liberty as any people on earth."[41] Similarly, in a mid-century essay, J. Sheridan Hogan stressed the peaceful nature of settlement in British North America. In commenting on the people who settled in Canada West, he observed, "And who and what are the people who divide among them this magnificent property? And how have they acquired it? Did they come in as conquerors, and appropriate to themselves the wealth of others? They came in but to subdue a wilderness, and have reversed the laws of conquest; for plenty, good neighbourhood, and civilization mark their footsteps."[42]

Hogan pointed to the violent upheavals that underpinned European history, and he posited that the colony's settlement represented a refuge from turmoil: "The wrongs of Princes, and the poverty of Nations, have been the chief causes of [Canada's] settlement."[43] Hogan's assertion, notwithstanding its melodramatic overtones and optimistic belief in the benefits that hard work and clean living would bring, became more pervasive as the nineteenth century unfolded. Interestingly, his ideas were echoed in another contemporary work. John McMullen's *The History of Canada, from Its First Discovery to the Present Time* emphasized the peaceful and orderly development of the colonies and highlighted the rejection of the rebellions and the embrace of Lord Durham's mission as exemplars of Canada's orderly coming of age.[44] The assumption that British North America, and then Canada, served as a beacon to peoples who sought refuge from bloodshed and the undemocratic nature of much of western Europe swiftly gained traction. Thus, the concept of the peaceable and orderly society was becoming a keystone to defining cultural identity and a compelling reason why settlers should be attracted to the British North American colonies.

The notion that Canada would represent a more peaceable alternative to European decadence and the tragically sundered United States, a country still engaged in the Civil War, was evident in the speeches of several of the Province of Canada's key political figures during the Confederation conferences and debates in 1864 and 1865.[45] Addressing the theme of harmonious relations between "Catholic and Protestant, English, French, Irish and Scotch," George-Étienne Cartier, one of the most influential francophone proponents of Confederation, envisioned a "diversity of races" that would "increase the prosperity and glory of the new Confederacy." He maintained that Canadians "were of different races, not for the purpose of warring against each other, but in order to compete and emulate for the general welfare."[46] Cartier and others saw Confederation as a way to solve the bickering and dissension that had plagued the British North American provinces earlier in the century. George Brown echoed, and expanded upon, Cartier's sentiments:

> We are striving to do peacefully and satisfactorily what Holland and Belgium, after years of strife, were unable to accomplish. We are seeking by calm discussion to settle questions that Austria and Hungary, that Denmark and Germany, that Russia and Poland, could only crush by the iron heel of armed force. We are seeking to do without foreign intervention that which deluged in blood the sunny plains of Italy. We are striving to settle forever issues hardly less momentous than those that have rent the neighboring republic and are now exposing it to all the horrors of civil war. Have we not then great cause of thankfulness that we have found a better way for the solution of our troubles than that which has entailed on other countries such deplorable results? Could the pages of history find a parallel to this?[47]

Direct comparisons with the United States, as well as warnings of imperial designs from below the border, underpinned the Confederation debates. In February 1865, Étienne-Paschal Taché addressed the ideas of American violence and echoed a cautionary note that resonated during the debates:

"We would be forced into the American union by violence, and if not by violence, would be placed upon an inclined plane which would carry us there insensibly."[48] Cartier noted the deleterious impact of violence on the American experiment, and the language of his arguments framed the underlying principle of an orderly society; Canada was born as a peaceful counterpart to the violent United States: "They had founded Federation for the purpose of carrying out and perpetuating democracy on this continent; but we, who had the benefit of being able to contemplate republicanism in action during a period of eighty years, saw its defects, and felt convinced that purely democratic institutions could not be conducive to the peace and prosperity of nations."[49] Not inconsequentially, "peace, order, and good government" has thereafter been compared with the Declaration of Independence's most cherished line: "life, liberty, and the pursuit of happiness."[50]

In the late nineteenth century, an intriguing dialogue unfolded about Canada's destiny in North America and its role, if any, in providing a model of an enlightened nation-state to the world. The American dynamic and the question of Canada's future in the British Empire framed the discussion among intellectuals. Irish-born Nicholas Flood Davin, a lawyer and newspaperman, highlighted the contributions of British civilization and constructed a comparative counterpoint to American violence. During a lecture in 1873, he took pains not to disparage his American neighbours. Nonetheless, he pressed the case for the superiority of a monarchy over the American form of elected government, which he argued had led to corruption and turmoil. He asserted that despotism was "an impossibility in Great Britain," and, in a dire warning about American might, he visualized "no moral forces that we can set against the hypothetical American despot of the future." In Canada, he maintained, a more respectful, law-abiding culture – based on the British model – had already taken root. In his estimation, British customs and not "rowdy traditions prevail."[51]

The English-born Goldwin Smith, the influential historian and political philosopher who constructed a counterpoint to the prevailing notion of a Canadian destiny that would continue to draw sustenance from the British Empire, sought to temper the stark differences between Canadians and Americans as he formulated a larger argument based on free trade and a geographic determinism that placed Canada firmly on the track of its North American destiny as an adjunct to the United States. Although he recognized the violent past of the United States, he argued that peaceful intercourse would be the hallmark of a North American union in the future: "Canada has the advantage of not having broken with her history or bearing on her political character, like the American, the trace of a revolution; but America is gradually renewing her historical associations, and since she has had herself to contend with rebellion and been threatened within by the Anarchists, the revolutionary sentiment has been losing force."[52] In an attempt to counteract the arguments of American violence, he noted: "Of conquest there is absolutely no thought. The Southern violence and the Western lawlessness which forced the Union into the War of 1812 are things of the past. The American people could not now be brought to invade the homes of an unoffending neighbor. They have no craving for more territory."[53] Today's observers would readily note Smith's deficiencies as a prognosticator of American hemispheric and global intentions, but we have the benefit of reviewing events that unfolded after the 1890s. Nonetheless, Smith's classic argument for a closer union of the two North American countries was predicated in large part on an ideal of orderly and peaceful intercourse.

In a review of Smith's book, an influential cleric and principal of Queen's University, George Monro Grant, argued that Canada's destiny was rooted to the British Empire and that it could indeed withstand a commercial and political union with the United States. In Grant's estimation, Canada's role was to provide a Christian model of peace and harmony. As historian Allan Smith argues, Grant's vision included notions that would be later defined as the ideal of order: "The vast edifice of universal peace and harmony, in whose construction Canada was to play so important a part, would finally come to rest, not on a genuinely pluralistic and synthetic foundation, but on a base provided by one civilization's view of what constituted humanity's purpose and destiny on earth."[54]

Investigators of the country's cultural issues also noted the struggle, if not the reality, of Canadians as they attempted to construct a peaceable domain with respect to law and order. The French observer André Siegfried commented extensively on the discordant relations between French and English in Canada in an oft-cited book published in 1906. Although he explored in detail the tensions between ethnic and religious groups in the country's past and present, Siegfried adopted a position that essentially supported an ideal that Canada's founders had carefully constructed and nurtured. Noting that political and cultural tranquility still eluded the grasp of Canada's leaders, he nonetheless celebrated the ways in which the country had avoided developing political parties along racial and religious divisions:

> We shall see how the Constitution of 1867, the basis of Confederation, endeavoured to combine national unity with the profound diversity of the provinces, separated as they are by distance, race, language and religion; and how rival peoples, forced by destiny to work in double harness, gradually arrived at an understanding in the fields of parliamentary business and general administration. The organization of parties upon the basis of compromise and not of racial strife will show us

> the wisdom of the leaders and the discipline of their followers. Nowhere else is the influence of British traditions to be found exerting itself more effectively or with better results.[55]

Although he concluded that the dynamic of resisting homogeneous parties for the sake of peaceful intercourse tended to make political debate lackluster, thus rendering the existing political parties "entirely harmless," Siegfried applauded the ideal of civilized discourse. Canada's phlegmatic political structure, therefore, provided a framework to avoid the "violent oppositions" of the country's past.[56] Notably, the British perspective of Canada, viewed through the lenses of numerous visitors in the late nineteenth and early twentieth centuries, also cast doubt on the universal ideal of perceiving Canada's development as orderly and benign. For many contemporary British writers, Canada's West was indeed "Wild and Wooly."[57] Thus a lively debate – one that turned in part on the principles of peaceful coexistence and the belief that Canada served as a counterweight to America and its violent tendencies – foreshadowed the historical and intellectual discussions of the twentieth century.

The aspiration that Canada's political and social experiment represented an amicable way to navigate potentially explosive differences gained more currency as the twentieth century unfolded. Intellectuals extolled the peaceful evolution of the nation-state as they considered the country's past, commented on its present, and pondered its future. This point can be most ably illustrated in the work of one of Canada's towering intellects of the late twentieth century. George Grant, a conservative professor of religion and philosophy, focused on the orderly and peaceful development of the Canadian state in his classic *Lament for Nation*. He proclaimed his fears that the Unites States had effectively triumphed in its protracted struggle to absorb Canada. "To be a Canadian," Grant asserted, "was to build a more ordered and stable society than the liberal experiment in the United States."[58] Through his interpretation of this profound distinction, he enunciated the positive ramifications of conducting an orderly society on a national scale: "The early leaders of British North America identified the lack of public and personal restraint with the democratic Republic. Their conservatism was essentially the social doctrine that public order and tradition, in contrast to freedom and experiment, were central to the good life ... In our early expansions, this conservative nationalism expressed itself in the use of public control in the political and economic spheres."[59]

Numerous academics wrestled with the ways in which the peace, order, and good government trope – and its "peaceable kingdom" corollary – shaped historiography.[60] Evidence strongly suggests that the peaceable kingdom myth, despite the anachronistic elements of its creation and emergence, essentially became synonymous with the peace, order, and good government ideal of the nineteenth century. By the late twentieth century, the peaceable kingdom ideal, as one scholar nimbly observed, had become "an anonymous unit of Canadian cultural currency."[61] As another academic maintained, historians often tend to choose subjects that "reinforce the great theme of Canadian history – the eventful but peaceful evolution of a Canadian nation based on a spirit of order and compromise."[62] R.C. Macleod reiterated this point in his introduction to a series of essays on criminal justice in Canada. He noted, and this was surprising given the importance attached to the criminal code by the Fathers of Confederation, that historians had consistently overlooked the subject of criminal behaviour in Canada's past. Although he did not explicitly delve into the reasons for this oversight, he implied that the avoidance was shaped by an overarching dedication to understanding the more flattering ethos of "peace, order, and good government."[63]

The overarching ideal of an orderly and peaceable society, with deep roots in the political debates and social milieu of the nineteenth century, has lost some if its luster.[64] There is little doubt that by 2019 those ideals or myths have become shopworn, or even debunked. For example, the acceptance and adaptation of those ideals varied greatly across the country and over time. The research avenues and sources for this study overwhelmingly reflect the orientation of political and intellectual elites from Ontario and anglophones in the Maritimes. Diverse political, social, and ethnic groups within those locations, as well as from other regions of Canada, would almost certainly temper or reject the more positivist components of the peace and order memes. Moreover, post-9/11 concerns with global terrorism, seemingly endless conflicts in the Middle East, unresolved and often contentious issues regarding land and social issues with Indigenous nations, and a more overt martial posturing and branding of modern Canadian nationalism during Stephen Harper's government (2006–15) exposed the myth of a uniform and unquestioned acceptance of the utility of the peace, order, and good government ideal in characterizing the country's national identity. Nonetheless, compelling evidence suggests that the phrase's sentiments continue to shape Canadian cultural perceptions and inform the scholarship of historians and social scientists.[65] For British North American and early Confederation eras, a case can be advanced that many Canadian elites sought to construct and nurture a durable – if not overwrought – tenet of national identity: the abiding respect for order, law, and peaceful behaviour. As they did so, they buttressed state authority, vigorously repressed dissent, and facilitated colonization that eroded the rights of Indigenous peoples. The impact of those aspirations on ordinary Canadians, including the often deleterious consequences of the hierarchical enforcement of a liberal order, is ably explored by the other contributors to this volume of essays.

NOTES

1 Portions of this chapter appear in Scott W. See, "The Intellectual Construction of Canada's 'Peaceable Kingdom' Ideal," *Journal of Canadian Studies* 52, no. 2 (Spring 2018): 510–37 (https://doi.org/10.3138/jcs.2017-0067.r1). Reprinted with permission from University of Toronto Press (https://utpjournals.press), ©2018 University of Toronto Press.
2 Rudyard Kipling, *Letters to the Family: Notes on a Recent Trip to Canada* (Toronto: Macmillan, 1908), 33–4.
3 Ibid., 68–9.
4 Historian Ian McKay convincingly argues that Canada's nineteenth-century political and social landscapes were contradictory and complicated, yet the country effectively became an archetype of the new liberal order. See "The Liberal Order Framework: A Prospectus for a Reconnaissance of Canadian History," *Canadian Historical Review* 81, no. 4 (December 2000): 616–78.
5 An excellent collection of essays that focus on the construction of a liberal order is Allan Greer and Ian Radforth, eds, *Colonial Leviathan: State Formation in Mid-Nineteenth-Century Canada* (Toronto: University of Toronto Press, 1992).
6 For a compelling analysis of the ideological parameters and conflicts that shaped the early development of British North America, see Michel Ducharme, *The Idea of Liberty in Canada during the Age of Atlantic Revolutions, 1776–1838* (Montreal and Kingston: McGill-Queen's University Press, 2014).
7 Journalists and other writers promulgated the ideals of peace and order as well, and the venues of newspapers, periodicals, and books merit attention. Given this chapter's overarching focus on the more formalized and elite aspects of the construction of national identity in the nineteenth century, however, a thorough analysis of those sources would necessitate a separate research project.
8 The author is mindful of Eric Hobsbawm's maxim that nationalism comes before nations. See *Nations and Nationalism since 1780: Programme, Myth, Reality* (Cambridge: Cambridge University Press, 1990), 10.
9 This borrows from Robert Wiebe's imaginative work on middle-class life in *The Search for Order, 1877–1920* (New York: Hill and Wang, 1967).
10 For a discussion of the relationship between the British imperial connection and a focus on order as an antidote to American cultural influences, see Carl Berger, *The Sense of Power: Studies in the Ideas of Canadian Imperialism, 1867–1914* (Toronto: University of Toronto Press, 1970). See also S.F. Wise, *God's Peculiar Peoples: Essays on Political Culture in Nineteenth-Century Canada*, ed. A.B. McKillop and Paul Romney (Ottawa: Carleton University Press, 1993); and Ramsay Cook, *Canada, Quebec, and the Uses of Nationalism* (Toronto: McClelland and Stewart, 1986). For the quintessential argument promoting the superior achievement of

Confederation, see Donald Creighton, *Canada's First Century, 1867–1967* (Toronto: Macmillan, 1970). The western expansion ideal and the Mountie myth are treated in Daniel Francis, *National Dreams: Myth, Memory, and Canadian History* (Vancouver: Arsenal Pulp Press, 1997), esp. 30. See also Keith Walden, *Visions of Order: The Canadian Mounties in Symbol and Myth* (Toronto: Butterworth, 1982), 8–9; and Doug Owram, *Promise of Eden: The Canadian Expansionist Movement and the Idea of the West, 1856–1900* (Toronto: University of Toronto Press, 1980).

11 For overviews of the revolutionary era, see Eric J. Hobsbawm, *The Age of Revolution, 1789–1848* (New York: New American Library, 1962); and Charles Tilly and Louise Tilly, *The Rebellious Century, 1830–1930* (Cambridge, MA: Harvard University Press, 1975). For a discussion of the literature on ethnic and religious clashes, consult Scott W. See, "Nineteenth-Century Collective Violence: Toward a North American Context," *Labour/Le travail* 39 (Spring 1997): 13–38, and Scott W. See, "'An Unprecedented Influx': Nativism and Irish Famine Immigration to Canada," *American Review of Canadian Studies* 30, no. 4 (Winter 2000): 429–53.

12 Janet Ajzenstat, *The Canadian Founding: John Locke and Parliament* (Montreal and Kingston: McGill-Queen's University Press, 2007), 63.

13 Col. Arthur Rankin, 10 March 1865, in *Parliamentary Debates on the Subject of the Confederation of the British North American Provinces* (Quebec: Hunter, Rose, 1865), 913.

14 Although this point is laden with the Whig interpretation of history that venerates liberty and democratic institutions, this essay is not intended to buttress that perspective. Beyond question, however, the viewpoints of many of the politicians and intellectuals cited in this study were grounded in this "Whiggish" orientation. For a thoughtful assessment of these issues, see John W. Burrow, *A Liberal Descent: Victorian Historians and the English Past* (Cambridge: Cambridge University Press, 1981), esp. 3.

15 One scholar even dubbed the phrase a "Canadian obsession." See George A. Rawlyk, *Wrapped Up in God: A Study of Several Canadian Revivals and Revivalists* (Burlington, ON: Welch Publishing, 1988), xiv.

16 It is likely that the phrase was commonly used in administrative documents in the eighteenth-century British Empire. Perhaps more importantly, there is no evidence to suggest that ideals embedded in the phrase were meant to apply exclusively to British North America.

17 Copy of Instructions for James Murray, Esquire, Governor of the Province of Quebec, dated 7 December 1763, in *Papers Relative to the Province of Quebec*, 21 April 1791 [Canadian Institute for Historical Microproductions, no. 40082].

18 An Act for the Union of Canada, Nova Scotia, and New Brunswick, and the Government thereof; and the Purposes connected therewith, 29 March 1867, s. 91.

19 Extract of the Instructions to John Parr, Esquire, Captain General and Governor in Chief of the Province of Nova Scotia, and the Islands of St John and Cape Breton,

dated 11 September 1784, in *Papers Relative to the Re-Annexation of the Island of Cape Breton to the Government of Nova Scotia* (London: House of Commons, 1823).

20 Petition from the Inhabitants of the Island of Cape Breton, in the Appendix to *Journal and Proceedings of Her Majesty's Legislative Council of the Province of Nova Scotia [Second Session]* (Halifax, 1844), 9.

21 For two examples, see An Act to Provide for the Government of British Columbia, 2 August 1858, and "Proclamation by His Excellency James Douglas, Governor and Commander-in-Chief of Her Majesty's Colony of British Columba and Its Dependencies," 22 December 1858.

22 An Act for the Temporary Government of Rupert's Land and the North-Western Territory When United with Canada, 22 June 1869.

23 Ajzenstat, *The Canadian Founding*, 81.

24 *Lord Durham's Report on the Affairs of British North America*, ed. Sir Charles Lucas, vol. 2 (Oxford: Clarendon Press, 1912), esp. 116–33, 183–4.

25 These themes are more thoroughly addressed in the author's monograph, *Affront to Peace and Order: Collective Violence in Nineteenth-Century Canada* (Toronto: University of Toronto Press, forthcoming). The most important grist for the book is a database of over four hundred riots that the author has constructed from primary and secondary sources, including government, military, and judicial records; newspapers; correspondence; and the personal papers of contemporaries. Important categories of violence include movements in opposition to immigration (nativism), religious conflict, political turmoil, racial confrontations, labour struggles, and vigilantism.

26 A more detailed discussion of the challenges of defining riots can be found in the author's *Riots in New Brunswick: Orange Nativism and Social Violence in the 1840s* (Toronto: University of Toronto Press, 1993), 7–8; and Paul A. Gilje, *Rioting in America* (Bloomington: Indiana University Press), 4–6.

27 An Act to Amend or Consolidate the Criminal Law of this Province, No. 11, 3rd Session, 3rd Parl., 13 Vic., 1850 (Toronto: Lovell and Gibson, 1850), 43–4; and W.C. Keele, *The Provincial Justice, or Magistrate's Manual, Being a Complete Digest of the Criminal Law of Canada* (Toronto: Henry Rowsell, 1858), 736–9.

28 An Act to Amend or Consolidate the Criminal Law, 44.

29 Ibid., 44–5.

30 Keele, *The Provincial Justice* 736–9; An Act to Amend or Consolidate the Criminal Law, 46.

31 An Act to Amend or Consolidate the Criminal Law, 45.

32 Ibid.

33 See Cap. LXX, An Act Respecting Riots and Riotous Assemblies, 22 May 1868, in *Statutes of Canada Passed in the Session Held in the Thirty-First Year of the Reign of Her Majesty Queen Victoria* (Ottawa: Malcolm Cameron, 1968), 283–6.

34 For a cogent assessment of the relationship between military and civil authorities, see Elinor Kyte Senior, *British Regulars in Montreal: An Imperial Garrison, 1832–1854* (Montreal and Kingston: McGill-Queen's University Press, 1981).

35 See the extensive rules governing this relationship in *Extracts from General Orders for the Guidance of the Troops, in Affording Aid to the Civil Power* (Quebec: Gilbert Stanley, 1851).

36 *Extracts from General Orders for the Guidance of Troops in Affording Aid to the Civil Power* (Quebec: G.T. Cary, 1868). For an analysis of the role of the militia in maintaining civil order, see Desmond Morton, "Aid to the Civil Power: The Canadian Militia in Support of Social Order," *Canadian Historical Review* 51, no. 4 (December 1970): 407–25.

37 John A. Macdonald, 6 February 1865, in *Parliamentary Debates on the Subject of the Confederation of the British North American Provinces, 3rd session, 8th Provincial Parliament of Canada* (Quebec: Hunter, Rose & Co., Parliamentary Printers, 1865), 44.

38 Janet Ajzenstat, Paul Romney, Ian Gentles, and William D. Gairdner, eds, *Canada's Founding Debates* (Toronto: Stoddart, 1999), 115. Brown's own prejudices and provocative behaviour make this point somewhat ironic. For the classic two-volume biography of the journalist and politician, see J.M.S. Careless, *Brown of the Globe* (Toronto: Macmillan, 1960, 1963).

39 George-Étienne Cartier, 7 February 1865, in *Parliamentary Debates on the Subject of the Confederation of the British North American Provinces*, 60. Nonetheless, Cartier applauded the benefits that a variety of racial and religious groups could bring to nation building.

40 John A. Macdonald, 6 February 1865, in *Parliamentary Debates on the Subject of the Confederation of the British North American Provinces*, 40–1.

41 Lt. Col. George T. Denison, "Presidential Address," in *Transactions of the Royal Society of Canada*, 2nd series, vol. 10 (Ottawa, 1904), reprinted in L.F.S. Upton, ed., *The United Empire Loyalists: Men and Myths* (Toronto: Copp Clark, 1967), 140.

42 J. Sheridan Hogan, *Canada: An Essay* (Montreal: B. Dawson, 1855), 8. The notion that the North American landscape constituted a wilderness is extremely problematic because it ignores the Indigenous presence. See the contributions of Thomas Peace, Émilie Pigeon and Carolyn Podruchny, Max Hamon, and John Reid in this volume for cogent studies of settler colonialism and Indigenous resistance to dispossession and cultural assaults.

43 Ibid., 8.

44 M. Brook Taylor, *Promoters, Patriots, and Partisans: Historiography in Nineteenth-Century English Canada* (Toronto: University of Toronto Press, 1989), 161. See John Mercier McMullen, *The History of Canada, from Its First Discovery to the Present Time* (Brockville, ON: J. McMullen, 1855). The impulse to establish and

maintain orderly colonies clearly shaped the British imperial design, so the British North American case would benefit from a comparative study of the empire's colonies that situates order, unrest, and violence at the analytical core.

45 David Chennells argued that Confederation served as a form of conflict resolution, in *The Politics of Nationalism in Canada: Cultural Conflict since 1760* (Toronto: University of Toronto Press, 2001), 131–2.

46 George-Étienne Cartier, 7 February 1865, in *Parliamentary Debates on the Subject of the Confederation of the British North American Provinces*, 60; and P.B. Waite, ed., *The Confederation Debates in the Province of Canada, 1865* (Montreal and Kingston: McGill-Queen's University Press, 2006), 51.

47 Waite, *The Confederation Debates*, 58.

48 Étienne-Paschal Taché, 3 February 1865, in *Parliamentary Debates on the Subject of the Confederation of the British North American Provinces*, 6.

49 George-Étienne Cartier, 7 February 1865, in *Parliamentary Debates on the Subject of the Confederation of the British North American Provinces*, 59.

50 This raises interesting questions about the centrality of liberalism and Toryism to the development of the two North American nations. For insightful discussions of these themes, see H.D. Forbes, "Hartz-Horowitz at Twenty: Nationalism, Toryism, and Socialism in Canada and the United States," *Canadian Journal of Political Science* 20, no. 2 (June 1987): 287–315; and Irving Lois Horowitz, "Louis Hartz and the Liberal Tradition: From Consensus to Crack-up," *Modern Age: A Conservative Review* 47, no. 3 (Summer 2005): 201–9.

51 Nicholas Flood Davin, *British versus American Civilization: A Lecture* (Toronto: Adam, Stevenson, 1873), 23, 24, 28.

52 Goldwin Smith, *Canada and the Canadian Question* (London: Macmillan, 1891), 272.

53 Ibid., 276.

54 Allan Smith, *Canada: An American Nation? Essays on Continentalism, Identity, and the Canadian Frame of Mind* (Montreal and Kingston: McGill-Queen's University Press, 1994), 378.

55 André Siegfried, *The Race Question in Canada* (Toronto: McClelland and Stewart, 1966), 16.

56 Ibid., 113–14.

57 For an insightful assessment of the British literary viewpoint of Canada in this era, see R.G. Moyles and Doug Owram, *Imperial Dreams and Colonial Realities: British Views of Canada, 1880–1914* (Toronto: University of Toronto Press, 1988).

58 George Grant, *Lament for a Nation: The Defeat of Canadian Nationalism* (Toronto: McClelland and Stewart, 1965), 4.

59 Ibid., 71.

60 Northrop Frye, an influential academic and critic, is often credited with advancing the peaceable kingdom ideal. In the penetrating conclusion to a *Literary History of Canada*, he discussed the country's search for a social ideal, which he defined as a "pastoral myth" with a "nostalgia for a world of peace and protection." See *The Bush Garden: Essays on the Canadian Imagination* (Toronto: Anansi Press, 1971), 238–9. See also William Kilbourn, ed., *Canada: A Guide to the Peaceable Kingdom* (Toronto: Macmillan, 1970). For an interesting discussion of the relationship between English-Canadian nationalism and the American model, see Ryan Edwardson, "'Kicking Uncle Sam Out of the Peaceable Kingdom': English-Canadian 'New Nationalism' and Americanization," *Journal of Canadian Studies* 37, no. 4 (Winter 2003): 131–50.

61 Philip Kokotailo, "Creating the Peaceable Kingdom: Edward Hicks, Northrop Frye, and Joe Clark," in *Creating the Peaceable Kingdom and Other Essays on Canada*, ed. Victor Howard (East Lansing: Michigan State University Press, 1998), 9.

62 Irving Abella, ed., *On Strike: Six Key Labour Struggles in Canada, 1919–1949* (Toronto: James Lewis and Samuel, 1974), xi.

63 R.C. McLeod, ed., *Lawful Authority: Readings on the History of Criminal Justice in Canada* (Toronto: Copp Clark Pitman, 1988).

64 For an exploration into the role of historians, intellectuals, and politicians in defining and critiquing the peaceable kingdom myth, see the author's "The Intellectual Construction of Canada's 'Peaceable Kingdom' Ideal," 510–37. The utility of the myth as an accurate metaphor for events in Canadian history, as well as a robust critique of the martial posturing of Stephen Harper's government in the early twenty-first century, can be found in Ian McKay and Jamie Swift, *Warrior Nation: Rebranding Canada in an Age of Anxiety* (Toronto: Between the Lines, 2012). For a decidedly different interpretation of the evolution and meaning of the peace, order, and good government trope, see John Ralston Saul, *A Fair Country* (Toronto: Viking Canada, 2008), esp. 111–40.

65 The same point can be made regarding the peaceable kingdom myth. Scholars continue to invoke the ideal for a ready frame of reference – often with the suggestion that it holds merit – and then critique or question its applicability. Examples range from scholarly works to popular tracts. For a recent example, see Dimitri Anastakis, *Death in the Peaceable Kingdom: Canadian History since 1867 through Murder, Execution, Assassination, and Suicide* (Toronto: University of Toronto Press, 2015). The author acknowledges Jerry Bannister's intriguing argument that "sentiment" might be a useful descriptor of the driving force behind the Confederation debates and Canada's search for order.

2 Loyalty, Order, and Quebec's Catholic Hierarchy, 1763–1867

D.C. BÉLANGER

After the Conquest, various policies designed to hamper the practice of Roman Catholicism in Quebec were central to British plans to assimilate the Canadiens. The British focused their efforts on Protestantizing the Canadiens, rather than on anglicizing them, because religious practice and identity were regarded as paramount before the twentieth century. However, in spite of their efforts to suppress the Catholic Church, British officials also believed that they could govern Quebec with the active collaboration of the clergy, which they sought and readily obtained. The clergy indeed played a key role in fostering the general acceptance of British rule that gradually came about in late eighteenth-century Quebec and that facilitated the colony's integration into the British Empire. Much like under the French regime, the Catholic clergy acted as the administrative and political auxiliaries of the colonial state under the British.

As part of this process, the clergy developed a loyalist discourse that urged French-speaking Catholics to accept and, later, to celebrate British rule. This discourse was present in clerical thought and writing for over a century, and it was especially prevalent among the higher clergy, whose responsibilities often required close interaction with British officials.[1] Many of these officials understood that clerical loyalty was a pillar of British rule, and they frequently turned to the clergy for support. In the context of the British regime, loyalty implied a faithfulness to the Crown. It could be active, expressing itself through a willingness to uphold and defend British rule, or passive, which involved eschewing movements that sought to undermine British power. In this sense, both the Canadiens who fought against the invading Americans in 1775–6 and those who merely refused to join or aid the rebels can equally be considered to have expressed their loyalty to the Crown.

Loyalism, by contrast, is a positive doctrine. It is the reasoned expression of the idea of loyalty and, in French Canada, it expressed a sincere devotion to the

Crown, to British rule, and to British institutions. It rested first and foremost on the idea that the British Conquest had been providential in nature; that it had been ordained by God and had proven to be a fortunate event. Loyalists also believed that the British authorities acted with reasonable munificence and that British political institutions were superior not only to the various republican systems that arose in continental Europe and the Americas but also to those of pre-revolutionary France.

Loyalism was first articulated by the clergy and the seigneurial class, and it was integral to nascent French-Canadian conservatism in the 1770s. However, as Jerry Bannister has noted, "loyalty to the Crown encompassed different political traditions" in British North America and it was not synonymous with reaction.[2] Indeed, by the beginning of the nineteenth century, a liberal loyalism was fast developing among the French-Canadian bourgeoisie and, for a time, a loyalist consensus characterized French Canada's middle and upper classes. This consensus was thrown into disarray in the 1830s, but loyalism remained present in liberal and conservative thought until the late nineteenth century, when the rise of imperialism in Britain and English-speaking Canada began to seriously undermine loyalist discourse in French Canada. Loyalist sentiment declined sharply during the conscription crisis of the First World War and had more or less disappeared by the Quiet Revolution. The Roman Catholic clergy's last great act of loyalty occurred in September 1914, when the bishops of Quebec issued a pastoral letter "sur les devoirs des catholiques dans la guerre actuelle."

The nature and intensity of loyalism differed significantly in English- and French-speaking Canada, and the loyalists of Quebec should not be confused with the United Empire Loyalists of Upper Canada and New Brunswick. The former adhered in a general sense to a doctrine, while the latter were a socio-political group born out of the turmoil of the American Revolution. As Donal Lowry notes, French Canadians can be counted among the "ethnic outsiders" of the British Empire; their loyalism could not contain an ethnic and racial element, and its religious component could not be based on a shared faith.[3] French Canadians could participate in the British imperial project, but only in an ancillary sense, and they were ultimately far more likely to suffer than to perpetrate British colonialism. And yet, loyalty to Britain was among the hallmarks of conservative thought in Quebec for well over a century. Even Henri Bourassa, the consummate anti-imperialist, admired British institutions and regarded the British Conquest as ultimately beneficial for French Canada.[4]

French-Canadian loyalists articulated a vision of Britishness that was essentially civic in character. Bourassa, for instance, was fond of referring to Canada as a "British community," by which he meant that the dominion was an

(Anglo-French) state whose fundamental institutions and liberties were British in nature. He believed, moreover, that "the very basis of our British institutions" rested not on racial or religious precepts but rather on the idea "that there shall be perfect equality before the law for all nationalities and for all religions."[5] This conception of Britishness was not widely shared among English-speaking Canadians, who tended to regard Canada's status as a "British community" as implying that the dominion was to be a Protestant and English-speaking nation, one whose leading citizens should be of British birth or ancestry. This logic was deployed relentlessly during the Jesuit Estates controversy, and also during the schools crises in Manitoba and Ontario, so that by the end of the First World War it had become painfully evident in Quebec that civic notions of Britishness were not likely to prevail in Canada. Loyalist sentiment withered accordingly.

The story of French-Canadian loyalism in many ways mirrors the Catholic experience in nineteenth-century Ireland, Scotland, and Newfoundland, where the clergy also generally upheld British rule. Moreover, as historian C.A. Bayly noted, "Irish patriots were desperate to reap the benefits of imperial expansion while Irish soldiers and savants were in the front-line of empire-building. In short, Irish nationalism arose from Ireland's perceived exclusion from empire, not her inclusion within it."[6] I would not follow Bayly and argue that French-Canadian nationalism emerged as a result of Quebec's exclusion from empire – French Canadians did not participate in the British imperial project nearly to the extent that the Irish did – but there is no doubt that the decline of French-Canadian loyalism was tied to the failure of civic notions of Britishness in late nineteenth- and early twentieth-century Canada.

Recent scholarly commentary on French-Canadian loyalism is reasonably sparse, which may be attributed to the doctrine's disappearance and current irrelevance within Quebec's intellectual debates. This was certainly not always the case, and the first scholars to examine loyalism were quite passionate about its role in Quebec history. For Thomas Chapais, who was in fact the last great exponent of the loyalist tradition in French Canada, the loyalism of Quebec's upper classes was the mainstay of order and British rule in the colony; it had prevented annexation and revolution on more than one occasion. Chapais furthermore believed that loyalty and patriotism were compatible. "Par une heureuse rencontre," he wrote in 1921, "il se trouvait que ce loyalisme inattaquable nous offrait un merveilleux point d'appui pour la défense de nos droits."[7]

Nationalist scholars disagreed. Among them, Lionel Groulx was no doubt the most caustic critic of loyalism. His early work was fiercely critical of the doctrine, which he regarded as one of the great ailments that afflicted French-Canadian political culture. He believed that the loyalty shown by the seigneurial class to the British Crown was nothing less than servility and that it had contributed to weakening the French-Canadian nation. The continuous betrayal of French Canada's lay elite is a recurring theme in Groulx's work. He argued in *Vers l'émancipation* (1921), for instance, that the seigneurs had acted, as a group, "avec ardeur, non pas tant au service de la patrie, qu'au service de George III."[8] Groulx was reasonably forgiving when it came to clerical loyalism, however. He believed that the clergy had been placed in a difficult position by the advent of British rule, that its loyalism had emerged under duress, and that it had not prevented leading clerics from lobbying London for greater freedom.

By the 1960s, few scholars were inclined to justify or excuse clerical loyalism. Anticlericalism was ascendant, and radicals like Pierre Vallières accused the clergy of having "collaborated" with the British, a term that of course had acquired a very sinister connotation during the Second World War.[9] A similar assessment of clerical loyalism can be found in the most recent work devoted to the subject, Adrien Thério's 1999 anthology of the loyalist *mandements* issued by Quebec's bishops. Thério, a literary scholar and notorious anticlerical, used the word "collusion" to describe the relationship between the clergy and the British authorities and implied that Quebec society would have been better off if London had shut down the Catholic Church in the eighteenth century.[10]

Recent scholarship on French-Canadian Catholicism has proved more indulgent of clerical loyalty. In his last great work, *Genèse de la société québécoise* (1993), sociologist Fernand Dumont noted that loyalism's roots could be traced to "la parenté des régimes monarchiques et des hiérarchies ecclésiastiques," but he also insisted that the church had actively sought to regain its autonomy in the face of British pressure. He argued that the ultramontane tradition in French-Canadian Catholicism expressed a long-standing desire to be free from state dominance, which the church had experienced under both the British and the French regimes.[11] Likewise, the authoritative *Histoire du catholicisme québécois* (1984–91) insists that there were clerical efforts to free the church from British oversight. Expressions of loyalty were sincere, since they voiced "le dogme de l'autorité établie par la volonté divine," but they should be understood as part of a complex strategy to ensure "la liberté de l'Église catholique."[12]

Most recent writing on Quebec during the "revolutionary era" tends to focus on conceptions of republicanism, liberty, and *américanité*.[13] My work seeks to include French Canada into the wider historiography of loyalism, which embraces the British Atlantic as a whole, and to better integrate the concept of loyalty into Quebec historical writing. Post-Conquest Quebec was not merely British by right; French Canadians participated in a loyalist framework that, according to Jerry Bannister, structured British North American political culture.[14] And loyalism in French Canada was not confined to the clerical hierarchy of the late eighteenth and early nineteenth centuries. It was expressed in liberal and constitutional discourse, as well as in conservative and traditionalist thought and writing. Even French-Canadian ultramontanism, which developed, among other reasons, as a reaction to British attempts to subjugate the Roman Catholic Church, could express loyalist notions. Quebec's two great ultramontane bishops, Msgrs. Ignace Bourget and Louis-François Laflèche, praised British institutions and regarded British power as a bulwark against annexation and upheaval.

Clerical loyalism expressed a complex and sometimes contradictory set of motivations. Yvan Lamonde perhaps put it best when he wrote that the Roman Catholic Church had followed a policy of loyalty "par conviction et par intérêt."[15] The church's woes under the British Regime are well documented, and I do not wish to delve too deeply into the factors that *forced* the clergy to cooperate with the British authorities.[16] Instead, I intend to explore the underlying convictions that fostered loyalty among the clergy.

To this end, I have examined the *mandements* and the circular and pastoral letters of the bishops of Quebec issued between the Conquest and Confederation that relate to British rule. These were public documents meant, for the most part, to be read out loud during church services; they reflected the official stance of the church on various matters, especially current events, but they could be issued under some measure of duress. For instance, Msgr. Briand's May 1775 *mandement* "au sujet de l'invasion des Américains" was originally intended to be a mere *lettre circulaire* until Governor Carleton pressed for a more authoritative statement to be issued.[17] For this reason, the *mandements* and *lettres* have been examined alongside relevant correspondence and secondary sources.

From the Conquest to Confederation, *mandements* and pastoral letters reveal a clerical hierarchy that increasingly regarded Britain as an ally in upholding Quebec's Catholic social order, most notably in the face of republicanism and revolutionary turmoil. By Catholic social order, I mean a social, legal, and political order structured according to Christian principles, and one in which the Roman Catholic Church plays a leading role – an order that likewise repudiates secularism and moral relativism. In the 1760s, assertions of loyalty rested on basic biblical principles; within a decade, however, leading clerics began to develop a more profound doctrine of loyalism, one which would persist in clerical writing for over a century.

As others have noted, the loyalty of the clergy can be attributed both to conviction and realism. Catholic doctrine advocates the submission to God's will and to legitimate authority. The church hierarchy in Quebec interpreted the British Conquest as divinely ordained and, once it became apparent that

London would not deport the Canadien population or outlaw Catholicism, the clergy began to preach submission to the British Crown. The clergy also viewed the power of the British authorities as divinely sanctioned. In Catholic doctrine, authority is sanctioned by God, and to refuse to submit to legitimate authority is to refuse submission to God.

Even before the formal cession of Canada, the higher clergy had called upon its flock to submit to British rule. In a *mandement* dated 14 February 1762, Jean-Olivier Briand, general vicar and future bishop of Quebec, quoted from the epistles of Peter and Paul, which would often be cited by the clergy to justify British rule. "Le Dieu des armées qui dispose à son gré des couronnes," he wrote, had decided that Canada was to fall "sous la domination de Sa Majesté Britannique." He reminded his flock that Saint Peter, "le prince des apôtres, dans sa première Épître ordonne d'être soumis au Roi et à tous ceux qui participent à son autorité," and he noted that Saint Paul had called upon Christians to honour and respect their sovereigns. There was little doubt in Briand's mind that British rule was divinely ordained and thus legitimate, and he ordered that prayers for the king said during Mass be amended to specifically refer to King George III.[18]

But the clergy's loyalty also reflected the Catholic Church's vulnerability in the face of British power. After the Conquest, the institution's legal status was in limbo. The British governor interfered with clerical appointments, and various restrictions were placed on clerical recruitment and on relations with France and Rome. The Crown had also interfered with clerical appointments during the French regime, but the long-standing Gallican policies of a Catholic monarchy were no doubt regarded as less invasive by the church than those formulated by a Protestant power.

Moreover, the church's title over its extensive property was not fully recognized by the colonial authorities. The Crown seized the Jesuit estates, for instance, in 1800. The clergy thus preached loyalty to Britain, in part, because it wished to ingratiate itself to the colonial authorities in the hope that London would eliminate or at least mitigate the various measures that constrained Catholicism in Quebec. Many clerics also reasoned that anything less than open loyalty would result in further constraints.

Clerical loyalism intensified after the 1774 Quebec Act expanded Catholic rights, and it intensified further still during the American and French Revolutions, when the divine nature of the British Conquest became more readily apparent to many clerics. It was assumed that British power protected Quebec from annexation and that the Conquest had spared the province the horrors of the French Revolution. Clerical loyalism thus acquired a new dimension. It no longer simply reflected basic theological imperatives and strategic calculations; leading clerics increasingly regarded British power and institutions as a means to uphold a Catholic social order in Quebec.

In the early 1770s, religious indifference was a growing problem in the colony. Sunday services were sparsely attended, and the Catholic Church, as an institution, was in shambles. Its financial situation was dire and future status uncertain. The Quebec Act brought with it the promise of redress, but the rebel invasion that soon followed struck fear in the heart of the clergy. The rebels held "des motifs qui choquent la raison, la justice, l'équité, l'ordre établi," wrote Msgr. Briand. Revolution, to be sure, represented a far more immediate threat to Quebec's Catholic social order than did religious indifference. The rebels proposed to abolish tithing and seigneurialism and sought to establish a secular and republican system of government in the St Lawrence valley. Moreover, noted the bishop of Quebec in a 1776 *mandement*, "nulle autre secte n'a persécuté les romains comme celle des Bostonnais."[19] The rebels threatened to upend the religious, social, and political order of Quebec, but British power had held back the tide of revolution.

Once the rebels had evacuated the province, Msgr. Briand made the return to Catholic communion for French Canadians who had supported invasion, whom he considered heretics, conditional on a royal pardon.[20] The bishop collaborated with the colonial authorities in repressing sedition and found the British to be effective allies in maintaining a Catholic social order. He successfully lobbied Governor Haldimand to close the republican *Gazette littéraire de Montréal*, for instance. Already, in late 1768, Msgr. Briand had convinced Governor Carleton to limit the number of cabarets in Quebec.[21]

Given the ambivalence expressed by many French Canadians towards the invading rebels, which Jeffers Lennox examines in his piece later in this volume, some clerics came to regard the British authorities as more politically reliable than was the general population. By the 1780s, they began to argue that the relationship between Quebec's Catholic Church and the British Crown had become symbiotic. In a 1787 address to Prince William Henry (the future William IV), whose naval vessel HMS *Pegasus* was visiting Quebec, the leading clerics of the city described the reciprocal nature of this relationship:

> Le zèle du Corps Ecclésiastique pour les intérêts de Sa Majesté reçoit une nouvelle activité par la présence de Son Auguste Fils; elle lui rappelle la protection condescendante dont le Roi a jusqu'ici favorisé la Communion Catholique et le Clergé qui la maintient. Si les principes rigoureux en ce point de cette communion ont contribué pour quelque chose à conserver la fidélité due à Sa Majesté, qui peut douter que réciproquement les bontés de Sa Majesté n'aient concouru à affermir pour toujours dans tous les cœurs catholiques les mêmes principes si favorables à l'État?[22]

The French Revolution furthered this logic among the clergy. Msgr. Joseph-Octave Plessis, bishop of Quebec from 1806 to 1825, argued, for instance, that the interests of the Catholics of Lower Canada "n'étaient pas distingués de ceux de la Grande-Bretagne."[23] His predecessor, Msgr. Pierre Denaut, did not hesitate to refer to the French as "nos ennemis" in a 1798 *mandement* celebrating the British victory in the Battle of Aboukir Bay, and to insist that God "s'est déclaré pour la justice de notre cause. Il a exaucé les vœux de son people, qui le priait d'humilier cette nation superbe qui ne veut que la guerre: Ps. 67. *dissipa gentes quae bella volunt.*"[24]

The advent of the French Revolution underscored the providential nature of the British Conquest. Clerics argued with increasing frequency that the Conquest was part of a divine plan to preserve Catholicism in Quebec. The French, like the American rebels before them, were portrayed as the agents not only of political mayhem but also of religious and social disorder. Revolutionary France, argued Msgr. Denaut in 1802, sought "la destruction de tous les trônes et de tous les autels." The clergy not only embraced and, indeed, celebrated British rule, it now clearly regarded British power as integral to the maintenance of Quebec's Catholic social order. Increasingly, official clerical documents referred to the protective nature of British rule. Msgr. Denaut exhorted his flock to remember, in the context of the Napoleonic Wars, that Lower Canada's peace and stability was not only the result of Divine Providence but also owed much to British power:

> ... en louant les bontés du Seigneur, n'oublions jamais qu'après lui nous devons cette longue suite de prospérités au monarque bienfaisant qui nous gouverne, à la nation généreuse qui nous protège; n'oublions jamais que tandis que nous jouissions dans nos foyers, de la sécurité la plus parfaite, le sang britannique coulait sur les champs de bataille pour protéger nos jours, que tandis que nous recueillons paisiblement les fruits de nos moissons et les richesses de notre commerce, les trésors de la mère-patrie s'épuisaient pour garantir nos propriétés; n'oublions jamais des bienfaits si signalés, et que nos vœux les plus ardents pour notre Auguste Souverain se mêlent aux actions de grâces que nous rendons à Dieu pour le don précieux de la paix.[25]

During the War of 1812, the protective nature of British rule was highlighted with even greater enthusiasm. Leading clerics by then regarded British power not only as integral to Lower Canadian order and stability but also as a global force for order and righteousness, indeed as a bulwark against global radicalism. In an 1812 *mandement*, which was issued at the prompting of Governor General Prévost, Msgr. Plessis mocked the ineptness of the

American military and praised God for Lower Canada's status as a British possession:

> Peut-être, Nos Très Chers Frères, qu'à nulle autre époque avant celle-ci, vous n'avez senti, comme vous le faites, combien la Divine Providence a été libérale envers vous, lorsqu'elle a permis que vous devinssiez sujets d'un gouvernement protecteur de votre sûreté, de votre religion, de vos fortunes; d'un gouvernement qui seul a su maintenir son honneur et sa gloire au milieu des débris de tous les autres; d'un gouvernement auprès duquel les peuples opprimés, les souverains détrônés, les victimes sans nombre de l'ambition et de la perfidie d'un conquérant insatiable, viennent chercher un asile et des moyens de recouvrer leur liberté ravie ou de défendre le peu qu'il en reste.[26]

Clerical loyalty reached its high-water mark in the years following the War of 1812. The church's adaptation to British rule, and especially to British institutions, was far-reaching. Msgr. Briand had praised British criminal justice, and most notably the presumption of innocence, in a 1776 *mandement*.[27] Later, Msgr. Plessis acclaimed the "constitution libérale, sur le modèle de celle du Royaume-Uni" that had been granted to Lower Canada in 1791.[28]

The church's loyalism nevertheless reflected the institution's natural distrust of democracy, by which I mean a system of government deriving its legitimacy from the people rather than from God. The church praised British parliamentarism, but it also benefited from Lower Canada's authoritarian structure of government because it hampered the growing power of the bourgeoisie. In the early nineteenth century, this class was beginning to challenge the leadership role that the clergy and seigneurs had assumed since the French regime. The bourgeoisie increasingly embraced democratism, a doctrine that the church held in very low regard. As early as 1810, Msgr. Plessis warned the clergy of Lower Canada against the "idées trompeuses d'une liberté inconstitutionnelle que chercheraient à lui insinuer certains caractères ambitieux."[29] As both a system of government and an ideal, democracy is disruptive to divinely ordained hierarchies. It promised most notably to lessen clerical power and influence.

The Roman Catholic Church condemned the 1837–8 rebels and refused them the sacraments. Most clergymen (a couple did voice support for the Patriotes) reminded their parishioners that to rebel against legitimate British authority was to rebel against God, since British rule was divinely sanctioned. "Ne vous laissez donc pas séduire," warned Msgr. Jean-Jacques Lartigue of Montreal, "si quelqu'un voulait vous engager à la rébellion contre le Gouvernement établi, sous prétexte que vous faites partie du *Peuple Souverain*."[30] The church had previously disapproved of the growing radicalism of the Patriotes, who had attempted to democratize parish administration – the measure was squelched by the Legislative Council – and promoted the separation of church and state. Patriote radicalism brought the church to collaborate ever more closely with the governor and the Château Clique (Lower Canada's largely English-speaking oligarchy), which, in turn, increasingly alienated the clergy from its flock. Msgr. Lartigue's October 1837 *mandement* against the Patriote agitation was coolly received in his diocese. In Montreal, radical leaders believed that the statement would hasten the coming revolution, while in Chambly a crowd gathered after the document was read in church and chanted "à bas le mandement."[31]

Clerical loyalty diminished after the rebellions, and this can be attributed, in part, to the 1840 Act of Union, which the clergy abhorred and lobbied against.[32] But it was also a result of actions taken by the Special Council of Lower Canada in the wake of the rebellions, which confirmed the title of the church's extensive property. The intensity of loyalist sentiment diminished along with the church's sense of vulnerability in the face of British power, but the sense of attachment to Britain did not disappear from clerical discourse until the twentieth century.

The clergy continued to view British rule and, especially, British institutions, as bulwarks against radicalism and revolution. As Jerry Bannister notes in another chapter in this volume, unease and outright fear at the prospect of revolutionary disorder were widespread and potent among nineteenth-century Canadian elites. This was especially true for Quebec's Catholic clergy, who regarded the Victorian era's emerging liberal order with far less anxiety than it viewed the radical challenge posed by republicanism, and most notably by the Parti rouge. The European turmoil of 1848 struck fear in the hearts of Quebec's leading clerics, as did the 1849 burning of the colonial parliament buildings at Montreal and the subsequent agitation in favour of annexation. The Archdiocese of Quebec, which had not issued an ultra-loyalist statement in several years, prepared an address of loyalty to Queen Victoria within a week of the attack on Parliament:

> Nous prions ... Votre Majesté de compter sur la loyauté, la fidélité et l'attachement de ses sujets catholiques de cette partie de la province du Canada, ci-devant appelée le Bas-Canada, et nous osons assurer Votre Majesté qu'ils regardent comme un bienfait de la divine providence de vivre sous le gouvernement de Votre Majesté, dans un temps où presque toutes les nations civilisées sont en proie aux révolutions, et à tous les malheurs qui en sont la suite inévitable.[33]

The protective nature of British power was highlighted again in a number *mandements* and pastoral letters issued during the turbulent 1860s, when annexation and the possibility of American aggression preoccupied leading clerics once more. In a letter reminding the clergy of his diocese to assist in the organization of militia levies, Msgr. Ignace Bourget of Montreal noted that the British army and navy formed the backbone of Canadian defence: "Notre gouvernement, après avoir donné à ce pays des institutions si libérales qu'il en a fait vraiment le plus heureux pays du monde, lui offre aujourd'hui pour l'aider à se protéger contre l'invasion ennemie dont il est menacé, sa puissante épée."[34] And Confederation gave several clerics the opportunity to reflect on the value of British rule and institutions. In a *mandement* calling upon his flock to accept the British North America Act, Msgr. Charles-François Baillargeon, the auxiliary bishop of Quebec, reminded Catholics "combien nous avons à nous féliciter de vivre sous l'égide de l'Empire Britannique. Il est peu de pays au monde qui ait marché aussi rapidement que le nôtre dans la voie du véritable progrès, et nous n'en connaissons aucun où la religion jouisse d'une plus grande liberté, et exerce une plus large part d'influence."[35]

Some bishops presented Canada's political future as a stark choice between confederation and annexation in the mid-to-late 1860s. "Des institutions républicaines ne nous iraient pas mieux qu'au grand peuple dont nous descendons, les Français!" exclaimed Msgr. Charles Larocque, bishop of Saint-Hyacinthe, and one of the most enthusiastic supporters of Confederation among the higher clergy, in an 1867 pastoral letter. As such, he continued,

> Défions-nous de ces esprits inquiets, de ces journaux à principes plus qu'équivoques, qui font si bon marché de la religion et de la patrie, et qui prennent pour des réalités les rêves de liberté, de gloire et de bonheur qu'ils croiraient goûter en passant sous la bannière étoilée: comme si les droits, les immunités et les privilèges dont nous jouissons sous le drapeau britannique, nous laissaient quelque chose à envier aux peuples les plus libres de la terre, politiquement, civilement et même religieusement parlant![36]

The Roman Catholic Church was nevertheless an ambiguous ally for the British. It acted as a bulwark against sedition and agitation, but it also lobbied for reform. As Denis McKim notes in his chapter in this volume, clerical submission did not preclude legitimate attempts to temper colonial rule. The church lobbied the colonial authorities on a number of matters, most notably in hopes of preventing the 1840 Union of the Canadas. The church resisted attempts to assimilate the Catholic population and colonial interference in clerical matters. When Governor Craig sought to further subjugate the church by forcing the bishop of Quebec to accept formal British control over ecclesiastical nominations – the bishop would have, in exchange, received greater recognition from the Crown and a generous salary – Msgr. Plessis refused to consent to this arrogation of power.[37] The appointment of an auxiliary bishop of Quebec by Msgr. Briand and his successors was designed, moreover, to limit British interference in the ecclesiastical hierarchy.

Yet clerical loyalism was alienating the church from the general population. At the beginning of the nineteenth century, the *habitants*, who, by and large, did not hate the British, appear nevertheless to have regarded the intensity of clerical loyalty with a measure of scepticism. Later, in the 1830s, democratic rhetoric and anger at British policies, most notably those related to immigration and settlement, drove an increasing wedge between the *habitants* and their clergy. The aftermath of the Lower Canadian Rebellions, however, led both the clergy and the general population to reconsider their relationship to British rule.

Clerical loyalism played a key role in fostering the wider adaptation of French Canadians to British rule and, especially, to British institutions. British power and institutions were largely accepted, indeed, often embraced, because they served the interests of various groups within French-Canadian society. For the Roman Catholic Church, loyalism was strategic, reflecting the institution's vulnerability in the face of British power, but it also proceeded from genuine belief. Many ultra-loyalist *mandements* were issued at the prompting of the British authorities, to be sure, but the available evidence generally indicates that these requests were acceded to with enthusiasm, and that their content was sincere. And the depth of this sincerity becomes more evident after the Special Council of Lower Canada solidified the legal status of church property and again when responsible government significantly diminished the power of the British authorities over Canadian affairs. Msgr. Bourget was not pressed to issue a *mandement* calling for prayers during the Indian Mutiny of 1857,[38] nor were the bishops of Quebec compelled to issue calls for loyalty in the 1860s; they did so because they genuinely believed that British power and institutions had become integral to the preservation of Quebec's Catholic social order.

NOTES

1 Indeed, the fervent loyalty of the higher clergy was not necessarily shared by many parish priests, especially during the 1760s. It is for this reason that Msgr. Jean-Olivier Briand of Quebec felt the need to include the following instruction in a 1768 letter to the clergy of his diocese: "Nous devons certainement soutenir les vérités de la foi, même au péril de notre vie, les prêcher et en instruire les peuples; mais il ne convient ni à la religion de la faire avec aigreur ni à la gloire de Dieu de le faire avec mépris. Vous éviterez donc soigneusement de vous servir de termes offensants et injurieux

pour ceux des sujets du Roi qui sont d'une autre religion; ceux de *protestants* et de *frères séparés* seront les seuls dont vous vous servirez, lorsqu'il sera absolument nécessaire de le faire pour expliquer notre croyance. Une autre conduite ne ferait qu'aliéner les cœurs, troubler la bonne harmonie qui doit régner entre les anciens et les nouveaux sujets, ne ferait pas de prosélytes, et pourrait engager le gouvernement à retirer la protection et la liberté qu'il veut bien accorder à notre sainte religion." Jean-Olivier Briand, "Lettre circulaire faisant connaître aux curés les intentions du gouverneur au sujet des cabarets, sur l'union entre les anciens et les nouveaux sujets du roi et sur le 1er rang à être accordé aux bailiffs (15 octobre 1768)," in *Mandements, lettres pastorales et circulaires des évêques de Québec*, vol. 2, ed. Henri Têtu and Charles-Octave Gagnon (Quebec City: A. Côté, 1888), 214. Please note that in all quotations modern French spelling and grammar have been employed.

2 Jerry Bannister, "Canada as Counter-Revolution: The Loyalist Order Framework in Canadian History, 1750–1840," in *Liberalism and Hegemony: Debating the Canadian Liberal Revolution*, ed. Jean-François Constant and Michel Ducharme, (Toronto: University of Toronto Press, 2009), 126.

3 Donal Lowry, "The Crown, Empire Loyalism, and the Assimilation of Non-British White Subjects in the British World: An Argument against 'Ethnic Determinism,'" *Journal of Imperial and Commonwealth History* 31 (2003): 99.

4 See, for instance, Henri Bourassa, *Les Canadiens-Français et l'Empire britannique* (Quebec City: Demers, 1903), 13–17.

5 Canada, House of Commons, *Debates* (1 March 1901), 747 (Henri Bourassa, MP).

6 C.A. Bayly, *Imperial Meridian: The British Empire and the World, 1780–1830* (London: Longman, 1989), 12.

7 Thomas Chapais, *Cours d'histoire du Canada*, vol. 2, *1791–1814* (Quebec City: Garneau, 1921), 220. A similar vision of the role of loyalism in Quebec history can be found in Jacques Monet, *The Last Cannon Shot: A Study of French-Canadian Nationalism, 1837–1850* (Toronto: University of Toronto Press, 1959).

8 Lionel Groulx, *Vers l'émancipation* (Montreal: Bibliothèque de l'Action française, 1921), 277–8.

9 Pierre Vallières, *Négres blancs d'Amérique* (Paris: Maspero, 1969), 30. In a similar vein, the FLQ Manifesto devoted a few choice words to the clergy's role in the Lower Canada Rebellions: "Il nous faut lutter, non plus un à un, mais en s'unissant, jusqu'à la victoire, avec tous les moyens que l'on possède comme l'ont fait les Patriotes de 1837–1838 (ceux que notre sainte mère l'Église s'est empressée d'excommunier pour mieux se vendre aux intérêts britanniques)." Front de liberation du Québec, Manifeste (October 1970), http://archives.radio-canada.ca/arts_culture/terrorisme/clips/322/.

10 Adrien Thério, *Un siècle de collusion entre le clergé et le gouvernement britannique: Anthologie des mandements des évêques* (Montreal: XYZ Éditeur, 1999), 52.

11 Fernand Dumont, *Genèse de la société québécoise*, 2nd ed. (Montreal: Boréal, 1996), 92.

12 Lucien Lemieux, *Histoire du catholicisme québécois: Les XVIIIe et XIXe siècles*, Tome 1, *Les années difficiles, 1760–1839* (Montreal: Boréal, 1989), 40, 401.

13 See Michel Ducharme, *Le concept de liberté à l'époque des Révolutions atlantiques, 1776–1838* (Montreal and Kingston: McGill-Queen's University Press, 2010); Allan Greer, *The Patriots and the People: The Rebellion of 1837 in Rural Lower Canada* (Toronto: University of Toronto Press, 1993); Louis-Georges Harvey, *Le printemps de l'Amérique française: Américanité, anticolonialisme, et républicanisme dans le discours politique québécois, 1805–1837* (Montreal: Boréal, 2005); and Yvan Lamonde, *Histoire sociale des idées au Québec*, vol. 1, *1760–1896* (Montreal: Fides, 2000).

14 See Bannister, "Canada as Counter-Revolution."

15 Lamonde, *Histoire sociale des idées au Québec*, 47.

16 For an overview of British interference with Quebec's Catholic Church, see Marcel Trudel, "La servitude de l'Église catholique du Canada français sous le Régime Anglais," *Report of the Annual Meeting of the Canadian Historical Association / Rapports annuels de la Société historique du Canada*, 42 (1963): 42–64.

17 Ibid., 47.

18 Jean-Olivier Briand, "Mandement pour faire chanter un *Te Deum* en action de grâce du mariage du roi George III (14 février 1762)," in Têtu and Gagnon, eds, *Mandements*, 2: 160–1. No doubt anticipating resistance to this change from some parish priests, Briand appended a revealing note to his *mandement*: "Monsieur ... Peut-être blâmerez-vous quelques-uns des articles de mon mandement; s'il m'avait été possible, j'eusse demandé sur une matière aussi difficile, le sentiment de messieurs les curés; je m'en suis rapporté à celui du clergé de la ville, qui pense presque unanimement qu'il n'est point défendu dans les prières publiques de nommer un hérétique non dénoncé. Au reste, je vous prie d'expliquer à vos paroissiens dans quel sens nous pouvons prier pour ceux qui sont hors de l'Église." Jean-Olivier Briand to the clergy of the Diocese of Quebec, in ibid., 162. In a subsequent letter to the general vicar of Montreal, Étienne Montgolfier, Briand acknowledged that he had hesitated before ordering the change and that it had been met with scepticism by various clerics. However, he wrote, "Je n'ai pas souffert qu'on m'apportât pour raison qu'il est bien dur de prier pour ses ennemis, etc., etc. Ils sont nos maîtres, et nous leur devons ce que nous devions aux Français lorsqu'ils l'étaient. Maintenant l'Église défend-elle à ses sujets de prier pour leur prince? Les catholiques du royaume de la Grande-Bretagne ne prient-ils point pour leur roy? C'est ce que je ne puis croire." Jean-Olivier Briand to Étienne Montgolfier, Quebec City, February 1762, *Rapport de l'archiviste de la province de Québec* (1929): 50.

19 Jean-Olivier Briand, "Mandement aux sujets rebelles durant la guerre américaine (juin 1776)," in Têtu and Gagnon, eds, *Mandements*, 2: 273, 275.

20 Jean-Olivier Briand to Jean-Baptiste Petit Maisonbasse, Quebec City, 25 October 1775, *Rapport de l'archiviste de la Province de Québec* (1929): 112.

21 Jean-Olivier Briand, "Lettre circulaire faisant connaître aux curés les intentions du gouverneur (15 octobre 1768)," in Têtu and Gagnon, eds, *Mandements*, 2: 213.

22 Louis-Philippe d'Esgly et al., "Adresse du clergé de Québec présentée le 21 août 1787 à Son Altesse Royale Guillaume-Henri, troisième fils de Sa Majesté Britannique," in Têtu and Gagnon, eds, *Mandements*, 2: 334.

23 Joseph-Octave Plessis, "Mandement pour des actions de grâces publiques (16 septembre 1807)," in *Mandements, lettres pastorales, et circulaires des évêques de Québec*, vol. 3, ed. Henri Têtu and Charles-Octave Gagnon (Quebec City: A. Côté, 1888), 31.

24 Pierre Denaut, "Mandement prescrivant des actions de grâces après la victoire de l'amiral Nelson (22 décembre 1798)," in Têtu and Gagnon, eds, *Mandements*, 2: 516. The *mandement* was issued at the suggestion of Governor General Prescott. It should be noted furthermore that Msgr. Denaut did not call for a high mass to celebrate the naval victory. In a letter written shortly after his *mandement*, he informed his auxiliary bishop, Msgr. Plessis, that he did not wish to create a precedent by ordering a high mass, and that a day of thanksgiving would do. Pierre Denaut to Joseph-Octave Plessis, Longueuil, 24 December 1798, *Rapport de l'archiviste de la province de Québec* (1931): 155; Plessis to Denaut, Quebec City, 27 December 1798, *Rapport de l'archiviste de la province de Québec* (1927): 220. For his part, Plessis would use the day of thanksgiving as an opportunity to deliver one of the most loyalist sermons in French-Canadian history, possibly to mollify the governor general, who appears to have urged the church to grant greater solemnity to the celebration. "Ne vous parait-il pas dur," he asked his congregation, "d'être obligés d'appeler ennemi un peuple auquel cette colonie doit son origine?" No, he continued, since revolutionary France was the quintessence of evil, while Britain, by contrast, had emerged as God's instrument on earth. The British Conquest of Canada was surely divinely ordained, Plessis concluded. His lengthy sermon was subsequently published and distributed by parish authorities at Quebec. Joseph-Octave Plessis, *Discours à l'occasion de la victoire remportée par les forces navales de sa majesté britannique dans la Méditérrannée le 1 et 2 août 1798, sur la flotte française, prononcé dans l'église cathédrale de Québec le 10 janvier 1799* (Quebec City, 1799), 3.

25 Pierre Denaut, "Mandement ordonnant des actions de grâces publiques pour la paix (1er août 1802)," in Têtu and Gagnon, eds, *Mandements*, 2: 532–3.

26 Joseph-Octave Plessis, "Mandement pour des prières publiques (29 octobre 1812)," in Têtu and Gagnon, eds, *Mandements*, 3: 95. Joseph-Octave Plessis to George Prévost, Quebec City, 24 October 1812, *Rapport de l'archiviste de la province de Québec* (1927): 291. Already, in a 1799 sermon, Msgr. Plessis had underscored Britain's new-found

role as a global barrier to revolution: "Au reste, messieurs, si d'un côté l'Angleterre tend une main secourable aux victimes de la révolution, et les comble de bienfaits et de largesses; elle arrête, de l'autre, une partie des désordres dont ses monstrueux instruments menacent l'univers entier." Plessis, *Discours à l'occasion de la victoire*, 14.

27 Briand, "Mandement aux sujets rebelles," 270–2.

28 Plessis, "Mandement pour des actions de grâces publiques," 30.

29 Joseph-Octave Plessis, "Lettre circulaire à messieurs les curés (21 mars 1810)," in Têtu and Gagnon, eds, *Mandements*, 3: 44. This *lettre* was issued in the midst of a political crisis orchestrated by Governor General Craig, who insisted that the bishop warn the clergy against supporting the Parti canadien in a forthcoming election. Msgr. Plessis, whose relationship with Craig was difficult, to say the least, allowed a proclamation from the governor general to be read in the Catholic churches of Lower Canada and warned his clerics not to appear disloyal to the administration. In a letter to the general vicar of Trois-Rivières, he noted tellingly that the clergy could not "encourir la disgrâce du gouvernement puisque c'est de sa protection que dépend la liberté du culte catholique dans la Province." Joseph-Octave Plessis to François Noiseux, Quebec City, 22 March 1810, *Rapport de l'archiviste de la province de Québec* (1927): 273.

30 Jean-Jacques Lartigue, "Premier mandement à l'occasion des troubles de 1837 (24 octobre 1837)," in *Le rouge et le bleu: Une anthologie de la pensée politique au Québec de la Conquête à la Révolution tranquille*, ed. Yvan Lamonde and Claude Corbo (Montreal: Presses de l'Université de Montréal, 1999), 121. Unlike many earlier counter-revolutionary *mandements* issued by the bishops of Quebec, this one does not appear to have been prompted by a request from the British authorities. In fact, during the rebellions, Msgr. Lartigue lobbied Rome to issue a statement to the Catholics of Lower Canada reminding them of their duty to obey civil authority. Jean-Jacques Lartigue to Msgr. Mai, Montreal, 15 October 1837, *Rapport de l'archiviste de la province de Québec* (1944): 255.

31 Jean-Jacques Lartigue to Jérôme Demers, Montreal, 30 October 1837, *Rapport de l'archiviste de la province de Québec* (1944): 57.

32 As early as February 1838, the clergy of the Diocese of Quebec petitioned Queen Victoria against a possible revival of the 1822 project to unite Upper and Lower Canada. See "Adresse du clergé du diocese de Québec au parlement imperial contre le projet d'unir la Bas et le Haut-Canada sous une même legislature," in Têtu and Gagnon, eds, *Mandements*, 3: 378–81.

33 "Adresse du clergé de Québec à la reine (2 mai 1849)," in Têtu and Gagnon, eds, *Mandements*, 3: 541–2.

34 Ignace Bourget, "Circulaire de Mgr l'évêque de Montréal à son clergé, sur les bruits de guerre et la nécessité de s'y préparer (25 décembre 1861)," in his *Fioretti vescovilli, ou extraits de mandements, lettres pastorales, et circulaires de monseigneur Ignace Bourget* (Montreal: Le Franc-Parleur, 1872), 121.

35 Charles-François Baillargeon, "Mandement à l'occasion de la confédération des provinces du Canada (12 juin 1867)," in *Mandements, lettres pastorales, et circulaires des évêques de Québec*, vol. 4, ed. Henri Têtu and Charles-Octave Gagnon (Quebec City: A. Côté, 1888), 581.

36 Charles Larocque, "Lettre pastorale concernant l'inauguration du gouvernement fédéral (18 juin 1867)," in *Mandements, lettres pastorales, et circulaires des évêques de St-Hyacinthe*, vol. 2, ed. Alexis-Xiste Bernard (Montreal: Beauchemin, 1889), 430. Among the bishops of Quebec, Msgr. Larocque along with Msgr. Louis-François Laflèche of Trois-Rivières were ardent supporters of Confederation. Others, like Msgr. Bourget, were sceptical of the scheme and merely accepted it as a fait accompli in mid-1867. On the episcopate's reaction to Confederation, see Walter Ullmann, "The Quebec Bishops and Confederation," *Canadian Historical Review* 44, no. 3 (September 1963): 213–34.

37 See Joseph-Octave Plessis, "Conversations entre son excellence sir James Henry Craig et l'évêque catholique de Québec (mai–juin 1811)," in Têtu and Gagnon, eds, *Mandements*, 3: 59–72.

38 See Ignace Bourget, "Mandement ordonnant des prières pour le succès de la guerre des Indes (21 novembre 1857)," in his *Fioretti vescovilli*, 97.

3 Anxious Anglicans, Complicated Catholics, and Disruptive Dissenters: Christianity and the Search for Social Order in the Age of Revolution

DENIS McKIM[1]

Shelves groan beneath the weight of scholarly works written on the religious dimension of early American history. Consequently, we know a great deal about such topics as the part played by Christian phenomena – the Great Awakening, the Episcopal controversy, the religious component of the Quebec Act – in sparking the Revolutionary War.[2] True, scholars' views on religion's role in early America are anything but monolithic. For example, Nathan O. Hatch has emphasized evangelicalism's emancipatory impact, while Amanda Porterfield has stressed its capacity for stifling critical inquiry and rationalizing racism. Still, they reveal that, for weal or woe, Christianity was integral to the emergence of the United States.[3]

We know less about Christianity's contribution to the development of a viable alternative to revolutionary republicanism in those North American colonies that remained within Britain's imperial orbit after 1783. This lack of knowledge presumably derives, at least in part, from the fact that American topics (including the religious factors that helped precipitate the Revolutionary War) almost invariably receive more attention than Canadian ones (including the relationship between Christianity and the persistence of British rule in polities that eventually became part of the Dominion of Canada). Yet it also derives from a long-standing habit among historians on both sides of the United States-Canada border to associate Christian loyalism – a fluctuating amalgam of religious and political sentiments and impulses – with reactionary conservatism, a tendency that is as misleading as it is persistent. This practice finds expression in the works of several scholars, including Christopher Adamson, who contrasted the "Christian loyalism" of Upper Canada's hidebound "elite" with the American-style "evangelical outlook and commitment to voluntaryism of many of [the colony's] early settlers"; George A. Rawlyk, whose essay on the intersection, in Canada, of religion and politics emphasized the Loyalists' introduction of a "conservative ideology and ... a deep-rooted antagonism towards the United States"; and S.F. Wise, whose writings stressed the toryism disseminated in British North America by eminent clergy who constituted part of a "small colonial upper class."[4]

Granted, this tendency is not wholly inaccurate. In the late eighteenth and early nineteenth centuries, Anglican clerics in several British North American colonies – including Nova Scotia's Charles Inglis, Lower Canada's Jacob Mountain, and Upper Canada's John Strachan – portrayed themselves as bulwarks of order and loyalty in a dangerously democratic North American context. Such notions lay at the heart of Anglican arguments in favour of religious establishments that bestowed benefits – including privileges regarding Crown lands, schooling, and the performance of marriage rites – on the English Church, which in turn strove to inculcate deferential principles in the colonial consciousness and quell threats posed to social order by such supposedly subversive (and allegedly interrelated) phenomena as unbridled evangelicalism and political radicalism.[5]

Yet in fixating on the correlation between Christianity (especially Anglicanism) and conservatism, scholars have obscured the fact that members of a wide variety of religious communities – including Roman Catholics and Protestant Dissenters from diverse linguistic, ethnic, and racial backgrounds – exhibited loyalist leanings in an equally wide variety of ways. As well, they have overlooked the fact that Christian loyalism was not synonymous with elite dominance and rank-and-file subservience, as the "Christian-loyalist-as-conservative" caricature suggests. To be sure, imperious Anglicans denounced criticisms of the status quo as treasonous and sinful, and took pains to promote docility and an unquestioning patriotism among the masses. However, members of other churches – who were cognizant of imperial authorities' reluctance to antagonize colonists – felt that their loyalist credentials permitted them to demand (and, often, obtain) redress from colonial authorities when they felt they had received short shrift. Thus, loyalism, despite being strategically invoked by elites eager to consolidate their grasp on power, could also be marshalled by comparatively disadvantaged peoples seeking equitable treatment regarding issues ranging from financial support for Roman Catholicism to the importance of honouring Indigenous treaty rights. One could plausibly contend, then, that in post-revolutionary British North America there was a mutually reinforcing relationship between colonial churches and British imperialism: the former burnished their loyalist *bona fides* in appealing to the latter for support, while the latter relied on the former to maintain authority without having to resort to costly, punitive displays of martial force.[6]

Historians have not ignored loyalism's resonance within British North American Christianity altogether. On the contrary, they have cast light on the existence of pro-British attitudes among members of several denominations within a single colony, and among members of a single denomination across several colonies.[7] As yet, however, there has not been a thorough examination of the intersection of Christianity and loyalty within multiple denominations dispersed over those North American colonies that remained within Britain's Empire after the Revolutionary War. This essay provides such an account through an analysis of the pervasiveness and malleability of religiously based support for the British regime within a multiplicity of northern North American communities and contexts, thereby highlighting the underappreciated complexity of loyalism's religious component. Although the most explicit examples of Christian loyalism appeared in the remarks of clerical elites, examples can also be found in appeals written by ordinary colonists to metropolitan authorities on behalf of their denominations, and in religiously charged processions involving large volumes of people through which members of the colonial populace made plain their pro-British orientations.

As several recent studies have shown, the flexibility of loyalism – a multifaceted phenomenon that encompassed diverse racial communities, ideological traditions, and socio-economic subgroups – was instrumental to the persistence of British imperial influence in various settings throughout the Age of Revolution, which ran from the late eighteenth to the early nineteenth century and witnessed radical uprisings on both sides of the Atlantic.[8] The enduring importance of British imperialism during (and after) this period was perhaps nowhere more evident than in the northern North American territories that eventually formed part of the Canadian nation-state. For, by 1825, Britain was the last European power to retain continental North American colonies, bespeaking its capacity for adapting to the revolutionary circumstances that triggered the unravelling of rival empires rooted in France and Spain.[9]

In response to the revolutionary maelstrom that manifested across the Atlantic world, conservative colonial Anglicans articulated a vision of society in which the English church was the indispensable defender of hierarchical order and British sovereignty. Members of other Christian groups, however, deployed a pro-British discursive strategy, or "language of loyalty," in enunciating alternative visions consonant with their denominations' priorities. Moreover, they backed the empire – for instance, by imploring their co-religionists to support the British regime – during such events as the American Revolution, the War of 1812, and the Rebellions of 1837–8. Rather than being threats to British rule, Dissenters and Catholics bolstered the pluralistic culture of loyalism that contributed to the abiding influence of empire in northern North America throughout the Age of Revolution.

Anxious Anglicans

The Anglican Church in post-revolutionary British North America was not monolithic. While it is often equated with conservatism, Anglicanism was actually quite diverse when it came to such issues as race (the first Protestant church in what became Upper Canada was built for Mohawk members of the Church of England);[10] political ideology (in addition to its conservative members, reformers such as Robert Baldwin belonged to the English Church);[11] and theology (Low Church evangelicals vied for influence within the denomination with their ritualistic High Church counterparts).[12] For all their heterogeneity, however, conservative instincts featured prominently within the Anglicans' ranks and were manifest in the belief that the English Church was uniquely capable of fostering order and loyalty.

This belief, which had important implications for British North America's politico-religious evolution, crystallized in early modern England. There, key politico-religious developments – especially the Henrician Reformation, through which England's monarch supplanted the pope as the English Church's head, and the Elizabethan Act of Supremacy, which affirmed the English monarch's authority over religious and civil spheres – buttressed the ancient idea that church and state are intrinsically entwined.[13]

The English Church's authority was reinforced in Restoration-era England, as non-Anglican groups – including Catholics, who were linked to the "gunpowder plot," and Puritans, who were associated with Charles I's execution – were denounced as threats to social order. Thus, the Test and Corporation Acts of the 1660s and 1670s curtailed both groups' civil liberties, as evidenced by the restrictions that prohibited the Roman Church's members from holding public office.[14] Anglicanism's privileged position was by no means unchallenged. Rather, in his *Letter Concerning Toleration* (1689), John Locke blamed state-aided religion for much of the conflict that beset English society in the seventeenth century, establishing a potent rationale for the separation of church and state that found a receptive audience in revolutionary America. Nevertheless, government-supported religion was central to a hierarchical social order that persisted until its foundations were abruptly undermined in the early nineteenth century due to such developments as the repeal of the Test and Corporation Acts, which eliminated civil disabilities against Catholics and Dissenters, and the Great Reform Act, which enfranchised segments of Britain's increasingly influential middle class.[15]

Bolstering the English Church's influence were arguments set forth in the mid-eighteenth century by William Warburton, who defended England's state church on utilitarian grounds, arguing that it buttressed civil authority by promoting social stability in exchange for the government assistance that facilitated its initiatives. Later in the century, Edmund Burke reasserted the idea that church and state are inherently fused, as reflected in his unequivocal contention that the English people viewed the national church "as the foundation of their whole constitution."[16]

When it came to British settler colonies, imperial authorities saw Anglican establishments as mechanisms through which an appreciation for loyalty and passivity could be instilled in colonists' minds by clerics acting as auxiliaries of the state. In embryonic polities that lacked conventional police forces and standing armies, elites saw conservative Christianity as an invaluable ally of civil authority; as Nova Scotia's first chief justice, Jonathan Belcher, put it in an address to a grand jury, absent state-aided religion, the colony's laws would be rendered "a Dead Letter."[17] Such views grew stronger after the Revolutionary War, which officials on both sides of the Atlantic attributed to the prevalence in colonial society of such subversive – and, as they saw it, mutually reinforcing – phenomena as Dissenting Protestantism and political radicalism.[18]

Thus, Anglican establishments were created in Nova Scotia in 1758; in New Brunswick in 1786; in Cape Breton (which was its own colony from 1784 to 1820) and the Canadas in 1791; and in Prince Edward Island in 1802. That these establishments were less restrictive than their counterparts elsewhere – Dissenters enjoyed freedom of worship and political equality with Anglicans across British North America, evidencing the Crown's desire to avoid antagonizing them – should not obscure the fact that powerful figures throughout the colonies, including civil officials such as New Brunswick's Thomas Carleton and Upper Canada's John Graves Simcoe, saw them as a vital means of buttressing hierarchy and promoting loyalty.[19]

Such beliefs were only reinforced by developments like the French Revolution, which Mountain denounced for "[dissolving] all the bonds of order ... and under the specious name of *Fraternity*, *Equality*, and *Liberty*, [letting] loose all the plagues of tyranny and oppression, of assassination and plunder, and debauchery and atheism."[20] Also culpable was the surge in radical evangelicalism associated with the New Light phenomenon in the Maritimes and the ascent of Methodism in the Canadas, whose ministers Strachan scorned as "uneducated itinerant preachers, who ... betake themselves to preaching the Gospel from idleness, or a zeal without knowledge, by which they are induced without any preparation, to teach what they do not know, and which, from their pride, they disdain to learn."[21] For all their differences – the French Revolution was associated with irreligion, while unbridled New Light and Methodist evangelicalism was associated with religious fanaticism – authorities in church and state felt that both phenomena threatened to unleash subversive forces that would imperil the status quo.[22]

Charles Inglis, who had served as rector of New York City's Trinity Church during the Revolutionary War and was consecrated as Nova Scotia's first Anglican bishop in 1787, articulated the essence of the conservative conception of Christian loyalty in a sermon delivered before the colony's legislature in the early 1790s.[23] Expounding on Proverbs 24:21 – "My son, fear though the LORD and the king: and meddle not with them that are given to change" – Inglis emphasized two themes. First was the Anglican belief in the intrinsic complementarity of church and state. From his perspective, "He that sincerely loves God, will be loyal to his earthly Sovereign, from a principle of Conscience," since religious and civil authority are mutually reinforcing. Though religion was ultimately focused on something far more important than the prosaic concerns of the everyday – "Salvation" – it "affords the most powerful aid" to the temporal realm by promoting "the peace and order of society." Inglis acknowledged that "the Gospel" was not concerned with particular regimes' constitutional intricacies, but felt that it "uniformly and strictly injoins [*sic*] obedience to the authority established in every government." For Inglis, "without obedience in the subject," government cannot exist, much less thrive; indeed, he was convinced that, without civil authority, "this earth would become a scene of the wildest disorder." Since government was indispensable to "the welfare of Society," God invariably fosters "the happiness of mankind" in the temporal, as well as the spiritual, sphere.[24]

Inglis's second theme involved denouncing unorthodox manifestations of Christianity. He informed his audience that, in asserting "the necessity of Religion for the welfare of society and Government," he was referring to "the pure, peaceable and rational Religion of Jesus Christ." This unimpeachable form of Christianity, he contended, "requires holiness and benevolence in its professors, and strongly inculcates order and subordination" in its adherents. It differed sharply from unconventional religiosity, which he associated with "the sallies of enthusiasm, the reveries of a disordered head, or a heated imagination." Alluding to the instability wrought by Puritans in Civil War–era England, he observed that "the history of mankind" yields abundant evidence of the tumult engendered by religious radicalism. Given the legacy of "Bloodshed and desolation" left in its wake, it was incumbent on "the rational, conscientious Christian and Loyal Subject" to combat both excessive religious enthusiasm and its "opposite extreme," the appalling tenets of "Infidelity and Atheism."[25]

Such ideas were transmitted to ordinary colonists who did not absorb conservative clerics' remarks in church via the medium of published sermons. Given that a popular press did not emerge in most British North American communities until the early nineteenth century, and that parliamentary proceedings were largely inaccessible before that era, published sermons occupied a privileged position in the nascent colonial public sphere as devices for shaping popular political and religious attitudes. Usually written by "churchmen" – that is, clergy affiliated with state-supported institutions like the Church of England and who tended to be unusually well educated and politically influential – they propagated a conservative conception of Christian loyalism across colonial society. Consequently, the conservative conception of Christian loyalism was by no means confined to the rarefied circles populated by conservative clergy such as Inglis.[26]

Complicated Catholics

Convinced though they were that they were the British regime's indispensable champions, Anglican Tories did not have a monopoly on loyalty. Quite the opposite – representatives of several other groups espoused pro-British sentiments. In addition, they backed the British regime during such events as the Revolutionary War, the War of 1812, and the Rebellions of 1837–8. For instance, certain British North American Catholics exhibited loyalty. This behaviour may seem counterintuitive. After all, by the early nineteenth century virtually all Catholic groups had ample reason to resent the British Empire. For some, the traumatic events had occurred in North America – Mi'kmaw Catholics had clashed with British settlers and experienced dispossession, Acadian Catholics had been deported. For others, hardships were experienced elsewhere in the British world: Scottish Catholics could recall the suppression of the Jacobite uprisings of "'15 and '45" and the upheaval wrought by the clearances, and Irish Catholics could recall any number of British-engineered humiliations, with the defeat of the 1798 Rebellion being only the most recent example.[27]

Also, many British North American Catholics suffered civil disabilities designed to minimize, if not eradicate, the Roman Church's influence in colonies that formed part of an expressly Protestant empire. This pattern of systemic persecution was especially pronounced in the Atlantic region. By contrast, in the British colony of Quebec and, after 1791, the Canadas, the Quebec Act guaranteed freedom of worship for the Roman Church's adherents and laid the groundwork for the realization of civil equality between Catholics and Protestants. The Quebec Act's religious dimension was informed by colonial authorities' desire, after the Conquest, to curry favour with clerical elites in hopes of neutralizing popular resistance to British rule. Grateful priests, the logic ran, would persuade their flock to revere – or, failing that, to tolerate – Protestant rulers. Designed to pacify the French-speaking Canadiens, the Quebec Act had important implications for Canadian Catholics from diverse backgrounds, as will be seen.[28]

In the Atlantic region, Catholics endured harsher treatment. Beginning in the mid-eighteenth century, priests were ordered to leave Nova Scotia "on pain of perpetual imprisonment," while the colony's Catholic laypeople were prohibited from owning land, among other civil disabilities. Such policies were not always enforced, and, from the 1780s onward, they were gradually eliminated. Yet certain anti-Catholic policies *were* consistently enforced and, in certain instances, they persisted beyond the early post-revolutionary period. For example, the Atlantic region's Catholics could not vote until 1789 in Nova Scotia, 1812 in New Brunswick, 1829 in Prince Edward Island, and 1832 in Newfoundland.[29]

What, then, accounts for the loyalism evinced by certain British North American Catholics, including ones in the Atlantic region? The pro-British sentiments that circulated in the denomination's ranks (which were never ubiquitous) can be attributed to three complementary factors. The first was a conservative theological outlook championed by members of the Catholic hierarchy – including figures from diverse backgrounds in several colonies – that stemmed from the apostles Peter and Paul and held that religious and civil authority were inseparably intertwined. To rebel against a civil ruler, even one whose authority had been obtained through conquest, was thus to rebel against a temporal order that was divinely ordained.

The second factor, which reinforced the Catholic clergy's conservative philosophical orientation, was the material benefits enjoyed by the Roman Church, in several colonies, under the British regime. The Quebec Act, for instance, was influenced by imperial authorities' desire to achieve harmonious relations with the Canadiens post-Conquest, which they hoped to accomplish, partially, by placating powerful Catholic figures.[30] Accordingly, it declared that the Roman Church's representatives "may hold, receive, and enjoy, their accustomed Dues and Rights" regarding such privileges as the collection of tithes.[31] The reliance of the Catholic hierarchy on Britain's support compelled an archbishop to inform Governor General Lord Gosford in 1838 that the demise of the British regime in North America would "destroy the clergy as well as its means of subsistence and influence."[32] (In an earlier chapter in this volume, Damien-Claude Bélanger sheds further light on the loyalism that circulated within Canadien Catholicism.)

Catholic figures also benefited under the British regime in the Atlantic colonies – certain missionaries, for example, received government salaries – even though the region's Catholics were subjected to civil disabilities. These arrangements bespeak the complicated relationship that existed in the region between Catholics and the colonial state. As in Quebec and, later, the Canadas, civil officials in the Atlantic colonies supported the Roman Church largely because they viewed it as a potential ally in their quest to promote social order. They valued its efforts to foster loyalty and obedience among the populace; to discourage behaviour such as Saturday night "frolics," social events that were notorious for drunkenness, violence, and illicit sex; and to foster diplomatic relations with Indigenous peoples, as seen in the efforts of the Acadian priest Joseph-Maturin Bourg, who helped colonial authorities secure the neutrality of Mi'kmaw and Wolastoqiyik Catholics amid the Revolutionary War.[33]

The third factor contributing to Catholic loyalty was an accommodative strategy employed by Catholic authorities throughout the north Atlantic world during the Age of Revolution. Through this strategy, which amounted to a coordinated response to the era's turbulence, the Roman Church's representatives cultivated constructive relationships with non-Catholic regimes in such places as British North America and the United States by cooperating, wherever possible, with Protestant civil authorities. Implemented at "[all] levels of the church's international organization," the strategy consolidated Catholicism's influence in uncongenial contexts and set the stage for denominational advances in terms of popularity and institutional influence in the future. Expressions of loyalty from British North American Catholics – whether they were based in Quebec/ Lower Canada, Upper Canada, or the Atlantic region – should therefore be seen not as rank capitulation, but rather as a far-seeing effort to forge links with non-Catholic powers amid unfavourable politico-religious circumstances.[34]

Owing to these factors, the Roman Church's representatives across British North America supported the empire throughout the Age of Revolution. For evidence, one need look no further than the views of Alexander Macdonell, a staunchly pro-British priest from the Scottish Highlands who had served as the first Catholic chaplain in Britain's military since the Reformation before immigrating to Upper Canada in 1804.[35] Macdonell's loyalty was borne out in his efforts to combat the growth, in Upper Canada, of the Friends of Ireland, a reputedly disloyal – and, so, potentially subversive – organization with branches in the United States and British North America that championed "Catholic emancipation" overseas.[36] By no means atypical, Macdonell's orientation is indicative of the pro-British views that came to permeate Highland society as a result of the decisive defeat, in 1746, of the Jacobites, and the subsequent pacification campaign orchestrated by Britain's government, which helped transform Scotland's hitherto unruly regions into "the arsenal of empire" as a result of their inhabitants' myriad contributions to imperial military victories.[37]

Macdonell, who was consecrated as bishop of Kingston in 1826, remarked on the fact that loyalist sentiments had accompanied Highland immigrants on their transatlantic journey to Upper Canada. He did so in an address given in the late 1830s to inhabitants of Glengarry County, many of whom were Catholics of Highland birth or extraction. Macdonell applauded these people for their "uncompromising attachment to Britain and the British constitution," witness to which was their willingness to defend the empire in various contexts on both sides of the Atlantic divide. He praised the county's Highland Catholics, some of whom had served in the British military alongside Macdonell before arriving in Upper Canada, for "restoring peace and tranquility to Ireland [in 1798]"; for "repelling the invasion of the Americans [during the War of 1812]"; and for "checking the progress ... of rebellion [in Upper Canada in 1837]."[38]

However, Roman Catholic loyalty did not automatically entail deference to imperial officials. Though he supported the British regime steadfastly, Macdonell was quite capable of behaving assertively when it came to his interactions with imperial authorities. For example, in his dealings with such figures as Colonial Secretary Lord Bathurst, Macdonell forthrightly demanded financial support for Upper Canadian Catholicism. A shrewd negotiator, Macdonell invoked the spectre of an expanding – and, he intimated, potentially rebellious – Irish Catholic population in Upper Canada to enhance his appeal's effectiveness. Macdonell told Bathurst that Irish Catholics had come to Upper Canada with "memories of tythes and rack rents" fresh in their minds, and with "mortal hatred of Orangeism which they find so rapidly spreading over this Province." Given these alienating circumstances, Upper Canada's Irish Catholics could easily fall prey to demagogues bent on fomenting discord. Thus, it was incumbent on imperial authorities (including Bathurst) to support Upper Canada's Catholic officials – including such pro-British figures as Macdonell – who, in turn, could promote among Irish Catholic immigrants a sense of "loyalty and grateful attachment to the British government."[39]

The Atlantic region's Catholics also exhibited imperial enthusiasm. Take, for example, the outpouring of loyalty from members of the Roman Church in Newfoundland in May 1829. Triggered by the passing, overseas, of the Reform Bill – legislation that eliminated barriers to Catholics' sitting in Parliament, signalling the demise of the Penal Laws under which, for centuries, the Newfoundlanders' Irish counterparts had languished – their exuberance threw into relief the existence of pro-British attitudes in their community. Thomas Scallan, the colony's Catholic bishop, responded to the bill's passing by requesting that 21 May be "a day of Public Thanksgiving to the Almighty, for the blessings conferred ... by the late Relief Bill."[40]

Ordinary Newfoundlanders, for their part, rejoiced. In St John's, for example, members of two voluntary societies – the Benevolent Irish Society and the Mechanics' Society – along with "a number of other respectable inhabitants of the town," gathered at the Orphan Asylum School. Intent on showing "the greatest possible respect for the day," these civic worthies led "a vast concourse of people, preceded by a band of music," to the Catholic church. Having reached their destination, the crowd – whose ranks swelled as the procession coursed through St John's, such that its proportions "became almost overwhelming" – absorbed a sermon by a priest, Michael Fleming, "characterized by sentiments purely loyal and patriotic."[41]

Fleming concluded by inviting his audience to join him in offering "three cheers" for King George IV; the Duke of Wellington, Britain's Prime Minister; and Robert Peel, a key supporter of the Relief Bill. He also urged the crowd to offer "as many cheers as lungs will permit for DANIEL O'CONNELL," iconic Irish proponent of Catholic Emancipation. Fleming's injunction, according to the *Newfoundlander*, "was complied with to the strict letter." Accentuating the celebratory atmosphere were the colours "displayed at several of the principal mercantile establishments, and by most of the vessels in port," and the ceremonial discharging of "canon and musquetry ... from the wharves."[42]

Like their co-religionists elsewhere in British North America, though, Newfoundland Catholics' sense of devotion to Britain did not render them servile. Instead, they were perfectly capable of expressing dissatisfaction with imperial authorities when circumstances warranted assertiveness. One such instance came on the heels of the aforementioned celebrations. In late 1829, members of Newfoundland's Catholic community learned, much to their chagrin, that the metropolitan ruling liberating Ireland's Catholics was inapplicable to British colonies, meaning that punitive legislation – for instance, anti-Catholic oaths that prevented the Roman Church's adherents from holding public office – persisted in Newfoundland even after it had been scrapped overseas. Compounding matters was the fact that, unlike other British North American colonies, Newfoundland did not have a House of Assembly, which rendered the colony unable to remedy the situation autonomously. Consequently, "angry and irritated" Newfoundlanders vented their frustrations by engaging in large protest meetings and dispatching a petition to Britain's Parliament via O'Connell.[43]

Disruptive Dissenters

Christian loyalism also circulated among British North America's Dissenters. This may seem unsurprising. After all, the argument has been made that Protestantism (including its Dissenting branches) was integral to the ethos of "Britishness" that crystallized in Britain between the Treaty of Union and the Great Reform Act. Moreover, by the early nineteenth century, metropolitan Dissenters responded to allegations of disloyalty – conservative intellectuals and "church and king" mobs alike had lashed out at them as a result of their opposition, in certain cases, to Britain's wars against the Thirteen Colonies and revolutionary France – by distancing themselves from political radicalism and insisting that they were unimpeachably patriotic "friends to the king and government."[44]

Yet, in British North America, elites viewed Dissenters with acute scepticism. Although, officially, they fared better under the British regime than Catholics – when Nova Scotia's Anglican establishment was crafted in the late 1750s, for example, civil officials ensured that Dissenters would be able to worship freely and would not be required to pay taxes to support the state church – conservative authorities (especially authoritarian churchmen) saw them as a greater threat to social order than the Roman Church's adherents, which underscores the latter institution's reputation for loyalty. Particularly anxiety-provoking were such radical evangelical groups as the Maritime New Lights and the Upper Canadian Methodists, as seen in Strachan's assertion that the latter were "filling the country with the most deplorable fanaticism."[45]

While jealousy of these groups' explosive growth (which, around the beginning of the nineteenth century, easily outpaced that of the English Church) likely informed the churchmen's views, their hostility towards the New Lights and the Methodists also reflected their belief that radical evangelicalism – notorious for emotional outbursts that flouted conventional etiquette – posed an existential threat to the hierarchical society they yearned to entrench. Such beliefs were especially pronounced between the Revolutionary War and the War of 1812, a period that witnessed a dramatic influx of New Light and Methodist preachers into British North America from the United States. Encapsulating the outlook of conservative Anglicans in other colonies, Nova Scotia's Charles Inglis saw radical evangelicals as a menace both politically – he denounced the New Lights as "violent republicans and democrats" – and socially – since their exuberant demeanour clashed with conservative attitudes towards such significant issues as gender and sexuality.[46]

From a political standpoint, the conservatives' anxieties were largely unfounded. While, in revolutionary America, many evangelicals embraced radical republicanism, their northern North American counterparts (who were more concerned with Doubting Thomas than Thomas Paine) typically eschewed politics. Though it is difficult to ascertain why this was the case, a persuasive interpretation holds that the evangelicals' apolitical orientation was largely attributable to the absence, in colonies such as Nova Scotia, of coercive religious establishments exalting Anglicans over other Protestants and compelling financial contributions for the English Church. This orientation, the interpretation runs, had important religious ramifications: unburdened by such political concerns as state-sanctioned religious inequality, Nova Scotia's evangelicals were free to dedicate themselves unreservedly to an especially enthusiastic form of revivalism that was arguably "more radical, more anarchistic, and more populist than its American counterpart."[47]

From a social standpoint, however, the conservatives' anxieties rested on firmer ground. The evangelicals' zeal contributed to the emergence of what Inglis described as "a host of newly assertive individuals," including women such as Sarah Bancroft of Onslow, Nova Scotia, and Mary Bradley of Saint John, New Brunswick, who challenged patriarchal authority by serving as lay preachers and denouncing backsliders, respectively. Inglis also observed that in New Light communities, "ignorant men and women ... were employed to pray and exhort, until the whole assembly groaned, and screamed, and finally ended with a falling down and rolling upon the floor of both sexes together," laying bare the conservative belief that radical evangelicalism elicited sexual debauchery.[48]

Disruptive though they may have been, radical evangelicals in the Atlantic region expressed sentiments that, in the aggregate, could plausibly be characterized as Christian loyalism. To be sure, such sentiments did not entail the extravagantly pro-British declarations of an Inglis or a Strachan. Rather, they conveyed a subtler appreciation for the British regime deriving from the fervent religiosity that flowed through their ranks.[49]

Central to the pro-British views enunciated by the radical evangelicals (specifically, the New Lights) was the belief, put forth by Nova Scotia Planters swept up in the frenzy of religious enthusiasm engendered by the iconic revivalist Henry Alline, that they were a divinely favoured people. The torrent of religious zeal that transformed their communities, coupled with the civil war into which their erstwhile home had descended, led many Planters to conclude that providence itself had spared them from the turmoil of the Revolutionary War and allowed them to experience an exhilarating religious revival in Nova Scotia. Such beliefs, in turn, led Planters to question – and, in some cases, shed – their sentimental attachments to New England and embrace the British colony to which they had moved. (Although factors that had little to do with religion – including the violence of the revolution itself, and the turbulent developments, like Shays' Rebellion, that occurred in its wake – conceivably contributed to these colonists' negative attitude towards the early republic as well.) Their Christian loyalism found expression not in the language of imperial chauvinism, but rather in a sense of gratitude to the empire for providing them with a setting in which they could concentrate on revivalism without being drawn into the sanguinary, fratricidal conflict that raged in the neighbouring colonies.[50]

Views expressed by inhabitants of Maugerville, Nova Scotia (later New Brunswick), during the American Revolution are illustrative of the Christian loyalism that circulated among Planters affected by radical evangelicalism.[51] During the early stages of the Revolutionary War, the community had been a veritable republican hotbed. Seth Noble, a Massachusetts-born Congregationalist minister, had dedicated himself to engendering support for the radical cause among the town's inhabitants. Thus, a Revolutionary Committee was struck, with ten of its twelve members belonging to Noble's church. Although their movement fizzled, the committee's activities threw into relief the existence of sympathy for the revolution among Maugerville's inhabitants.[52]

Noble, who returned to the United States following the movement's collapse, contacted the committee's erstwhile members shortly after the revolution ended. He invited them to leave their home, which was experiencing an influx of Loyalists, and immigrate to the United States, where they could revel in republican liberty. They rejected his request. That people who had shared Noble's republican ardour during the revolution's early phases reacted this way in the conflict's aftermath is suggestive of the extent to which they had grown attached to Nova Scotia – and, by extension, the British Empire – in the intervening years. It is not a coincidence that this was also the era in which many Nova Scotians (including inhabitants of Maugerville) were galvanized by New Light evangelicalism and came to see themselves as beneficiaries of providential favour. Accordingly, religious themes featured prominently in the response sent to Noble by the people to whom he had reached out. Maugerville's one-time revolutionary sympathizers stated that they lived in "a place where God in his providence had smiled upon us," and doubted whether there could be more "vital piety" in the American republic than there was in Nova Scotia. Such statements encapsulate the radical evangelicals' belief that they were a divinely favoured people who had experienced an uplifting religious revival under British rule.[53]

Evangelicals' attachments to Britain would only intensify in the nineteenth century. This was the case because the Baptist Church that absorbed many New Light adherents, whose links to New England Congregationalism had been severed as a result of the revolution, strove to distance itself from reputedly uncouth religious radicalism. Influential figures within the church – including clerics such as Edward Manning and laymen such as J.W. Johnston – downplayed the denomination's associations with unrestrained religiosity and gravitated towards political conservatism and conventional expressions of British patriotism in hopes of gaining recognition for their denomination as a "respectable" pillar of society.[54]

Much like their Catholic counterparts in the Atlantic region and the Canadas, Maritime evangelicals' Christian loyalism was not synonymous with deference to imperial authorities. Evidence can be gleaned from Alline's response to the outbreak of the Revolutionary War. In late 1775, when Nova Scotia's government called up the colonial militia, officers urged Alline to accept a commission. After mulling their recommendation, he opted not to take up the position, declaring that the only commission he would accept would be "[one] from heaven to go forth, and enlist my fellow-mortals to fight under the banners of King Jesus." More than any other figure, Alline was responsible for promulgating the notion that Nova Scotia's New Lights were divinely favoured. This idea, as we have seen, seemingly undergirded their favourable view of the empire. That Alline elected not to acquiesce to the military officials' solicitations reveals that, for all his contributions to the British regime, he was capable of behaving assertively when it came to his interactions with colonial authorities.[55]

Comparable, though not identical, attitudes circulated among the Maritime region's black Dissenters. Debate over the term "black Loyalist" – Barry Cahill has rejected the label because slaves who sided with Britain during the Revolutionary War and migrated north sought "refuge from slavery, not from rebellion" – should not obscure the fact that peoples of African heritage in British North America, many of whom were Dissenters, manifested loyalty to Britain.[56] Christianity's capacity for according "equality to all men before a welcoming God" helps to account for its resonance among black colonists, with the especially egalitarian ethos of such Dissenting traditions as Baptism and Methodism proving particularly appealing.[57] While, in some cases, their loyalty may have sprung from a genuine sense of patriotism, black Maritimers could also deploy that sentiment tactically as a means of securing rights for their communities. Whatever the underlying motivations, the pro-British language of loyalty employed by certain black Maritimers often downplayed Britain's extensive involvement with slavery in the region, where the number of people living in bondage had peaked at approximately two thousand in the 1780s due to the influx of slaves imported by elite Loyalists.[58]

The outlook of Richard Preston, one of the black refugees who relocated to Nova Scotia from the United States during the War of 1812, is indicative of the pro-British views espoused by certain black Maritimers. Preston was instrumental to the founding, in 1854, of the African Baptist Association (ABA), a popular organization that brought together members of that denomination, which boasted more black adherents than any other religious group in the colony. He conveyed fondness for Britain towards the end of his life – Preston died in 1861 – while reflecting on his youth. Preston observed that, after arriving in Nova Scotia at age twenty-five, he felt

> doubly free, free from sin and free from slavery; – thanks be to my God, and thanks be to Old England for thy good laws. The slave that gets his foot upon thy shore, his chains fall, and binds him no more ... [causing him to say] I must go and show [African Americans] the way to heaven and England.[59]

Preston's remarks accord with sentiments that circulated extensively within the black Maritime community. For example, in 1838 members of the African Friendly Society expressed gratitude to the recently installed Queen Victoria "for the blessings of civil and religious liberty we have enjoyed under your illustrious house." And, shortly after the institution's formation in 1854, members of the ABA sang the praises of "Old England, God Bless her, forever," because donations obtained in that nation had been instrumental to the founding of Halifax's first African Baptist church.[60]

Like their white Dissenting counterparts, black Dissenters' sympathy for Britain did not render them subservient. Quite the reverse; they exhibited assertiveness in interactions with imperial authorities. For example, in the early 1830s, Preston travelled to England in hopes of being ordained, and of raising funds that could be used to buy land and build the aforementioned church. During his trip, Preston also became actively involved in the metropolitan abolitionist movement, rubbing elbows with such eminent figures as William Wilberforce and Thomas Fowell Buxton. Rather than deferring to these metropolitan luminaries, Preston availed himself of the opportunity to denounce the evils of slavery forthrightly while in their company. So eloquent were his remarks that an English newspaper (haughtily) observed that Preston's "manner of delivery is exceedingly pleasing, and in his dissertations he evinces much clearness and perspicuity."[61] Admittedly, he was not explicitly challenging imperial authorities. Still, Preston's vigorous involvement in the British abolitionist movement reveals that his loyalist leanings were compatible with assertive behaviour vis-à-vis metropolitan figures. The same could be said for Henry Jackson, a black Methodist who travelled from Nova Scotia to Britain in the 1850s in search of financial aid for his denomination. In addition to his fund-raising activities, Jackson took advantage of the opportunity to discuss with a metropolitan audience issues pertinent to the "black community," not the least of which was slavery.[62]

Despite Simcoe's allegation that they were "hostile ... to the British constitution," Canadian Dissenters – including supposedly subversive denominations like the Methodists, who were linked to radical evangelicalism in the Age of Revolution – contributed to British North America's highly diverse culture of Christian loyalism.[63] Around 1807, a group of Lower Canadian Methodists wrote to one of their metropolitan co-religionists in an effort to obtain for their community the services of a British preacher. The figure to whom they had written responded by encouraging the colonists to direct their request to one of the denomination's branches in the United States, largely because itinerant Methodist preachers from the American republic had been integral to the denomination's growth in the Canadas since the 1790s, crisscrossing the border on myriad occasions and nurturing the growth of a vibrant evangelical culture. Undeterred, the colonists wrote to the metropolitan official again a few years later, reiterating their desire to gain access to a British preacher. In doing so, these Lower Canadian Methodists made plain their ardent loyalism. American preachers, they explained,

> are in general bitter enemies of our good old King and Government ... Therefore we are often stigmatized as a set of Jacobins, when in fact only our [American] spiritual guides are so; but they being our head, we the body are supposedly defiled and corrupted in the Sorbonian Bog of Democracy which we abhor.[64]

As in the Atlantic region, Canadian Dissenters' pro-British bent grew stronger over time. In the upper provinces, this pattern occurred mainly as a result of such developments as the War of 1812, which weakened links between Canadian Methodists and their American counterparts (for instance, during the war's first year, only one Methodist preacher entered Upper Canada from the United States, signalling a dramatic departure from the prewar years), and the post-1815 surge of British immigrants into the Canadas (especially Upper Canada), which reinforced links between metropolitan churches (including Methodism, which increasingly came under the influence of conservative British Wesleyans) and their colonial North American offshoots.[65]

In the early nineteenth century, Egerton Ryerson, an influential journalist, educator, and minister, captured the pro-British views that percolated in the colonial Methodist community of which he was a leader. Evidence can be gleaned from a series of letters Ryerson wrote to Edward Stanley, Britain's colonial secretary, in the early 1830s. The catalyst for the letters was Ryerson's frustration regarding Anglican efforts to monopolize the Clergy Reserves, Crown lands set aside for the benefit of a notoriously ill-defined "Protestant clergy" under the Constitutional Act. Through the letters, Ryerson rejected the English Church's claim that state aid in the form of control over the reserves constituted "a tie" that bound its members to "His Majesty's Paternal Government," and a vehicle for promoting imperial patriotism. For Ryerson, "'the tie which binds' the great body of the inhabitants of Upper Canada to the British Government" was not the self-interested machinations of the colony's "state-paid priests," but rather the spontaneously occurring loyalty that originated within the colonists, most of whom were Dissenters, suffusing society of its own accord. "Their attachment and fidelity to the King's Government," he explained, "are established, and have, in every season of trial, been ... [secured] by nobler ties" than the activities of grasping Anglicans who happened to be the recipients of civil largesse.[66]

Loyalty, for Upper Canadian Dissenters such as Ryerson, was not synonymous with meek acquiescence. Thus, he warned Stanley that, instead of forging links between Upper Canadians and metropolitan authorities, government-supported Anglicanism could jeopardize the genuine ethos of loyalty that permeated the colony's Dissenting majority. He wondered "whether the proposed means to 'tie' the loyalty of the *few*" to Britain through the mechanism of Anglican establishments "will not have a tendency to mortify, to irritate ... and alienate the affections of the *many*." State support for the Church of England, in other words, could function not as a means by which to draw colonial and metropolitan Britons together, but rather as a destabilizing wedge that threatened to drive them apart.[67]

Christian loyalism also existed among the Canadas' Indigenous Dissenters. Consider the remarks, in the early nineteenth century, of Peter Jones (also known as Kahkewaquonaby, or Sacred Feathers). The mixed-race son of an Indigenous man and a white woman, Jones became a successful Methodist missionary to the Ojibwe peoples of Upper Canada's Credit River region after a life-altering conversion experience in the early 1820s.[68] Although many Ojibwe warmed to Christianity, they clung to their linguistic and cultural traditions, and eschewed imported phenomena – social hierarchy, for example – that they found unappealing, testifying to the complex interplay between Indigenous and Western religiosities in colonial North America.[69] Along with other converted "Credit Indians," he espoused pro-British views in an appeal submitted to Queen Victoria in 1837. It observed that "We have been happy and contented to live under the protection of such a great and powerful empire" and expressed "gratitude ... [for] the good we have enjoyed under the British Government," which was lauded for "civilizing and educating" the region's Indigenous inhabitants and exposing them to soul-saving "the Gospel of Jesus Christ."[70]

Anything but obsequious, Jones used loyalism adroitly as a means of pressuring colonial authorities to honour land grants allocated by the Crown to the Credit River region's Indigenous peoples, and curb settlers' encroachments on their territories. "Will your Majesty be pleased," the appeal declared, "to assure us that our lands shall not be taken away from us, or our people ... [and] permit us to go on dividing our lands among our people as our [leaders] in council think best."[71] Jones's rhetorical strategy fits comfortably in a venerable tradition of Indigenous individuals – including ones who happened to be Dissenters – strategically deploying loyalism in hopes of persuading the Crown to honour treaty commitments, whether because of a gnawing sense of obligation, a compelling sense of appreciation, or an irresistible blend of the two.[72]

Historians have debunked the notion, espoused by figures such as Seymour Martin Lipset, that post-revolutionary British North America amounted to a monolithic bastion of conservatism.[73] Yet this notion's religious equivalent – that "Christian Loyalist" invariably meant "reactionary conservative" – remains stubbornly persistent.[74] This interpretation is not entirely erroneous, as conservative clergy in the late eighteenth and early nineteenth centuries took pains to portray themselves as the British Empire's staunchest North American supporters, while denouncing expressions of religious and political dissent as intolerable threats to social order. Yet these figures had neither a monopoly on loyalty nor a majority of colonists on their side. Rather, members of a wide variety of Christian groups, including Catholics and Dissenters from diverse backgrounds, expressed pro-British views for an equally wide variety of reasons. Furthermore, they supported the empire during the American Revolution, the War of 1812, and the Rebellion of 1837–8. By no means synonymous with deference to imperial authorities, these individuals' words and deeds attest to the religious aspect of loyalism, a pluralistic cultural phenomenon that was integral to the persistence of empire in British North America during the Age of Revolution and beyond.

NOTES

1 For their assistance, I would like to thank Michel Ducharme, Michael Lanthier, Elizabeth Mancke, Thomas Peace, Stephanie Pettigrew, and Laura J. Smith.

2 See, for example, James B. Bell, *A War of Religion: Dissenters, Anglicans, and the American Revolution* (London: Palgrave Macmillan, 2008); and Patricia U. Bonomi, *Under the Cope of Heaven: Religion, Society, and Politics in Colonial America*, updated ed. (New York: Oxford University Press, 2003).

3 Nathan O. Hatch, *The Sacred Cause of Liberty: Republican Thought and the Millennium in Revolutionary New England* (New Haven, CT: Yale University Press, 1977); and Amanda Porterfield, *Conceived in Doubt: Religion and Politics in the New American Nation* (Chicago: University of Chicago Press, 2012).

4 Christopher Adamson, "God's Continent Divided: Politics and Religion in Upper Canada and the Northern and Western United States, 1775 to 1841," *Comparative Studies in Society and History* 36, no. 3 (July 1994): 431–2; George A. Rawlyk, "Politics, Religion, and the Canadian Experience: A Preliminary Probe," in *Religion and American Politics: From the Colonial Period to the 1980s*, ed. Mark A. Noll (New York: Oxford University Press, 1990), 261; and S.F. Wise, "Sermon Literature and Canadian Intellectual History" in *God's Peculiar Peoples: Essays on Political Culture in Nineteenth-Century Canada*, ed. A.B. McKillop and Paul Romney (Ottawa: Carleton University Press, 1993), 6.

5 On Anglican establishments in British North America, see Peter M. Doll, *Revolution, Religion, and National Identity: Imperial Anglicanism in British North America, 1745–1795* (Madison, NJ: Farleigh Dickinson University Press, 2000); and Curtis Fahey, *In His Name: The Anglican Experience in Upper Canada, 1791–1854* (Ottawa: Carleton University Press, 1991). Throughout the nineteenth century, Anglicans battled with Methodists, Presbyterians, and (to a lesser extent) Baptists for numerical dominance among British North American Protestants. These denominations exerted tremendous influence within the primarily English-speaking colonies, while Roman Catholicism was predictably dominant in overwhelmingly French-speaking Lower Canada / Quebec. Michael Gauvreau, "Protestantism Transformed: Personal Piety and the Evangelical Social Vision, 1815–1867," in *The Canadian Protestant Experience 1760 to 1990*, ed. George Rawlyk (Burlington, ON: Welch, 1990), 96–7.

6 On the centrality of institutions, including churches, to the development of a statist Canadian political culture that differed from the libertarian model that took root in the United States, see Elizabeth Mancke, "Early Modern Imperial Governance and the Origins of Canadian Political Culture," *Canadian Journal of Political Science* 32, no. 1 (March 1999): 3–20.

7 See, respectively, David Mills, *The Idea of Loyalty in Upper Canada, 1784–1850* (Montreal and Kingston: McGill-Queen's University Press, 1988); and Mark G. McGowan, "Canadian Catholics, Loyalty, and the British Empire, 1763–1901," in *Loyalism and the Formation of the British World, 1775–1914*, ed. Allan Blackstock and Frank O'Gorman (Woodbridge, UK: Boydell Press, 2014), 201–22.

8 On the flexibility of loyalism, see Blackstock and O'Gorman, eds, *Loyalism and the Formation of the British World*; and Jerry Bannister and Liam Riordan, eds, *The Loyal Atlantic: Remaking the British Atlantic in the Revolutionary Era* (Toronto: University of Toronto Press, 2012). On the Age of Revolution, see David Armitage and Sanjay Subrahmanyan, eds, *The Age of Revolutions in Global Context* (London: Palgrave Macmillan, 2010); and Michel Ducharme, *The Idea of Liberty in Canada during the Age of Atlantic Revolutions, 1776–1838* (Montreal and Kingston: McGill-Queen's University Press, 2014).

9 Elizabeth Mancke, "The American Revolution in Canada," in *A Companion to the American Revolution*, ed. Jack P. Greene and J.R. Pole (Malden, MA: Blackwell, 2000), 503.

10 John Webster Grant, *Moon of Wintertime: Missionaries and the Indians of Canada in Encounter since 1534* (Toronto: University of Toronto Press, 1985), 72–3.

11 Michael S. Cross, *A Biography of Robert Baldwin: The Morning-Star of Memory* (Don Mills, ON: Oxford University Press, 2012), 105–7.

12 John Kenyon, "The Influence of the Oxford Movement upon the Church of England in Upper Canada," *Ontario History* 51, no. 2 (Spring 1959): 79–88.

13 Doll, *Revolution, Religion, and National Identity*, 15–16.

14 Michael R. Watts, *The Dissenters* (Oxford: Clarendon Press, 1995), 2: 417–18.

15 J.C.D. Clark, *English Society, 1660–1832: Religion, Ideology, and Politics during the Ancién Regime*, 2nd ed. (Cambridge: Cambridge University Press, 2000).

16 Edmund Burke, *Reflections on the Revolution in France*, ed. L.G. Mitchell (Oxford: Oxford University Press, 1993), 99.

17 D.G. Bell, "Religious Liberty and Protestant Dissent in Loyalist New Brunswick," *University of New Brunswick Law Journal* 36 (1987): 147–8.

18 Judith Fingard, *The Anglican Design in Loyalist Nova Scotia, 1783–1816* (London: SPCK, 1972), 2–11.

19 J.M. Bumsted, "Church and State in Maritime Canada, 1749–1807," Canadian Historical Association *Historical Papers* 2, no. 1 (1967): 41–2; John S. Moir, "The Upper Canadian Roots of Church Disestablishment," *Ontario History* 60, no. 4 (December 1968): 247–58; and Denis McKim, "Upper Canadian Thermidor: The Family Compact and the Counterrevolutionary Atlantic," *Ontario History* 107, no. 2 (Autumn 2014): 253–6.

20 Jacob Mountain, *A Sermon Preached at Quebec ... Being the Day Appointed for a General Thanksgiving* (Quebec: John Neilson, 1799), 29–30.

21 John Strachan, *A Sermon, Preached at York, Upper Canada, Third of July, 1825, on the Death of the Late Lord Bishop of Quebec* (Kingston: James MacFarlane, 1826), 19.

22 John S. Moir, *The Church in the British Era: From the British Conquest to Confederation* (Toronto: McGraw-Hill Ryerson, 1972), 87–9; and Fingard, *The Anglican Design in Loyalist Nova Scotia*, 29–30 and 124–9.

23 Charles Inglis, *Steadfastness in Religion and Loyalty Recommended...* (Halifax: John Howe, 1793).

24 Ibid., 8–10.

25 Ibid., 16.

26 Wise, "Sermon Literature and Canadian Intellectual History," 3–18. Examples include the sermons written by Inglis, Mountain, and Strachan cited elsewhere in this essay.

27 McGowan, "Canadian Catholics, Loyalty, and the British Empire," 202.

28 Mark G. McGowan, "Rendering unto Caesar: Catholics, the State, and the Idea of a Christian Canada," Canadian Society of Church History *Historical Papers* (2011): 67–8; Moir, *Church in the British Era*, 38–62. Relations between Catholics and Protestant authorities in British North America were by no means purely harmonious. On the conflict that occasionally characterized this relationship, see Jean-Pierre Wallot, "Religion and French-Canadian Mores in the Early Nineteenth Century," in *Prophets, Priests, and Prodigals: Readings in Canadian Religious History, 1608 to Present*, ed. Mark G. McGowan and David B. Marshall (Toronto: McGraw-Hill Ryerson, 1992), 60–2.

29 Terrence Murphy, "The English-Speaking Colonies to 1854," in *A Concise History of Christianity in Canada*, ed. Terrence Murphy and Roberto Perin (Toronto: Oxford University Press, 1996), 164–5; and Bumsted, "Church and State in Maritime Canada," 47.
30 Gilles Chaussé, "French Canada from the Conquest to 1840," in Murphy and Perin, *A Concise History of Christianity*, 59–71; and McGowan, "Canadian Catholics, Loyalty, and the British Empire," 204.
31 Adam Shortt and Arthur G. Doughty, eds, *Documents Relating to the Constitutional History of Canada, 1759–1791* (Ottawa: King's Printer, 1907), 1: 403
32 Jacques Monet, *The Last Cannon Shot: A Study of French-Canadian Nationalism, 1837–1850* (Toronto: University of Toronto Press, 1969), 52; and Yvan Lamonde, *The Social History of Ideas in Quebec, 1760–1896* (Montreal and Kingston: McGill-Queen's University Press, 2013), 41.
33 Terrence Murphy, "The Emergence of Maritime Catholicism, 1781–1830," *Acadiensis* 13, no. 2 (Spring 1984): 42; Éloi Degrâce, "Joseph-Mathurin Bourg," *Dictionary of Canadian Biography*, vol. 4, http://www.biographi.ca/en/bio/bourg_joseph_mathurin_4E.html, accessed 18 April 2016; Murphy, "The English-Speaking Colonies," 125–6; and Chaussé, "French Canada from the Conquest," 61.
34 Luca Codignola, "Roman Catholic Conservatism in a New North Atlantic World, 1760–1829," *William and Mary Quarterly*, 3rd series 64, no. 4 (October 2007): 717–56.
35 Kathleen M. Toomey, *Alexander Macdonell: The Scottish Years, 1762–1804* (Toronto: Canadian Catholic Historical Association, 1985), 103–58.
36 Brandon S. Corcoran and Laura J. Smith, "Bishop Macdonell and the Friends of Ireland: Mixing Politics and Religion in Upper Canada," *Historical Studies* 79 (2013): 7–23.
37 Linda Colley, *Britons: Forging the Nation, 1707–1837* (New Haven, CT: Yale University Press, 1992), 119–20.
38 Alexander Macdonell, "The Address of Bishop Macdonell, to the Inhabitants of the County of Glengarry," in *A Short Account of the Emigration from the Highlands of Scotland, to North America; and the Establishment of the Catholic Diocese of Upper Canada* (Kingston: 1839), 26–8.
39 J.E. Rea, *Bishop Alexander Macdonell and the Politics of Upper Canada* (Toronto: Ontario Historical Society, 1974), 76–7, 191–2.
40 *Newfoundlander*, 7 May 1829, n.p. See also John P. Greene, *Between Damnation and Starvation: Priests and Merchants in Newfoundland Politics, 1745–1855* (Montreal and Kingston: McGill-Queen's University Press, 1999), 48–50.
41 *Newfoundlander*, 28 May 1829, n.p. Similar celebrations took place in Carbonear and Harbour Grace.

42 Ibid. Irish Catholics exhibited loyalism elsewhere in the Atlantic region, as evidenced by the beliefs and behaviour of Nova Scotia's Irish-born vicar general, Edmund Burke. See Burke, *Letter of Instruction to the Catholic Missionaries of Nova Scotia and Its Dependencies* (Halifax: A. Gay, 1804), 3–7; McGowan, "Canadian Catholics, Loyalty, and the British Empire," 205–6; and Murphy, "The English-Speaking Colonies," 125–6.

43 Greene, *Between Damnation and Starvation*, 65–6. Maritime Catholics – for example, Angus MacEachern, one of Prince Edward Island's most powerful priests – also asserted themselves in dealings with colonial officials. Murphy, "The Emergence of Maritime Catholicism," 13.

44 Linda Colley, "Britishness and Otherness: An Argument," *Journal of British Studies* 31, no. 4 (October 1992): 327; Watts, *The Dissenters*, 2: 350–3.

45 George W. Spragge, ed., *The John Strachan Letter Book, 1812–1834* (Toronto: Ontario Historical Society, 1946), vii; and Moir, *Church in the British Era*, 12–13, 19–20.

46 G.A. Rawlyk, *The Canada Fire: Radical Evangelicalism in British North America, 1775–1812* (Montreal and Kingston: McGill Queen's University Press, 1994), 126–31; and Adamson, "God's Continent Divided," 125.

47 Elizabeth Mancke, "Another British America: A Canadian Model for the Early Modern British Empire," *Journal of Imperial and Commonwealth History* 25, no. 1 (January 1997), 23–4; and Rawlyk, *The Canada Fire*, 131.

48 G.A. Rawlyk, *Ravished by the Spirit: Religious Revivals, Baptists, and Henry Alline* (Montreal and Kingston: McGill-Queen's University Press, 1984), 84–5; Rawlyk, *The Canada Fire*, 131–2; and Jo-Ann Carr Fellows, "Mary Coy," in *Dictionary of Canadian Biography*, vol. 8, http://www.biographi.ca/en/bio/coy_mary_8E.html, accessed 23 April 2016.

49 On the resonance of loyalty within diverse colonial communities, including Dissenting Protestantism, see Keith Shepherd Grant, "Enthusiasm and Loyalty: Emotions, Religion, and Society in British North America" (PhD diss., University of New Brunswick, 2017).

50 Gordon Stewart and George Rawlyk, *A People Highly Favoured of God: The Nova Scotia Yankees and the American Revolution* (Toronto: Macmillan, 1972), 154–88; and Rawlyk, *The Canada Fire*, 137.

51 On affect in the Age of Revolution see Grant, "Enthusiasm and Loyalty."

52 M.W. Armstrong, "Neutrality and Religion in Revolutionary Nova Scotia," in *Historical Essays on the Atlantic Provinces*, ed. G.A. Rawlyk (Toronto: McClelland and Stewart, 1967), 33–43; and Stewart and Rawlyk, *A People Highly Favoured of God*, 58.

53 Stewart and Rawlyk, *A People Highly Favoured of God*, 180–1.

54 Rawlyk, *Ravished by the Spirit*, 84–99.

55 Mark A. Noll, "The American Revolution and Protestant Evangelicalism," *Journal of Interdisciplinary History* 23, no. 3 (Winter 1993): 622.

56 Barry Cahill, "The Black Loyalist Myth in Atlantic Canada," *Acadiensis* 29, no. 1 (Autumn 1999): 79.

57 James St G. Walker, *The Black Loyalists: The Search for a Promised Land in Nova Scotia and Sierra Leone, 1783–1870* (New York: Africana, 1976), 66–7, 70–86.

58 Harvey Amani Whitfield, *Blacks on the Border: The Black Refugees in British North America, 1815–1860* (Burlington: University of Vermont Press, 2006), 104; and Harvey Amani Whitfield, *North to Bondage: Loyalist Slavery in the Maritimes* (Vancouver: UBC Press, 2016), 8–10, 45.

59 Whitfield, *Blacks on the Border*, 96.

60 Ibid., 84–95.

61 Frank S. Boyd Jr, "Richard Preston," *Dictionary of Canadian Biography*, vol. 8, http://www.biographi.ca/en/bio/preston_richard_8E.html, accessed 24 April 2015); and P.E. McKerrow, *A Brief History of the Coloured Baptists of Nova Scotia ...* (Halifax: Nova Scotia Printing Co., 1895), 19–24.

62 Whitfield, *Blacks on the Border*, 97–8.

63 E.A. Cruikshank, ed., *The Correspondence of Lieut. Governor John Graves Simcoe* (Toronto: Ontario Historical Society, 1923), 1: 251–2.

64 Goldwin French, *Parsons and Politics: The Role of the Wesleyan Methodists in Upper Canada and the Maritimes from 1780 to 1855* (Toronto: Ryerson Press, 1962), 70. See also Todd Webb, *Transatlantic Methodists: British Wesleyanism and the Formation of an Evangelical Culture in Nineteenth-Century Ontario and Quebec* (Montreal and Kingston: McGill-Queen's University Press, 2013), 51–3.

65 Elizabeth Jane Errington, "British Migration and British America, 1783–1867," in *Canada and the British Empire*, ed. Phillip Buckner (New York: Oxford University Press, 2008), 140–1; Webb, *Transatlantic Methodists*, 15; and French, *Parsons and Politics*, 67.

66 *Christian Guardian*, 30 October 1833, 202.

67 Ibid.; see also 23 July 1831, 146.

68 Peter Jones, *The Sermon and Speeches of the Rev. Peter Jones ...* (Leeds, UK: n.d. [1831?]), 8.

69 Donald B. Smith, *Mississauga Portraits: Ojibwe Voices from Nineteenth-Century Canada* (Toronto: University of Toronto Press, 2013), 19; and Nancy Christie and Michael Gauvreau, *Christian Churches and Their Peoples, 1840–1965: A Social History of Religion in Canada* (Toronto: University of Toronto Press, 2010), 107–8.

70 Peter Jones, *History of the Ojebway Indians: With Especial Reference to Their Conversion to Christianity* (London, 1861), 266.

71 Ibid. See also Donald B. Smith, *Sacred Feathers: The Revered Peter Jones (Kahkewaquonaby) and the Mississauga Indians* (Toronto: University of Toronto Press, 1987), 164–6.

72 Sarah Carter, "Aboriginal People of Canada and the British Empire," in Buckner, *Canada and the British Empire*, 205–18. For Indigenous peoples, employing the "language of loyalty" in exchanges with imperial authorities did not preclude other discursive strategies. Rather, as Jennifer Reid has demonstrated, in addition to utilizing the vocabulary of "Britishness," Mi'kmaw peoples in the Maritimes asserted their right to the region's territory in exchanges with metropolitan officials by stressing such factors as history (asserting that "Our Fathers" had "possessed" the land before Europeans arrived) and spirituality (informing British authorities that "God [gave them] the land first"). See Jennifer Reid, *Myth, Symbol, and Colonial Encounter: British and Mi'kmaq in Acadia, 1700–1867* (Ottawa: University of Ottawa Press, 1995), 78–83.

73 Seymour Martin Lipset, *Continental Divide: The Values and Institutions of the United States and Canada* (New York: Routledge, 1990). Alternative interpretations include E. Jane Errington, *The Lion, the Eagle, and Upper Canada: A Developing Colonial Ideology* (Montreal and Kingston: McGill-Queen's University Press, 1987); and D.G. Bell, *Early Loyalist Saint John: The Origin of New Brunswick Politics, 1783–1786* (Fredericton: New Ireland Press, 1983).

74 For a recent example, see Jonathan Den Hartog, "Trans-Atlantic Anti-Jacobinism: Reaction and Religion," *Early American Studies* 11, no. 1 (Winter 2013): 142.

4 Liberty, Loyalty, and Sentiment in Canada's Founding Debates, 1864–1873

JERRY BANNISTER

Among the recent trends in pre-Confederation Canadian political history, two stand out. The first is the interest in using intellectual traditions – particularly liberalism, but also republicanism and others – as the primary means for explaining the formation of Canada. Practitioners of this approach propound a range of ideologies, but they share a common belief that ideas shape loyalties. Whereas Jeff McNairn emphasizes the intellectual influence of the public sphere, for example, Michel Ducharme stresses the role of different concepts of liberty. And, while Ian McKay and Janet Ajzenstat advocate starkly different interpretations of liberalism and its impact on society, they both share a faith that its rise in the nineteenth century explains Canada. Whether conceptualized as a (unjust) liberal order or a (just) Lockean founding, this framework favours ideas such as liberty over factors such as loyalty. The second trend is the interest in using imperial and colonial influences – particularly loyalty, but also Britishness and Protestantism – as the principal vehicle for assessing the development of British North America. Like their colleagues in intellectual history, practitioners of this approach are far from united in their politics, but they share a common understanding that loyalties and identities shape political ideas and opinions. Whereas Elizabeth Mancke emphasizes the impact of state institutions on regional political cultures, for example, Geoffrey Plank stresses the effects of geopolitics and raw imperial power on colonial societies. While John Mack Faragher and Phillip Buckner embrace radically different visions of the British Empire, for instance, they both share a faith that its influence explains the development of British North America. Whether conceived as a (malignant) agent of settler colonialism or a (benign) engine of migration and settlement, this framework favours identities and institutions over ideas and intellectual traditions.[1]

My goal in this chapter is to explore ways to bridge the gap between these two trends. This goal stems from a number of concerns and questions. The first is my own disappointment in the attempts (including my own) to use McKay's liberal order framework to generate fresh debates in Canadian history. In retrospect, the belief that the *Liberalism and Hegemony* project would move the field forward proved naive.[2] Rather than open up debate, the "liberal turn," if you will pardon a neologism, runs the risk of creating new orthodoxies that are just as stifling as the old ones. The promise of intellectual history carries with it the peril of draining the history of British North America of the emotion and fear that animated so much of nineteenth-century public life, such as in response to cholera epidemics. I understand and appreciate the desire of intellectual historians to raise Canadian political history above the quotidian muck of venality, corruption, and avarice. But I worry that, in focusing so intently on the bourgeois public sphere, we give too much credit to ideas and too little to emotions.[3] On the other hand, the rise of settler colonialism as an explanatory framework brings with it the risk of simplifying the complex public sphere that political historians have painstakingly unearthed.[4] Colonialism was, like liberalism, central to the making of Canada; settler colonialism, like the liberal order framework, should be a starting point for inquiry, rather than a destination. As with liberalism, one of the most important aspects of colonialism is the way it was publicly explained and legitimized. Re-examining the logics and the languages of Confederation will help us to understand more fully why it received sufficient political support to become enacted in 1867–73.

Our reliance on intellectual traditions to explain the political history of North America would strike many nineteenth-century intellectuals as odd. In his study of American pragmatism, Louis Menand summarized the perspective of Charles Peirce, William James, Oliver Wendell Holmes, Jr, and John Dewey this way: "We don't act because we have ideas; we have ideas because we must act, and we act to achieve ends."[5] Recoiling from the horrors of the Civil War, American pragmatists came to view ideas not as the animating source for politics but rather as the tools we use to pursue the ends we want. The Civil War played, of course, a significant role in the debates surrounding Confederation, and, when I started work on this paper, my initial impulse was to track how fear of the United States shaped colonial politics in the 1860s.[6] The Confederation debates are littered with references to the threat of invasion, but what is striking about those references is how they are tied so intimately to the connection with Great Britain. For example, in a speech to the Canadian Legislative Assembly in February 1865, John A. Macdonald repeatedly invoked the spectre of war, but in doing so he stressed that pro-Confederates were willing to face the sacrifices of war with the United States in order to preserve their link with Britain:

> At the very mention of the prospect of a war some time ago, how were the feelings of the people aroused from one extremity of British America to the other, and preparations made for meeting its worst consequences? Although the people of this country are fully aware of the horrors of war – should a war arise, unfortunately, between the United States and England, and we pray it never may – they are still ready to encounter all perils of that kind for the sake of the connection with England.[7]

Macdonald was, in other words, invoking war as something that Confederation could make more, not less, likely, as relations between Britain and the United States remained tense. A year later, in a speech to the Nova Scotia House of Assembly, Charles Tupper used the dangers posed by the Fenians to offer the more familiar argument that Confederation offered security:

> Holding the sentiments I do – believing that the crisis has come when we must decide whether we shall be annexed to the United States or remain connected to the parent state, I would be the blackest traitor that ever disgraced a country if I did not by every means in my power urge upon this legislature to prove equal to the emergency and take that course which, in a few months, will secure that consolidation of British North America and the connection with the crown of Great Britain which I believe, which I know, it is the sincere wish of the people to secure, and which can alone place these provinces in a position that will at once give them dignity of position and ensure their safety.[8]

In making this argument, Tupper's goal was to attack his opponents, particularly Joseph Howe, as much as it was to build up his own base of support.

In assessing this type of argument, several points are worth noting. First, as Macdonald himself was careful to claim, the rights enjoyed by Canadian subjects were conditional on the connection with Britain. Liberty was, in other words, dependent on loyalty. "So long as that alliance is maintained," Macdonald argued, "we enjoy, under her protection, the privileges of constitutional liberty according to the British system."[9] After affirming the loyalty of the people of Canada East and West, he quipped, "But, if they can by [any] possibility be exceeded in loyalty, it is by the inhabitants of the Maritime provinces. Loyalty with them is an overruling passion."[10] I do not think that Macdonald's word choice here was accidental, because it fits a broader pattern in how politicians invoked and described loyalty. Macdonald and Tupper wanted to connect Confederation and loyalty in the public mind, but they also sought to make important distinctions between policies and feelings. As Tupper was careful to point out, he held sentiments that shaped his principles towards Confederation.

Tupper's use of *sentiment* was not mere window dressing or hollow rhetoric that clouded the substantive debate over principle. My point is that such language itself formed an important part of Canada's founding debates.[11] Tupper and his peers used such language frequently yet self-consciously: while they linked notions of sentiment to questions of liberty, their discussions of loyalty and the connection to Britain were, in important ways, qualitatively different from discussions of liberalism. Invocations of sentiment were not restricted to conservatives, nor were they used solely in support of Confederation. As John Robson, a radical in British Columbia, put it, "Depend on it, sir, the people are seldom wrong in their opinions; in their sentiments they are never mistaken."[12] Politicians who used such language were careful to distinguish it from the language of materialism. As James Johnston argued in the Nova Scotia Assembly in 1864:

> What is it ... that creates this marked distinction between ourselves and the neighbouring states? It is the sentiment we breathe – the influence that we have derived from our connection with the parent state. The influences of monarchical institutions have permeated through us and given a marked colour to all our sentiments. It is, however, a distinction that exists in sentiment, and not one that exists in any material or real form. But is this sentiment to be perpetuated?[13]

Contemporaries were well aware of the risks of emphasizing sentiment too much. In British Columbia, the pro-Confederate Joseph Trutch argued, "I say that loyalty is no exploded idea, call it a sentiment if you will; life is nothing without sentiment; everyone whose soul is not dead must cling to love of country and attachment to her flag, as one of the most cherished sentiments of the heart, and I regard loyalty as one of the most deep-rooted and highly prized treasures of the human breast."[14]

Trutch was being rather melodramatic, but his statement fits well with mainstream liberal thought. In the introductory chapter to *On Liberty*, John Stuart Mill invoked sentiment as a way to frame his argument on the need to guard against what he called the tyranny of the magistrate and the tyranny of the majority. For Mill, sentiment was not a synonym for feeling or emotion, nor did he equate it with sentimentality, which was a term that he used only once, pejoratively, in *On Liberty*. In his formulation of liberty, Mill invoked the term alongside opinion: "This, then, is the appropriate region of human liberty. It comprises, first, the inward domain of consciousness; demanding liberty of conscience, in the most comprehensive sense; liberty of thought and feeling; absolute freedom of opinion and sentiment on all subjects, practical or speculative, scientific, moral, or theological."[15] In his discussion of opinion, Mill observed that sentiments emerged out of morality, but he did not view them through the lens of the private world of the individual. Unlike liberty, which Mill associated with the individual, sentiments were associated with the social. Sentiments formed part of the public ties that bound society together, while liberty gave individuals the protection from social oppression. According to Mill, "education brings people under common influences, and gives them access to the general stock of facts and sentiments."[16] "Why then should tolerance," Mill asked, "as far as the public sentiment is concerned, extend only to tastes and modes of life which extort acquiescence by the multitude of their adherents?"[17]

When Mill turned to the question of nationalism in his *Considerations on Representative Government*, he opened the chapter by referring to the "sentiment of nationality."[18] In his analysis of the "common sympathies" that formed the essential core of nationality, Mill argued that they could flow from different sources. On the one hand, Switzerland had a strong sense of nationhood yet encompassed different languages, denominations, and ethnicities. On the other hand, Sicily shared a common language, religion, and history with Naples yet constitituted a different nationality. The point for Mill, and for many of participants in the Confederation debates, was that "fellow-feeling" was essential for the proper functioning of free institutions and representative government.

This sense of connectedness emanated from neither a Lockean social contract nor a principled calculation of utility. It was neither a base emotion nor a popular enthusiasm. The use of sentiment by Mill and the politicians of British North America accorded with a usage that became common in the seventeenth and eighteenth centuries and was employed by a variety of writers, from Jonathan Swift and Daniel Defoe to Charles Dickens. The *Oxford English Dictionary* defines it this way: "What one feels with regard to something; mental attitude (of approval or disapproval, etc.); an opinion or view as to what is right or agreeable. Often *pl.* with collective sense."[19] Though the precise meaning could vary, the term was commonly used in a positive sense to denote a viewpoint believed to be genuine, common, and deeply held.[20] Appealing to a person or group's sentiments meant appealing to more than their self-interest. It offered a way for politicians across British North America to find rhetoric and arguments that crossed colonial, regional, ethnic, and linguistic borders. It also provided an important means to circumvent divisive political issues, such as legislative union versus federalism, and to blunt opposition. While it was used in the context of threats, such as the Fenian attacks, it was not deployed (at least not explicitly) to pander to fears or to stoke prejudices. By invoking sentiments, politicians most often invoked the historic and emotive ties to England, particularly the Crown, rather than to the policies of the British government.[21]

They were participating in a public debate over the links between ethics and social bonds that stretched back to Adam Smith's influential treatise.[22]

Contemporaries who employed patriotic language knew that they could be criticized for waving the flag too much. According to W.H. Pope, who was speaking to the House of Assembly in Prince Edward Island in 1865, there existed a clear understanding of how patriotic appeals were viewed:

> I feel, sir, that I am approaching what my eloquent friend, the member for Charlottetown, Mr. Brecken, is pleased facetiously to designate the "*glory argument*." I attach great importance to this glory argument. I desire to live under monarchical institutions and the glorious flag of old England. Sir, there are in this house honourable members who smile when the glory argument is mentioned. Their fathers made great sacrifices in order that they might enjoy those privileges which are the inheritance of British subjects.[23]

As important as the "glory argument" was, there were clear limits to how far it could be taken. As Archibald McLelan said in response to pro-Confederates in the Nova Scotia in 1866, "I have no hesitation in telling the honourable gentleman that he is tampering with the loyalty and allegiance of the people. He knows our attachment to the mother country is strong, but he must not count too much on it."[24] Loyalty, like liberalism, was always mixed to varying degrees with other beliefs and traditions, according to shifts in colonial politics.[25] For McLelan, the loyalty of the British subject was conditional on the principle that "[he] be consulted in all changes affecting his rights and privileges and the constitution under which he lives."[26] The evidence from the debates indicates that participants understood the bipartite nature of the social contract, which depended on both consent and allegiance. "By adhering to the monarchical principle," John A. Macdonald claimed, "we avoid one defect inherent in the constitution of the United States."[27] This was because an elected president could, as a mere politician, never be "the sovereign and chief of the nation," but Canadians had a sovereign "whom you respect and love."[28]

Macdonald's link of nation and sovereign was echoed in many of the exchanges in colonial legislatures. For French Canadians, this pairing of nation and sovereign raised the spectre of the Conquest. Joseph Perrault's speech in 1865 took what was the hardest line that I have found in the debates: "Yes, Mr. Speaker, the policy of England has ever been aggressive," Perrault said, "and its object has always been to annihilate us as a people."[29] Such views attracted limited support in the Legislative Assembly. In response to Perrault, Joseph Dufresne questioned, to cheers from his fellow members, "What good can result from thus ransacking history in order to hold up a single page, the record of an evil deed ... Why bring up that matter now? What good can it do? Does the honourable member desire to provoke the prejudices of a sensitive and powerful nation against us?"[30] Alexander Mackenzie recognized that national sentiment was both a stumbling block to the negotiations yet an inseparable part of the process: "I believe that that feeling of nationality has been our sole difficulty in working our present political system. But I do not believe for one moment that it would be possible or perhaps desirable to extinguish that strong feeling of nationality."[31] In a later exchange, Mackenzie took this point further. Responding to an earlier speech by George-Étienne Cartier that emphasized the loyalty of French Canadians to the British Crown during the American and French Revolutions, Mackenzie said, "The honourable gentleman's claim was perfectly just. But I believe that they were actuated by another feeling beyond the feeling of loyalty – that they felt their only safeguard as a distinct people, the only way to preserve their nationality, was to remain attached to Great Britain."[32] In Mackenzie's view, the Crown was the guarantor of both liberty and identity.

In their discussions of identity and nationalism, participants in the Confederation debates drew directly on Mill. Ambrose Shea, in a speech to the Newfoundland Assembly in 1865, quoted Mill's *Considerations on Representative Government*, which considered the roles of identity and memory in the formation of a nation.[33] Mill's argument on the role of national sentiment struck at the heart of the debate over unitary versus federal forms of government. While Cartier did not quote Mill directly, his speech to the Legislative Assembly in February 1865 tackled the question of the differences between French and English Canada. He did so by making a distinction between "political nationality" – that is, the proposed union – and the "races" that lived within it. Cartier asked rhetorically, "Look for instance at the United Kingdom, inhabited as it was by three great races. Had the diversity of race impeded the glory, the progress[,] the wealth of England?"[34] His question echoed Mill's point about the composition of Switzerland.

Cartier's point lies at the heart of Janet Ajzenstat's thesis about the Canadian founding. For Ajzenstat, what is most important about the views of the "Fathers of Confederation" is that "although there was no *social* vision, there was a *political* one." "They devised, and bequeathed to us today," Ajzenstat continues "a collective *political* identity, a civic identity, or as they called it a *political nationality*."[35] One limitation of this interpretation is that it keeps the role of the Crown in protecting liberties but drops the role of sentiment. It sheds light on the importance of Lockean ideas of consent, but does little to explain the cultural identities in which Confederation was debated. It does not account for the continued role of imperialism, the rise of English-Canadian nationalism, or the deeply racist governments that colonialism produced. For Ajzenstat, the purity of the Lockean founding remains above and separate from the feelings, biases, and sentiments that fed federal politics. While Ian McKay rejects Ajzenstat's fondness for Locke, he shares her faith that the abstract concepts of individualism and property rights explain the formation of Canada.[36]

Nineteenth-century liberals did not share this view. *Lord Durham's Report* is known popularly for three things – prejudice against French culture, advocacy of responsible government, and a call for colonial union – but Durham paid particular attention to issues such as taxation, the administration of justice, and the allocation of power. His section on Upper Canada covered many of the causes of discontent among the colonists, including the challenges of geography to fostering national sentiment:

> Its inhabitants scattered along an extensive frontier, with very imperfect means of communication, and a limited and partial commerce, have, apparently no unity of interest or opinion. The Province has no great centre with which all the separate parts are connected, and which they are accustomed to follow in sentiment and action; nor is there that habitual intercourse between the inhabitants of different parts of the country, which, by diffusing through all a knowledge of the opinions and interests of each, makes a people one and united, in spite of the extent of territory and dispersion of population.[37]

Durham advocated legislative union not only as a way to spur French Canadians to "abandon their vain hopes of nationality,"[38] but also to increase the ties between the colonists and Great Britain. At the end of his *Report*, Durham laid out his case emphatically: "I am, in truth, so far from believing that the increased power and weight that would be given to these Colonies by union would endanger their connexion with the Empire, that I look to it *as the only means of fostering such a national feeling* throughout them as would effectually counterbalance whatever tendencies may now exist towards separation."[39] Only by "raising up for the North American colonist some nationality of his own" could the extension of American influence be countered. National identities were, for Durham, both the cause and the effect of colonial union.

Durham's comments raise important questions about interpreting political identities. It brings us back to Carl Berger's classic formulation of the link between British imperialism and Canadian nationalism.[40] The question was not so much pro- or anti-empire, or pro- or anti-nation, but about what *type* of nationality and empire politicians in British North America advocated. Was it an ethnic nationalism tied to British ancestry, or a civic nationalism linked to constitutional bonds? Was it based on a shared loyalist history, or allegiance to a constitutional monarchy? Was the polity to be, as P.B. Waite asked, a *British* or a *British-American* empire? For Waite, "The most pervasive characteristic of British Americans was their passionate desire for a place in the world."[41] What divided politicians was not so much constitutional principles as how to achieve that place. These politicians "were still adolescent with high dreams and fancies; nationality was the most golden of them all," Waite concluded.[42] When opponents of the Quebec Resolutions realized that the tide was turning against them, they naturally returned to the question of identity and empire.

More than anyone else, Joseph Howe represented the conundrum that faced politicians who opposed Confederation while stressing their loyalty to Britain. Knowing that he was fighting a losing battle, in 1867 Howe and two allies appealed directly to Lord Carnarvon. Their long letter recounted every conceivable objection to Confederation – from concerns over taxation and revenue to defence and economic development – but it culminated with an overwrought claim to identity and loyalty. "It is said that the tendencies of modern political life are to the consolidation into large states of people having one origin, or speaking a common language," they noted. Germans and Italians were, they observed, breaking down the barriers that divided them into separate polities. They then launched their final appeal:

> This is true; but let it be remembered that what the Germans and Italians dream for and fight for we now have. We are in full communion with all who speak our language in every part of the world (the United States excepted)[,] we have one Sovereign, one flag, with the most populous, wealthy, and powerful city, the fountainhead of our civilization, and the Pantheon where our sacred dust reposes for a capital.[43]

By invoking a religious metaphor, they were making it clear that the connection to Britain transcended trade, security, or constitution. For them, the tie to the mother country was their very lifeblood.

Howe's gambit failed because the pro-Confederates had already circumvented his argument. Even past his prime, Howe could still wield eloquence and command attention, but John A. Macdonald had taken great pains to prevent anyone from successfully using the glory argument against him. He did this in what is generally viewed as his most important speech in the Confederation debates, held in the Canadian Assembly in 1865. On 6 February, Attorney General Macdonald rose in the Legislative Assembly to make his case for a federal union. In his lengthy speech, which encompasses twenty dense pages of double-column text, he covered a wide range of issues – including the need to protect minority rights, the impracticalities of legislative union, the benefits that Confederation would bring for trade and defence, and the need to avoid the errors of previous colonial systems – but woven throughout his speech was the connection to Britain. Halfway through, he returned to the imperative of remaining true to the monarchical principle: "I believe it is of the upmost importance to have that principle recognized, so that we shall have a Sovereign who is placed above the region of party – to whom all parties look up to – who is not elevated by the action of one party nor depressed by the action of another."[44] The sentiment associated with having a monarch whom they could "respect and love" was important because it acted as a counterbalance to the passions of deliberative democracy. The tie to Britain represented, therefore, a higher ideal. Macdonald pointed out that the "public mind" of England wanted to maintain the connection with British North America, though Britons were generous enough to allow the colonists to sever their ties if that was their desire.[45] He argued that, in order to signal the imperative of maintaining those ties, the first of the Quebec Resolutions of 1864 had made it clear that the federal union would be under the Crown of Great Britain. Macdonald claimed that keeping this imperial link would, in fact, help to strengthen connections between the colonies and to ensure that they did not fall prey to the divisions that led to the American Revolution.

As Macdonald built his argument, he was careful to diffuse opposition. He argued that the proposed federation would not override local interests or interfere with the interests and culture of minorities. He reiterated that there would be no money votes unless introduced into the popular branch of the federal legislature. Macdonald then returned to the Quebec Resolutions. He reminded everyone of the penultimate resolution, 71, which states "That Her Majesty the Queen be solicited to determine the rank and name of the Federated Provinces."[46] Macdonald used this as a springboard to return to the queen and the connection to Britain, in a critical part of his speech:

> One argument, though not a strong one, has been used against this Confederation, that it is an advance towards independence. Some are apprehensive that the very fact of our forming this union will hasten the time when we shall be severed from the mother country. I have no apprehension of that kind. I believe it will have the contrary effect. I believe that as we grow stronger, that, as it is felt in England we have become a people, able from our union, our strength, our population, and the development of our resources, to take our position among the nations of the world, she will be less willing to part with us than she would be now, when we are broken up into a number of insignificant colonies, subject to attack piece-meal, without any concerted action or common organization of defence. I am strongly of opinion that year by year, as we grow in population and strength, England will

> more see the advantage of maintaining the alliance between British North America and herself.[47]

Moving to his conclusion, Macdonald emphasized that the imperial connection brought with it all the constitutional liberties of the British system, which protected minority rights. Yet, for Macdonald, the benefits were not merely constitutional or even material. The connection would ensure that "our public men will be actuated by principles similar to those which actuate the statesmen at home." "These although not material, physical benefits, of which you can make an arithmetical calculation, are of such overwhelming advantage to our future interests and standing as a nation," he asserted, "that to obtain them is well worthy of any sacrifices we may be called upon to make, and the people of this country are ready to make them (Cheers)."[48] And then, before sitting down at 11:00 pm, Macdonald warned of the dangers of missing such a great opportunity to create a nation under the fostering care of Queen Victoria.

Macdonald's speech comprised an amalgam of liberal ideology and loyal sentiment. He was careful to emphasize the principle of consent, the protection of minority rights, and the rule of law. In doing so, he was drawing on the Lockean tradition that Janet Ajzenstat sees as so central to the Canadian founding. But, for Macdonald, loyalty to the Crown was more than the means to an end, whether constitutional or economic. It was a goal in and of itself, something that brought more than material benefits, something worth sacrifice to obtain. Macdonald said relatively little about the people or their rights, and even less about justice or equality. Nor did he rely, as Tories such as John Beverley Robinson had a generation earlier, on a Lockean social contract whereby men consented to be governed by a government so long as their property was protected.[49] Macdonald's rhetoric was more romantic and more rooted in sentiment. It was populist in the sense of being calculated to appeal to legislators, but he was doing much more than pandering to prejudices by waving the union flag. Confederation represented a lofty ideal because it would unite British North Americans and strengthen their ties to Britain. More than any other argument, this is the selling point to which he kept returning and on which he chose to end. He thus made it virtually impossible for figures such as Howe to use arguments about loyalty against the cause of Confederation.

What does this have to do with unrest, violence, and the search for social order? How does focusing on *sentiment* help us to understand the political culture of British North America? My first response is to acknowledge the limits of focusing on the language and rhetoric in the founding debates. It tells us precious little, maybe next to nothing, about what the majority of people living in British North America thought, felt, or did.[50] Even in the realm of high politics, it does not fundamentally alter the conventional wisdom that liberalism was central to the public debates in the nineteenth century. In reading the debates over Confederation, I was repeatedly struck by the loud silences on issues such as women's rights, poverty, injustice, or Indigenous peoples. What focusing on sentiment does offer, however, is a way to bridge the divide between studies of liberty and loyalty. It shows that participants in the debates over Confederation self-consciously made explicit arguments based on sentiments, and that they recognized distinctions between those arguments and other arguments as they discussed the socio-political order. It demonstrates the different ways that politicians invoked the connection to Britain, both for and against a legislative union, and how they understood the distinction between "nations" and "races." It illuminates how politicians negotiated the tangled politics of identity and loyalty in ways that both McKay's liberal order and Ajzenstat's Lockean founding cannot capture.

By getting us closer to the actual language used in the colonial legislatures, this approach helps us understand the arguments on which public men relied. When Macdonald quipped that Maritimers had an "overruling passion" for loyalty, he was referring, I believe, as much to a social vision as a political one. Macdonald and others portrayed this vision as more noble than the gritty negotiations over taxes or representation by population. The language of loyalty intersected with the language of liberalism – sentiment formed a type of connective tissue that bound together different strains of thought – but it could also operate on a separate plane. As Frederick Brecken put it in a speech to the Nova Scotia Assembly in 1865, questions of allegiance raised questions of sacrifice. After raising serious objections to the report of the Quebec Conference, Brecken said, "If ... the choice is between a union with the sister provinces and a severance with the mother country, I would say, let us be united, *even at a sacrifice of our local interests*."[51] For Brecken, as for many propertied men in British North America, severing the connection with Britain represented their ultimate fear.

NOTES

1 There is not space here to cite all the relevant studies, but see, for example, Jeffrey L. McNairn, *The Capacity to Judge Public Opinion and Deliberative Democracy in Upper Canada, 1791–1854* (Toronto: University of Toronto Press, 2000); Michel Ducharme, *Le concept de liberté au Canada à l'époque des Révolutions atlantiques, 1776–1838* (Montreal and Kingston: McGill-Queen's University Press, 2010); Ian McKay, "The Liberal Order Framework: A Prospectus for a Reconnaissance

of Canadian History," *Canadian Historical Review* 81, 4 (2000): 617–46; Janet Ajzenstat, *The Canadian Founding: John Locke and Parliament* (Montreal and Kingston: McGill-Queen's University Press, 2007); Janet Ajzenstat and P.J. Smith, eds, *Canada's Origins: Liberal, Tory, or Republican?* (Ottawa: Carleton University Press, 1995); Elizabeth Mancke, *The Fault Lines of Empire: Political Differentiation in Massachusetts and Nova Scotia, 1760–1830* (New York: Routledge, 2004); Geoffrey Plank, *Rebellion and Savagery: The Jacobite Rising of 1745 and the British Empire* (Philadelphia: University of Pennsylvania Press, 2006); John Mack Faragher, *A Great and Noble Scheme: The Tragic Story of the Expulsion of the French Acadians from Their American Homeland* (New York: Norton, 2005); and Phillip Buckner, "Defining Identities in Canada: Regional, Imperial, National," *Canadian Historical Review* 94, 2 (June 2013): 289–311.

2 Jean-François Constant and Michel Ducharme, eds, *Liberalism and Hegemony: Debating the Canadian Liberal Revolution* (Toronto: University of Toronto Press, 2009).

3 See Barbara Rosenwein, "Worrying about Emotions," *American Historical Review* 107, no. 3 (June 2002): 821–45.

4 Lorenzo Veracini, "'Settler Colonialism': Career of a Concept," *Journal of Imperial and Commonwealth History* 41, no. 2 (2013): 313–33.

5 Louis Menand, *The Metaphysical Club: A Story of Ideas in America* (New York: Farrar, Straus and Giroux, 2001), 364.

6 Greg Marquis, *In Armageddon's Shadow: The Civil War and Canada's Maritime Provinces* (Montreal: McGill-Queen's University Press, 1998).

7 *Canada's Founding Debates*, ed. Janet Ajzenstat, Paul Romney, Ian Gentles, and William D. Gairdner (Toronto: University of Toronto Press, 2003), 206.

8 Ibid., 175.

9 Ibid., 206.

10 Ibid., 205.

11 On the role of sentiment in debates over colonial legal reform, see Jeffrey L. McNairn, "'The Common Sympathies of Our Nature': Moral Sentiments, Emotional Economies, and Imprisonment for Debt in Upper Canada," *Histoire sociale / Social History* 49, no. 98 (May 2016): 49–71.

12 *Canada's Founding Debates*, 35.

13 Ibid., 168.

14 Ibid., 215.

15 John Stuart Mill, *On Liberty* (1859; Kingston: Batoche Books, 2001), 15.

16 Ibid., 68.

17 Ibid., 63.

18 John Stuart Mill, *Considerations on Representative Government* (1861; Kingston: Batoche Books, 2001), 181.

19 *Oxford English Dictionary Online*, http://www.oed.com.ezproxy.library.dal.ca/view/Entry/176056?redirectedFrom=Sentiment#eid.

20 Michael Bell, "The Cult of Sentiment and the Culture of Feeling," *Representations of Emotions* 3 (1999): 87–98; and Marie Banfield, ed., "Special Issue: From Sentiment to Sentimentality: A Nineteenth-Century Lexicographical Search," *Interdisciplinary Studies in the Long Nineteenth Century* 19, no. 4 (2007).

21 There is not space here to cite all the relevant studies of imperialism in Canadian history, but see, for example, D.R. Owram, "Canada and the Empire," in *Oxford History of the British Empire,* vol. 5, *Historiography*, ed. Robin Winks (Oxford: Oxford University Press, 1999), 146–8; Phillip Buckner, "Introduction: Canada and the British Empire," in *Canada and the British Empire*, ed. Phillip Buckner (Oxford: Oxford University Press, 2008), 1–20; Jane Errington, *The Lion, the Eagle, and Upper Canada: A Developing Colonial Ideology,* 2nd ed. (Montreal and Kingston: McGill-Queen's University Press, 2012); Kathleen Wilson, "Histories, Empires, Modernities," in *A New Imperial History: Culture, Identity, and Modernity in Britain and the Empire, 1660–1840*, ed. Kathleen Wilson (Cambridge: Cambridge University Press, 2004); Nancy Christie, ed., *Transatlantic Subjects: Ideas, Institutions, and Social Experience in Post-Revolutionary British North America* (Montreal and Kingston: McGill-Queen's University Press, 2008); and Maya Jasanoff, *Liberty's Exiles: American Loyalists in the Revolutionary World* (New York: Alfred A. Knopf, 2011).

22 Adam Smith, *The Theory of Moral Sentiments* (London: A. Millar, 1759).

23 *Canada's Founding Debates*, 197.

24 Ibid., 245.

25 This point is developed further in Jerry Bannister and Liam Riordan, "Loyalism and the British Atlantic, 1660–1840," in *The Loyal Atlantic: Remaking the British Atlantic in the Revolutionary Era*, ed. Jerry Bannister and Liam Riordan (Toronto: University of Toronto Press, 2012), 3–36.

26 *Canada's Founding Debates*, 245.

27 Ibid., 281.

28 Ibid., 282.

29 Ibid., 350.

30 Ibid., 353.

31 Ibid., 344.

32 Ibid., 345.

33 Ibid., 257.

34 Ibid., 230.

35 Janet Ajzenstat, *The Canadian Founding: John Locke and Parliament* (Montreal and Kingston: McGill-Queen's University Press, 2007), 81 (emphasis in original).

36 Ian McKay, "Canada as a Long Liberal Revolution: On Writing the History of Actually Existing Canadian Liberalisms," in Constant and Ducharme, *Liberalism and Hegemony*, 347–52.
37 *Lord Durham's Report on the Affairs of British North America*, ed. C.P. Lucas (1839; Oxford: Clarendon Press, 1912), 146.
38 Ibid., 307.
39 Ibid., 310 (emphasis added).
40 Carl Berger, *The Sense of Power: Studies in the Ideas of Canadian Imperialism, 1867–1914*, 2nd ed. (Toronto: University of Toronto Press, 2013).
41 P.B. Waite, *The Life and Times of Confederation, 1864–1867: Politics, Newspapers, and the Union of British North America* (Toronto: University of Toronto Press, 1962), 327.
42 Ibid., 328.
43 *Letter Addressed to the Earl of Carnarvon by Mr Joseph Howe, Mr William Annand, and Mr Hugh McDonald: Stating Their Objections to the Proposed Scheme of Union of the British North American Provinces* (London: G.E. Eyre and W. Spottiswoode, 1867), 21.
44 *Parliamentary Debates on the Subject of the Confederation of the British North American Provinces, 3rd session, 8th Provincial Parliament of Canada* (Quebec: Hunter, Rose & Co., Parliamentary Printers, 1865), 33.
45 Ibid.
46 *The Quebec Resolutions, October, 1864*, Library and Archives Canada, https://www.collectionscanada.gc.ca/confederation/023001-7104-e.html
47 *Parliamentary Debates on the Subject of the Confederation of the British North American Provinces*, 43.
48 Ibid., 44.
49 This argument is developed in Jerry Bannister in "Canada as Counter-Revolution: The Loyalist Order Framework in Canadian History, 1750–1840," in Constant and Ducharme, *Liberalism and Hegemony*, 98–146.
50 On the contested social dimensions of royalism in public life, see Ian Radforth, *Royal Spectacle: The 1860 Visit of the Prince of Wales to Canada and the United States* (Toronto: University of Toronto Press, 2004).
51 *Canada's Founding Debates*, 223 (emphasis added).

SECTION II

From Tory Imperialism to Liberal Settler Colonialism

Colonization and wars of the long eighteenth century (1688–1815) dramatically accelerated the global visibility of the military and ministry in the imperial governance of the British Empire, which in turn triggered strong reactions from colonists, a constitutional crisis over Parliament's role in legislating for the colonies, and ultimately a War for Independence (1775–83) by thirteen colonies and the founding of the United States.

Colonists who chose not to support the war were accused by rebels of supporting Tory imperialism against settler interests. Loyalists, however, were concerned about the constitutional problems inherent in the ministry and military's enhanced power, yet they also decried the turn towards militarized violence by both their fellow colonists and the British government as an appropriate tactic for resolving the constitutional problems engendered by rapid territorial expansion. Although scholars have shown that the Loyalists' ideological differences with the rebels were fewer than the commonalities, the myth remains strong that Loyalists contributed a Tory touch to post-1783 British North America.

The chapters in this section explore aspects of the shifting balance from the ascent of a kind of Tory imperialism in the mid-eighteenth century to its eclipse after the Napoleonic Wars (1803–15) and the emergent agendas set by liberal settler colonialism. Jeffers Lennox argues that the Continental Congress's failed invasion of Quebec in the fall and winter of 1775–6 made it decide to focus on securing the colonies already committed to resistance, including declaring independence in July 1776. The Continental Congress had believed that the recently conquered Canadiens would embrace rebel liberators, and were surprised to find that they did not. The ignominy of military failure in Canada contributed, Lennox shows, to the Continental Congress's moving to a higher stakes War of Independence, thereby embedding militarized revolution in the metanarrative of modernity. Ironically, the Canadian indifference to the Americans' invitation by invasion to join the resistance contributed to the push towards independence.

John G. Reid shows how the British military needed Indigenous friends and allies, especially in the vast parts of North America with few colonists. Treaties and policies of peace and friendship, coupled with the Royal Proclamation of 1763, shaped Indigenous-imperial relations through the Napoleonic Wars and provided more protection to Indigenous peoples than would settler colonialism. The rising tide of settlers, first with Loyalist refugees and then after 1815 with waves of settlers out of Britain and Ireland, led to the dispossession of Indigenous peoples from their lands. Civilian authorities in the colonies also gained power, and, in the shift towards liberal settler colonialism, prior commitments to Indigenous peoples were neglected by settlers but remembered by Indigenous peoples.

The next two chapters offer close analyses of settler society in the Canadas. Elsbeth Heaman focuses on the transition from the Tory imperial state to the liberal colonial state, as manifested in the Canadian Indian Department in the 1820s and 1830s. Through an analysis of the 1828 Darling Report on Indigenous Affairs, Heaman demonstrates that Darling, a Tory appointee, still thought that Indigenous nations were important to the empire, and recognized that their interests, particularly their lands, needed protecting. She argues that this Tory "policing" of ethnic boundaries was replaced by the liberal settler state with a commitment to "civilizing" Indigenous peoples, a policy that blurred boundaries and made Indigenous people increasingly vulnerable to dispossession.

Jane Errington explores the challenges of incorporating thousands of immigrants, some of whom were sick and destitute, into settler society. The large numbers of immigrants relative to the existing population and the small colonial state in Upper Canada strained resources and threatened that the people who were supposed to be a blessing to the growing colony might be a destabilizing force. Anxious to impose a modicum of order, in 1833 the lieutenant governor appointed Anthony Hawke as the colony's "chief emigrant agent." Assisted by agents, Hawke undertook to establish a system for immigrant reception, recording who was arriving and their condition, identifying the sick and indigent, and moving healthy settlers on to their final destinations. Errington shows the critical role of even a small colonial state to the maintenance of order.

Collectively, these essays offer ways to understand why the Tory imperial state of the late eighteenth and early nineteenth centuries, despite its reliance on the military and the ministry, often provided better protection to minority peoples in the British Empire than did its successor liberal settler state, which displayed greater confidence in the processes of civilization producing modern order, even if it meant assimilation through cultural destruction.

5 Revolution Expected: The Invasion of Quebec and American Independence

JEFFERS LENNOX

Canada is perhaps one of the last things brought to mind by the Declaration of Independence. The declaration is a quintessentially American document, born of either practical necessity or the product of a divine plan, depending on one's perspective. But the revolution that gave birth to the Declaration of Independence is American only if we read the outcome backwards.[1] The "Thirteen Colonies" so readily presented by historians as the building blocks of the United States existed in a continent without hard and fast borders, and the revolutionary spirit could be found not only in Boston, Philadelphia, and Savannah, but also in Halifax, Montreal, and many places in between. By shifting the focus of the revolution slightly north, past loyalist New York along the Hudson River to Albany, and north from there beyond the Mohawk River and Iroquioa to Lake Champlain and, eventually, to the St Lawrence and Quebec, new connections that link the Declaration of Independence to revolutionary ideas about Canada come into focus.[2]

The American invasion of Quebec, which began in the summer of 1775 and lasted through the spring of 1776, is hardly ignored historical territory. Historians have documented and described the various ways in which revolutionary Americans failed to win over the French Canadians.[3] American historians pay less attention to this episode, though it features in most sweeping narratives of the era because it explains Richard Montgomery's death and demonstrates that Benedict Arnold was not all bad.[4] Yet, Canada features more heavily in the revolutionary mind than is often understood. From the Quebec Act (1774) to the American invasion to negotiations in Paris (1782–3), both the British province of Quebec (colloquially known as Canada at the time) and the colonies that formed the nucleus of British North America were a constant source of concern among leading revolutionary politicians, military leaders, and civilians.[5]

Even the Declaration of Independence has a Canadian history.[6] Recent studies have demonstrated that alternative interpretations of the revolutionary era and a continental approach illuminate just how entangled was the development of British North America and the United States.[7] There emerged in northern North America a geographic and ideological borderland in which events, ideas, and ideologies impacted patriots and loyalists alike.[8] Although triumphalist national narratives tend to focus on how Thomas Paine's *Common Sense* and patriot victories in the Northeast helped shaped the path towards independence, there are many ways to understand the early months of 1776. To Paine's words and American military victories, we should add the patriot losses in Canada to the list of factors that culminated in Thomas Jefferson's most famous document.[9] I argue in this chapter that the failure of the American invasion of Quebec, and the patriots' inability to push the revolution north forced politicians and citizens in the rebelling colonies to focus on independence. In turn, the Declaration of Independence took some of the sting out of the failure of the Canadian campaign.

The American invasion of Canada did not turn out as the revolutionaries had hoped. Patriots directed most of their attention towards the province of Quebec, even though a small but vocal group in Nova Scotia sent repeated requests for an invasion of that province.[10] Convincing the French inhabitants to commit to the patriot cause was ultimately unsuccessful. As Gustav Lanctot notes, "The Canadian was a good Norman ... quite capable of distinguishing who was master at the moment; and of serving him for his own profit."[11] H.V. Nelles calls this response "the Acadian option."[12] As Damien Bélanger argues in this collection, and others have explored elsewhere, there is an important difference between loyalty and loyalism.[13] The French in Quebec teetered between loyalty to the British and ambivalence towards the patriots, which posed a significant obstacle for the invaders who believed the Canadians would happily upset the social order to exact revenge for the Conquest of 1763.[14]

The invasion of Canada, and the tepid Canadian response, served as a pivotal moment in the American Revolution. What had been defined by British Americans as a defence of liberty was transformed into an offensive campaign against Canada. Leading revolutionaries hoped that social unrest in places such as Boston and Philadelphia would be mirrored in Montreal and the city of Quebec. American military success in capturing Montreal and the Americans' expectation that revolutionary violence and disorder would sweep across the province were blunted by the inability to conquer Quebec. Patriot efforts met with Canadian ambivalence, forcing the rebels to reconsider their options and surrender – temporarily, at least – the hope of increasing to fourteen the number of colonies taking up arms against king and Parliament.[15] Ultimately, colonial leaders and most of their subjects in Quebec rejected the idea of breaking away from the British, favouring social order and loyalty over unrest and violence. In return, British officials invested money and manpower to protect their loyal provinces.[16] This episode sheds light on revolutionary goals and Canada's wider influence on American independence. A fuller understanding of this relationship requires an examination of the invasion of Quebec, the Canadian response, and the reaction of revolutionaries to an abject failure. The Canadian theatre put its stamp on the revolutionary movement in both practical and ideological ways. Ultimately, the "radicalism" of the American Revolution was hastened by its Canadian experiences.[17] Failures in (and second thoughts about) Canada nudged Americans closer to independence by forcing military and diplomatic leaders to focus their efforts not on attacking British tyranny wherever they believed it existed, but rather on fighting for American liberty where it could be won.[18]

Interest in Canada among American politicians was common after the British Parliament passed the Quebec Act, extending the colony's borders into territory coveted by British American settlers. In 1774, 1775, and 1776, the Continental Congress meeting at Philadelphia published addresses to the citizens of Quebec, hoping to encourage unrest by convincing them to join the revolutionary cause. The first letter was drafted over the course of September and October 1774 and then published in Philadelphia newspapers.[19] It informed Canadians that they were being denied important British rights and encouraged them to send delegates to the next meeting of Congress.[20] None arrived. The second address, published in May 1775, was shorter than the first but worked harder to inspire social upheaval. Coming shortly after Lexington and Concord, Congress invited Canadians "to join with us in resolving to be free, and in rejecting, with disdain, the fetters of slavery, however artfully polished." Slavery served as a central theme in the letter: "By the introduction of your present form of government, or rather present form of tyranny, you and your wives and your children are made slaves." Relying on the Canadians' sense of their past, and the history of animosity between the French and the British, Congress explained that they could not presume "that you are so lost to all sense of honor. We can never believe that the present race of Canadians are so degenerated as to possess neither the spirit, the gallantry, nor the courage of their ancestors."[21] For American patriots reading these letters, which the colonial press published, Canadian recalcitrance was infuriating.

Within months of the second letter, the American attack on Canada signalled an important shift in revolutionary ideology. Attacks on British forts near or in Canada, including Ticonderoga on Lake Champlain and Saint Jean on the Richelieu River south of Montreal in the late spring of 1775, provided spoils, including much-needed armaments for the siege of Boston. These were minor campaigns, not planned offensives meant to expand revolutionary ideals. George Washington was concerned about what aggressive moves would mean for the patriot cause. Writing to the Massachusetts General Court in August 1775 in response to a request from the people of Machias, Maine, for an attack on Nova Scotia, Washington noted the difference between offensive and defensive measures. Congress included no representatives from Nova Scotia, and consequently the province was subject to the commercial restrictions imposed on British goods. But neither had Nova Scotians launched hostilities against the United Colonies, and, so, "to attack them therefore is a Step of Conquest rather than Defence, & may be attended with very dangerous Consequences."[22]

Perceived British perfidy made it easier for Washington to jettison his concerns about taking offensive measures. The British seemingly refused to attack American positions around Boston once they were completed, and Washington knew that the British were so entrenched "as to render our approaches almost impossible without great Slaughter." So he sent Benedict Arnold up the Kennebec River to attack Quebec and, importantly, to divert attention from a second attack on Montreal to be led by Philip Schuyler and Richard Montgomery. "If these Expeditions succeed," Washington confided to his brother, "the Ministry will make a glorious figure with their Canada Bill, & the Regiments which they proposed to raise in that Government for the purpose of Deluging our Frontier Settlements in Blood."[23]

The first stage of the American invasion of Quebec gave patriots reason to celebrate the expansion of their cause. Richard Montgomery marched his forces to Montreal (Schulyer remained at Albany), and the city fell without resistance on 13 November 1775.[24] Just days earlier, American forces had captured the strategically important sites of Chambly and St Johns. Washington and Congress received the news with great joy, and the Americans were optimistic that Montgomery and Arnold would work together effectively in Canada.[25] The two had a formidable task ahead of them. General Carleton had barely escaped from Montreal and had fled to Quebec before Montgomery's arrival. The American general followed shortly after, meeting Benedict Arnold and his troops, who had travelled from Cambridge, Massachusetts, via the Kennebec, Chaudière, and St Lawrence Rivers. This was no easy voyage, and reports circulated in the colonies of men "subsisting upon dead dogs, devouring their shoes ... to complet the grand work of the subduction of Canada."[26] Arnold's "Little Army" had completed a march "equal to Hanibals over the Alps."[27] The American forces camped outside Quebec for several weeks before launching an attack. Members of Congress remained optimistic, but the bombardment of Quebec over the course of several days in December resulted in only two Canadian casualties: one non-combatant and a turkey (also unarmed). After the unsuccessful onslaught, the Americans launched an ill-fated attack during a stormy night on 30 December. Montgomery was killed quickly, and Arnold was badly wounded. Without the aid of the Canadians, most of whom refused to raise arms for the Americans, the city remained in British hands. News of the failed attack trickled slowly to Philadelphia. In a 12 January letter, John Hancock declared, "by the last advices from Canada we are flattered with the hopes of a fortunate issue of the Campaign in that quarter." But, just five days later, a more somber Hancock reported "we have this day rec'd disagreeable accotts. from Canada, poor Montgomery & severall officers kill'd, Arnold Wounded, &c."[28]

After the failed attack, Congress issued a third letter to the Canadians, which was meant to bolster support for the invasion. If the first letter was meant to educate, and the second to scare, the final address was a humbler plea. Congress, having learned of Montgomery's death, assured Canadians that "the best of causes are subject to vicissitudes; and disappointments have ever been inevitable." "Such is the lot of human nature," but "we will never abandon you to the unrelenting fury of your and our enemies."[29] In support of that end, Canadians were called upon to raise regiments and to appoint delegates to Congress. With Montgomery's defeat at Quebec and the lack of specie to pay Canadians for their supplies, what little support the Americans did enjoy waned, though many in Congress remained convinced of Canada's importance. "No Cost or pains must be Spared to Secure the important Province of Canada," blustered Josiah Bartlett, the New Hampshire delegate.[30]

Even facing the formidable challenges of Montgomery's death and Canadian ambivalence, Washington and Congress remained dedicated to the Canadian campaign. Washington emphasized the need to send more troops and reiterated that "no person can be more sensible of the importance of securing Canada than I am."[31] Congress agreed and did its best to keep troops and supplies marching north. In a letter to Washington, John Hancock argued, "The most vigorous Measures should be adopted, as well to defend our Troops against the Canadians themselves, as to ensure Success to the Expedition." Controlling Quebec was important "for Reasons too obvious to be mentioned," and Congress would do whatever it could to send troops to "quiet the Minds of the Canadians and to remove the Sources of their Uneasiness & Discontent."[32] For John Adams, these efforts came much too late. "That we have been a little tardy in providing for Canada is true – owing to innumerable Difficulties," he wrote to Horatio Gates. "However," he continued, "We have been roused at last, and I hope have done pretty well."[33] Quebec was still in British hands; American troops were tired, ravaged by smallpox, and wanted to return home; and the Canadians clung to their judicious neutrality. It would take a small miracle for Canada to join the American colonies.

Though no miracle could bring Richard Montgomery back from the dead, he lived on in the pages of colonial newspapers, which voiced his wishes for an independent American future. Montgomery's death was also celebrated in the increasingly vocal opposition press in England, which hailed the fallen general as a hero.[34] His death shocked and saddened Americans who had hoped that he would prove instrumental in winning Canadian support, and it did not take long before he acquired martyr status.[35] Reports of Montgomery's fate circulated widely within the rebelling colonies, and interested readers became aware of Canada's impact on the revolutionary cause. In early May 1776, the *Virginia Gazette* published Thomas Paine's imagined dialogue between the ghost of General Montgomery and a delegate for Congress. The spectral encounter took place in a wooded area near Philadelphia. Readers would not have been surprised to learn that death had not dampened Montgomery's zeal for the American cause. "I am glad to see you," he began. "I still love liberty and America," Montgomery informed the delegate, "and the contemplation of the future greatness of this continent now forms a large share of my present happiness."[36] Yet the dead general was concerned that the American colonies might consider terms of accommodation from Britain. The delegate voiced his worry that independence would bring "domestick wars without end." Montgomery replied that delaying independence by fifty years would not prevent "the supposed contensions between sister colonies," if they existed at all. It was the weakness of the colonies that would preserve the union, because each needed the other. Canada served as an important example: "Had the colony of Massachusetts Bay been possessed of the military resources which it would probably have had fifty years hence, would she have held out the signal of distress to her sister colonies, upon the news of the Boston port bill? No; she would have withstood all the power of Britain alone, and afterwards the neutral colonies might have shared the fate of the colony of Canada."[37] The only thing worse than death in Canada, apparently, was for the British American colonies to remain in the empire.[38]

Military leaders, soldiers, and even revolutionary ghosts were unable to convince Canada to join the American colonies, so Congress turned to Benjamin Franklin.[39] There had been rumblings for months from a pro-American faction in Montreal that more diplomatic efforts were required to convince French inhabitants to support the Americans fully. In February 1776, Canadian Prudent Lajeunesse, a resident of Longueuil who had campaigned for the American forces in the Richelieu valley, appeared before Congress and requested that they send delegates to explain the American position.[40] Congress agreed and named Benjamin Franklin, Samuel Chase, and Charles Carroll of Carrollton as the "Commissioners to Canada." Chase was a member of the Maryland legislature and future Supreme Court justice, while Carroll (who added "of Carrollton" to his name as a way of distinguishing himself from relatives) was a Roman Catholic planter, businessman, investor, and politician.[41] Invited to accompany the commissioners was John Carroll, Charles Carroll's cousin, who was a Catholic priest. The Carrolls knew only too well the challenges facing Catholics in the American colonies compared to their brethren in Canada.[42] Unlike Catholics in Ireland and in British colonies such as Maryland, Catholics in Quebec after 1774 (like those in Grenada after 1768) looked to Britain to protect their religious freedoms.[43] For his part, John Carroll was not optimistic about the commission, though he fretted less about religion than about the proper process of revolution. He laid out his concerns over neutrality and social order in a letter drafted (unfinished and never sent) shortly after learning of his appointment:

> From all the information I have been able to collect concerning the State of Canada, it appears to me, that the inhabitants of that country are no wise disposed to molest the united colonies, or prevent their forces from taking & holding possession of the strong places in that province, or to assist in any manner the British arms. Now if it be proposed that the Canadians apprehend it will not be in my power to advise them to it. They have not the same motives for taking up arms against England, which render the resistance of the other colonies so justifiable. If an oppressive mode of government has been given them, it was what some of them chose, & the rest have acquiesced in. Or if they find themselves oppressed they have not tried the success of petitions & remonstrances, of all which ought, as I apprehend, to be ineffectual before it can be lawful to have recourse to arms & change of government.[44]

For John Carroll, then, any Canadian unrest or violence, regardless of American encouragement, was illegitimate until all other options had been exhausted.

Congressional delays hurt the diplomatic mission to Canada. The commissioners were named in February, and Franklin hoped to set out for Montreal shortly thereafter; however, it took weeks to get instructions drafted and they were not approved until 20 March.[45] In the interim, members of Congress discussed the mission's prospects. John Adams, writing to his wife, Abigail, on 18 February expressed his desire to participate in the commission. "I wish I understood French as well as you," he admitted, "I would have gone to Canada, if I had."[46] That same day, Adams wrote to James Warren, president of the Massachusetts Provincial Congress, noting "the Unanimous Voice of the Continent is Canada must be ours, Quebec must be taken." Adams was satisfied that Congress had done everything in its power to accomplish this laudable goal, and, if the mission fell short "I shall be easy because I know of nothing more or better that We can do." Canada was important, according to Adams, because it could do so much damage if left under British control. "In the Hands of our Enemies," he warned, "it would enable them to inflame all the Indians upon the Continent, and perhaps induce them to take up the Hatchet, and commit their Robberies and Murders upon the Frontiers of all the southern Colonies as well as to pour down Regulars, Canadians and Indians together upon the Borders of the Northern."[47] Franklin, Chase, and the Carrolls were tasked with preventing this danger. The commissioners were to assure Canadians that they would be welcomed into the union, enjoy the free practice of their Catholic religion, and have the same laws and freedoms as the other colonies.[48]

Franklin and his co-commissioners left for Montreal in mid-April 1776 and reached their destination by the end of the month. Perhaps the most troublesome issue they encountered upon their arrival was the dire economic realities facing Americans in Montreal. Their first two letters sent to Congress detailed just how grave the situation had become. Many French Canadians had initially welcomed the patriot invaders as potential customers in need of food and goods and carrying hard currency. Within months, however, the low opinion of American credit was leading Canadians to question whether Congress had much power at all, and the fact that soldiers resorted simply to taking what they wanted from the inhabitants did little to win Canadian favour. Of course, lack of money was in no small part what caused soldiers to behave as they did, as "it is very difficult to keep soldiers under proper discipline without paying them regularly."[49] Without an infusion of hard money (Canadians had long since tired of Congressional scrip used after specie ran out), it would be best to withdraw the army and fortify the lakes against possible attack from the British and, quite possibly, the Canadians themselves.[50] Their third letter lamented that "the Tories will not trust Us a Farthing and some who perhaps wish Us well, conceiving that We shall thro' our own poverty, or from superior Force be soon obliged to abandon the Country, are afraid to have any Dealings with Us, least they should hereafter be called to Account for Abetting our Cause." What goodwill had existed among the Canadian inhabitants was evaporating as a result of the violence they endured at the hands of patriot soldiers who took what they needed without paying: "A Conduct towards a people, who suffered Us to enter their Country as Friends, that the most urgent Necessity can scarce excuse, since it has contributed much to the Changing their good Dispositions towards Us into Enmity, makes them wish our Departure."[51]

The mission to Canada was a failure. Over the course of the next few days, John Carroll attempted to win over the clergy, with little success. As Damien Bélanger argues in this volume, a 1776 *mandement* from Bishop Briand outlined for French Catholics the dangers (temporal and spiritual) of supporting the Americans. Carroll's assurances that patriots would welcome French Catholics were challenged by the presence of John McKenna, an Irish Catholic priest from the Mohawk Valley who had been chased out of the colonies; Franklin had no luck with merchants or politicians at Montreal; and Chase and Charles Carroll could do little to improve military prospects.[52] The situation was dire, and, less than two weeks after their arrival, Franklin and John Carroll returned to Philadelphia. Chase and Charles Carroll remained in Canada and oversaw military affairs as best they could, while smallpox and a lack of supplies continued to devastate the American troops. In a report to Schuyler, Chase and Charles Carroll emphasized the need for food: "The army here is suffering from want of Provisions particularly Pork. None, or next to none, is to be procured in Canada," they complained, adding, "For God sake send off Pork."[53] With so few things going well for the Americans, it is hardly surprising that officials were growing worried. Washington fretted that holding on to Canada, a region he considered so valuable to the American cause, was becoming impossible.[54]

Members of Congress spent May, June, and July dissecting the Canadian debacle and convincing themselves that a military defeat was in fact a strategic victory. Part of the process was assigning blame, and there was plenty to go around. John Adams pointed the finger at American politicians, who had been hoodwinked. "This Day has brought us the Dismals from Canada. Defeated most ignomininiously," he fumed to James Warren. "Where shall We lay the blame?" he asked rhetorically before providing the answer: "America, duped and bubbled with the Phantom of Commissioners, has been fast asleep and left that important Post undefended, unsupported."[55] Adams was referring to rumours of a possible peace negotiation that had, so he argued, distracted colonial leaders from the task at hand. "The Ministry have [*sic*] caught the Colonies, as I have often caught a Horse," he quipped, "by holding out an empty Hat, as if it was full of Corn."[56]

Loyalty and social order had prevailed over the revolutionary sentiment that patriots expected would sweep across Canada. In the face of such dismal reports on the failures of the campaign, members of Congress worked to cast the entire episode in a more favourable light. These arguments generally fell into two categories: first, that it was unnecessary to hold Canada if the Americans could control the waterways leading into the colonies; and second, that the campaign itself was useful for other purposes, even if the ultimate goal of winning Canadian support had failed. In early June, Richard Henry Lee described how the

Americans could benefit from what they held, despite not having taken Quebec. The forces had retreated from the town and were fortifying a region about thirty miles away, at the falls of Richelieu. "If they can maintain that Post," Lee argued, "which commands 8 tenths of Canada, we shall do almost as well as if we had Quebec [the city], as we [there]by effectively cut off all communication with the upper Country, or Western Indians, and prevent the West Indies receiving supplies from that fertile Province."[57] Richard Morris agreed, suggesting a few days later that although the entire affair had been badly managed: "I dont think we have any occasion to hold that Country, if we maintain the passes on the Lakes it is sufficient for our purposes and the Garrison that defend[s] those passes will always be ready to rush into Canada if the Enemy quit it."[58] The country itself was less important than controlling points of entrance and exit, which could be done as long as a few key posts were maintained.

The American defeat in Canada closed the door on an expansive revolution northward. As a result, challenging British imperial tyranny was no longer sustainable as a sufficient revolutionary cause. Benedict Arnold – somewhat ironically, given his ultimate career path – seemed to have realized that Americans needed to look to their own colonies and derive a strategy from within. "Shall we sacrifice the few men we have, by endeavouring to keep possession of a small part of the country, which can be of little or no service to us?" he asked in a letter to General John Sullivan. "The junction of the Canadians with the Colonies, an object which brought us into this country, is now at an end," the beleaguered general admitted. But from this loss came a new opportunity: "Let us quit them, and secure our own country, before it is too late."[59] We should not misread Arnold's use of the word "country." Like Jefferson and others who spoke fondly of their "country" before independence or the ratification of the Constitution, Arnold was talking about his "native land" or colony. Yet he suitably crystallized what Canada had meant for the revolution itself: it had not been conquered, it would not fall to the Americans, and thus it was better to focus on securing American liberties within the rebelling colonies themselves rather than fight for British liberties throughout North America. Some disagreed. "Our repeated Misfortunes in Canada have greatly chagrind every Man who wishes well to America," fumed Sam Adams just a few days after signing the Declaration of Independence. "To be acting merely on the defensive at the Time when we should have been in full possession of that Country is mortifying indeed. The Subject is disgusting to me," he continued, "I will dismiss it."[60] He had little choice but to do just that.

Those who signed the Declaration of Independence had just spent months worrying about Canada, and the subject naturally shaped opinions on independence. In early 1776, Joseph Hawley, a prominent associate of Samuel

Adams and James Otis and member of the Massachusetts Provincial Assembly, wrote to Elbridge Gerry to warn him of a potential British attack from Quebec. He suggested that the American forces send their best-trained troops to Canada, warning that Britain would likely send "their land forces for the reduction of America ... chiefly ... by the way of Quebeck and New-York." Hawley followed this advice with an opinion on independence. "I beg leave to let you know that I have read the pamphlet, entitled, 'Common Sense, addressed to the Inhabitants of America,' and that every sentiment has sunk into my well prepared heart for good seed."[61] Others made more direct connections between *Common Sense* and Canada. In an open letter to Thomas Paine, one colonial resident suggested, "Let it be the work of your Continental Conference to set the bounds to their claim as an associated Continent, which ought to include, at least, the thirteen at present associated Colonies, with those of Quebec and Nova-Scotia."[62] For some, including Canada (and Nova Scotia with its access to valuable fisheries) in American independence was common sense indeed.

A counter-argument to this logic suggested that the failures at Quebec demonstrated how unprepared Americans were for independence. "Should the Army be compelled to evacuate Canada," Hancock wrote to the Massachusetts Council, "it is impossible to say what will be the consequences, or where the mischief may end. It becomes us, therefore, as we regard our country and its best interests, to exert every nerve to guard against so fatal an event." He continued to argue that the inability to carry on such an offensive "furnishes a most striking proof of the weakness or wickedness of those who charge [the colonists] with an original intention of withdrawing from the Government of Great Britain, and erecting an independent Empire. Had such a scheme been formed, the most warlike preparations would have been necessary to effect it."[63] Meshech Weare agreed, arguing that independence was "a measure the British Administration have long and very unjustly charged the Americans with having in view, but now we conceive are driven thereto by them."[64] Weare's next sentence concerned how best to reinforce the army in Quebec. The fact that Canada could not be taken hinted that independence was never at the root of rebellion, though, rather paradoxically, independence made failures in Canada easier to swallow.

The very act of drafting the Declaration of Independence had a Canadian influence. Richard Henry Lee's resolution of 7 June, which argued "that these United Colonies are, and of right ought to be, free and independent States," pushed Congress to consider seriously the ideas promoted earlier in Thomas Paine's *Common Sense*.[65] On 10 June, Congress appointed the drafting committee, known as the Committee of Five, made up of Thomas Jefferson, John Adams, Roger Sherman, Robert R. Livingston, and Benjamin Franklin. Franklin, who was still suffering from the gout that had plagued him during his voyage to Montreal, had returned from Canada less than two weeks earlier.[66] The writing of the Declaration fell to Jefferson. Given the ultimate importance of the document, it might be imagined that he would have been afforded the time to retire and dedicate himself solely to the task of crystallizing the American decision to break from Great Britain. Such was not the case, as Canadian issues kept him at his seat in Congress. On 15 June, he was named to a committee concerned with sorting out a number of issues, complaints, and logistics related to the failed attack on Quebec. On 24 June, he joined yet another committee convened "to enquire into the causes of the miscarriages in Canada." It is entirely likely, as Pauline Maier has suggested, that Jefferson kept a draft of the Declaration at his desk as he served on committees charged with untangling the Canadian mess, hoping for the opportunity to "poke at it in dull moments" when not fretting over prisoner exchanges, Montgomery's death, and the American failure outside Quebec.[67]

As debate over independence increased, the Canadian theatre remained a primary concern among delegates at Congress. The patriot defeat in May 1776 at the Battle of the Cedars, west of Montreal, was reported to much horror in the American colonies. Canada was linked to Indigenous "savagery" that put both Canadians and Indigenous peoples outside the "common cause" around which patriots rallied. Published responses to accounts from the battle, including one from Jefferson, included "themes the Declaration would make famous just one month hence."[68] These connections continued. In a jubilant letter the day before Congress adopted the Declaration of Independence, John Adams recorded his excitement for the future of the united colonies. "This morning is assigned for the greatest debate of all," he enthused. "A Declaration, that these Colonies are free and independent States," Adams continued, "has been reported by a Committee, appointed some weeks ago for that purpose, and this day or to-morrow is to determine its fate. May Heaven prosper the new-born Republick, and make it more glorious than any former Republicks have been!" From such an excited pronouncement, Adams then fixed his attention on matters to the north of the rebelling colonies: "The small-pox has ruined the American Army in Canada, and of consequence the American cause ... The small-pox, which infected every man we sent there, completed our ruin, and compelled us to evacuate that important Province. We must, however, regain it some time or other." Any future attempts on Canada, however, would be undertaken not as rebelling British colonies but as newly united states. Adams remained optimistic, suggesting that "a little more wisdom, a little more activity, or a little more integrity, would have preserved us Canada." He concluded, however, that "irretrievable miscarriages ought to be lamented no further than to enable and stimulate us to do better in future."[69]

John Dickinson, in notes that he took to prepare for a speech in Congress regarding independence, used Canada to triangulate the British-French-American relationship that might result from a permanent separation from Great Britain. He was against declaring independence until proper articles of confederation were drafted and foreign alliances secured. "Suppose on this Event G.B. should offer Canada to France & Florida to Spain with an Extension of the old Limits. Would not France & Spain accept them?" he mused. "Gentlemen say the Trade of all America is more valuable to France than Canada," he continued, "I grant it but suppose she may get both." Dickinson believed that independence would put France in too powerful a position, having only to intimidate Great Britain (which would be occupied fighting in America) until Canada "is put into her hands," at which point France could then "intimidate Us into a most disadvantageous Grant of our Trade."[70] Though his vision would not come to pass exactly as predicted – although Florida was returned to Spain – Dickinson absented himself from voting on independence.

Hours after Dickinson's speech, Adams wrote to Samuel Chase, one of the commissioners to Canada. Adams reported that Congress, in the Committee of the Whole, had debated and agreed to independence, though the vote had been postponed to the following day, 2 July. He immediately turned his attention to Quebec, lamenting "Alas, Canada! We have found misfortune and disgrace in that quarter – evacuated at last." After a short description of what had gone wrong, Adams compared the Canadian failure and the Declaration of Independence to ancient Roman strategies surrounding peace and power. "The Romans made it a fixed rule never to send or receive Ambassadors to treat of peace with their enemies, while their affairs were in an adverse or disastrous situation," he noted. Independence seemed to have buoyed the Americans after the Canadian debacle. "There was a generosity and magnanimity in this becoming freemen," Adams declared. "It flowed from that temper and those principles which alone can preserve the freedom of a people. It is a pleasure to find our Americans of the same temper. It is a good symptom, foreboding a good end."[71]

The Declaration itself illuminated just how deeply Canadian affairs influenced the American Revolution. For all it has come to represent, the Declaration of Independence is primarily a list of complaints levelled by Congress at the king and Parliament of Great Britain. Two of those complaints, both of which are found in the bottom third of the list, directly relate to Canada. First,

Parliament was accused of "abolishing the free System of English Laws in a neighbouring Province, establishing therein an Arbitrary government, and enlarging its Boundaries so as to render it at once an example and fit instrument for introducing the same absolute rule into these Colonies." This was a specific reference to the Quebec Act that so angered the colonists. The second complaint was directed at Indigenous nations, many of which fought alongside the British in Canada and throughout the northern theatre. Although the Americans signed treaties, met with various Indigenous groups, and had their own Indigenous allies, the Declaration painted all Indigenous people with the same brush: the king had "excited domestic insurrections amongst us, and has endeavoured to bring on the inhabitants of our frontiers, the merciless Indian Savages, whose known rule of warfare, is an undistinguished destruction of all ages, sexes and conditions."[72] These two complaints encapsulated the problems Canada caused: it was a safe haven for French Catholics and Indigenous peoples, two groups long perceived as enemies to the British colonies and, after 1776, the American states.

Some argued that, if independence had been adopted earlier, Canada would have fallen to the American forces. In a letter to his wife, John Adams celebrated the Declaration but lamented that it came too late: "Had a Declaration of Independency been made seven Months ago, it would have been attended with many great and glorious effects. We might before this Hour, have formed alliances with foreign States." In addition, Adams suggested, "We should have mastered Quebec and been in Possession of Canada." Adams remained frustrated by how slowly Congress had moved and how haphazard had been the execution of the Canadian campaign. He was sure that many leading figures had been duped by the promise of an early peace with Britain, which, consequently, distracted them from taking real measures to support and supply the Canadian mission. Those who might not have been distracted sincerely wished that the American forces would be defeated because, had they been successful, perhaps it "should elevate the Minds of the People too much to hearken to those Terms of Reconciliation which they believed would be offered Us." The combination of these two positions, both of which, as far as Adams was concerned, would have been eliminated had independence been declared earlier, had, in the end, "lost Us the Province."[73]

The Declaration of Independence raised morale but did not change military prospects. Viewed from a different perspective, however, it helped soften the blow of the failures in Canada. Rather than joining the American future, Canada would serve as a reminder of the united colonies' imperial past. As weary soldiers straggled south from their failed campaigns, members of Congress ensured that they were returning to colonies focused on achieving full independence. This symbolism was not lost on Abraham Clark, one of the delegates for New Jersey. "At the Time our Forces in Canada were retreating before a Victorious Army, while Genl. Howe with a Large Armament is Advancing towards N. York, Our Congress Resolved to Declare the United Colonies Free and independent States," he informed Elias Dayton, who led the third New Jersey Regiment. The decision to declare independence had "gone so far that we must now be a new independent State, or a Conquered Country."[74] Perhaps this new independent state could later do some conquering of its own. Benjamin Rush, the noted Philadelphia physician, believed this might happen. He lamented the loss of Canada and believed that it should have been won on the merits of Arnold's march and Montgomery's sacrifice alone. He allowed himself to believe that "the banner of liberty will be planted on some future day by the States of America upon the walls of Quebec."[75] Canada would continue to shape the way Americans viewed themselves and their relationship with the British Empire.

❧

The standard trope that the American Revolution created two countries – the United States and, ninety years later, Canada – is a useful reminder that all the colonies and territories in British America felt the impact of the struggles for independence. But there were immediate and consequential continental experiences during the revolutionary era that, when explored without the blinders of nationalist narratives, demonstrate the deep interconnections between the revolution and the loyal colonies to the north. The process of declaring independence offers a window into the Canadian influence on the American Revolution. The invasion of Canada and the challenges faced by American troops outside Quebec brought revolutionary ambitions into stark relief. Attacking a loyal British colony was a risky venture aimed at expanding the geography of American liberties into a society of French-speaking Catholics. The failure of this campaign helped revolutionary leaders reorient their efforts on the more plausible – yet audacious – goal of breaking free from the British Empire. Americans expected their revolution – fuelled by unrest, social disorder, and violence – to spread north, but they were disappointed. When the military leaders and politicians who had planned and executed the failed campaign against Canada turned their attention towards an independent American future, they helped to reframe the intent, outcome, and significance of the invasion of Quebec. In turn, Quebec and Canada became integrated into the many histories of the Declaration of Independence.

NOTES

1 For a broad interpretation of the Declaration's influence, see David Armitage, *The Declaration of Independence: A Global History* (Cambridge, MA: Harvard University Press, 2007).
2 This is, as Eliga H. Gould suggests, American history from "the outside in." Eliga H. Gould, *Among the Powers of the Earth: The American Revolution and the Making of a New World Empire* (Cambridge, MA: Harvard University Press, 2012), 13. For the purposes of this essay, I will use the terms "Canada" and "Quebec" interchangeably, as was the practice at the time. Nova Scotia, Newfoundland, and St John Island (Prince Edward Island) were not considered to be part of Canada in the eighteenth century.
3 Mark R. Anderson, *The Battle for the Fourteenth Colony: America's War of Liberation in Canada, 1774–1776* (Hanover, NH: University Press of New England, 2013); Pierre Monette, *Rendez-vous manqué avec la Révolution américaine* (Montreal: Québec Amérique, 2007); George A. Rawlyk, *Revolution Rejected, 1775–1776* (Scarborough, ON: Prentice-Hall, 1968); Gustave Lanctot, *Canada and the American Revolution, 1774–1783*, trans. Margaret M. Cameron (Toronto: Clarke, Irwin, 1967); Hilda Neatby, *Quebec: The Revolutionary Age, 1760–1791* (Toronto: McClelland and Stewart, 1966); and George M. Wrong, *Canada and the American Revolution: The Disruption of the First British Empire* (New York: Macmillan, 1935). Recent works on the revolution's influence on Canada, including Mark Anderson's, have breathed new life into both the revolution and the history of early Canada. See also Elizabeth Mancke, *The Fault Lines of Empire: Political Differentiation in Massachusetts and Nova Scotia, ca 1760–1830* (New York: Routledge, 2005); and Michel Ducharme, *Le concept de liberté au Canada à l'époque des Révolutions atlantiques, 1776–1838* (Montreal and Kingston: McGill-Queen's University Press, 2009).
4 There are too many surveys to list. Recent works that take Canada as a serious revolutionary subject include Alan Taylor, *The Divided Ground: Indians, Settlers, and the Northern Borderland of the American Revolution* (New York: Vintage, 2007); and Maya Jasanoff, *Liberty's Exiles: American Loyalists in the Revolutionary World* (New York: Knopf, 2011).
5 The Quebec Act was the subject of an Omohundro Institute for Early American History and Culture workshop, "The Quebec Act of 1774: Transnational Contexts, Meanings, and Legacies," 4–5 October 2013, Montreal.
6 A recent, and excellent, article on this topic is Amy Noel Ellison, "Montgomery's Misfortune: The American Defeat at Quebec and the March toward Independence, 1775–1776," *Early American Studies* 15, no. 3 (2017): 591–616. Ellison successfully combines military and diplomatic history to argue, as I do here, that we must

consider Canada's influence on American independence. However, while Ellison argues that the Quebec theatre "forces us to reconsider the historiographical divide between the American Revolution and the War for Independence" (p. 595), I am pushing for a broader reconfiguration of the revolutionary era that accounts for the impact of the loyal British colonies on the American experiment, more generally. There is a difference, of course, between a Canadian history and a British history. Recent scholarship has begun to emphasize the British influence on the Declaration of Independence specifically and the American Revolution generally. See Steve Pincus, *The Heart of the Declaration: The Founders' Case for an Activist Government* (New Haven, CT: Yale University Press, 2016); Justin du Rivage, *Revolution against Empire: Taxes, Politics, and the Origins of American Independence* (New Haven: Yale University Press, 2017); Eric Nelson, *The Royalist Revolution: Monarchy and the American Founding* (Cambridge, MA: Harvard University Press, 2014); and Andrew Jackson O'Shaughnessy, *The Men Who Lost America: British Leadership, the American Revolution, and the Fate of the Empire* (New Haven, CT: Yale University Press, 2013).

7 Robert G. Parkinson, *The Common Cause: Creating Race and Nation in the American Revolution* (Chapel Hill: University of North Carolina Press, 2016); Alan Taylor, *American Revolutions: A Continental History, 1750–1804* (New York: W.W. Norton, 2016); Lawrence B.A. Hatter, *Citizens of Convenience: The Imperial Origins of American Nationhood on the US-Canadian Border* (Charlottesville: University of Virginia Press, 2016); and Robert Bothwell, *Your Country, My Country: A Unified History of the United States and Canada* (New York: Oxford University Press, 2015).

8 Jeffrey L. McNairn, *The Capacity to Judge: Public Opinion and Deliberative Democracy in Upper Canada, 1791–1854* (Toronto: University of Toronto Press, 2000); Ducharme, *Le concept de liberté au Canada*; J.I. Little, *Borderland Religion: The Emergence of an English-Canadian Identity, 1792–1852* (Toronto: University of Toronto Press, 2004); and Jane Errington, *The Lion, the Eagle, and Upper Canada: A Developing Colonial Ideology* (Montreal and Kingston: McGill-Queen's University Press, 1987).

9 It is also important to understand the loyalist responses to Thomas Paine, which have been too easily discounted by historians. See Philip Gould, "Loyalists Respond to *Common Sense*: The Politics of Authorship in Revolutionary America," in *The Loyal Atlantic: Remaking the British Atlantic in the Revolutionary Era*, ed. Jerry Bannister and Liam Riordan (Toronto: University of Toronto Press, 2012), 105–27.

10 On the desire for rebellion within Nova Scotia, see Régis Brun, A.J.B. Johnston, and Ernest Clarke, *Fort Beauséjour – Fort Cumberland: Une histoire / A History* (Memracook, NB: Parks Canada and Société du Monument Lefebvre, 1991); Ernest Clarke, *Siege of Fort Cumberland, 1776: An Episode in the American Revolution* (Montreal and Kingston: McGill-Queen's University Press, 1995); James S. Leamon,

Revolution Downeast: The War for American Independence in Maine (Amherst: University of Massachusetts Press, 1995); and Mancke, *The Fault Lines of Empire*, 83–107.

11 Lanctot, *Canada and the American Revolution*, 116.

12 H.V. Nelles, *A Little History of Canada*, 2nd ed. (Don Mills, ON: Oxford University Press, 2011), 62. Nelles is referring to Nova Scotian neutrality but frames this response as a comparison to that of Quebec. The impact of Acadian neutrality on French Canadian responses to the revolution are worth exploring further.

13 See the chapter by D.C. Bélanger in this volume.

14 John G. Reid and Elizabeth Mancke, "From Global Processes to Continental Strategies: The Emergence of British North America to 1783," in *Canada and the British Empire*, ed. Phillip A. Buckner (Oxford: Oxford University Press, 2010), 40.

15 On the history of French-Canadian ambivalence, see Colin M. Coates, "French Canadians' Ambivalence to the British Empire," in *Canada and the British Empire*, ed. Phillip A. Buckner (Oxford: Oxford University Press, 2008), 181–99.

16 P.J. Marshall, *The Making and Unmaking of Empires: Britain, India, and America, c. 1750–1783* (Oxford: Oxford University Press, 2005), 353.

17 Gordon S. Wood, *The Radicalism of the American Revolution* (New York: Vintage Books, 1993).

18 Edmund S. Morgan put it a little more bluntly. When discussing the failed Canadian expedition, he noted, "Americans reassured one another that no such thing could occur among themselves. If the Canadians lacked the noble urge to be free, if they would not help themselves, then they deserved slavery. Meanwhile American patriots would establish their rights on battlefields closer to home." See Edmund S. Morgan, *The Birth of the Republic, 1763–89*, 3rd ed. (Chicago: University of Chicago Press, 1992), 77–8. Morgan also discounts the impact of neutrals, claiming that "the war itself sooner or later obliged men to get off the fence on one side or the other," 78.

19 Monette, *Rendez-vous manqué*, 60–1.

20 "Letter to the Inhabitants of the Province of Quebec," 26 October 1774, https://en.wikisource.org/wiki/Letter_to_the_Inhabitants_of_the_Province_of_Quebec. Unfortunately, Congress was working at diplomatic cross purposes, sending, around the same time, an "Address to the People of Great Britain" in which they expressed astonishment at the Quebec Act: "Nor can we suppress our astonishment that a British Parliament should ever consent to establish in that country a Religion that has deluged your Island in blood, and dispersed impiety, bigotry, persecution, murder, and rebellion, through every part of the world," https://en.wikisource.org/wiki/Address_to_the_People_of_Great_Britain

21 "Letter to the Oppressed Inhabitants of Canada," 29 May 1775, http://avalon.law.yale.edu/18th_century/contcong_05-29-75.asp.

22 George Washington to the Massachusetts General Court, Cambridge, 12 August 1775, available at National Archives (US), Founders Online, https://founders.archives.gov (hereafter FA). By the summer of 1775, King George III had already refused the olive branch petition and was busy securing German mercenaries to fight in America. Britain itself was divided over the conflict, and Lord North, the prime minister, was leading an increasingly divided cabinet. Opposition to the war was similarly divided and could not rally against the king and ministry. See O'Shaughnessy, *The Men Who Lost America*, 17–82; Kathleen Wilson, *The Sense of the People: Politics, Culture, and Imperialism in England, 1715–1785* (Cambridge: Cambridge University Press, 1995), 237–53; and Eliga H. Gould, *The Persistence of Empire: British Political Culture in the Age of the American Revolution* (Chapel Hill: Published for the Omohundro Institute of Early American History and Culture by the University of North Carolina Press, 2000), 148–80. On the revolutionary's northeastern frontier, see Mancke, *The Fault Lines of Empire* and Leamon, *Revolution Downeast.*

23 George Washington to the Massachusetts General Court, Cambridge, 12 August 1775, FA.

24 I draw the narrative in this section from Neatby, *Quebec*, 145–54; also Lanctot, *Canada and the American Revolution*, 93–106.

25 George Washington to John Hancock, Cambridge, 28 November 1775, FA.

26 North Carolina Delegates to Samuel Johnson, Philadelphia, 2 January 1776, *Letters of Delegates to Congress, 1774–89*, ed. Paul H. Smith (Washington: Library of Congress, 1976) 3: 18 (hereafter LOD).

27 Joseph Hewes to Robert Smith, n.d. [8 Jan 1776?], LOD, 3: 58.

28 John Hancock to Johnathan Trumbull, Sr, Philadelphia, 12 January 1776, LOD, 3: 85; John Hancock to Thomas Cushing, Philadelphia, 17 January 1776, LOD, 3: 105.

29 Letter to the Inhabitants of the Province of Canada, 24 January 1776, https://en.wikisource.org/wiki/Letter_to_the_Inhabitants_of_the_Province_of_Canada

30 Josiah Bartlett to the New Hampshire Committee of Safety, Philadelphia, 20 January 1776, LOD, 3: 118.

31 George Washington to Richard Henry Lee, 4 April 1776, FA.

32 John Hancock to George Washington, Philadelphia, 23 April 1776, FA.

33 John Adams to Horatio Gates, Philadelphia, 27 April 1776, FA.

34 O'Shaughnessy, *The Men Who Lost America*, 59.

35 "Never was any City so universally Struck with grief, as this [Philadelphia] was on hearing of the Loss of Montgomery," Thomas Lynch informed Philip Schuyler. The delegate from South Carolina continued, "Every lady's Eye was filled with Tears. I happened to have Company at Dinner but none had Inclination for any other Food than sorrow or Resentment." Thomas Lynch to Philip Schuyler, Philadelphia, 20 January 1776, LOD, 3: 125. In a letter from Mercy Otis Warren to Janet

Livingston Montgomery on the subject of her husband's death, Warren wrote, "It may still further brighten the clouded moment to reflect that your friends are not confined to the limits of a province, but by the happy union of the American colonies (suffering equally by the rigor of oppressions) the affections of the inhabitants are cemented and the grave of the companion of your heart will be sprinkled with the tears of thousands who revere the character of the commander at the gates of Quebec." Quoted in Kate Davies, *Catharine Macaulay and Mercy Otis Warren: The Revolutionary Atlantic and the Politics of Gender* (New York: Oxford University Press, 2005), 203.

36 "A Dialogue between the Ghost of General Montgomery and a Delegate, in a Wood near Philadelphia," 8 March 1776, *Virginia Gazette*. This was a reprint of Thomas Paine's *A Dialogue between the Ghost of General Montgomery Just Arrived from the Elysian Fields; and an American Delegate, in a Wood Near Philadelphia* (Philadelphia: R. Bell, 1776). See also Ellison, "Montgomery's Misfortune," 613–14.

37 Ibid.

38 This point Montgomery's ghost makes explicitly: "It was no small mortification to me, when I fell upon the plains of Abraham, to reflect that I did not expire like the brave general Wolfe, in the arms of victory. But I now no longer envy him his glory. I would rather die in attempting to obtain permanent freedom for a handful of people than survive a conquest which would serve only to extend the empire of despotism." Ibid.

39 This decision had a lasting influence on Canada's connection to the revolution right up until 1783. Franklin's trip to Montreal, according to Samuel Flagg Bemis, "had the result of fixing Canada as a quest in Franklin's subtle mind." Samuel Flagg Bemis, *The Diplomacy of the American Revolution* (1935; Bloomington: Indiana University Press, 1957), 197, 201n34.

40 Lanctot, *Canada and the American Revolution*, 126–7; Anderson, *Battle for the Fourteenth Colony*, 229.

41 For short biographies of the commissioners, see *American National Biography Online*, www.anb.org

42 See Robert Emmett Curran, *Papist Devils: Catholics in British America, 1574–1783* (Washington, DC: Catholic University of America Press, 2014); and Maura Jane Farrelly, *Papist Patriots: The Making of an American Catholic Identity* (New York: Oxford University Press, 2012).

43 Vincent Morley, *Irish Opinion and the American Revolution, 1760–1783* (Cambridge: Cambridge University Press, 2002), 86; and Pauline Maier, *From Resistance to Revolution: Colonial Radicals and the Development of American Opposition to Britain, 1765–1776* (New York: W.W. Norton, 1991), 185.

44 John Carroll, Thomas O'Brien Hanley, and Association American Catholic Historical, *The John Carroll Papers*, vol. 1 (Notre Dame: University of Notre Dame Press, 1976), 46.

45 Benjamin Franklin to General Schuyler, Philadelphia, 11 March 1776, FA. In early March, Richard Smith noted in his diary that a discussion over part of the instructions for commissioners going to Canada took up three or four hours. The debate over whether Canadians should form a constitution and government for themselves led to "much Argumt. on this Ground." Richard Smith's Diary, [9 March 1776], LOD, 3: 364.

46 John Adams to Abigail Adams, 18 February 1776, LOD, 3: 272.

47 John Adams to James Warren, 18 February 1776, LOD, 3: 275.

48 "Instructions, &c.," *Journals of the Continental Congress, 1774–89*, ed. Worthington Chauncey Ford (Washington, DC: Government Printing Office, 1906), 4: 215–16 (hereafter JCC). Mark R. Anderson does an excellent job of detailing the commissioners' daily activities, in Anderson, *Battle for the Fourteenth Colony*, 290–332.

49 Commissioners to Canada to [John Hancock], Montreal, 6 May 1776, FA.

50 Ibid.

51 Commissioners to Canada to [John Hancock], Montreal, 8 May 1776, FA.

52 Anderson, *Battle for the Fourteenth Colony*, 305–15.

53 Commissioners to Canada to Philip Schuyler, 16 May 1776, LOD, 4: 4. An account of the inspections performed by Chase and Carroll after Franklin and Carroll departed can be found in *Journal of Charles Carroll of Carrollton, during His Visit to Canada in 1776, as One of the Commissioners from Congress* (Baltimore: Maryland Historical Society, 1876), 93–100.

54 George Washington to Major General Philip Schuyler, New York, 17 May 1776, FA.

55 John Adams to James Warren, 18 May 1776, FA.

56 Ibid.

57 Richard Henry Lee to Landon Carter, Philadelphia, 2 June 1776, LOD, 4: 118.

58 Robert Morris to Silas Deane, Philadelphia, 5 June 1776, LOD, 4: 147.

59 General Benedict Arnold to General John Sullivan, Chambly, 13 June 1776, in *Correspondence of the American Revolution*, ed. Jared Sparks, vol. 1 (Boston: Little, Brown, 1853), 528–9.

60 Sam Adams to Joseph Hawley, Philadelphia, 9 July 1776, LOD, 4: 416.

61 Major Hawley to Elbridge Gerry, Watertown, 18 February 1776, *American Archives: Documents of the American Revolutionary Period, 1774–1776*, 4th series, 4: 1191, www. http://amarch.lib.niu.edu/.

62 To the Author of Common Sense, 26 February 1776, ibid., 4: 1496.

63 President of Congress to Massachusetts Council, Philadelphia, 30 April 1776, ibid., 5: 1139.

64 Meschech Weare to the New-Hampshire Delegates in Congress, Exeter, 18 June 1776, 6: 1029.

65 Pauline Maier, *American Scripture: Making the Declaration of Independence* (New York: Vintage, 1997), 41–5.

66 While it was impossible to blame Canada for Franklin's corporal ailments, his sister, Jane, suggested a specifically Canadian source for his foul mood: "The Raiseing the seige of Quebeck, the Ignorance of the Canadans, there Incapasity and Aversnes to have any thing to do in the war and his [?] Indisposition I beleve Affected His Spirets." Jane Mecom to Catherine Green, Philadelphia, 1 June 1776, FA. On Mecom's life and her letters, see Jill Lepore, *Book of Ages: The Life and Opinions of Jane Franklin* (New York: Knopf, 2013).

67 Maier, *American Scripture*, 99–103.

68 Parkinson, *The Common Cause*, 235–41; the quote is from 241.

69 John Adams to Archibald Bullock, Philadelphia, 1 July 1776, *American Archives*, 4th series, 6: 1193–4.

70 John Dickinson's Notes for a Speech in Congress, 1 July 1776, LOD, 4: 353–4.

71 John Adams to Samuel Chase, Philadelphia, 1 July 1776, *American Archives*, 4th series, 6: 1194.

72 Declaration of Independence, 1776.

73 John Adams to Abigail Adams, Philadelphia, 3 July 1776, LOD, 4: 375.

74 Abraham Clark to Elias Dayton, Philadelphia, 4 July 1776, LOD, 4: 378.

75 Benjamin Rush to Patrick Henry, Philadelphia, 16 July 1776, LOD, 4: 474.

6 Empire, Settler Colonialism, and the Role of Violence in Indigenous Dispossession in British North America, 1749–1830

JOHN G. REID[1]

The 175th anniversary of the establishment in Mi'kma'ki of the British imperial outpost of Halifax was celebrated in proper style. On 5 August 1924, the battlecruiser HMS *Hood* – pride of the Royal Navy, with its complement of almost 1,500 – entered Halifax Harbour with two other warships on the latest stop of a world cruise that had taken it to all the major settler dominions. The emblematic status of the mighty vessel was emphasized by the *Halifax Herald* under the portentous headline, "Puissant Sign of an Empire United in an Enterprise of Universal Law and Order."[2] To welcome the *Hood* and to "entertain the visiting naval men in a fitting manner, and show them Halifax in gala attire," the city deployed all of its major symbols of the glories of settler colonialism. The Memorial Tower on the Northwest Arm, commemorating the opening of the first Nova Scotia assembly in 1758 and thus the inauguration of representative government throughout the empire as it would exist after 1783, was illuminated.[3] Among the varied sporting events that customarily accompanied a naval visit, the Wanderers – Nova Scotia's most socially exclusive cricket club – entertained "a Naval XI" to a friendly match, thus underlining the sport's contribution to the cultural normalization of settler colonial society.[4]

The main historical content of the festivities came in the form of a pageant held on the afternoon of 6 August. A re-enactor playing the role of Governor Edward Cornwallis (in everyday life, a major of the Royal Canadian Ordnance Corps) stepped ashore from a replica of the eighteenth-century warship HMS *Sphinx*. Conveniently, "two friendly Indians awaited the arrival of the party to guide them to a 'grassy glade' some distance inland" – in reality, a locale on the campus of Dalhousie University. A crowd of some ten thousand watched as the red-uniformed officers made their way uphill, while "striding stolidly ahead" were their two "armed and silent" Indigenous guides. Eventually, "headed by their chieftain, wearing a gaudy head-dress of gay feathers ..., [a] little band of Mic Mac Indians approached the Governor's party with upraised hands in signal of greeting," and the smoking of a pipe of peace brought a harmonious close to the proceedings.[5] In the evening, the circle of celebration was closed in suitably anachronistic fashion, as the reanimated Cornwallis visited the Memorial Tower to honour the legacy of the provincial assembly, the calling of which the actual governor of the day – Charles Lawrence – had opposed so implacably.[6]

The anachronism also had to do in part with the conflation of a settler colonial monument with the realities of an era in which the British, with their tiny and insecure group of would-be colonists in the 1750s, controlled very little outside of Halifax itself and the previous headquarters at Annapolis Royal. More broadly, the notion of peaceful settlement with the friendly compliance of Indigenous inhabitants was one that, in the Canada of the Victorian era and stretching from the late nineteenth century far into the twentieth, was made to carry a substantial amount of freight. This essay suggests that, even if outright physical and military violence was the exception rather than the rule, settlement was far from peaceful, in that environmental transformation and demographic pressures represented in themselves a form of violence, often lethal to Indigenous groups. Yet for Sir John George Bourinot, writing at the beginning of the twentieth century in the Cambridge Historical Series, the Royal Proclamation of 1763 had especial significance as "the beginning of that honest policy which has distinguished the relations of England and Canada with the Indian nations for a hundred years, and which has obtained for the present Dominion the confidence and friendship of the many thousand Indians, who roamed for many centuries in Rupert's Land and in the Indian Territories where the Hudson's Bay Company long enjoyed exclusive privileges of trade."[7] In an earlier work, Bourinot had praised the treaties that provided "for the transfer to Canada of immense tracts of prairie lands where we now see wide stretches of fields of nodding grain," while at the same time "the Indians ... find their interests carefully guarded by treaties and statutes of Canada, which recognise their rights as wards of the Canadian Government."[8] Another imperialist of the early twentieth century – J. Castell Hopkins, who, as Carl Berger once remarked, was "seldom at a loss for illustrative detail" – put the matter more fulsomely:

> The Indian was a natural monarchist, a born believer in aristocracy, and it is probable that the English system, as it evolved to the north of the Great Lakes, was far more suited to his tastes and inclinations than the democracy of the new Republic. He saw and felt the forms of British institutions, liked the principle of loyalty to a great King or Chief, and also admired, as time went on, the strength of British love for law and order and for justice between different races. His day of power

> had gone, it is true, but he all the more appreciated kindness and just treatment, and ... Canada has no prouder or more satisfactory page in her history than the treatment of her Indian wards and their immunity from strife and bloodshed and corrupt government.[9]

Although Hopkins was not a member of the Royal Society of Canada, Bourinot and other leading imperialist scholars – of an avocational bent – had been closely associated with that organization's founding in 1882 as a national academy that spanned a broad range of literary and historical studies, as well as others in mathematics and the natural sciences. That empire and its manifestations formed a frequent preoccupation of the anglophone historians of this era – and, with greater complexities, also of the francophones – and that empire itself was a link between the still-ongoing process of settler colonization and the current and prospective imperial roles of Canada and other dominions, put a premium on portraying peacefulness and scrupulous legality as central characteristics of the dominion's dealings with Indigenous populations. From this perspective, attaching significance to the Indigenous past in its own right had much less to recommend it, and the small though gradually increasing number of professional historians did little to disturb the pattern. It was true that, in 1937, Alfred Goldsworthy Bailey's profoundly innovative *The Conflict of European and Eastern Algonkian Cultures, 1504–1700: A Study in Canadian Civilization* struck a note that was decidedly less benign.[10] In the work's preface, Bailey explained that the conflict of cultures that was inseparable from imperial expansion "resulted in most cases in the obliteration of those [cultures] of the Indian," following which remaining Indigenous inhabitants had no choice but to adapt to "the immigration of an alien race." Although one of the results was *métissage* – "a fusion of Indian and European elements often occurred, with the result that a new culture which was neither European nor Indian was built up" – Bailey was deeply pessimistic regarding the chances of autonomous survival of Indigenous culture and identity.[11] The book's conclusion was omitted from the first edition for financial reasons, but, when published a year later in *Canadian Historical Review*, it offered a blunt assessment of the results of colonial settlement: "When a people migrates into an already inhabited area, a conflict almost inevitably arises between the culture of the immigrants and that of the indigenous population. The result of such a conflict may amount both in intensity and magnitude to nothing less than an economic and social revolution."[12]

So much for grassy glades and natural monarchism. Yet Bailey was an isolated voice, an ethnohistorian before his time whose approach resonated little with historians or anthropologists of the day.[13] Among academic historians more broadly, the influence of those whom Tamson Pietsch has defined as the "settler professors" of the late nineteenth and early-to-mid twentieth century, exerting enormous influence over faculty recruitment within and to Canada and the other dominions, long continued to give the intellectual reach of the empire a remarkable breadth.[14] While membership within an imperial intellectual community did not in any crude sense constrain the inquiries of individual scholars, a pervasive sense of "imperial loyalty" in "settler universities" was sufficient to channel the scholarship well away from critical analysis of colonization in an Indigenous context.[15] Canada, Pietsch notes, had a distinctive element in that its geographical proximity to the United States enabled it "to function as something of a 'hinge' between the British and American academic worlds."[16] In Canadian history, such a robust hinge brought substantial reinforcement to the settler-centred narrative. Thus, as late as 1972, E Palmer Patterson was another scholar isolated in pointing out to Canadian historians that workable strategies were available for mitigating this tendency, based both on placing the Indigenous experience in a global context of colonialism and on adopting a periodization suited to Indigenous rather than settler history. "The white man of Western culture," Patterson observed in 1972, "sees himself as the norm in Canada, the United States, Australia, and New Zealand, in relation to the aborigines of those nations. In the total world picture, however, white civilization and the white man himself, while very influential and penetrating everywhere, are not the norm."[17]

Yet, as Lorenzo Veracini has observed, "paradoxically, settler colonialism was most recognisable when it was most imperfect – say, 1950s Kenya or 1970s Zimbabwe."[18] Conversely, where settler colonialism has been realized most completely – as in the major settler dominions – normalization of the emergence of settler societies and of accompanying narratives of peace and justice may thrive at the expense of more critical perspectives. In Canada, despite the emergence of a strong, extensive, and sophisticated literature in Indigenous history and Indigenous studies since Patterson wrote in 1972, the image of the "peaceable kingdom" has continued to resonate in many contexts of public discourse. Popularized by William Kilbourn in the title of and introduction to an anthology published in 1970 that drew on the work of major Canadian authors of (mainly) the 1960s,[19] the term originated from a painting by the Pennsylvania Quaker folk artist Edward Hicks, who painted multiple works entitled "The Peaceable Kingdom" over the course of his lengthy career. It was Northrop Frye who identified Hicks's image as applicable to Canadian values and characteristics. While the foreground consisted of stylized depictions of various animal species coexisting harmoniously with one another and with human children (as in Isaiah 11:6–9), a large body of water in the background – representing the Delaware River – takes the viewer's eye to a ceremony at which William Penn and others are signing a 1682 treaty with the Lenni Lenape.[20] For Frye, writing the conclusion to *The Literary History of Canada*, the painting was "a pictorial emblem of ... the reconciliation of man with man and of man with nature." It captured "the haunting vision of a serenity that is both human and natural which we have been struggling to identify in the Canadian tradition. If we had to characterize a distinctive emphasis in that tradition, we might call it a quest for the peaceable kingdom."[21]

It is true, of course, that Frye saw the notion of the peaceable kingdom in aspirational terms. It is also true that discussion of the term in the twenty-first century is more likely to focus on competing views of Canada's military role – muscular interventionism or peacekeeping – than on Indigenous matters.[22] Not that the two are entirely disconnected. As Ian McKay and Jamie Swift have commented, "The peaceable kingdom was always something of an illusion because its many Anglo subjects were so often captivated by rather warlike visions of the White Man's Burden. It was a vision they applied rigorously to the indigenous societies located within the Dominion's borders, and also to many racialized peoples they encountered outside them. And especially after 1885, Canadians were very much inclined to see themselves reflected in the exploits of the British Empire's soldiers, the bearers of Anglo-Saxon freedom and civilization throughout the world."[23] Nevertheless, the concept endures, and the Indigenous context associated with it continues by some authors to be defined by a scrupulous regard for propriety and legality. In 2008, for example, John Ralston Saul emphasized the Indigenous elements of Canada's origins, going so far as to define Canada as "a métis civilization." In this view, an ethical commitment to "colonial fairness" – even though Saul did admit that such measures as the eighteenth-century Indigenous treaties and the Royal Proclamation of 1763 may also have owed something to imperial weakness – underlined the peaceful and inclusive character of the British North America that was emerging, later lapses notwithstanding, during the late eighteenth and early nineteenth centuries.[24]

Thus, a paradox emerges between, on the one hand, the continuing strength of the notion of Canada as having dealt ethically and, on the whole, peacefully with Indigenous populations, and, on the other hand, the reality of the ruthless and systematic dispossession that occurred from the late eighteenth century onwards. In an intellectual sense, a partial resolution of this paradox can be found in the inherent contradiction between the imperialist idealizations of peaceful relations that were advanced by the late nineteenth-century theorists and historians of settler dominions and the earlier reality summarized by Jane Errington that "to many emigrants, the very presence of Aboriginal people in the Canadas and the Maritimes was a romantic anachronism. British America was, by definition, a white settler society."[25] In the British North America of the era discussed in this essay, there was indeed a relative lack of overt violence that distinguished imperial-Indigenous relations in British North America from those that existed in other areas of the world affected by intensive colonial settlement. Of course, neither state violence nor violent aggression by settler colonists was absent. The question of violence in Indigenous dispossession is, unsurprisingly, a sensitive one in public discourse, and controversies over the roles of imperial officers such as the aforementioned Edward Cornwallis, the first Halifax-based governor of Nova Scotia, and the offering of bounties for Indigenous scalps, provide one example.[26] Violence against children in residential schools had its origins in schooling long before Confederation, even though systematic residential schooling, as it is normally understood, had later beginnings, as Judith Fingard demonstrated in contrasting the at least nominally humanitarian intentions of the New England Company in the Sussex Vale School in New Brunswick with their "perversion" by settler colonial leaders and institutions.[27] Taking examples such as these together with other instances of intermittent hostilities and violent harassment directly by settlers, and of course with the later use of state violence – military and judicial – in suppressing Metis and Indigenous resistance on the Red River and during the insurgency of 1885,[28] it would be foolish to argue that Indigenous dispossession, of any era, in what became Canada was a process free of outright violence.

It remains true nevertheless that wars of conquest waged against Indigenous inhabitants were largely absent from the history of British North America. There was no northerly equivalent of the Pequot War or (in its southern New England context, as opposed to the very different outcome in Maine) King Philip's War. Moreover, the nineteenth-century deployment of imperial force in the long succession of frontier wars in Australia, in the New Zealand wars that for decades went unrestrained by the Treaty of Waitangi, in African conflicts such as the British campaigns against the Xhosa and the overlapping and later Zulu wars, and of course – by a different empire – in the many conflicts in the western United States, had no obvious parallel in British North America. Certainly, even in these other imperial contexts, it is important to heed the warning offered by the historian James Belich about the historiographical and popular-memory implications of giving exclusive emphasis to the victimization of Indigenous nations through imperial violence, even when violence incontestably took place, at the expense of acknowledging other elements of interaction that may also have prevailed at certain times and places, including "the success of indigenous resistance, and coexistence."[29] Yet British North America remains anomalous, and significant questions accordingly arise. How to account for the lesser levels of sustained and outright physical violence in British North America? And how to account, in turn, for the thorough and callous dispossession of Indigenous inhabitants that nevertheless took place in most areas?

The balance of this essay addresses these questions, contending that, in British North America from 1749 to 1830, Indigenous dispossession was carried out by force of the demographic and environmental kind – with, of course, the active complicity of the nascent settler colonial state – rather than principally by the application of direct physical violence. Much depends, of course, on how *violence* is defined. The delineation of violence against individuals is debated among criminologists who advocate narrower definitions that focus on the infliction of physical harm and those who prefer broader definitions that extend to actions that cause injury – including physical injury – without administering it directly.[30] Similarly, although a narrow definition of collective violence in British North America might be used to apply a benign veneer to Indigenous dispossession, a broader view reveals a more sombre reality. It is also essential to give attention to the sequencing of, respectively, imperial and settler-centred assertions of power. Thomas Peace and I have recently argued that in northeastern North America there were a number of distinctive routes towards the assertion of settler sovereignty but that, by the early part of the nineteenth century, they were coalescing into a pattern by which settler colonialism was increasingly entrenched throughout this broad region of the continent.[31] In an earlier analysis of the preceding era in Mi'kma'ki and Wulstukwik – corresponding essentially to the area later occupied by Canada's Maritime provinces – I have also argued that the era preceding the decisive shift to settler colonialism was characterized by imperial-Indigenous friendship. During the earlier phase, violence was restricted, though not averted altogether, by a political relationship that, to varying degrees, would be replicated in other areas of British North America. By the time settler colonialism came to prevail, the route towards dispossession through environmental change had been largely identified and cleared by the principles of friendship, and by the time it became evident that friendship had been erased by settler actions and settler authorities, there was no way back.

The era of friendship in Mi'kma'ki and Wulstukwik can be dated from the period immediately following the Treaty of Utrecht (1713) to the beginning of the major phase of the loyalist migration (1782). Friendship did not signify any abandonment of a position of strength on the part of Indigenous leaderships, any more than it involved land surrender, but it did offer a basis for coexistence.[32] As practised by and with French governors at Louisbourg (until the ultimate fall of that fortified town to the British in 1758), it involved annual meetings held in various parts of Mi'kma'ki at which matters of mutual concern could be resolved, while at the same time the legitimacy of toleration for the

French presence was reaffirmed.[33] As practised by and with British governors, it involved a series of treaties that spanned the era from 1725 to 1779, sometimes punctuated by hostilities but highlighted most centrally by the comprehensive treaty making of 1760–1 – following the deportation of most Acadian inhabitants and the capture of the French islands by British forces during the late 1750s – after which violence on any significant scale largely disappeared. Whether with the French or the British, friendship was neither a vague concept nor a comforting fiction. Rather, it was a well-defined ethic and a political relationship that rested on a rare principle that brought together European and Indigenous values: that of reciprocity. As early as in 1719, royal instructions had obliged the Nova Scotia governor to "cultivate and maintain a strict Friendship and good Correspondence with the Indian Nations inhabiting within the precincts of Your Government." The governor was to make explicit promises of friendship and make gifts accordingly.[34] As the eighteenth century went on, the instruction underwent periodic revisions, including the addition in 1749 of a phrase requiring governors to "enter into a treaty with them," but it retained its central meaning and survived into the 1780s.[35] At all times, it carried the promise of the Crown that its support, service, and benevolence would be extended, with regular gift giving intended to symbolize this commitment. The French at Louisbourg too had been assiduous in gift giving, recognizing that sufferance of the French in Mi'kma'ki was itself a gift that deserved reciprocity.[36]

With British claims to the entire region confirmed by the Treaty of Paris (1763), a limited number of new British settlers entered Nova Scotia, many of them taking over areas vacated by deported Acadians. Mi'kmaw and Maliseet spokespeople never hesitated to remind imperial officials of the continuing Indigenous geographic centrality and military capacity. A succession of British governors, in turn, were blunt in informing London that the security of the British presence in the region depended on maintaining Indigenous friendship. Thus, the era of friendship that had begun with the treaty making of 1725 persisted during the American Revolutionary War. The transition to a new era of dispossession began towards the close of that conflict, with the influx into Mi'kma'ki and Wulstukwik of some thirty-five thousand loyalist refugees and discharged military personnel. The loyalist migration was reinforced and soon exceeded by longer-lasting migrations from the British Isles, notably of Scots.[37] The pressures of sheer demography – a settler population in Nova Scotia alone of some ninety thousand by 1817, more than tripling by the time of the 1851 census – ensured encroachment everywhere on land that had agricultural or commercial possibilities.[38] This process irrevocably changed the physical environment through clearance, with depletion of resources, as well as obstructing Indigenous transportation routes. New fisheries disrupted harvesting patterns in coastal areas and on rivers. Indigenous protests were vigorous, but they were largely premised on appeals to the Crown and its officials, bracketed with references to the treaties, while, by the early nineteenth century (and especially after the establishment of peace between empires in 1815), the real problem centred on settler colonialism, expressed institutionally by the provincial assemblies and the courts and extending even to encroachments on the meagre reserves that had been established for Indigenous communities. Imperial-Indigenous relations had minimized overt violence on either side, but at the expense of the environmentally driven and institutionally reinforced violence of dispossession through settlement. The confinement of Indigenous communities to small and resource-barren reserves, surrounded and often encroached upon by ever-growing numbers of settlers, was the logical and profoundly destructive outcome.

In the Canadas, known with varying boundaries from 1763 to 1791 as the Province of Quebec, matters were complex. The St Lawrence valley itself, of course, was the seat of a long-established settler population. While debate among historians persists as to the degree to which settler colonialism is a viable characterization of a society in which the imperial institutions of ancien régime France had been overlaid by elements of British governance after 1760, there is no doubt that this was a mature settler space.[39] It was adjoined, however, by extensive areas that were Indigenous in terms of occupancy and environment. There were considerable areas of continuity and comparability with the earlier history of Mi'kma'ki and Wulstukwik. The Royal Proclamation of 1763, which also applied to Nova Scotia but must there be interpreted in the context of the treaties, had a particular application in Quebec in that it not only regulated alienations of Indigenous land but also provided the initial governance structure for the new province. As Denys Delâge and Jean-Pierre Sawaya have recently argued, the proclamation can be taken in its provisions confining sales of territory only to the Crown as applying to all Indigenous peoples within Quebec.[40] The key instruction that since 1719 had bound governors of Nova Scotia to pursue friendship was quickly adapted for transmission to successive governors of Quebec from 1763 onwards, who were likewise enjoined "to cultivate and maintain a strict friendship and good correspondence" with "the several nations and tribes of Indians" by whom Quebec was "in part inhabited and possessed," with the delivery of "such presents as shall be sent to you for that purpose" being central to the relationship.[41] Precedents from the French regime also offered avenues of justification for allowing settlement without Indigenous agreement, and Alain Beaulieu has argued convincingly that, over a period of several decades, a hybrid process emerged by which gift giving assumed the character of a notional form of indemnification for land appropriation. It was, as Beaulieu observes, “a syncretic model that coated dispossession without treaties with the varnish of compensation.”[42] Although, as Thomas Peace has pointed out, Indigenous communities experienced the consequences of the Conquest of Canada in diverse ways,[43] the model that Beaulieu observes was – as in the Maritime colonies, although with somewhat different roots in law and governance – an effective imperial process for attaining peace and friendship in advance of new waves of settlement.

The western portions of the Province of Quebec (as bounded by the Quebec Act of 1774 and modified by the Treaty of Paris of 1783), known from 1791 as Upper Canada, embraced a wide variety of Indigenous groups, including large proportions of the Haudenosaunee as well as a multiplicity of Algonkian-speaking peoples. Here, as in what was by then designated Lower Canada but to a greater and more direct degree, there was a further historical influence. A separately evolved model of friendship had long characterized English and British relationships with Haudenosaunee and other groups, culminating in the appointment of Sir William Johnson as superintendent of Indian affairs for the northern colonies in 1756. Although Johnson’s entangled personal and political affairs make him a complex figure,[44] his politic commitment to values of friendship and alliance was central to his relations with the Indigenous leaders and representatives with whom he regularly dealt. Johnson’s diplomacy and the broader evolution of, especially, British-Haudenosaunee relations are the subjects of large historiographies that cannot be reviewed here, but his papers are filled with references to British-Indigenous friendship. Johnson reacted sceptically to any suggestions that the empire’s Indigenous friends were either subject to the Crown or liable to arbitrary deprivation of their lands. On the first of these issues, Johnson observed to General Thomas Gage in 1764 that “you may be assured that none of the Six Nations, Western Indians &[ca]. ever declared themselves to be subjects, or will ever consider themselves in that light whilst they have any Men, or an open Country to retire to, the very Idea of Subjection would fill them with horror.”[45] On the second, he informed a correspondent in 1765 that “I grant it is the policy of our Constitution that Where-So-Ever the Kings Dominions extend, he is the fountain of all property in Lands &c. But how can this be made to extend to the native rights of a people whose property none of our Kings have claimed a right to invade, and to whom the Laws have never Extended without which Dominion cannot be said to be Exercised.”[46]

Into the 1820s, as J.R. Miller has noted, the Indian Department was headed by successors who, like Johnson, were “experienced forest diplomats” who had experience of working with Indigenous allies in a military context.[47] Their actions were grounded on pragmatism and not on ideals. Like the military officials, or governors who frequently were themselves serving or retired officers, in other areas where Indigenous leanings were militarily important, they valued friendship for strategic reasons. But friendship could also be an effective prelude for inserting the thin end of the wedge of land surrender. During the late eighteenth century, starting with the relatively limited goal of acquiring land for the comparatively small number of loyalist refugees who came to Upper Canada, treaties that involved land surrender were negotiated by the Indian Department. In 1830 came a shift to civil rather than military officials as treaty negotiators – in an era accompanied by the decline of an earlier humanitarian tradition in the British Colonial Office that had at times imposed limits on settler ambitions – and, since the incoming officials were beholden to settler institutions, this marked in effect the closing of the trap of settler colonialism.[48] Large-scale settlement, again, had been camouflaged by the previously existing political relationships of peace and friendship. As E.A. Heaman shows in this volume, the related shift to an officialdom that envisaged Indigenous people as poverty-stricken wards of the state, and yet operated through corrupt or predatory Indian agents, deepened Indigenous vulnerability and entrenched a damaging pattern of localized violence against Indigenous communities.[49] Moreover, as Thomas Peace demonstrates, also in this volume, the increasing demographic imbalances and the hardening of settler colonial pressures came at the expense of suppressing the subtle but fragile relationships between Indigenous leaderships and certain religious and political reformers in the emerging non-Indigenous society.[50] And all the while, environmental change through agriculture and non-Indigenous resource harvesting continued to effect dispossession with ineluctable force.

As the nineteenth century progressed and the geographical reach of colonial settlement expanded, the onset of settler colonialism in what became the Dominion of Canada took on divergent patterns and more variable sequencing. In extensive areas of the North and Northwest, settlement remained largely absent, even though the fur trade had unleashed inter-Indigenous conflicts by the beginning of the nineteenth century that were compounded by epidemic disease.[51] In the more westerly areas of the Great Lakes region and across the Plains, the development of settler colonialism was accompanied by the conclusion of the early numbered treaties during the 1870s. As J.R. Miller has shown, the choice of treaty making was effectively imposed on the Dominion government by the clarity of Indigenous demands that agreement must be reached before any outsiders would be permitted to use the resources of the territories concerned, as well as by the priority placed by the settler state on clearing the path for agricultural settlement and railway development without the debilitating expense of military conflict as exemplified south of the border.[52] The early numbered treaties, despite including explicit land surrenders that would lead directly to settlement and ultimately to settler colonialist institutional development, showed the continuing negotiating strength of Indigenous participants. Treaty 7 – pertaining to what became southern Alberta, and the first to be negotiated following the passage of the federal Indian Act – saw that strength eroded by continuing environmental change and, as a result, key concessions were made in favour of the settler state that had not characterized the previous numbered treaties.[53] While the numbered treaties originated from the ample precedents offered by earlier treaties further east and embodied much of the protocol and the discourse of ceremonial Crown-Indigenous relationships, their association with settler colonialism and its impositions was direct and increasingly explicit over time. For Indigenous populations, famine, disease, and the manipulation of treaty-mandated relief by federal state officials in the interests of clearing land for settlement were quick to follow.[54]

To the east and to the west, different patterns obtained. Both British Columbia and Newfoundland experienced settlement long before the era of the numbered treaties. In British Columbia, Indigenous dispossession proceeded from a complex and incremental process of land surrenders. "The Native land problem," Cole Harris summarizes, "grew out of settler society itself: it elected the provincial governments that did its bidding and contributed, within a federal system, to another settler government at one remove. In the final analysis the reserve map of British Columbia maps the mind and values of a settler society."[55] The island of Newfoundland followed a different pattern of imperial administration, as Jerry Bannister's study of naval governance has shown, and the withdrawal of Beothuk occupancy from the path of non-Indigenous colonial settlement – as well as the isolation from settlement of the Mi'kmaw presence on the south coast of the island – largely obviated the possibility of either explicit conflict or effective negotiation over land issues. As the late Ralph Pastore convincingly argued, the results for the Beothuk showed, in the shorter term, the wisdom of minimizing the risks of epidemic disease and of consolidating key coastal communities, as well as, in the longer term, the disasters associated with the inland removal that became the logical result of further settler encroachment.[56] Yet, in a broad sense, the study of other areas of British North America demonstrates that Pastore's key argument that the demise of the Beothuk was prompted by settlement but ultimately was environmentally imposed – rather than stemming from persistently lethal non-Indigenous physical violence, even though such aggression undoubtedly existed – was no isolated observation but rather a prescient insight that is capable of wider application.[57] Indigenous dispossession in British North America from 1749 to 1830 was associated largely with the application of demographic and environmental – rather than physical or military – force. By any broadly realistic definition, it was nonetheless violent.

Thus, while the escorting of the personifier of Edward Cornwallis to the grassy glade in 1924 was misleading in a literal sense – Mi'kmaw leaders, in reality, communicated bluntly to Cornwallis the unacceptability of British settlement on the harbour of Kjipuktuk[58] – nevertheless it had some symbolic reality of a more general nature. Imperial friendship, binding the Crown to Indigenous nations through diplomacy in which the Indigenous negotiators were active and powerful participants and – at least in the case of the peace and friendship treaties – land surrender was not involved, represented a practical and productive option for either side, in the absence of intensive colonial settlement. Trade could be facilitated, while Indigenous toleration of imperial enclaves enabled the economic and strategic interests of the empire to be safeguarded. However, when settler colonialism came to prevail, and the face of the Crown accordingly turned in a different direction, the inability of friendship to restrain settler excesses – despite the much later legal actionability of its obligations – meant that friendship itself became an instrument of dispossession. While the eighteenth century was marked by a chronological separation of imperial friendship from the encroachment of settler colonialism, the nineteenth saw the increasing identification of one with the other, both chronologically and in the erosion of the distinction between empire and colonization. Later phases of treaty making showed the intensifying dangers for Indigenous societies when assertions of friendship – and kinship – by the Crown operated as direct and immediate precursors to environmental depredation.

Canadian writers of the imperial bent, in the late nineteenth and early twentieth centuries, chose to focus on the relative scarcity of overt violence and to infer that all was peaceful and even harmonious between Indigenous peoples and settler populations. Their contention has shown remarkable durability in the century or so that has followed, even though it has been increasingly, and rightly, contested. The reality, as can be shown in many contexts through the study of unrest and violence in British North America, is that Canada's forerunner societies and institutions were far from peaceful. The point from which Canada is challenged to move towards a bleaker awareness regarding the Indigenous past, or at least to recognize that, as J.R. Miller has argued, "we are all treaty people,"[59] is represented by the obligations assumed during the era of friendship, through the treaties that were concluded before settler colonialism established its grip. Separated historically from the populous Thirteen Colonies by geography and environment, and from the other settler dominions by a chronological sequence from which conquest of a military kind was absent, Canada continues to struggle with unfulfilled and as yet often unacknowledged obligations towards the Indigenous peoples who chose to place some faith in imperial friendship and minimized physical violence accordingly, but were then confronted by the demographic, environmental, and spatial violence that was inseparable from colonial settlement.

NOTES

1 I am grateful to colleagues in the "Unrest, Violence, and the Search for Social Order" project for valuable comments on an earlier version of this essay, and also to my research assistant, Courtney Mrazek.

2 *Halifax Herald*, 1 July and 6 August 1924.

3 *Halifax Herald*, 31 July and 5 August 1924; see also Paul Williams, "Erecting an 'Instructive Object': The Case of the Halifax Memorial Tower," *Acadiensis* 36, no. 2 (Spring 2007): 91–112.

4 *Halifax Herald*, 31 July 1924; *Morning Chronicle*, 9 August 1924. The naval cricketers also took on "the local West Indian team," *Halifax Herald*, 8 August 1924. See also John G. Reid, "Cricket, the Retired Feather Merchant, and Settler Colonialism: The Troubled Halifax Sojourn of A.H. Leighton, 1912," *Acadiensis* 46, no. 1 (Winter/Spring 2017): 73–96. On the world cruise of HMS *Hood*, 1923–4, see Bruce Taylor, *The Battlecruiser HMS Hood: An Illustrated Biography, 1916–1941* (London: Chatham Publishing, 2005), 69–74.

5 *Halifax Herald*, 7 August 1924. To judge from the names (John Newell, Peter Newell, Peter Thorne, and John Paul), at least three of those who played Mi'kmaw characters were themselves drawn from the Mi'kmaw community, and an equivalent observation can be made of the three who played Acadians (Herbert M. Aucoin, C. Boudreau, and F. Deveau) in a related ceremony. Cornwallis was played by Major Philip Edward Prideaux.

6 *Halifax Herald*, 5 August 1924.

7 Sir John G. Bourinot, *Canada under British Rule, 1760–1905*, 2nd ed. (Cambridge: Cambridge University Press, 1909), 41–2. See also Margaret A. Banks, "Sir John George Bourinot," *Dictionary of Canadian Biography*, vol. 13, http://www.biographi.ca/en/bio/bourinot_john_george_13E.html.

8 J.G. Bourinot, *Canada* (London: T. Fisher Unwin, 1897), 276, 400.

9 J. Castell Hopkins, *The Story of Our Country: A History of Canada for Four Hundred Years* (Philadelphia: John C. Winston, 1912), 65; and Carl Berger, *The Sense of Power: Studies in the Ideas of Canadian Imperialism, 1867–1914* (Toronto: University of Toronto Press, 1970), 165. See also Jeffrey A. Keshen, "John Castell Hopkins," *Dictionary of Canadian Biography*, vol. 15, http://www.biographi.ca/en/bio/hopkins_john_castell_15E.html.

10 Alfred Goldsworthy Bailey, *The Conflict of European and Eastern Algonkian Cultures, 1504–1700: A Study in Canadian Civilization* (Saint John: New Brunswick Museum, 1937); see also Bruce G. Trigger, "Alfred G. Bailey: Ethnohistorian," *Acadiensis* 18, no. 2 (Spring 1989): 3–21.

11 Bailey, *Conflict of European and Eastern Algonkian Cultures*, ix.

12 Alfred Goldsworthy Bailey, "Social Revolution in Early Eastern Canada," *Canadian Historical Review* 19, no. 3 (September 1938): 264. For the curtailment of the first edition of the book, see Bailey, *The Conflict of European and Eastern Algonkian Cultures, 1504–1700: A Study in Canadian Civilization*, 2nd ed. (Toronto: University of Toronto Press, 1969), xi.

13 See Alfred G. Bailey, "Retrospective Thoughts of an Ethnohistorian," Canadian Historical Association *Historical Papers / Communications historiques* 12 (1977): 14–29; Trigger, "Alfred G. Bailey."

14 Tamson Pietsch, *Empire of Scholars: Universities, Networks, and the British Academic World, 1850–1939* (Manchester: Manchester University Press, 2013), 65, 110. See also M. Brook Taylor, *Promoters, Patriots, and Partisans: Historiography in Nineteenth-Century English Canada* (Toronto: University of Toronto Press, 1989); and Carl Berger, *The Writing of Canadian History: Aspects of English-Canadian Historical Writing, 1900 to 1970* (Toronto: Oxford University Press, 1976), esp. 11–13.

15 Pietsch, *Empire of Scholars*, 1–4.

16 Ibid., 7.

17 E Palmer Patterson, *The Canadian Indian: A History since 1500* (Don Mills, ON: Collier Macmillan, 1972), 5. In the author's name, 'E' is not an abbreviation but a name.

18 Lorenzo Veracini, "'Settler Colonialism': Career of a Concept," *Journal of Imperial and Commonwealth History* 41, no. 2 (June 2013): 325.

19 William Kilbourn, *Canada: A Guide to the Peaceable Kingdom* (Toronto: Macmillan, 1970), esp. "Introduction," xvii.

20 See "Edward Hicks: The Peaceable Kingdom," http://www.worcesterart.org/collection/American/1934.65.html.

21 Northrop Frye, "Conclusion," in Carl F. Klinck, general editor, *Literary History of Canada: Canadian Literature in English* (Toronto: University of Toronto Press, 1965), 847–8.

22 See, for example, Eric Wagner, "The Peaceable Kingdom? The National Myth of Canadian Peacekeeping and the Cold War," *Canadian Military Journal* 7, no. 4 (Winter 2006–7): 45–54.

23 Ian McKay and Jamie Swift, *Warrior Nation: Rebranding Canada in an Age of Anxiety* (Toronto: Between the Lines, 2012), 62.

24 John Ralston Saul, *A Fair Country: Telling Truths about Canada*, 2nd ed. (Toronto: Penguin Canada, 2009), 3, 117.

25 Elizabeth Jane Errington, "British Migration and British America, 1783–1867," in *Canada and the British Empire*, ed. Phillip Buckner (Oxford: Oxford University Press, 2008), 154.

26 See John G. Reid, "The Three Lives of Edward Cornwallis," *Journal of the Royal Nova Scotia Historical Society* 16 (2013): 19–45.

27 Judith Fingard, "The New England Company and the New Brunswick Indians, 1786–1826: A Comment on the Colonial Perversion of British Benevolence," *Acadiensis* 1, no. 2 (Spring 1972): 29–42; see also J.R. Miller, *Shingwauk's Vision: A History of Native Residential Schools* (Toronto: University of Toronto Press, 1996), esp. 74–6.

28 For recent perspectives, see the essays in Hans V. Hansen, ed., *Riel's Defence: Perspectives on His Speeches* (Montreal and Kingston: McGill-Queen's University Press, 2014), esp. Nicole C. O'Byrne, "'Through the Grace of God I Am the Founder of Manitoba': Louis Riel's Constitutional Thought," 90–105.

29 James Belich, *Replenishing the Earth: The Settler Revolution and the Rise of the Anglo-World, 1783–1939* (Oxford: Oxford University Press, 2009), 552–3.

30 See Willem de Haan, "Violence as an Essentially Contested Concept," in *Violence in Europe: Historical and Contemporary Perspectives*, ed. Sophie Body-Gendrot and Peter Spierenburg (New York: Springer, 2009), 27–40; Steve Tombs, "'Violence,' Safety Crimes and Criminology," *British Journal of Criminology* 47, no. 4 (July 2007): 531–50.

31 Thomas Peace and John G. Reid, "Settlement and Settler Colonialism in Northeastern North America, 1450–1850," in *Routledge History of Settler Colonialism*, ed. Edward Cavanagh and Lorenzo Veracini (London: Routledge, 2017), 79–94.

32 For a fuller discussion, see John G. Reid, "Imperial-Aboriginal Friendship in Eighteenth-Century Mi'kma'ki/Wulstukwik," in *The Loyal Atlantic: Remaking the British Atlantic in the Revolutionary Era*, ed. Jerry Bannister and Liam Riordan (Toronto: University of Toronto Press, 2012), 75–102.

33 See William C. Wicken, *Mi'kmaq Treaties on Trial: History, Land, and Donald Marshall Junior* (Toronto: University of Toronto Press, 2002), 51–2.

34 Instructions to Richard Philipps, 14 July 1719, National Archives of the United Kingdom (hereafter UKNA), CO5/189, 427–8.

35 Revisions in the wording of the instruction can be traced in Leonard W. Labaree, *Royal Instructions to British Colonial Governors, 1670–1776,* 2 vols. (New York: American Historical Association, 1935), 2: 469–70. On the use of the wording for other colonies, see Reid, "Imperial-Aboriginal Friendship," 79–80.

36 See Bernard Pothier, "Joseph de Monbeton de Brouillan, *dit* Saint-Ovide," *Dictionary of Canadian Biography*, vol. 3, http://www.biographi.ca/en/bio/monbeton_de_brouillan_joseph_de_3E.html.

37 For fuller discussion, see John G. Reid, "Scots in Mi'kma'ki, 1760–1820," *Nashwaak Review* 22–3, no. 1 (Spring/Summer 2009): 527–57; John G. Reid, "Empire, the Maritime Colonies, and the Supplanting of Mi'kma'ki/Wulstukwik, 1780–1820," *Acadiensis* 38, no. 2 (Summer/Autumn 2009): 78–97; and John G. Reid, "Scots, Settler Colonialism, and Indigenous Displacement: Mi'kma'ki, 1770–1820, in Comparative Context," *Journal of Scottish Historical Studies* 38, no. 1 (May 2018): 178–96.

38 For population numbers, see Julian Gwyn, *Excessive Expectations: Maritime Commerce and the Economic Development of Nova Scotia, 1740–1870* (Montreal and Kingston: McGill-Queen's University Press, 1998), 25, 153. The figure for 1817 includes an estimated population for Cape Breton Island, even though it was at the time (until 1820) an autonomous colony.

39 For an especially revealing analysis of the wary and pragmatic adaptations that followed the conquest, see Donald Fyson, "The Conquered and the Conqueror: The Mutual Adaptation of the *Canadiens* and the British in Quebec, 1759–1775," in *Revisiting 1759: The Conquest of Canada in Historical Perspective*, ed. Phillip Buckner and John G. Reid (Toronto: University of Toronto Press, 2012), 190–217.

40 Denys Delâge and Jean-Pierre Sawaya, "La Proclamation royale vaut-elle pour tous les Indiens de la Province de Québec?" *Canada Watch* (Fall 2013), 9–10.

41 Labaree, *Royal Instructions to British Colonial Governors*, 2: 478–9. The wording was also contained in the governors' instructions for East and West Florida, and (applied to "Caribbeans or wild Negroes") Grenada. A version of the same had also been applied in the meantime to Georgia. Ibid., 474.

42 Alain Beaulieu, "'An Equitable Right to Be Compensated': The Dispossession of the Aboriginal Peoples of Quebec and the Emergence of a New Legal Rationale (1760–1860)," *Canadian Historical Review* 94, no. 1 (March 2013): 27.

43 Thomas Peace, "The Slow Process of Conquest: Huron-Wendat Responses to the Conquest of Quebec, 1697–1791," in Buckner and Reid, eds, *Revisiting 1759*, 115–40.

44 See Julian Gwyn, "Sir William Johnson," *Dictionary of Canadian Biography*, http://www.biographi.ca/en/bio/johnson_william_4E.html.

45 Sir William Johnson to Thomas Gage, 31 October 1764, in James Sullivan et al., eds, *The Papers of Sir William Johnson*, 13 vols. (Albany: University of the State of New York Press, 1921–62), 11: 395.

46 Johnson to John Tabor Kempe, 7 September 1765, ibid., 11: 925.

47 J.R. Miller, *Compact, Contract, Covenant: Aboriginal Treaty-Making in Canada* (Toronto: University of Toronto Press, 2009), 104.

48 Ibid., 101–6. See also Cole Harris, *Making Native Space: Colonialism, Resistance, and Reserves in British Columbia* (Vancouver: UBC Press, 2002), 4–15; and Sarah Carter, "Aboriginal People of Canada and the British Empire," in Buckner, ed., *Canada and the British Empire*, 204–8.

49 See the chapter by E.A. Heaman in this volume.
50 See the chapter by Thomas Peace in this volume.
51 See James Daschuk, *Clearing the Plains: Disease, Politics of Starvation, and the Loss of Aboriginal Life* (Regina: University of Regina Press, 2013), esp. 41–57.
52 Miller, *Compact, Contract, Covenant*, 152–6.
53 Ibid., 182–3.
54 See Daschuk, *Clearing the Plains*.
55 Harris, *Making Native Space*, 323.
56 Jerry Bannister, *The Rule of the Admirals: Law, Custom, and Naval Government in Newfoundland, 1699–1832* (Toronto: University of Toronto Press, 2003); and Ralph Pastore, "The Collapse of the Beothuk World," *Acadiensis* 19, no. 1 (Autumn 1989): 52–71.
57 Pastore, "The Collapse of the Beothuk World," esp. 68–71.
58 See Mi'kmaq of Cape Breton and Antigonish to Cornwallis, 23 September 1749, UKNA, CO217/9, 116.
59 Miller, *Compact, Contract, Covenant*, 283–309.

7 Space, Race, and Violence: The Beginnings of "Civilization" in Canada

E.A. HEAMAN

"Protection, Civilization, Assimilation": thus did John Tobias magisterially sum up Canadian Indian policy.[1] The "founding document of the British civilizing project" was a report on the Canadian Indian Department, penned by Henry Charles Darling in 1828 on instructions from the Colonial and War Office, transmitted to him via Governor General George Ramsay, Lord Dalhousie.[2] The British fiscal-military state, continuously in Tory hands since 1804, was beset by a coalition of liberal reformers demanding that it reduce spending, especially military spending. The Canadian Indian Department was under military oversight: could costs be cut, and could they be cut by curtailing the annual distribution of presents, an obligation that was written into eighteenth-century peace treaties? In December 1822, Dalhousie agreed to reduce expenses but insisted on more fortifications and a continued military presence at Sault Ste Marie to protect the frontier and maintain communications with the numerous tribes there. He also warned that any curtailment of presents would be a dangerous breach of faith.[3] But Whitehall needed more cutbacks and demanded an extensive report on the "exact" condition of the Indian Department of Canada, both Upper Canada and Lower Canada. Asked whether the Colonial Office should reinforce or close down the Indian Department, Darling responded in 1828 with a recommendation for civilization.[4]

Darling's report has generally been read with hindsight, in terms of its impact on and relevance for subsequent policies and events. But hindsight obliterates the Tory tilt that inflected this first iteration of civilization policy. In the 1820s, demilitarization was first and foremost a question of police: of the civil and state mechanisms that, overlapping like Venn diagrams, conduced to public order and social stability. The question as to whether "Indians" should be governed according to a military or a non-military paradigm emerged amidst complex challenges to the demilitarization of the state and the constitution of civil society in Britain. Darling's strategic goal, I argue, did not anticipate liberal assimilation but was a covert prop to the waning fiscal-military state. In this chapter, I aim at a reading of the Darling report that raises a methodological question: how broadly should we understand the historical context within which Darling compiled his report and his understanding of the audiences for it? Precisely because much of the new imperial history neglects the British North American colonies,[5] I argue that we should read that context very broadly; that the object of Darling's report, the impoverished Indigenous subject in the backwoods of Canada, genuinely mattered across the imperial spectrum. To that end, I sketch the wider imperial context of the waning military state, beset by partisan attack and widespread threat of violent disorder. I then discuss Darling and his report in terms of how it channelled the ambitions and perplexities of the Tory project of rule on the eve of its capitulation to liberal hegemonies.

A quarter century of on-and-off warfare, from the onset of the French Revolutionary Wars in 1792 to the Peace of Vienna in 1815, had seen a massive escalation of the taxing and intervening state. Once the Napoleonic Wars were over, the British state, but more particularly the army and navy, seemed too big and expensive. An adverse postwar economy engendered widespread disaffection and resistance to the various state and state-protected mechanisms of rent, tithe, and tax exaction. The British population was worryingly restive, as signalled by the bloody "Peterloo" confrontation of 1817 and the Lancashire uprisings of the late 1820s. A loose Whig opposition was channelling such grievances into an increasingly organized political party in its campaign for "cheap, economic, civil government" as against "large, expensive military government."[6] Tory cabinets were replete with military officers, especially that of the Duke of Wellington, prime minister from January 1828 to November 1830. For three decades, the governing Tories – the Earl of Liverpool, George Canning, Viscount Goderich, the Duke of Wellington, Sir Robert Peel – walked a fine line between maintaining and dismantling their armies and their veteran-staffed bureaucracies.[7]

The Tories, a loose coalition ranging from moderate to ultra conservatives, were weak in Parliament. They had only a few strong debaters, primarily Wellington in the Lords and Home Secretary Robert Peel and Chancellor of the Exchequer Henry Goulburn in the Commons. Peter Jupp tallied spoken interventions by cabinet members during Wellington's administration and found 259 interventions by Wellington, 860 by Peel, and 785 by Goulburn. Those three men carried the burden of defending the government, while strong Whig opponents ceaselessly harried them. Joseph Hume, the leading radical critic on colonies among other subjects, spoke 1,434 times. According to Jupp, the picture that emerges "is of a Parliament in which a small number of senior ministers, only modestly supported by their colleagues, battled to control an agenda that was determined in each House by a hard core of activists drawn principally from a broad spectrum of members from the opposition benches."[8]

Colonial rule was a central piece in the increasingly politicized perplexities of Tory government in the 1820s.[9] Soldiers remained indispensable props to imperial rule. The numbers of imperial subjects governed were unprecedented and almost unimaginable to previous generations: C.A. Bayly estimates them at 200 million people.[10] Governing so many, very different peoples provoked, both indirectly and directly, administrative and political experimentation. Bayly sees an "imperial meridian," a long phase of political conservatism, militarization, and repression that was more than just a plateau between two liberalisms. Colonial rule in the empire and cabinet rule at home were remarkably intertwined. Leading British politicians cut their teeth on the perplexities of imperial rule and, indeed, on the rule of British North America in particular. They reformed the Colonial and War Office to make it an efficient node for exercising power that was at once both military and administrative, as they sought to depoliticize it. (In the 1830s, Peel quietly advised the Whig government to adopt colonial policies he could support, because he did not want to ride colonial grievances into office.)

Boyd Hilton observes, "Canada's experience supports the argument that Britain's fiscal-military state was not so much dismantled as exported to the colonies."[11] There, citadels and Martello towers were going up, canals were going down, and veterans, including Dalhousie himself and much of his staff, filled offices. Indeed, Canada was not a distant and abstract problem but a known, vital concern for Tory ministers, Wellington, Lord Bathurst, Robert Peel, Henry Goulburn, and especially George Murray. As the minister responsible for colonies from 1812 to 1827, Bathurst was credited with the modern reconstruction of the Colonial Office. Both Peel and Goulburn served as his undersecretaries before transferring to the Irish office, in 1812 and 1821, respectively. Peel then went to the Home Office, while Goulburn got the Exchequer in Wellington's cabinet. As undersecretary, Goulburn had largely overseen the North American theatre of the War of 1812, including the efforts of Murray, lieutenant governor of Upper Canada from December 1814 to May 1815 (when Napoleon's escape summoned him back to Europe). In May 1828, Wellington chose Murray as his colonial minister because the Canada question "was becoming a major colonial issue."[12] In fact, Wellington relied on Peel for political advice and on Bathurst and Goulburn for colonial advice, and he tended to dictate colonial policy to Murray, treating him as a "senior clerk."[13] These men were well situated to reason from colonial to metropolitan perplexities and to encompass Canada as a part of that process. So were their enemies. The colonies were fodder for attack everywhere that governors and settlers fell out, but they fell out so spectacularly in the 1820s in the Canadas as to make those colonies particularly interesting. They were the object of a special investigation by a twenty-one-member Select Committee of the House of Commons on the Civil Government of Canada, established in 1828, which investigated the militia question as well as other grievances related to land tenure, clergy reserves, and constitutional questions. In 1830, the leading Whig, Earl Grey advised his son, Lord Howick, to build his career on the colonial question.[14] People cared about Lower Canada and Upper Canada in the late 1820s, not for the Canadas' sake but because they saw in the two colonies a synecdoche of the larger political perplexities of post-war Britain. Was the imperial state a war-mongering, fiscally predatory autocracy or was it the guardian and exemplar of British political liberty and fairness?

The Colonial and War Office was a good place to make a stand for the Tory state, but it had to be reconstructed to make it defensible. Governing at a distance required bureaucratic innovations that were then expanded through the civil service more generally. Links within the department were crucial: administrative capacity became most highly developed in the military branch of the state during the Napoleonic Wars. Military men were among the best administrators of their day, and the postwar era saw those capacities being extended into the civil state, a process that began with the colonies because they were viewed first as a military and second as a civil-society problem.[15] Generating an informed and efficient Colonial Office required something like a revolution in government. Under Bathurst (1812–27), it was transformed from neglectful and uninformed into a competent and informed administrative apparatus, at the vanguard of modern state formation.[16] Pre-Ireland, Peel exemplified the old regime: in 1812, when ceding the undersecretaryship to his friend Goulburn, Peel advised him to rely on delaying tactics as he took over "the superintendence of the correspondence with all the British colonies on the face of the globe on all subjects military and civil." "Collisions of the governor and assemblies" were the greatest difficulty, Peel warned, not easily resolved politically or administratively.[17] Over the 1820s, the two-way flow of correspondence over civil governance of even small colonies increased enormously. Precisely because Bathurst preferred to delegate administration, he made his department a model of administrative efficiency under men such as Wilmot Horton and James Stephen. In short, modern state formation was having an intense moment around the growing capacity of the Colonial Office of the 1820s, prompted by both internal reorganization and partisan attacks in Parliament.

The Colonial Office of the 1820s had a "rage for order," according to a new analysis by Lauren Benton and Lisa Ford. They see a "middle power" project whereby colonial officials would gather and submit information, negotiate conflicts, rein in petty despotisms and abuses of legal authority, and uphold not "rights," not a positive rule of law, but multiple vernacular forms of stability and order, in projects that had "less to do with universal principles than with efforts to remake the interface between imperial and municipal structures of authority."[18] In the early nineteenth century, commissions of inquiry were a privileged and preferred mechanism for intervention by the Colonial Office, Henry Darling's report on the Canadian Indian Department not least among them. It fits perfectly into the framework described by Benton and Ford and the larger trajectory of imperial governance in the 1820s, as the work of a military officer and a veteran of the War of 1812, with evolving and expanding colonial and civilian responsibilities, gathering information to serve a centralizing administrative project.

For Darling, military forms and mechanisms were not a "state of exception" to civilian rule but an indispensable branch of stable civilian rule and executive mandate.[19] Henry Darling owed his career to his brother: both were career soldiers, sons of a sergeant in the 45th Foot Regiment and quartermaster, originally from Durham but long stationed in Ireland. Ralph Darling enlisted as a private at age fourteen and, with the patronage of the Duke of York, rose to important offices in the military and colonial office; Ralph, in turn, obtained positions for Henry Charles Darling and later his son Charles Henry Darling. The brothers saw military action in various arenas, and Ralph rose to administer both recruitment and demobilization (he signed Dalhousie's commission papers), then becoming an acting governor of Mauritius and governor of New South Wales. Henry, like his brother, began in his father's 45th Foot Regiment, serving in the West Indies and in Nova Scotia with the Fencibles. He went on half-pay at the end of the war before finding employment with Dalhousie as his military secretary from 1820 and was also, from 1826, a superintendent of the Indian Department in the Canadas. In later life, Henry and his son Charles emulated Ralph Darling's career: both were knighted and both served as colonial governors (Sir Henry in Tobago and Sir Charles in Newfoundland, the Cape Colony, and finally Victoria, Australia). The Darlings were Tories, with a genuinely imperial as well as a military outlook, better connected within military networks than colonial ones: administrators in the Colonial Office described Ralph as a martinet and a "plodder."[20]

But to be too military in one's orientation was to be a magnet for liberal attack. If Ralph and Henry Darling brought personal and partisan coherence to colonial governance, it was because they faced similar challenges. In the Canadas and New South Wales, the key problem was land-hungry settlers determined to exercise local despotisms against Indigenous peoples and to justify them by discrediting the governor, along with his retinue, as a high-spending petty, overly military despot; thus they could expect support from Whigs and liberals across local and imperial stages. The Darlings could hope to fend off such attacks only if they could make the special needs or problems associated with Aboriginal peoples cohere with the legitimate exercise of state authority.

Were "Indians" a threat to or an adjunct of civil order and authority? There was no simple answer, and the question was, in effect, one of "civilization" more generally. For Tory purposes, the two concepts were virtually interchangeable. Civilization, as an immediate practical policy in Canada, meant the Bible and the plough; but as an abstract political principle, it meant a governable population. Where liberals wanted to remake pre-liberal subjects into modern liberal citizens, Tories, more modestly, sought something more commensurate with what Michel Foucault described as the concept of police in the eighteenth century: "the ensemble of mechanisms serving to ensure order, the properly channeled growth of wealth and the conditions of preservation of health in general."[21] There was some scope for legal and civilizational pluralism, at least according to a handful of Enlightenment theorists, but the broader trend on both sides of the Atlantic was towards a Eurocentric reading.[22] Increasingly, policing became bureaucratically distinct, while civilization became racially distinct. The 1820s were a key moment in that transformation, and Canada a key place for their reconfiguration, according to a logic that helps us understand both the ambitions and the failings of that Tory project of rule.

Civilization and police connected; their opposite was violence, running the gamut from petty to revolutionary forms. Across different British domains, varying kinds of actual and threatened violence suggested diverse solutions. Soldiers remained the gold standard for open violence everywhere, including mainland Britain: they were deployed against the Lancashire weavers' "rising" of 1826 that saw ten people killed, scores injured, and much damage to property.[23] There, the classic municipal mechanism of civil order, the magistracy, entirely broke down. Perhaps because his mill-owning grandfather had once been threatened by such an uprising, Peel readily deployed soldiers to the Midlands, though he resented the expenditure, believing that such an "opulent" place should pay for policing as a local and civil expense.[24] The magistracy was more obviously inadequate in Ireland, as was the volunteer militia force known as the "Yeomanry": it was too Protestant to maintain order, and tended rather to provoke than restrain violence, especially during the "Captain Rock" movement of the early 1820s that saw widespread agrarian violence. Peel struggled, during his years at Dublin Castle, to create and sustain a more autonomous instrument of police, a "Peace Preservation Force" introduced in 1814 that became, under his successors, an autonomous and increasingly trustworthy and trusted constabulary.[25] Moving to the Home Office, Peel was establishing yet another police force in London, beginning in 1829. The new "Met" police would be less military than the Irish version: uniformed, so as not to be feared as spies, but their uniform, complete with top hat and wooden truncheon, was tailored to signal civilian oversight.[26] That was also the year that Peel, spurred by the worsening political crisis in Ireland, reversed his position on Catholic emancipation and forced it through Parliament.

Canada was not yet an acute problem in the same way as Ireland, but the potential was there for all to see. Lower Canada had the religious divisions that made Ireland so ungovernable, divisions deep and politicized enough to make neutral bureaucratic instruments of police unobtainable; the thousands of Irish immigrants arriving each year intensified such concerns. The whole able-bodied male population was supposedly organized into a militia, led by officers who served as the necessary aid to government when some civilian show of force was needed, for such occasions as arrest or transportation of prisoners. But the militia was considered by state officials to be unreliable and too likely to let prisoners escape, according to historian Donald Fyson. Magistrates preferred to rely on a quasi-professional constabulary and watch.[27] Dalhousie expressed his disappointment with such arrangements in early dispatches to Bathurst, regretting the absence of something like a uniformed yeomanry, found in almost every other part of the British Empire.[28] In 1827, distressed by what he saw as disloyal sentiments expressed at public meetings frequented by militia officers, Dalhousie "dismissioned" some prominent French-Canadian officers, including thirteen current and three former members of the Legislative Assembly. Where Dalhousie saw a branch of the colonial state behaving as "active agents of a party hostile to His Majesty's Government," the colonial perspective was that, in a world where all able-bodied men were in the militia, a ban on their participation in partisan public meetings amounted to martial law.[29] The London *Times* avidly reported the "very serious" dispute between governor and governed in Lower Canada as showing "alarming symptoms of apparent alienation" and of "anger and distrust towards this country." The *Times* blamed the disaffection on overly military rule: "we doubt very gravely, whether military men ought ever to be employed as civil governors over any portion of a free people. They have one and all an instinctive jealousy of privileges which set their own power at defiance; they are habituated to command, but not to persuade or reason: they dread freedom of speech, and hate a deliberative assembly."[30]

But British North America had other wellsprings for violence than internal faction. Above all, the border with the United States, with many sections contested, fostered complex incitements to violence. It was more like a frontier than a border – that is, a place of limited state authority and, indeed, of counter-hegemony.[31] Smuggling and counterfeiting were regular cross-border activities, as American counterfeiters set up shops in Montreal, prompting retaliatory cross-border raids organized by bankers rather than by state officials.[32] Local officials along the borderlands regularly negotiated local resolutions to crises around the extradition of criminals or escaped prisoners and refugee slaves, tending more towards a legal continentalism, in the assessment of Bradley Miller, than towards formal adherence to constitutional centralization.[33] Those counter-hegemonic negotiations were not just on the fringes of settler society but influenced its core governing institutions. The Anglican bishop of Toronto, John Strachan, who was also the leading ideologue of Upper Canadian conservativism (he had marshalled the civilian response to the American taking of York in 1813 and peppered officers like Murray with ultrapatriotic squibs), came around to support popular schooling after the War of 1812 only because he saw settlers in the borderlands taking their children to American schools.[34]

The American border was both a threat and a seductive lure. Its proximity escalated the perceived dangers from internal violence within Canada. The American Revolution had turned social violence into revolutionary and military violence and the danger was of paradigm formation. Lord Liverpool, prime minister from 1812 to 1827, worried that an alliance of English radicals and "factious and disaffected colonials" would see the American experience repeated in other settler societies.[35] Both Canadas seemed worryingly riddled with potential republicans. Upper Canadians had grounds for concern during the War of 1812, as the colonial elite, suspicious of the largely American-born population in the Niagara peninsula, demanded martial law there. Such concerns prompted the disenfranchisement of American-born settlers in 1818, and over the next decade debates over its repeal polarized Upper Canadian politics.[36]

But what most distinguished this North American border from European borders was the Indigenous peoples who frequented it. Indigenous and Metis peoples claimed territory on both sides, moved back and forth across it, and played British and American authorities against one another.[37] Their cultural and political otherness continually challenged European policing mechanisms. France had never managed to master borderlands diplomacy in North America: Brett Rushforth shows that its Indigenous allies west of New France continually made "use of intervillage violence to limit and direct France's commercial and territorial ambitions in North America."[38] Rival imperial powers stirred up local violence throughout North American borderlands in the eighteenth century as part of their "search for sovereignty,"[39] and new lexicons of race, space, and violence were deployed around accusations of "savagery."

Conceptions of violence were spatialized and racialized in North America in a way not seen in Britain. For example, in an important article written in 1760 to persuade the British not to return New France to the French government, Benjamin Franklin argued for keeping Canada, because, so long as there was a border, so long would it nurture violence and war. "If the *French* remain in *Canada* and *Louisiana*, fix the boundaries as you will between us and them, we must border on each other for more than 1,500 miles. The people that inhabit the frontiers, are generally the refuse of both nations, often of the worst morals and the least discretion, remote from the eye, the prudence, and the restraint of government. Injuries are therefore frequently, in some part or other of so long a frontier, committed on both sides, resentment provoked, the colonies first engaged, and then the mother countries." Even slights *between* "the people of our own colonies have frequently been so exasperated against each other in their disputes about boundaries, as to proceed to open violence and bloodshed."[40] Borders in North America were uniquely violent, for Franklin, because of the liminal figure of Indigenous peoples.

> The wide extended forests between our settlements and theirs, are inhabited by barbarous tribes of savages that delight in war and take pride in murder, subjects properly neither of the *French* nor *English*, but strongly attach'd to the former by the art and indefatigable industry of priests, similarity of superstitions, and frequent family alliances. These are easily, and have been continually, instigated to fall upon and massacre our planters, even in times of full peace between the two crowns, to the certain diminution of our people and the contraction of our settlements. And tho' it is known they are supply'd by the *French* and carry their prisoners to them, we can by complaining obtain no redress, as the governors of *Canada* have a ready excuse, that the Indians are an independent people, over whom they have no power, and for whose actions they are therefore not accountable. Surely circumstances so widely different, may reasonably authorise different demands of security in *America*, from such as are usual or necessary in *Europe*.[41]

Franklin's descriptions of vulnerable Britons were denounced by interests advocating keeping Guadeloupe as "phantoms of a piece with such as are hatched by old women to frighten children in the nursery." The plea of insecurity veiled a bellicose project aimed at independence.[42]

Mendacious or not, Franklin's arguments had a long afterlife with huge implications for Canadian security. Andrew Jackson parlayed borderland threats into a bellicose nationalism. A lawyer from the borders of North and South Carolina, Jackson worked as a prosecutor and also traded in Cherokee lands around present-day Memphis, Tennessee, in anticipation of their becoming available. Federal treaties with the Cherokees in 1790–1 stipulated that only federal authorities, not territorial ones, could cross the border. Years later, as treaty provisions were enforced, Jackson found it increasingly difficult to cross the border. In 1811, a federal official refused him permission, provoking Jackson to brandish his guns, describing them as "General Jackson's passports." Jason Opal sees in Jackson the epistemology of war hawks: "Bitterly rejecting a Federalist model of citizenship that assumed clear territorial limits, they invented a new 'protection covenant,' whereby the people themselves, imagined within a brutal state of nature, retained full sovereignty to deploy violence."[43] That is to say, while engaging in some unsavoury commercial projects, Jackson claimed a right to violence and state warrant – a thoroughly American version of "l'état c'est moi." The borderlands underwrote this epistemology: "Instead of dwelling in a civil society, where they had to continually perform certain laws, they were an inherently lawful people living in a pitiless, indeed savage, world. To protect the American people it was necessary to stop pretending that anything like civil order existed beyond national borders and deploy violence accordingly." Jackson's rising political fortunes worked to disseminate his outlook across American frontiers more generally. The American invasion of Canada had been repelled in the War of 1812, but Jackson, who resoundingly beat the main British army in New Orleans in the final battle of that war, continued to mobilize frontier violence and to escalate his political ambitions after the war, with a failed presidential bid in 1824 and a successful one in 1828. Jackson exaggerated the threat of Indigenous violence to engage in extreme forms of retaliatory violence, including warfare and removal, that served an expansionary American nationalism.[44] Jackson's logic of frontier violence was a paradigmatic expression of settler colonialism. Even as it threatened British North American security, it also recapitulated tensions felt along settlement frontiers. The 1820s have been described as a key decade of global settler sovereignty: on the one hand, it saw violent aggressions against Indigenous populations; on the other, aggressors claimed to impose positive law on Indigenous populations to ensure security of property and person and thereby attract new settlers.[45] Canadians (including Loyalists) proved remarkably immune to violent incitements during the Revolutionary War and the War of 1812.[46] Positive law and dispossession were imposed less spectacularly in the Canadas, and legal pluralism remained widespread through the 1820s.[47]

Canadian settlers similarly coveted Indigenous lands, but their governing officials were much less likely to license an overtly republican, bottom-up warrant to violence. Indigenous dispossession was carefully managed as a prop to, rather than as defiance of, metropolitan authority, according to a British legal-political framework that, Elizabeth Mancke has argued, created distinctive political cultures in British North America.[48] Nonetheless, by the mid-1820s, violent confrontations on settlement frontiers from Seven Oaks in Rupert's Land to Red Indian Lake in Newfoundland, revealed that a Jacksonian-like logic could find fertile ground in British North America, as it did elsewhere in British settler societies.

Therein lay one of the greatest perplexities of the Colonial Office in the 1820s: how to interpose stabilizing British political mores and bureaucratic middle power. The Darling brothers were at the heart of that confrontation, and distinctively politicized as such, amidst real ambiguity about who or what interest they served. In New South Wales, debates around violence and rule of law in settler-Aboriginal relations were framed around the extension of positive law and its suspension in favour of martial law to let the Crown "exercise its severities, against rebels." Governor Thomas Brisbane declared martial law in 1824, but his successor, Ralph Darling, refused to declare martial law in 1826, resisting the arguments from his attorney general that the government must "take the lead in a decisive manner and on a large scale ... in the coercion ... of the aborigines." Responding to settler demands for violent repression at Hunter River, Darling instead blamed "irregularities on the part of your own people which I apprehend is in many cases the causes of the disorders committed by the Natives."[49] Darling interposed himself between settlers and Aboriginal-held land in much the way that Britain had done in North America with the Royal Proclamation and the Quebec Act, and earned similar hostility from settlers as those "intolerable acts" had done and as any serious protections for Indigenous peoples in the Canadas of the 1820s must also do.

Henry Darling wrote his report within that highly politicized context, addressing both the grievances and misgovernance of Indigenous people and also reflecting on the political stakes of settler resistance. Lord Goderich, who served successively as chancellor of the Exchequer, minister for war and the colonies, and prime minister between 1823 and 1828 (when he ceded leadership to Wellington), sought to abolish the Canadian Indian Department entirely, something Darling and Dalhousie strenuously fought. If they did not bend the Indian Department to party purposes, they knew their enemies would. In 1824, the two men reflected in their correspondence about the deprivations inflicted by metropolitan austerity, especially around the determination of the Wendat chiefs at Lorette, Lower Canada, to take their grievances to the throne: "perseverance in the pursuit of their object is the most conspicuous trait in the Indian character." Amidst Indigenous peoples' genuine grievances were supposedly spurious ones stirred up by machinating political rivals. Darling dismissed one from Kahnawà:ke, remarking that "little confidence is placed in any paper purporting to contain the real sentiments of the Indians for as these unfortunate

People are destitute of education, and little acquainted with any language but their own, they are necessarily at the mercy of designing Persons, who they may consult in their Affairs." He instanced rival petitions from Oka from two different translators that shared signatures.[50] Darling dismissed Indigenous criticisms in the same way Dalhousie did French-Canadian criticisms, as drafted by a small fractious minority playing on widespread popular ignorance. No report written by such a man could be other than politically strategic. Although evidence was not made up, it was not neutrally presented.

Darling sought to make "Indians" a crucial prop to the high-stakes government of the Canadas. A mounting alliance of Whigs and radicals, including evangelical interests and other "humanitarians," that organized initially around the abolition of slavery was broadening its scope and compounding pressure on the Colonial Office to protect Indigenous peoples from quasi-genocidal attacks by land-hungry settlers. The key events in that story occurred in the mid-1830s: the genocidal projects of Sir Francis Bond Head, lieutenant governor of Upper Canada; the formation of the Aborigines' Protection Society; and publication of the parliamentary *Report of the Select Committee on Aborigines*, which drew upon the Darling report for evidence of predation in Canada. Consequently, scholars have read the Darling report retrospectively, promiscuously intermingling developments from the 1820s and 1830s.[51] That's a mistake.

Both colonialism and its enemies in the 1830s were heavily invested in racializing Indigeneity. Darling's Tory civilization project, in contrast, was less vested in parsing race and more vested in parsing the state. For the Tory coalitions of the 1820s, the key Canadian question was: How do you get a secure and economically prospering state, with minimal violence and minimal constitutional change? "Indians" were, from that perspective, as much a solution as a problem, because they seemed to reverse the American paradigm. Where the American political logic tended towards a trajectory of rebellion, militarization, and separation, the Indigenous trajectory was from bellicose autonomy to loyal subjecthood. Indigenous peoples had discontents and grievances, just like anybody else, but their grievances were a serious concern only if they found common cause with Americans. Violence on the Jacksonian settlement frontier south of the border meant they were not likely to find common cause there unless, Darling observed, serious mistreatment in Canada drove them there.

Darling organized his report around two axes – military violence and extramilitary violence – that spoke to two major concerns. Did the British government in Canada any longer need to cultivate the Indigenous peoples as military allies? And did those Indigenous peoples pose another kind of threat than a military one? Darling analysed relations with each Indigenous nation, paying special attention to their record of military service, their proximity to the border, and their proclivity to join an opposing side. In short, were they useless, useful, or dangerous in the event of another American war? Whereas some groups of people around Oka or the eastern border of Lower Canada were dismissed as too corrupted to be useful, Darling insisted on the usefulness of the Kahnawà:ke Mohawks, the Six Nations at Brantford, and the Algonquin and Abenaki at Three Rivers, St Francis, and Beçancour. To keep them useful and loyal, however, the government must protect their lands and encourage their civilization. Darling made that observation repeatedly. Speaking of the peoples around Three Rivers, Darling observed that they were losing their land to squatters and other encroachments and that this "cruel" plundering was *the* Indian question. Concerning

> all the Indian tribes having lands assigned to them for their support; viz. That if by vigilant superintendence and effectual legal protection they are not maintained in the possession of their lands, one of three results must follow, as the consequence of the rapid progress making in the clearing and settling of the forest through which they have been accustomed to hunt.
>
> 1st. They must be entirely maintained and supported by Government:
> 2d. Or they will starve in the streets of the country towns and villages, if they do not crowd the gaols of the larger towns and cities:
> 3d. Or they will turn their backs with indignation on their father, in whose promises of protection they have with confidence for so many years relied, and will throw themselves, with vengeance in their hearts, into the arms of the Americans, who are ever ready to receive them, and who are now endeavouring to induce the tribes in Upper Canada, with whom they have the readiest intercourse, to accept of lands on the Mississippi. The Abenaquais and Algonquins now particularly under consideration were much employed last war, and in case of a renewal of hostilities, their services would again be valuable.[52]

A few pages later, regarding the Six Nations at Brantford, Darling observed that they had been faithful and useful in the past. To keep them so would "depend upon the conduct of the British Government during this period of peace, to improve that feeling and rivet their attachment." That objective, Darling contended, "will be best promoted by taking advantage of the disposition now so rapidly spreading amongst them to advance in civilization; by creating and improving in them, by every means, a love of the country, of the soil in which they are settled, and a respect for the Government which protects them." Again, his closing words restated the argument: the choices were protection of or ruin to "the Indian" in Canada.[53]

Darling defended the Indian Department with an argument for non-military militarization of both Indigenous-settler boundaries and the British North American-United States boundary. Indigenous peoples were borderlands peoples who could reinforce the international border; they would be a non-military but unmistakably martial presence. In return, the British government must firm up and honour the boundaries between settlers and Indigenous communities. That firming up was also best done in non-military fashion, with agents, missionaries, and teachers appointed and administered from the civil rather than the military branch of the British state. That policy change did indeed follow from the Darling report: the Indian Department became a civil expense in 1830. Darling did not engineer the relational transition from military alliances to demilitarized civilization projects; rather, he aimed at maintaining a veiled military-style presence in an expanding civil society increasingly resentful of military warrants and expenses. Wellingtonians, as a military state within the imperial state, tended to see Indigenous warriors as a potential praetorian guard – a view later borne out by their role in the rebellions. Civilization for Darling was not so much a liberal project as a conservative and clientelist one.

Darling's solution reflected the kind of negotiation around policing seen in other British jurisdictions. The Tory viewpoint was that, if you could maintain order, liberal prosperity should naturally follow – in contradistinction to the reform viewpoint that, if you could get liberal prosperity, order should naturally follow. Tories preferred statist solutions; reformers preferred to dismantle the state; where the former would blur state-society distinctions, the latter would sharpen them.

Henry Darling's civilization project had two key precedents. First, his brother recommended a civilization policy in New South Wales in 1826. Soon after arriving there in December 1825, Ralph Darling instructed a local archdeacon to report on ways that Aboriginal peoples might be converted and educated. In turn, the archdeacon commissioned a report from a naval lieutenant, Richard Sadleir, who had served on the Great Lakes from July 1815 to 1819 and was counted an expert on Indigeneity. Ralph Darling forwarded those reports to the Colonial Office and recommended civilization but also warned that "a very considerable expense must be incurred to do anything effectually," to which the minister, Lord Goderich, responded with approval that fell short of committing resources to the project.[54] Henry Darling proceeded more strategically: his civilizing project would be cheap and would rely primarily on the Anglican Church; it could oversee civilization without increasing military spending by drawing on metropolitan subscriptions and a colonial church establishment. "It appears to me that this would not be attended with much expense. A small sum by way of salary to a schoolmaster wherever a school may be formed, say four or five in the whole," plus small sums added to the salary of an existing English missionary and a second if the lord bishop of the diocese appointed one, as well as "some aid in building school-houses."[55]

But the Anglican role in the civilizing project collided with the other precedent for its recommendation. Henry Darling built his civilization project atop a *self-civilization* project launched by Indigenous peoples themselves, when he urged civilization as commensurate with "liberality of the British Government," which should encourage "the disposition now shown generally amongst the resident Indians [of Canada] to shake off the rude habits of savage life, and to embrace Christianity and civilization."[56] Indigenous peoples were not simply pawns to be moved around an imperial chessboard. They had their own ideas on violence, the state, and civilization, and their own ways of managing them. Among their own projects of self-civilization was the conversion to Methodism of Peter Jones or Kahkewaquonaby, a Mississauga chief at the Credit Reserve (in present-day Toronto) with close ties to the Six Nations at Brantford. Jones rapidly converted much of his community – an event that struck not just Darling but many others as a remarkable and promising new tendency. Conversion was a principled act on Jones's part, but it was also a strategic one aimed at ensuring for the Mississauga political rights and secure land tenure.[57] Jones decided that "civilization" could be relatively easy to demonstrate, with evidence of church going and settlement – the Bible and the plough – and the repudiation of alcohol, which he blamed for the growing weakness of his people.

For Jones, civilization was performance art: he made surprise visits to private households to assess and record their state of cleanliness. On a visit to Grape Island in 1830, he recorded: "Joseph Skunk's. – Floor clean – cupboard poor – table good but dusty – beds tolerably good. A woman was making light bread like a white woman. James Indians. – Floor rather dirty – one curtain bed – cupboard poor – one woman making light bread." Several pages record women at work: sewing, making brooms, making baskets, boiling pumpkins, splitting spruce roots to fasten birch canoes; only very occasionally was one described as idle. According to Jones, "The object of my going around and making remarks, was to stir the Indian sisters in cleanliness and in industry" and to prove that Indigenous women were as much "improved in the arts of civilized life" as the men.[58]

Jones understood civilization as an empirical category; instead, it would prove a reifying and "Orientalizing" one. Jones's early success posed problems for any Tory civilization project. Evangelicals, such as Methodists, were generally not good Tories; they tended, rather, towards the other side of the emerging party divide. If the Indigenous peoples of Canada were converting to Methodism en masse, they threatened to form a partisan, anti-Tory faction, even perhaps an anti-Tory *race*. In Canada, Methodists were particularly dangerous because they were seen as American levellers in fact or spirit: they carried the borderlands into the heart of loyalist society.[59] The Anglican establishment, led by Bishop Strachan, was irreducibly hostile to Peter Jones and his Mississauga civilizing project and lent his influence to their dispossession. Peter Jones's strategy failed in a dramatic and definitive confrontation in January 1828 when he and his brother met with Lieutenant Governor Sir Peregrine Maitland's inner governing circle: Bishop Strachan, Attorney General John Beverley Robinson,[60] Civil Secretary Sir George Hillier (who served with Maitland in the wars), and James Givins, Superintendent of Indian Affairs for the Home District since 1797. Givins, a military officer, had spent two years of the Revolutionary War as a prisoner in American hands; he fought the 1813 American invasion, and his house, looted by American soldiers (who stole a picture of the Battle of Trafalgar among other items), still bore bloodstains of soldiers wounded in that fight. The four men informed Jones that the governor "did not feel disposed to assist the Indians so long as they remained under the instruction of their present teachers [i.e., Methodists], who were not responsible to the Government for any of their proceedings and instructions." Forced to choose, Jones chose Methodism and dispossession over Anglicanism and patronage.[61] The Canadas, like Ireland, were too factionalized to generate neutral bureaucracies. In Ireland, Peel had rebuffed efforts to insinuate Protestant oversight into Irish Catholic emancipation in 1829; in Canada, Anglicans were not so restrained.

Without patronage and assistance, Indigenous peoples, as wards of the state, could not protect their land from the predations of neighbouring settlers and squatters. Darling forcefully described the situation as "plunder": "the active interposition of the Government is urgently called for on behalf of these helpless individuals, whose landed possessions (where they have any assigned to them,) are daily plundered by their designing and more enlightened white brethren."[62] Indigenous peoples could not defend themselves against asset stripping by squatters, tenants, and all sorts of scofflaws who congregated near their reserves. If they leased a plot of land to a farmer, they were liable to lose both rents and title. Legal hybridity, as when a non-Indigenous man married an Indigenous woman and laid claim to common rights and usages, thereby privatizing them through legal forms, provided another dangerous encroachment on Indigenous commons.[63] The problem also reflected a process of dispossession that Allan Greer has described as an overlay of a non-Indigenous commons on an existing Indigenous commons, where settlers let their livestock roam freely and encroached upon Indigenous resources. Elsewhere, by contrast, livestock owners were responsible for damages done by their livestock.[64] The process also reflected a broader failure of the state to police and protect Indigenous lands and rights to anything like accepted standards in areas settled by Europeans. Rather than police the interface between Indian and non-Indian lands and land uses, the local settler state left things to run themselves, after the model of a frontier, a Franklinesque racialized, spatialized borderlands. Indigenous lands, by dint of their special legal status, functioned as an internal borderland, a place where state authority did not stretch and where, therefore, illicit profits and predations attracted scofflaws and squatters. Wherever the state created Indian reserves, it generated hard-wired geographies of disorder, lawlessness, and violence. To be an "Indian" in settler Canada was to be perpetually on an unstable, if not violent, frontier.

As Darling recognized, this disorder emanated not from Indigenous inhabitants but rather from "enlightened" settlers. Darling's sardonic remark reflects a central irony of the interplay of violence and Euro-Canadian civilization. Civilization for Tories constituted a disciplined respect for rule of law and consensual restrictions on violence. By the 1820s, Indigenous communities in places like Brantford, Mississauga, and Kahanwà:ke were already too "civilized" to respond violently to the encroachments on their lands by less-restrained neighbours. But even as land-hungry settler society defied such restraints, it also claimed a monopoly on higher civilization and denounced "Indians" as uncivilized savages, the better to rob them. The source of the disorder was not the cultural traits of Indigenous peoples living on reserves but the legal limbo of differences of legal title to reserve property. Because Indigenous people had legally anomalous property and no vote, the colonial state could be put to work to prise their property from them. So long as settlers accompanied the process with intense, vituperative racialization, other kinds of property relations could not be threatened in that process of predation. Where Jones thought he could demonstrate visibly orderly use of property as empirical proof of civilization, the emerging settler colonial state would reify civilization as the antithesis of disorder understood not as violence but as an underlying, primitive or pre-liberal, racialized threat to "liberal" property relations and values.

Although the Canadian colonial state did not engage in Andrew Jackson's populist appeals to sovereign political violence, it quietly tolerated petty violence and illegal predations on Indigenous property, violations that wrought similar damage in the long run. Whereas the military retinue around Dalhousie sought to interpose barriers between settlers and Natives, colonists – patrician and reformer alike – dismantled them. Paul Romney maintains that settlers also experienced disenfranchisement and dispossession under John Beverley Robinson, but Indigenous people were uniquely vulnerable because of their lack of independent political and legal agency.[65] Sidney Harring shows, for example, how Robinson overcame his distaste for squatters enough to claim that their unstoppable encroachments and his inability to police them added up to a logic of land surrender.[66] The patricians of Upper Canada made disorder and predation their allies in the project of dispossessing Indigenous peoples settled in Canada. The Colonial Office proved no more effective a protector after 1828 than before.

Indeed, as policing became increasingly understood as a local and civil project, rather than an imperial and military project, it would become impervious to imperial interventions and obligingly subsidiary to the agenda of settler colonialism.

Henry Darling did not remain in Canada to see his report enacted but, on Dalhousie's advice, proceeded to England in September 1828 to present it personally to the colonial authorities. He coveted but did not get the office of superintendence in the reformed Indian Department; nor was he appointed governor of the Bahamas, his next choice; nor did he get the Treasury of New South Wales that brother Ralph Darling tried to secure for him in 1829.[67] Both of Henry Darling's patrons were too discredited: Dalhousie was replaced in September 1828 and Ralph Darling was embattled through 1829. Sir Ralph had aroused hostility in New South Wales for harsh treatment of a prisoner who died after being sentenced to a chain gang, for trying to repress the "republicans" in the local newspapers with taxes and restraining laws, and for other acts typical of excessively military rule, according to complaints voiced by such critics as Joseph Hume and Daniel O'Connell: "Mr. O'Connell said, that unless the Governors of our distant colonies were kept under proper control, there was no extent of despotism which they would not practice."[68] Pamphlets also accused Ralph Darling of overspending and of dispensing patronage to a troop of relations that included Henry Darling's son, Charles Darling, who served as his uncle's assistant private secretary and later his military secretary.

With the governor attacked in absentia, with Sir George Murray weakly defending Sir Ralph in the Commons and quietly casting about for a replacement, Henry Darling took up the cause, reprinting some of his brother's self-exculpatory despatches to the Colonial Office and adding his own arguments. The first charge against Sir Ralph, cited by Henry Darling, specified "that the progress of extravagance has been most enormous in every department; – for instance, the Police Establishment in 1828 cost £8,000, and that now it is doubled." In fact, Henry Darling responded, the "Police Establishment" had increased from £20,556 8.s. 2½d to £21,632, 3s. 5½d between 1828 and 1829. But his broader line of defence was that governors naturally aroused local resentments when they did their jobs, and that they could hardly do them well when "the Editors of the opposition papers and a few factious individuals, were eagerly looking out for every pretence to abuse and vilify the Government, and whose object has been to magnify or distort every occurrence, and to persuade these people that they have been treated with unnecessary severity ... If the Governor of such a colony is to be arraigned on the information of every factious malecontent, or by individuals dismissed for improper conduct, no man who regards either his peace or his reputation, would accept the situation."[69] As ever, Darling was not just describing a particular situation but simultaneously defending an equally embattled and discredited Dalhousie and recapitulating a defence of the Tory state more generally. He could not save his brother from recall in March 1831: that was inevitable under the newly elected Whig administration, to whom Ralph Darling "symbolized much that was wrong with the colonial system of government."[70] But Henry Darling was acceptable enough to the government of Earl Grey to be named governor of Tobago in 1833, where he oversaw the dismantling of slavery, fought accusations of misgovernance around high infant mortality rates, and died in office in 1845. By that time, the scene was set for a very different iteration of the civilization project in Canada.

In the 1820s, state officials thought hard about how to govern within the remnants of the fiscal-military state, and Henry Darling's report of 1828 spoke strategically from that insider perspective. The 1830s, in contrast, was a decade of Whig-reform hegemony: it saw reformers thinking hard about how to do things through the medium of civil society. Tories had sought to construct intermediary gradations between the state and civil society that could variously, and usually ambiguously, reflect military and/or civilian branches as required by the situation, given enough political discretion. Their critics and successors wanted more utilitarian and theoretically driven reforms that would more starkly distinguish state from society. These reformers believed that the heavily armed, heavily taxing state was the major obstacle to improvement, and they demanded a smaller, cheaper civilian state as the best avenue to economic and social improvement.

But the persistence of violence through the 1830s forced a reconsideration of the logic of civil society. The writings of Alexis de Tocqueville reflect the transition. Tocqueville's theory of the tyranny of the majority posited that, in modern, egalitarian societies, physical violence was superseded by moral violence: "Monarchs had, so to speak, materialized oppression; the democratic republics of the present day have rendered it as entirely an affair of the mind as the will which it is intended to coerce. Under the absolute sway of one man the body was attacked in order to subdue the soul; but the soul escaped the blows which were directed against it and rose proudly superior. Such is not the course adopted by tyranny in democratic republics; there the body is left free, and the soul is enslaved."[71] If public opinion could force majoritarian change, then armies need not.

Lord Durham soon translated Tocqueville's theories into a project for non-coercive assimilation of French Canada, while largely ignoring the consequences for the Indian Department. The logic of civil society came to that department from another quarter: the emergence of social statistics and the investigation of poverty around the London Statistical Society, formed in 1834. Poverty appeared as a concern in the Darling report but primarily as the consequence of lawlessness and as a potential cause of further lawlessness. Public order, not poverty, was the statesman's primary concern. In 1830s Britain, that emphasis began to reverse, and poverty began to draw more attention, as the deeper threat to British well-being, according to Malthusian calculations. Violent rebellion in the Canadas in 1837–8 slowed the transmission of such reasoning to the Canadas, but the Indigenous peoples of Canada were, during this period, Brian Gettler observes, reconceptualized in the image of the pauperism that the New Poor Law of 1834 was designed to eradicate.[72] The next iteration of Tory civilization policy in the early 1840s would see the newer strategic reasoning around social statistics and civil society applied very directly to the Canadian Indian Department, when an experienced investigator of social statistics and urban poverty, Rawson W. Rawson, came to Canada and produced a major report on the causes and consequences of Indigenous poverty. Rawson's Tory tilt was very different from Darling's, of course, but it was no less representative of emerging new tropes of civilization, police, poverty, and race in play across the imperial spectrum.

NOTES

1 John L. Tobias, "Protection, Civilization, Assimilation: An Outline of Canada's Indian Policy," *Western Canadian Journal of Anthropology* 6, no. 2 (1976): 13–30.

2 Olive P. Dickason, *Canada's First Nations: A History of Founding Peoples from Earliest Times*, 2nd ed. (Oxford: Oxford University Press, 1997), 206.

3 Library and Archives Canada (hereafter LAC), MG24-A12, R4950-0-3-E, George Ramsay, 9th Earl of Dalhousie fonds, Dalhousie to Bathurst, 22 December 1822; Canada, *Report of the Public Archives for the Year 1938* (Ottawa: King's Printer, 1939), 38.

4 Henry Darling, "Report upon the Exact State of the Indian Department," 24 July 1828, enclosed in Earl of Dalhousie to Sir George Murray, Secretary of State for the Colonies, 27 October 1828, in British Parliamentary Papers, *Papers Relative to the Aboriginal Tribes in British Possessions* (London: House of Commons, 1834), vol. 5, no. 617, 22–35.

5 Phillip A. Buckner, "Was There a 'British' Empire? The Oxford History of the British Empire from a Canadian Perspective," *Acadiensis* 32, no. 1 (Autumn 2002), 110–28.

6 Boyd Hilton, *Corn, Cash, Commerce: The Economic Policies of the Tory Governments, 1815–1830* (Oxford: Oxford University Press, 1977), 246–7.

7 Martin Daunton, *Trusting Leviathan: The Politics of Taxation in Britain, 1799–1914* (Cambridge: Cambridge University Press, 2001).

8 Peter Jupp, *British Politics on the Eve of Reform: The Duke of Wellington's Administration, 1828–30* (Basingstoke, UK: Macmillan, 1998), 202–3.

9 Philip Buckner, *The Transition to Responsible Government: British Policy in British North America, 1815–1850* (Westport, CT: Greenwood Press, 1985), 20.

10 C.A. Bayly, *Imperial Meridian: The British Empire and the World, 1780–1830* (London: Longman, 1989), 21.
11 Boyd Hilton, *A Mad, Bad, and Dangerous People? England, 1783–1846* (Oxford: Clarendon, 2006), 567.
12 Jupp, *British Politics*, 85.
13 D.M. Young, *The Colonial Office in the Early Nineteenth Century* (London: Longman, 1961), 110.
14 Buckner, *Transition to Responsible Government.*
15 Ibid., 57; Bayly, *Imperial Meridian*, 129.
16 Young, *Colonial Office*; W.P. Morrel, *The British Colonial Office in the Age of Peel and Russell* (London: Routledge, 1966).
17 Norman Gash, *Mr Secretary Peel: The Life of Sir Robert Peel to 1830*, 2nd ed. (London: Longman, 1985), 93.
18 Lauren Benton and Lisa Ford, *Rage for Order: The British Empire and the Origins of International Law, 1800–1850* (Cambridge, MA: Harvard University Press, 2016), 5 and passim.
19 See the discussion in Giorgio Agamben, *State of Exception*, trans. Kevin Attell (Chicago: University of Chicago Press, 2005).
20 Brian H. Fletcher, *Ralph Darling: A Governor Maligned* (Oxford: Oxford University Press, 1984); H. Manners Chichester, "Sir Ralph Darling," *Dictionary of National Biography* 5 (London: Smith, Elder, 1908), 5: 508–11 contains a short note distinguishing Sir Ralph's brother Henry from another Henry Darling (who served in Upper Canada in the 1790s).
21 Michel Foucault, *Power/Knowledge: Selected Interviews and Other Writings, 1972–1977*, ed. and trans. Colin Gordon (New York: Pantheon, 1972), 170.
22 Jennifer Pitts, *Boundaries of the International: Law and Empire* (Cambridge, MA: Harvard Unversity Press, 2018).
23 David Walsh, "The Lancashire 'Rising' of 1826," *Albion* 26, no. 4 (Winter 1994): 601–21.
24 Gash, *Mr Secretary Peel*, 602.
25 Galen Broeker, *Rural Disorder and Police Reform in Ireland, 1812–36* (London: Routledge and Kegan Paul, 1970), 239; and James S. Donnelly Jr, *Captain Rock: The Irish Agrarian Rebellion of 1821–1824* (Madison: University of Wisconsin Press, 2009).
26 Clive Emsley, *The English Police: A Political and Social History*, 2nd ed. (London: Routledge, 1996), 26.
27 Donald Fyson, *Magistrates, Police, and People: Everyday Criminal Justice in Quebec and Lower Canada, 1764–1837* (Toronto: University of Toronto Press, 2006), ch. 4, "The Police before the Police."
28 "The Militia of Lower Canada," Canadian Military History Gateway, Online Reference Books, vol. 2 (1755–1871), http://www.cmhg.gc.ca/cmh-pmc/page-418-eng.aspx.

(accessed 15 November 2018); Dalhousie to Bathurst, 19 December 1823, summarized in *Report on Canadian Archives 1896* (Ottawa: Queen's Printer, 1897), 378.

29 *Report from the Select Committee on the Civil Government of Canada* (Quebec: House of Assembly, 1829; reprint from Britain, House of Commons), esp. 118–19, 316–17; Christian Dessureault, "La crise sous Dalhousie: Conception de la milice et conscience élitaire des réformistes bas-canadiens, 1827–1828," *Revue d'histoire de l'Amérique française* 61, 2 (Autumn 2007): 167–99; and Louis-Georges Harvey, *Le printemps de l'Amérique française: Américanité, anticolonialisme, et républicanisme dans le discours politique québécois, 1805–1837* (Montreal: Boréal, 2005).

30 *The Times*, London, 31 December 1827; Michel Ducharme, *Le concept de liberté au Canada à l'époque des Révolutions atlantiques, 1776–1838* (Montreal and Kingston: McGill-Queen's University Press, 2010).

31 John C. Weaver, *The Great Land Rush and the Making of the Modern World, 1650–1900* (Montreal and Kingston: McGill-Queen's University Press, 2003).

32 Stephen Mihm, *A Nation of Counterfeiters: Capitalists, Con Men, and the Making of the United States* (Cambridge, MA: Harvard University Press, 2007); and J.I. Little, *Loyalties in Conflict: A Canadian Borderland in War and Rebellion* (Toronto: University of Toronto Press, 2008).

33 Bradley Miller, *Borderline Crime: Fugitive Criminals and the Challenge of the Border, 1819–1915* (Toronto: University of Toronto Press, 2016).

34 J.H.L. Henderson, ed., *John Strachan: Documents and Opinions* (Toronto: McClelland and Stewart, 1969); George W. Spragge, ed., *The John Strachan Letter Book, 1812–1814* (Toronto: Ontario Historical Society, 1946); and Anthony Di Mascio, *The Idea of Popular Schooling in Upper Canada: Print Culture, Public Discourse, and the Demand for Education* (Montreal and Kingston: McGill-Queen's University Press, 2012).

35 Brian Jenkins, *Henry Goulburn, 1784–1856: A Political Biography* (Montreal and Kingston: McGill-Queen's University Press, 1996), 67.

36 Paul Romney, *Getting It Wrong: How Canadians Forgot Their Past and Imperilled Confederation* (Toronto: University of Toronto Press, 1999), 34–6.

37 Michel Hogue, *Metis and the Medicine Line: Creating a Border and Dividing a People* (Regina: University of Regina Press, 2015).

38 Brett Rushforth, *Bonds of Alliance: Indigenous and Atlantic Slaveries in New France* (Chapel Hill: University of North Carolina Press, 2012), 221.

39 Lauren Benton, *A Search for Sovereignty: Law and Geography in European Empires, 1400–1900* (Cambridge: Cambridge University Press, 2009).

40 *The Interest of Great Britain Considered with Regard to Her Colonies and the Acquisitions of Canada and Guadeloupe* (London: T. Becket, 1760), 8–9. On attribution to Franklin, see National Archives (US), Founders Online, *The Interest of Great Britain Considered*, https://founders.archives.gov/documents/Franklin/01-09-02-0029, accessed 10 May 2017.

41 *The Interest of Great Britain*, 5–7.

42 *Reasons for Keeping Guadeloupe at a Peace, Preferable to Canada* (London, 1761); and Philip Lawson, *The Imperial Challenge: Quebec and Britain in the Age of the American Revolution* (Montreal and Kingston: McGill-Queen's University Press, 1989).

43 J.M. Opal, "General Jackson's Passports: Natural Rights and Sovereign Citizens in the Political Thought of Andrew Jackson, 1780–1820s," *Studies in American Political Development* 27 (October 2013): 69–85.

44 J.M. Opal, *Avenging the People: Andrew Jackson, the Rule of Law, and the American Nation* (Oxford: Oxford University Press, 2017); and Nicole Eustace, *1812: War and the Passions of Patriotism* (Philadelphia: University of Pennsylvania Press, 2012).

45 Lisa Ford, *Settler Sovereignty: Jurisdiction and Indigenous People in America and Australia, 1788–1836* (Cambridge, MA: Harvard University Press, 2011).

46 Elizabeth Mancke, "Stewarding a Canadian Culture of Comity," *Borealia* 12 December 2016, https://earlycanadianhistory.ca/2016/12/06/stewarding-a-canadian-culture-of-comity/; E.A. Heaman, "Constructing Innocence: Representations of Sexual Violence in Upper Canada's War of 1812," *Journal of the Canadian Historical Association* 24, no. 2 (2013): 114–55.

47 Mark D. Walters, "The Extension of Colonial Criminal Jurisdiction over the Aboriginal Peoples of Upper Canada: Reconsidering the Shawanaksiskie Case (1822–26)," *University of Toronto Law Journal* 46, no. 2 (Spring 1996): 273–310; see also essays in G. Blaine Baker and Donald Fyson, eds, *Essays in the History of Canadian Law: Quebec and the Canadas* (Toronto: University of Toronto Press, 2013).

48 Elizabeth Mancke, *The Fault-Lines of Empire: Political Differentiation in Massachusetts and Nova Scotia, c. 1760–1830* (New York: Routledge, 2005).

49 Ford, *Settler Sovereignty*, 173–4; Fletcher, *Ralph Darling*, 185–6.

50 LAC, R4950-0-3-E, George Ramsay, 9th Earl of Dalhousie Fonds, Canadian Documents, subject files, file 508, letters and report from Col. Darling, letters of 12 November and 10 October 1824.

51 For example, Jule Evans, Patricia Grimshaw, David Philips, and Shurlee Swain, *Equal Subjects, Unequal Rights: Indigenous Peoples in British Settler Colonies, 1830–1910* (Manchester: Manchester University Press, 2003), 27, 44–9.

52 Darling, "Report upon the Exact State of the Indian Department," 24.

53 Ibid., 29–30.

54 Fletcher, *Ralph Darling*, 184–5.

55 Darling, "Report upon the Exact State of the Indian Department," 29

56 Ibid.

57 Donald B. Smith, *Sacred Feathers: The Reverend Peter Jones (Kahkewaquonaby) and the Mississauga Indians* (Toronto: University of Toronto Press, 1997).

58 *Life and Journals of Kah-ke-wa-quo-na-by (Rev. Peter Jones)* (Toronto: Anson Green, 1860), 284–7; see also Michael Ripmeester, "'It Is Scarcely to Be Believed...': The Mississauga Indians and the Grape Island Mission, 1826–1836," *Canadian Geographer* 39, no. 2 (1995): 157–68; see also Mark D. Walters, "'According to the

Old Customs of Our Nation': Aboriginal Self-Government on the Credit River Mississauga Reserve, 1826–1847," *Ottawa Law Review* 30 (1998–9): 1–46.

59 Nancy Christie, "'In These Times of Democratic Rage and Delusion': Popular Religion and the Challenge to the Established Order, 1760–1815," in *The Canadian Protestant Experience, 1760–1990*, ed. George A. Rawlyk (Montreal and Kingston: McGill-Queen's University Press, 1990), 3–41.

60 Patrick Brode, *Sir John Beverley Robinson: Bone and Sinew of the Compact* (Toronto: University of Toronto Press, 1984).

61 Smith, *Sacred Feathers*, 100–3. Givins figures in the Dalhousie-Darling correspondence as a political enemy.

62 Darling, "Report upon the Exact State of the Indian Department," 22.

63 See the discussion of Claude Delormier in Daniel Rueck, "Enclosing the Mohawk Commons: A History of Use-Rights, Landownership and Boundary-making in Kahnawá:ke Mohawk Territory" (PhD diss., McGill University, 2013), 96–9.

64 Allan Greer, "Commons and Enclosure in the Colonization of North America," *American Historical Review* 117, no. 2 (2012): 365–86. See also Allan Greer, *Property and Dispossession: Natives, Empire, and Land in Early Modern North America* (Cambridge: Cambridge University Press, 2018).

65 Paul Romney, *Mr Attorney: The Attorney General for Ontario in Court, Cabinet, and Legislature* (Toronto: University of Toronto Press, 1986); and Paul Romney, "From the Rule of Law to Responsible Government: Ontario Political Culture and the Origins of Canadian Statism," Canadian Historical Association *Historical Papers* 23 (1988).

66 Sidney L. Harring, *White Man's Law: Native People in Nineteenth-Century Canadian Jurisprudence* (Toronto: University of Toronto Press, 1998).

67 *Annual Report of the Department of Indian Affairs for the Year Ended March 31, 1921* in Canada, *Sessional Papers*, no. 27 (1922), 9–11; Dalhousie papers, December 1828; Fletcher, *Ralph Darling*.

68 Great Britain, House of Commons, *Debates*, 8 July 1830, 114; 7 and 17 June 1830, 436–50; Thomas Keneally, *Australians: Origins to Eureka* (Crows Nest: Allen and Unwin, 2009), 364–9.

69 Henry C. Darling, *Statement in Refutation of Accusations Made by Mr Hume, MP, and Others, against Lieut.-Gen. Darling, Governor of New South Wales* (London: I. McGowan, 1831).

70 Fletcher, *Ralph Darling*, 297.

71 Alexis de Tocqueville, *Democracy in America*, trans. Henry Reeve (1835; New York: Barnes and Noble, 2003), 239.

72 Brian Gettler, "En espèce ou en nature? Les présents, l'imprévoyance, et l'évolution idéologique de la politique indienne pendant la première moitié du XIXe siècle," *Revue d'histoire de l'Amérique française* 65, no. 4 (2012): 409–37.

8 Worthy and Industrious or a Burden? Managing Migration in Upper Canada, 1815–1845

JANE ERRINGTON

In 1818, members of the House of Assembly of Upper Canada declared that they shared the Crown's "expectation" of the "great benefits [that would] result from the accession of an industrious and loyal population from the United Kingdom" to the colony.[1] And a year later, the assembly undertook to do all in its power to help "defray the expense" of settlement for these new arrivals.[2] Upper Canadians' support for British emigration was tempered with some disquiet, however. In 1817, an anonymous Kingstonian had called on local residents to assist new arrivals who "are now literally starving through want of food and shelter."[3] In the colonial capital, York, the Society of Friends to Strangers in Distress had begun to help those who were reduced to begging for bread "for their perishing families,"[4] and soon after the Kingston Compassionate Society was formed to assist bewildered and needy migrants "to procure employment."[5]

For thirty years or so after the end of the Napoleonic Wars, Upper Canadians confronted a dilemma. As frequent testimonies from the House of Assembly and imperial agents in the colony, and countless numbers of articles in the local press declared, Upper Canadians welcomed the arrival of "worthy and industrious" Britons who would enhance the colony's "march to improvement"[6] and promote prosperity and security. As John G. Reid and Thomas Peace explain in their chapters in this volume, British America in the first half of the nineteenth century exhibited all the hallmarks of settler colonialism. Most of the colony was, after all, apparently "untouched," just waiting for British subjects to subdue the wilderness and make it their home. The Indigenous population would, it was assumed, soon disappear, and the "arrival of settling peoples" would create a new Britain, or what Cecilia Morgan has characterized as a better Britain in North America.[7] But colonial officials and local leaders soon discovered that not all new arrivals were "worthy and industrious." Some, and it seemed an increasing number, were unable or unwilling to cope in the new environment; others did not have the capital or the skills necessary to succeed. Indeed, in some years, the colony was inundated by a deluge of hungry, bewildered, and often penniless men, women, and children who needed immediate assistance just to survive. Wholesale emigration[8] could be a boon, but it also had the potential to become a serious burden on local residents and to threaten the social fabric of the colony.

Upper Canadians' ability to resolve this dilemma was limited. The colony was, as J.K. Johnson has recently reminded us, a "dependent state,"[9] and officially the responsibility to control or regulate the flow of emigration to the North American colonies rested in London. Colonial leaders had to manoeuvre within imperial policies that were intended to secure peace and security at "home" but that often compromised local aspirations and needs. Moreover, for much of the first half of the nineteenth century, the ability of the colonial state to know and control its own population was at best limited,[10] and it struggled to manage the arrival of thousands of new subjects who had the potential to overwhelm the colony. Initially, in a spirit of benevolence laced with an underlying unease about what would happen if they did nothing, individual communities took on the task of assisting the "strangers" in their midst. But as the numbers of emigrants who landed at Quebec and made their way up the St Lawrence grew in the 1820s, local efforts were increasingly strained. By the early 1830s, the lieutenant governor was forced to become directly involved, and the appointment of Anthony Bewden Hawke in 1833 as chief emigrant agent for Upper Canada (and, after 1841, for Canada West) marked the beginning of a rudimentary, colony-wide system to manage the influx of new subjects and to protect the integrity of local communities. Hawke's letter books of 1835–45 and the reports he submitted to various authorities reflect, I think, his determination to bring order to the situation and a spirit of utilitarianism that valued efficiency and uniformity. His records also chronicle, however, an often-overlooked attempt of the early colonial state to manage its people and, at the same time, to further its own development. At the heart of what is rather dry correspondence is Hawke's determination to assist new arrivals but, as importantly, to maintain order and protect the well-being and stability of the colony.[11]

There is a rich and illuminating scholarship on the migration of the Scots, the Irish, and the English and their settlement in British North America and particularly Upper Canada in the first half of the nineteenth century.[12] How these new settlers were received has been given somewhat less systematic attention.[13] A number of studies consider the impact of land policies on settlement[14] or various attempts to cope with the growing number of paupers in the colonies, many of whom were new arrivals.[15] What most of these studies overlook is the underlying tension that the arrival of thousands of new subjects created in the colony. The work of Scott See and others has illustrated how host communities sometimes responded violently to the arrival and settlement of migrants whom they feared threatened the social, political, or economic order.[16] But colonial authorities wanted, if at all possible, to avoid situations that could lead to such violence. As See discusses in his chapter earlier in this volume, colonial authorities placed great value on maintaining peace and order in the colony. And they were well aware that the "Great Land Rush," as John Weaver has so aptly termed it, created not only untold opportunities but also had the potential to rupture the social fabric.[17] Even before the colony was almost overwhelmed by the arrival of the tens of thousands fleeing famine in Ireland in 1847–8, Upper Canadians' determination to forestall the potential for unrest led them to develop various mechanisms to manage migration.

The situation that Upper Canadians confronted after 1815 was unprecedented. Certainly, the colony had received tens of thousands of emigrants – American settlers in search of land – in the twenty years before the War of 1812, and some leaders had been concerned that not only were the original loyalist residents outnumbered but the political leanings of these "late" Loyalists posed a serious threat to the integrity of the young colony.[18] But the numbers and nature of emigrants who arrived after the end of the Napoleonic Wars presented even greater potential problems. As James Belich has evocatively argued, the nineteenth century witnessed an "Anglo Explosion"[19] and was, as one Scottish newspaper proclaimed, "a spectacle without precedent since the time of the crusades."[20] About twelve million Britons left home for North America, Australia, and South Africa during this period, and, by 1845, a significant portion of these restless Britons had settled in Upper Canada.[21] Moreover, as Upper Canadians soon realized, unlike the late Loyalists, the majority of these new arrivals had neither the skills nor the knowledge needed to succeed in the North American environment.

For the first few years after the War of 1812, it appeared that the British government intended to take an active part in promoting emigration. In addition to offering disbanded soldiers and their families land in the colonies, London selectively supported the departure and resettlement of a few parties of artisans and farmers. These "experiments" were expensive, however, and roundly criticized for draining the nation of its most industrious citizens. Despite strong recommendations from Wilmot Horton's parliamentary committee in 1826 that Britain should systematically assist the country's "surplus" population to emigrate to the colonies, London in the end decided to leave emigration "to the enterprises of private or associated speculators" and to individuals who were willing and able to cover their own expenses.[22] The government did bring in various administrative measures to try to direct the flow of migration and to keep its subjects in the empire (instead of going to the United States, as so many were doing). Among other things, beginning in the mid-1820s, revisions to the Passenger Acts substantially lowered the cost of travel to Quebec, although this meant that conditions on-board many ships were horrendous. The Colonial Office also appointed agents in Quebec and Saint John, New Brunswick, to assist emigrants to find work or to travel to join friends or family, and, if absolutely necessary, to provide them with emergency food and lodgings.[23] And, by the early 1830s, when, as Eric Richards has persuasively argued, "emigration had moved up a gear" and "the prevailing opinion [in Britain] ... held that emigration was beneficial, especially for the poor,"[24] the government had stationed agents in major British ports to provide would-be emigrants with advice on where to go and how best to get there. At about the same time, although some in Britain and Upper Canada were arguing that "to excite and encourage Emigration" of particularly the unemployed, the displaced, and the destitute was absurd,[25] landlords and parish authorities had begun to subsidize the passage of tenants and residents, the unemployed and apparently unemployable, to various parts of the empire, including Upper Canada.

Only a small minority of those who landed at Quebec and made their way up the St Lawrence were supported by parish programs, tenant organizations, or their landlords. Most Britons caught up in "the rage of emigration" that swept across the country funded their own passage, and this was not a decision that was taken lightly.[26] Britons who left home came from all walks of life and for a variety of personal reasons. There were artisans, common labourers, farmers, and even a few "gentle" folk. Most were propelled by their immediate circumstances – unemployment, seeking a better life for their children, marriage (or marriage breakdown), or just to escape an untenable situation. The availability of transport often factored into their decision, as well as the knowledge that they could travel in the company of neighbours and friends. Some were undoubtedly enticed by colonial promoters who actively extolled the virtues of settling in Upper Canada; and an untold number were encouraged by reports of opportunities in the colony that they had received from those already there, and they turned to the increasing number of emigrant guides for advice on how to proceed.[27]

Britons left home with a mixture of trepidation and high expectations. As Weaver and others have argued, most hoped to acquire their own piece of land and gain the independence that accompanied it. Yet many, and in some years most, did not have the skills or the funds to realize their dreams, at least in the short term. And although the vast majority of British emigrants were not paupers being "shovelled" out of Britain, many arrived in strained circumstances, having expended all their resources on the journey. As boatloads of British migrants, who had little or no knowledge of the local environment, arrived at ports along the inland route, it was left to receiving authorities to make what they could of the situation.

In the first decade or so after the end of the Napoleonic Wars, Upper Canadians celebrated the opening of the emigrant season in May or early June each year. The recent war had graphically illustrated the danger of encouraging American settlers to move north; what the colony needed was British subjects who would bring not only their capital and skills but also their British sensibilities and allegiance to Crown and country. Colonists quickly realized that, although most new arrivals seemed "worthy and industrious" – God fearing, willing to work hard, and totally committed to making Upper Canada their new home – at least some new arrivals would need help to make the transition from emigrant to settler. In the spirit of reform that was gripping the British world, local communities established various benevolent societies explicitly intended to meet this need. Initial reports of the Kingston Compassionate Society, its sister organization, the Female Benevolent Society (which ran a seasonal hospital from May to November, from 1820 to 1839), the York Society for Strangers in Distress, and other aid organizations were optimistic that, with only a little assistance, new arrivals would quickly establish themselves and enhance the well-being of all. At the same time, these same reports hinted at an underlying concern that the arrival of so many men and women with no ties to the community who were not settled quickly could spell trouble – an increase in beggars on the streets, in property crime, and even violence, as disoriented strangers, often with nothing to lose, scrambled to find their place.[28]

To avert such problems, local organizations established informal protocols that would frame the general colonial response to emigration for the next thirty years. Those emigrants in the greatest and immediate need (who were expected to be only a small portion of new arrivals) were afforded temporary relief and, as required, medical attention; emigrants with capital were offered advice about the availability of land and how best to get there. But central to the work of local aid organizations was to assist that majority who came with goodwill, but limited or no funds, to find employment; if work was not available locally, they were directed to other parts of the colony where it might be found.[29] For the first few years, private community efforts seemed sufficient to meet the need. But as the numbers arriving increased, local organizations began to find their resources stretched to the limit.

By 1830, the situation had become acute. As the Commission of Emigration reported to the colonial secretary in London, the numbers of emigrants landing at Quebec that year was twice that of 1827 and ten times greater than in 1821.

After a tour of the Canadas, Commissioner J. Richards concluded that the policy of "unregulated emigration" and the relaxation of the Passenger Act in the previous few years, together with the shipment by local parishes of paupers to British America, was creating "a general dissatisfaction in the colonies." Local townsfolk "manifested liberality and kindness" to new arrivals, he wrote, but rather than moving on to find work or take up land, many emigrants hung about the towns until all their resources were exhausted and then turned to local charity for assistance. As serious, he continued, were the difficulties that the emigrants encountered when trying to take up land. Altogether the situation was "sowing the seeds of disorder and disaffection to the Government," and "it is to be feared that it may end in the passing of some provincial law to check the future indiscriminate shipment of paupers."[30]

Neither the Lower nor Upper Canadian government was in any position to check "the indiscriminate shipment of paupers," and London quickly rejected colonial proposals that it initiate some rudimentary vetting of migrants before they left home to ensure they were suitable candidates to succeed in North America. The Lower Canadian Assembly did, over the opposition of the House of Assembly in Upper Canada, introduce an emigrant tax to help fund the reception of new arrivals in Quebec and Montreal. In 1831, the lieutenant governor of Upper Canada, Sir John Colborne, appointed temporary agents to help "disperse" emigrants throughout the colony. But at the end of that season, the governor general warned London, if the number of pauper emigrants were not capped and the terrible conditions on-board many ships that bred disease and destitution not addressed, any benefits that could be accrued from emigration would be far outweighed by the burden it placed on the colonies and the danger it posed to the health and safety of local communities.[31]

The urgency of the situation was forcefully brought home to both London and colonial authorities the following year when cholera accompanied the emigrants. In an effort to protect colonists as well as emigrants, the government, following the example of New Brunswick, established a quarantine station at Grosse Isle, manned by British soldiers, and created temporary boards of health at various ports that tried to isolate and treat the sick to prevent the spread of the infection.[32] In Upper Canada, Lieutenant Governor Colborne settled "destitute" but "worthy" emigrants on small plots of land, and he appointed an agent to oversee the management of emigration into Upper Canada.[33] A.B. Hawke was first stationed in Lachine in 1832; a year later he was formally appointed chief emigrant agent for Upper Canada and stationed in York, becoming one of the few full-time employees of the colonial state. Officially, Hawke worked under the authority of A.C. Buchanan, chief agent in Quebec; he reported, however, directly to the lieutenant governor. Over the next thirty years, he ran a department that included increasing numbers of seasonal agents scattered throughout the colony, that developed and implemented a rudimentary program to receive emigrants, and that tried to ensure the welfare of both new arrivals and of the communities that received them.[34]

In the beginning, Hawke's department was not intended to replace the work of community-based charity groups. When Colborne prorogued the House in 1832, he urged members as they returned home to organize societies "for the purpose of affording information to emigrants which they so much require at the ports where they first disembark, and facilitating their dispersion in the districts in which they may readily obtain employment."[35] There is no question that Hawke spent considerable time corresponding with the leading residents of various port towns, urging them to continue helping new arrivals find work and, if necessary, providing those in need with provisions and shelter. Initially, I think that Hawke was expected to bring some order to managing emigration and to supplement work at the local level. By the early 1840s, however, it appears that the Emigrant Agency was assuming greater and greater responsibility for implementing an overall policy. With the arrival of Governor Sydenham and the subsequent reform of the colonial administration, Hawke's department and his responsibilities became increasingly formalized and bureaucratic.[36] By then, Hawke had become the official face of the state with respect to the reception and management of migrants.

Hawke's primary concerns were to ensure that local ports of entry were not overwhelmed by the arrival of exhausted emigrants and to help such people find work and begin to establish their new homes. Of particular importance was that these soon-to-be-settlers not be allowed to congregate in one place. Time and again, Hawke advised his agents that "it is desirable to prevent the accumulation" of healthy migrants and that the "sooner" they "are scattered, the better."[37] Dispersal was no easy task. Many arrived at Prescott or Kingston or other ports in Upper Canada without the funds to go on; others landed with no means whatsoever to cover the cost of provisions or accommodations; and some were too ill to proceed. Then there were those who sought to take advantage of the largess of residents or government agents. The task was, at times, daunting.

Hawke usually began his yearly preparations in the spring with a tour of ports and communities on the St Lawrence and Lake Ontario to assess their readiness to receive the new arrivals. He also took the opportunity to consult with officials and shipowners in Quebec and Montreal about the numbers of emigrants expected that year and opportunities for employment.[38] One of the persistent problems that Hawke confronted was not knowing how many emigrants to expect and where they intended to go once they arrived in the colony.

Indeed, there seemed to be no particular pattern to the extraordinary "sporadic and frenetic" movement of peoples.[39]

The numbers landing in 1830 had caught the colony completely unprepared, and Hawke tried to ensure that that situation did not happen again. But he was not always successful. In 1837, for example, authorities in London told Hawke to expect about forty thousand emigrants, most of them paupers. But, as he explained to the lieutenant governor's secretary, the actual number was much lower.[40] Two years later, as a result of the bad press the colony had received after the rebellion, Hawke did not appoint agents until well in July, in anticipation that the numbers would be very low. But the colony received an unexpected number of indigent emigrants, and he and his agents had to scramble to cope.[41] In 1845, even though Hawke expected "good immigration this season," boat-loads began to arrive much earlier than anticipated and "before we are prepared for them."[42]

Once Hawke assessed the colony's readiness for the upcoming emigrant season, he made recommendations to the government as to the facilities that each port of call would need and who to appoint as local agents to oversee and administer government policies. With the exception of Hawke, emigrant agents were employed for only five or six months of each year, although, when the numbers of emigrants were low or the budget was tight, their term could be shortened with little notice. Agents were respected members of their communities, and the remuneration they received supplemented their income from their "full-time" employment, often as merchants or physicians. Between 1835 and 1845, many appointments were renewed annually, although, if an agent did not meet with Hawke's expectations, he was replaced.

Not every community on the St Lawrence and Great Lakes was eligible for an agent. And needs changed over the years. Between 1833 and 1845, only Kingston and York (Toronto) always had an agent, as well as emigrant sheds for short-term accommodation. In the early years, Prescott also had an agent, but in 1840 Hawke decided that, as most emigrants travelled by way of the Rideau Canal, he needed one in Bytown.[43] That same year, although he appointed a part-time agent in Hamilton, for he expected the numbers of arrivals to be high, he refused to appoint one in Picton, but instead thanked a Mr Rorke and "the kind hearted population" there for their ongoing assistance in finding work for new arrivals.[44] Some communities were insistent on their need for an agent. In June 1840, the good fathers of Cobourg requested that Hawke open an agency in the community to take responsibility for those who arrived at their port. Hawke refused and told them that "I should suppose you could find little difficulty in getting employment for so small a number in your wealthy and prosperous district."[45] A month later, he received a second petition from the gentlemen of Cobourg reiterating their request. Hawke again refused. Their petition had not included any details about how many emigrants had needed assistance or any account of "the evils complained of," he noted with some exasperation. As a concession, he agreed to authorize a "small supply of food for the indigent," but anyone who needed medical assistance should go to Belleville or Picton. With the "present state of the Emigrant fund, it would be impossible for one to appoint Agents at every port at which a few hundred Emigrants may land and at the same time grant free passage and food to the destitute."[46] Two years later, Hawke did propose that a part-time agent be appointed at Cobourg; but he also reported to the governor general that "several of the leading gentlemen" there had organized an association to assist emigrants to find work.[47] In a letter to Charles Green of Cobourg, he noted that he was "happy to hear that the good people [of the town] have been so kind to the immigrants. I wish the inhabitants of all other places which they land at would follow so praiseworthy an Example."[48]

Hawke never assumed that his office could or should take sole responsibility for managing migration into the colony. Local communities were expected to do their part, and this periodically led to some acrimony. For example, Hawke refused to provide any additional funds to William Cattermole, the agent in Hamilton in 1836. Hawke judged that "most of the cases" of assistance that Cattermole had written about "might be easily provided for by a little exertion on your part, in such a flourishing Town as Hamilton, through the medium of private charity."[49] A year later, Hawke received "complaints made by a portion of the Inhabitants of Hamilton" that "the system of transporting Emigrants" to that community was "a burden upon them." He was unrepentant. "I can only say they are unjust," he wrote to Dr Thomas, the new emigrant agent. The community had in the past benefited from the arrival of new settlers and workers. The current extraordinary state of affairs (by which he was referring to the lack of employment in the colony as a whole) had created some "evils," but the government "has done and is doing all in its power to mitigate them."[50] Hawke believed that well-established and wealthy Hamiltonians too had responsibilities and it was time they realized it. In contrast were the efforts of the Western Emigration Society, recently formed west of London, Upper Canada. "I hope every District in the Province will follow your example," he concluded his letter of appreciation. "There can be little doubt the effect produced at a distance by showing our readiness to receive our fellow subjects and to furnish them information and employment must have a beneficial effect."[51]

Even in ports with an agent, Hawke worked with local organizations and authorities. He did not hesitate to use a local hospital to treat ill emigrants, if one existed in the community.[52] In 1835, Hawke turned to the local British

Emigration Society in Toronto to "provide services" to his agency, although, when it came time to pay their account, he objected to some of their charges.[53] After he moved to Kingston, the new capital of the unified province, in 1841, Hawke again turned to the British Emigration Association of Toronto to assist him in supporting emigrants in that city.[54] He also called on local emigration societies in Kingston and Toronto to use their networks to gather and forward to him information about opportunities for emigrants to find work.[55]

Most of Hawke's time and energy was spent managing and monitoring the work of agents stationed throughout the colony. Each spring he sent them detailed instructions. They were to provide emigrants with general information about the colony and, if need be, about where they might find work or, if they had the means, about land on which to settle; to assist the destitute; and, if there was no work in the immediate vicinity, to send emigrants on their way.[56] Agents had considerable discretion, as, in the end, they were the ones to decide who would receive any form of assistance and who would not. At the same time, Hawke demanded that his agents provide him with detailed reports, not only on the numbers who had arrived and the specifics on assistance provided, but also on the funds expended. He often refused to pay subcontractors if their vouchers were incomplete. Soon after the union of the Canadas and the institution of various administrative reforms of government departments, the system became increasingly formal. By 1842, Hawke expected to receive, in addition to their accounts, standardized monthly reports from each agent, which he compiled and send on to the governor general.[57]

The agents' responsibilities began as soon as parties of emigrants arrived. By 1842, Hawke had a regular system worked out, as he explained to the governor general's secretary. After recording their names, occupations, and proposed destination Hawke then grouped the most recent arrivals based on their apparent needs. Those who had sufficient funds to proceed on their own were given information about possible routes and prices and sent on to their final destination. Others were examined as to what relief they had already received, whether they continued to require assistance, and, if so, what to provide. The basic purpose, Hawke stated, was to "endeavour to discover whether their [the emigrants'] poverty is real or pretended."[58] Many emigrants, even those with some funds, who landed at various colonial ports of call needed at least temporary accommodation while they waited for transportation – whether it was a steamship to take them further into the colony or friends to arrive to take them on.

Only communities that regularly received large numbers of emigrants had purpose-built emigrant sheds. In 1835, these included Prescott, Kingston, and Toronto.[59] Building even rough accommodation was costly, and Hawke periodically refused to authorize government funds for such local projects.[60] In these cases, emigrants looking for work or waiting to go on into the colony had to find local accommodation or camped near the wharf. Most sheds were only rough, temporary buildings, often with an open front. In 1840, for example, Hawke told agent Burke in Bytown to build a small shed of twenty feet by fifteen. It only needed to have "a board shed roof."[61] The sheds in Kingston and Toronto were considerably larger but no more accommodating. Time and again Hawke reminded his agents that "the healthy should not suffer to remain in the shed more than a few days and it is not a place for the sick – mere shelter is all that is desirable to afford."[62] Providing anything more would only encourage emigrants to stay and would leave little room for those who were following. This would lead to unrest as individuals and families would become discontented and disheartened with their lot. And it could have even worse effects. Hawke told Anthony Manahan, the agent in Kingston, "If you erect a building with separate rooms," as Manahan seems to have suggested, "it would, I fear, be perverted as at this place [to which he seems to be referring to York] and to very bad purposes."[63] A month later, Manahan repeated his request, and Hawke was even more emphatic in his response: "I know of no better nuisance than a permanent shed affording extensive and separate accommodation. Your streets would soon be infested with beggars and your office besieged by applications for food from those who would avail themselves of its shelter."[64]

Hawke was always conscious of the fine line between providing temporary shelter to those in need and ensuring that they did not take advantage of the government's largess or disrupt life in local communities. At the same time that Hawke was admonishing Manahan for his grandiose plans, he was coping with his own difficulties in York. The numbers of emigrants in 1840 was particularly high, and many had gravitated to the colonial capital to look for work and assistance. As a result, in June that year, Hawke sought permission to build a new shed there. The existing accommodations had apparently been the source of problems in the past, and Hawke informed the lieutenant governor that he intended to place the new shed "under the protection and supervision of city authorities."[65] Yet, when he contacted the mayor of Toronto to request the town's cooperation and to arrange a suitable site for the shed, Hawke reassured him that the emigrant office would continue to oversee emigrants' conduct. Among other things, the new shed would be visited two or three times each day by someone from his office "whose duty will be to see that it is not perverted to other purposes than those contemplated."[66]

When numbers warranted, Hawke authorized local agents to engage a shedkeeper to ensure that emigrants conducted themselves appropriately. In 1842, the mayor and council of Toronto complained about "the insufficiency of accommodation for destitute settlers" and "the want of cleanliness and order at the Emigrant sheds."[67] Hawke proposed to appoint a keeper to oversee those housed in the shed and to have the local agent, Mr Bradley, "distribute" healthy emigrants outside the city. He further authorized Bradley to extend the current shed by forty feet and to "enclose the space" with a fence – one presumes to keep emigrants from roaming about the community.[68] Hawke also authorized that the sheds in Kingston be fenced, and he appointed a keeper there "whose duty it will be to keep the place and people in Order" (emphasis in original).[69] But 1842 had been an exceptional year. As Hawke told Bradley when he refused to authorize an assistant in 1843, "The duty of seeing that the inmates of the sheds conduct themselves properly has ..., except last year, devolved on the agent."[70]

There was no question that, most of the time, the sheds needed close supervision. Not only could they be used for unspecified nefarious purposes, but, in addition, a persistent problem was that some emigrants had nowhere else to go and stayed in the sheds for as long as possible. In 1839, for example, Hawke reported to S.B. Harrison, the civil secretary, that a number of widows with children were living in the shed in Toronto.[71] A similar situation occurred in Kingston in October 1842. Several families had taken up residence in the shed and, although they knew that it would be closed shortly, agent Roy feared "they have been indulged so long, that they will not remove until compelled to leave."[72]

The sheds were intended to accommodate only healthy migrants and for a short time. The cholera epidemic that had swept through the colony in 1832 had taught the colonial government and local leaders that emigrants who were ill needed to be segregated and treated. In Kingston and Toronto, sick emigrants who were feared to be infectious were sent to the local hospital; non-infectious cases were treated as outpatients. In communities without a hospital, Hawke authorized agents to find suitable and separate accommodation for sick emigrants. By 1840, Hawke had assumed personal responsibility for engaging local doctors, as he found that his agents often either overlooked or did not pay sufficient attention to medical accounts. He also set their rate of remuneration and often corresponded directly with the medical personnel to assess their needs.[73]

The problems created by emigrants who were reluctant to leave the sheds – or, as sometimes happened, who feigned illness – were compounded by those who came to depend on the emergency rations that agents distributed. There was always a question of who was eligible to receive such assistance and how much. Local agents had to exercise their own judgment for, as Hawke explained to Mr Burke in Bytown, "I cannot establish any specific rate of assistance. That must depend on the state of the party." But, he continued, "Assistance is to be rendered only when it is imperatively necessary and must cease the moment the object can do without it."[74] The agents were authorized to provide only a little bread or oatmeal, whichever was cheaper, and even this was only in "extreme cases" and only after the agent had assiduously investigated the situation and was "satisfied that such help is indispensably necessary."[75] Hawke believed that "an able bodied man or woman can always obtain food for their labour."[76] As he explained to Manahan in Kingston, "If food is to be obtained for nothing, you will find but little disposition in many of the Emigrants to work for it." Such aid would "become an evil and not a benefit."[77] In 1841, Agent Bradley in Toronto appears to have had growing numbers of emigrants seeking provisions. Hawke was emphatic that he should never give meat, tea, or sugar, but only bread or biscuits, and only for a day or two. Otherwise, he warned Bradley, he would never be rid of some: "If the idler finds that he can live better by begging than by work, he will never exert himself. The sooner such people are thrown upon their own resources the better, for themselves and for the community amongst whom they reside."[78] An agent could and should only do so much. Even the old, the infirm, and widows were to be treated firmly. Despite entreaties from the agent in Cobourg in 1840, Hawke refused to authorize any further assistance to a recent widow: "When this happens," he wrote, "I give the family a few days food and a certificate stating their condition and particular claims on the charity of the public. A sufficient number of benevolent persons have been found to give the widow employment and to provide places for such of their children as are old enough to work."[79] To Agent Bradley in Toronto, Hawke advised that he give only a small supply of bread to those who persisted in seeking provisions and then "scatter them over the country." Hawke judged that their children would soon find work. He acknowledged that such situations posed "a perpetual problem," but, he continued, "by adopting this system I think you may relieve the City and benefit the Emigrants."[80]

One of the fundamental aspects of Upper Canada's attempt to manage migration was to ensure that new arrivals were quickly dispersed from their port of entry. Congregations of hungry and dispirited emigrants with high expectations could be dangerous. Officially, neither the imperial nor the colonial governments assumed any financial responsibility for emigrants' travel once they landed in Quebec. Government information made available to would-be emigrants in Britain included only the names and locations of agents in the colonies. It made no mention of any monetary aid that might be available. As Hawke explained to Chief Secretary Murdoch in 1840, to even mention the possibility of aid for travel "would be to invite the idle and improvident to take advantage of the liberality of the Government."[81] A growing number of emigrants arrived, however, without the means to pay for transportation, and many knew that family and friends already in the colony had received some assistance on their arrival.

In the first half of the 1830s, the Quebec and Montreal Emigrant Societies provided indigent emigrants with free passage up the St Lawrence River and along the Great Lakes. In the spring of 1836, however, the Montreal society informed Hawke that it could afford only to assist emigrants to get to Prescott; it was up to Upper Canadian authorities to assume responsibility from thereon.[82] For the next few years, Hawke was clear that such assistance was to be granted only "in extreme cases," which included widows, orphans, or women with children who were joining friends or family.[83] And free passage was to be granted only if there was no work in the immediate area. In 1836, he denied a request from the agent in Hamilton to send a party of Scots to join friends. They should get local work, Hawke declared, and only if they could not find any would he reconsider his decision.[84] One of Hawke's persistent concerns was that at least some and perhaps many emigrants would try to take advantage of the government's and local communities' largess. In 1836, Hawke asked Agent Scott in Prescott why his travel costs were so high. Hawke agreed that the number of indigent emigrants was up over the previous year, but "on close investigation, I find that many of the applications for relief at Toronto are imposters." They had sold their tickets and now wanted additional aid.[85] Scott was instructed to investigate each claim closely before he gave out any more travel vouchers. Three years later, Hawke again complained of the "much fraud practised ... in procuring passage." He reported to Secretary Murdoch in 1840 that a few families had received free passage from Montreal to anywhere in Upper Canada but had managed to obtain a further ticket from the agent in Bytown and had then sold it to others.[86] Hawke appreciated "the difficulty of discerning the destitute Immigrants from those who may have hidden means," he told Palmer in Hamilton in 1843. It was a situation that all agents confronted. But, if after investigation he was in any doubt about an individual's need, then the applicant should receive no aid and be sent away. Only if he returned in two or three days in similar straits, then should the case be reconsidered.[87] In 1840, a group of Highland emigrants were apparently reluctant to take up work in the Kingston area. They were being "mischievous" Hawke judged, and should receive no further assistance from the government.[88]

At times, agents found that the numbers of emigrants in the sheds or camped out in the open were unmanageable, and the only way to alleviate the situation was to send some on to the next port of call with little investigation. In 1836, Hawke told W.J. Scott, then agent in Prescott, "As it is desirable to prevent the accumulation of such Persons" who had not funds, "you are at liberty to grant them free Passages to any British Ports on Lake Ontario or to the Long Sault."[89] In 1841, Kingston became "very crowded" with new arrivals, and Hawke, himself now located in the new colonial capital, was inundated "with an outcry against the Government agent for forcing such bodies of destitute persons upon public charity."[90] The number of emigrants who had arrived penniless was much larger than expected. Many had no particular destination in mind, and others who wanted to join family or friends had no place to rest even for a few hours while waiting for their transport. "I am assailed by the inhabitants of the Town for permitting Emigrants to accumulate in such numbers," he complained.[91] The situation was no better in Toronto and Hamilton. Agents could do little but send emigrants to where they might find work.

Providing transportation took up a large portion of Hawke's annual budget, and each year he tried to negotiate what he considered "reasonable rates" from local shipmasters (and often complained to the lieutenant governor about captains' sharp practices). But, in some years, the need to send parties on resulted in Hawke going over budget. At the end of the 1840 season, for example, Hawke explained to Secretary Harrison that his account was in deficit because "an unusually large number of Emigrants this year had landed in great distress and many in a state of starvation owing to the long passage they have had."[92] These emigrants had needed not only free passage but also emergency rations. Hawke faced a similar situation in 1845. As he told Chief Agent Buchanan, there was no work for the "pennyless" emigrants who were now in Kingston "and I am obliged to send them on." And, he continued, "Indeed, they would think it an act of cruelty after having crossed the Atlantic to join their relatives if Agents were to refuse to assist them to reach their destination."[93]

Providing emergency provisions and free passage were only short-term measures to address the problems emigrants and local communities faced. The long-term solution was for emigrants to find work, or to take up land and become settlers and fully productive members of the society. Hawke's reports to his agents and to the colonial secretaries regularly included information about lots for sale or opportunities for employment, whether on the canals, as farm servants, or on government projects. That small proportion of emigrants with capital was of no concern. According to Hawke, however, their numbers decreased after 1837, in part because many had found that they could not sustain their previous mode of living. Those who arrived with particular skills – for example, mechanics and farm labourers – or those suited to become servants in town also never had a problem finding employment.[94] The growing numbers of common labourers presented the greatest difficulties for Hawke and his agents. In this respect, 1837 appears to have been a particularly bad year. As Hawke reported to the colonial secretary, with the failure of local crops in 1836, "large portions of the settlers in the new Townships" looked for "employment in the Old Settlements," and this left nothing for new arrivals. At the same time, no government projects that might provide work were then underway. He anticipated that "considerable numbers of immigrants" were likely "to remain idle" for some time and would become "a burthen to the community."[95] Hawke faced a similar situation four years later. Early in the 1841 season, he reported that he expected "very extreme emigration this year" and "a very troublesome season."[96] Not only did a very high proportion of new arrivals need immediate assistance, but there was little work to be had. "I fear," he wrote to the agent in Hamilton, that "I am entered for a troublesome service one which will occupy the whole of my time, from day light till dark until the Emigration closes."[97]

A particular concern in the 1840s was the arrival of growing numbers of poor, young Irish labourers. As Ian Radforth's study in this volume illustrates, groups of young men had a reputation for creating problems, and those who arrived without family or any attachments to the community were worrying. Hawke judged that members of this class of emigrants "are not calculated to make good settlers."[98] Although most seemed to be law abiding and upright and were good with a shovel, they did not have the skills or temperament to take up the work available. They had no idea how to tend livestock or clear the bush and would not make good farm servants – and there was little else for them to do. In 1840, he reported to A. Lachlan, the agent in Bytown that year that, "generally speaking [they] ... belong to the better class of labourers" and had "strong arms and willing hearts."[99] But they were still not fit to become settlers. Moreover, many were clearly "idle and improvident" and posed a threat to peace in the colony.[100]

Hawke's ability to find work for the hundreds and sometimes thousands of emigrants arriving in the colony was often compromised by the emigrants themselves. Time and again, Hawke reported that emigrants refused work because the wages being offered in a particular place were not high enough or the work was not to their liking. In the bad year of 1837, Hawke discovered that a number of emigrants had refused work in the Quebec region because they had expected higher wages in Upper Canada. On their arrival in Toronto and finding wages even lower there, they had complained, he wrote to the lieutenant governor's secretary, "of being deceived by the Government."[101] In 1841, Hawke discovered, after a tour of Cobourg, Port Hope, and Toronto, "where there was an accumulation of unemployed," that many had sought work only in the immediate community or were looking for higher wages.[102] He advised his agents that those who refused work were to be left "to shift for themselves."[103] Only emigrants who really wanted to work were to be supported. Hawke devised his own test for this standard. He told the governor general's secretary that he had put some unemployed emigrants in Kingston to work breaking stone and paid them very low rates: "It enables me to distinguish the willing workmen from the idlers."[104]

Like many of his class, Hawke had little sympathy for "idlers" but was more than willing to assist those he deemed worthy. He was also the consummate bureaucrat and wanted to make the system work. A good deal of his correspondence details his attempts to get reports from his agents. "I have been anxiously expecting to hear from you and I am in utter ignorance of what is passing at your agency," an exasperated Hawke wrote to his new agent in Hamilton in July 1840.[105] At the end of each year, as he was preparing his own consolidated accounts for the government, Hawke frequently had to urge agents to submit their local ledgers and vouchers. Hawke's attention to detail is astounding. When an agent did not meet Hawke's standards, he did not hesitate to admonish him. Manahan, the agent in Kingston until the mid-1840s, frequently received curt notes from Hawke about his failure to adequately account for rations distributed, his unreasonable desire for a new shed, the contracts that he entered into without authority, and his failure to submit reports.[106] Hawke was more patient with Bradley, the agent in Toronto. That port was undoubtedly the busiest and was known to be "one of the most troublesome" in the colony.[107] Bradley had originally been chosen as the agent in 1840, as he was not only highly recommended as competent and caring but was also Irish.[108] Bradley clearly had difficulties "in the discharge of his duties," and the two men did clash over the lateness of his reports and his apparently lax accounting. But, as Hawke told Buchanan, Bradley was good with his charges and well meaning.

One of the questions that Hawke repeatedly asked his agents was how many emigrants had gone through their port, and where they intended to settle. In an apparent attempt to maintain efficiency and some control, he frequently asked agents to confirm their own records, particularly when emigrants seemed to have disappeared between one station and another. At the heart of this determination to keep track of new arrivals was, I think, Hawke's desire to ensure that immigration proceeded in an orderly fashion. There is no question that Hawke's letterbooks reflect, in part, what Bruce Curtis had termed "the cult of numbers."[109] As a colonial administrator, Hawke was expected to collect detailed information about those arriving from "home" and to provide officials in London with an inventory of local resources. But Hawke's correspondence also chronicles his and others' attempts to control the movement of people and to ensure that new arrivals did not have the opportunity to create trouble. He shared the concerns and sensibilities of community leaders that only the deserving – the "worthy" – should receive assistance, and he went to considerable lengths to secure peace and harmony.

Managing migration was an ongoing concern in Upper Canada between 1815 and 1845. One can imagine what chaos must have existed at some of the ports, as tired, dishevelled, often hungry, and sometimes desperate men, women, and children landed in a world that was truly foreign. And one can imagine the response of local residents as they watched hopeful emigrants straggle off the boats often disappointed that this was not the land of milk and honey promised in the promotion literature. These newcomers represented growth and a prosperous colonial future. At the same time, they could be, and sometimes were, disruptive and difficult to manage and could pose a serious problem for communities that did not have the means to accommodate them. By the early 1840s, when the apparatus of a colonial state with the ability to really "know" its residents began to emerge, Hawke and his agents had already established a constellation of policies and organizations to cope with the situation. These were by no means integrated into one seamless system, and indeed, there was no colonial immigration "policy" that was entirely enforceable. Neither the imperial nor the colonial government had any means of selecting who could either leave home or enter the colony (other than for reasons of public health). As Upper Canadians realized, there was no guarantee that all, or even most, new arrivals were industrious, loyal, or worthy subjects, or that there were not those who would pose a threat either individually or collectively to the well-being of the colony. Nonetheless, between 1815 and 1845, community leaders and, increasingly, representatives of the "state" did what they could to maintain social stability and peace while taking advantage of the thousands of new settlers in their midst.

NOTES

1 *Journals of the House of Assembly* (Upper Canada), Ninth Report of the Bureau of Archives for the Province of Ontario (Toronto, 1912), 7 February 1818, 434 (hereafter *Journals of the Assembly*).
2 Ibid., 5 February 1818, 432.
3 *Kingston Gazette*, 11 November 1817.
4 *Upper Canada Gazette*, 30 October 1817, for a report of a meeting five days earlier.
5 *Kingston Gazette*, 9 December 1817.
6 *Journals of the Assembly*, 7 February 1818.
7 John G. Reid and Thomas Peace, "Colonies of Settlement and Settler Colonialism in Northeastern North America, 1450–1850," in *The Routledge Handbook of the History of Settler Colonialism*, ed. Edward Cavanagh and Lorenzo Veracini (London: Routledge, 2017), 79–94, 80; and Cecilia Morgan, *Building Better Britains? Settler Societies in the British World, 1783–1920* (Toronto: University of Toronto Press, 2017).

8 "Emigration" and "emigrant" (and not "immigration" and "immigrant") were the terms that were consistently used throughout this early period in colonial records and by both local residents and authorities, and this chapter reflects this usage.

9 J.K. Johnson, *In Duty Bound: Men, Women, and the State in Upper Canada, 1783–1841* (Kingston and Montreal: McGill-Queen's University Press, 2014), 7.

10 Bruce Curtis, *The Politics of Population: State Formation, Statistics, and the Census of Canada, 1840–1875* (Toronto: University of Toronto Press, 2001).

11 Archives of Ontario, Ontario Immigration Records, Chief Emigrant Agents Letterbooks, RG 11-1-0-1 and -2, Hawke Papers (also known as Records of the Toronto Emigration Office, although after the union of the Canada's in 1841, Hawke was stationed in Kingston). Unless specifically noted, all references in this paper to Hawke's correspondence are taken from this collection and will include recipient and date only.

12 See Elizabeth Jane Errington, *Emigrant Worlds and Transatlantic Communities: Migration to Upper Canada in the First Half of the Nineteenth Century* (Montreal and Kingston: McGill-Queen's University Press, 2007), particularly the Note on Sources.

13 One exception is Lisa Chilton's article "Managing Migrants: Toronto, 1820–1880," *Canadian Historical Review* 92, no. 2 (June 2011): 231–62, which includes a brief discussion of the early period. See also Morgan, *Building Better Britains?* 42.

14 Beginning with the still-classic Lilian Gates, *Land Policies of Upper Canada* (Toronto: University of Toronto Press, 1968), and discussion in Johnson, *In Duty Bound*, particularly ch. 1.

15 See Richard Splane, *Social Welfare in Ontario, 1791–1893: A Study in Public Welfare Administration* (Toronto: University of Toronto Press, 1965); Rainer Baehre, "Paupers and Poor Relief in Upper Canada," in *Historical Essays on Upper Canada: New Perspectives*, ed. J.K. Johnson and Bruce Wilson (Ottawa: Carleton University Press, 1989); Baehre, "Pauper Emigration to Upper Canada in the 1830s," *Histoire sociale / Social History* 14, no. 28 (1981): 339–67; Cheryl Des Roches, "A Place to Call Home: A Comparison of the Development of State Funded Institutional Care ..." (PhD diss., Queen's University, 2008); and Johnson, *In Duty Bound*, ch. 7.

16 Scott W. See, *Riots in New Brunswick: Orange Nativism and Social Violence in the 1840s* (Toronto: University of Toronto Press, 1993); Laura J. Smith, "The Ballybiglins: British Emigration Policy, Irish Violence, and Immigration Reception in Upper Canada," *Ontario History* 108, no. 1 (2016): 1–23; and Dan Horner, "'Shame upon you as men!' Contesting Authority in the Aftermath of the Montreal's Gavazzi Riots," *Histoire sociale / Social History* 44, no. 87 (2011): 29–52.

17 John Weaver, *The Great Land Rush and the Making of the Modern World* (Montreal and Kingston: McGill-Queen's University Press, 2003).

18 See Jane Errington, *The Lion, the Eagle, and Upper Canada: A Developing Colonial Ideology*, 2nd ed. (Montreal and Kingston: McGill-Queen's University Press, 2012), particularly ch. 2.

19 James Belich, *Replenishing the Earth: The Settler Revolution and the Rise of the Anglo-World, 1783–1939* (Oxford: Oxford University Press, 2009), 9. See also Eric Richards, *Britannia's Children: Emigration from England, Scotland, Wales, and Ireland since 1600* (London: Hambledon and London, 2004).

20 From Edinburgh *Scotsman*, quoted in *Kingston Gazette*, 8 September 1818, as quoted in Errington, *Emigrant Worlds*, 15.

21 As Eric Richards, *Britannia's Children*, 131 ff., and many others have noted, it is also impossible to determine with any accuracy the numbers of Britons who left home or who arrived in Upper Canada. The population figures for Upper Canada during this period are only estimates.

22 "Bandana on Emigration," *Blackwood's*, September 1826, 474, as quoted in Errington, *Emigrant Worlds*, 16.

23 After reports in 1828 that conditions on-board many ships were horrendous, and under pressure from colonial authorities, the act was further amended to afford migrants some protection from unscrupulous emigrant agents and ship captains. The classic study of the Passenger Acts is Oliver MacDonagh, *A Pattern of Government Growth, 1800–60: The Passenger Acts and Their Enforcement* (London: MacGibbon and Kee, 1961). See also discussion in Errington, *Emigrant Worlds*, 188n55.

24 Richards, *Britannia's Children*, 117.

25 See, among others, Errington, *Emigrant Worlds*, ch. 1; Eric Richards, *Britannia's Children*, particularly for the debates about pauper immigration that engaged the British press and Parliament.

26 *Scots Times*, Glasgow, 26 June 1832; *Manchester Guardian*, 17 April 1830, as quoted in Errington, *Emigrant Worlds*, 13. See also John Darwin, *Unfinished Empire: The Global Expansion of Britain* (London: Allen Lane, 2012), 99.

27 See Errington, *Emigrant Worlds*, ch. 1, for a more detailed discussion of factors that influenced Britons' decisions to emigrate.

28 For a preliminary discussion of these efforts, see Errington, *Wives and Mothers, School Mistresses and Scullery Maids* (Montreal and Kingston: McGill-Queen's University Press, 1995), ch. 7.

29 See, for example, the report "The Meeting of the Society for Relief of Strangers in Distress," *Upper Canada Gazette*, 13 April 1820, found in Edith Firth, ed., *The Town of York, 1815–1834: A Further Collection of Documents of Early Toronto* (Toronto: Champlain Society, 1966), 224–5.

30 *Canada Waste Lands: Return of an Address to His Majesty Dated 13 September 1831 for a Copy of the Report of Mr Richards to the Colonial Secretary, Respecting the Waste Lands in the Canadas and Emigration* (London, HMSO, 1832), 23, 24. Taken from Early Canadiana online, http://eco.canadiana.ca/view/oocihm.9_01677/2?r=0&s=1.

31 Extract of a despatch from Lord Alymer to Lord Gorderich, 12 October 1831, in *Emigration Report of Commissions' Return to an Address to His Majesty ...*, (London: HMSO, 1832), dated 11 August 1832, 16–19.

32 C.M. Godfrey, *The Cholera Epidemics of Upper Canada, 1832–1866* (Toronto: Seccombe House, 1968); and Geoffrey Bilson, *A Darkened House: Cholera in Nineteenth Century Canada* (Toronto: University of Toronto Press, 1980).

33 Colborne's policies have been explored and evaluated in numerous works. For an overview, see Alan Wilson, "Colbourne, John, Baron Seaton," in *Dictionary of Canadian Biography* (online) 2003, http://www.biographi.ca/en/bio/colborne_john_9E.html.

34 Anthony Hawke was himself an emigrant who, with his family, had arrived in the colony soon after the end of the Napoleonic Wars. Known as a staunch Tory supporter, in 1827 he was appointed a JP for the Midland District. As chief emigrant agent, Hawke maintained considerable autonomy, to the disquiet of A.C. Buchanan, the chief agent in Quebec. Wesley B. Turner, "Hawke, Anthony Bewden" *Dictionary of Canadian Biography* (online) 1976, http://www.biographi.ca/en/bio/hawke_anthony_bewden_9E.html.

35 "From the Lieutenant Governor," *Kingston Chronicle*, 4 February 1832.

36 See, among others, Ian Radforth, "Sydenham and Utilitarian Reform," in *Colonial Leviathan: State Formation in Mid-Nineteenth-Century Canada*, ed. Allan Greer and Ian Radforth (Toronto: University of Toronto Press, 1992), 64–102.

37 Hawke to Anthony Manahan, (Kingston) 14 July 1840.

38 See, for example, Hawke to John Joseph, secretary, 28 March 1836, explaining his role. Then each year, he sought authority to tour the province. See Hawke to Joseph, 10 May 1837; Hawke to Harrison, private secretary, 6 May 1840; Hawke to Buchanan, 3 June 1842.

39 Belich, *Replenishing the Earth*, 87.

40 Hawke to Joseph, 24 July 1837. In a letter to A.C. Buchanan, 30 November 1837, Hawke estimated that approximately 22,000 emigrants had landed at Quebec that season, and of those he could account for 14,690 who had passed through Prescott and Bytown, with another 1,500 who had arrived by way of the United States. See also letter to Joseph, 23 May 1836, that they were to expect more in 1836 than in 1835, but that this was not looking to be the case.

41 Hawke to Harrison, 15 July 1839.

42 Hawke to Buchanan, 12 May 1845, 20 May 1845.

43 Hawke to Harrison, 26 May 1840. In this report of his spring trip to assess needs for the current season, Hawke also reiterated the duties of all of his agents and explained their terms of service.
44 Hawke to Mr Rorke, 29 June 1840; Hawke to Harrison, 19 June 1840, in which Hawke recommended Dr E.C. Thomas.
45 Hawke to the Gentlemen of Cobourg, 26 June 1840.
46 Hawke to Rev. Bethune and others, 14 July 1840. In the 1840s, Hawke was increasingly conscious that he did not have sufficient funds to cover the cost of the various agencies. For example, he informed Buchanan on 27 July 1843 that he intended to visit Cobourg and Hamilton and expected to close down the agencies there early.
47 Hawke to Murdoch, 13 June 1842.
48 Hawke to Charles Green, 25 June 1842.
49 Hawke to Cattermole, 6 September 1836.
50 Hawke to Thomas, 7 July 1837.
51 Hawke to R. Lachlan, 3 August 1840.
52 See Hawke to Bradley in Toronto, 17 October 1843, authorizing him to pay the hospital account (which they agreed was too high); Hawke to Thomas Dick, 9 December 1843, arranging the accounts for municipal services.
53 Hawke to Mr Cull of the British Emigration Society of Toronto, 7 December 1835, 8 December 1835, 18 December 1835.
54 Hawke to S.B. Jarvis, 2 July 1841.
55 See Hawke to Jarvis of the Toronto Emigrant Society, 22 May 1841 and 2 June 1841; letter to Murdoch, 25 May 1841.
56 For a sample of these instructions, see Hawke to S.B. Harrison (private secretary to the lieutenant governor), 26 May 1840; Hawke to Manahan (agent in Kingston), 24 May 1836; Hawke to Bradley (new agent in Toronto), 7 June 1841.
57 See, among others, Hawke's standard letter to all agents in Bytown, Kingston, and Hamilton, 16 October 1840 and 14 November 1840. This was repeated each year, and in 1843 Hawke and his agents were required to fill out a standardized form. See Hawke to W. Rawson, civil secretary, 12 July 1843. At Hawke's suggestion, financial reports were also standardized. See his letter to Buchanan, 14 March 1842. See letter to agents informing them of the new system, 26 October 1842.
58 Hawke to W. Rawson, 21 December 1842. Hawke provided considerable detail about the procedures that he had developed over the years.
59 There had been a shed at York at least as early as 1830. See report in *Kingston Chronicle*, 29 August 1830 about building an "emigrant asylum," ninety feet by twenty feet to accommodate "destitute emigrants."
60 See Hawke correspondence with G.W. Ridley and the other gentlemen of Belleville, 13 July 1837, refusing to fund the renovation of a local building at the cost of £300 as not enough emigrants landed there to warrant it.

61 Hawke to Burke, 13 June 1840.

62 Ibid.

63 Hawke to Manahan, 13 June 1840. There was considerable correspondence on the matter. See also 22 June 1840.

64 Hawke to Manahan, 14 July 1840.

65 Hawke to Harrison, secretary of the lieutenant governor, 15 June 1840.

66 To His Worship the Mayor, 17 June 1840. Hawke informed the mayor that the shed would be removed in November, at the end of the emigrant season.

67 Hawke to Murdoch, 13 June 1842.

68 Hawke to Bradley, 10 June 1842; Hawke to Murdoch, 26 April 1842.

69 See Roy, the agent in Kingston, to Hawke, 17 October 1842.

70 Hawke to Bradley, 24 May 1843.

71 Hawke to Harrison, 2 September 1839.

72 Roy to Hawke, 17 October 1842.

73 Hawke to Harrison, 13 June 1840, outlined Hawke's proposal for dealing directly with local doctors in Kingston. A similar practice was instituted in Bytown and Hamilton.

74 Hawke to Chatterton in Cobourg, 17 July 1840. See also Hawke to Chas. Green, 18 June 1841, to give only to young families.

75 Hawke to Burke, 29 June 1840; see also Hawke to Burke, 16 May 1843; Hawke to Palmer, 17 July 1843 citing the need to keep expenses down.

76 Hawke to E.C. Thomas, Hamilton, 15 June 1837.

77 Hawke to Manahan, 18 July 1837.

78 Hawke to Bradley, 17 July 1841.

79 Hawke to Chatterton, 17 July 1840.

80 Hawke to Bradley, 26 July 1841.

81 Hawke to Murdoch, 27 May 1840. This echoed the sentiments of A.C. Buchanan almost ten years earlier, when he reported that many had who landed at Quebec in 1832 had expected the government to pay their passage to the upper province. The result, he had continued, was to check "the industry of that portion of the Emigrant population already too prone to seek any means of support rather than work." "Mr. Buchanan's Report" in "Copies of Extracts of the Correspondence between the Secretary of State for the Colonial Office and the Governors or Lieutenant Governors of the British Colonies in North America and Australia, since the Last Returns, in so far as Relates to the Question of Emigration." Ordered by the House of Commons, 1 April 1833, 5–25, 23, in Early Canadiana online http://eco.canadiana.ca/view/oocihm.9_07182/2?r=0&s=1.

82 Hawke to Joseph, 23 May 1836, reporting on his recent trip to Montreal.

83 Hawke to Scott, 24 May 1837.

84 Hawke to Cattermole, 8 September 1836.

85 Hawke to Scott, 12 September 1836.
86 Hawke to Murdoch, 22 June 1840.
87 Hawke to Palmer, 16 May 1843.
88 Hawke to Roy, 29 August 1840.
89 Hawke to W.J. Scott, 24 June 1836.
90 Hawke to Buchanan, 11 June 1841; see also 17 June 1841.
91 Hawke to Buchanan, 17 June 1841.
92 Hawke to Harrison, 16 October 1840.
93 Hawke to Buchanan, 8 August 1845.
94 Hawke to Rawson, 17 November 1843. He noted in a report to Harrison, 2 September 1839, "I have never experienced any difficulty in getting work for good farm servants, unless encumbered with large families."
95 Hawke to John Joseph, 7 June 1837. Hawke expressed similar concerns in the 1840s, as American workers flooded north and took most jobs before emigrants even arrived. Hawke to Bradley, 15 May 1842; see also Hawke to Buchanan, 10 September 1842.
96 Hawke to Jarvis in Toronto, 2 June 1841; Hawke to Bradley, 9 June 1841.
97 Hawke to Forbes, 4 June 1841.
98 Hawke to Harrison, 16 October 1840. See also 19 August 1840.
99 Hawke to A. Lachlan, 3 August 1840.
100 Hawke to T.W.C. Murdoch, chief secretary, Montreal, 7 May 1840.
101 Hawke to John Joseph, 3 May 1837.
102 Hawke to Murdoch, 30 September 1841. In a letter to Buchanan, 28 September 1841, Hawke judged that there was work, but "it is quite evident that most of them prefer Idleness to industry and they had made little or no effort to provide for themselves."
103 Hawke to Burke, 2 October 1841.
104 Hawke to Murdoch, 28 June 1841.
105 Hawke to Manahan, 27 July 1840.
106 The accounts were perhaps the most serious. "You are well aware that I can pay nothing that is not covered by your instructions or for which special authority had not been obtained," Hawke wrote, 10 August 1840. In the end, Manahan precipitously resigned, to be replaced by the assistant agent, a Mr Roy. Hawke to Manahan, 24 August 1840.
107 Hawke to Buchanan, 14 February 1845.
108 Hawke to Buchanan, 8 May 1844, explaining what he wanted to appoint another Catholic to the post and had received advice from the bishop.
109 Curtis, *Politics of Population*, 18.

SECTION III

Resisting Dispossession

A conceit accompanying colonization in the Americas and reinforced by the Enlightenment was that Europeans could build new – and some believed better – societies in the "New World." For the British, these societies embraced traditional English rights, as well as newer rights such as expanded political participation. Those British aspirations, however, were predicated on colonial societies' having relative cultural homogeneity. To "manage" the peoples who did not conform culturally, colonists devised programs of assimilation and "civilization," or for those thought incapable of being civilized to the level of political participation, discrete marginalization. Within the settler communities of British North America, with their Enlightenment visions of orderly civic society, Indigenous peoples had few autonomous places.

People who did not fit – whether Indigenous, of African descent, or even French or Celtic Catholics – understood these social visions as intrinsically disruptive to their lives, if not outright violent when executed. The four essays in this section explore how marginalized peoples responded to the agendas of the settler and imperial worlds, the disruptions that accompanied them, and their attempts to make sense of them in ways that preserved cultural integrity.

Indigenous nations that had long associations with Europeans recognized how education could be both beneficial and a vehicle of unwanted transformation. Thomas Peace shows how the Wendat in Lower Canada and the Mississauga in Upper Canada worked with local colonial elites to establish schools in which their own people taught. This move to education on their own terms coincided with Wendat and Mississauga petitions for title to their lands. Peace argues that these initiatives by two separate nations were not just coincidental but were part of a broader set of attempts by nations of the Seven Fires Confederacy to respond proactively to pressures from rapidly growing settler societies.

Harvey Amani Whitfield examines the struggle over visions of social order that can be discerned in close readings of advertisements for runaway slaves. When Loyalists left the United States and took refuge in the Maritimes, among them were people of African descent: some had obtained their freedom by fighting with the British; some were free black servants; others were slaves. Revolutionary disorder allowed some blacks to grasp their freedom, but, as Whitfield shows, it also made blacks vulnerable to re-enslavement and sale to the West Indies. Running away was another avenue of freedom, and the large numbers of advertisements shows blacks used it frequently. Whitfield suggests that frequent public notices of runaways, together with the movement to end the British slave trade, if not slavery itself, may have contributed to the unwillingness of the New Brunswick and Nova Scotia assemblies to legitimate slavery in statute law and thus helped to bring about its end.

Two papers address Metis culture centred in the Red River area, the political authority of which included both women and men. Émilie Pigeon and Carolyn Podruchny offer a compelling analysis of the role of Metis women in bison brigades. Earlier commentators described them as military units, but, as Pigeon and Podruchny show, women were central to maintaining social order in the brigades, which were structured as mobile villages. Women played a critical leadership role within the brigade camps and in driving the carts, but also in diplomacy on the Great Plains. Max Hamon re-examines the political thought of Louis Riel and how he sought to restructure the public sphere in the face of settler colonialism. Unlike earlier studies of Riel that anticipated violence, Hamon shows how Riel reshaped the public sphere in Red River around consensus and negotiation. Both of these essays demonstrate that nineteenth-century settler society emphasized the political roles of men at the expense of women and, in turn, interpreted Metis culture as being more masculine and militarized than settler society and thus a threat to it. Hamon revivifies Riel's injunctions in 1869 and 1885 to honour the mothers of the Metis, who were descended from Indigenous nations, as well as Riel's struggle not to concede too much to settler society and its vision of a masculine public sphere.

9 Searching for Order in a Settlers' World: Wendat and Mississauga Schooling, Politics, and Networks at the Beginning of the Nineteenth Century

THOMAS PEACE[1]

The long eighteenth century (1688–1815) marked a radical transformation in the political geography of northeastern North America and the lower Great Lakes. Beginning in the early seventeenth century along the Atlantic coast in the territory of Wabanaki, Mohican, and Leni-Lenape peoples, among others, European empires gradually expanded inland up river valleys and along the shores of the Great Lakes. By the 1680s, key nodes of European expansion in the region, such as Albany and Montreal, had formed. Settlement, of course, was not the only influence spreading across the continent in these early years. At a much faster pace than European farmers, Catholic missionaries and fur traders also entered the region, bringing with them disease and fuelling conflict among Indigenous nations. These forces sparked significant waves of migration and political realignment among Indigenous and colonial peoples. Indigenous resistance to foreign incursions, and warfare between European empires, slowly brought these diverse imperial and colonial influences together, culminating in the Seven Years' War. From 1760 onwards, settlement, the fur trade, and missionary work became increasingly aligned as tools of dispossession; at the same time, Indigenous nations responded with resilient strategies to maintain their cultures, communities, and relationship to the land.[2]

At first, then, it may seem odd to compare Wendat and Mississauga experiences of this transition. The Wendat, after all, left their homelands on the shores of Georgian Bay in the 1650s due to disease, famine, and warfare, moving to the outskirts of Quebec, among other places. The Mississauga confronted these challenges nearly one hundred and fifty years later. As Neal Ferris amply demonstrates in *Native Lived Colonialism*, despite the fur trade and missionary efforts, Europeans minimally affected Anishinaabe and Haudenosaunee lives in the Lower Great Lakes until the early-to-mid-nineteenth century.[3] By this time, Wendat peoples at Lorette (their community near Quebec) had been living closely with Jesuit missionaries for nearly two hundred years. Nonetheless, the coalescence of previously fragmented imperial interests, the end of imperial warfare, and the rising influence of settler colonial power – with its increasing emphasis on centralized policies of "civilization" and assimilation – created conditions whereby Indigenous peoples found themselves in similar situations despite their diverse histories. The period from 1760 to 1840 was one of considerable direct and indirect violence, within which both colonial and Indigenous peoples sought to establish or, in the case of First Peoples, to recover social order. In doing so, there were moments when the interests of Indigenous nations and settlers aligned, if only imperfectly and somewhat problematically.

At the end of the eighteenth century, the politics of schooling and the strategic use of alphabetic literacy was one arena where some settler and Indigenous men found common ground. Settlers saw in the school an important institution with which to order their emerging society as well as control the people living on the lands they coveted; at the same time, some Indigenous communities saw in these institutions a strategy for survival in the face of radical environmental, political, and cultural pressures. Within this context of similar interest in the promise of schooling emerged a set of personal relationships – perhaps even friendships – between some prominent Wendat and Mississauga intellectuals and a handful of colonists active in resettling, redefining, and re-ordering the region's culture and politics during the first half of the nineteenth century.

This chapter examines the social and political relationships of two men, Louis Vincent Sawatanen and Kahkewaquonaby (Peter Jones), with the emerging colonial elite, to point a way forward for future studies of violence, settler colonialism, and the perception of social order. In comparing the long-standing relationships that developed between these two men and prominent colonists involved in shaping early education policy, such as Andrew Stuart, John Neilson, and Egerton Ryerson, we can see more clearly the role Indigenous peoples played in shaping, and being shaped by, Lower and Upper Canada's settler colonial development. Similar to Maxime Gohier's work, whose dissertation on Laurentian Indigenous people's petitions during this period demonstrates that "the State was not a foreign entity for Indigenous peoples, but rather they formed an important part of it; in their participation, they shaped its nature and its form,"[4] this chapter argues that, for a brief period between 1810 and 1830, the interests of these men in public schooling, the administration of land, and the nature and behaviour of government aligned, bringing about strategic partnerships. These partnerships, however, were soon eroded in the decades after 1830, as the demographic balance in both colonies shifted attention away from First Peoples and led to deliberate strategies (sometimes proposed by the very settler men discussed here) to isolate Indigenous nations from the emerging settler colonial society.

Schooling and Petitioning the Crown

The Royal Proclamation of 1763 established a new culture of negotiation for land in North America, but it was not until the very end of the eighteenth century that the pressures of settlement became increasingly apparent for many Indigenous communities. In the St Lawrence valley, the proclamation's impact was somewhat muted. Though it was posted in Laurentian Indigenous communities, its direct manifestation in the form of territorial treaties never developed.[5] Further west, however, along the banks of the upper St Lawrence and in the lower Great Lakes, the proclamation required negotiation and treaty making before colonists could expand onto Indigenous lands. This shift in policy was noticed, causing Laurentian Indigenous nations – known at the time as the Seven Fires Confederacy – to demand of the Indian Department why they were not similarly compensated for settlers' expansion onto their lands.[6] Despite these differences, the waves of British colonization that followed the loyalist migrations of the 1780s began to redefine Indigenous spaces throughout Lower and Upper Canada, creating a context for increasingly common responses from Indigenous nations.

In the aftermath of the Conquest of Quebec, the Wendat political position was uncertain. Allied with the Jesuits for over a century, they faced newly imposed British restrictions on the Jesuit Order that made it clear that this relationship was endangered. The Jesuits played an important role in liaising between the Wendat and imperial officials during the French and early British regime. As Jesuit practices intermixed politics, language, religion, and culture, they had come to play an important role within town life. Long after the order's demise in Quebec, manuscript dictionaries, grammars, and religious texts created by Jesuits continued to be used within the Wendat community.[7] Compounding this substantial cultural and political transition, nearly a century and a half of living near the expanding French settlement at Quebec had also begun to take its toll. Community members increasingly complained about their declining access to local resources. Although the dynamics of the relationship between the Jesuits and Wendat remain somewhat uncertain – especially as they relate to territory – by the mid-1760s it was clear that the Wendat needed to adopt new strategies vis-à-vis the British to maintain their distinct presence on the land they had called home for at least a century.[8]

At the Credit River, this process was different. Also anchored in the practices set out in the Royal Proclamation, from the late 1780s the British had negotiated treaties with Anishinaabe peoples for permission to begin importing colonists onto their lands.[9] Although Europeans had been visiting the area since the mid-seventeenth century, active and intensive agricultural settlement did not occur until the early nineteenth century. The transformation of space in that region from an Indigenous to colonial landscape was much more rapid and profound. With the creation of Upper Canada in 1791, the region went from having a relatively non-existent non-Indigenous population to, by the early-1830s, rivalling in size its Lower Canadian counterpart.[10] By bringing these two contexts into conversation with each other, this period reveals the flattened experiences in what had been a heterogeneous space in the St Lawrence valley and lower Great Lakes during the eighteenth century.

In response to these pressures, both the Wendat and Mississauga started schools. At Lorette, Louis Vincent Sawatanen, who had graduated from Dartmouth College about a decade earlier, started a school in the 1790s. He had already taught for at least a few years in the Mohawk community on the Bay of Quinte before returning home in 1791 or 1792. General descriptions of the school at Lorette tend to paint a consistent picture. Most of the village's boys and girls, between twenty-five and thrirty-five students in total, attended the school between 1790 and 1843.[11] Not all students in the school were Wendat. A visitor in the 1820s commented that some Algonquin, Mi'kmaw, Mohawk, and Wabanaki students also attended.[12] According to Louis Fortier, the missionary living in the community in the 1840s, the curriculum at the school was similar to that of the Wendat's Canadien neighbours. Importantly, Mathieu Chaurette's research suggests that some instruction continued to be delivered in the Wendat language. Overall in Lower Canada, this school was unique. Scholars of colonial schooling and alphabetic literacy in the colony have observed that, by mid-century, few Canadien parishes had schools; those that did had teachers who were poorly trained and were focused mostly on religious piety.[13]

Some of the school books used at this time by François-Xavier Picard, who would later become the nation's grand chief, are held at the Bibliothèque et Archives nationales du Québec. They demonstrate that, while he was a student of Sawatanen's in the late 1810s, Picard studied *The Spelling-Book or Introduction to Reading of the General Sunday-School Society, Heures Nouvelles pour les enfans à l'usage des écoles*, as well as *Neuvaine a l'honneur de St Francois Xavier*; according to Bruce Curtis, the latst text was also used by Elie Paré in her school on Île d'Orléans in the 1830s.[14] These texts tell us two important things about the school's curriculum. First, in addition to French and Wendat, training in English – which was not available to most people living outside of

Quebec, Montreal, and Trois Rivières – was deemed an important skill. Second, Sawatanen's pedagogy had some religious overtones. Too much should not be made of this second point, however, because Sawatanen was accused of heterodoxy when he first started teaching in 1792 and, when Thaddeus Osgood visited the school in 1825, he was quick to point out the absence of Bibles.[15]

The school at Credit River was similar in some respects. It was started by Kahkewaquonaby and his brother Thayendanegea (John Jones) in the mid-1820s. Like Sawatanen, the two men had some formal education, having attended a colonial school in Stoney Creek during their youth. Thayendanegea also trained as a surveyor (as had François-Xavier Picard), the profession of his British father, in the early 1820s.[16] After their conversion to Methodism and the creation of a Methodist Mississauga village on the Credit River, a schoolhouse was completed in 1826. About forty students attended the new institution. Thayendanegea taught the boys in the school, while a Miss Rolph taught the girls. Egerton Ryerson, one of the first Methodist missionaries to live with the Mississauga on the Credit River, emphasized that "about twenty Indian children have learned those catechisms which teach the first principles of the Christian religion, and a number of Watt's hymns for children. About the same number can read the Holy Scriptures – twelve of these can repeat the greatest part of our Saviour's Sermon on the Mount, and are beginning to write intelligibly."[17] Three years later, Ryerson extended his observations, noting about fifty students in attendance, with separate instruction for boys and girls.[18] Though it was the first of such schools, Hope MacLean's research demonstrates that similar institutions, also led by Indigenous schoolteachers, were built at Lake Simcoe, Sault Ste-Marie, Saugeen, and Munceytown from 1820 to 1850.[19]

The development of the day schools at both Lorette and the Credit occurred while both communities were directly petitioning the Crown over their declining access to land and resources. Wendat petitioning grew slowly from oral appeals to the Indian Department made in the 1770s and 1780s, and were anchored in that tradition.[20] Once oral approaches were found ineffective, they brought their concerns before the governor in writing. The date of the first formal petition – in the summer of 1791 – marks when the Wendat at Lorette began their school.[21] Schooling, in the form of access to higher education at the Petit Séminaire in Quebec, was a key concern in this petition. By the 1810s, Wendat complaints were taken up by the Lower Canadian Assembly, which held formal hearings in 1819. Sawatanen was central to these petitions, often serving as a translator, but also seen by many as one of their lead instigators.[22] Supporting the Wendat in the assembly, and playing an important role in their achieving an audience with the British monarch, were two prominent members of the Parti canadien / Parti patriote: Andrew Stuart, a well-known lawyer at

Quebec, and John Neilson, perhaps the city's best-known printer and bookseller and editor of the *Quebec Gazette*.[23] Though both men would later leave the party in the 1830s as it radicalized, at this time they were central players in its social and political life, and in the colony more generally.

Mississauga petitions were similar. Beginning with in-person complaints to Indian Department officials and then gradually deploying more formal petitions, Mississauga diplomats protested settler violations of their treaty agreements.[24] As noted, although it did not apply to the Wendat, the 1763 Royal Proclamation required the British to negotiate treaties before settlers could occupy Indigenous lands. The period 1790–1820 witnessed continual treaty making and treaty breaking as Mississauga lands rapidly transformed into the pastoral landscape known as Upper Canada.[25] The first written Mississauga petition was filed in 1829, just three years after the school was started and nearly fifty years after the first terms of these treaties were agreed upon. Much like the Wendat petition forty years earlier, this one was sent to the lieutenant governor, Sir John Colborne, focused on the depletion of resources and the importance of schooling for the nation. Like the Wendat petition, Mississauga concerns were taken relatively seriously and investigated by an assembly committee.[26]

Unlike in Lower Canada, where Stuart and Neilson spearheaded the investigation as members of the colonial assembly, in Upper Canada Egerton Ryerson testified before the committee. Ryerson was a moderate reformer, Methodist missionary at the Credit River, and newspaper publisher at nearby York. Many in the colony took him quite seriously.[27] Based on the evidence Ryerson presented on the Mississauga's behalf, William Warren Baldwin, who, along with his son Robert (both prominent Upper Canadian assemblymen), was advocating for responsible government, concluded "the complaints made by the petitioners are too well founded."[28] Seven years later, Ryerson was involved in another Mississauga petition to the Crown. This time, though, Kahkewaquonaby consulted with him about how best to bring Mississauga grievances before the imperial government in anticipation of a trip to England. Kahkewaquonaby wrote to Ryerson that "it is the intention of the Credit Indians to forward by me, a petition to the Home Government respecting the uncertain tenure by which they hold their lands at this place, and to apply for a Deed, securing their Reserve to them and their descendants forever."[29] Ryerson followed up on Kahkewaquonaby's letter with an introduction to Lord Glenelg, the secretary of state for war and the colonies, noting especially that "it will be impracticable to improve the civil condition of our much injured aboriginal fellow countrymen unless the lands on which it is proposed for them to settle are properly and legally secured to them, an object which I have no doubt would have been accomplished had Sir John Colborne remained in Upper Canada."[30] In writing back from Britain to the Credit River in the spring of 1838, Kahkewaquonaby advised that, as the Mississauga consider how best to acquire title-deeds to their lands, they consult with Ryerson and Joseph Stinson, another prominent Methodist in the colony, about how best to meet their political and territorial goals.[31]

In heading to Britain, Kahkewaquonaby followed dozens of other Indigenous leaders in bypassing the increasingly settler-focused colonial government in favour of appealing directly to the Crown.[32] Begun in 1710, when three Mohawk leaders and one Mohican crossed the Atlantic to appeal their treatment before Queen Anne, this practice became increasingly common in the nineteenth century. In April 1825, four Wendat chiefs – Nicolas Vincent, André Romain, Michel Sioui, and Stanislas Koska – had an audience with King George IV during a trip coordinated partially by Andrew Stuart, who was also in Europe at the time, and John Neilson, who remained in Quebec.[33] Their visit built upon nearly three decades of petitions and an earlier visit to the British Parliament in 1814 by Joseph Bouchette, another close friend of the two Lower Canadian assemblymen.[34] Mi'kmaw chief Andrew Meuse was also in England in 1825 to petition the Crown for an extensive tract of land on the shores of the Annapolis Basin in the colony of Nova Scotia.[35]

Nor was Kahkewaquonaby's 1837 trip to Britain his first. During a fundraising tour in 1832, Kahkewaquonaby petitioned the Crown over Mississauga grievances, meeting with King William IV just before his return home.[36] During the trip that followed six years later, the introduction for which was facilitated by Ryerson, he met with the newly crowned Queen Victoria; his efforts this time focused on opposing Lieutenant-Governor Francis Bond Head's proposal to remove Indigenous peoples to Manitoulin Island.[37] Three decades later, a Mississauga woman, Nahnebahnwequay (Catharine Sutton), who accompanied Kahkewaquonaby during his first visit, had an audience with Queen Victoria as well as other imperial officials in order to discuss settler encroachment on lands around Lake Simcoe and Georgian Bay.[38]

The alignment between schooling and dispossession can be traced as Anglo-American settlers moved inland following the Seven Years' War.[39] Between 1760 and 1776, about fifty thousand colonists in what would soon become Vermont and New Hampshire created nearly three hundred new towns; within a decade following the American Revolution, an even larger number expanded further into British North America and the Indigenous territories south of Lakes Ontario and Erie.[40] Indigenous engagement with colonial schooling – as opposed to colonial or missionary engagement with Indigenous communities through schools – followed this trajectory of resettlement. In the 1750s in southern New England, where the colonial population was the densest, schools attended by Indigenous students and led by Indigenous teachers existed at Stockbridge, Massachusetts; Mashantucket, Connecticut; and Narragansett, Rhode Island.[41] Colonial observers noted that these schools had fifty-five, thirty, and fifty-three students, respectively. This amounted to nearly 150 Indigenous peoples with some type of settler-society formal schooling in mid-eighteenth-century New England. Similar schools were built in Haudenosaunee communities in the 1760s. After the revolution, as some of these Indigenous people relocated to British North America, Mohawk communities at Grand River and on the Bay of Quinte started schools as early as 1785.[42] In 1792, a visitor to Grand River reported that the school there was attended by sixty-six students, who were taught English and arithmetic, "some of whom had excellent capacities for learning, and read distinctly and fluently."[43] As we have seen, around 1791, the school was founded at Lorette.[44] Twelve years later, another school was created in the Abenaki community of Odanak (with a history similar to Lorette, linking schooling and petitioning to the Crown).[45] As the eighteenth century progressed, similar endeavours began in Anishinaabe communities north of the Great Lakes in communities like Kahkewaquonaby's at Credit River.[46]

A cursory total suggests that well above three hundred Indigenous students in the region had some form of schooling in the period before colonial school systems developed. This was, of course, highly contested terrain. Even though many of these schools were taught by members of their communities, they were all tied in one way or another to European missionary efforts that shared as least some sympathies with Eleazar Wheelock, the president of Moor's Indian Charity School and Dartmouth College, who believed that the work of the school was to send off "godly and faithful [missionaries], as well as learned ministers into these parts of our country, till, the whole continent be filled [by colonists]."[47] In situating these efforts beside the petitions that developed at the same time, it is possible to see how formal petitioning and schooling were tightly bound together. Between 1760 and 1840 – the period when settler colonial hegemony was eventually achieved but was also highly contested – there existed a complex world where schooling in the Canadas was a key site of cultural encounter and contest. This was a period when both Indigenous peoples and colonists were in search of social order. Schools and formal written petitions became two important sites where this contest played out vigorously.

Friendships, Networks, and Strategic Alliances

The Wendat and Mississauga schools and petitions were fuelled by the relationships that developed between prominent colonists and members of the Wendat and Mississauga nations. These relationships had three qualities to them. First, they were personal. Though the degree to which we might use the term *friendship* to describe them can be debated, an expansion of this concept towards its eighteenth-century meanings – described by John Reid elsewhere in this collection – suggests that the term is appropriate in this context. Second, they were anchored in knowledge of the land. Neilson, Ryerson, and Stuart were all familiar with Wendat and Mississauga homelands, having lived nearby the villages at Lorette or Credit River for much of their adult lives. Third, they were strategic, strengthening colonial political, personal, and religious goals within the region. Drawing on Reid's study of friendship, environmental force, and dispossession, we can see in these relationships the complex processes through which settler colonialism gained hegemony in this part of North America.

It is tempting to frame Stuart and Neilson's support for Wendat petitions in light of the Parti canadien / Parti patriote's broader political goals during the 1820s and 1830s vis-à-vis the executive powers of the governor and the so-called Chateau Clique.[48] It seems quite likely that Wendat territorial claims were useful in pitting the assembly against the governor and Legislative Council as the Lower Canadian assembly lobbied for greater political control. Aside from being a response to the executive's tactical use of funds from the Jesuit Estates to offset those frozen by the assembly, Stuart's and Neilson's interactions with the Wendat do not appear to be part of a broader political strategy.[49] Instead, what we see in the archives is a much more personal and local set of connections that drew Wendat and Parti canadien / Parti patriote interests together. The world in which both men lived – and a good number of prominent members of the Parti canadien / Parti patriote as well – was one in which the Wendat played an active part. The point of connection between these two groups was one of the defining set of institutions of settler colonial society: the school and colonial college.

Wendat connections to the Stuart family were long-standing and developed out of the relationship that Sawatanen developed with Andrew Stuart's father, John, following the American Revolution. In late May 1784, Stuart recommended Sawatanen, with a degree from Dartmouth in hand, to the Society for the Propagation of the Gospel as the schoolteacher for the Mohawk who had recently moved to the Bay of Quinte. Outlining Sawatanen's qualifications, Stuart emphasized that he "understands their language, and has had a tolerable education and a competent knowledge of the French and English languages."[50] During this time, Sawatanen also helped Stuart with a translation of the Gospel of Matthew into Mohawk.[51] This relationship was expanded at the turn of the century after Sawatanen returned to Lorette to open a school, and Andrew Stuart, alongside his older brother, James, began to practise law in Quebec. Sawatanen's return to Lorette marked the beginning of the series of formal petitions that led to the Wendat meeting with George IV, but, as early petitions went unresolved during the 1790s and early 1800s, Andrew's social and political network increasingly played a role in keeping Wendat concerns on the political agenda.[52] As we have already seen, when we look at the key players involved in supporting Wendat grievances, Andrew Stuart was at the centre. In addition to John Neilson, who was a business and political associate, Andrew's good friend Joseph Bouchette, the colony's surveyor general, also represented Wendat claims before the Crown.[53] Though we cannot be certain, the earlier relationship between Sawatanen and Stuart's father seems to be the one factor that made Stuart unique among his colleagues. That Andrew's son and namesake was photographed wearing Wendat fashions in the late nineteenth century suggests the possibility of a multigenerational relationship between these families.[54]

We know less about the Wendat relationship with John Neilson. In the early nineteenth century, Sawatanen sent Neilson a series of three letters requesting supplies from the Quebec City printer; he also subscribed to Neilson's newspaper, the *Quebec Gazette*.[55] In all three of the letters, the Wendat schoolteacher referred to Neilson as "the patron and protector of the Huron school."[56] Nearly two decades later, correspondence between the two men reappears. In this case, Sawatanen himself (or perhaps his son, also named Louis Vincent) was active in Neilson's political work with the Parti canadien / Parti patriote. In 1820, an election year, he informed Neilson about the political meeting of an adversary:

> At the Bonhomme Etienne [Dydacouvant], the son of Monsr. McCallum hosted a great dinner for many men, the tavern keepers from the neighbourhoods of St. Jean and St. Roche where the electors of the county come most often, in order to most easily gain the residents' votes, through the counsel of these men during the next election of representatives ... For their recreation, they had the people from our village – the singers and their wives – dance for them a native dance. ha! ha! ha! ha! There were 15 sleighs and at the end of the night they yelled hurrah! For McCallum. I am your servant. Louis Vincent.[57]

The context needed to understand this letter is that Neilson had lost a by-election in 1817 to James McCallum. Neilson had the victory overturned by demonstrating that McCallum had used bullies and bribery to win.[58] This letter was sent less than a month before the next electoral contest between the two (which Neilson won), and it seems that Sawatanen served here as a political informant. Finally, though well after Sawatanen's death in 1825, the Wendat

9.1 Andrew Stuart, John Stuart's grandson (date unknown). Source: Library and Archives Canada/Collection de la famille Aubert de Gaspé/MG18-H44.[59]

lined the streets of their town and fired their minute guns in early winter 1848 as Neilson's casket made its way from St Andrew's Presbyterian Church in Quebec's old city to the village of Valcartier, about thirty kilometers away.[60] The relationship between these men and the Wendat was much deeper than the political intrigue at play in petitioning the Crown.

Kahkewaquonaby and Ryerson did not have as long-standing a relationship as that between Sawatanen and Stuart, but their relationship was stronger. Donald Smith, Kahkewaquonaby's biographer, considers Ryerson to have been the Mississauga man's "best British Canadian friend," and indeed it seems quite reasonable to consider the two friends in a more modern sense than the eighteenth-century understanding outlined in Reid's chapter.[61] Though Ryerson claimed to have been present when Kahkewaquonaby converted to Methodism in 1823, it seems that the two men did not really become acquainted until Ryerson became the missionary at the Credit River in 1826.[62] During his time in the Credit River community, Ryerson was given the name "Cheechock" or "Chechalk" (bird on the wing) and considered the Mississauga as his "own people."[63] Over the subsequent years, their friendship blossomed. By 1833, Kahkewaquonaby wrote to his future wife that she should "have frequent interviews with the Rev. E. Ryerson & that you will talk freely to him, he is a friend in whom I have the greatest confidence."[64] Over the next three decades, the men interacted relatively frequently. During this time, Ryerson worked closely with others from the community, having hired two young boys, William Wilson and John Sawyer, as apprentices to work in his print shop.[65] After leaving his work with Ryerson, Wilson went on to attend Cobourg College (which eventually became the University of Toronto's Victoria University) and Cazenovia College, a centre for people training to become Methodist missionaries.[66] Ryerson supported Wilson throughout his studies, sending him books over the course of the 1830s.[67] In 1847, Ryerson baptized Kahkewaquonaby's son George (Wuhyahsakung).[68] And, as Donald Smith so evocatively demonstrates in *Mississauga Portraits*, the men spent the last couple weeks of Kahkewaquonaby's life together, and Ryerson delivered the eulogy at the Mississauga leader's funeral.

The stories of these two sets of relationships come together through Joseph Brant, after whom Kahkewaquonaby's brother John was named Thayendanegea. The older Thayendanegea (Brant) had been active in liaising between the Mississauga and the British, and it was through his friendship with Augustus Jones, Kahkewaquonaby's father, that the boys' parents were introduced. At the ages of fourteen and eighteen, Kahkewaquonaby and his older brother moved from their mother's Mississauga community to live with their father, who had married a Mohawk woman. For the rest of their youth, their relationship with these people strengthened, eventually leading to Kahkewaquonaby's adoption into Mohawk society, where he was given the name Desagondensta.[69] Kahkewaquonaby's brother John had an even closer relationship: in addition to sharing this name, he was also married to the elder Thayendanegea's granddaughter Kayatontye (Christina Brant).[70]

Although there is little direct evidence placing the elder Thayendanegea as the lynchpin connecting Sawatanen and the Stuarts, there is plenty of circumstantial evidence suggesting that this was the case. John Stuart was the Anglican missionary who served the Mohawk living at Canajoharie, where Thayendanegea grew up.[71] This community was tightly associated with Indian Department Superintendent William Johnson through Thayendanegea's sister Koñwatsi'tsiaiéñni (Molly Brant). It was through Johnson that Thayendanegea and Stuart began to collaborate. During the 1770s, Thayendanegea helped Stuart evangelize and learn the Mohawk language, eventually – like Sawatanen – translating the gospel of Mark into Mohawk; their relationship continued after Stuart moved to what would soon become Upper Canada.[72] The connection between Thayendanegea and Sawatanen is more opaque, but still plausible. Most likely, the two men connected through Moor's Indian Charity School. Though they did not attend at the same time – Thayendanegea was a student there between 1761 and 1763 while it was located in Connecticut – both men retained a meaningful connection to the institution. Thayendanegea sent his two sons, Joseph Jr and Jacob, Kayatontye's father, to the school between 1800 and 1803, while another Vincent from Lorette, perhaps Sawatanen's son, attended briefly in 1807, suggesting a certain degree of continued institutional affiliation on both sides of the relationship.[73]

The relationships between these men were not without their complications. Neilson, Ryerson, and Stuart were all heavily involved in developing and supporting the new colonial regime being imposed along the St Lawrence and lower Great Lakes. Neilson and Stuart not only were important members of the Parti canadien / Parti patriote but were equally involved in the colonization of new lands north of the censives and seigneuries of New France.[74] The two men were partners in establishing and settling the township of Valcartier, located just ten kilometers north of Lorette on land that the Wendat had likely used for well over a century.[75] As figures of local prominence, Stuart and Neilson had plenty of opportunity to encounter members of the Wendat nation. In the early nineteenth century, Stuart, for example, owned land much closer to the Wendat village than Valcartier; it was neighboured by Wendat landholders.[76] His family papers contain a number of copies of notarial records that relate to Wendat landholding.

At Valcartier, the two men employed Wendat men as they began to colonize the region. In an undated note, the manager of Neilson's farm complained that "no Indians appeared last week to assist me," suggesting that he was using Indigenous labour to run the farm.[77] Reinforcing this observation, in 1818 Neilson paid at least four members of the community for constructing a house on his property.[78] And, in 1837, François-Xavier Picard was contracted to survey a road up a local mountain (Mount Tsonotoanne).[79] The irony in all of this is that, although champions of the Wendat cause in the assembly, Stuart and Neilson (and Bouchette as surveyor general) were equally active in bringing about the settlement-related hardships complained about in the Wendat petitions. Michel Lavoie and Maxime Gohier suggest that both men acted in their own self-interest in supporting the petitions in order to facilitate their own political agendas and land acquisition in the region, but the long-standing personal relationships between these men and some Wendat suggest a much more complicated story.[80] What is clear from these interactions is that, in addition to the personal connection between Stuart and Sawatanen, this relationship took on critical economic and political dimensions at the same time as Stuart and Neilson pushed the Wendat claims in the assembly.

Though less involved in the physical expansion of the colony, Ryerson was, as a Methodist missionary, deeply implicated in the colony's evangelical expansion and assimilationist drive. For Ryerson, schooling was central to the missionary project. "The schools to the missions are as important as a foundation is to a building," Ryerson wrote in 1832. "I conceive that the missions may as well be relinquished by the missionaries, as for them to abandon their schools."[81] As time progressed, Ryerson put forward the first report arguing for the development of a system of Indigenous boarding schools somewhat akin to the system that was developed by the Canadian government in the 1880s and 1890s. We must be careful, though, not to draw links too tightly between Ryerson and the later residential school system. Manual labour schools, which were the foundation for Ryerson's planned "industrial schools," were an important curricular movement in the nineteenth century, especially in missionary circles; at least initially, Kahkewaquonaby and many Anishinaabe communities supported the creation of these types of institutions.[82]

Relationships with men such as Stuart, Neilson, and Ryerson were the most significant, but they were not the only relationships with the colonial elite in which the Wendat and Mississauga entered. In addition to that with Ryerson, Kahkewaquonaby and his community maintained other important relationships. Most prominent, perhaps, were Methodist missionaries such as William Case, Conrad Van Dusen, and Joseph Stinson, though the prominent colonist William Lyon Mackenzie also took up their cause in his newspaper, the *Colonial Advocate* and other writings.[83] Around Quebec, the Wendat integrated local leaders into their community's political structure by creating honorary chiefs in recognition of colonists who had assisted the community in a particular way. Actor Edmund Kean was adopted in 1826; later, the community adopted Robert Symes, a justice of the peace who helped the Wendat during an outbreak of cholera, and it recognized the Swedish consul general Folke Cronholm in 1905.[84] At these ceremonies, the Wendat grand chief would address those who had gathered, while the newly inducted honorary chief would receive a bark document inscribed in both Wendat and French with the grand chief's words.[85] It seems quite possible, given the photograph of Andrew Stuart in Wendat honorary clothing, that his photo was taken in this type of context.

Although these honorary relationships were clearly political and likely not indicative of a particularly close relationship between Wendat and Canadian societies, they had substance. In 1844, Robert Symes ordered four pairs of shoes from François-Xavier Picard, who would soon become the nation's grand chief. His letter invokes proximity to the community: "Dear Xavier," he begins after making his order for shoes, "I am sorry to hear of the Death of our Grand Chief. I would have gone to his funeral if I had known of the Event in sufficient time. I very much want to go out to Lorett to see my old friend Madam Laurent who I understand is very sick give my love to her as well as Mary Ann and Thomas and tell them I will try and go to see her soon. with my best Compliments to your Father & Mother and your wife."[86] In addition to these sentimental statements about the nation's members, Symes's language and concern for some members of the community demonstrates a deep attachment.

Nor were Stuart and Neilson likely alone in linking Parti canadien / Parti patriote and Wendat interests. In the first petition written to Lord Dorchester in 1791, in addition to making a clear claim on the seigneury of Sillery, the Wendat also asked that some of their children attend the Petit Seminaire, a school in Quebec that was somewhat akin to Dartmouth (though it was francophone and Catholic). In all, as many as six Wendat boys attended the school during the 1790s and early 1800s. The people that these Wendat students would have encountered at the *seminaire* went on to become some of the colony's most important political players. Names in the school's account books ring out as a veritable who's who of Lower Canadian politics during the 1820s and 1830s: Aubert de Gaspé, Pierre Baby, Antoine Bernard Panet, Michel-Louis Juchereau Duchesnay, Joseph-Rémi Vallières de Saint-Réal, Louis Plamondon, and Louis-Joseph Papineau.[87] In fact, both Papineau – the famed leader of the Parti canadien / Parti patriote – and, Vallières, who helped Stuart and Neilson establish Valcartier, and were similarly involved in facilitating the Wendat petitions, attended the seminaire in the same years that Wendat students attended the school.[88] Duchesnay, who came from one of the region's most established families and later became the colony's superintendent of Indian Affairs, also attended the *seminaire* at this time.[89] His family had a long-standing relationship with the Wendat. They were the seigneurs of the neighbouring seigneury of Gaudarville, where a number of Wendat held land over the course of the eighteenth century.[90] The central point here is that, even if we were to set aside the connections with Andrew Stuart and John Neilson, the Petit Seminaire was a place where many prominent Lower Canadiens would have encountered members of the Wendat community, if only in their youth. In addition to the political stakes, we must consider the legacy of these encounters when thinking about the party's broader support for the Wendat petitions.

There is also an important point to be made here about the influence of Dartmouth College in shaping the Canadas during the early nineteenth century. In marrying Kayatontye (Christina Brant), the younger Thayendanegea (John Jones) married a woman whose father and grandfather had attended Moor's Indian Charity School (the precursor to the college), providing a loose connection between the Mississauga day school on the Credit River and similar schools at Odanak and Lorette that were also started by alumni of the school. Perhaps more importantly, though, was the connection that all of the people discussed in this chapter had with Thaddeus Osgood, another Dartmouth alumnus. While Osgood attended Dartmouth between 1799 and 1803, Kayatontye's father (Jacob Brant) was also in Hanover, attending Moor's Indian Charity School.

Upon graduation, Osgood made Lower and Upper Canada the focus of his missionary work. Turning his emphasis quickly to non-sectarian free schooling, Osgood soon found himself in the company of the five men whose relationships form this chapter's focus. In an 1815 letter, for example, Osgood wrote to John Neilson – one of many letters between the two men – suggesting that funds be allocated to the schoolmaster at "Indian Lorette."[91] Did it matter for Osgood that both he and Sawatanen were Dartmouth alumni? Similarly, was Osgood informed by a relationship with Sawatanen when, in the former's *The Canadian Visitor*, he observed that, during the chiefs' audience with the king in 1825, the Wendat diplomats were assured "that their lands, of which they had been deprived, should be restored, or other lands of equal value granted to them"?[92] Another letter between Osgood and Neilson, dated 21 November 1825 in London, suggests that it was delivered to Neilson in Quebec by "Mr. Stuart, the kind friend who bears this," indicating both that Osgood was himself in Britain during the same year as the Wendat chiefs and that he may also have been with Andrew Stuart at the time, although this is conjecture based on the similarity of the name and the fact that Stuart was in Europe at the time.[93] That same year, though, Stuart's brother, George Okill Stuart, provided a written endorsement for Osgood's written tract *Appeal to Christian Benevolence for the Promotion of Education among the Indians and Destitute Settlers in Canada.*[94] Two years later, in June 1827, Osgood spoke at a Methodist camp meeting twelve miles north of York attended by twenty-five settlers, including Ryerson, and seventy-five Mississauga, for whom Kahkewaquonaby translated and to whom he also preached.[95] This visit was not a single event; Osgood reports having started a Sunday school in the area in the middle of the second decade of the nineteenth century and meeting with William Case and Kahkewaquonaby again at Newmarket during the 1829 winter.[96] Alhough the connections between all of these people remain tenuous, they demonstrate the shared commitment all of these men had to the promise of schooling and their Christian faith, ideas that periodically brought them together over the first decades of the nineteenth century.

This comparison of Wendat and Mississauga relationships with prominent colonial figures focuses our attention on the prominence of Indigenous peoples within some of the major historiographical topics and relationships of nineteenth-century Canadian state formation. Specifically, the argument laid out here builds on Maxime Gohier's work, which makes a similar point about the importance of integrating the historiographies of Indigenous North America and colonial state formation.[97] The commitments to political reform espoused by Ryerson (although he later became a moderate Tory), Neilson, and Stuart, as well as the periodic reference to other reformers such as Louis Joseph Papineau, William Lyon Mackenzie, and William Warren Baldwin, point us towards broader questions about the role of Indigenous peoples during the heady debates of the 1820s and 1830s.[98] Although Indigenous leaders are more often noted for their loyalty to the Crown during the rebellions and for their increasing political marginalization, their alliances with moderate reformers point to a more complex set of interactions and nuanced political perspectives.[99] Far from being marginal to the political debates of the day, the relationships explored in this chapter reinforce Gohier's conclusions about Indigenous petitioning, that, at least for the crusaders for public education, some members of the colonial elite were active in important debates taking place in these Indigenous communities.[100] Perhaps the reverse was also true, especially as it relates to the development of colonial school systems.

Neither these relationships nor the diverse Indigenous perspectives on colonial politics are apparent in more general colony-focused historiography on the Lower and Upper Canadian past. With few exceptions, historians have tended to assume that Indigenous peoples were not present or concerned with the events, people, or intellectual currents that shaped their studies of each colony's development and, for the most part, they have therefore not included them in their discussions of broader patterns of colonial development.[101] Though not an exhaustive study, a cursory glance at some key books underpinning the historiography of this period, the rise of public schooling, or the broader historiographies of Lower and Upper Canada suggests at least some inattention to the relationships outlined in this chapter or the presence of Indigenous schools within the colonies.[102] This absence is no doubt reflective of broader silences in the historical record and source material available to study this time and place, rather than any wilful inattention or simplistic historical methods. In any case, what this chapter has tried to demonstrate is that the limitations of the archive do not necessarily mean absence. The historiographies of Indigenous peoples and the colonial states developing on their lands need not be so isolated from each other.

Looking at the colonies from the biographical perspective of Wendat and Mississauga intellectuals, we see important historiographical themes differently. First, it is easier to see how the Wendat and Mississauga actively protested settler encroachment on their lands. Second, in the process of doing so, and well before colonial systems of education were put into place, these communities built schools where children were taught by members of their own communities. And third, in the alliance between schooling and colonial politics over land, a handful of moderate reformers and key pillars of the developing Upper and Lower Canadian school systems not only had personal relationships with Indigenous peoples but also advocated and intervened on their behalf. None of these men were isolated from nearby Indigenous communities and the pressing concerns of rapid colonial-driven environmental transformation; rather, they were embedded within that context. Likewise, as they advocated for popular schooling, Neilson, Ryerson, and Osgood interacted with men such as Kahkewaquonaby and Sawatanen, who saw in schooling one possible solution to the devastation colonial settlement brought to their communities.

In sum, this alignment between personal relationships, education, and petitioning for land demonstrates the complex and contradictory relationships that developed during this formative period in the history of the settler state. In the similarities between the Wendat and Mississauga, we can see how colonial schooling, formal petition-making, and settler colonialism were deeply intertwined in both Lower and Upper Canada. Looking at these relationships through this lens suggests a need to rethink how we discuss this period, to consider more carefully the role of Indigenous peoples within the colonies' political life, and to ask questions about the relationship among day schools, alphabetic literacies, and the widespread European resettlement of Indigenous lands during the late eighteenth and early nineteenth centuries.

That both the Wendat and Mississauga had such diverse histories up until this time is telling of the uniform nature of this newly arrived settler social order. Indigenous experiences of British settler colonialism became increasingly common as the nineteenth century progressed. And yet these diverse peoples also existed within a settler society that, though aligned in the act of dispossession, was far from united in its politics or religion. The complex ways that Wendat and Mississauga peoples engaged with day schools, and the developing systems of colonial education that Neilson, Ryerson, and Osgood espoused, point us towards a moment in time when there was considerable possibility for crafting the future social and political fabric of both colonies. Those possibilities began to close in the 1830s and were sealed shut following the 1837–8 rebellions.

After that time, a more deliberate colonial strategy of assimilation and "civilization" developed, anchored, as Elsbeth Heaman argues elsewhere in this volume, in the ideas found within the 1828 Darling Report (and, later, in those of the Bagot Commission). Heaman suggests a more complicated transition, emphasizing a continued military emphasis and the role of violence; yet we might similarly muddy the waters by turning our attention to the role played by these personal relationships in crafting the colonial policies of the mid-nineteenth century. Nowhere is this clearer than in Ryerson's own call for a colonial system of education for Indigenous peoples anchored in removing children from their families.[103] Although prominent members of the colonial elite had been interacting with the Wendat and Mississauga for decades, they increasingly espoused a push away from day schooling, and therefore community-based schooling on the land.

Ryerson's prescriptions resonate with those made in the Darling Report and by the Bagot Commission, but they must also be placed within the more specific relationship between Ryerson and Kahkewaquonaby. From this perspective, the technology of the state – as it was deployed to control Indigenous peoples – becomes clearer. At the end of the eighteenth and beginning of the nineteenth centuries, Wendat and Mississauga peoples used schools, alphabetic literacies, and social and political networks as aligned strategies to resist the resettlement and re-ordering of their lands; by mid-century, the settler state – and some of the Wendat's and Mississauga's key allies – worked to separate and isolate these processes, inevitably reducing each nation's social and political influence.[104] The trajectory of this shift was neither clear nor straightforward; it was, rather, complicated by the complex interweaving of individual life courses and the broader patterns of nineteenth-century empire and migration.

NOTES

1 I am very grateful to Donald Smith both for the research notes he has left at the E.J. Pratt Library at Victoria University (University of Toronto) and for the lengthy correspondence that we have begun on these topics. Much of the material about Kahkewaquonaby and Egerton Ryerson comes from our correspondence, Smith's papers or his two books on Mississauga history. See Donald B. Smith, *Sacred Feathers: The Reverend Peter Jones (Kahkewquonaby) and the Mississauga Indians* (Toronto: University of Toronto Press, 1987); and *Mississauga Portraits: Ojibwe Voices from Nineteenth-Century Canada* (Toronto: University of Toronto Press, 2013). I am also grateful to Jerry Bannister, Elizabeth Mancke, Denis McKim, and Scott See for coordinating the two workshops in which this chapter was developed. Finally, Donald Fyson offered significant and substantive advice on this chapter as it developed; it is substantially better for his counsel.

2 This chronology is more fully developed in Thomas Peace and John Reid, "Colonies of Settlement and Settler Colonialism in Northeastern North America," in *Routledge History of Settler Colonialism*, ed. Edward Cavanagh and Lorenzo Veracini (London: Routledge, 2016); and Thomas Peace, "Two Conquests: Aboriginal Experiences of the Fall of New France and Acadia" (PhD diss., York University, 2011).

3 Neal Ferris, *The Archaeology of Native-Lived Colonialism: Challenging History in the Great Lakes* (Tuscon: University of Arizona Press, 2009), 45.

4 Maxime Gohier, "La pratique pétitionnaire des Amérindiens de la Vallée du Saint-Laurent sous le Régime britannique: Pouvoir, représentation, et légitimité (1760–1860)" (PhD diss., Université du Québec à Montréal, 2014), 43. The original citation reads: "l'État n'est pas une entité 'étrangère' aux Autochtones, mais que ceux-ci font partie intégrante de son existance, qu'ils participant à définir sa nature et sa forme."

5 Denys Delâge, Jean-Pierre Sawaya, and Alain Beaulieu have discussed the differences in how the British treated Indigenous peoples in each colony. See Denys Delâge and Jean-Pierre Sawaya, *Les traités des Sept-Feux avec les Britanniques: Droits et pièges d'un héritage colonial au Québec* (Sillery: Septentrion, 2001), 227–33; and Alain Beaulieu, "'An Equitable Right to Be Compensated': The Dispossession of the Aboriginal Peoples of Quebec and the Emergence of a New Legal Rationale (1760–1860)," *Canadian Historical Review* 94, no. 1 (March 2013): 1–27.

6 Recit du Conseil adressé à Monsieur le Colonel Campbell Surint Genl des Affaires Sauvages, 16 December 1791, Library and Archives Canada (hereafter LAC), Superintendent of Indian Affairs, series 2, MG 19 F35, lot 694.

7 Thomas Peace, "Borderlands, Primary Sources, and the Longue Durée: Contextualizing Colonial Schooling at Odanak, Lorette, and Kahnawake, 1600–1850," *Historical Studies in Education* 29, no. 1 (2017): 8–31.

8 Thomas Peace, "The Slow Process of Conquest: Huron-Wendat Responses to the Conquest of Quebec, 1697–1791," in *Revisiting 1759: The Conquest of Canada in Historical Perspective*, ed. Phillip Buckner and John G. Reid (Toronto: University of Toronto Press, 2012), ch. 6; and Alain Beaulieu, Stephanie Bereau, and Jean Tanguay, *Les Wendats du Quebec: Territoire, economie, et identité, 1650–1930* (Quebec City: Les Editions GID, 2013), chs. 5 and 6.

9 See chapter 2 of Victoria Freeman's dissertation on how the so-called Toronto Purchase should be considered an act of outright deception. Victoria Jane Freeman, "'Toronto Has No History!' Indigeneity, Settler Colonialism, and Historical Memory in Canada's Largest City" (PhD diss., University of Toronto, 2010).

10 Although the towns of Quebec and York remained substantially different, the region surrounding each town (York County and the Quebec District) comprised about the same number of people, just over 36,000. See the 1831 census for the Quebec population and 1832 census for York. Government of Canada, *Censuses of Canada, 1665 to 1871* (Ottawa: I.B. Taylor, 1876), 107 and 112.

11 Requête de Louis Vincent, maître d'école à la Jeune-Lorette, adressée aux commissaires des biens des Jésuites, 9 December 1800, Bibliothèque et Archives nationales du Québec à Québec (hereafter BANQ-QUE), Fonds Ministère des Terres et Forêts (E21), Gestion des terres publiques (S64), Biens des Jésuites (SS5), Administration générale gouvrnementale (SSS2), D1623.

12 J.G. Kohl, *Travels in Canada and through the States of New York and Pennsylvania*, vol. 1, trans. Mrs Percy Sinnett (London: George Manwaring, 1861), 177.

13 Réponses du Missionnaire des Hurons de la Jeune Lorette aux questions des Commissaires au Département Indien, Marc 1843, Archives de l'Archidiocèse de Québec (hereafter AAQ), 62 CD Mission Notre Dame-De-Lorette, I-2; see also Appendice du Quartrième volume des journaux de l'Assemblée Législative de la Province du Canada du 28 Novembre 1844 au 29 mars 1845, ces deux jours compris et dans la Huitième année du Règne de Notre Souveraine Dame La Reine Victoria: Première session du second Parlement Provincial du Canada, appendix EEE. For use of the Wendat language, see Mathieu Chaurette, "Les premières écoles autochtones au Québec" (MA thesis, Université du Québec à Montréal, 2011), 36. On schooling in Lower Canada, see Bruce Curtis, *Ruling by Schooling Quebec: Conquest to Liberal Governmentality. A Historical Sociology* (Toronto: University of Toronto Press, 2012), 52–7 and 286–91; Allan Greer, "The Pattern of Literacy in Quebec, 1745–1899," *Histoire sociale / Social History* 11, no. 22 (1978): 334; Roger Magnuson, *Education in New France* (Kingston and Montreal: McGill-Queen's University Press, 1992), 86; and Michel Verrette, *L'alphabétisation au Québec, 1660-1900* (Sillery: Septentrion, 2002), 95–6, 161.

14 Fonds Famille Picard, BANQ-QUE, P883. The full bibliographic references for the texts in this collection are *The Spelling-Book or Introduction to Reading, of The General Sunday-School Society,* 35th ed. (London: T. Smith: No. 19, Little Moorfields, Secretary to the Society, 1811); *Heures nouvelles pour les enfans, à l'usage des écoles* (Chez L. Hovius, Imprimeur-Libraire, place de la Paroisse, Nos 589–90, 1817); and *Neuvaine a l'honneur de St Francois Xavier* (Quebec: J. Neilson, 1814). See Curtis, *Ruling by Schooling Quebec*, 287.

15 Lettre de Mr Derome, ptre, 30 March 1792, AAQ, 61, Charlesbourg, CD I-8; Thaddeus Osgood, *The Canadian Visitor Communicating Important Facts and Interesting Anecdotes respecting the Indians and Destitute Settlers in Canada and the United States of America* (London: Hamilton and Adams, n.d.[1829?]), 23–4.

16 Biographical information taken from Donald B. Smith's *Dictionary of Canadian Biography (DCB)* entries for Kahkewaquonaby and Thayendanegea. See "Peter Jones," http://www.biographi.ca/en/bio/jones_peter_8E.html, accessed May 2016; and "John Jones," http://www.biographi.ca/en/bio/jones_john_1798_1847_7E.html, accessed May 2016.

17 Letter from Egerton Ryerson, 18 April 1827, *Methodist Magazine*, 10, 27, in Donald B. Smith Collection (hereafter Smith), E.J. Pratt Library, box 24, file 9: Ryerson, Aboriginal Peoples, 1803–1829.

18 "The Rev. Mr Ryerson's Evidence on Indian Petitions," *Colonial Advocate*, Parliament of Upper Canada, 4 June 1829, in Smith, b24, file 9.

19 Hope MacLean, "A Positive Experiment in Aboriginal Education: The Methodist Ojibwa Day Schools in Upper Canada, 1824–1833," *Canadian Journal of Native Studies* 22, no. 1 (2002): 46.

20 Maxime Gohier's doctoral dissertation demonstrates well the culture of petitioning that developed in the St Lawrence valley at the end of the eighteenth and beginning of the nineteenth century. Though he does not fully explore the importance of social networks (which he recognizes as a gap in historians' interest, "La pratique pétitionnaire," 59), nor the role of dispossession and the Upper Canadian context (which he somewhat dismisses), in shaping some Lower Canadian petitions, his work well situates Indigenous nations and individuals within the pivotal and considerably complex political transitions of the early nineteenth century. For Gohier, the evolution of Indigenous political identities and state formation must go hand-in-hand – a conclusion similar to the arguments made here about more individual social and political networks.

21 For more detail, see Peace, "The Slow Process of Conquest," 132.

22 House of Assembly, Committee Room, 29 Jan 1819. *Eighth Report of the Committee of the House of Assembly, on That Part of the Speech of His Excellency The Governor in Chief Which Relates to the Settlement of the Crown Lands with the Minutes of Evidence Taken before the Committee* (Quebec: Neilson and Cowen,

1824), 11–12; see also "Timeline of the Huron Community," n.d., Archives du Conseil de la nation huronne-wendat (ACNHW), Collection Francois Vincent, FV/104/6/b6; see also Georges Boiteau, "Les chasseurs hurons de Lorette," (MA thesis, Université Laval, 1954), 56–7, 61; and Denis Vaugeois, *The Last French and Indian War: An Inquiry into a Safe-Conduct Issued in 1760 That Acquired the Value of a Treaty in 1990* (Montreal and Kingston: McGill-Queen's University Press, 2002), 74. Boiteau went so far as to suggest that Sawatanen became someone on whom all of the hope of the community was placed (61). This is clearly an exaggeration; many of his contemporaries were equally involved in these claims and, based on some of their signatures, may have been similarly educated. Nonetheless, his role in the community was important, as was the emphasis that he placed on education.

23 See Ginette Bernatchez, "Andrew Stuart," *DCB online* http://www.biographi.ca/en/bio/stuart_andrew_7E.html, and Sonia Chassé, Rita Girard-Wallot, and Jean-Pierre Wallot, "John Neilson," *DCB online*, http://www.biographi.ca/en/bio/neilson_john_7E.html

24 See Smith, *Sacred Feathers*, ch. 2; Smith, *Mississauga Portraits*, 44–51.

25 For examples, see Toronto Purchase, 1787; 13a in 1805; Treaty 19 in 1818; Treaties 22 and 23 in 1820, in Government of Canada, *Indian Treaties and Surrenders from 1680 to 1890* (Ottawa: B. Chamberlain, 1891), available online, http://eco.canadiana.ca.proxy1.lib.uwo.ca/view/oocihm.91942, accessed May 2016.

26 "Report of the Select Committee to Which Was Referred the Petition of the Indians Residing on the River Credit," *Appendix to Journal of the House of Assembly of Upper Canada* (Toronto: F. Collins, 1829), http://eco.canadiana.ca/view/oocihm.9_00942_5, A-88 to A-90. The petition described here was transcribed by William Lyon Mackenzie in *Sketches of Canada and the United States* (London: E. Wilson, 1833), 133–5.

27 "The Rev. Mr Ryerson's Evidence on Indian Petitions," 4 June 1829; "Report of the Select Committee to Which Was Referred the Petition of the Indians Residing on the River Credit," *Journal of the House of Assembly of Upper Canada*, 8 January to 20 March 1829 (York, UC: Francis Colins, 1829), appendix.

28 W.W. Baldwin, "Report of the Select Committee to Which Was Referred the Petition of the Indians Residing on the River Credit," May 28, 1829, *Colonial Advocate*, 4 in Smith, box 24, file 9.

29 Peter Jones to Egerton Ryerson, 29 Aug 1837, LAC RG10, v. 1011, [transcription] in Smith, box 24, file 10: Ryerson: Aboriginal Peoples, 1830–1839.

30 Ryerson to Rt. Hon. The Lord Glenelg, 2 Oct 1837, LAC RG10, v. 1011, T-1456, 121–2 in Smith, box 24, file 10.

31 Peter Jones, *History of the Ojebway Indians* (London: A. W. Bennett, 1861), 263.

32 See Alden Vaughan, *Transatlantic Encounters: American Indians in Britain, 1500–1776* (Cambridge: Cambridge University Press, 2006); Jace Weaver, *The Red Atlantic: American Indigenes and the Making of the Modern World, 1000–1927* (Chapel Hill: University of North Carolina Press, 2014).

33 Nicolas Vincent to John Neilson, 4 January 1825; Andrew Stuart to John Neilson, 23 July 1825; Butterworth to John Neilson, 27 July 1825; Butterworth to John Neilson, 2 Aug 1825 in Neilson Collection, LAC MG24-B1, vol. 5, 19–22, 124–30, 138–41, and 142–5.

34 *Eighth Report of the Committee of the House of Assembly.*

35 L.F.S. Upton, "Andrew Meuse," *DCB online*, http://www.biographi.ca/en/bio/meuse_andrew_james_7E.html, accessed May 2016.

36 Smith, "Peter Jones," *DCB.*

37 Smith, *Mississauga Portraits*, 75.

38 Ibid., 86, 90.

39 Here I have focused mostly on community schools created within Indigenous communities and taught by Indigenous schoolteachers. Alongside these schools, colonial officials and missionaries also sought to use schooling more directly as a tactic of dispossession. For one nuanced example, see Jean-Pierre Sawaya, "Les Amérindiens domiciliés et le protestantisme au XVIIIe siècle: Eleazar Wheelock et le Dartmouth College," *Historical Studies in Education / Revue d'histoire de l'éducation* 22 (Fall 2010): 18–38.

40 David Jaffee, *People of the Wachusett: Greater New England in History and Memory, 1630–1860* (Ithaca, NY: Cornell University Press, 1999), 163; see also Peace and Reid, "Colonies of Settlement and Settler Colonialism."

41 Linford Fisher, *The Indian Great Awakening: Religion and the Shaping of Native Cultures in Early America* (New York: Oxford University Press, 2012), 163.

42 Charles M. Johnston, ed., *The Valley of the Six Nations: A Collection of Documents on the Indian Lands of the Grand River* (Toronto: Champlain Society, 1964), 46, 52, 93, 245.

43 Ibid., 60.

44 Jonathan Lainey and Thomas Peace, "Louis Vincent Sawantanan, premier bachelier autochtone canadien," in *Vivre la Conquête*, vol. 1, ed. Gaston Deschênes and Denis Vaugeois (Sillery: Septentrion, 2013), 204–14. A modified English version of this essay appears as "Louis Vincent Sawatanen: A Life Forged by Warfare and Migration," in *Aboriginal History: A Reader*, ed. Kristin Burnett and Geoff Read (Toronto: Oxford University Press, 2016), 106–16.

45 Jean Barman, *Abenaki Daring: The Life and Writings of Noel Annance* (Montreal and Kingston: McGill University Press, 2016), ch. 2; Gohier, "La pratique pétitionnaire," 222–3.

46 MacLean, "A Positive Experiment in Aboriginal Education," 46.

47 Eleazar Wheelock, *A Continuation of the Narrative of the Indian Charity School* (1771), 26. For a related but somewhat different take on the influence of Wheelock's schools on the St Lawrence valley, see Sawaya, "Les Amérindiens domiciliés."

48 Gohier, "La pratique pétitionnaire," 262 and 521; Michel Lavoie, "'C'est ma seigneurie que je réclame': Le lutte des Hurons de Lorette pour la seigneurie de Sillery, 1760–1888" (PhD diss., Université Laval, 2006), 230.

49 Lavoie, "'C'est ma seigneurie,'" 244.

50 *Journal of the Society for the Propagation of the Gospel*, vol. 23, 379–81, as cited in John Wolfe Lydekker, "The Rev. John Stuart, D.D. (1740–1811): Missionary to the Mohawks," *Historical Magazine of the Protestant Episcopal Church* 11, no. 1 (March 1942): 44–5.

51 See C.M. Johnston, "John Deserontyon," *DCB online*, http://www.biographi.ca/en/bio/deserontyon_john_5E.html, accessed May 2016.

52 It is important to also note that, by the end of the 1820s, Andrew Stuart's older brother James – who was for a brief time the leader of the Parti canadien – had also become involved in these claims. By this time, however, the elder Stuart had become a more stalwart supporter of the executive, being appointed the colony's attorney general in 1825. In this capacity, he most actively opposed the Wendat claims. See Attorney General Stuart's opinion on the claim of the Lorette Indians, 28 April 1829 and Attorney General Stuart to Lieut. Col. Yorke, civil secretary to James Kempt, 17 Aug 1830, in *Continuation of the Appendix to the XLIInd Volume of the Journals of the House of Assembly of the Province of Lower Canada, session 1832–3*, appendix OO, 2, 24. See Vaugeois, *The Last French and Indian War*, 74–6 and 161–4; also Lavoie, "C'est ma seigneurie,'" 271–84; Gohier, "La pratique pétitionnaire," 260–4.

53 Reference to Stuart's friendship with Bouchette can be found in Bernatchez, "Andrew Stuart." Bouchette's claim to have represented the Wendat in England can be found in the *Eighth Report of the Committee of the House of Assembly*, 16 and 53.

54 Collection de la famille Aubert de Gaspé, LAC, MG18-H44.

55 Fonds Imprimerie Neilson, BANQ-QUE, P193.

56 Louis Vincent to John Neilson, 2 November 1799, Fonds Famille Neilson, BANQ-QUE, P192; see also, in the same collection, Louis Vincent to John Neilson, 2 December 1795, and Louis Vincent to John Neilson, 19 November 1800.

57 Neilson collection, LAC, MG24-B1, vol. 190, 5012-5014, author's translation. The original text reads: "Chez le Bonhomme Etienne Dydacouvant, Monsr McCallum fils a donné un grand diner a plusieurs Messieurs des (Tavern Keepers) des Fauxbourgs de St Jean et de St Roche ou les Electeurs du Conté frequent le plus, pour se procurer plus facilement les votes des habitants de l'endroit, par l'entremise de ces Messieurs, a la prochaine election du Répresantants, a ce qu'il est [supposé] et dans leurs[bale] ils ont eu les gens de notre village pour leur dancer une [danse]

sauvage pour recréation de ces messieurs les Cantonniers et de leurs Dames aussi. // ha ! ha ! ha ! ha ! // ils étoit 15 carioles, et le soir en partant ils crioient, hora ! pour Mccallum. // Je suis votre Serviteur. // Louis Vincent."

58 James H. Lambert, "James McCallum," *DCB online*, http://www.biographi.ca/en/bio/mccallum_james_6E.html, accessed May 2016.

59 Thanks to Jonathan Lainey for bringing this photograph to my attention.

60 "Death of the Hon. John Neilson," *Globe*, 16 February 1848.

61 Smith, *Mississauga Portraits*, ch. 1.

62 Egerton Ryerson, *Christian Guardian*, 30 July 1871, in Smith, box 24, file 9.

63 Smith, *Mississauga Portraits*, 19–21.

64 Peter Jones to Eliza Freed, 10 April 1833 in Smith, box 24, file 9.

65 See Peter Jones, *Life and Journals of Kah-ke-wa-quo-na-by* (Toronto: Anson Green, 1860), 266, and William Case, *Christian Advocate*, 2 April 1830 in Smith, box 24, file 10.

66 Smith, notes, box 24, file 10.

67 Wilson to Ryerson, 5 March 1838, United Church of Canada Archives, in Smith, box 24, file 10.

68 Louise Thorp, Family bible of Peter Jones, August 1847, in Smith, box 24, file 9.

69 Smith, *Sacred Feathers*, chs 1–3.

70 Smith, "John Jones."

71 T.R. Millman, "John Stuart," *DCB online*, http://www.biographi.ca/en/bio/stuart_john_1740_41_1811_5E.html, accessed May 2016.

72 Barbara Graymont, "Thayendanegea," *DCB online*, http://www.biographi.ca/en/bio/thayendanegea_5E.html, accessed May 2016.

73 For a detailed list of Indigenous students at the school, see Colin G. Calloway, *The Indian History of an American Institution: Native Americans and Dartmouth* (Hanover, NH: Dartmouth College Press, 2010), appendix 1 and 2.

74 Gohier, "La pratique pétitionnaire," 263; Vaugeois, *The Last French and Indian War*, 161.

75 Lavoie, "'C'est ma seigneurie,'" 233. See also Peace, "Two Conquests," 271–3.

76 Vente par Genevieve Barbeau veuve de Louis Cliche à André Stuart, 6 July 1816; Echange et permutation entre Jean Baptiste Sébastien et Judith Sébastien, sa fille, 18 August 1836, Fonds Famille Stuart, BANQ-QUE, P294.

77 Neilson collection, LAC, MG24-B1, vol. 191, 5131.

78 Ibid., 5146–7. See also 5169, which references field work; 5233 for road building; and 5216 for survey work.

79 Ibid., vol. 38, 959.

80 Gohier, "La pratique pétitionnaire," 263–4; Lavoie, *The Last French and Indian War*, 233; In noting that Stuart and Neilson's support for the 1835 petition occurred after both had left the increasingly radical Parti patriote, Gohier alludes

to there being broader factors at play than just the financial politics between the assembly and executive. He does not, however, examine these additional factors in his dissertation. See Gohier, "La pratique pétitionnaire," 524.

81 Ryerson, *The Christian Guardian*, 22 Feb 1832, 59; cited in MacLean, "The Hidden Agenda: Methodist Attitudes to the Ojibwa and the Development of Indian Schooling in Upper Canada, 1821–1860," (MA thesis, University of Toronto, 1978), 30.

82 Paul Axelrod, *The Promise of Schooling: Education in Canada, 1800–1914* (Toronto: University of Toronto Press, 1997), 72–3. An interesting point of comparison that remains to be done would be to situate the founding of the Indigenous-focused Mount Elgin Institute at Munceytown in 1850, an institution championed by Kahkewaquonaby, beside the founding of the British American Institute at the relatively nearby Free-Black Dawn settlement eight years earlier. For similarities, compare Smith, *Mississauga Portraits*, 235–7, with Paul Goodman, "The Manual Labor Movement and the Origins of Abolitionism," *Journal of the Early Republic*, 13, no. 3 (Autumn 1993): 366–7. Both works emphasize the importance of Philip Emanuel von Fellenberg's school at Hofwil, near Berne, Switzerland in shaping ideas about manual labour schooling. It was upon visiting Fellenberg's school that Ryerson's ideas about industrial schooling for Indigenous peoples took shape.

83 See Smith, *Mississauga Portraits*, 50; Mackenzie, *Sketches*, 133.

84 Annette de Stecher, "Wendat Arts of Diplomacy: Negotiating Change in the Nineteenth Century," in *From Huronia to Wendakes: Adversity, Migrations, and Resilience, 1650–1900*, ed. Kathryn Labelle and Thomas Peace (Norman: University of Oklahoma Press, 2016), 189. For Symes, see McCord Museum, M20009; LAC, R9266-2676 & R9266-2677; and LAC, W.H. Coverdale Collection acc. no. 1970-188-641. See also http://www.donaldheald.com/pages/books/19496/after-henry-daniel-thielcke/the-presentation-of-a-newly-elected-chief-of-the-huron-tribe-canada#sthash.UWLnESYP.dpuf, accessed May 2016.

85 de Stecher, "Wendat Arts of Diplomacy," 189.

86 Letter from R. Symes to Picard, 7 November 1844, BANQ-QUE, Fonds Famille Picard, P883.

87 Centre de reference de l'Amérique française, Séminaire de Québec, c. 36 and c. 37.

88 On Saint-Réal's involvement in the petitions see Gohier, "La pratique pétitionnaire," 260.

89 See LAC, MG24-B1, Neilson Collection, vol. 20, files 168–69 and files 188–202

90 See Céline Cyr, "Michel-Louis Juchereau Duchesnay" *DCB* online, http://www.biographi.ca/en/bio/juchereau_duchesnay_michel_louis_7F.html, accessed May 2016; Peace, "Two Conquests," 269–70; and Benoît Grenier, *Marie-Catherine Peuvret: Veuve et seigneuresse en Nouvelle-France, 1667–1739* (Sillery: Septentrion, 2005), 128, 218.

91 See LAC, MG24-B1, Neilson Collection, vol. 2, files 508–11.

92 Osgood, *The Canadian Visitor*, 23.

93 Thaddeus Osgood to John Neilson, 21 November 1825, LAC, MG24-B1, Neilson Collection, vol. 17, file 37.

94 Thaddeus Osgood, *Appeal to Christian Benevolence for the Promotion of Education among the Indians and Destitute Settlers in Canada* (1825), in LAC, MG24-B1, Neilson Collection, vol. 17, file 32.

95 Egerton Ryerson, *The Story of My Life*, 74–5; Thaddeus Osgood, *The Canadian Visitor* (1829), 38.

96 Osgood, *The Canadian Visitor*, 70.

97 Gohier, "La pratique pétitionnaire" ch. 1.

98 David Mills, *The Idea of Loyalty in Upper Canada, 1784–1850* (Montreal and Kingston: McGill-Queen's University Press, 1988), ch. 4 (esp. 66–7).

99 On Indigenous loyalty to the Crown, see Colin Read and Ronald J. Stagg, eds, *The Rebellion of 1837 in Upper Canada* (Ottawa: Carleton University Press, 1985), lvi–lvii.

100 For articulations of his historiographical framing, see Gohier, "La pratique pétitionnaire," ch. 1, specifically section 1.1.4, which begins on page 51.

101 Aside from Maxime Gohier's recent thesis, the sole exception that I have come across is Jeffrey L. McNairn, *The Capacity to Judge: Public Opinion and Deliberative Democracy in Upper Canada, 1791–1854* (Toronto: University of Toronto Press, 2000), 219–20. Here McNairn points to three addresses written by the Mohawk on the Bay of Quinte; Chippawas, Munsees, Oneidas, and Delawares of the Thames River; and thirteen chiefs from the Western District. They wrote in support of the governor, Charles Metcalfe. In his analysis, McNairn observes, "These addresses signalled both native awareness of colonial political debate and the different stances assumed by observers of that debate and its full participants" (p. 219).

102 Here is an assessment of coverage of Indigenous people is the more general colonial-focused historiography of this period, based on book indexes. An asterix indicates that the index has an entry for Ryerson, Neilson, or Stuart. On the Rebellions, see Michel Ducharme, *Le concept de liberté au Canada à l'époque des Révolutions atlantiques, 1776–1838* (Montreal and Kingston: McGill-Queen's University Press, 2010), no references*; Allan Greer, *The Patriots and the People: The Rebellion of 1837 in Rural Lower Canada* (Toronto: University of Toronto Press, 1993), 320–1, 344, 346–9 (7 pages)*; Colin Read, *The Rising in Western Upper Canada, 1837–38* (Toronto: University of Toronto Press, 1982), 12, 19–20, 22, 34, 75–6, 87, 99–100, 105, 115, 130, 138–9, 142, 146–7, 155, 169, 206 (21 pages)*; on education, see Axelrod, *The Promise of Schooling*, 4, 27, 70–8 (14 pages)*; Curtis, *Ruling by Schooling Quebec*, 100–1 (2 pages)*; Bruce Curtis,

Building the Educational State: Canada West, 1836–1871 (London, ON, Althouse Press, 1988), no references**; Anthony DiMascio, *The Idea of Popular Schooling in Upper Canada* (Montreal and Kingston: McGill-Queen's University Press, 2012), 14 and 84 (2 pages)*; Susan E. Houston and Alison Prentice, *Schooling and Scholars in Nineteenth Century Ontario* (Toronto: University of Toronto Press, 1988), 6, 29, 37–8, 45, 57 (6 pages)*; in the broader historiography of Lower and Upper Canada, see Jane Errington, *The Lion, the Eagle, and Upper Canada: A Developing Colonial Ideology* (Montreal and Kingston: McGill-Queen's University Press, 1987), no references*; Donald Fyson, *Magistrates, Police, and People: Everyday Criminal Justice in Quebec and Lower Canada, 1764–1837* (Toronto: University of Toronto Press, 2006), 22–3, 81, 290, 302–4, 308, 349, 361, 397n77 (10 pages)*; F. Murray Greenwood, *Legacies of Fear: Law and Politics in Quebec in the Era of the French Revolution* (Toronto: University of Toronto Press, 1993), no references**; J.I. Little, *Loyalties in Conflict: A Canadian Borderland in War and Rebellion, 1812–1840* (Toronto: University of Toronto Press, 2008), vii, 3–4, 107 (4 pages); McNairn, *The Capacity to Judge*, 80n40, 104n115, 131, 219–20, 347, 435–6 (8 pages); Cecilia Morgan, *Public Men and Virtuous Women: The Gendered Languages of Religion and Politics in Upper Canada, 1791–1850* (Toronto: University of Toronto Press, 1996), 5–6, 10, 16–8, 26, 32–4, 69, 93, 98–9, 121, 133–9, 153, 165–6, 171–2, 175, 181–2, 185, 196, 221 (32 pages)*; Carol Wilton, *Popular Politics and Political Culture in Upper Canada, 1800–1850* (Montreal and Kingston: McGill-Queen's University Press, 2000), no references*; total pages in the fifteen books covered: 106 pages.

103 Government of Canada, *Statistics Respecting Indian Schools with Dr Ryerson's Report of 1847 Attached* (Ottawa: Government Printing Bureau, 1898), appendix A.

104 Though his analysis is complicated somewhat by the personal and intercolonial contexts outlined here, Gohier's dissertation "La pratique pétitionnaire" well outlines the reflexive way this process worked.

10 Runaway Advertisements and Social Disorder in the Maritimes: A Preliminary Study

HARVEY AMANI WHITFIELD[1]

The Context of Runaways

After the American Revolution, New York Loyalist Frederick William Hecht moved to Saint John, New Brunswick, and found employment at Fort Howe as an assistant commissary.[2] In July 1784, he placed an advertisement in the *Royal St John's Gazette* complaining that his "negro man slave, named Hector," had recently escaped.[3] Hecht unwittingly left historians plenty of information about Hector, and therefore scholars can partially reconstruct some of this slave's life. First, Hector worked as a cooper, so he had an important skill that would have been valuable in Saint John. Second, he had travelled throughout the Atlantic world and along the North American coast. Hecht noted, "[Hector] came from St. Augustine [Florida] to this place, via New-York." Moreover, aside from being "very talkative," Hecht noted that Hector, "speaks English much like the West-India negroes."[4] This detail indicates that Hector might have been from Africa and that he almost certainly had lived in the Caribbean. Thus, Hector was a well-travelled slave, having possibly lived in Africa and the West Indies and then St Augustine, briefly New York, and finally Saint John. Lastly, Hecht described his slave as being slender and tall with "a lazy gait."[5]

This runaway slave advertisement is also notable because it raises questions about unrest, violence, and the search for social order in the new loyalist city of Saint John. These are worthy topics to be explored in the context of runaway slaves and their tenuous place in the Maritimes, but the most important aspect of these advertisements is what they say about the slaves. They were living and breathing people, and historians must try to recover as much as possible about their lives: who they were, where they lived, what work they did, who they married, their physical appearance and personality traits, and if they secured freedom. The sources will not allow us to answer all of these important questions about an individual slave's life, but runaway notices illuminate the lives of slaves in ways that historians might not otherwise be able to document.[6] In terms of societal unrest, runaway slaves in the Maritimes challenged the prevailing and emerging social order by taking advantage of the unrest caused by the American Revolution, and the subsequent resettlement of approximately thirty thousand Loyalists.[7] In running away, slaves asserted their autonomy, rejected the violence that was inherent in the system of slavery, reunited with and protected their families, and cast doubt on the place of slavery in the Maritime colonies.

While they escaped for a variety of reasons, including concerns about their family, desire for autonomy, and protest against violence or other forms of mistreatment, the foundational reason was freedom. Yet their quest for freedom should not blind historians to the fact that some runaways also used temporary escape as a way to negotiate for improved conditions *within* slavery, such as more freedom to visit a relative or improved working circumstances. Historian Billy Smith captures this type of negotiation between slaveholders and female slaves, arguing that "some women [and, I would add, men] employed escape and other forms of resistance as bargaining devices to assert some control over their own lives and to curtail the power of their owners. This strategy might not gain their freedom, but it could improve the lives of slaves who desired a different master or wanted to live closer to kin and friends."[8] Runaway advertisements depict black people challenging the social order envisaged by their owners. Whatever the case, running away fundamentally disturbed and challenged the status quo of a relationship between slave and owner and also between slaves and the wider society. In challenging the social order, runaway slaves and runaway black servants anticipated a series of reforms in the legislatures of Nova Scotia and New Brunswick that consistently blocked any statutory recognition of slavery, despite the best efforts of slave owners to secure such laws.

The complex formation of Maritime slavery happened in the crucible of war, migration, and resettlement. After the influx of American Loyalists and their slaves to the Maritimes, slavery became widespread, and racism increasingly entrenched. It is a mistake, however, to see the region as monolithically dedicated to slavery and racism. Though slavery remained common, it was also highly contested by anti-slavery legislators, judges, lawyers, and religious groups. The number of slaves increased after the loyalist influx, but slavery remained legally insecure and somewhat unstable because, although it was recognized under common law as a form of private property ownership, it had no statutory basis (such as a slave code) in Nova Scotia or New Brunswick. In Prince Edward Island, an act that dealt with slave baptism gave statutory recognition to slavery.[9]

But the tenuousness of slavery elsewhere in the Maritimes is highlighted by the numerous attempts by owners to gain statutory protection for their property (in 1787, 1789, 1801, and 1808 in Nova Scotia, and in 1801 in New Brunswick). They were defeated each time.[10] Yet Maritime slavery seems to have lasted into the early 1820s, and owners constantly fought in the courts and legislatures to protect their rights to their human property.

The runaway advertisements, especially those from the 1780s and 1790s, must be understood as part of the wider loyalist diaspora after the American Revolution. Between 1783 and 1785, individuals from a complex constellation of American slaveries, from East Florida to northern Massachusetts, settled in the Maritimes. Slave owners and slaves struggled to redefine what slavery meant by relying partially on past experiences while confronting the pressing realities of settlement, climate, soil, and economy. The first years after the loyalist influx to the Maritimes were devoted to defining a system of slavery that was complicated by the large population of free black Loyalists, the lack of clarity regarding slavery's legal status, and the willingness of loyalist slaves to abscond and challenge the emerging social order so that they could win freedom, gain autonomy, and reunite their families or protect them from predatory owners.[11] On the other side, local whites regularly re-enslaved free blacks and sold them into slavery in the West Indies.

In the Maritimes, the labels of *free*, *servant*, and *slave* could quickly change through running away or re-enslavement. These categories, and their permeability, are probably the most significant issue related to black life in the Maritimes in the late eighteenth and early nineteenth century. A black person might arrive in New Brunswick as a slave, only to escape from her owner before being recaptured and sold to the West Indies. Another individual might begin his sojourn in Nova Scotia as a free person, be subjected to indentured servitude followed by re-enslavement, eventually escape, and finally enjoy freedom in Sierra Leone. The case of Lydia Jackson is instructive. Originally, she settled at Manchester (Guysborough Township, Nova Scotia) with other free blacks. As a result of poverty and desertion by her husband, Jackson indentured herself to a Loyalist for what she thought would be a short time. It turned out that this person had tricked Jackson into signing an indenture that essentially made her a servant for life. This man then sold her as a slave to a Dr Bulman. As a slave of the doctor, Jackson suffered from the most brutal mistreatment. Bulman regularly beat "her with the tongs, sticks, pieces of rope &c. about the head and face." John Clarkson, a Royal Navy officer and organizer of the black loyalist exodus to Sierra Leone in 1792, noted that, eventually, Jackson escaped to Halifax. Jackson's owner planned on "selling her to some planter in the West Indies to work as a slave."[12] Lydia Jackson's story must be considered in the context of

Clarkson's comment, "I do not know what induced me to mention the above case as I have many others of a similar nature; for example, Scott's case, Mr. Lee, Senr. case, Smith's child, Motley Roads child, Mr. Farish's negro servant, &c."[13]

In the case of re-enslavement, historians can only speculate about how many black people who were kidnapped and sold to the West Indies never had their stories come before a court.[14] The kidnapping of black people in Nova Scotia became widespread enough that legislators attempted in 1789 to pass An Act for the Regulation and Relief of the Free Negroes within the Province of Nova Scotia. Although the bill failed, it affirmed that "attempts have been made to carry some of them out of the Province, by force and Strategem [*sic*], for the scandalous purpose of making property of them in the West Indies contrary to their will and consent."[15] Based on information from a local observer (possibly his brother John), the anti-slavery advocate Thomas Clarkson outlined the problems that free blacks faced in the Maritimes: "It was not long till these loyalists, many of whom had been educated with all the ideas of the justice of slavery, the inferiority of negroes, and the superiority of white men, that are universal in the southern provinces of America, began to harass and oppress the industrious black settlers, and even wantonly to deprive them of the fruits of their labour, expelling them from the lands they had cleared."[16] Clarkson continued by noting that whites reduced "again to slavery those negroes who had so honourably obtained their freedom. They hired them as servants, and, at the end of the stipulated time, refused payment of their wages, insisting that they were slaves: in some instances they destroyed their tickets of freedom, and then enslaved the negroes for want of them; in several instances, the unfortunate Africans were taken onboard vessels, carried to the West Indies, and there sold for the benefit of their plunderers."[17]

The line between black servants and black slaves was extremely fluid and could easily be transgressed, crossed, and manipulated. Even those blacks who were indentured servants were often treated as slaves and consistently faced the fear of being sold to the West Indies or elsewhere. How much did white Loyalists truly distinguish between an indentured black servant and a black slave? More importantly, did indentured black servants and slaves see each other as having different statuses? Black servants and black slaves sometimes ran away together, usually from the same master. For example, South Carolina Loyalist Nathaniel Bullern complained about the loss of, "TWO NEGRO – the Property of Mr. Nath. Bullern, the One an indented Servant, the Other a Slave."[18] These two people, servant and slave, were both part of a world of "unfreedom."[19] In running away together, they saw their status as similar, if not the same. The fugitives, Jupiter and Clarinda, had both arrived in Nova Scotia as slaves, but shortly after their arrival Bullern had freed one of them.[20] Several court cases in Shelburne in the 1780s and 1790s show how easily black people could fall victim to re-enslavement but also the ways in which they could go to court, defeat attempts at re-enslavement, and ultimately achieve freedom. The first years after the loyalist influx were, at best, confusing and complicated in terms of the changing status of free black, black servant, and black slave. Runaway advertisements included black indentured servants and black servants. Does that mean that these people were virtually enslaved? Obviously, it would depend on their masters, but black servants operated in a world where they could easily be sold as slaves to the United States or West Indies. Were their lives any different than their enslaved brethren? Again, the answer varied by individual.

After the loyalist influx, runaway slaves were enmeshed in a region where black bondage had existed from the time of early European settlement. For a century before the loyalist arrival, the Maritimes were intimately connected through commerce, migration, and trade to the wider trends of the Atlantic world. Slavery existed in both the French and English spheres of interest in the region. Historian Ken Donovan has illuminated the lives of over four hundred slaves in Île Royale (Cape Breton) between 1713 and 1815. After the founding of Halifax in 1749, the British government wanted to encourage the settlement of Protestants, and this resulted in an influx of New England planters who brought slaves to various parts of the Maritimes. Although the absolute numbers of slaves in the region were not large, there were several basic trends among slaves and slaveholders that would be greatly expanded after the loyalist settlement. In both Île Royale and New England planter settlements, slavery was defined by close interactions between owners and slaves, due to the small number of slaves per household, multi-occupational slaves who worked with their owners in a mixed economy, and trading connections with the British Atlantic, especially in the West Indies. Thus, before the arrival of possibly 1,500 to 2,000 loyalist slaves, structures of black labour exploitation, racism, and trade connections to the West Indies were already well established.[21]

Runaways, Agency, and Autonomy

Slaves absconded for an array of reasons, including the desire for freedom, hope for greater autonomy, the desire to escape the horrors of physical abuse, and attempts at family reunification. In running away, slaves challenged their owners, asserted their autonomy, and attempted to gain freedom. As the American historiography so poignantly shows, runaway slaves were examples of the enduring goal of freedom, dignity, and the taking of their humanity back from owners who wished to extinguish any aspirations for liberty. Each runaway notice is a testament to an individual's declaration of personal independence.[22]

The advertisements also show how black slaves and servants rejected a social order that stole their labour and attempted, but failed, to destroy their humanity. The print culture that benefited from slave notices inscribed black people's rejection of the social order and how they fought against their bondage. As historian David Waldstreicher notes, "individual acts of running away proved to be profoundly destabilizing, even comparable over the long term to the slave rebellions and other collective acts of resistance in the South and the Caribbean."[23] In the Maritimes, this type of resistance challenged local white politicians, judges, and other elites to think about the place of slavery in the region. The instability caused by runaway blacks made slavery itself seem troublesome and perhaps even untenable. Although the runaway notices reflect the opinion of slave owners, they also represent "the first slave narratives – the first published stories about slaves and their seizure of freedom," precisely because masters had good reason to be accurate in their portrayal of the escaped slave if they hoped to recapture her or him.[24] When read carefully, runaway notices highlight various aspects of an individual slave's personality. Sometimes, masters grudgingly admitted that a slave was daring and intelligent. For example, New Brunswick master John Agnew complained that his "NEGRO MAN slave" Prince, "is artful, has a gloomy and malevolent look – is a daring liar, and has attempted twice before this to RUNAWAY."[25]

Still, runaway advertisements have limitations as primary sources for historians. They do not come close to recording all people of African descent who absconded from their owners. The runaway notices also must be distinguished from the slave-for-sale advertisements that percolated throughout Maritime newspapers.[26] For-sale notices quite often provided a decent description of a slave but almost never provided the name of the slave, which makes them quite different from runaway advertisements. These nameless black slaves in for-sale notices say something about the control and victimization of black personhood, reducing their complex and worthy lives to a description of stolen labour. For example, in 1786, the printer of the *Royal American Gazette* described a young teenager as "A Healthy, stout, NEGRO BOY, about fourteen Years of Age. – He has been brought up in a Gentleman's Family, is very handy at Farming, House-Work, or attending Table, is strictly honest, and has an exceeding good Temper."[27] One New Brunswick owner described a slave for sale as a "healthy negro wench, of about 17 years of age, [who] is well calculated for the country."[28] Another New Brunswick slave owner offered to sell his female slave who "is well acquainted with all kinds of household business, and [in] particular is an excellent COOK."[29]

Despite the limitations of runaway notices, we can draw some general conclusions about runaways in the Maritime region. The most striking aspect of runaway advertisements is their stunning diversity. In this sense, Maritime runaways were very similar to their American counterparts. In their important study, *Runaway Slaves: Rebels on the Plantation*, John Hope Franklin and Loren Schweninger note that "the profile of a runaway reveals a diversity in origin, appearance, language, skills, color, physique, gender, and age."[30] In Nova Scotia and New Brunswick, runaways included men and women; both African- and American-born slaves; carpenters and less skilled individuals; those who spoke "Good English" and others who conversed like "West-India" blacks; the very young child to much older women and men; those who were "quick-spoken" and others slow of speech; and many who had escaped alone and others who had decided to abscond with loved ones or friends. Other common features of regional runaways mirrored broader patterns of runaways in North America. For example, the majority of runaways were relatively young, healthy men. They were usually under thirty and probably did not have children. It should be noted that a significant minority of female slaves also absconded, but usually within the context of group or family escape attempts.[31]

Runaway advertisements represented a battle between slave (and sometimes black servant, whether free or indentured) autonomy and the master's authority. Absconding sent a clear message to the owner that there were things that a slave would not tolerate. Slave owners responded to runaways by publishing notices threatening to use the law or other measures to retain the services of their escaped human property. They were reasserting their authority and attempting to restore the social order, which slaveholders thought sanctioned and supported black bondage – whether as slaves or indentured servants. The runaway notices were also an attempt by slave owners to define and regularize black slavery in the Maritimes. In reality, the protean character of Maritime slavery allowed plenty of space for slaves to escape successfully but also provided whites with the opportunity to re-enslave free blacks.

Some cases of slave escape involved clear contests and debates over the terms of enslavement as understood by the master. In these cases, slaveholders were faced with a form of rebellion within their own households. This caused stress, financial expenditure (for the runaway notice and perhaps a reward), and time re-establishing control. In 1781, Abel Michener placed an advertisement in one of Nova Scotia's newspapers, complaining that his "Negro Man" James had escaped. Michener described James's apparel and noted that he had a "lively countenance." James was a valuable slave, and Michener offered "Five Pounds" reward for anyone willing to capture him and put him in "His Majesty's Goals [Jails]." Although he warned others about concealing or harbouring the fugitive, Michener also noted that, if "the said JAMES, will return to his Master, he shall be forgiven."[32] Michener's blunt offer of forgiveness is extremely rare. James had rejected not only his enslavement but also some form of the treatment within his relationship with Michener. Although James's agency was limited, he should not be understood as having been completely devoid of the abililty to make some choices and carve out a space to control his own life. James's escape put Michener on the defensive, and he felt compelled to make an offer rather than simply threaten punishment.

Michener either recaptured James, or he returned to his owner. Yet five years later, Michener paid for another advertisement to find James, who had absconded again. In 1786, his owner gave a more descriptive account of the runaway, portraying him as having a "Smooth Face, a Nose rather acqueline [*sic*], [and as speaking] Good English."[33] However, Michener's tone had changed from relatively gentle persuasion to blunt coercion. Michener no longer offered to forgive James should he return. Instead, he simply offered a reward of forty shillings and cautioned anyone against protecting James or helping him board a vessel to leave the region.

On two different occasions, then, James left his owner in hopes of finding freedom, independence, and autonomy. Abel Michener wanted to control James and used the newspaper to try to coerce him back into slavery. As Scott See has noted, one aspect of understanding social order and disorder is looking at the ways the powerful governed and how less powerful people might challenge the emerging system.[34] James and other runaway slaves challenged the emerging system of slavery in the late eighteenth century. Runaway advertisements attest to the profound destabilizing influence that black runaways had in a society attempting to find order in the postwar world of the 1780s and beyond.

Running away left a powerful impression on slaveholders, and the shrewd ones who recaptured their slaves knew that, if they wanted to continue to benefit from their slaves' labour, they had to make concessions or face other runaway attempts. On the other hand, slaves knew the possibilities and pitfalls of absconding. As a result, South Carolina–born Bill, in his pursuit of freedom and autonomy and his rejection of his owner's treatment, carefully planned his escape down to the very last detail. His owner, Michael Wallace, left a highly detailed portrait of Bill in his runaway notice. The notice portrays two men, one using the coercion of slavery and the other using the weapons of the powerless – his wit and craftiness – struggling to gain the upper hand. This battle for control and order began with Wallace's name for Bill. Wallace attempted to call him "Belfast," but he had to admit that his property "commonly goes by the name of Bill."[35] Wallace hired Bill out to another man, William Forsyth. Recognizing an excellent opportunity to escape, Bill attempted to board a vessel bound for Newfoundland, but, for reasons that are unclear, he did not manage to do so. Wallace described Bill as twenty-seven years of age, possessing a "mild good countenance" and an ability to speak "good English." Wallace believed Bill would "endeavor to escape" onboard one of the many vessels that entered and left Halifax Harbour. He also noted that Bill "will no doubt endeavour to pass for a free man, and possibly by some other name." Wallace offered an in-depth description of Bill's clothes but admitted that his runaway had "other cloaths secreted in town, he may have changed his whole apparel." Bill's repeated attempts to escape and Wallace's lengthy description and "Twenty Dollars" reward represented an encounter between an unfree man and a master.[36] They were fighting to define their own relationship but also the place of slavery and black freedom in Nova Scotia. Ten years after the loyalist influx, slave owners and slaves were still negotiating and battling over the meaning of bondage.

Although most individual runaways were like James and Bill – young and male – several female slaves attempted to escape on their own from abusive and overbearing masters. These slaves faced more obstacles in attempting to escape than did their male counterparts. Yet historians must carefully understand the context of escapes to account for the reasons why this was largely a male activity.[37] Moreover, historian Amani Marshall makes the point that slaveholders assumed that female runaways would "either return voluntarily or be captured easily" and thus did not pay for runaway notices for women as quickly or as often as they did for men.[38] It is certainly true that the number of runaway female slave advertisements greatly underestimates the actual number of total female runaways. Even so, there are several reasons why women did not abscond as often as men. Traditionally, historians have pointed to the fact that the formation of meaningful family units among slaves discouraged running away, especially for female slaves. While this argument carries some weight, one of the best historians on the topic, Billy Smith, points out that family ties could also encourage women to escape with their children (as we see with the example of Bet and Statia, described below).[39] Indeed, some women took children with them to escape predatory owners or an increasingly violent situation.[40] Instead, Smith points to other factors that influenced female slaves' decisions to escape, including sexual abuse by owners, proximity to cities, work patterns, reproductive burdens, and places where they could escape.[41] Another reason female slaves could not escape their owners was their limited options after running away. In the Maritimes, one of the favoured routes of escape was boarding a vessel and going to work in the seafaring industry. The majority of runaway women simply did not have this option. In contrast, seafaring had long been an outlet for free black men and male slaves.[42]

In the Maritimes, black women sometimes encountered predatory and potentially sexually abusive, if not obsessive, owners who seemed particular determined to prevent their escape. An example of this is John Ryan's shocking advertisement in New Brunswick's *Royal Gazette*:

> CAUTION. THE Subscriber hereby cautions all persons against attempting in future to seduce from his Service his Female Negro Slave DINAH, (for whom he has a good legal title) – as he is determined to punish by all legal ways and means, every offender of that description. – And that no one may plead ignorance of the person of the Slave in excuse, he informs all concerned, that she is about 26 years of age – 4 feet 9 inches high-has a small scar upon her forehead – and lately belonged to MR. JAMES TAYLOR, of Maugerville.[43]

Ryan's stark warning to any anti-slavery individuals and his pre-emptive advertisement for a woman before she had actually attempted to escape are remarkable. It is telling that Ryan put this notice in a paper for a female slave. What was actually going on between Dinah and Ryan? Why did Ryan think he needed to exercise so much control over this woman? The advertisement reeks of personal issues and an abusive relationship (beyond the typical abuse inherent in the master/slave encounter) between Ryan and Dinah. Whatever the case, Ryan eventually took Dinah and her children to Newfoundland. In his will (probably drawn up well before his death in 1847), Ryan freed Dinah and also freed her two children, Cornelius and Rachel, when they reached the age of twenty-one.[44] The "Dinah" advertisement is unique – I have not come across something similar for a male slave.

In trying to escape from bondage, slaves wanted their freedom, but they were also rejecting the terms of their enslavement. This is especially clear when families absconded together, which usually meant that the owner planned to sell a husband, wife, or child. Among the reasons Maritime slaves ran away was in defiance of attempts to destroy slave families. Although young men were the majority of runaways, families made up a significant minority of escapees. In addition, slaves of different owners often ran away in groups for mutual support and protection. These groups of runaways tell us two important things about Maritime slavery. First, slaves developed close networks and together devised careful plans to escape. Second, they carefully weighed the possibilities of freedom and whether the risk involved in escape was worth it. Group escapes included men, women, and sometimes young children. For example, in summer 1786, Isaac, Ben, Flora, Nancy, and Lidge, who was only four years of age,

> RAN AWAY FROM the Subscriber living at Nashwakshis [New Brunswick], in the county of York, between the 15th and 21st days of this instant July, the following bound Negro slaves, viz. ISAAC about 30 years old, born on Long Island near

> New-York, had on when he went away, a short blue coat, round hat and white trowsers. BEN, about 35 years old, had on a Devonshire kersey jacket lined with Scotch plad, corduroy breeches, and round hat. FLORA, a Wench about 27 years old, much pitted with small-pox, she had on a white cotton jacket and petticoat. ALSO, NANCY about 24 years old, who took with her a Negro child about four years old called LIDGE. The four last mentioned Negroes were born in Maryland, and lately brought to this country.[45]

What precipitated this escape? Were the men and women married, siblings, or unrelated? Was Nancy Lidge's mother? If so, who fathered the young boy? The advertisement simply does not provide enough information to answer these important questions.

There are two things going on in this slave advertisement – one explicit and another rather implicit. First, these slaves wanted freedom, increased autonomy, and better treatment. Perhaps, they saw other free blacks in the area and knew quite well that there was a possibility of black freedom. More subtly, they were attempting to negotiate with their owner Caleb Jones about the contours of slavery in their new homeland. The migration from Maryland had opened up new possibilities and problems for the owner, but also for the slaves. In running away, especially as a group, they were making a clear statement about what they would not tolerate. If Jones captured them, he knew that pushing his slaves too far could result in further escape attempts. Second, there was the larger question of social disorder and the place of black people in the changing society of New Brunswick. Jones believed he had to restore order through the capture of the runaways. He offered a reward of "TWO GUINEAS" for each man and "SIX DOLLARS" for each woman. In typical slave-owner practice, Jones threatened anyone who might help his five runaways: "ALL persons are hereby forbid to harbor any of the above Negroes, and all masters of vessels are forbid to take any of them on board their vessel as they shall answer the consequences."[46] This stark threat illuminates that slaveholders were very concerned that "their Negroes" would receive help from local anti-slavery supporters. It also reveals that owners felt it was within their rights to threaten legal consequences as a way to restore what they thought to be the proper social order, even if slaveholding was not necessarily supported by the majority of local inhabitants. Jones recovered his slaves, despite their best efforts, although Lidge attempted to escape again thirty years later.[47]

Slaves and free blacks attempted to keep their families together by absconding from their owners. At times, running away could be an attempt to reunite families; other slave families absconded to escape a difficult or unhappy situation. Reasons for leaving included mistreatment and possibly forced sexual relations between a master and an unfortunate slave. Slaves ran away as families because of the importance of these relationships. Although most slaves would have had a better opportunity to escape and hide as individuals, families preferred to remain together, even if this lessened their chance of gaining permanent freedom. For example, in 1787, two enslaved siblings escaped from their owner, along with a free black servant. According to their owner, Thomas Lester, "two negro Men and one Wench" had run away "in a BIRCH CANOE." He described the brother, Sam, as around seventeen or eighteen years of age, "between a black and dark Mulatto" and "quick spoken," and even notes that he "attempts to play the VIOLIN." His sister, Beller, was dark skinned and sixteen years of age. According to Lester, she had formerly lived with Judge Peters and was "slow in her speech." He also claimed that they "were raised in the family." They were accompanied by Tony Smith (alias Joe), who had dark skin and "speaks broken." Lester admitted that Smith was "a free fellow, but hired for a time," which indicates that Beller and/or Sam were unfree and likely slaves.[48] This escape attempt shows the planning and careful execution of a group of black people who secured a canoe and escaped by water. It also underlines, perhaps, the similarities between unfree and free black labour, in that they all chose to escape Lester. Clearly they were experiencing the same type of mistreatment. Again, the line between the enslaved, indentured, and free (but heavily exploited) black labourer remained tenuous and thin.

Two years earlier, in Shelburne, Nova Scotia, "A Man, his Wife, and two Children, *James, Bet, Frank, and Judy*," escaped from their owner, Samuel Andrews.[49] The father, James, a skilled slave, would have had a much better opportunity for freedom if he had left on his own. This slave family may have absconded because of their treatment at Andrews's hands or perhaps because he planned to sell some of them out of the region. Unfortunately, Andrews recaptured them. A few years later, New Brunswick Loyalist Joseph Clarke placed an advertisement complaining about the loss of his slave family:

> RAN-AWAY, FROM the subscriber on the night of the 9th instant, an indented [*sic*] Servant Man, named DICK HOPEWELL; about 5 feet 9 inches high – very active, and supposed to be near 40 years of age ... At the same time went off a Negro Woman Slave, named STATIA, who he claim'd as a Wife, with two small children – a boy about five years old and a girl about 15 months – she is about 30 years of age, and now pregnant ... She is of the mulatto cast, and speaks very fluently.[50]

Statia and Dick were escaping to better protect their family from the predatory Joseph Clarke. They feared he would break apart the family and prevent the couple from being together. Clarke recaptured the runaways and then immediately sold Statia to another man, thus separating her from her husband and children.[51] The case of Statia did not end there, as her son became part of an important legal case thirteen years later.

In 1805, anti-slavery attorney Samuel Denny Street went before the New Brunswick Supreme Court and filed for a writ of *habeas corpus* for Richard Hopefield, Jr, who had allegedly been detained by Stair Agnew "for the space of Three years and fifty five Days." The case focused on Patience (also known as Stacey or Statia), who had been brought to New Brunswick as a slave, eventually married Richard Hopefield Sr, and had several children, including the younger Hopefield, whom Agnew claimed to own. During the case, Hopefield Sr gave a deposition that outlined his personal life history. Born in Virginia, he had served his owner during the Revolutionary War before escaping to the British. Shortly thereafter, he married Patience and had several children, including Richard Hopefield Jr, who was born in New Brunswick. Hopefield claimed that his wife "had been put on board a vessel by one Phineas Lovitt [a member of the House of Assembly] in order as the deponent was informed to send her to the West Indies to be sold – when she was relanded [*sic*] by order of Governor Carleton who set her at liberty." It seems that Patience and Hopefield lived together for several years as free people before Joseph Clarke "forcibly seized" her.[52] In 1792, as discussed above, Clarke placed an advertisement in a local paper complaining about the loss of a female slave named Statia and her five-year-old son and fifteen-month-old daughter. Clarke also noted that she had run away with an indentured servant named Dick Hopewell (probably Richard Hopefield), who claimed to be married to her. It seems probable that Statia was actually Patience.[53]

Stair Agnew denied the charges against him and benefited from the advice and legal representation of Ward Chipman, who admitted that his client had beaten Hopefield Jr, but claimed it resulted from "disobedient and refractory and insolent" behaviour and neglect of "duty." Agnew did not dispute that he prevented "Richard from absenting himself." Agnew justified his actions, however, because Richard was "a Negro Servant, the property of the said Stair ... bound to serve the said Stair for the said Richard's life time."[54] Agnew's claims were damaged by the testimony of other witnesses. In 1801, the York County Court of General Sessions had indicted him for "Cruel Treatment" of "two Negro Boys" in his service. At the court, Agnew "publickly pledged" that "he would manumitt and make free a certain Negro Boy named or called Richard Hopefield" when he turned twenty-one years old.[55]

Samuel Denny Street argued that, since Hopefield Sr was a free man, his son ought to be free as well. The defence "countered by attempting to show that Hopefield's parents had never been formally married, so that he had taken the status of his mother rather than of his [free] father."[56] After a court battle, the younger Hopefield's writ of *habeas corpus* failed. Also, a civil suit against Agnew for battery and false imprisonment did not proceed past an early stage.[57] In sum, Hopefield's case for freedom had failed. As David Bell notes, "*Hopefield's* case was undoubtedly a legal triumph for the slave-owning interests. They had received a clear legal verdict in favour of the continuance of Negro slavery."[58] The case is also an example of how the differences between black slaves and black servants could be thin in the protean world of Maritime slaves and slaveholders in the late eighteenth century. Although the case of Statia and her family illuminate this point brilliantly, the question of slavery, servitude, and freedom is also elucidated through the story of several black "servants" who attempted a mass escape in 1784.

The sliding scales of slavery and freedom defy and challenge historians to acknowledge the textured and multilayered experiences of free blacks and slaves in the Maritime colonies. In the Maritimes, free people of African descent were prone to suffering re-enslavement at the hands of local whites who had promised to gainfully employ them and provide wages. Vulnerable in this regard were several free black people who boarded the *Aurora* in New York which was bound for the Saint John area in July 1783. According to the Book of Negroes, Ed Morris (called Ned in Bon, though his name seems to have been Edward), his wife, Charity Morris, their three children (Isaac, Edward, and Mary Ann), and Peter Cock were free, as the adults had "General Birth Certificates," which supposedly guaranteed their liberty.[59] Yet they were listed as being in the "possession" of Thomas Rogers.[60] (The Book of Negroes often listed free blacks as being in the "possession" of a white Loyalist, thus exacerbating the potential for re-enslavement among the black Loyalists who migrated to the Maritimes.) Then, less than a year after their arrival in New Brunswick, Thomas Rogers placed an unusually lengthy runaway notice complaining about the loss of his "Negroes," whom he described as "belonging to the subscriber." In addition to the individuals listed above, he also possessed Andrew Bush and his wife. The runaway advertisement demonstrates the lengths that escaped unfree people were willing to go to obtain their freedom, but also how Rogers had taken away their freedom:

> HARBOURED, or otherwise CONCEALED. THE following Negroes belonging to the subscriber, viz. Edward Morris, an elderly negro about five feet five inches high, by trade a mason, has a remarkable wound in his forehead which shews a hole resembling a bullet shot, is a celebrated methodist preacher among the negroes, was bred at Fairfield in Connecticut; also Charity his wife, a half bred Indian of the tribe on Long Island, province of New York, and a small boy about seven years of age, son of the said wench by an Indian father. Andrew Bush, a comely stout negro, remarkable high forwarded, generally called the Widow's Peek, formerly the property

> of Doctor Bush, in Connecticut, is a remarkable *good miller*, which practice he has been used all his life to, also his wife Eanus, a yellow mustee [octoroon or a person of mixed ancestry]. And, Peter Cock, a young negro, comely countenance.[61]

Thomas Rogers continued his runaway notice with a long accusatory epistle about runaway servants and slaves. He identified one of the major difficulties facing loyalist slaveholders, stating that "for the better security of indented [*sic*] servants, slaves, &c there [should be] a law of the province enacting that any person harbouring, concealing, or otherwise encouraging indented [*sic*] servants, apprentices or slaves from their master or their service, for every such offence shall forfeit the sum of ten pounds, &c."[62] The problem, as Rogers saw it, rested with New Brunswick's failure to have enacted laws preventing local residents from protecting fugitive slaves and runaway indentured servants. Rogers also noted that "a certain Mr. Dibble, has encouraged some of the aforesaid servants."[63] Apparently, Dibble had told Rogers's unfree black servants to lodge a complaint with local magistrates "to have them[selves] liberated," but this complaint failed, mostly due to the magistrate, John Coffin (he probably also owned slaves), who "judiciously" decided in Rogers's favour. Without question, Edward Morris, his wife, and the other unfree labourers were quite capable of wanting their freedom without encouragement from Dibble, but his help would have been appreciated. Rogers claimed that Dibble had enticed his "indebted" servants away "under pretense of purchasing them," but that Rogers informed him that "he [Rogers] will not have any bargain, or other negociation whatever touching the above servants, with him, and hereby once more forwarns him from farther harbouring, concealing, or otherwise preventing said negroes from returning to their duty."[64] Although, as noted, these runaways had general birth certificates, which guaranteed their freedom, Rogers claimed that they were unfree labourers.[65] In this particular case, less than one year from their arrival in New Brunswick, the Morrises had gone from free black Loyalists to unfree indentured servants, and the next step easily could have been enslavement, if they were not already being treated as slaves.

Reflecting on white treatment of free blacks, African-American Baptist preacher David George noted that "white people in Nova Scotia" had "treated many of us as bad as though we [free blacks] had been slaves."[66] Edward Morris, his wife Charity, their child, Peter Cock, Andrew Bush, and his wife had lost their freedom and were being treated as slaves despite their legal status as free. They absconded from Rogers because he had deprived them of their freedom and could easily have planned to break up their families through sale. Perhaps these people realized that they were about to be re-enslaved by an unscrupulous master or sold to the West Indies, and this is why they absconded as a group.

It was rather common for white Loyalists not to pay wages they owed to black workers – in effect re-enslaving them. Three black Loyalists fell into this sort of enslavement with a loyalist officer in Nova Scotia. Moses Reed and Jameson Davis were "two years in the Service of Colonel Hamilton" and "received no wages." Phebe Martin claimed that she "was never [Hamilton's] slave, or ever received any Wages from him." After two years of being re-enslaved, these captive labourers resorted to escaping from their would-be master by travelling to distant Halifax, where they hoped to be safe.[67] At this point Hamilton, along with Captain Daniel McNeil, organized a slave patrol, which attempted to recapture the escaped labourers. The slave catchers found the four runaways, put them in irons, and locked them in a ship's hold, but not before they beat Jameson Davis with a "Cudgell." Molly Sinclair recalled "she was Chained to Moses Reed when put on the vessell."[68] The re-enslaved black Loyalists were taken to Shelburne, but, before they could be shipped away, local officials got word of their condition and ordered McNeil to bring them ashore for an inquiry and court investigation. McNeil claimed that he had been told to take the re-enslaved black Loyalists to Shelburne and give them to a Mr Dean, who "was to give him a Receipt for them, and, as he understood, was to carry them to the Bahamas." After hearing the testimony of these people along with McNeil's statement, the Shelburne court considered whether the blacks were the rightful property of Hamilton (there was no evidence such as a bill of sale) or should go free. The majority of the court (five in favour of freeing them and two against) decided that "the aforesaid Negros" would be allowed to "go where they pleased."[69]

The similarities between this case and that of individuals re-enslaved by Thomas Rogers are striking. It is certainly plausible that Rogers had turned free blacks into de facto slaves by not paying them any wages, and this might have resulted in their decision to abscond. Another possible reason behind their escape is that Rogers might have taken and sold some of their children. Charity Morris had three children when she left New York in 1783, but, by May 1784, the runaway notice mentions only one of her children with Edward Morris.[70] What happened to the other two? Had they died earlier in the winter, or did Rogers illegally sell them to the West Indies?

Black children were at extreme risk for re-enslavement and, without the intervention of the local authorities, could easily be sold to the West Indies. In November 1791, two young black boys faced re-enslavement by their alleged owners, whom they regarded as having no right to their service as slaves. In the first case, a black woman named Susannah Connor "came here personally into Court" and complained that John Harris intended to take her son out of the province. Her son (Robert Gemmel or Gammel) worked as Harris's indentured apprentice. The court ordered Harris to come in immediately and answer for his alleged plans. Harris readily admitted that he planned to leave the province but claimed that the only reason he planned to take the boy was because there were no other available owners to teach Gemmel the art of butchery. The court cancelled the indenture. If Susannah Connor had not intervened on behalf of her son, Gemmel would have been taken out of the province – to the United States or elsewhere – and no doubt enslaved. In the other case, a sympathetic local citizen told the court that Timothy Mahan "detains, a Negro Boy, who he hath attempted to sell, and Dispose of, without having property therein." The court ordered Mahan to appear before it along with five-year-old John Simmons. Mahan claimed that Simmons's parents had given him the boy three years earlier. The court found that Mahan had treated the child "kindly, and humanely" but ruled that Simmons's parents had no right to give him away and Mahan had no "property in the said Boy." What is unclear is whether Mahan originally stole the child from his parents – certainly, saying they "gave" the child to him was a convenient answer. Nevertheless, the boy escaped sale to another owner. The cases of Robert Gemmel and John Simmons again underline the tenuous nature of the line between slavery and freedom that black people faced in the Maritimes, even – perhaps especially – if they were small children.[71]

At best, the potential freedom of Thomas Rogers's servants was extremely precarious, while their de facto enslavement seemed rather likely. Slaves and indentured black servants regularly married and ran away together, underlining the similarity of their status and the dangerous situation they confronted in a society that sometimes allowed their sale to the West Indies. Preventing "owners" from selling black people out of the region as slaves depended almost wholly on the government's willingness to enforce certain laws and black people's ability to escape and find sustenance among other free people of African descent or anti-slavery whites. In escaping from Rogers, his "servants" were asserting their freedom and autonomy. Rogers's runaway advertisement also illuminates the challenges to the social order in the disagreements between anti-slavery whites and those who supported black bondage. Dibble, for example, seemingly wanted to provide some sort of escape for the Morris family and their companions. Rogers's runaways did not accept his claims on them, and they escaped only to have their master prevail upon the court system to have them returned to him. Yet they absconded again. Although there were multiple reasons for their escape, Rogers's black unfree labourers wanted their liberty and were willing to try different types of escape to break free of his suffocating grasp.

Runaway advertisements are important tools for examining slavery, servitude, and social disorder in the Maritimes. In the late eighteenth century, the social disorder created by the mass migration of Loyalists allowed slaves from various parts of the United States an opportunity to escape from abusive owners, but at the same time local whites attempted to re-enslave free black Loyalists through various schemes. The result of this changing and complicated context was a slew of runaway advertisements that underline the sense of social disorder that defined Maritime slavery and black-white relations in the 1780s and 1790s. These runaway notices illuminate family relationships, occupational skill, colour, physical appearance, and personality traits, and also say something about the relationship between individual slaves and owners. Slave owners – and would-be owners – used print culture to try to reassert control over their runaway slaves, but these advertisements are also testaments to the lengths black people went to achieve their freedom or carve out more autonomy within their labouring situation. Labels such as black slave, black indentured servant, free black servant, and free black Loyalists were very fluid and could change quickly, with some individuals losing their freedom and being re-enslaved while others escaped slavery and constructed a narrative of black loyalist freedom and liberation. Runaway advertisements are essential to understanding social order and disarray in this region of British North America. They reveal the battle between slaveholders and enslaved people to determine the contours of the emerging system of bondage after the loyalist influx. While masters attempted to create order through slaveholding, labourers of African descent challenged them at every turn, including by running away, thereby creating disorder for the individual owner and also for society at large. Absconding remained a weapon that slaves could use to fight against the emerging social order.

NOTES

1 This chapter includes sections that were reprinted with permission of the Publisher from *North to Bondage* by Harvey Amani Whitfield © UBC Press 2016. All rights reserved by the Publisher.

2 Scholars can find a full listing and discussion of the historiography of Maritime slavery, black Loyalists, and Canadian slavery in Harvey Amani Whitfield, *North to Bondage: Loyalist Slavery in the Maritimes* (Vancouver: UBC Press, 2016), 131–74. See also Gregory Palmer, *Biographical Sketches of Loyalists of the American Revolution* (Westport, CT: Meckler Publishing, 1984), 375; and Harvey Amani Whitfield, *Black Slavery in the Maritimes: A History in Documents* (Peterborough, ON: Broadview Press, 2018).

3 *Royal St John's Gazette* (NB), 15 July 1784.

4 Ibid.

5 Ibid.

6 The works mentioned here are important but do not come close to listing all significant treatments of this subject. See Antonio T. Bly, *Escaping Bondage: A Documentary History of Runaway Slaves in Eighteenth-Century New England, 1700–1789* (Lanham, MD: Lexington, 2013); John Hope Franklin and Loren Schweninger, *Runaway Slaves: Rebels on the Plantation* (Oxford: Oxford University Press, 1999); Billy G. Smith, "Black Women Who Stole Themselves in Eighteenth-Century America," in *Inequality in Early America*, ed. Carla Gardina Pestana and Sharon V. Salinger (Hanover, NH: University Press of New England, 1999), 134–59; David Waldstreicher, "Reading the Runaways: Self-Fashioning, Print Culture, and Confidence in Slavery in the Eighteenth-Century Mid-Atlantic," *William and Mary Quarterly* 56 (April 1999): 243–72; Amani Marshall, "'They Will Endeavor to Pass for Free': Enslaved Runaways' Performances of Freedom in Antebellum South Carolina," *Slavery and Abolition* 31 (June 2010): 161–80; and Amani Marshall, "'They Are Supposed to Be Lurking about the City': Enslaved Women Runaways in Antebellum Charleston," *South Carolina Historical Magazine* 115 (July 2014): 188–212. Also, the important project Freedom on the Move is dedicated to runaway slaves: http://freedomonthemove.org.

7 Whitfield, *North to Bondage*, 31–45.

8 Smith, "Black Women," 152.

9 See note 2.

10 *Journal and Proceedings of the House of Assembly* (hereafter *JHOA*) (Halifax: King's Printer, 1787), 17 and 22, Nova Scotia Archives (hereafter NSA); An Act for the Regulation and Relief of the Free Negroes Within the Province of Nova Scotia, In Council, 2 April 1789, RG 5, Series U, Un-passed Bills, 1762–1792, NSA; *JHOA*, 1801, 72, NSA; A Bill relating to Negroes, 6 February 1801, Legislative Assembly Records, RS 24, S 14-B 9, Provincial Archives of New Brunswick (hereafter PANB); An Act for regulating Negro Servants within and throughout this Province, 1808, RG 5, Series U, Un-passed Bills, NSA.

11 For a full listing of works related to the Black Loyalists, see *North to Bondage*, 132–4.

12 C.B. Fergusson, ed., *Clarkson's Mission to America, 1791–1792* (Halifax: Public Archives of Nova Scotia, 1971), 89–90.

13 Ibid., 90.

14 Ibid.

15 An Act for the Regulation and Relief of the Free Negroes Within the Province of Nova Scotia.

16 Thomas Clarkson "Some Account of the New Colony at Sierra Leone," *American Museum; or Universal Magazine* (May 1792), 229. Ellen Wilson believed that the information he used came from Thomas Peters's petition; Wilson, *Loyal Blacks* (New York: G.P. Putnam's Sons, 1976), 181.

17 Clarkson "Some Account of the New Colony at Sierra Leone," 229–30.

18 *Nova Scotia Gazette and Weekly Chronicle*, 21 September 1784. Also see, *Royal Gazette* (New Brunswick), 10 July 1787; *Saint John Gazette and Weekly Advertiser* (NB), 29 June 1792.

19 Jared Ross Hardesty, *Unfreedom: Slavery and Dependence in Eighteenth-Century Boston* (New York: New York University Press, 2016).

20 Book of Negroes, Sir Guy Carleton Papers, the National Archives [Britain], microfilm copy at NSA. Clarinda (age 19) and Jupiter (age 33) are listed one after the other. Clarinda seems to have been the property of Henry Boyd before becoming the property of Dr Bullern. The way Bullern wrote his runaway advertisement makes it somewhat unclear exactly which one was enslaved.

21 Whitfield, *North to Bondage*, 36–45; Kenneth Donovan, "Slaves and Their Owners in Ile Royale, 1713–1760," *Acadiensis* 25 (Autumn 1995): 3–32; and Kenneth Donovan, "Slaves in Île Royale, 1713–1758," *French Colonial History* 5 (2004): 25–42.

22 See note 6.

23 Waldstreicher, "Reading the Runaways," 245.

24 Ibid., 247; also see Smith, "Black Women," 136.

25 *Saint John Gazette* (NB), 29 June 1792.

26 Robert E. Desrochers, "Slave-for-Sale Advertisements and Slavery in Massachusetts, 1704–1781," *William and Mary Quarterly* 3rd ser., 59 (July 2002): 623–64.

27 *Royal American Gazette* (NS), 19 June 1786.

28 *Royal Gazette* (NB), 11 September 1787.

29 Ibid., 21 August 1787.

30 Franklin and Schweninger, *Runaway Slaves*, 233.

31 Runaway advertisements used for this chapter include those found in the following: *Saint John Gazette* (NB), 29 June 1792; *Royal St John's Gazette* (NB, 15 July 1784; *Royal Saint John's Gazette* (NB), 13 May 1784; *Nova Scotia Gazette and Weekly Chronicle* , 21 September 1784; *Royal Gazette* (NB), 10 July 1787; *Nova Scotia Gazette and Weekly Chronicle*, 12 July 1785; Royal Gazette (NS), 7 September 1790; *Nova Scotia Gazette and Weekly Chronicle*, 9 December 1783; *Royal Gazette* (NB), 15 December 1802; *Nova Scotia Gazette and Weekly Chronicle*, 22 May 1781; *Royal Gazette* (NB), 12 October 1787; *Royal Gazette* (NB), 17 June 1788; *Royal Gazette* (NS), 10 July 1792; *Nova Scotia Packet and General Advertiser*, 12 October 1785; *Saint John Gazette* (NB), 5 and 12 May 1797; *Saint John Gazette* (NB), 6 January 1797; *Royal Gazette* (NB), 17 August 1787; *Royal Gazette* (NB), 16 May 1786; *Royal Gazette* (NB), 20 August 1799; *Nova Scotia Gazette and Weekly Chronicle*, 20 May

1783; *Royal Gazette* (NB), 25 July 1786; *Royal Gazette* (NB), 7 March 1786; *Royal Gazette* (NB), 9 July 1816; *Nova Scotia Gazette and Weekly Chronicle*, 22 August 1786; *Weekly Chronicle* (NS), 15 March 1794; *Nova Scotia Packet and General Advertiser,* 3 August 1786; *Saint John Gazette* (NB), 30 September 1791; *Royal Gazette* (NB), 15 December 1802; *Royal Gazette* (NS), 10 July 1792; *Saint John Gazette* (NB), 5 May 1797; *Royal Gazette* (NS), 9 December 1783; *New Brunswick Courier*; 5 September 1818; *Nova Scotia Packet and General Advertiser*, 28 February 1785; *Nova Scotia Packet and General Advertiser*, 26 October 1786.

32 *Nova Scotia Gazette and Weekly Chronicle*, 22 May 1781.

33 Ibid., 22 August 1786.

34 Scott See, "Concluding Remarks," Unrest, Violence, and the Search for Social Order in British North America, 1749 to 1876 Conference, Fredericton, June 2015.

35 *Weekly Chronicle* (Nova Scotia), 15 March 1794.

36 Ibid.

37 Smith, "Black Women," 137.

38 Amani Marshall, "'They Are Supposed to Be Lurking,'" 192.

39 Smith, "Black Women," 137.

40 The following advertisements were for individual female runaways: *Nova Scotia Packet and General Advertiser*, 3 August 1786; *Royal Gazette* (NB), 21 August 1787; *Saint John Gazette* (NB), 30 September 1791; *Nova Scotia Gazette and Weekly Chronicle*, 4 October 1785.

41 Ibid., 151–2.

42 Jeffrey Bolster, *Black Jacks: African American Seamen in the Age of Sail* (Cambridge, MA: Harvard University Press, 1997).

43 *Royal Gazette* (NB), 24 December 1806.

44 KAW, "Ryan, John D. (1761–1847)," in *Encyclopedia of Newfoundland and Labrador*, vol. 4, ed. Cyril F. Poole and Robert H. Cuff (St John's: Henry Cuff, 1993), 668.

45 *Royal Gazette* (NB), 25 July 1786.

46 Ibid.

47 Ibid., 25 July 1786 and 9 July 1816.

48 Ibid., 10 July 1787.

49 *Nova Scotia Packet and General Advertiser*, 5 October 1785.

50 *Saint John Gazette and Weekly Advertiser* (NB), 29 June 1792.

51 Whitfield, *North to Bondage*, 104–6.

52 *Richard Hopefield v. Stair Agnew*, 1802/1805, RS 42, Supreme Court Original Jurisdiction Records, PANB.

53 *Saint John Gazette* (NB), 29 June 1792.

54 *Richard Hopefield v. Stair Agnew.*

55 Ibid.; D.G. Bell, "Slavery and the Judges of Loyalist New Brunswick," *University of New Brunswick Law Journal* 31 (1982): 24–5.

56 Ibid., 24.

57 Ibid., 25.

58 Ibid.

59 These certificates were issued at the end of the Revolutionary War, primarily to slaves who had escaped from Patriot owners during the conflict and fled to British lines. Many of them worked as labourers for the British Army or Royal Navy, while others took part in military engagements. The certificate allowed the holder to travel or relocate freely.

60 Book of Negroes, NSA.

61 *Royal Saint John's Gazette* (NB), 13 May 1784. It is interesting to note that the Book of Negroes states that Edward (or Ned) Morris was only thirty-six, but in this runaway advertisement he's described as elderly. The age in the Book of Negroes may be an error.

62 *Royal Saint John's Gazette* (N B), 13 May 1784.

63 There is a strong possibility that the Mr Dibble in the source was Frederick Dibblee, a clergyman who represented the Society for the Propagation of the Gospel. See Darrel Butler, "Dibblee, Frederick," in *Dictionary of Canadian Biography*, vol. 6 (University of Toronto/Université Laval), 2003.

64 *Royal Saint John's Gazette* (NB), 13 May 1784.

65 Ibid.

66 David George, "An Account of the Life of Mr David George, from Sierra Leone in Africa; given by himself in a Conversation with Brother Rippon of London, and Brother [Samuel] Pearce [1766–1799] of Birmingham," cited in *Unchained Voices: An Anthology of Black Authors in the English-Speaking World of the Eighteenth Century*, ed. Vincent Carretta (Lexington: University Press of Kentucky, 2004), 340.

67 Special Sessions at Shelburne, NS, 5 August 1786, Shelburne Records, MG 4, vol. 141, NSA; Carole Watterson Troxler, "Hidden from History: Black Loyalists at Country Harbour, Nova Scotia," in *Moving On: Black Loyalists in the Afro-Atlantic World*, ed. John W. Pulis (New York: Garland, 1999).

68 Ibid.

69 Ibid.

70 Book of Negroes, NSA.

71 General Sessions at Shelburne, N S, 1 and 3 November 1791, Shelburne Records, MG 4, vol. 141, NSA.

11 The Mobile Village: Metis Women, Bison Brigades, and Social Order on the Nineteenth-Century Plains

ÉMILIE PIGEON AND CAROLYN PODRUCHNY

Bison are large animals. Adult plains bison can weigh from 700 to 2,200 pounds (318 to 1,000 kg). Hunting them, butchering them, and transporting their meat and hides necessitated collective labour. Plains Metis hunting parties in the nineteenth century numbered up to two thousand people and included men, women, and children who travelled in extended kin networks and communities.[1] These mobile villages that followed the bison herds assembled hundreds of people on horseback and hundreds more driving Red River carts pulled by horses or oxen. Observers and scholars have generally represented these hunting brigades as strict and hierarchical armies ruled with martial authority by hunt leaders. Some argue that militaristic discipline was necessary to implement and maintain such large and well-organized camps. Historian George Colpitts calls them "war parties that hunted buffalo and buffalo hunters travelling as armies."[2] Metis studies scholar Adam Gaudry contends that "the hunt, as a constitution, legitimized the formation of a military force which could compel hunt participants to follow its laws," and sees them as essential to "the development of a coherent Métis political collectivity."[3]

These characterizations of hunting brigades as regimented militias seem paradoxical. Metis families cherished and celebrated principles of freedom. They descended from freemen, former employees of fur trade companies who married First Nations women, but chose to live outside of fur trade posts and First Nations communities.[4] Metis families tended to form independent economic units not subject to tribal or mercantile dictates.[5] Observers called Metis "the free people," "the people who own themselves," or "the people who are their own bosses."[6] Alexander Ross, fur trader and Red River settler and local official, observed that Metis men were keenly interested in politics and valued free society: "They cherish freedom as they cherish life."[7] While commemorating the Metis victory in the Battle of Seven Oaks, hunter and songwriter Pierre Falcon wrote, "We are the Bois-Brûlés, Freemen of the plains / We choose our chief! We are no man's slave!"[8] Indeed, Gaudry identifies *kaa-tipeyimshoyaahk* (independence) as a central tenant of Metis political thought.[9]

Building on these widely acknowledged traits shared by Metis families, we argue that the Metis organized their hunting brigades as mobile villages with a gendered distribution of power between men and women. Mobile villages reflected the governing practices of sedentary communities. Our approach challenges existing histories of Metis bison hunting, which have favoured portrayals of brigades as strict patriarchies, with women subordinate to men, despite Metis women's active roles in the fur trade, working as guides, interpreters, traders, hunters, and household managers.[10] Recently, however, historians Brenda Macdougall and Nicole St-Onge have shifted the conversation with their analysis of three Metis women, the Laframboise sisters, highlighting their central position in the Trottier family brigade.[11] Our investigations show that women played a central role in bison-hunting parties by acting as the primary drivers of the Red River carts, regulating social order in hunting encampments, and helping facilitate the mostly peaceful diplomacy between Metis brigades and neighbouring First Nations.

By focusing on the role of women and children, we explain how brigades formed mobile villages committed to peaceful and democratic social governance and diplomacy with all neighbouring First Nations, be they relatives, friends, or enemies. We first explore the primarily non-violent social order within the mobile communities. Women were the main drivers of Red River carts, they governed the space inside encampments after the Red River carts were circled (including organizing food and shelter), and they processed bison products after the hunt. Men ruled the space outside the encampment circles, where they scouted for enemies and bison herds, guarded the group, and hunted for bison and other food. Second, we turn our attention to external relations, looking at how Metis bison hunters interacted with outsiders. Since the Metis homeland extended into what we now call the United States, we analyse the Battle of Grand Coteau, an 1851 dispute between Metis bison hunters and the Yanktonais[12] in the Minnesota Territory. Traditional rivals for plains resources paid little attention to nation-state lines when harvesting natural resources in the mid-nineteenth century. We explain the low rate of casualties (a sole Metis death) in this conflict and the flamboyant roles played by Metis women, using their clothing to distract their enemies.

The polyethnic character of Metis bison hunting brigades shaped their movements and their relations with outsiders. Histories that focus on ethnic conflicts rather than inter-ethnic collaborations on the plains ignore the complex kin connections that stretched across thousands of miles and hundreds of communities. The brigades studied in this essay include Anishinaabe (Saulteaux or Ojibwe), Nakoda (Assiniboine or Stoney), and Cree, as well as the Metis. Nicholas Vrooman's history of the Little Shell Tribe emphasized that, for Metis families, "the whole country was ... 'one robe.'"[13] Many layers of kinship constituted and influenced Metis families, and peace among nations was necessary for posterity. Although the Battle of the Grand Coteau was a conflict between Indigenous peoples on the plains, its origins were triggered by the gendered violence of colonialism that increasingly restricted the movement of Indigenous peoples in their traditional territories. The emergence of foreign political borders and their increasing enforcement by settlers shaped Metis lifeways.[14]

The absence of women from analyses of the hunting brigades and from narratives of the Battle of Grand Coteau was not an accident. Most Metis bison-hunt descriptions and memoirs come from men. Male historians then reinforced a gender bias by relating the actions of the men involved in bison hunting. Historians entrenched an imperial perspective by emphasizing Indigenous peoples warring with one another and thus necessitating the "civilizing" hand of the British Empire. These scholarly trends derive from Euro-North Americans' patriarchal framework that elevated white, Protestant, Anglo-Saxon persons of the male gender to the highest echelons of relevance, while relegating persons of the female gender and all non-white male persons to scholarly details. Historical works attributing the July 1851 Metis victory solely to men and/or the Christian God suffer from a myopic patriarchal lens, neglecting to explain how brigades constructed social order and handled unrest and violence. Inspired by the robust historiography highlighting the gendered nature of colonialism,[15] we amplify women's voices to illustrate both a fuller context of Plains Metis social governance and how it affected the outcome of the Battle of Grand Coteau.

Social Governance in Bison-Hunting Brigades

For centuries, Indigenous peoples worked together hunting bison, driving them over cliffs or jumps, or herding them into pens.[16] In the sixteenth century, escaped or traded Spanish horses began spreading north, dramatically changing hunting tactics and life on the plains. People travelled greater distances to hunt bison, and some Indigenous groups moved onto the plains, engendering new Plains ethnicities organized around horse-mounted bison hunting.[17] The smallpox epidemics from 1775 to 1782 and the contraction of bison herds and diminishing resources encouraged new and mixed bands made up of Nakoda, Cree, Anishinaabeg, and Metis to form on the plains, occupying spaces vacated by those who had succumbed to diseases.[18] The Plains Metis, according to Michel Hogue, "emerged amid these displacements in the first decades of the nineteenth century as powerful new players in this changed world."[19] The explosion of the bison-robe trade and the dramatic increase in the consumption of pemmican (a very old Indigenous food) among fur traders led to decreases in bison populations by the late 1840s.[20]

Shifting tribal boundaries and blurred territorialities defined the northern plains in the seventeenth, eighteenth, and nineteenth centuries. George Colpitts observes that "the shrinking of the bison herds brought groups even further into contact and competition in smaller spaces." Some regions became war zones where only large hunting parties dared to venture.[21] Metis bison-hunting brigades would travel southwest from the Red and Assiniboine river valleys and follow plains bison herds as they migrated throughout the spring, summer, and autumn on the northern Great Plains, coalescing into large groups in contentious areas. Initially, Metis organized two or three separate seasonal expeditions, travelling back and forth from home to hunt, but they shifted to wintering on the plains when the bison herds moved farther away from Red River and diminished further in size in the 1850s.[22]

When a brigade struck camp, the men chose captains, officers, or chiefs of the hunt. An 1840 hunt that Alexander Ross accompanied had 1,630 participants; ten captains were named, and, among these ten, one was recognized as the overall head of the hunt.[23] Each captain had ten soldiers at his disposal to guard the camp and enforce the rules of the hunt.[24] Ten guides were appointed; these men led the carts when travelling, and each day one served as flag-bearer.[25] Metis elder Louis Goulet recalled at the beginning of the twentieth century that the number of captains, soldiers, and guides could vary depending on the number of people in a brigade, with sentinels specifically responsible for encampment security. Scouts were the eyes of the caravan, travelling on horseback in pairs to keep a look out for enemies and bison herds. Novices were always paired with old hands to ensure that knowledge and skills were passed down through generations.[26] Although primary sources are vague about brigade elections, most likely a simple majority of adult men elected the annual chief and captains. Those elected then selected scouts. The collective agreed on the laws that would apply to that hunt.[27] Metis Peter Erasmus (1833–1931) recalled that, in the winter of 1869–70, "As was customary when two or more groups joined together, a meeting was called to elect a leader for the whole group ... The leader was chosen by the total vote of all the heads of families and any of the young men who were old enough to take responsible positions of trust in the duties of guards in camp or scouting for the camp."[28]

Metis elder Auguste Vermette recounted that brigade elders were consulted when electing the council.[29] According to Goulet, "The leader and members of council were chosen with such care ... [and] settled according to a kind of semi-religious ceremony usually presided over by the missionary who went along with the caravan. The council's decisions were law, entirely and everywhere, for the duration of the journey."[30] Although Goulet is the only source who mentions priests participating directly in elections, most sources show that priests played a large role in the social functioning of the brigades. In 1850, Father Albert Lacombe's preparations for the "Great Hunt" involved maintenance of his mission cart and spiritual council. Before departing for the hunt, Lacombe called the hunters, women, and children to prayer. Afterwards, the women left the men to their assembly to organize the hunt structures.[31]

In addition to hunters and their families, small-scale Metis traders accompanied the brigades; these men and women with extensive trading ties facilitated trade between the brigades and the First Nations they passed in their travels.[32] Antoine Vermette describes his 1860s brigades as accompanied by twenty to thirty First Nations men, presumably to help with diplomacy and trade.[33] Women were among the experts and specialists found in the brigade. Victoria (Belcourt) Callihoo (1861–1966) related that her grandmother was a medicine woman who travelled with the brigades to treat all those injured during bison hunts.[34]

Before every morning departure, the Metis families attended mass.[35] The flag-bearer then would hoist the flag, which was the signal for breaking camp.[36] Council chose the order of the wagons, explained Goulet, and "these travelled single file in one, two, three or more parallel lines. Every line was divided into equal sections, each under the command of a marching captain."[37] When the flag-bearer raised the flag, he acted as the chief guide of the expedition, directing the captains and soldiers, who ensured that no one wandered off or fell behind. Because most men rode their horses alongside the lines of carts to provide extra security, the organization and transport of the carts fell into the domain of women. Most families had more than one cart, so both women and children acted as cart drivers.[38] Depending on the trail, a camp could travel twenty to thirty miles a day, including pauses so the animals could rest and drink water.

In the evening, the lowering of the flag signalled the striking of camp for the night. Women drove the carts into a large circle, while the men helped raise tents within. Metis families could strike or dismantle their camps within thirty minutes. Goulet described such camps as fortresses: "Some caravan leaders had a habit of forming a circle at every stop so that the people would get used to the manoeuver and learn with practice how to do it quickly. *Former la ronde* meant to place the carts parallel, side by side, wheel to wheel, in a line, with the shafts lifted in the air so that the carts tipped backwards and rested on the rear bottom edge forming a circular enclosure."[39] The wheels of the carts were tied together to create a barricade.

At day's end, the council of captains, soldiers, and guides assembled to hear reports, discuss crimes and contraventions of the rules, and plan for the next day. They met outside the camp circle, presumably for privacy and quiet, but perhaps also because inside the encampment was the social space controlled by Metis women. Hunters left their horses and oxen to graze outside the circle if they perceived no threats, and the night watch kept a close eye to ensure they did not wander too far.[40]

Inside the cart circle, families pitched their tents, and women prepared the evening meal of flatbread and game or birds that were caught during the day's march.[41] After dinner, larger watch fires and smaller smudge fires to combat insects replaced the cooking fires. Monsieur was very impressed by the "well ordered, and well arranged camp" and by the "courteous and kindly bearing towards each other" exhibited by Metis in the camps.[42] The head captain would call everyone to prayers, and, if a priest accompanied the brigade, he would begin an evening service, weather permitting.[43] Storytellers and singers brought the day to a close.[44]

When bison herds were spotted, the camp mobilized quickly. Mounted hunters, primarily men, readied their guns, waiting for the captain to issue the order to start. Auguste Vermette remembers that hunters gathered to pray before launching the attack: "Ils se disaient un *Pater*, un *Ave Maria*, puis un *Gloire soit au Père*. Au oui, ah oui, ah oui ! C'était pour se mettre sous la protection de Dieu pour qu'ils n'aient pas de malchances. C'étaient des chrétiens !"[45] Ross counted four hundred mounted hunters on his 1840 trip. It was important to act in unison, to avoid warning the herd of the impending attack. When bison noticed the hunters were approaching, the herd took flight, kicking up dust, noise, and chaos. The hunters galloped into the fray and looked for the fattest to target. Ross marvelled at the sight:

> Those who have seen a squadron of horse dash into battle, may imagine the scene, which we have no skill to depict. The earth seemed to tremble when the horses started; but when the animals fled, it was like the shock of an earthquake. The air was darkened; the rapid firing at first, soon became more and more faint, and at last died away in the distance. Two hours, and all was over; but several hours more elapsed before the result was known, or the hunters reassembled.[46]

Antoine Vermette remembered that "the roar from the impact of the thousand of hoofs was like the rumbling of thunder ... And above the roar you could hear the excited shouts of the hunters. When we were in the thick of it we did not fear anything and we used to ride right into the heart of the herd."[47] Depending on the speed and agility of a horse and rider, a skilled hunter could hope for ten kills, while the less experienced could manage two or three. Common accidents included falling off horses, being trampled by bison, and gunfire injuries.[48]

Although the vast majority of bison hunters were men, women could participate. Monsieur's female Nakoda guide and translator, Josette, surprised the brigade when she announced her intention of joining in the hunt:

> We will take our horse and gun and go with you. Maybe we will kill a buffalo, maybe we will not. We are very sorry for the buffalo anyway. The white man hunts them[,] the Indian hunts them, the half breed hunts them. They [?] no rest at all, but we will go with you. Monsieur, you will hire some of the women of the camp or the small boy and girl to drive the carts with the pack horses and the travois, and we will all go together. We do not like to stay in the camp. We are not one of them.[49]

Josette distinguished herself from the Metis women of the camp by joining the male hunters on horseback, revealing that Metis women did not normally hunt. Yet, Josette was not prohibited. Her directives also reveal that women and children had full charge of the Red River carts and pack horses in retrieving the meat of the fallen bison. Later during the same trip, while under immediate threat from the Dakota, Monsieur notes that Josette and at least twenty other women left the carts in the charge of older children. The women then rode horses into battle, with rifles and cartridge belts slung over their shoulders, even while they carried babies on their backs.[50]

After the hunt, some women took charge of processing the fallen bison, bringing some of the carts to the kill site, where men had immediately begun dismembering carcasses. Other women remained behind in the camp to take care of young children and elders and to prepare for the carts' return, readying stretchers and fires to dry the hides. Runners helped direct carts to the owners' kills. Everyone worked quickly to harvest as much meat as possible before sundown, though sometimes work continued through the night. Leftovers fed the wolves and scavengers. Soldiers kept a careful guard against enemies, as the best time to attack was immediately after a hunt in the chaos of the initial butchering. After loading the meat and robes, women drove the carts back to camp while men followed alongside them on horseback.[51]

Back at camp, the hunters rested while women organized the preparing of hides and meat for preservation.[52] Then all pitched in to help with curing the meat and drying and dressing the hides.[53] The hides were scraped, removing meat, fat, and any impurities. Women hung the hides on stretchers to dry in the sun and then smoked them until they were stiff. Some hides became the leather for tents, bags, thongs, whips, drums, and shields. Next the meat was butchered into thin strips to dry quickly in the sun. Women placed the meat on grids of branches and positioned them over smoking fires of buffalo chips to drive away the flies and hasten the drying.[54] Young girls tended the smoky fires and gathered the bison chips for fuel.[55] Meat usually took two days to dry, after which women stored it in skin bags or baskets made of wicker, rushes, or leather.[56]

After each hunt was complete, women began transforming the meat into pemmican. They placed dried meat on a buffalo hide and pounded it into a fine powder before adding melted fat to create a paste and adding dried and crushed berries to the mix. While still hot, the pemmican was poured into airtight bison-skin bags and left to cool and dry in the sun.[57] According to Sarah Nolin, women shared the labour of preparing pemmican. Some pounded the meat. Others melted the tallow and boiled bison bones to extract fat from their marrow. Another group packed the pemmican into bison-hide pouches that would have likely been prepared in the winter.[58] These bags of pemmican were heavy, according to Callihoo, and required two men to load into a cart.[59]

Bison-hunting brigades governed themselves by formal rules that were developed early in Metis practice and universally employed until the hunts declined with the virtual extinction of bison in 1885. These rules included not hunting on the Sabbath; having brigades operate as single and unified entities without side parties branching off or lagging behind; not hunting until the captain gave permission; and having all brigade members taking turns guarding and patrolling the camp.[60] Goulet remembers that the first rule forbade the use of alcohol on the hunt as well as "immorality of any kind, even blasphemy, the mildest. Leaving the camp without authorization from that council was forbidden, and one always have to wait for a signal from the guide before undertaking anything."[61] Hunting brigades did not stay longer than three days in one place, presumably to ensure fresh grazing for their animals.[62]

A moral economy ensured that all participants could share in the spoils of the hunt, even those families whose hunters did not manage a kill because of lack of experience, poor horses, poor quality rifles, or little ammunition. Successful hunters happily shared meat with the less fortunate. They often held races on horseback, charging an admission fee, given to the needy. Indeed, members of brigades freely shared ammunition and tools, as well as food.[63] Metis brought this long-standing ethic of sharing with them from their farming communities. "Whenever some building needed to be done," Goulet explained, "people would have a *corvée*. It was a long-standing custom with us. If a job was too much for one man's strengths or talents, everyone was ready to lend a hand. That way, people shared their skill or labour automatically and an entire house could be built from scratch in one day with spontaneous help from neighbours. Nobody ever had to be asked."[64] He continued to explain that, on the hunts, it was very common for families and neighbours to share food, and people looked for any excuse to hold parties and invite everyone to feast.[65] The Plains Metis also cared for the condition of the bison. According to Antoine Vermette, hunters could not shoot a female bison after 15 July, presumably because they might be pregnant, and those found guilty would be fined. In addition, men who could not skin all the bison they killed would be fined.[66]

Rule breakers met punishment, ranging from fines to execution, depending on the severity. Ross reported that hunters punished first-time offenders by slashing their saddle and bridle, second-time offenders by cutting up their coat, and third-time offenders by flogging. Thieves were subject to public identification, loud announcement, and humiliation. Yet Ross thought these punishments were nominal, implying that Metis seldom broke the rules because they "lived honestly and fairly."[67] Goulet, however, remembers punishments differently:

> There was one instance of a whole family put to death. The story had more than one version, but the only one I know said the Deschamps were well-known as a bad lot. It seems they'd been caught red-handed breaking all the rules including the ones about robbery and immorality. Apparently, one of them had even tried to lay hands on certain members of the council. One evening the family went to bed as usual, like everyone else. Next morning they were all found dead. Nobody every [sic] knew how, nor by whom, they'd been wiped out. The massacre of the Deschamps has become a legend on the plains, but the mystery has never been solved.[68]

This chilling tale underscores the seriousness of the hunt for Metis sustenance and prosperity. Maintaining social order was crucial for a successful hunt, and the cost of security could be high. Indeed, Hogue interprets the rules as "tempering the market motivations that might drive ... hunters to ruin resources and livelihoods." The chief and council gave the Metis brigades a form of community governance as well as martial discipline.[69] Erasmus observed that the camp leader "enforce[ed] rules and regulations for the general good. The safety of the camp depended largely on the experience and good judgement of the man elected." He remembered an incident when the elected chief overrode the council: when John Whitford realized that the brigade was on a southward route towards a party of Blackfoot, he ordered everyone to immediately turn west to avoid a direct meeting. Some Saddle Lake Cree in the brigade opposed Whitford's decision, arguing that the Cree and Blackfoot had negotiated a peace treaty. "John Whitford wheeled his horse and levelled his gun at the [Cree] man's chest," related Erasmus, "and in a voice like a crack of a whip said, 'You will follow my orders or die! It is better for one of us to die than risk the lives of everyone in this party. Turn your cart around now.' The man swung his horse around and headed for the west, lashing his horse unmercifully to show his anger." It turned out that the camp of Blackfoot was infected with smallpox, and Whitford managed to avert a tragedy.[70]

Indigenous Diplomacy and the Battle of Grand Coteau

Metis bison brigades often included members of various First Nations, particularly the Nakoda, Anishinaabe, and Cree, who had a long history of alliances with one another, and with fur traders in the northern Great Plains.[71] Many mixed bands emerged on the plains, which included Metis.[72] Robert Innes explains that Nakoda, Anishinaabe, Cree, and Metis "operated as sets of linked bands, which were politically autonomous units lacking tribal-level political organization. A band's membership was highly fluid, relatively small in size and highly mobile, usually dispersing and gathering with the seasons ... By the early 1800s, [they] ... had formed a formidable military alliance,"[73] called the Nehiyaw-Pwat or "Iron Alliance," symbolizing their military might. They often acted as middlemen in the fur trade and became major players in the bison trade.[74]

Traditional enemies of the Nakoda, Anishinaabe, and Cree entered into conflict with the Metis, which included Dakota (Yankton Sioux), Blackfoot, Gros Ventre, and Mandan/Hidatsa.[75] Struggles for access to European trade goods, bison, and horses determined much of the warfare on the northern plains. The Nakoda broke off from other Siouan-speakers, including the Dakota, to form an alliance with the Cree and Anishinaabe because of their secure connections to European fur traders.[76]

Metis recollections of the bison hunt include tales of terror and warfare, as the groups clashed over resources and access to land. Hogue explains that "informal agreements and more formal peace treaties negotiated between Metis and Dakota often helped avert or minimize conflict." Each group tried to curtail the fighting, and individuals from various bands sought good relations through gift giving, covering the dead, extending fictive kin relations, and sharing peace pipes.[77]

The forty-ninth parallel, determined in 1818 as marking the international boundary between British territory and the United States, clearly cut across Metis bison-hunting territory. The Metis used the boundary to promote their economic empowerment and political sovereignty, often playing the Hudson's

Bay Company and US-based competitors against one another and securing political rights depending on which side of the border they claimed.[78] As long as their source of economic wealth, namely, the bison herds, remained stable, Metis could use their numbers, hunting prowess, and alliances to prosper. The forty-ninth parallel was named "the medicine line" because of its ability to mark newcomer jurisdictions and to keep those national players (like soldiers and fur traders) on their side of the line. September 1851 witnessed the signing of the Treaty of Fort Laramie between American treaty commissionaires and members of the Sioux, Assiniboine, Cheyenne, Mandan, Hidatsa, Arikara, Arapaho, and Crow nations. The significance for all bison hunters on the plains was the growing number of wagon trains headed to Oregon and California across what is now southern Wyoming. Their presence increased stress on the environment and among peoples.[79]

Our analysis of the Battle of Grand Coteau begins by reconstructing the events of 12–14 July 1851 from six Metis accounts of the event, some written shortly after, others transmitted through oral history. They include those of "*Le vieux*" Simon Blondeau (1827– ?), a bison hunter accompanying the St François Xavier / White Horse Plain brigade; ChWeUm Davis (1845–1937), a bison hunter from Pembina and early Turtle Mountain historian; Gabriel Dumont (1837–1906), the military leader of 1885 resistance, accompanying the St François Xavier brigade; Jean-Baptiste Falcon (1826– ?), leader of the St François Xavier brigade; Isabelle (Fayant) McGillis (1838–1933), member of the Saint-Boniface brigade; and Jean Baptiste Laframboise (1806–70), a member of the St François Xavier brigade.[80] We also consulted two missionary accounts written in French.[81] Our final source is Rudolph Friedrich Kurz, a Swiss artist and writer who travelled along the Missouri River in 1851, relayed Metis men's voices in a travelogue, and drew images of the people he encountered.[82] Only one of these sources is a woman's voice. In the rest we have to listen carefully to find the active and diverse roles of women in diplomacy.

The St François Xavier brigade departed on 15 June 1851 from their home on the Assiniboine River. After a four-day walk, their two hundred carts joined the Pembina and Saint-Boniface groups, which were already assembled at the launching point for the hunt southwest of the Red River valley. Combined, the groups had 1,300 carts, ready to haul the year's bounty.[83] Two days later, on 21 June, this large hunting party encountered bison and, after the hunt, filled their carts with fresh meat, delighted to be ending a period of forced fasting. Laflèche remarked that the two groups comprised 700 men, 200 of whom were Anishinaabe.[84] Women and children inflated the numbers in the brigade, but Laflèche did not count them, considering them as passive witnesses to masculine achievements. This seasonal trek marked the beginning of the summer hunting season, where polyethnic brigades of Metis crossed the Medicine Line, met with their extended kin, and began their hunt for bison.[85]

Brigades from north of the Medicine Line joined their Pembina counterpart in council to finalize their summer plans. Their pre-arranged meeting point was usually Lodge Pole Valley, west of St Joseph (present-day Walhalla, North Dakota).[86] In 1851 Jean-Baptiste Falcon, captain of the St François Xavier brigade,[87] and Jean-Baptiste Wilkie, renowned captain of the hunt from Pembina / St Joseph, led the combined group.[88] During the council meeting, hunters agreed not to let the "Sioux" penetrate their camps under any circumstances.[89] After hunting together for a few days, the brigades parted ways to maximize their potential bison yield for the summer. Splitting up was an insurance strategy: should a brigade encounter violence or theft on a large scale, some of their relatives in other brigades would be share their profits with the unfortunate victims. The larger party, accompanied by missionary Albert Lacombe, headed west towards Dog Den Butte.[90] The smaller brigade, accompanied by Father Louis-François Richer Laflèche, headed towards Grand Coteau and reached their destination Saturday evening. As soon as the brigade climbed over the first hill of the Missouri Coteau, scouts spotted a large Indigenous encampment in the distance.

The missionaries' allegations that the brigade stumbled onto the large encampment by accident or misjudgment are false. Since the scouts were prepared to open diplomatic channels with peace offerings, they were well aware that they were heading towards a large party of Yanktonais.[91] Metis buffalo hunters were proud of their expertise at reading the prairie landscape. Explaining the deep roots of Metis geographical knowledge, Elder Gabriel Lafournaise dit Laboucane bragged to lost nineteenth-century surveyors about his connection to land: "Messieurs, c'est mon pays ici. Je lis dans les prairies comme vous lisez sur vos petites machines et votre papier."[92] On 12 July 1851, as the St François Xavier brigade approached Grand Coteau, scouts were dispatched to gather information on the Yanktonais encampment of over six hundred lodges and two thousand people.[93]

The brigade chose a defendable position to set up its carts in a circle for protection. The goal was not to attack the Yanktonais on the open plain but rather to draw them to their encampment so they would be forced to deal with the whole village, women and children included, thus encouraging peaceful diplomacy. Presumably the Metis hoped the Yanktonais would be less inclined to attack a village than a party of men on horseback. Nonetheless, ramparts were reinforced with pieces of buffalo meat obtained during their earlier summer hunt.[94] Laflèche, the priest accompanying the brigade, recited evening prayers, and, at some point in the night, the lunar eclipse Laflèche had predicted darkened the prairie sky. The eclipse was remembered in Metis oral history because it foreshadowed a calamity: it was an "omen of impending doom."[95]

The calamity materialized when the Metis learned that the Yankontais had captured their scouts.[96] A Yanktonais party then approached the makeshift Metis village. Ten Metis cavaliers rode up to intercept and engaged them in pipe ceremonies, respecting protocols of Indigenous diplomacy. During this exchange, the brigade learned that the captured scouts – James Whitford, Jean-Baptiste Malaterre, and Jérôme McGillis (sometimes identified as "Macdalise") – would be fed and looked after overnight.[97] In exchange for their safe return, the Metis pledged gifts of tobacco, gunpowder, and ammunition.[98] As a precaution, Metis men, women, and children began to dig trenches under the Red River carts and continued reinforcing their defensive position throughout the night. Laflèche spent the rest of the night hearing the confessions of the sixty to eighty men and youth preparing themselves for defensive warfare and possible death.[99] The next morning, 13 July, the brigade dispatched two men to inform the Pembina and Saint-Boniface group of their dangerous predicament and need for reinforcement.[100]

Shortly after the departure of their envoys, hundreds of Yanktonais, with the three Metis prisoners in tow, approached the encampment. Laflèche comforted the Metis and urged them to pray: "Courage, courage, mes amis! ... Souvenez-vous surtout que Dieu est de votre côté et que vous avez un père dans le ciel qui voit combien est injuste l'attaque de ces gens contre vous. Battez-vous courageusement, c'est Lui qui vous commande de défendre vos femmes et vos enfants et de protéger vos vies."[101] An American man travelling with the Yanktonais urged the captives to flee and provided cover by pretending to fire in their direction.[102] One of the three scouts did not have a strong horse and became an easy target for the Yanktonais during the escape. Jean-Baptiste Malaterre was killed, his mutilated remains displayed for all to see, while McGillis and Whitford made it to the Metis encampment.[103] The Yanktonais party continued to approach, ignoring Metis warnings, and insisted on "parlamenting" once again.[104] Brigade members equipped with guns fired in self-defence to prevent the large party from overtaking their position.[105]

At that point, the Metis had no choice but to engage in a battle. The armed split into two groups. One was tasked with the defence of the cart camp, the other comprised men on horseback, who divided into three lines of attack. Some women joined this assault. Kurz recorded Metis men's memories of "a Chippewa woman" who "was beside herself in her desire to do battle."[106] Likely the spouse of a bison hunter, the unnamed woman attempted to launch into battle with the oncoming assailants all by herself, instead of following the defence plan agreed to in council the previous night. After brigade members failed to stop her, she charged towards the Yanktonais and "took off all her clothes and, standing naked, waved her skirt at the enemy with jeering words." Three other women joined her, and the four sang and whooped at their enemy.[107] Perhaps these women were trying to show the Yankontais that they were not members of the settler wagon trains and instead were Indigenous neighbours who could coexist in peace. Irene Ternier Gordon tentatively identified two of the women as Madeleine Wilkie, future spouse of Gabriel Dumont, and Isabelle Falcon. An unknown source credits the women with ending the battle.[108] A similar combat strategy appeared in Gabriel Dumont's life story based on Metis oral history collected by Thomson. In this account, the young Gabriel Dumont engaged in the battle by waving a large red flag around to distract the Yanktonais attack, much like the women waving their skirts in the air.[109]

These descriptions suggest that women and youth gave the brigades' cavaliers opportunity to organize assaults by distracting the enemy. Missionary accounts made no mention of Anishinaabe women at the Battle of Grand Coteau, perhaps because of their nudity and because women's labour in a war effort transcended the realm of acceptability for Roman Catholic gender prescriptions. Reporting naked women waving their skirts in the battle would have discredited Laflèche's alleged control over his faithful and would have placed him in serious moral dilemmas with the church.

The Metis eventually pushed the assault away from their encampment.[110] Every shot fired was accompanied by cries of joy.[111] Laflèche hid in a pit dug out for him, reportedly praying to the God of armies and singing loudly.[112] Warfare paused on the first day when heavy rain and fog set in.[113] Families in the brigade encampment sang to remain awake through the night.

By the evening of 13 July, the two men dispatched to seek help from the Pembina and Forks groups reached their destination and shared the bad news. Jean-Baptiste Wilkie's brigade met in council and decided to send reinforcements at dawn on their fastest horses while the rest of the brigade would begin walking towards the group under attack. Father Lacombe spent the night hearing the confessions of the men who would be dispatched in the morning. He recommended a general fast for all present in his camp and promised two high masses to God should the Metis escape unharmed.[114]

Some Metis remembered the miraculous weather events on 14 July, specifically the heavy fog, which allowed the White Horse Plain brigade to move its camp southwest, following the Cheyenne River towards the Missouri Coteau. Members hoped the move would increase the chance of a prompt reunion with their relatives and provide them with much-needed respite.[115] After the fog faded, the battle resumed between the two groups until mid-afternoon. Again, the Metis arranged their carts into a defensive circle formation, this time, *à double rang*.[116]

11.1 Kurz contemporary (1851) drawings of Anishinaabeg women in various outfits. Source: Rudolph Friedrich Kurz, *Journal of Rudolph Friedrich Kurz: An Account of His Experience among Fur Traders and American Indians on the Mississippi and the Upper Missouri Rivers during the Years 1846 to 1852*, Plate 23, p. 389, NAA MS 2522-b. National Anthropological Archives, Smithsonian Institution.

Metis women were more prominently featured in the often-recounted narratives of the Battle of Grand Coteau than their Anishinaabe counterparts. Two historical accounts, in particular, highlight the role of armed women on equal footing with men. First, the oral accounts of the Falcon family noted that, since Jean-Baptiste was busy with his brigade captain duties, "his sister Isabelle was fighting in his place."[117] Isabelle Falcon, a lauded markswoman, ensured that her brother rested and covered his position. Isabelle, the wife of André Trottier, was thirty-two years of age at the time of the encounter.[118] Isabelle, her husband, and her family's relatives were affiliated with the Trottier brigade.[119] Isabelle Falcon's skill set was not unlike that of other Metis women. They were agile shooters and indispensable contributors to hunt profits, and they took care of their family members in times of difficulty.

The second woman named as an active participant in the conflict was James Whitford's mother. This account is more problematic, however, as it is impossible to determine *which* James Whitford was the scout that escaped Yankton capture – there were two and historical analyses do not distinguish between them.[120] In this published account from 1906, Dugas reported that, when Whitford's mother learned of her son's escape, she was jubilant. On seeing her son again, she approached him, and offered to take over his weapon so he could rest and recover from his ordeal as a prisoner and escapee.[121]

Unarmed men, women, and children participated in the battle in a variety of ways besides waving their clothing to distract the Yanktonais warriors. They continued to dig trenches, prepare ammunition, and care for the wounded. The oral history of Isabelle McGillis (née Fayant) relays that she and her relatives were tasked with healing the three wounded members of the brigade, including Isidore Ekapow Dumont, Gabriel Dumont's father.[122]

The battle ended about forty-five minutes before the Metis reinforcements arrived when the Yanktonais retreated following a final skirmish after another false pretence of peace. The Metis had prevailed. The polyethnic brigade of hunters did not suffer additional human losses besides captive Jean-Baptiste Malaterre, but lost twelve horses and four oxen, while reports indicate that the Yanktonais lost between eighteen and eighty people.[123] The Yanktonais attributed their defeat to the singing Manitou, or Father Laflèche. His presence incited the Metis's opponents to abandon the fight altogether, even though they greatly outnumbered the Metis, fearing the missionary's prayers and "medicines" were too strong to defeat.[124] Most Metis sources attributed the defeat to their marksmanship and military skill. Only a few scant references acknowledge the central role played by women. When all three brigades reunited, they agreed to continue hunting together for the safety of numbers.[125]

Even though the Yanktonais had started the fight, the Metis left a letter of apology written in English addressed "to the Sioux" at the site of the second day's attack, assuming that the American who liberated the captured scouts would translate it.[126] The letter denounced the Metis's use of violence and described their victory as repugnant. The Metis wished for an alliance, reminding the Yanktonais that they could act as a buffer with their Saulteux (Anishinaabe) relatives, who were long-time enemies of the Yanktonais. The Metis forgave the Yanktonais for the attacks and called them "good brothers."[127] Metis hunters likely felt sympathy for an Indigenous nation increasingly suffering from settler encroachment on their territory. In addition, the two nations shared kinship bonds via intermarriage. The three prisoners from the brigade encampment were sheltered in the lodge of an acquaintance of Jérôme McGillis's, indicating space for friendships between members of the two groups.[128] Jean-Baptiste Wilkie, captain of the Pembina/Forks brigade, wished to take the responsibility for the well-being of the orphans and widows the violent altercation created.[129] Taking responsibility for victims was part of a relationship-building process initiated by the letter, demonstrating what Gaudry called the "common, international political language, based on the symbolism of kinship, which determined how families, bands and nations were to behave towards one another."[130] Evidently, bison hunters had long-term, vested interests in ensuring good diplomatic relations with the Yanktonais. By claiming responsibility for the widows and orphans the conflict created, accepting them, perhaps, into Metis families, they might encourage peaceful encounters in the future.

Yet not all Metis shared the sentiments expressed in the letter of apology. Gabriel Dumont, for example, could not trust the Yanktonais's word.[131] Some Metis families approached a Yanktonais encounter with extreme caution because of past conflicts, such as that with the Sisitou-Dakota in 1844–5. Peaceful relations facilitated a good hunt, but the Metis had trouble trusting their long-term enemies.[132] Although she joined the St François Xavier party the next day, Isabelle Fayant's recollections reflect the same mistrust: when the two groups met, "the Metis offered the customary gift of tobacco and suggested the Sioux depart in peace after the release of the other prisoners they had taken. They scorned the gifts and scoffed at the idea of retreat."[133]

Despite the diversity of views on Metis and Yanktonais relations, Indigenous diplomatic practices shaped the conflict and resolution. Both missionaries' written accounts stress the presence of Indigenous ceremony. Laflèche recounted that the first encounter following the capture of the three scouts involved "many ceremonies" that opened avenues of communication, after which they agreed the prisoners would be exchanged for tobacco, gunpowder, and ammunition.[134] The following day, when the hundreds of Yanktonais advanced towards the brigade encampment with the three captives, Laflèche states that Metis approached the party with gifts, hoping to avoid conflict.[135] Lacombe's recollection emphasized the Yanktonais' desire to enter the brigade encampment to smoke the pipe and make peace, as they were accustomed to doing.[136]

Warfare, Indigenous protocols, and treaty-making practices included both men and women. Women made up close to half of the 1851 brigade encampment and must have played a significant role in a conflict where the Yanktonais outnumbered and threatened Metis hunters. Women present at this event could shoot, fight, defend themselves, and voice political opinions. Women also protected their children, healed the wounded, and engaged in religious ceremonies and rituals. The four distinct accounts of women's activities in the battle show the range of roles they played, including shooting, singing, healing, digging pits, and waging war. The mention of caring for women and children in the apology letter illustrates the family nature of Metis mobile villages.

The role of youth and children at Grand Coteau needs further investigation. According to calculations made by Laflèche, the White Horse Plain brigade had as many as thirteen youths, which meant that young males, whether adolescent or prepubescent, had access to weapons and sufficient battle training to directly engage the enemy.[137] Their words and experiences were recorded mostly through the eyes of others. The sole youth experience detailed in historical scholarship on Grand Coteau was Gabriel Dumont's. Thirteen years old at the time, he wanted to take an active role in the battle and the diplomatic processes that preceded it, but his father, Isidore "Ekapow" Dumont, prevented him.[138] Since his injury on 13 July, Isidore Dumont watched from inside the corral and encouraged his relatives.[139] Although Gabriel was too young to train for battle, he was familiar with Indigenous diplomatic protocols. Dumont was an expert "buffalo caller/taunter," a skill he used against his opponents by forcing them into the line of fire, much like he could incite a bison herd to move in a particular direction. Dumont relied on his agility, speed, polyglot mastery of insults, and bison-hunting knowledge to help the White Horse Plain brigade declare victory.[140] He was likely not alone in using these methods of distraction.

The tactics deployed by Dumont were similar to those used by the unnamed women who removed their skirts and taunted the Yanktonais. Over a dozen unnamed adolescents, between twelve and fifteen, followed in Dumont's footsteps in this battle. Although he was only thirteen, some Metis historical accounts of the event suggest that Dumont played a larger role in the victory than did Jean-Baptiste Falcon. Gabriel Dumont was related to the chief of the Pembina Brigade, Jean-Baptiste Wilkie, who "was conferring on [Dumont] some of [his] prestige."[141] Dumont's kin connection to Wilkie gave him significant influence among the White Horse Plain brigade. As with women, finding the contributions of youth require that we look beyond the limits of patriarchal myopia in primary sources and historiography.

Metis bison-hunting brigades were mobile villages that travelled great distances across the plains in pursuit of their prey. Their well-organized formations, careful adherence to rules, and strong social order do not mean they were militaristic patriarchies looking to wage wars on their competitors. The village model of the hunt encouraged all to avoid violence both outside and within the brigade. The strict rules of the hunts helped secure community order.

Women played a central part in the social order of Metis brigades, both on hunts and in battles. As primary drivers of the Red River carts and in charge of the space inside the large encampment circles of carts, women were central to the smooth functioning of internal social order. Although men were the primary agents in negotiating war and peace, women participated in battles and diplomatic ceremonies to help facilitate the mostly peaceful diplomacy with other Metis brigades and neighbouring First Nations. Travelling as a village, with women and children present, helped keep men safe and helped keep peace on the plains.

Men and women had separate responsibilities in the hunting brigades. Men elected into leadership of the brigades controlled the hunt and relations with neighbours, both friend and foe. Women's authority resided on the carts and inside the cart circle as they managed sustenance, healing, and children. Yet, the gendered lines of labour and responsibility were not harshly drawn. Women hunted and fought, often alongside their male kin, when they desired and necessity required. Although women remained outside of council meetings, and few became hunt leaders, ties of kin meant that women could influence the political actions of their husbands and sons. When battle became necessary, women's participation – especially, in the case of the Battle of Grand Coteau, their flamboyant nudity and skirt waving – communicated to enemies that they were attacking not just male hunters but a whole village of men and women, young and old. Both Metis men and women were prepared to take up arms and fight, but peace ensured the success of the hunt. Sharing the wealth of bison required collective action within brigades and cooperation with neighbours. After all, processing thousands of pounds of bison takes a village.

NOTES

1 See, for example, "The Summer Hunt," *Nor-Wester*, 14 August 1860, 2.

2 George Colpitts, *Pemmican Empire: Food, Trade, and the Last Bison Hunts in the North American Plains, 1780–1882* (Cambridge: Cambridge University Press, 2014), 193.

3 Adam Gaudry, "Kaa-Tipeyimishoyaahk – 'We Are Those Who Own Ourselves': A Political History of Metis Self-Determination in the North-West, 1830–1870" (PhD diss., University of Victoria, 2014), 102.

4 John E. Foster, "Wintering, The Outsider Adult Male, and the Ethnogenesis of the Western Plains Metis," *Prairie Forum* 19, no. 1 (Spring 1994): 1–13.

5 Brenda Macdougall, *One of the Family: Metis Culture in Nineteenth-Century Northwestern Saskatchewan* (Vancouver: UBC Press, 2010); and Nicole St-Onge, *Saint-Laurent, Manitoba: Evolving Metis Identities, 1850–1914* (Regina: Canadian Plains Research Center, 2004).

6 Heather Devine, *The People Who Own Themselves: Aboriginal Ethnogenesis in a Canadian Family, 1660–1900* (Calgary: University of Calgary Press, 2004); Diane Payment, *"Les gens libres – Otipemisiwak," Batoche, Saskatchewan, 1870–1930* (Ottawa: Parks Canada, 1990); and Michel Hogue, *Metis and the Medicine Line: Creating a Border and Dividing a People* (Chapel Hill: University of North Carolina Press, 2015), 23–4.

7 Alexander Ross, *The Red River Settlement: Its Rise, Progress, and Present State. with Some Account of the Native Races and Its General History, to the Present Day* (London: Smith, Elder, 1856), 252.

8 Pierre Falcon, "The Buffalo Hunt," in *Songs of Old Manitoba*, ed. Margaret Arnett MacLeod (Toronto: Ryerson Press, 1959), 20, also cited by Hogue, *Metis and the Medicine Line*, 44–5.

9 Gaudry, "Kaa-Tipeyimishoyaahk," 1–2, quote on 97–8.

10 Sylvia Van Kirk, *'Many Tender Ties': Women in Fur-Trade Society, 1670–1870* (Winnipeg: Watson and Dwyer, 1980); Jennifer S.H. Brown, *Strangers in Blood: Fur Trade Company Families in Indian Country* (Vancouver: UBC Press, 1980); and Susan Sleeper-Smith, *Indian Women and French Men: Rethinking Cultural Encounter in the Western Great Lakes* (Amherst: University of Massachusetts Press, 2001).

11 Brenda Macdougall and Nicole St-Onge, "Rooted in Mobility: Metis Buffalo-Hunting Brigades," *Manitoba History* 71 (Winter 2013): 24. One sister, Ursule, married Charles Trottier, elected captain of the brigade. The other two sisters, Angélique and Philomène, married Antoine Trottier and Moise Landry, leading members of the same brigade.

12 Yanktonais are part of the Western Dakota (a Souian group), who, with the Yankton, call themselves Wičhiyena. David Grant McCrady, *Living with Strangers: The Nineteenth-Century Sioux and the Canadian-American Borderlands* (Toronto: University of Toronto Press, 2010), 13. Lawrence Barkwell states that the conflict was between the Metis and "Cut Head (Pabaksa) Yanktonais (Ihanktonwanna), Dakota, led by Chief Medicine (Sacred) Bear," based on the geographic location of the encounter at Dog Den Butte in "Grand Coteau, Metis Veterans and Families" (Louis Riel Institute, 22 January 2015), Gabriel Dumont Institute of Native Studies and Applied Research, Virtual Museum of Métis History and Culture,

http://www.metismuseum.ca/resource.php/15067, accessed 13 June 2016. Gaudry, in contrast, prefers the name "Yankton" in "Kaa-Tipeyimishoyaahk," 159.

13 Nicholas C.P. Vrooman, *The Whole Country Was ... One Robe: The Little Shell Tribe's America* (Great Falls, MT: Drumlummon Institute and Little Shell Tribe of Chippewa Indians of Montana, 2013), 387.

14 Sarah Carter and Patricia Alice McCormack, eds, *Recollecting: Lives of Aboriginal Women of the Canadian Northwest and Borderlands* (Edmonton: Athabasca University Press, 2011).

15 Gendered colonialism is a rapidly growing field; here, we highlight only a few relevant studies: Ann Stoler, ed., *Haunted by Empire: Geographies of Intimacy in North American History* (Durham, NC: Duke University Press, 2006); Myra Rutherdale and Katie Pickles, eds, *Contact Zones: Aboriginal and Settler Women in Canada's Colonial Past* (Vancouver: UBC Press, 2005); and Adele Perry, *On the Edge of Empire: Gender, Race, and the Making of British Columbia* (Toronto: University of Toronto Press, 2001).

16 Colin G. Calloway, *One Vast Wintercount: The Native American West before Lewis and Clark* (Lincoln: University of Nebraska Press, 2003), 34, 37–42.

17 Calloway, *One Vast Wintercount*, 267–312; and Andrew C. Isenberg, *The Destruction of the Bison: An Environmental History, 1750–1920* (Cambridge: Cambridge University Press, 2000), 42–4, 50–3, 65–75.

18 On diseases in the northwest plains, see Calloway, *One Vast Wintercount*, 224–5, 255, 257–8, 342, 415–26; Elizabeth A. Fenn, *Pox Americana: The Great Smallpox Epidemic of 1775–82* (New York: Hill and Wang, 2001); and James Daschuk, *Clearing the Plains: Disease, Politics, and the Loss of Aboriginal Life* (Regina: University of Regina Press, 2013), 11–77. On new/mixed bands, see John S. Milloy, *The Plains Cree: Trade, Diplomacy, and War, 1780 to 1870* (Winnipeg: University of Manitoba Press, 1990); Laura Peers, *The Ojibwa of Western Canada, 1780–1870* (Winnipeg: University of Manitoba Press, 1994); and Robert Alexander Innes, *Elder Brother and the Law of the People: Contemporary Kinship and Cowessess First Nation* (Winnipeg: University of Manitoba Press, 2013), 43–69.

19 Hogue, *Metis and the Medicine Line*, 13, 34, quote on 4.

20 Isenberg, *The Destruction of the Bison*, 93–4, 104, 108–9.

21 Colpitts, *Pemmican Empire*, 192–3, quote on 192.

22 Louis Goulet, *Vanishing Spaces: Memoirs of Louis Goulet*, recorded by Guillaume Charette and translated by Ray Ellenwood (Winnipeg: Editions Bois-Brûlés, 1976, originally recorded in 1903), 16, 53, 57, 67; Gerhard J. Ens, *Homeland to Hinterland: The Changing World of the Red River Metis in the Nineteenth Century* (Toronto: University of Toronto Press, 1996), 77–9; and Hogue, *Metis and the Medicine Line*, 28.

23 Ross says they were elected, but he does not describe the process of the election.

24 It is not clear whether these were elected or appointed. Goulet notes that councillors were named "after careful deliberation." Goulet, *Vanishing Spaces*, 22.

25 Ross, *Red River Settlement*, 248.

26 Goulet, *Vanishing Spaces*, 21–2.

27 Katherine Hughes, *Father Lacombe: The Black-Robe Voyageur* (Toronto: McClelland and Stewart, 1920), 25.

28 Peter Erasmus, *Buffalo Days and Nights*, as told to Henry Thompson in 1920 (Calgary: Fifth House, 1999), 200–1.

29 Auguste Vermette, *Au temps de la prairie: L'histoire des Mêtis de l'Ouest canadien racontée par Auguste Vermette, neveu de Louis Riel*, recorded by Marcien Ferland (Saint-Boniface, MB: Blé en Poche, 2006), 112.

30 Goulet, *Vanishing Spaces*, 21.

31 Hughes, *Father Lacombe*, 25.

32 Goulet *Vanishing Spaces*, 21.

33 Antoine Vermette, "Antoine Vermette, Red River Pioneer, Tells of Manitoba's Buffalo," *Manitoba Free Press*, 26 August 1905, typescript in Charles D. Denney Papers, Glenbow Archives, Calgary, pp. 6–7.

34 Victoria Callihoo, "Our Buffalo Hunts," *Alberta Historical Review* 8, no. 1 (Winter 1960), 24–5.

35 Hughes, *Father Lacombe*, 26.

36 Ross, *Red River Settlement*, 249.

37 Goulet, *Vanishing Spaces*, 23.

38 Ibid., 24–5; Father Georges-Antoine Belcourt, letter written 25 November 1845 to the Secretary of War transmitting report of Major Wood, United States War Department (1850), House of Representative, 31st Congress, 1st Session, Ex. Doc no. 51, 44–52 (later published in *North Dakota History* 38, no. 3 (1971): 334–48), 2 (hereafter Belcourt to Wood).

39 Goulet, *Vanishing Spaces*, 23.

40 Ross, *Red River Settlement*, 249–51, 254; Goulet, *Vanishing Spaces*, 22.

41 Auguste Vermette, *Au temps de la prairie*, 113; Goulet, *Vanishing Spaces*, 23–4. For an example of women hunting ducks on the brigade, see Heather Devine, ed., *The Buffalo Hunters of Pembina* (manuscript in preparation for publication), 15 September 1866. Original typescript: Gordon J. Keeney, "The Buffalo Hunters of Pembina" 1862–1865, Ms. 10431, State Historical Society of North Dakota, Bismark, microfilm roll 12193. Devine describes the manuscript as "the personal diary of an anonymous traveler, a young British nobleman who had spent the larger portion of a year on the plains with a party of Métis buffalo hunters originating at Pembina, North Dakota, around 1871." See Heather Devine, "New Light on the Plains Metis: The Buffalo Hunters of Pembina, 1870–71," in *The Long Journey of a Forgotten People: Metis Identities and Family Histories*, ed. Ute

Lischke and David T. McNab (Waterloo: Wilfrid Laurier University Press, 2007), 198. Note that she now believes the manuscript to have been written in 1866. We thank Heather Devine for her generosity in sharing her edition of the manuscript and for her counsel in understanding its contents.

42 Devine, ed., *The Buffalo Hunters of Pembina*, 18 August 1866.

43 Father Georges-Antoine Belcourt commented that he always accompanied the bison brigades on their hunts; Belcourt to Wood, 25 November 1845, 6; also see August Vermette, *Au temps de la prairie*, 110–11; John E. Foster, "Le Missionnaire and le chef métis," *Western Oblate Studies 1 / Études oblates de l'ouest 1*, ed. Raymond Huel (Edmonton: Western Canadian Publishers and l'Institut de recherche de la Faculté Saint-Jean, 1990), 117–27.

44 Goulet, *Vanishing Spaces*, 26–7.

45 Auguste Vermette, *Au temps de la prairie*, 123. Also see Devine, ed., *The Buffalo Hunters of Pembina*, 22 August 1866.

46 Ross, *Red River Settlement*, 256.

47 Antoine Vermette, "Red River Pioneer," 4–5.

48 Ross, *Red River Settlement*, 254–7; also see Belcourt to Wood, 25 November 1845, 2–4.

49 Devine, ed., *The Buffalo Hunters of Pembina*, 21 August 1866.

50 Ibid., section called "We Are Attacked by the Sioux in Force."

51 Sarah Nolin, "Mrs William Davis WPA Making Pemmican," n.d., MSS 10035, Reel 5905 (scans 2331–2333.pdf), State Historical Society of North Dakota.

52 Ross, *Red River Settlement*, 257–62; Goulet, *Vanishing Spaces*, 55; Auguste Vermette, *Au temps de la prairie*, 126–7; Antoine Vermette, "Red River Pioneer," 8.

53 Devine, ed., *The Buffalo Hunters of Pembina*, 22 August 1866.

54 Goulet, *Vanishing Spaces*, 53–5; Auguste Vermette, *Au temps de la prairie*, 127–9.

55 Callihoo, "Our Buffalo Hunts," 25.

56 Goulet, *Vanishing Spaces*, 55.

57 Ibid., 56; also see also see Belcourt to Wood, 25 November 1845, 5.

58 Nolin, "Mrs William Davis WPA Making Pemmican."

59 Callihoo, "Our Buffalo Hunts," 25.

60 Ross, *Red River Settlement*, 249–50. Also see a discussion of the law of coordinated killing of bison in Auguste Vermette, *Au temps de la prairie*, 119–22, and in Antoine Vermette, "Red River Pioneer," 8.

61 Goulet, *Vanishing Spaces*, 21; Auguste Vermette also asserted that drinking was not permitted on brigades in *Au temps de la prairie*, 114.

62 Ross, *Red River Settlement*, 246.

63 Ibid., 286–7. Also see Erasmus, *Buffalo Days and Nights*, 229.

64 Goulet, *Vanishing Spaces*, 4.

65 Ibid., 43.

66 Antoine Vermette, "Red River Pioneer," 5.

67 Ross, *Red River Settlement*, 249–50.

68 Goulet, *Vanishing Spaces*, 21.

69 Hogue, *Metis and the Medicine Line*, 33.

70 Erasmus, *Buffalo Days and Nights*, 201–4, quotes on 201, 203.

71 Arthur J. Ray, *Indians in the Fur Trade: Their Role as Hunters, Trappers, and Middlemen in the Lands Southwest of Hudson Bay, 1660–1870* (Toronto: University of Toronto Press, 1974); William R. Swagerty, "Indian Trade in the Trans-Mississippi West to 1870," in *Handbook of North American Indians*, vol. 4, *History of Indian-White Relations*, ed. William C. Sturtevant (Washington, DC: Government Printing Office, 1978), 351–74; and W. Raymond Wood and Thomas D. Thiessen, eds, *Early Fur Trade on the Northern Plains: Canadian Traders among the Mandan and Hisatsa Indians, 1738–1818* (Norman: University of Oklahoma Press, 1985).

72 Peers, *The Ojibwa of Western Canada*, 152–4, 187–8; Innes, *Elder Brother*, 70–89.

73 Innes, *Elder Brother*, 58, 60. Also see Robert Alexander Innes, "Multicultural Bands on the Northern Plains and the Notion of 'Tribal' Histories" in *Finding a Way to the Heart: Feminist Writings on Aboriginal and Women's History in Canada*, ed. Robin Brownlie and Valerie J. Korinek (Winnipeg: University of Manitoba Press, 2012), 122–45; Hogue, *Metis and the Medicine Line*, 20–1; and Gaudry, "Kaa-Tipeyimishoyaahk," 128–59.

74 The best description of Nehiyaw Pwat, especially concerning Metis, is Vrooman, *"The Whole Country Was ... 'One Robe,'"* 23–38, 53–4, 57–8, 61–3, 83–9. Also see Innes, *Elder Brother*, 60–4, 75–6.

75 We note that some Anishinaabeg became allies of Dakota. See Michael Witgen, *An Infinity of Nations: How the Native New World Shaped Early North America* (Philadelphia: University of Pennsylvania Press, 2013).

76 Raymond J. DeMaillie and David Reed Miller, "Assiniboine" in *Handbook of North American Indians*, vol. 13, *Plains*, ed. Raymond J. DeMallie (Washington, DC: Smithsonian Institution Press, 2001), pt. 1, 572–95.

77 Hogue, *Metis and the Medicine Line*, 36–7; Gaudry, "'Kaa-Tipeyimishoyaahk," 137.

78 Hogue, *Metis and the Medicine Line*, esp. 51–2.

79 Melinda Marie Jetté, *At the Hearth of the Crossed Races: A French Indian Community in Nineteenth-Century Oregon, 1812–1859* (Corvallis: Oregon State University Press, 2015), 122; Isenberg, *The Destruction of the Bison*, 109.

80 For the accounts of the battle and biographical information on Jean-Baptiste Laframboise, Isabelle Fayant, and Gabriel Dumont (translated into English) see Barkwell, "Grand Coteau, Metis Veterans, and Families." Another account of Gabriel Dumont's experience based on Metis oral history is Charles Duncan Thomson, *Red Sun: Gabriel Dumont the Folk Hero* (Winnipeg: Author, 1995),

31–8. The French language accounts translated in Barkwell's research include B.A.T. de Montigny, "Biographie et récit de Gabriel Dumont sur les événements de 1885," in *La vérité sur la question métisse au Nord-Ouest*, by Adolphe Ouimet (Montreal: n.p., 1889), http://peel.library.ualberta.ca/bibliography/1517.html, accessed 12 June 2016. This source is a longer, French-language version of the English text attributed to the Belleau Collection (p. 2 n. 2) in Barkwell's research. The other French-language source translated by Barkwell is Georges Dugas's *Histoire de l'Ouest canadien de 1822 à 1869: Époque des troubles* (Montreal: Librairie Beauchemin, 1906). For the oral account left by Simon Blondeau, see Pierre Picton, "Témoignage du vieux Blondeau, notes de Mgr Langevin: La bataille du Grand Coteau 13 et 14 juillet 1851," 1937, Fonds 0001, box 6, file 211, Société Historique de Saint-Boniface, Winnipeg. For the account by ChWeUm Davis, see William Davis, "The William Davis Diaries, Book 5," n.d., MSS 10035, reel 5905 (scans 2475–88.pdf), State Historical Society of North Dakota, Bismark, 11–12.

81 Albert Lacombe, "Deux lettres du P. Lacombe écrites en 1852," *Les cloches de Saint-Boniface* 16, no. 5 (1 March 1917): 73–8; Louis-François Richer Laflèche, "Lettre de M. Richer Laflèche, missionnaire à un de ses amis, le 4 septembre 1851" in *Rapport sur les Missions du Diocèse de Québec (mars 1853)* 10 (Quebec: Presses à Vapeur d'Augustin Côté, 1853), 44–70.

82 Rudolph Friedrich Kurz, *Journal of Rudolph Friedrich Kurz: An Account of His Experience among Fur Traders and American Indians on the Mississippi and the Upper Missouri Rivers during the Years 1846 to 1852*, ed. J.N.B. Hewitt, Smithsonian Institution Bureau of American Ethnology Bulletin 115 (Washington, DC: United States Government Printing Office, 1937).

83 Lacombe, "Deux lettres."

84 Laflèche, "Lettre," 54, 76.

85 Barkwell's 2015 unpublished manuscript "The Battle of Grand Coteau" explains that this was "a battle between the Cut Head (Pabaksa) Yankton and a hunting group of the *Nehiyaw Pwat* (literally Plains Cree-Nakoda) alliance which was also known as the Iron Alliance. This historic polyethnic group comprised of Metis, Plains Cree, Plains Ojibwa (Chippewa), and Assiniboine (Nakoda or Stoney) peoples. Most of the hunters of this group were descendants of either Plains Cree, Assiniboine (Nakoda) or Chippewa parents or grandparents." See Barkwell, "Grand Coteau, Metis Veterans and Families," 1.

86 Thomson, *Red Sun*, 31.

87 His leadership was contested by Gabriel Dumont's contributions to warfare. Francis Falcon, "Battle of the Grand Coteau with the Sioux 85 Years of Age This Coming July," 23 May 1938, Belleau Collection, roll 2, slides 180–1, Assumption Abbey, Richardton, ND.

88 Thomson, *Red Sun*, 31.

89 Lacombe, "Deux lettres," 76–7.

90 Laflèche, "Lettre," 54.

91 Ibid., 56.

92 "Les voix de la colonie: Un ancien chasseur de buffalos. Noces d'or," *Les cloches de Saint-Boniface* 1, no. 8 (July 1902): 240.

93 Laflèche's account states the Sioux had 2,000 people, or 600 loges ("Lettre," 57). Lacombe, whose party met up with the White Horse Plain brigade after the two days of battle, estimated 800 lodges and 2,000 men ("Deux lettres," 76). When Gabriel Dumont dictated his memoirs to Ouimet, when he was fifty-one years old, he stated that the Grand Coteau battle involved "1000 warriors." The account attributed to Dumont in the Belleau Collection states that there were 3,000 warriors. Simon Blondeau's account, as told to Mgr. Langevin, reported 800 lodges of Sioux. In contrast, the account of the battle published by Kurz, who obtained his factual information from the Metis in the fall of 1851, reported 2,500 Sioux in 800 tents, with another 600 "farther back" (see Kurz, *Journal*, 191). This extensive list of total number Yanktons encountered by the Metis on 12 July 1851 highlights the fact that all of these numbers are estimates and that, because the number of Metis soldiers armed with guns was estimated at between 60 (Falcon) and 80 (Laflèche), the ratio of brigade member to Yanktons in this conflict varies from 1:12 (80 Metis vs. 1,000 Yanktons) to 1:31 (63 Metis vs. 2,000 Yanktons) to 1:47 (63 Metis vs. 3,000 Yanktons).

94 Kurz, *Journal*, 191.

95 Melvin Beaudry, "Isbelle Fayant McGillis Eyewitness Account of Battle of Grand Coteau," ca 2000, 3, http://www.metismuseum.ca/resource.php/11684, accessed 9 November 2018.

96 Falcon, "Battle of the Grand Coteau."

97 Picton, "Témoignage du vieux Blondeau."

98 Laflèche, "Lettre," 57.

99 The importance of lived religion in this event, specifically Metis Catholicism, is explored at length in Émilie Pigeon, "Au nom du Bon Dieu et du buffalo: Metis Lived Catholicism on the Northern Plains" (PhD diss., York University, 2017).

100 Laflèche, "Lettre," 59.

101 Ibid., 60.

102 Picton, "Témoignage du vieux Blondeau."

103 Falcon, "Battle of the Grand Coteau." Also, Laflèche recorded the event in the St François Xavier parish register as follows: "Le 13 juillet 1851 Nous soussignés avons inhumé près de la Rivière des Chayennes le corps de l'infortuné Jean-Baptiste Malaterre, masacré le même jour par les Sioux. Il fut inhumé les pieds et les mains coupés, la chevelure levée, la cervelle répandue sur la terre et ayant dans le corps autant que trois coups de fusil, soixante-sept flèches et trois couteaux

plantés. Furent présents à l'inhumation Pascal Breland, Charles Montour." (on 13 July 1851, we the undersigned inhumed the body of the unfortunate Jean-Baptiste Malaterre near the Chayenne River, massacred the same day by the Sioux. He was buried with missing hands and feet, his head scalped and his brains spread out on the ground. He had in his body as many as three bullets, sixty-seven arrows, and three knifes still implanted. Also present at the burial were Pascal Breland, Charles Montour).

104 de Montigny, "Biographie et récit de Gabriel Dumont," 172.

105 Thomson, *Red Sun*, 35.

106 Kurz, *Journal*, 191.

107 Ibid., 191–2.

108 Irene Ternier Gordon, *A People on the Move: The Metis of the Western Plains* (Victoria, BC: Heritage House Publishing, 2009), 145. Gordon does not provide a source for this information. If true, Wilkie would have been fourteen years old at the time, and Falcon thirty-two.

109 Thomson, *Red Sun*, 34.

110 de Montigny, "Biographie et récit de Gabriel Dumont," 101–2.

111 Laflèche, "Lettre," 61.

112 Lacombe, "Deux lettres," 76. Although there is no Catholic "god of armies," there are numerous military saints that Laflèche could have called upon to protect the Metis brigade. It is unknown if Lacombe meant to say patron saints instead of "Dieu des armées" but the letter in question used the latter vocabulary.

113 Ibid., 77.

114 Ibid., 75.

115 According to the oral history account of Gene "Chip" Lafromboise to Lawrence Barkwell on the Turtle Mountain Reservation in Belcourt, ND. See Barkwell, "Grand Coteau, Metis Veterans and Families," 33.

116 Laflèche, "Lettre," 64.

117 Falcon, "Battle of the Grand Coteau."

118 "Scrip Affidavit for Trottier, Isabelle; Born: June 1819; Claim No 3005; Scrip No: 12567," 10 November 1879, RG15-D-II-8-a Reel C-14934, Library and Archives Canada, http://collectionscanada.gc.ca/pam_archives/index.php?fuseaction=genitem.displayItem&lang=eng&rec_nbr=1504360, accessed 9 November 2018.

119 Macdougall and St-Onge, "Rooted in Mobility."

120 Barkwell, "Grand Coteau, Metis Veterans and Families," 40.

121 Abbé Georges Dugas, *Histoire de l'Ouest canadien*, 126.

122 Beaudry, "Isbelle Fayant McGillis Eyewitness Account," 4.

123 Ibid.; Laflèche's "Lettre," states that there were 50 Sioux dead, 18 wounded, and 9 dead horses (69–70). In contrast, Lacombe, "Deux lettres," states there was a total of 16 Sioux dead (77). Dumont's accounts in *Red Sun* lists 18–80 Sioux losses

(37), whereas Kurz recorded 80 dead men and 65 horses lost (Kurz, *Journal*, 192). Whatever the losses, they were significant enough to trigger a withdrawal from the Metis encampment.

124 Falcon, "Battle of the Grand Coteau"; Lacombe, "Deux lettres," 77. Some Metis people agreed that the priests' connection to God led to their victory. See Barkwell, "Grand Coteau, Metis Veterans and Families," 33.

125 William Davis, "The William Davis Diaries, Book 5," n.d., 11–12, MSS 10035, reel 5905 (scans 2475–88.pdf), State Historical Society of North Dakota.

126 Laflèche, "Lettre," 65.

127 Ibid., 66.

128 Picton, "Témoignage du vieux Blondeau."

129 Thomson, *Red Sun*, 38.

130 Gaudry, "Kaa-Tipeyimishoyaahk," 134.

131 de Montigny, "Biographie et récit de Gabriel Dumont," 101. Dumont states: "il fallait être sur ses gardes et ne pas trop se fier à la parole des Sioux qui approchaient avec des propositions de paix, sous prétexte de négocier pour des provisions qu'ils avaient prises."

132 Gaudry, "Kaa-Tipeyimishoyaahk," 153–9. In 1844, "the Sisitou Dakota sent an emissary to the Métis Chief Cuthbert Grant ... lamenting the loss of young men during a series of deadly skirmishes between Sisitou warriors and Métis soldiers." In this conflict, the Sisitou opened diplomatic channels with the Metis, hoping that they could offer the prestige of the deceased to build kinship links and "behave as good relatives." Gaudry notes there were no written record of the outcome of this diplomatic encounter.

133 Beaudry, "Isbelle Fayant McGillis Eyewitness Account," 4; Gaudry, "Kaa-Tipeyimishoyaahk," 162.

134 Laflèche, "Lettre," 57.

135 Ibid., 59.

136 Lacombe, "Deux lettres," 76.

137 Laflèche, "Lettre," 58.

138 Old Simon Blondeau relates: "un Métis veut aller voir les Sioux, son fils veut l'accompagner, son père refuse" in Picton's "Témoignage du vieux Blondeau." This account corroborates the oral history collected synthesizing Gabriel Dumont's life in Thomson, *Red Sun*, 31.

139 de Montigny, "Biographie et récit de Gabriel Dumont," 101–3.

140 Thomson, *Red Sun*, 34.

141 Ibid., 33.

12 "Recognize Us as a People and Not as Buffaloes": Louis Riel and the Gendering of the Red River Public Sphere

M. MAX HAMON[1]

One imagines that Charles Mair entered Mr Bannatyne's store in Red River in February 1869 with a strong sense of trepidation. He was met with an angry reception. Joseph Hargrave, the local historian and public commenter, recorded: "The female part of the population got very angry. One lady pulled the poet's nose, while another used her fingers rudely about his ears. A third, confining herself to words, said his letters would be productive of serious mischief by circulating doubts about the reality of the destitution [in the settlement]." The source of their anger was the publication in the Toronto *Globe* of Mair's comments on the settlement of Red River. Hargrave, for one, was pleased to report that they had put the run to Mair: "I am happy to be able to record that, since the arrival of the objectionable series, a long letter from the pen of Mr. Mair, has appeared in the 'Globe' which, as it was expressly written for publication, forms a strong contrast to the others, and has recommended itself to a critical Prairie public as being, on the whole, a very creditable effort."[2]

The actions of these Metis women represent an enduring tradition of feminine authority in Red River. As Carolyn Podruchny and Émilie Pigeon argue in their chapter in this collection, women in Metis communities exercised significant authority within the "wagon circle" of the Metis hunt: they were cultural brokers, but they were also capable of violent opposition.[3] By the late 1860s, however, settler colonialism was shifting public authority away from governance based on matrilocal kinship ties to the Enlightenment ideal of "public opinion."[4] This shift revolutionized gender relations because "public opinion" was, at least in a theoretical sense, framed according to settler ideology, a male activity.

Louis Riel knew that to defend the rights of Indigenous women was a critique of a liberal empire and thus it served as a powerful means of anti-colonial resistance. On 28 November 1885, the Montreal paper the *Daily Star* published one of his letters. Riel explained that the Metis claimed rights to the Northwest Territories as an inheritance from Indigenous mothers. Riel rejected the "politeness" of people who minimized the degree of Indian blood in their veins: "Voici comment les Métis pensent là-dessus en eux-mêmes: 'C'est vrai que notre origine sauvage est humble, mais il est juste que nous honorions nos mères aussi bien que nos pères' ... Le sang indien de leurs veines établissait le droit ou le titre qu'ils avaient à la terre."[5] Indigenous women literally grounded the Metis nation, through their ties of blood and soil, in a logic of territorial rights. The "droit d'indien aux terres du pays" was central to Riel's national program, and Metis political independence relied on the ownership of land by the female heads of Metis families. In other words, Riel's justification for Metis rights to the land required him to consider how gender was "a primary way of signifying power."[6] Through an examination of Riel's political career, this essay provides a case study of the shifting ideas of gender in the Red River public sphere and the stakes involved in defining that space.[7]

As an exemplar of violence in Canada's history of settler colonialism, Riel has attracted much attention. However, by focusing on the violence of his career, Canadian history has ignored the much more significant fact that Riel established a new social order in the Northwest based primarily upon consensus and negotiation. The fact that the first minister of the province of Manitoba wore moccasins adds useful complexity to the history of peace, order, and good governance in Canada. It demonstrates the possibility of modern, yet alternative, forms of social order in British North America.

Cultivating Manliness

Studies of Indigenous masculinity make clear that Indigenous men played an important part in the process of resisting and accommodating settler colonialism.[8] Previous historians of male leadership in Red River, John Foster, George Stanley, and Margaret MacLeod, have emphasized the physicality and potential for violence among leaders such as Cuthbert Grant and Paul Paulet.[9] By contrast, Louis Riel, who aspired to public influence, cultivated a "manliness" that depended less on physical force and kinship authority than on his ability to discuss and organize public opinion.

Riel cultivated a manliness,[10] and corresponding beliefs about gender, derived from two sources: his family and the Collège de Montréal. His father and mother would have provided role models for gender divisions that had a lasting effect. During the 1840s, Louis Riel Sr (hereafter referred to as Jean-Louis) was frequently at odds with the Hudson's Bay Company (HBC) and commanded significant authority in the community through his public opposition to the HBC and Adam Thom, the company's appointed magistrate. Julie, Louis's mother, brought land from the powerful Lagimodière family into the marriage and played a key role in the management of the property. In the 1850s, through the intervention of Curé Louis-François Laflèche, Jean-Louis obtained the reluctant support of the HBC for a water mill, and, as a miller, he was an influential source of public opinion. Upon the death of her husband, Julie did not remarry, so the family was organized on a matrilocal principle. While it is unclear whether the land was legally transferred to the widow or the son, it was likely managed by the widow, and someone had to attend to the sale and management of the mill and several pieces of land.[11] Julie consulted Louis about the management and sale of Lots #50 and #51 in St Vital, even though they were in her name.[12] In 1875, she sent a letter to Louis, requesting that he send her a power of attorney and suggesting that she apply on his behalf for a land grant, and providing details about the local harvest.[13]

With the death of his father in 1865, despite his distance from home and his intention to become a priest, Louis was expected to take up the role of the *pater familias* and care for his younger sisters accordingly. In his private letters to his sister Sara, we see paternalistic advice: "La vertu qui te convient est l'humilité. Tu l'as déjà, je le sais. Mais aie-la encore plus."[14] His letters home are paternalistic and include much advice to his younger siblings about family affairs. In 1873, he attended to his sister Marie on her deathbed; he later explained to Sarah that this experience culminated in a vision of his father and confirmed for him his divine mission.[15] This familial authority extended into the Red River public sphere because Louis spoke as a representative for his extended kin network, which included the Proulx, Sauvé, Lagimodière, and Nault families.

The other influence on Riel's manliness was the Collège de Montréal. Riel accepted the Sulpicians in Montreal as his new "fathers": "Vraiment pour moi, les bons M.M. de Montréal sont ici de véritables pères."[16] These words are more remarkable when we note that he wrote them on 21 March 1864, less than a month after the news of his father's death reached him. The Collège, with its exclusive humanist curriculum of Latin, Greek, and classical literature, was the training ground for the most influential of French-Canadian political leaders.[17] As a bulwark of Christian civilization, it modelled its social relations according to the idealized Catholic patriarchal family.[18] By reading conservative thinkers such as Louis Bonald, César Guillaume de la Luzerne, Joseph de Maistre, and René Chateaubriand, students were taught to analyse the social order as a reflection of the "natural bonds" of the family and see the revolutionary state as a threat to true liberty and the foundation of social order.[19] The teachers, part of a counter-revolutionary Atlantic culture described by Nancy Christie, spun the words of the freethinking *philosophes* on their head: "La paternité et l'autorité sont une seule chose et même chose dont découlent la Liberté, l'Égalité et la Fraternité."[20]

At the Collège, formal groups like the Académie française (a literary and debating society), the congregational association (charged with care of the altar), and even a militia encouraged a vibrant student culture that cultivated manly leadership. Riel took active part in the student associations; he was even elected prefect for the congregational association in 1864.[21] At the Collège, worldly ideas about bourgeois individuality and society jostled with spirituality and selflessness. Ollivier Hubert has pointed out that a dynamic of oscillation between tradition and modernity characterized the discipline at the Collège.[22] To some degree, transgressions were tolerated; a certain independence from the "Rule" was part of being a student and an assertion of manliness.[23] The careful framing of self-presentation can be inferred from the common practice of students posing for a *carte de visite* photograph to send home. These "chemically produced portraits" provided subjects with the means to project masculine self-control and middle-class respectability.[24] Riel learned early on to control his appearance to gain public authority. Like British public schools that trained other imperial subjects, the Collège encouraged self-government.[25] At the same time, a daily regime of classes, prayer, and regulations about combing hair, uniforms, and clean shoes promoted self-discipline.[26]

When Riel faced the Red River public, he simultaneously spoke with the authority of Canadian classical learning and as the head of a Red River family. Bringing these two repertoires together was a performance of what Brendan Hokowithu has called a "hybridised masculine leadership."[27] By fusing them together, Riel was changing the paradigm of leadership and providing a fruitful argument for Indigenous sovereignty. However, at the same time, the frontier public sphere was increasingly exposed to colonialism and was being transformed in ways that would dramatically undermine Indigenous governance. In order to understand the particular historical context according to which this "public sphere" evolved, it will be helpful to present a brief overview of public authority in Red River and some of the forces, particularly settler colonialist ones, that were reshaping this space.

Gendered Politics

In Red River, public authority had always been a tense tango between the colonial officials and Indigenous publics composed of a mixture of groups variously defined as French Metis, English Halfbreed, Cree, Saulteaux, and other peoples. However, by the 1850s, the Metis had become the proximate brokers of hegemony.[28] Through their labour in the buffalo hunt, both men and women held significant power to resist an arbitrary state.[29] The government – or rather the HBC, which appointed the government – had been forced to accept that it could not rule by imperial fiat, and its presence, while welcomed by many, was possible only through the grace of the Metis. In 1849, the HBC governor, overwhelmed by public outcry at the trial of Guillaume Sayer, who was charged with illegally selling furs, renounced the company's policy on a fur trade monopoly. This decision effectively demonstrated that the company could not afford to lose Metis support for social order.[30] The Metis could assert themselves and would insert their people into the apparatus of office-holding individuals who constituted the state.[31] On 31 May 1849, the HBC, considering ways to "restore the tranquillity of the Settlement," agreed that Metis and Canadians should be given a certain proportion of the seats on the Council of Assiniboia.[32] By the 1860s, the Metis, serving as translators, ferry operators, bridge contractors, mailmen, and police, constituted a significant portion of the state personnel. Furthermore, the security of the territory depended heavily on Metis muscle. When, for instance, large numbers of Sioux arrived in the settlement, retreating in the face of American aggression in 1862–4, the Metis provided the security force keeping order.[33]

In Red River, like other colonial settings, spiritual and political authority were interwoven by both colonizers and colonized.[34] The Anglican bishop, David Andersen, and the Catholic bishop, Antonin-Alexandre Taché, had great influence in the community and the government. The HBC saw the church as an important agent to "civilize" and "settle" the unruly Metis.[35] However, as with the colonial state, relations between the Metis and the colonial church were subject to negotiation. The church was unable to dominate the Metis, who subverted ecclesiastical authority for their own interests. Catholic priests, such as Antoine Bellecourt and Louis-François Laflèche, discovered that they had to follow the Metis out into the plains, where they were dependent on Metis hunters for security and sustenance.[36] The Metis allied themselves intentionally: as a symbol of moral and religious authority, clergy were deployed strategically in Metis relations with other bands. Clergy helped draft petitions, educated their children, and defended Metis interests in council. The importance of the church to Metis power is illustrated by the "kidnapping" of a Grey nun who had been ordered to return to Ottawa. Jean-Louis Riel led a posse of Metis and Indians who intercepted "their sister" and escorted her back to the settlement.[37] Bishop Taché also recognized the importance of Metis involvement in the church when he defended the right of Metis women to become nuns, despite the racist protests of the mother superior in Ottawa.[38]

The primary means for the Metis to exert their influence over the church and the state was through kinship ties and extended family networks. These intimate relations provided coherence to Metis social order and the authority necessary for governance and active civil society.[39] The role of Indigenous women in establishing kin relationships was critical. Women were the "tender ties" that bound Metis society together,[40] and family relations were politically relevant in sustaining Metis identity and independence.[41] Biographical work on Sara Riel and Marie Rose Delorme shows the complicated intertwining of patriarchal society and feminine agency in Red River.[42] Lucy Eldersveld Murphy writes that these "public mothers," as cultural brokers in "mixed-blood" relationships, determined colonial publics.[43] Because they were decentralized, these relations, while patriarchal, facilitated feminine authority and influence in social and political affairs. Without a clear separation between formal and informal public spaces, women's authority in the mess hall and in the town stores was well recognized as politically influential. The court cases of Sarah Ballenden (who accused HBC men and their wives of gossip and slander) and Maria Thomas (who accused an English clergyman of rape and attempted abortion) illustrate how women negotiated the "pure patriarchy" of the European legal systems.[44] By becoming full sisters in the Order of the Grey Nuns, women also formed a basis for Metis cultural and political independence in the religious sphere.[45] As was seen in the opening of this essay, the influence of women in the prairie public could also be physical and direct.

Prior to 1860, law and order in Red River were subject to a delicate alliance between colonial governance and kinship ties. In prairie politics, there was no universal public sphere, but rather, manifold publics challenged and interrupted any discourse that claimed universal authority.[46] As Scott Stephen's study of master-servant relations concludes, the principle of the "household" in HBC governance overlapped with Indigenous relations.[47] It was the overlap between these two systems that allowed for reasonable efficiency in the first institutions of government.[48] During the 1860s, however, new forces associated with settler colonialism upset this delicate intimacy. According to the *Nor'wester*, "A new class of people is coming amongst us, with widely different tastes and habits, and both for good and evil are leavening our population."[49] These changes were not just demographic; settler colonialism involved a cultural and institutional shift.[50] New conceptions of public authority and the principle of state authority would radically disrupt the existing relations that guaranteed social order.

The process of state building in Red River intertwined with transformations of the public sphere as "public opinion," the interface between the liberal state and society, transformed in the wake of the settler revolution. Immigrants viewed the older colonial relations as tyrannical, corrupt, and inefficient, and called for a reform of governance that would grant responsible government in the form of a Crown colony. Agitators for reform challenged the authority of the HBC courts, broke open the jails, and organized public petitions to change the system of government.[51] Earlier agreements about authority were overturned and new ideas about liberal governance gained traction.

The Indigenous peoples of Red River recognized this shift and participated in it. They formed the Ouevre de la propagation de la foi, which collected donations for the Holy See and a temperance society. By 1855, the latter had a thousand enrolled members.[52] As Jeffrey McNairn argues, such institutions, "by developing distinctive norms and sociability," created a space autonomous from family, economic activity, and the state.[53] In 1859, the arrival of a printing press along with the steamboat provided new means of communication for this increasingly formal public sphere. These new technologies did not entirely replace older forms of communication, but they extended the reach and increased the speed at which information was communicated. Frequently, Indigenous opinions, because they were "uncivilized," were deemed unreasonable and illegitimate by jealous and fearful colonists.[54] Consider James Ross's attempt to embarrass and thereby delegitimize the opinions of Riel's father, in a scathing review in the *Nor'wester*: "Is he head man among the French people? We regard as the leading men the Bruneaus, the Amelins, the Marions, the Gentons, the Ducharmes, the Fishers, the Deases, the Brelands, the Delormes and many others too numerous to mention; these are principle men and they are a credit to the Settlement; but as for L. Riel, pray, who or what is *he?*"[55] Ross critiqued Riel's grammar, as if it were a marker of his ability to express a reasoned and logical public opinion. Significant obstacles of education, race, and class tended to deepen social gulfs, with drastic implications for kinship authority.[56]

Newspapers capture only a slice of the Red River public sphere. Indigenous voices resisted colonial institutions by maintaining the older spheres of the prairie public, such as buffalo hunt councils and horse races, and continued to exert significant influence on political decisions. Furthermore, Indigenous groups increased their efforts to participate in the new public spaces. For instance, Peguis, a leader from the "Indian settlement" at St Peter's Parish, wrote in the paper to protest settlement on his lands. In 1849, Louis Riel's father was reported to have started the movement to defend Sayer with a speech from the church steps.

Colonialism had a greater impact on the authority of Indigenous women than it did on men. The work of Nathalie Kermoal and Diane Payment shows that colonization of Metis societies entailed the replacement of gender egalitarianism with a patriarchal hierarchy.[57] The impact of patriarchal and imperialistic culture on a cooperative system was devastating because it targeted the power of women.[58] The dispossession of Indigenous peoples was achieved through the disempowerment of women. Reformers resented the informal (and, to them, tyrannical) influence women had in places like the fort mess hall and the settlement stores. As Nancy Fraser argues, the gender subtext of "societal rationalization" tends to exclude those considered non-rational, especially women, from the public sphere.[59] Her analysis holds for the settler revolution in Red River, where legislative councils, legal courts, and other modern institutions of the state marginalized women. While petitions were increasingly used as a means of public pressure, women, at least officially, did not participate.[60] The gendered institutions of the Catholic Church offered different opportunities to men and women in Red River. Consider the experience of Louis's sister, Sara Riel. By taking the veil, Sara, like her Quebec counterparts, found that religion provided an opportunity for public service in an increasingly patriarchal environment.[61] But her choice was a "great sacrifice" for the family, while Louis's failure to become a priest was a disappointment.[62] With the death of his father in 1865, and despite the geographic distance and his intentions to become a priest, Louis was expected to take charge of his family's affairs. Sara, by contrast, lost control over her property when she joined the Grey Nuns. When she attempted to use her Manitoba Act allowance lands to fund an orphanage, her superiors blocked her, arguing that the financial needs of the Riel family outweighed her religious work.[63]

Prescriptive ideas about "separate spheres" became increasingly powerful in the 1860s, but it was in combination with changes in the economy that the authority of women was marginalized. The decline of the buffalo hunt and the emergence of a settler colonial order would undermine the independence of women and dramatically change gender relationships in the community.[64] Women had played an important role in the proto-capitalist buffalo robe industry. But, as labour relations shifted, women were increasingly marginalized while men found other work.[65] Moreover, changing demographics intensified racialized ideas about "civilization." The arrival, in 1830, of Frances Simpson, the white, teenage bride of the HBC governor, signalled shifting attitudes about imperialism.[66] Catholic apologists had touted the arrival, earlier in the century, of Marie-Anne Gaboury, the "First White woman," as a sign of the progressive march of civilization.[67] In the 1850s, James Douglas, the HBC governor in Victoria and himself married to a Red River Metis woman, referred to this preference for white women as a "strange revolution."[68] Importing white women served as an "alibi of exclusion" that allowed settlers to claim autonomy from Indigenous social bonds and to stabilize colonial rule.[69]

The impact of separate spheres ideology was that, while women's public presence was increasingly restricted, men were able to move between private and public spheres.[70] Even as we acknowledge its complex social reality, we ought not to disregard its power as an ideological metaphor.[71] These prescriptive parameters, which attempted to isolate feminine influence from the public sphere, were vigorously resisted in Red River, but they carried sufficient weight to disrupt Indigenous gender relations, with a domino effect on Indigenous governance. As "public opinion" replaced relations of kinship as the organizing principle of society, the autonomy of Indigenous governance was short-circuited, in a way similar to that described by Susan Sleeper-Smith in the Great Lakes area.[72]

Riel in Red River's Public Sphere

The Canadian disruption of the prairie public presented an opportunity for Louis Riel. His first intervention in the public sphere was a response, published in *Le Courrier de St-Hyacinthe*, to Charles Mair, the Canadian annexationist who had raised the ire of the women of Red River. It is worth emphasizing that this paper was in Quebec: by publishing his opinion there, Riel demonstrated an understanding of how the stakes of public engagement had changed. While the greater part of the letter, addressed to the public, is a refutation of his opponent's views, towards its close, Riel shifts voice to address Mair directly: "Vous parlez bien d'autres choses que vous n'avez pas eu le temps de voir ni de connaître; ça vaudrait bien autant que le reste de votre lettre; tout autant que les terms peu courtois, et je dirai même peu civilisés, dont vous vous servez en parlant des dames du pays, qui certes sous tous les rapports, valent bien les dames de votre pays."[73] Riel, quick to validate Metis women, began to play with a thread in the discursive fabric that would become a recurring theme: Canadian disrespect for Indigenous women. Frequently, Riel would argue that Canadians threatened Metis women, and Metis men needed to be able to defend their homes.

Unfortunately, Riel, unlike his contemporaries John Stuart Mill and Louis Veuillot,[74] did not leave us a clear statement of the role he expected women to play in public; we must tease out his sexual politics from fragments.[75] Riel's public engagement was framed within a political discourse of manliness that corresponded to settler ideas of a separation of spheres. As Stephen Smith argues in this volume, the language of respectability was about creating categories of who belonged, and gender was a key category. On 8 February 1870, at a meeting of the Convention of Forty (which agreed to form a provisional government in Red River), William B. O'Donoghue, an Irish American, defended the Metis choice of Riel as president because he was "a man who forced Canada to recognize us as a people, and not as buffaloes."[76] Leadership by "free and spirited men" was part of Riel's own platform of legitimacy. Galled by the hesitation of the English delegates to commit to a plan of action during the Convention of Forty, Riel burst out in anger: "Allez ... retournez-vous-en paisiblement sur vos fermes. Restez dans les bras de vos femmes. Donnez cet exemple à vos enfants. Mais regardez-nous agir. Nous allons travailler et obtenir la guarantie de nos droits et des vôtres."[77] To gain legitimacy in a newly emerging formal public sphere, he employed appropriate gendered terms to describe the influence of public opinion. In this, he was careful to monitor the media. By January 1870, he had closed the *Nor'wester* and put political allies in charge of the *New Nation*. Even then, he kept close tabs on the paper and warned the editor when it ran an unfavourable article on Bishop Taché.[78] Through his declarations of loyalty to the British Crown, Riel also justified his demands for self-determination in accordance with British ideas of manliness. As Cecilia Morgan argues for Upper Canada, the language of loyalty to the British monarch and constitution legitimated "public activities by those who might otherwise be considered private individuals."[79] Riel's enemies were described as effeminate by friendly newspapers. Following the defeat of a Canadian insurrection against the provisional government, rumours abounded in the public press that Colonel Dennis, the Canadian officer, had dressed as an "Indian squaw" and been forced to carry "leggins'" to disguise himself and escape the Metis patrols. Riel also framed his actions as a response to hostile Canadian media that employed rhetoric to delegitimize the rebellion as "rule by violence and bloodshed ... rebellion and murder."[80] Riel's detractors claimed that he was "just an ordinary town loafer" who "lived with his mother" and imagined himself as a "Napoleon," and that he was an egotist with fluffy hair to boot![81]

It is significant that women were not enfranchised in the political order determined by the provisional government:

> Every man in the country (except uncivilized and unsettled Indians) who has attained the age of 21 years, and every British subject, a stranger to this country, who has resided three years in this country and is a householder, shall have a right to vote at the election of a member to serve in the Legislature of the country and in the Dominion Parliament; and every foreign subject, other than a British subject, who has resided the same length of time in the country, and is a householder, shall have the same right to vote on condition of his taking the oath of allegiance.[82]

Because Riel did not contribute to the question of women's enfranchisement (when the idea was proposed by Alfred Scott, the delegate from Winnipeg, it was met with laughter), we cannot be sure of his ideas on the subject. Riel was more concerned with opposing restrictions based upon class, and he argued for a more republican version of citizenship. "Suppose a man's house were burned down, is he to be deprived of his vote? Does he lose his intelligence, because his house happens to be burned down? To advocate a property qualification is to speak in the interests of the rich as against the poor. Are there more honest men among the rich than among the poor? Are we not honest, though poor?" Riel also proposed a motion, which failed to carry, that would have allowed men who were recent immigrants the right to vote. He argued it was a means of preventing violence: "My own opinion is that the system prevailing in the States is better than that in Canada. I have seen more disturbances in Montreal at elections than ever I have seen in the United States. Liberty to vote is what would be best for us. There should be no discrimination against foreigners."[83] The violence of Montreal elections, as Colin Grittner discusses in his chapter in this volume, served as an extreme lesson that allowed Riel to speak from a position of experience and to demonstrate the knowledge and control expected of male leadership.

Control of violence was a key aspect of authority in Red River's political culture. Riel demonstrated his ability to act as Leviathan, most famously in the execution of Thomas Scott. In his pamphlet on the amnesty issue, Riel wrote, "Le ... 4 Mars 1870, cette autorité de gouvernement qui nous avait été provisoirement confiée pour le bonheur d'une colonie anglaise ..., fait usage que pour désarmer nos ennemis, nous l'exerçâmes enfin dans toute sa sévérité: Scott fut exécuté, notre motif étant celui de faire triompher l'ordre."[84] But, overall, restraint was more important to his legitimacy as a political leader. Consider his management of the "Sioux Scare" when Chief "Grand Oreilles" and a party of "50 Sioux Indians, well armed" from Portage la Prairie threatened violence if the Metis were disloyal to the Crown. Alexander Begg had reported "that they were all well supplied with arms and ammunition, at the expense, it was said of the Canadian Government; even the squaws being armed with knives and guns."[85] (It is interesting to note that Begg framed the potential violence of "squaws" as an instance of the depths to which Canadian agitators had sunk.) Riel defused the situation by presenting tobacco and assuring Grand Oreilles that the Metis remained loyal to the Crown. By restraining violence and staring down this threat of "squaws" armed with guns by the Canadian government, Riel ensured social order in the settlement while simultaneously reasserting a Metis monopoly on violence.

The "civilizing" presence of women could also justify the avoidance of violence when Riel needed to appear conciliatory. In February, to celebrate the formation of the Provisional Government and to ease tensions in the settlement, Riel released hundreds of prisoners being kept in Fort Garry. But there was a gendered aspect to this clemency. By portraying the decision to release the prisoners as the result of feminine influence, Riel demonstrated that he was a man with civilized sensibilities. The *New Nation* printed the following story of Victoria MacVicar's entreaty for clemency from the president in February 1870:

> Determined to see the last man set free, if that were possible, she sat there for hours in order to effect her resolve. Where words of counsel or kindness would be effective with the prisoners or President, she used them freely and with effect. The prisoners were assured with a word from her – and the President – young and a bachelor – of course he could withhold nothing. All the prisoners were liberated, even the four who were at one time sentenced to be sent across the line as too dangerous to be at large.[86]

The *realpolitik* of the affair was that the release of the prisoners defused the tensions in the settlement and removed the excuse that Canadian agitators were using to organize a counter-insurgency. But, carefully advertised in the pages of the government-supported paper, this feminine intervention provided an explanation for Riel's clemency without making him appear weak. In fact, it reinforced his manliness, as he responded appropriately to the virtue and beauty of a young woman. Similarly, on 11 March, the *New Nation* reported that the petition of a Mrs McLean for the release of her husband and son from the prison had been granted.[87] Clemency, when advocated by women, and the integrity of the family were a more useful means of securing a reputation for manliness and political authority than was unreasonable violence.

The protection and dependence of female subjects was the basis of a social order founded upon a separate spheres ideology. By constructing feminine dependency, Riel could argue that independent Metis men must act in the defence of those who were dependent upon them. Representations of women in the public sphere also served as important symbols in Riel's attempt to legitimize his political movement in a manner which Joan Landes might have called the "eroticization" of the nation.[88] "La Metisse," sung by the Metis guardsmen, was likely written by the Metis president.[89] It provides a window into the oral culture and popular politics of a largely illiterate population and shows how gender was constructed not just for the literate elite but more broadly.[90] The song opens, "Je suis métisse et je suis orgueilleuse / D'appartenir à cette nation ..." The refrain declares the singer's desire to find a lover among the soldiers of the "petite armée," which is commanded by the proud adjutant, Ambroise Lepin. The fictional Metisse does not represent a woman so much as the desires of the soldiers. Like the careful constructions of Madeline de Vercheres and Laura Secord, who undertook military actions,[91] "La Metisse" does not threaten the gendered division but "captures" female sexuality and refashions it to support the heterosexual patriarchal order.

In his interventions in the public sphere, Riel largely benefited from and employed a political culture that relied on patriarchal order. But he also understood how Metis society functioned and the importance of kinship ties. His anger at the betrayal by his relatives in 1869 was an attempt to reform those relationships or at least to discredit their reasons for opposing him (the papers suggested that his relatives had been bought).[92] By April of the following year, Riel and Nolin, a cousin estranged in the events of 1869, had achieved some level of reconciliation. Riel's response to one of Nolin's letters is revealing of the diplomatic openings that family metaphors could provide. Addressing Nolin as "cher cousin," he continued, "de nous regarder de la même façon qu'avant les troubles. Oui! Assurément je le veux de tout mon coeur. Soyons deux bons amis comme nous sommes parents."[93] Metis depended upon "parents," or relatives, for political recognition.

The role of women in forging family ties was of paramount importance for Metis sovereignty. It was through marriage to or birth by Indigenous women that the Metis acquired their rights to land: as shown above, this was a point that Riel formally spelled out in 1885. But, already in 1873, he argued, in a document entitled "Programme national des Métis canadiens français" and in two undated private letters, for "le droit que notre sang sauvage nous donne aux terres du pays."[94] The Manitoba Act, which Riel considered a "treaty" between the Metis and the Canadian government,[95] was based on territorial sovereignty inherited from Indigenous women. In addition, the impulse towards matrilocal governance was rooted in the land claims derived from connections with Indigenous women. That's why Riel had to defend the rights of women in an increasingly patriarchal public sphere.

When the HBC government collapsed in the face of pressure for reform, Riel reconstituted Metis governance based on the authority of public opinion and successfully constructed a new political order. Riel understood that violence alone would not be enough to preserve the coherence and independence of the Metis. In many respects, his engagement in the public sphere arose from an understanding of manliness that was connected to settler ideas of a separation of spheres, and his formal use of women in the public sphere was symbolic. But he also understood how Metis society was founded on kinship ties rooted in feminine authority. He thus cultivated family ties and left open the possibility for feminine influence.

Settler colonialism and the rise of public opinion are rarely explicitly linked in Canadian historiography, yet their histories overlap. Since at least the 1830s, public opinion played a significant role in determining official colonial policy and local governance.[96] At the same time, the fallout from the War of 1812 marks a notable decline in the recognition of Indigenous sovereignty by the settler society and a steady encroachment on Indigenous political independence.[97] The decline in colonial acknowledgment of Indigenous sovereignty is linked to the growing influence of settler public opinion and the growth of the settler state. Older forms of public authority, which were grounded in kinship ties and which had proven effective in mediating the disruption of colonialism, were no longer viable. As kinship declined in public influence, so too did the authority of women, a development that proved to be an effective way of dispossessing Indigenous people of their land.

In the nineteenth century, the Metis were confronted with an increasingly powerful settler state that drew its legitimacy from public opinion. This story is typically told as one of conflict and violence: modernity, with all its trappings of a state, a formalized market, and a public sphere, was a disruptive force shredding Red River traditional society. A more useful metaphor for understanding the emergence of the modern settler colonial order is that of the trading blanket. The threads of a blanket can be picked apart and then rewoven into a new fabric by Indigenous people. In Red River, where undisguised state violence was increasingly unsustainable, the Metis responded to settler colonialism by establishing a state based on Indigenous public opinion. Riel's manipulation of the weave of public opinion provided a powerful check to Canadian expansionism while positing his own vision of a modern state.

In this new weave, gender relations were profoundly redefined with respect to public authority. Riel's interaction with the shifting understanding of gender in the public sphere was not straightforward. In many regards, Riel assumed the patriarchal role for which he had been conditioned by his parents and his education in Montreal. Yet, for Riel, violence and the authority that women commanded in the public domain were a potent combination for resisting domination. Whether in 1869, in response to Charles Mair, or in 1885, in defence of rebellion, when he spoke about the need to honour the mothers of the Metis, it was with an awareness of a depth to Metis governance that Canadian annexationists did not possess.

Violence overshadows the significance of the consensus of December 1869, when forty delegates agreed to form a provisional government that would represent the interests of the public. The Canadian state, interested in delegitimizing this agreement, stressed the violence in its historical narrative in order to justify its own version of peace, order, and good governance. This history, framed as traditional versus modern, colonizer versus native, is too simple. A history of the Indigenous public sphere offers us a glimpse at a more complex history in which Indigenous peoples attempted to define an alternative to the Canadian social order. Riel's interventions show us how the struggle against colonialism was by no means clear and frequently involved complex negotiation of new political culture and social values.

NOTES

1 I am grateful to Elizabeth Mancke and the entire Unrest, Violence, and Search for Social Order team for their appraisal of earlier versions of this chapter. I also benefited from the comments and critiques of Colin Grittner, Émilie Pigeon, as well my McGill reading group, Andrew Dial, Colin Gilmour, Carolynn McNally, Sonya Roy, and Catherine Ulmer. Thanks to my supervisors Elsbeth Heaman and Elizabeth Elbourne for their helpful remarks and critical support.
2 Joseph Hargrave, *Red River* (Montreal: Lovell, 1871), 456 and 458.
3 Such scenes invite sharp critique of the Pocahontas-like myth that Indigenous women passively accepted outsiders. John Gyles's account of women humiliating and beating male captives reveals the role they could play in determining who and what would be accepted into their community. See Ann M. Little, *The Many Captivities of Esther Wheelwright* (New Haven, CT: Yale University Press, 2016), 58. The *Jesuit Relations* also refers to female torture of captives; see J.R. Miller, *Skyscrapers Hide the Heavens: A History of Indian-White Relations in Canada*, 3rd ed. (Toronto: University of Toronto Press, 2000), 73.
4 By *public opinion* here, I refer to the metaphor or concept frequently used in political debates as an argument for legitimacy. It does not refer to any objective or social reality. As Jeffrey McNairn, *The Capacity to Judge: Public Opinion and Deliberative Democracy in Upper Canada, 1791–1854* (Toronto: University of Toronto Press, 2000), 7, puts it: "Rather than an aggregate of individual opinions, 'public opinion' of the Kantian enlightenment was a collective entity – the outcome of prolonged public deliberation among diverse individuals listening to and participating in the free, open and reasoned exchange of information and argument."
5 Louis Riel, "Les Métis du Nord-Ouest" doc. 3-156 in *The Collected Writings of Louis Riel* (hereafter *CWLR*), ed. George Francis Gillman Stanley and Thomas Flanagan (Edmonton: University of Alberta Press, 1985), 3: 278–9.
6 Joan Wallach Scott, *Gender and the Politics of History*, rev. ed. (New York: Columbia University Press, 1999).

7 The idea of the "public sphere" according to Jürgen Habermas in *The Structural Transformation of the Public Sphere: An Inquiry into a Category of Bourgeois* (Cambridge, MA: MIT Press, 1989) is that public opinion, and its relative weight on political decision-making, evolves according to a broad constellation of social, technological, and economic forces. While Habermas's formulation has undergone extensive criticism, I believe that his approach offers a useful foothold in a complex field. Cf, Nancy Fraser, "What's Critical about Critical Theory? The Case of Habermas and Gender," in *Feminism as Critique: On the Politics of Gender*, ed. Seyla Benhabib and Drucilla Cornell (Minneapolis: University of Minnesota Press, 1987); and Harold Mah, "Phantasies of the Public Sphere: Rethinking the Habermas of Historians," *Journal of Modern History* 72, no. 1 (March 2000): 153–82.

8 Kim Anderson and Robert Alexander Innes, *Indigenous Men and Masculinities: Legacies, Identities, Regeneration* (Winnipeg: University of Manitoba, 2015). For an interesting study of Anishinaabe leadership see Anton Treuer, *The Assassination of Hole in the Day* (St Paul, MN: Borealis Press, 2011).

9 Margaret Arnett MacLeod, "Cuthbert Grant of Grantown," *Canadian Historical Review* 21, no. 1 (March 1940): 25–39; and John Foster, "Some Questions and Perspective on the Problems of Metis Roots," in *The New Peoples: Being and Becoming Metis in North America*, ed. Jacqueline Peterson and Jennifer Brown (Winnipeg: University of Manitoba Press, 1985).

10 Gail Bederman, *Manliness and Civilization: A Cultural History of Gender and Race in the United States, 1880–1917* (Chicago: University of Chicago Press, 2000), convincingly argues that *masculinity* is tied up in ideological concerns with civilization, and that *manliness* is a more accurate, and historically neutral, term.

11 For example, Louis wrote to his mother: "Chère Maman, veuillez donc demander à Nanin [Andre Nault] s'il veut aller, au plus vite qu'il pourra, labourer un arpent ou deux de terre sur ma terre au pied du lac à Norman et y semer de l'orge bien clair. Vous le payerez vous-même ou je lui enverrai moi-même l'argent." "Lettre à Julie Riel. St Paul. 17 May 1870," doc. 1-138 in *CWLR*, 1: 211–12.

12 Thomas Flanagan, "Louis Riel's Land Claims," *Manitoba History* 21 (Spring 1991): 2–12.

13 Julie Riel to Louis Riel, St Vital, 14 August 1875, MG3 D2. file #10, Provincial Archives of Manitoba (hereafter PAM).

14 "Lettre à Sara Riel," doc. 1-163 in *CWLR*, 1: 261.

15 "Lettre à Sarah Riel," doc. 1-173 in ibid., 1: 273–5.

16 "Lettre à Très chère maman ...," doc. 1-004 in *CWLR* 1: 6–8. In 1885, in a letter to the archbishop of St Boniface, A.A. Taché, Riel recalled his good fortune to have attended the college. See "Lettre à A.-A. Taché," doc. 3-077 in *CWLR*, 3: 140–51.

17 Ollivier Hubert, "De la diversité des parcours et des formations dans les collèges du Bas Canada: Le cas de Montréal," *Historical Studies in Education* 21, no. 1 (2009): 41–65.

18 "Responsible paternalism" captures the role men play in the "compassionate patriarchy" of nineteenth-century Montreal. See Bettina Bradbury, *Wife to Widow: Lives, Laws, and Politics in Nineteenth-Century Montreal* (Vancouver: UBC Press, 2011), 61–86. Brian Young *Patrician Families and the Making of Quebec: The Taschereaus and McCords* (Montreal: McGill-Queen's University Press, 2014), 93, employs the term "benevolent patriarchy" to describe such relations.
19 Cahier de Thèmes en Rhétorique, I2:6.2.2.1, Archives des Prêtres de Saint-Sulpice de Montréal.
20 *Essai Philosophique sur la Revolution en général*, Lole Marceau, 6 March 1873, Plaidoyer et discourse d'élèves, I2:6.3.3-3 1-6, APSSM. Nancy Christie, "'He Is the Master of His House': Families and Political Authority in Counterrevolutionary Montreal," *William and Mary Quarterly* 70, no. 2 (April 2013): 341–70.
21 Past attempts of biographers to portray Riel as inward looking and morose are unjustified. They based their interpretations on the much later reflections of one classmate, L.O. Mousseau, in *Une page de l'histoire* (Montreal: W.F. Daniel, 1886). Other classmates such as Eustache Prud'homme disagree: see "Louis Riel," *L'opinion publique*, 19 February 1870. Archival evidence of Riel's activity in the student associations seems to contradict Mousseau.
22 Hubert, "De la diversité des parcours," 41–65.
23 Louise Bienvenue and Christine Hudon, "'Pour devenir homme, tu transgresseras ...': quelques enjeux de la socialisation masculine dans les collèges classiques québécois (1880–1939)," *The Canadian Historical Review* 86, no. 3 (2005): 485–511.
24 Andrea Volpe, "Cartes de Visite Portrait Photographs and the Culture of Class Formation," in *The Middling Sorts: Explorations in the History of the American Middle Class*, ed. Burton Bledstein and Robert Johnston (New York: Routledge, 2001).
25 Patrick Joyce, *The State of Freedom: A Social History of the British State since 1800* (Cambridge: Cambridge University Press, 2013), 263–307.
26 Ollivier Hubert, "Collèges classiques et bourgoisies Franco-Catholiques (XVIIe–XXe Siècles)," in *Le collège classique pour garçons: études historiques sur une institution québécoise disparue*, ed. Louise Bienvenue and Christine Hudon (Montreal: Fides, 2014), 124; and Christine Hudon and Louise Bienvenue, "Entre franche camaraderie et amours socratiques: l'espace trouble et ténu des amitiés masculines dans les collèges classiques (1870–1960)," *Revue d'histoire de l'Amérique française* 57, no. 4 (2004).
27 Brendan Hokowhitu, "Producing Elite Indigenous Masculinities," *Settler Colonial Studies* 2, no. 2 (2012): 23–48.
28 Dale Gibson, *Settlement and Governance, 1812–1872*, vol. 1 (Montreal and Kingston: McGill-Queen's University Press, 2015); and Darren O'Toole, "The Red River Resistance: The Machiavellian Moment of the Red River Metis of Manitoba" (PhD diss., University of Ottawa, 2010).

29 Gerhard Ens, *Homeland to Hinterland: The Changing Worlds of the Red River Metis in the Nineteenth Century* (Toronto: University of Toronto Press, 1996).

30 At the trial, the presence of armed Metis, including Louis Riel's father, prevented the HBC from enforcing its claim to a monopoly on the fur trade. O'Toole, "The Red River Resistance," 107–10.

31 For Metis involvement in the state, see Michel Hogue, *Metis and the Medicine Line: Creating a Border and Dividing a People* (Regina: University of Regina Press, 2015), 107. Elsbeth Heaman, *A Short History of the State in Canada* (Toronto: University of Toronto Press, 2015), 1–4, characterizes the state as "a series of office-holding individuals who took certain actions in the name of the crown but who drew upon a complex material and cultural infrastructure that predisposed other people to accept their claims and enactments."

32 Over the course of the 1840s, the company added Metis to the HBC council. In 1839, Cuthbert Grant was appointed "Warden of the Plains" and then to the council in 1842. In 1853, three new "half-breed" councillors were appointed. See Gibson, *Settlement and Governance, 1812–1872*, 145; Lionel Dorge, "'The Metis and Canadien Councillors of Assiniboia' [1835–1856]," *The Beaver* (Summer 1974).

33 David G McCrady, *Living with Strangers: The Nineteenth-Century Sioux and the Canadian-American Borderlands* (Lincoln: University of Nebraska Press, 2006); Alvin Gluek, "The Sioux Uprising: A Problem in International Relations," *Minnesota Historical Society* 34 (Winter 1955): 317–24. The sovereignty of the government was a key issue; as Gluek notes, the "Hudson's Bay Company hesitated to establish a local military force whose loyalty to its interests might not be as great as its devotion to the free traders of Rupert's Land" (318).

34 See the discussion by Tolly Bradforth and Chelsea Horton in "Introduction," *Mixed Blessings: Indigenous Encounters with Christianity in Canada*, ed. Tolly Bradforth and Chelsea Horton (Vancouver: UBC Press, 2016), 6–8.

35 Frits Pannekoek, *A Snug Little Flock: The Social Origins of the Riel Resistance of 1869–70* (Winnipeg: Watson and Dwyer, 1991); and Raymond Huel, *Archbishop A.-A. Taché of St Boniface the "Good Fight" and the Illusive Vision* (Edmonton: University of Alberta Press, 2003), 63.

36 Raymond Huel, *Proclaiming the Gospel to the Indians and the Metis: The Missionary Oblates of Mary Immaculate in the Canadian North West* (Edmonton: University of Alberta Press, 1996).

37 According to the community annals, Sister Sainte-Thérèse was ordered "to get into the cart which was [carrying] Mlle Céleste Lagimodière [cousin to Louis Riel], who returned to St Boniface with the prisoner." Geneviève Rocan, "McDonell, Teresa" *DCB*, vol. 14, http://www.biographi.ca/en/bio/mcdonell_teresa_14E.html, accessed 30 January 2016.

38 Huel, *Archbishop A.-A. Taché*, 95–6.

39 Brenda Macdougall *One of the Family: Metis Culture in Nineteenth-Century Northwestern Saskatchewan* (Vancouver: UBC Press, 2010), 8, has argued that Metis family connections, or *wahkootowin*, "influenced the behaviours, actions, and decision-making processes that shaped all a community's economic and political actions."

40 Sylvia Van Kirk, *Many Tender Ties: Women in Fur-Trade Society, 1670–1870* (Norman: University of Oklahoma Press, 1983); and Jennifer S.H. Brown, *Strangers in Blood: Fur Trade Company Families in Indian Country* (Norman: University of Oklahoma Press, 1980). For an overview of their work, see Robin Jarvis Brownlie and Valerie Korinek, eds, *Finding a Way to the Heart: Feminist Writings on Aboriginal and Women's History in Canada* (Winnipeg: University of Manitoba Press, 2012). See also Susan Sleeper-Smith, *Indian Women and French Men: Rethinking Cultural Encounter in the Western Great Lakes* (Amherst: University of Massachusetts Press, 2001); Lucy Eldersveld Murphy, *Great Lakes Creoles: A French-Indian Community on the Northern Borderlands, Prairie du Chien, 1750–1860* (New York: Cambridge University Press, 2014); and Jean Barman, *French Canadians, Furs, and Indigenous Women in the Making of the Pacific Northwest* (Vancouver: UBC Press, 2014).

41 Macdougall, *One of the Family*; Nicole St-Onge, *Saint-Laurent, Manitoba: Evolving Metis Identities, 1850–1914* (Regina: Canadian Plains Research Center, 2004); Nathalie Kermoal, "Le 'temps de Cayoge': La vie quotidienne des femmes métisses au Manitoba de 1850 à 1900" (PhD diss., University of Ottawa, 1996); and Diane Payment, *Riel Family: Home and Lifestyle at St Vital, 1860–1910* (Ottawa: Parks Canada, 1980).

42 Doris Jeanne MacKinnon, *The Identities of Marie Rose Delorme Smith: Portrait of a Metis Woman, 1861–1960* (Regina: Canadian Plains Studies Press, 2012); and Lesley Erickson, "'Bury Our Sorrows in the Sacred Heart': Gender and the Metis Response to Colonialism. The Case of Sara and Louis Riel, 1848–83," in *Unsettled Pasts: Reconceiving the West through Women's History*, ed. Sarah Carter et al. (Calgary: University of Calgary Press, 2005).

43 Lucy Eldersveld Murphy, "Public Mothers: Native American and Metis Women as Creole Mediators in the Nineteenth-Century Midwest," *Journal of Women's History* 14, no. 4 (2003): 142–66; and Sleeper-Smith, *Indian Women and French Men.*

44 In 1850, Captain Christopher Vaughan Foss accused HBC traders Pelly and Davidson and their wives of slandering Sarah Ballenden, the wife of the chief factor. Foss accused the defendants of causing a scandal by spreading rumours of a sexual affair between himself and Ballenden. *Foss vs Pelly*, 16 July 1850, Quarterly Court Records, PAM. Sylvia Van Kirk, "The Reputation of a Lady: Sarah Ballenden and the Foss-Pelly Scandal," *Manitoba History* 11 (Spring 1986): 4–12. In 1863, the father of Maria Thomas, a young Metis woman, charged a Methodist preacher,

the Reverend William Corbett, with the rape and repeated attempts to abort the pregnancy of his daughter. Maria, who had been hired by Corbett to clean house, demonstrated her own agency by taking her own place on the stand and describing the crimes in detail. Erica Smith, "'Gentlemen, This Is No Ordinary Trial': Sexual Narratives in the Trial of Reverend Corbett, Red River, 1863," in *Reading Beyond Words: Contexts for Native History*, ed. Jennifer Brown and Elizabeth Vibert (Peterborough, ON: Broadview Press, 1996), 364–403; and Sharron Fitzgerald, "Hybrid Identities in Canada's Red River Colony," *Canadian Geographer* 51, no. 2 (2007): 186–201.

45 Lesley Erickson, "Repositioning the Missionary: Sara Riel, the Grey Nuns, and Aboriginal Women in Catholic Missions of the Northwest," in *Recollecting: Lives of Aboriginal Women of the Canadian Northwest and Borderlands* (Edmonton: Athabaska University Press, 2011).

46 Habermas's "official" public sphere has been critiqued as deaf to the subaltern and other heterogeneous voices that contested authority. See Iris Marion Young, "Impartiality and the Civic Public: Some Implications of Feminists Critiques of Moral and Political Theory," in *Feminism as Critique: On the Politics of Gender*, ed. Seyla Benhabib and Drucilla Cornell (Minneapolis: University of Minnesota Press, 1987), 56–76; and Michael Gardiner, "Wild Publics and Grotesque Symposiums: Habermas and Bakhtin on Dialogue, Everyday Life, and the Public Sphere," in *After Habermas: New Perspectives on the Public Sphere*, ed. Jürgen Habermas, Nick Crossley, and John M. Roberts (Oxford: Blackwell Publishing: 2004), 38.

47 Scott Stephen, "Master's and Servants: The Hudson's Bay Company and Its Personnel, 1668–1782" (PhD diss., University of Manitoba, 2006), 8.

48 Gibson, *Settlement and Governance*, 18, challenges Bumsted's observation that Red River "lacked a political dimension"; rather, the problem was competing claims of "*several different* legal structures" (emphasis in original). See also Norma Jean Hall, "'Perfect Freedom': Red River as a Settler Society, 1810–1870" (MA thesis, University of Manitoba, 2003).

49 *Nor'wester*, 14 September 1861.

50 According to recent critiques, settler colonialism is "a specific mode of domination" based on dispossession of land. Rather than an event, it is a process of creating a political organization that premises the sovereign capacity of settlers and requires Indigenous people to vanish. See Edward Cavanagh and Lorenzo Veracini, eds, *The Routledge Handbook of the History of Settler Colonialism* (New York: Routledge, 2016). My approach is particularly informed by the research of Elizabeth Elbourne, who rejects an a priori commitment to dialectical oppositions, even while investigating the creation and maintenance of categories of difference that shape colonial politics. See *Blood Ground: Colonialism, Missions, and the Contest for Christianity in the Cape Colony and Britain, 1799–1853* (Montreal and

Kingston: McGill-Queen's University Press, 2002). For Elbourne, the colonial encounter is a problem of interpretation and a contest to establish ideological hegemony of one interpretation of that encounter. Similarly, Susan Neylan defines settler colonialism as a "dialogue," albeit one characterized by imbalances in power. In her study of Tsimshian encounter with Christianity, Neylan stresses the co-existence and interaction of colonial and Indigenous forms of knowledge and expression: see *The Heavens Are Changing: Nineteenth-Century Protestant Missions and Tsimshian Christianity* (Montreal and Kingston: McGill-Queen's University Press, 2003).

51 Gibson, *Settlement and Governance,* 170–98.

52 Huel, *Archbishop A.-A. Taché*, 63.

53 McNairn, *The Capacity to Judge*, 109.

54 As a key indicator of the independence of a political subject, upon which British ideas of liberal rule depended, "irrationality" eliminated the possibility for responsible participation in politics. Uday Mehta, "Liberal Strategies of Exclusion," in *Tensions of Empire: Colonial Cultures in a Bourgeois World*, ed. Frederick Cooper and Ann Laura Stoler (Berkeley: University of California Press, 1997), 59–86.

55 "A Cure for the Blues" *Nor'wester*, 14 September 1861.

56 Fiona Paisley and Kirsty Reid, eds, *Critical Perspectives on Colonialism: Writing the Empire from Below* (New York: Routledge, 2014); and Maureen Konkle, *Writing Indian Nations: Native Intellectuals and the Politics of Historiography* (Durham: University of North Carolina, 2004).

57 Kermoal, "Le 'temps de Cayoge'"; Diane Payment, "La Vie en Rose: Metis Women at Batoche, 1870–1920," in *Women of the First Nations: Power, Wisdom, Strength*, ed. Christine Miller and Patricia Chuchryk (Winnipeg: University of Manitoba Press, 1996).

58 Jeannette Armstrong, "Invocation: The Real Power of Aboriginal Women," in *Women of the First Nations: Power, Wisdom, Strength*, ed. Christine Miller and Patricia Chuchryk (Winnipeg: University of Manitoba Press, 1996).

59 Nancy Fraser, "What's Critical about Critical Theory," in *Feminism as Critique: On the Politics of Gender*, ed. Seyla Benhabib and Drucilla Cornell (Minneapolis: University of Minnesota Press, 1987).

60 For studies of female participation in petitions, see Gail Campbell, "Disenfranchised but Not Quiescent: Women Petitioners in New Brunswick in the Mid-19th Century," in *Separate Spheres: Women's Worlds in the 19th-Century Maritimes*, ed. Janet Vey Guildford and Suzanne Morton (Fredericton: Acadiensis Press, 1994), 39–66.

61 Marta Danylewycz, *Taking the Veil: An Alternative to Marriage, Motherhood, and Spinsterhood in Quebec, 1840–1920* (Toronto: McClelland and Stewart, 1987).

62 Quoted in Erickson, "Repositioning the Missionary," 119. See also Erickson, "'Bury Our Sorrows.'"

63 Erickson, "'Bury Our Sorrows,'" 35.

64 Kermoal, "Le 'temps de Cayoge,'" 265: "Nous pouvons conclure en affirmant que la disparition du bison a entraîne une transformation des activités féminines à partir des années 1870. Le expertise des femmes pour la préparation et le tannage des peaux et la confection des produits manufacturés dérivés de la chasse a été peu à peu supplantée par d'autres activités économiques. Il est évident que l'expérience des familles métisse après 1870 n'est pas uniform et que le travail des femmes dépend essentiellement de leur maris."

65 Ens, *Homeland to Hinterland*, 114–21.

66 Adele Perry, *Colonial Relations: The Douglas-Connolly Family and the Nineteenth-Century Imperial World* (Cambridge: Cambridge University Press, 2015).

67 L'Abbé George Dugas, *The First Canadian Woman in the Northwest, or the Story of Marie Anne Gaboury, Wife of John Baptiste Lajimonière, Who Arrived in the Northwest in 1807, and Died at St Boniface at the Age of 96 Years* (Winnipeg: Manitoba Press, 1902).

68 Adele Perry, "'Is Your Garden in England, Sir': James Douglas's Archive and the Politics of Home," *History Workshop Journal* 70, no. 1 (September 2010): 86.

69 Ann Laura Stoler, *Race and the Education of Desire: Foucault's History of Sexuality and the Colonial Order of Things* (Durham, NC: Duke University Press, 1995).

70 John Tosh, *A Man's Place: Masculinity and the Middle-Class Home in Victorian England* (New Haven, CT: Yale University Press, 2007).

71 The tropes of separate spheres were "just not intriguing literary devices but were instead strategies whereby relations of power were produced, organized and maintained": Cecilia Louise Morgan, *Public Men and Virtuous Women: The Gendered Languages of Religion and Politics in Upper Canada, 1791–1850* (Toronto: University of Toronto Press, 1996), 10. Janet Vey Guildford and Suzanne Morton, eds, *Separate Spheres: Women's Worlds in the 19th-Century Maritimes* (Fredericton: Acadiensis Press, 1994). See especially the articles by Rusty Bitterman, Bonnie Huskins, and Gail Campbell.

72 Susan Sleeper-Smith, "'[A]n Unpleasant Transaction on This Frontier': Challenging Female Autonomy and Authority at Michilimackinac," *Journal of the Early Republic* 25, no. 3 (Fall 2005): 417–43.

73 "Lettre à Monsieur le rédacteur," doc. 1010 in *CWLR*, 1: 13–15.

74 I am thinking here of Mill's *On the Subjection of Women* (1869) and Veuillot's *L'honnête femme* (1858).

75 There are no other studies of Riel's view of women during the 1869 resistance. Through a study of Riel's writings while in Beauport mental asylum between 20 May 1876 and 23 January 1878, Thomas Flanagan has argued that Riel, inspired

by Mosaic Law, argued for the restoration of polygamy, and was therefore anti-democratic. Flanagan, "Sexual Politics of Louis Riel," *Dorchester Review* (Winter 2013): 60–4. Elsewhere, Flanagan confusingly suggests that Riel's love for his sister reflected incestuous desire. For a critical engagement with Flanagan, see Lesley Erickson, "'Bury Our Sorrows.'"

76 *New Nation,* 11 February 1870.

77 "Compte rendu incomplet de la convention de novembre–décembre 1869," doc. 1-017) in *CWLR,* 1: 23–31.

78 "Letter to H.M. Robinson,"(doc 1-41, in ibid., 64. On the same day, the editor, Henry Robinson, resigned and became the American consul. Robinson was replaced by Thomas Spence.

79 Cecilia Morgan, "Of Slender Frame and Delicate Appearance: The Placing of Laura Secord in the Narratives of Canadian Loyalist Tradition," in *Settling and Unsettling Memories: Essays in Canadian Public History*, eds Peter Hodgins and Nicole Neatby (Toronto: University of Toronto Press, 2012), 25.

80 A.I. Silver, "Nineteenth-Century News Gathering and the Mythification of Riel," in *Images of Louis Riel in Canadian Culture*, ed. Ramon Hathorn and Patrick Holland (Lewiston, NY: Edwin Mellen Press, 1992), 76. See also Lyle Dick, "Nationalism and Visual Media in Canada: The Case of Thomas Scott's Execution," *Manitoba History* 48 (Autumn/Winter 2004–5): 2–13.

81 Morgan, *Public Men and Virtuous Women*, 79–80. George B. Winship Papers, Memoires, box 321905, series 10011, North Dakota Historic Society.

82 *New Nation*, 11 February 1870.

83 Ibid.

84 Published by *Le Nouveau Monde* in Montreal, January 1874. See also "L'Amnistie: mémoire sur les causes des troubles du Nord-Ouest et sur les négotiations qui ont amené leur règlement amiable," doc. 1–188 in *CWLR*, 1: 310.

85 Alexander Begg, J.M. Bumsted, and Joseph James Hargrave, *Reporting the Resistance: Alexander Begg and Joseph Hargrave on the Red River Resistance* (Winnipeg: University of Manitoba Press, 2003), 206–8.

86 "A Lady on the Case," *New Nation*, 18 February 1870, 3.

87 "Acknowledgement," *New Nation,* 11 March 1870, 2.

88 Joan B. Landes, *Visualizing the Nation: Gender, Representation, and Revolution in Eighteenth-Century France* (Ithaca, NY: Cornell University Press, 2003), 168.

89 Riel, "La Métisse," doc. 4–041 in *CWLR*.

90 Elizabeth Elbourne argues that literate and non-literate forms overlap. See "Orality and Literacy on the New York Frontier: Remembering Joseph Brant," in *Critical Perspectives on Colonialism: Writing the Empire from Below*, ed. Fiona Paisley and Kirsty Reid (New York: Routledge, 2014).

91 Colin Coates and Cecilia Morgan, *Heroines and History: Representations of Madeleine de Verchères and Laura Secord* (Toronto: University of Toronto Press, 2002).

92 He threatened them: "As for you Charles Nolin, Tom Harrison and Geo. Kyne – two of you relatives of my own – as for you, your influence as public men is finished in this country." *New Nation*, 11 February 1870.

93 "Lettre à Charles Nolin," doc. 1-090 in *CWLR*, 1: 138.

94 "Programme national des Métis canadiens français," doc. 1-183; "Lettre à mes chers amis," doc. 1–184; and "Lettre a John Macdougall, doc. 1-185, all in ibid., 1: 289–95.

95 Adam Gaudry, "Kaa-Tipeyimishoyaahk – 'We Are Those Who Own Ourselves': A Political History of Metis Self-Determination in the North-West, 1830–1870" (PhD diss., University of Victoria, 2014).

96 McNairn, *The Capacity to Judge*; Morgan, *Public Men and Virtuous Women*. Studies of public opinion are not usually framed within the context of settler colonialism; for exceptions, see Lesley Erickson, *Westward Bound: Sex, Violence, the Law, and the Making of Settler Society* (Vancouver: UBC Press, 2011); and Adele Perry, *On the Edge of Empire: Gender, Race, and the Making of British Columbia, 1849–1871* (Toronto: University of Toronto Press, 2001). Elsbeth Heaman argues that the Canadian state attempted to engage Indigenous communities in settler politics through exhibitions. Elsbeth Heaman, *The Inglorious Arts of Peace: Exhibitions in Canadian Society during the Nineteenth Century* (Toronto: University of Toronto Press, 1999). Scholarship on the British Empire has argued that the public sphere was a means of excluding Indigenous voices. See Mrinalini Sinha, "Britishness, Clubbability, and the Colonial Public Sphere: The Genealogy of an Imperial Institution in Colonial India," *Journal of British Studies* 40, no. 4 (October 2001): 489–521; and Julie Evans et al., *Equal Subjects, Unequal Rights: Indigenous People in British Settler Colonies, 1830–1910* (Manchester: Manchester University Press, 2003).

97 The importance of kinship to Indigenous governance has been explored. For example, see Peter Cook, "Onontio Gives Birth: How the French in Canada Became Fathers to Their Indigenous Allies, 1645–73," *Canadian Historical Review* 96, no. 2 (June 2015): 165–93; Heidi Bohaker, "'Nindoodemag': The Significance of Algonquian Kinship Networks in the Eastern Great Lakes Region, 1600–1701," *William and Mary Quarterly* 63, no. 1 (January 2006): 23–52; and Gilles Havard, "'Protection' and 'Unequal Alliance': The French Conception of Sovereignty over Indians in New France," in *French and Indians in the Heart of North American, 1630–1815*, ed. Robert Englebert and Guillaume Teasdale (Winnipeg: University of Manitoba, 2013).

SECTION IV

Legitimating and Contesting the Public Sphere

Many avenues can be taken to understand the ways in which individuals experienced disorder – including violent episodes – and sought ways to bring a measure of order to their institutions. The chapters in this section tackle the intersections between the private and public worlds of British North America and early Confederation Canada; they explore public spaces, election campaigns, contentious street activities, and membership in fraternal organizations. These interactions illustrate complicated themes that were based on notions of the common good and perceptions of what was acceptable for the maintenance of public order.

At the core of many of these public-private interactions was a difficult question of the threshold, if any, of the societal tolerance for disorder. Colin Grittner's research on disruptive and sometimes violent behaviour at the hustings and attempts by governing elites to implement franchise reforms demonstrates the disorder that could be corralled by groups to advance political agendas. The impulse to define and construct public spaces that could be accessed and enjoyed by popular classes as well as elites in urban spaces, as Dan Horner explores in his history of the evolution of Montreal's Viger Square, alerts us to core ideals of modernity in the nineteenth century. Reformers sought to wrest control over public spaces from working-class people in order to achieve their vision of social harmony. Other agendas of municipal reform were at play in Toronto as well, as Ian Radforth's exploration of the disruptive activities of boys and young men in the city's public spaces in the Victorian era illustrates. Middle-class and elite citizens sought to solve the problem of rowdy and potentially criminal elements by developing and maintaining industrial schools and reformatory homes. Bonnie Huskins takes a different path, to explore the fault lines between institutions and public disorder. She identifies the paradoxical role of Masonic lodges in Saint John, New Brunswick, and Shelburne, Nova

Scotia, in the late eighteenth and early nineteenth centuries. Freemasons often employed disruptive tactics in public spaces to achieve hegemony over other elements of colonial society, while simultaneously espousing an Enlightenment ideal that championed the positive dynamics of regulatory institutions.

This section comes to grips with the important question of who has the right to pursue social and political agendas in the public sphere. It complements the essays in section III that addressed Indigenous attempts to engage in and define the public sphere in ways that would accommodate them. It also complements and complicates the contributions and machinations of political and religious elites – the focus of section I's essays – by demonstrating the equally important give and take of ordinary actors in the arenas of community spaces and organizations. Those activities provide another lens through which to view individual and institutional anxieties and sometimes-violent reactions. Moreover, they served as a catalyst for elites to craft regulations, legal codes, and architectural plans – all with an express purpose of deepening their reach into institutions of social, political, and economic order. Taken together, these chapters provide an exemplar of liberalism in practice: a belief in the beneficial role of government and organizations in suppressing conflict in public spaces.

13 Discontents and Dissidents: Unrest among Loyalist Freemasons in the 1780s and 1790s

BONNIE HUSKINS

Introduction

American Loyalists, upon their flight into exile, set up Freemasonic lodges throughout British North America, including in Shelburne, Nova Scotia, and Saint John, New Brunswick, sites of the largest urban concentrations of Loyalists on the Atlantic coast. Two of these lodges – Solomon's Lodge No. 5 in Shelburne and Hiram Lodge No. 17 in Saint John – were rent by considerable conflict and contestation. Little has been written about the unrest generated by Freemasonry in a Canadian context in the late eighteenth century.[1] This paper analyses the general relationship between fraternal orders and colonial unrest, as well as the types of unrest generated by Freemasonry in particular. Freemasonic unrest did not resemble the ethnic, racial, and religious violence generated by the Orange Order in later decades,[2] but rather was of a more interpersonal and political nature. In Shelburne, for instance, members of Solomon's Lodge jockeyed for leadership of the fraternity, which degenerated quickly into internecine conflict,[3] while Hiram Lodge members actively protested the colonial elite's manipulation of New Brunswick's first election in 1785.[4] This paper also highlights the irony of Freemasonry's relationship to unrest. On the one hand, Freemasons, like Orange Lodge members, actively fomented unrest. On the other hand, their Enlightenment roots and organizational structure channelled and regulated that unrest, a significant function in a pioneer society that had relatively few regulatory institutions.

An important clue in understanding Freemasonic disorder in Saint John and Shelburne lies in the socio-economic and political makeup of the loyalist Freemasons. Although loyalist elite families from the Atlantic seaboard did settle in the Maritimes, we have known for some time that the Loyalists who made their way to this region were a diverse lot, ethnically, racially, culturally, and economically. Commentators of the period observed that many of the Loyalists who arrived in Shelburne and Saint John were primarily artisans and shopkeepers with urban backgrounds.[5] What is not effectively articulated in the literature is the class tension that many loyalist arrivals brought with them. I argue elsewhere that many Loyalists migrated to Shelburne looking for social mobility and subsequently set up the infrastructure of polite society.[6]

Similarly, the Freemasons who made their way to British North America after the revolution have been described as "social climbers."[7] The reason for this overlap is that Loyalists and Freemasons shared a similar social profile. The Freemasons who came to the Maritimes as Loyalists were primarily Ancients, an order that had split from the original Grand Lodge in London because they disapproved of its exclusivity and demanded a "more genuine egalitarianism." The Ancients tended to recruit among the middling and lower orders and, because of the fraternity's openness and flexibility, successfully expanded in the American colonies. Empowered by the destabilization of the American Revolution and the rise of an embryonic middle class throughout the Atlantic world,[8] Ancients were dedicated to the ideals of merit and virtue and, in turn, were more sensitive to issues of privilege and corruption.[9] Members often joined the fraternity to negotiate social, cultural, and economic advancement. Those who resettled in places like Saint John and Shelburne came to view the establishment of new lodges as a "passport" to social betterment.[10] Mark A. Tabbert notes that "Ancient Freemasonry became a pathway to extend a man's business contracts, confirm his honour and integrity, improve his manners and knowledge, and further his aspirations of becoming an affluent and respected gentleman."[11] These efforts to enhance social standing through fraternalism generated interpersonal and political unrest. They also engendered elite responses from government and Freemasonic leaders who attempted to regulate the behaviour of the rank and file. Analysing this dynamic contributes to our understanding of how fraternities and voluntary associations attempted to regulate governance and morality in the late eighteenth century and, in turn, responded to attempts to regulate the behaviour of their members.

The cohort of loyalist Freemasons who migrated to Saint John engaged in political dissent informed partly by their socio-economic profile as well as by contested definitions of loyalty. Loyalists functioned as agents of discontent, carrying with them a host of grievances against fellow Americans, local officials, and British authority.[12] The members of Hiram Lodge in Saint John thought that their rights as British subjects had been compromised. Thus, they saw no contradiction between engaging in political opposition to established authority and remaining Loyalists and Freemasons. The governing elite in New Brunswick defined *loyalty* as obedience to constituted authority, while lower-class Loyalists, many of them Freemasons, "maintained that their status as loyal subjects allowed them to take issue with imperial authorities and agitate for reform."[13] This conflict between loyalist Freemasons and the New Brunswick government over what it meant to be a Loyalist also suggests that loyalty was defined not so much by ideology as by the appropriate relationship between governors and the governed. This definitional tension reveals that loyalism can be "sufficiently broad to be a tool of governance or an instrument of opposition."[14] It also illustrates that, although a Freemason was supposed to be "a peaceable subject, never to be concerned in plots against the state," the fraternity was also elastic enough in the post-revolutionary period to "house divisive or oppositional political perspectives."[15]

British Freemasonry and the Rise of the Ancients

British Freemasonry emerged from the ruins of the medieval stonemasons' guilds. These guilds, which had regulated the conditions of work, fell upon hard times in the sixteenth and seventeenth centuries due to the decline of castle and cathedral building, the rise of the market economy, urbanization, rapid population growth, and the transiency of workers. In order to survive, the guilds turned to the patronage of aristocrats and gentlemen, and incorporated them as "free and accepted" brothers. In 1717, a non-mason was elected as grand master, marking the transition from "operative" to "speculative" masonry, from a concern with "building better edifices" to "building better men."[16]

Speculative masons revamped the structure, regulations, rituals, history, and "secrets" of the stonemasons' guilds to their own more "metaphoric" ends.[17] They adapted the guilds into a system of local, regional, and national lodges with parent or "grand" lodges in England (1717), Ireland (1725), and Scotland (1736). The guilds' lists of rules or "charges" became Freemasonic constitutions. Their hand signals, grips, and handshakes, initially used to identify each other and retain trade secrets, helped to transform Freemasonry into a secret society.[18] Speculative masons incorporated the symbols of their predecessors' tools of the trade into their rituals: the square symbolized honesty; the level equality; the plumb rectitude; and the trowel the tool used to spread the "cement of brotherly love." The operative masons' three basic degrees – Entered Apprentice, Fellowcraft, and Master Mason – which had initially marked a mason's initiation and passage through the trade, was adapted by their Freemasonic brothers as a means of progressing by degrees towards a "veiled yet constantly unfolding wisdom and enlightenment."[19]

Speculative Freemasonry evolved over the course of the eighteenth century in tandem with the Enlightenment. Fraternal brothers attempted to understand the universe by melding the stonemasons' interest in buildings and architecture with the Enlightenment practice of looking to the ancients for inspiration. They espoused that the architecture and ornaments of ancient structures like Solomon's Temple were mathematical and geometric "keys" central to understanding the nature of God and creation. This "history" was included in the Freemasonic constitution published by James Anderson in 1723.[20] The first systematic attempt to codify and give deeper meaning to the fraternity's rituals was William Preston's *Illustrations of Masonry* (1772), which was reprinted many times. He organized the material into a lecture system to be delivered to new initiates, and it was widely read in British North America and the United States.[21]

Many of the ideals of British Freemasonry also emerged out of the Glorious Revolution (1688–9), which led to the fall of James II and the rise of constitutional and parliamentary governance. After 1689, we see the emergence in England of new voluntary societies and reading clubs that constituted a "newly emergent civil society." According to German philosopher Jürgen Habermas, the rapid spread of Freemasonry anticipated the adoption of what he calls the "public sphere," a "virtual space" created to regulate civil society and composed of "private people gathered together as a public and articulating the needs of society." This public sphere, of which Freemasonry was an early embodiment, provided an "alternative to absolutism."[22]

Moreover, emerging as it did in the wake of political and religious sectarianism, Freemasonry promoted religious toleration and political cosmopolitanism in an effort to attain a new form of political and social regulation. The lodges were not established explicitly as political entities, but Margaret C. Jacob argues that "more than any other new form of sociability, the lodges became schools of government, places where the reformist impulses of the Enlightenment [and the Glorious Revolution] could be focused on one's immediate surroundings." She notes that the "most startling aspect of masonic day-to-day living" was the invention of "forms of governance." These bodies had constitutions, which "made them capable of being transformed into microscopic, and contractually founded and constitutionally governed, civil societies." They also "naturalized" constitutional practices such as holding elections, forming representative assemblies, imposing taxes (dues), and convening courts where disputes could be heard.[23]

This establishment of reformist governance in the lodges is also part of the Enlightenment search for harmony and social order. The earliest records of the London lodges illustrate an insistence that their officers be properly appointed and that their grand lodges and grand masters be recognized as constituting legitimate authority. The authority of masters and other officers on the local level was also to be recognized and respected by lodge members. If individuals did not follow the rules, they were subjected to fines and sometimes expulsion.[24]

Despite this insistence on respecting authority, hierarchy, and proper procedure, a schism developed in British Freemasonry in the mid-eighteenth century between the Ancients and the Moderns. It was precipitated by Irish Masons in London who complained that they were often denied admission to the local lodges. Thus, they constituted their own grand lodge in 1751 as a rival to the "Premier" Grand Lodge. They labelled the latter the Moderns and themselves the Ancients, arguing that they embodied the more traditional notions of "fraternal equality." This development essentially pitted "newly risen men of artisan background" against what they perceived to be the "decadence into which many of the London lodges had fallen." Their main spokesperson, Grand Secretary Laurence Dermott, an Irish journeyman painter and later wine merchant, published *The True Ahiman Rezon, Or, a Help to All That Are, or Would Be Free and Accepted Masons* in 1756 as a guide for the Ancients. He began by reminding his readers of the many ancient and biblical personalities who had emerged from humble beginnings to attain success. He also revised the standard mythology, glorifying the builders, as opposed to the architects, of Solomon's Temple. He went so far as to claim a "secret cabalistic wisdom transferred from original guild" to the artisans of the Ancient lodges. The literature of the Ancient Freemasons generally attempted to balance deference for church and state with a "lionization" of the trades and a disdain for privilege.[25]

Loyalist Freemasons

The British expeditiously exported Freemasonry throughout the empire. This imperial expansion was facilitated through widespread emigration and by the formation of a network of military lodges.[26] Outside of Britain, the Ancients spread more widely than their rivals, as they used travelling warrants more effectively and recruited actively among the Irish, Scottish, and English lower and middling classes. Artisans and small merchants in the American colonies joined the lodges in large numbers, using them to "negotiate an expanded role in economic and cultural life in eighteenth-century urban centres."[27]

While the destabilization of the American Revolution continued to empower the lower and middling strata, it also created confusion in the fraternity, which in turn increased the chance of power struggles. It has been assumed that Freemasons played an important role in the American Revolution, as a number of the Founding Fathers, including George Washington and Benjamin Franklin, were Masons. One Masonic publication notes: "It would almost seem that the Revolution which gave the American colonies their freedom was planned in the anteroom of some Masonic Lodge."[28] However, according to Jessica Harland-Jacobs in her path-breaking book on Freemasons in the British Empire, Freemasonry had a "significant presence among Loyalists, a point that eighteenth-century historians have insufficiently addressed."[29] Ultimately, there seems to have been no linear connection between lodges and political loyalties: "Moderns and Ancients, Masons and non-Masons, ended up on both sides of the Revolution."[30] The war certainly disrupted meetings and divided lodges.[31] Those lodges with large numbers of Loyalists either disbanded or relocated in exile.[32] There was a fair amount of confusion in Nova Scotia over Freemasonic authority until the Ancient Provincial Grand Lodge of Nova Scotia was established in 1784. Within two years of its founding, the Loyalists had formed ten lodges.[33]

The first lodges formed in Nova Scotia, outside of Annapolis Royal and Halifax, were created in Shelburne. Some of these lodges were ambulatory military lodges created by British military regiments sent to aid in the process of loyalist resettlement. The 17th Regiment (1784–6) and the 6th Regiment (1786–91) contained a couple of lodges each.[34] Sion Lodge No. 3, containing members from the 57th Regiment of Foot, and Lodge No. 52, with members from the 37th Regiment, also spent time in Shelburne.[35] Three civilian lodges were constituted in September 1784 by the Loyalists: Solomon's Lodge No. 5 Provincial; Parr Lodge No. 3 Provincial, Ancient York Masons; and Lodge No. 4, which, due to a mix-up with warrants, was never established – instead, many of its members formed Hiram Lodge No. 10 Provincial in March 1785.[36] The application to organize Hiram Lodge No. 17 in Saint John was made at Halifax on 6 March 1784 by Elias Hardy, a barrister who would become deeply embroiled in the unrest that would unfold in Saint John. A dispensation was granted by three Halifax lodges meeting in quarterly communication, and, on 1 September 1784, Hiram Lodge No. 17 was formally opened, the first Freemasonic lodge in New Brunswick. On 6 December 1786, members of Hiram Lodge applied for and received a warrant from the Nova Scotia Grand Lodge.[37]

A significant number of the Freemasons in Shelburne and Saint John migrated directly from New York City, the main point of departure for the loyalist fleets to Shelburne and Saint John, and the "centre of Masonic loyalism" during the American Revolution.[38] Of the twenty members of Saint John's Hiram Lodge No. 17 identified by Masonic researcher A.J.B. Milbourne, four had been members of the New York City Lodge No. 169. Similarly, of the thirty-seven members of Shelburne's Parr Lodge No. 3 identified by the author, seven had been members of Boston's No. 169, twelve had been members of New York City's Lodge No. 169, and four had been members of both. Ancient Lodge No. 169 had received its warrant from London in 1771 and became one of the most militantly loyalist lodges in Boston. But as Loyalists were evacuated from Boston in 1776, they carried the warrant with them to Nova Scotia, accompanying General Howe's troops. Two or three years later, the Boston lodge was moved to New York City, where several lodge members formed the nucleus of the Provincial Grand Lodge in New York City.[39] Milbourne has suggested that approximately 115 members of New York's No. 169 became Loyalists, and, of that number, thirty-three joined lodges in New Brunswick, eighteen in Nova Scotia, and four in Lower Canada.[40]

Freemasons in Saint John and Shelburne had also been members of New York City's Lodge No. 210 E.R., including thirteen individuals from Saint John's Hiram Lodge No. 17, three members of Shelburne's Solomon's Lodge No. 5 Provincial, three members of Hiram Lodge No. 10, and at least one member of Parr's Lodge No. 3 Provincial. Milbourne estimates that eighty-one members of the Lodge No. 210 were Loyalists, and of that number, twenty-five joined lodges in Nova Scotia, twelve in New Brunswick, two in Lower Canada, and one in Upper Canada.[41] Other New York City lodges to which Shelburne and Saint John Freemasons belonged included No. 168, No. 212, No. 213, Sion's Lodge No. 3, and Union Lodge No 8. Loyalists clearly carried Freemasonry with them as part of their cultural baggage, transplanting it in the Maritime colonies, and reinforcing the pre-existing Masonic culture percolating among earlier military and civilian lodges. Freemasonry helped to mitigate the challenges of resettlement, providing comfort, opportunities for sociability and intellectual development, and mutual support for members.

Discontents: Solomon's Lodge No. 5 in Shelburne

In Shelburne, rank-and-file Freemasons jockeyed for the leadership of Solomon's Lodge No 5. Elsewhere I have argued that this manoeuvring reflected a larger tension within American Freemasonry, between working for the common good of the fraternity and using the lodges to further personal interests and ambitions.[42] It also illustrates the desire of middling Loyalists for upward mobility. Both Shelburne and Saint John were hardscrabble communities during this period. Shelburne, on the southwest coast of Nova Scotia, grew very rapidly with the arrival of approximately eleven thousand Loyalists by late September 1783, as did Saint John, which attracted ten thousand Loyalists to the mouth of the St John River.[43] Many of these new arrivals, with their shiny loyalist dreams, took advantage of the fluidity of pioneer society to advance themselves socially, culturally, and politically.

In Shelburne, much of the controversy took the form of interpersonal conflict among three members: the first master of the lodge, Philip Lenzi, a confectioner and caterer from New York City;[44] Hugh Hay, a tavern keeper from New York City;[45] and John Stewart. The enmity began with the original warrant in 1784, on which Hay's name was erased as master, due to "unmason like behavior," and Lenzi's substituted.[46] Hay was angry enough to draw a sword on lodge members, but, by March 1785, the lodge was meeting at Hay's residence.[47] Stewart had gotten himself into trouble by speaking "very degrading speeches" about the lodge, for which he was found guilty and suspended for four months.[48] The lodge eventually reconsidered his suspension "on account of his being a young Br[other]," perhaps taking into account the reputation of young men as "unruly youth," as discussed by Ian Radforth in this volume. The lodge secretary was about to read a memorial from Stewart regarding his reinstatement when Lenzi snatched the memo from his hands and attacked Stewart with a sword and then turned on Hay.

The Masters Lodge launched an investigation into the internal affairs of Solomon's Lodge No. 5. Although the investigation was initially requested by Lenzi, most lodge members, in their interviews with the Masters Lodge, complained that Lenzi was the problem: he was "passionate, fiery & outrageous, and irregular in his behavior." Lenzi's conduct had allegedly led some members to apply for their certificates to leave the lodge.[49] The masters recommended that Lenzi be deprived of the privileges associated with the rank of past master but remitted the initial recommendation of a six-month suspension. In November 1786, Lenzi wrote to the Grand Lodge, "praying that he may be restored to the Privileges of a Past Master," but he was refused.[50]

The Masters Lodge also recommended that the lodge's warrant be recalled, but the Grand Lodge decided to give the branch one last chance by launching another inquiry. Nonetheless, members continued to fight among themselves. Eventually the Grand Lodge resolved that Solomon's Lodge No. 5 be "absolutely and *bona fide*, excluded, their Number Erased from the Grand Lodge Books, and their Warrant withdrawn."[51] Lenzi moved to Halifax, where, in 1785, he was investigated for threatening the life of Adam Fife, a member of Artillery Lodge No. 2 in Halifax. The Grand Lodge found him guilty, but they also acknowledged that there had been an "unintentional provocation," and they recommended "mutual apologies."[52] In 1790, Lenzi applied for and received 40s in assistance from the Grand Lodge, and the next year he received £3 10s "to assist him in procuring a Passage to Jamaica."[53]

The multiple interventions of the Nova Scotia Grand Lodge in this affair are in part an elitest response to disorder. Despite the celebrity of genteel Freemasons such as Archibald Cunningham, Shelburne postmaster and grand master of the Nova Scotia Grand Lodge, and Gideon White, a prominent merchant, judge, and politician, most Shelburnian Freemasons tended to be modest in rank and social status: teachers, shopkeepers, bookbinders, printers, tailors, and carpenters. The provincial Grand Lodge, on the other hand, still recruited military officers, colonial, and respectable citizens as leaders and patrons.[54] One of the main conclusions of the colonial elite sitting on the Grand Lodge was that the Shelburne fiasco was a function of the members' lower status and pretensions: their manners were "strongly replete with all that vulgar and disgusting pomposity inseparably attached to ignorance and low breeding when acting beyond its sphere."[55]

They also concluded that the members of Solomon's Lodge had clearly been "unacquainted" with the "most simple forms" of Freemasonry.[56] This is inaccurate when one considers the combined Masonic experience of the ringleaders. Both Lenzi and Hay had served together in New York City's No. 210, often meeting in Hay's tavern. Perhaps Lenzi and Hay brought tension with them when they emigrated to Shelburne, for No. 210 followed a similar trajectory to that of Solomon's Lodge, becoming so divided that it was eventually dissolved and its members were expelled.[57] The Grand Lodge, in its dismissive remarks about Shelburne's brothers, may have been referring to irregularities in how the members of Solomon's Lodge governed themselves. In any case, the elites of the provincial Grand Lodge proceeded in proper form by holding court to hear the relevant grievances and then rendering their verdict. Although lodges attempted to screen "men with bad reputations," sometimes they slipped through. Under such circumstances, officers had to use "due process."[58] It has been suggested that this "force of Lodge-administered justice" was powerful in British North American society.[59]

Freemasons were also emerging as arbiters of moral order in a pioneer society that had few formal regulatory institutions. It appears that late eighteenth-century Freemasonry was transitioning between Enlightenment concerns to a focus on morality that would later dominate in Victorian lodges. Upon the recall of the warrant for Solomon's Lodge No. 5, the Halifax elites, in their response to local lodge members, presented themselves as embodiments of Enlightenment concepts such as harmony and toleration: "Honor and dignity can never be supported by feuds, quarrels, contentions, dissentions, pride, Obstinancy, party-rage, self-will, Malicious Strifes & Debates, envy, hatred &&, but with all lowliness and meekness; let each esteem others better than themselves, holding the faith in Unity of the Spirit & in the bond of peace."[60] In other words, they instructed members to transcend partisanship. They also articulated a clear sense of moral order, not only within the lodge, but outside of it as well. The minutes of Solomon's Lodge were replete with details about various improprieties. For example, Peter Taylor was accused of stealing from the lodge, while the aforementioned John Stewart was guilty of being an "acessary [*sic*] to the Elopement" of brother Walter Dunn's wife. The subcommittee charged with investigating this behaviour recommended that Stewart "be Put upon his Oath of Obligation whether he had any Carnal Dealings with Br Dun's [*sic*] wife are as Courrantly [*sic*] Reported." Freemasons put in place a series of fines and punishments for "immoral behavior" such as theft and "sleeping away from home."[61] Brother Hay noted that Stewart was bound in the sum of £20 for the appearance of Dunn's wife in court. Stewart responded that he was "guilty of Convaying [*sic*] away Mrs Dunn" but ignorant of being bound for her appearance. In the press, Hay had also advertised a reward for the apprehension of Ann Dunn, for whom he had posted bail and who had absconded. Walter Dunn and Hugh Hay eventually forfeited their £20 "in consequence of non-appearance of Ann Dunn."[62] Moreover, Stewart seems to have been a volatile man, appearing before the Court of General Quarter Sessions in November 1784 on charges of "Riott [*sic*] and Assault." He was also there to answer for contempt during his previous appearance. On examination, he again "uttered words of additional Contempt and proceeded so far as to impeach the Honour & integrity of Two of his Majesty's Justices then sitting in Sessions." Not long after, on 14 July 1785, he was charged with firing a pistol at a "Negro Man," wounding him "in diverse parts of his body."[63] Hay also appeared in the Shelburne County court on the charge of assault and battery; his wife, Magdelen, launched a complaint against William Summers in 1786 for defamation of character.[64] Since these matters were a matter of public record in the courts and in the newspapers, the Grand Lodge was undoubtedly aware of them when they deliberated over the fate of Solomon's Lodge. Such acts of immorality were not considered proper behaviour for Freemasons.

Dissidents: Hiram Lodge No. 10 in Saint John

While the Nova Scotia Grand Lodge assumed that its moral code would apply to life outside of the fraternity, so too did the members of Hiram Lodge No. 10 think it appropriate to participate in political unrest outside of the lodge. Governor Thomas Carleton called the first provincial election in New Brunswick in 1785. The election was hotly contested, characterized by violence in the local taverns and corruption, including an unsuccessful attempt to allow the garrison to vote in an effort to drum up supporters for the government slate. Much to the surprise of the ruling elites, the non-government slate won by a margin of more than 10 per cent.[65] How did Governor Carleton's administration respond to this upset of the status quo? They held a recount and disallowed almost two hundred votes, enough to permit the installation of only the government candidates. After an emotional protest letter was published in the *Saint John Gazette*, printer John Ryan and his colleague William Lewis were charged with seditious libel and the newspaper was shut down. Petitions against the election results were widely circulated throughout the province. Dissidents called on the British monarch to dissolve the assembly and call a new election. Governor Carleton responded by passing legislation that essentially made petitioning illegal. When four men appealed to the assembly, they were arrested and went to trial with detained election rioters and the newspaper printers, all of whom were "severally convicted and punished."[66]

How did Saint John Freemasons participate in this unrest? First of all, they ran as candidates in the election: four of the six challengers on the non-government slate were Freemasons. David Bell also suggests that approximately 70 per cent of the fifty or so Freemasons in Saint John signed the anti-government petitions.[67] Moreover, Freemasons were among the men detained. Besides printer John Ryan, a letter from Hiram Lodge to the Grand Lodge of Nova Scotia on 1 May 1786, notes that another brother, Joseph Montgomery, was confined under military guard for nearly three months with three other citizens "only for presenting a petition for redress of Grievances at the late Election, which was resented so highly that the Writ of Habeas Corpus has been refused. Tomorrow their Trial comes on, the Event of which will determine whether we are to have a British Constitution or not."[68]

The involvement of fraternal brothers in partisan politics runs counter to the Ancients' charge that "we are resolved against political disputes, as contrary to the peace and welfare of the lodge."[69] So why did these Freemasons feel it was appropriate to engage in political unrest? First, they were acting within the environment of British Freemasonry, which, during this period, promoted political cosmopolitanism, and thus accepted the legitimacy of radical politics. This tolerance was embodied in the "escape clause" contained in the 1723 constitution: that if a brother did engage in a challenge to the state, his relationship to the lodge would "remain indefeasible." In other words, the brother would not be expelled, although he should be "discountenanced" for his action. This suggests that an Ancient Freemason in the eighteenth century could "justify opposing the state in open rebellion."[70]

Loyalist Freemasons in Hiram Lodge believed that their treatment warranted opposing the state. Many Loyalists arrived in Saint John with "instincts ... sharpened by a generation of revolutionary agitation." During the American Revolution, the "patriots had outfoxed them. In war the generals had misdirected them. At the peace table their government had betrayed them. They came ashore wounded, reluctant and sullen."[71] New arrivals soon assembled a series of concrete local grievances as well, ranging from receiving blankets with holes in them to corruption in the distribution of lands and lots.

Their political action was also a product of their social make-up. Most rank-and-file Freemasons in Saint John resembled the more general profile of the Ancients. Of the first forty-one members of Hiram Lodge who joined between 1784 and 1786, 60 per cent were in skilled and middling occupations. Although ten of the members were merchants, they may have been modest shopkeepers. Only four members were recorded as gentlemen.[72] Most of the Freemasons also lived in the section of town called Lower Cove, a commercial neighbourhood along the waterfront, which was inhabited by shopkeepers, artisans, and seafarers, who had been denied commercial lots in the Upper Cove. The Upper Cove was situated on higher ground near Fort Howe, and its population comprised professionals, officeholders, and other gentlefolk. Because of the social profile of the Freemasons, the "Lower Cove leaders were Freemasons; Upper Cove leaders were not."[73]

As Lower Covers, Loyalists, and Ancients, Saint John Freemasons were sensitive to issues of privilege and corruption. Many ordinary Loyalists had already been disillusioned by the favouritism shown towards elite Loyalists in the case of the "petition of fifty-five," wherein fifty-five prominent Loyalists in New York City petitioned Governor Thomas Carleton's brother Guy Carleton, the British commander-in-chief, for assistance in procuring grants of 5,000 acres each in Nova Scotia. These gentlemen Loyalists argued that they had lost much for the king and needed large landed estates to regain their former status. They would also "add polish" to the new province. When word of this circulated, especially to those awaiting evacuation to Nova Scotia, 628 loyalists signed a counter-petition at Roubalet's Tavern. These common loyalists worried that a land grab in Nova Scotia would mean that they would either receive poor land or none at all, reducing them to the status of tenants on the lands of the wealthy. Elias Hardy, who had petitioned for the formation of Hiram Lodge, was one of the four scribes chosen at Roubalet's Tavern to pen the "savagely sarcastic counter-petition." [74]

Loyalist Freemasons' involvement in the election unrest, as well as the government's response to it, manifests competing definitions of loyalty. Lower Cove Loyalists believed that their status as loyal subjects gave them the right to protest a violation of their liberty. After absorbing the results of the election, "Americanus" pled the following in the *Saint John Gazette*: "My distressed Countrymen, Be firm in the protection of the Birth Right handed down to you, and supported by our happy Constitution ... Upon no account ... lose sight of what you are. In Fine, let the world know, as you know, the Rights you are jealous of [as] Descendants of Britons." Loyalists believed in the principle of British liberty. Just as American patriots had invoked the British constitution in "pleading for just representation," Saint John Loyalists protested the political process in New Brunswick as a "violation of their rights as British subjects."[75]

Indeed, in the late eighteenth century, loyalty often involved allegiance to a "constitutional monarchy and parliament."[76]

But the most significant aspect of their loyalism was the belief that their actions were justified because they had been treated shabbily by the established authorities. As Elizabeth Mancke has recently suggested, Loyalists "deplored elite manipulation of ... populous disenchantment for political ends."[77] The largest opposition petition, which was signed by nearly one-third of the electors of Saint John, including many Freemasons, detailed this elite manipulation of the political process:

> We have publicly seen British Subjects confined in Irons ... The Military introduced & unnecessarily & unlawfully patrolling the streets, during an Election ... Taxes levied by the Incorporation Contrary to Law ... The freedom of Election violated ... In the most public manner ... We must positively affirm these Proceedings to be unjust, Injurious to the Freedom of Election, manifest Violations of the Rights of the People & Subversive of the first Privileges of the British Constitution.[78]

Governor Carleton, however, accused the Saint John Loyalists of disloyalty. He contended that Loyalists were supposed to support constituted authority. In fact several of the dissidents were branded by Carleton and his entourage as "rebels."[79] Of course, office-holding Loyalists such as Edward Winslow and Ward Chipman were very pleased by this turn of events. They wanted loyalist New Brunswick to be a "stable hierarchical alternative to the seeming anarchy of the republican United States."[80]

The Freemasons of Hiram Lodge were similarly branded as disloyal. A government supporter, "Mr. Sower," noted in the *Royal Gazette* on 24 January 1786 that the opposition dissidents of Lower Cove were members of a "republican craft." Moreover, their principles "correspon[d] exactly with those of the rebels ... They brought with them all that restless turbulence and leveling disposition, that characterized the enemies of loyalty." The use of "craft" is undoubtedly an allusion to Freemasonry; "leveling disposition" is not only a reference to a democratizing tendency, but to a mason's level, and thus to the members of Hiram Lodge.[81] By this time, the colonial elite had probably developed an ingrained suspicion of Freemasonry. Since the 1730s, Roman Catholics and some Protestants had portrayed the Freemasons as a "rival, parallel or false religion." Moreover, conservatives suspected the "whig affiliations" of British Freemasons and accused them of sporting a "form of republicanism" and participating in revolutionary conspiracies.[82]

Loyalist Freemasons in Shelburne and Saint John were a discontented lot, fomenting interpersonal and political unrest in the late eighteenth century. Part of this unrest was generated by their status as Loyalists and their belief that they had been treated unfairly by the Americans, the British, and local authorities. Their membership in the Freemasonic order also contributed to dissension. Loyalist Freemasons in Shelburne and Saint John were primarily Ancients from the lower and middling strata who saw their fraternity as a conduit to advancement. This set the stage for power struggles, as members jockeyed for leadership in their fraternities and in their communities.

Masonic lodges in the late eighteenth century functioned as schools of governance, wherein members debated the practices of reformist government and the parameters of loyalty and morality. Margaret Jacob contends that the "eighteenth-century lodges have left the most remarkable records we possess for tracing the prehistory of nationally identified formal institutions of representative government."[83] Freemasonry was one of the first vehicles to spread the ideas and practices of constitutionalism throughout the British Empire and ultimately throughout continental Europe in the late eighteenth and early nineteenth centuries. One must remember, however, that elites used the fraternity to channel unrest by challenging egalitarian ideas and practices and regulating proper behaviour. In that sense, Freemasonic lodges are embodiments of a transition between Enlightenment values and Victorian morality. As Michael Eamon notes for the colonial print community in Halifax and Quebec City, Freemasonic lodges became "hybrid spaces of sociability and social control," which increasingly "favoured consensus and balance over discord and radical change."[84] In this regard, Freemasonic lodges were at once bulwarks of and challenges to the social order.

NOTES

1 See Bonnie Huskins, "'Ancient' Tensions and Local Circumstances: Loyalist Freemasons in Shelburne Nova Scotia," *Journal for Research into Freemasonry and Fraternalism*, 5, no. 1 (2014): 47–72. Michael Eamon, in his recent book, *Imprinting Britain: Newspapers, Sociability, and the Shaping of British North America* (Montreal and Kingston: McGill-Queen's University Press, 2015), discusses the Freemasons in Halifax: see ch. 5. Jackie Logan provides an interesting analysis of Hiram's Lodge No. 8 in Sheet Harbour, Nova Scotia, during the Loyalist era in "The Sheet Harbour Loyalist Settlement of 1784 and Hiram's Lodge No. 8," *Nova Scotia Historical Review* 15, no. 1 (1995): 118–26. Another work on Freemasonry in Maritime Canada is Hannah M. Lane, "Evangelical Churches and Freemasonry in Mid-Nineteenth Century Calais, Maine and St Stephen, New Brunswick," *Journal of Research into Fraternalism and Freemasonry* 2, no. 1 (2001): 60–78. For a recent analysis of Freemasonic

lodges in Canada today, see J. Scott Kenney, *Brought to Light: Contemporary Freemasonry, Meaning, and Society* (Waterloo, ON: Wilfrid Laurier University Press, 2016); and J. Scott Kenney, "Paths to Masonry Today: Social Factors behind Joining the Craft among Twentieth and Twenty-first-century Canadian Freemasons," *Journal for Research into Freemasonry and Fraternalism* 3, no. 2 (2012): 152–84. W. McLeod, "Freemasonry, as a Matter of Fact," *Canadian Historical Review* 69, no. 1 (1988): 51–61, is merely a tirade against Freemasons. Stephen C. Bullock's work provides a myriad of insights into the evolution of revolutionary and post-revolutionary Freemasonry within the United States, but he does not extend his focus to the Loyalist lodges which were established by American exiles in British North America: *Revolutionary Brotherhood: Freemasonry and the Transformation of the American Social Order, 1730–1840* (Chapel Hill: University of North Carolina Press, 1998); "The Revolutionary Transformation of American Freemasonry, 1752–1792," *William and Mary Quarterly*, 3rd series, 47, no. 3 (July 1990): 347–69; and "'A Pure and Sublime System': The Appeal of Post-Revolutionary Freemasonry," *Journal of the Early Republic* 9, no. 3 (1989): 359–73. Masonic historians have written useful institutional histories of Loyalist lodges: Ronald S. Longley and Reginald V. Harris, *A Short History of Freemasonry in Nova Scotia, 1738–1966*, written for the Centennial of the Grand Lodge of Nova Scotia, available at https://www.kingsolomonlodge54.com/history/freemasonry-nova-scotia/history-of-freemasonry-in-nova-scotia-chapter-1-beginnings/; J. Plimsoll Edwards, "The History of Freemasonry," *Transactions of the Nova Scotia Lodge of Research* 1, no. 2 (13 January 1916): 14–19; and A.J.B. Milbourne, "Loyalist Masons in the Maritimes," *Canadian Masonic Research Association* 112 (September 1974): 1955–95.

2 The work of Scott W. See is of particular interest here: *Riots in New Brunswick: Orange Nativism and Social Violence in the 1840s* (Toronto: University of Toronto Press: 1993); "'A Colonial Hybrid': Nineteenth-Century Loyalism as Articulated by the Orange Order in the Maritime Colonies of British North America," in *Loyalism and the Formation of the British World, 1775–1914*, ed. Allan Blackstock and Frank O'Gorman (Woodbridge, UK: Boydell Press, 2014); "Variations on a Borderlands Theme: Nativism and Collective Violence in the Mid-Nineteenth Century," in *New England and the Maritime Provinces: Connections and Comparisons*, ed. Stephen J. Hornsby and John G. Reid (Montreal and Kingston: McGill-Queen's University Press, 2005); "The Fortunes of the Orange Order," in *New Ireland Remembered: Historical Essays on the Irish in New Brunswick*, ed. Peter Toner (Fredericton, NB: New Ireland Press, 1988), 90–105; and "The Orange Order and Social Violence in Mid-Nineteenth Century Saint John," *Acadiensis* 13 (Autumn 1983): 68–92. Gregory Klages has compared Freemasons to the Orange Order in late nineteenth-century Ontario: "Freemasonic and Orange Order Membership in Rural Ontario during the Late 19th-Century," *Ontario History* 103, no. 2 (Autumn 2011): 192–214.

3 See Huskins, "'Ancient' Tensions."

4 I am greatly indebted to the research of David Bell for his work on the Saint John Freemasons: *Loyalist Rebellion in New Brunswick: A Defining Conflict for Canada's Political Culture* (Halifax: Formac, 2013), 151–2, and "The Republican Craft and the Politics of Loyalist Saint John," conference paper presented to the Atlantic Canada Studies Conference, University of New Brunswick at Saint John, 5 May 2012.

5 See the commentary of Benjamin Marston, surveyor in Shelburne, in Bonnie Huskins, "'Shelburnian Manners': Gentility and the Loyalists of Shelburne Nova Scotia," *Early American Studies* 31, no. 1 (Winter 2015): 177.

6 Ibid., 157–8.

7 Jessica Harland-Jacobs, *Builders of Empire: Freemasons and British Imperialism, 1717–1927* (Chapel Hill: University of North Carolina Press, 2007), 165.

8 The rise of the middling sort and middling manners in eighteenth-century America is addressed by C. Dallett Hemphill, "Manners and Class in the Revolutionary Era: A Transatlantic Comparison," *William and Mary Quarterly* 63, no. 2 (April 2006): 354–72, and *Bowing to Necessities: A History of Manners in America, 1620–1860* (New York: Oxford University, 1999).

9 Margaret C. Jacob, *Living the Enlightenment: Freemasonry and Politics in Eighteenth-Century Europe* (New York: Oxford University Press, 1991), 59–65; and Bullock, *Revolutionary Brotherhood*, 39.

10 Harland-Jacobs, *Builders of Empire*, 29, 34; Bullock, "'A Pure and Sublime System,'" 368–9; and Bullock, *Revolutionary Brotherhood*, 91.

11 Mark A. Tabbert, *American Freemasons: Three Centuries of Building Communities* (Lexington, MA: National Heritage Museum, 2005), 27.

12 Maya Jasanoff, *Liberty's Exiles: American Loyalists in the Revolutionary World* (New York: Knopf, 2011), 11.

13 See the chapter by Denis McKim in this volume.

14 Frank O'Gorman and Allan Blackstock, "Loyalism and the British World: Overviews, Themes, and Linkages," in *Loyalism and the Formation of the British World, 1775–1914*, ed. Allan Blackstock and Frank O'Gorman (Woodbridge, UK: Boydell Press, 2014), 17.

15 Tabbert, *American Freemasons*, 12; and Jacob, *Living the Enlightenment*, 50–1.

16 Tabbert, *American Freemasons*, 7.

17 Margaret C. Jacob, *The Origins of Freemasonry: Facts and Fictions* (Philadelphia: University of Pennsylvania Press, 2006), 87.

18 Ibid., 99.

19 Ibid., 87; Tabbert, *American Freemasons*, 16–25, 43.

20 James Anderson, *The Constitutions of the Free-Masons; Containing the History, Charges, Regulations, &c of the Most Ancient and Right Worshipful Fraternity.*

For the Use of Lodges. London. In the Year of Masonry 5723, Anno Domini 1723 (London, 1723); the volume was reprinted in Philadelphia in 1734.

21 William Preston, *Illustrations of Masonry; A Reprint of the Rare 1772 Edition* (London: Forgotten Books, 2016); also see Tabbert, *American Freemasons*, 25–7.

22 Jacob, *The Origins of Freemasonry*, 60, 77–8; and Jürgen Habermas, *The Structural Transformation of the Public Sphere: An Inquiry into a Category of Bourgeois Society*, trans. Thomas Burger with Frederick Lawrence (Cambridge, MA: MIT Press, 1991), 176.

23 Jacob, *The Origins of Freemasonry*, 14–16, 22, 25, 132–3; Jacob, *Living the Enlightenment*, 33–4.

24 Jacob, *Living the Enlightenment*, 46, 57.

25 Laurence Dermott, *The True Ahiman Rezon, or, a Help to All That Are or Would Be Free and Accepted Masons: With Many Additions* (London: Southwick and Hardcastle, 1805); Jacob, "Temples of Virtue," 60–1; and Tabbert, *American Freemasons*, 26–7.

26 Jessica Harland-Jacobs, "Worlds of Brothers," *Journal for Research into Freemasonry and Fraternalism* 2, no. 1 (2011): 19; and Harland-Jacobs, *Builders of Empire*, 2.

27 Harland-Jacobs, *Builders of Empire*, 29, 34; and Huskins, "Ancient Tensions and Local Circumstances: Loyalist Freemasons in Shelburne, Nova Scotia," 51.

28 James Fairbairn Smith, "Masons Who Made America: Interesting Story. The Boston Tea Party," *Masonic World*, 8 September 1974, in Milbourne Masonic Collection, RG 3052-0-6-E, box 14, file 776, Library and Archives Canada (hereafter LAC).

29 Harland-Jacobs, *Builders of Empire*, 116.

30 Bullcock, "According to Their Rank: Masonry and the Revolution, 1775–1792," in *Freemasonry on Both Sides of the Atlantic: Essays Concerning the Craft in the British Isles, Europe, the United States, and Mexico*, ed. R. William Weisberger, Wallace McLeod, and S. Brent Morris (New York: East European Monographs, 2002), 492. Neil L. York notes, "Not every Mason became a Revolutionary, and some became or remained Loyalists" in "Freemasons and the American Revolution," *Historian*, 55, no. 3 (Winter 1993): 231.

31 Bullcock, "According to Their Rank," 490.

32 Tabbert, *American Freemasons*, 39–40.

33 Longley and Harris, *Short History of Freemasonry in Nova Scotia*, chs. 3–4; and Harland-Jacobs, *Builders of Empire*, 50, 167–8.

34 Marion Robertson, *King's Bounty: A History of Early Shelburne, Nova Scotia* (Halifax: Nova Scotia Museum, 1983), 111–12.

35 Ibid., 185; Howard P. Nash, "Origins of the Grand Lodge of New York," *Transactions [of] the American Lodge of Research Free and Accepted Masons* 4, no. 3 (30 April 1946–29 October 1947): 571, 576–7; and Harland-Jacobs, *Builders of Empire*, 37.

36 Nash, "Origins of the Grand Lodge of New York," *Transactions [of] the American Lodge of Research Free and Accepted Masons* 3, no. 2 (December 1939–31 October 1940): 323–5, and Nash, "William Walter's Associate Officers in Grand Lodge," *Transactions [of] the American Lodge of Research Free and Accepted Masons* 2, no. 2 (6 January 1939–28 May 1936): 295.

37 William F. Bunting, *History of the St John's Lodge, F & AM of Saint John* (Saint John: J. & A. MacMillan, 1895).

38 Harland-Jacobs, *Builders of Empire*, 118.

39 Bullock, "According to Their Rank," 494.

40 Milbourne, "Loyalist Masons."

41 Author's calculations; see also ibid.

42 Bullock, "'A Pure and Sublime System.'"

43 Huskins, "'Shelburnian Manners,'" 160; Bell, *Loyalist Rebellion*, 34.

44 Some identify Lenzi as posting the first advertisement offering ice cream for sale in a public advertisement in the *New York Gazette* in 1774. Biographical overview of Lenzi in Nash, "Origins of the Grand Lodge of New York," *Transactions* 4, no. 3 (30 April 1946–29 October 1947): 496–8; see advertisement for Monsieur Lenzi, confectioner, in *Rivington's New York Gazeteer*, 25 November 1773 and 22 June 1774. I am indebted to Christopher Minty for providing this reference. For more on Lenzi as an ice cream maker, see http://www.idfa.org/news-views/media-kits/ice-cream/the-history-of-ice-cream.

45 Shortly after his arrival in Shelburne, Hay paid a fine of £2 in 1785 for selling liquor without a licence, but a year later he was operating a legitimate tavern on St Patrick's Lane. He is also listed in the tax assessment rolls and other sources as a shopkeeper, schoolmaster, and constable. Nash, "Origins of the Grand Lodge of New York," *Transactions* 4, no. 3 (30 April 1946–29 October 1947): 480–3, 584–7. For reference to him operating an unlicensed tavern and being a constable, see Nova Scotia Court of General Quarter Sessions of the Peace, Shelburne County, 1784–1800, vol. 1, 7 February 1785, 7 July 1785, 27 April 1791, in the Loyalist Collection, Harriet Irving Library, University of New Brunswick (hereafter HIL). Hay is listed in the Shelburne poll tax rolls for 1791–3 as a shopkeeper: https://novascotia.ca/archives/census/returnsTax.asp?ID=3163

46 Letter from Michael Gordon to Grand Master Thomas Alexander, 7 December 1784, Grand Lodge of Nova Scotia Ancient Free and Accepted Masons fonds, MG 20, vol. 2005, no. 9.4, Nova Scotia Archives (hereafter NSA); letter from Philip Lenzi to George Pyke, 8 June 1785, Grand Lodge of Nova Scotia Ancient Free and Accepted Masons fonds, MG 20, vol. 2005, no. 9.15, NSA.

47 Letter from Grand Secretary Peters to Philip Lenzi, 22 January 1785, Nova Scotia Grand Lodge Ancient Free and Accepted Masons fonds, MG 20, vol. 2005, no. 9.7,

NSA; Minutes of Solomon Lodge No 5, 21 December 1784, Nova Scotia Grand Lodge, Ancient Free and Accepted Masons fonds, MG 20, vol. 2005, no. 9.6, NSA; Minutes of the meeting of the Grand Lodge, 23 June 1785, Nova Scotia Grand Lodge Ancient Free and Accepted Masons fonds, MG 20, vol. 2005, no. 9.18, NSA; letter from Archibald Cunningham to Grand Secretary Peters, 12 March 1785, Grand Lodge of Nova Scotia Ancient Free and Accepted Masons fonds, MG 20, vol. 2005, no. 9.12, NSA.

48 Letter from Archibald Cunningham to Grand Secretary Peters, 12 March 1785, Nova Scotia Grand Lodge Ancient Free and Accepted Masons fonds, MG 20, vol, 2005, no. 9.12, NSA; letter from John Stuart [Stewart] to offices of Solomon's Lodge, 20 April 1785, Nova Scotia Grand Lodge Ancient Free and Accepted Masons fonds, MG 20, vol. 2005, no. 9.14, NSA; letter from Archibald Cunningham to Grand Secretary Peters, 7 April 1785, Nova Scotia Grand Lodge Ancient Free and Accepted Masons fonds, MG 20, vol. 2005, no. 9.12, NSA.

49 Letter from Grand Secretary Peters to William Walter, 10 June 1785, Nova Scotia Grand Lodge Ancient Free and Accepted Masons fonds, MG 20, vol. 2005, no. 9.16, NSA; letter from Grand Secretary Peters to Archibald Cunningham, 10 June 1785, Nova Scotia Grand Lodge Ancient Free and Accepted Masons fonds, MG 20, vol. 2005, no. 9.17, NSA; Minutes of Meeting of Grand Lodge, 23 June 1785, Nova Scotia Grand Lodge Ancient Free and Accepted Masons fonds, MG 20, vol. 2005, no. 9.18, NSA.

50 Meeting of the Grand Stewards Lodge, 15 November 1786 and Meeting of the Grand Lodge, 6 December 1786, Nova Scotia Grand Lodge Minute Book, 24 September 1784–28 December 1795, Nova Scotia Grand Lodge Ancient Free and Accepted Masons fonds, MG 20, vol. 2133, no. 1, 72, 74, NSA.

51 Emergency Meeting of the Nova Scotia Grand Lodge, 2 March 1785 and 7 September 1785, Nova Scotia Grand Lodge Minute Book, 24 September 1784–28 December 1795, Nova Scotia Grand Lodge Ancient Free and Accepted Masons fonds, MG 20, vol. 2133, no. 1, 34, 49, NSA.

52 On 3 July 1785, Solomon's Lodge No. 5 agreed to Lenzi's request for his certificate "by reason of his going to Halifax": Minutes of the Grand Lodge, 23 June 1785, Nova Scotia Grand Lodge Ancient Free and Accepted Masons fonds, MG 20, vol. 2005, no. 9.18, NSA; letter from Walter Dunn to Grand Lodge, 3 July 1785, Nova Scotia Grand Lodge Ancient Free and Accepted Masons fonds, MG 20, vol. 2005, no 9.19, NSA. For information on Lenzi's trial in Halifax and an overview of Fife, see Milbourne, "Loyalist Masons in the Maritimes," 1977; Nash, "Origins of the Grand Lodge of New York," *Transactions* 4, no. 3 (30 April 1946–29 October 1947): 498, 533–5. Also see Meeting of the Grand Lodge, 28 October 1788, Nova Scotia Grand Lodge Minute Book, 24 September 1784–28 December 1795, Nova Scotia Grand Lodge Ancient Free and Accepted Masons fonds, MG 20, vol. 2133, no. 1, 116–17, NSA.

53 Re the assistance of 40s, see Meeting of the Grand Lodge, 1 November 1790, Nova Scotia Grand Lodge Minute Book, 24 September 1784–28 December 1795, Nova Scotia Grand Lodge Ancient Free and Accepted Masons fonds, MG 20, vol. 2133, no. 1, 149–50, NSA; Jamaica: Meeting of the Grand Lodge, 21 October 1791, Nova Scotia Grand Lodge Minute Book, 24 September 1784–28 December 1795, Nova Scotia Grand Lodge Ancient Free and Accepted Masons fonds, MG 20, vol. 2133, no. 1, 169, NSA.

54 Huskins, "'Shelburnian Manners,'" 59.

55 Letter from Archibald Cunningham to Grand Lodge, 29 September 1785, Nova Scotia Grand Lodge Ancient Free and Accepted Masons fonds, MG 20, vol. 2005, no. 9.22, NSA.

56 Ibid.

57 Peter Ross, *A Standard History of Freemasonry in the State of New York* (New York: The Lewis Publishing Company, 1899), 1: ch. 5.

58 Tabbert, *American Freemasons*, 8–9.

59 Klages, "Freemasonic and Orange Order Membership," 206.

60 Letter from Grand Secretary Peters to James Taylor, 17 December 1785, Nova Scotia Grand Lodge Ancient Free and Accepted Masons fonds, MG 20, vol. 2005, no. 9.27, NSA.

61 Jacob, *The Origins of Freemasonry*, 75.

62 On Priscilla Lancaster also named as forfeiting £20, see See Nova Scotia Court of General Quarter Sessions of the Peace, Shelburne County Minutes, 28 July 1785; forfeited their £20 "in consequence of non-appearance of Ann Dunn": 4 August 1785; on petition from Hugh Hay that penalty be remitted: 11 August 1785, HIL. Archibald Cunningham to Grand Lodge, 29 September 1785 and Committee of Emergency Report, Solomon's Lodge, 6 October 1785, Nova Scotia Grand Lodge Ancient Free and Accepted Masons fonds, MG 20, vol. 2005, nos. 9.22 and 9.25, NSA.

63 Nova Scotia Court of General Quarter Sessions of the Peace, Shelburne County Minutes, 1784–1800, 14 July 1785 and 21 January 1789, vol. 1. Loyalist Collection, HIL; General Quarter Sessions of the Peace for the District of Shelburne, 1784–1785, reel 3, 4 November 1784, 8 November 1784, 22 November 1784, 30 March 1785, HIL.

64 Nova Scotia Court of General Quarter Sessions of the Peace, Shelburne County, Minutes, 1784–1800, 6 December 1787, vol. 1, HIL. Magdelen's complaint against William Summers for defamation of character on 23 August 1786: Nash, "Origins of the Grand Lodge of New York," *Transactions* 4, no. 3 (30 April 1946–29 October 1947): 482–3.

65 Bell, *Loyalist Rebellion in New Brunswick*, 151.

66 Jasanoff, *Liberty's Exiles*, 187.

67 Bell, "The Republican Craft," 6.
68 Hiram Lodge to Grand Lodge of Nova Scotia, 1 May 1786, records of Nova Scotia Grand Lodge, MG 20, vol. 2001, no. 10, NSA.
69 *Charges and Regulations of the Ancient and Honourable Society of Free and Accepted Masons, Extracted from Ahiman Rezon, &c. Together with a Concise Account of the Rise and Progress of Free Masonry in Nova-Scotia, from the First Settlement of It to this Time; and a Charge Given by the Revd. Brother Weeks, at the Installation of His Excellency John Parr Esq; Grand Master. Designed for the Use of the Brethren, and Published by the Consent and Direction of the Grand Lodge of this Province* (Halifax: John Howe, 1786), 9.
70 Harland-Jacobs, *Builders of Empire*, 99, 113.
71 Bell, *Loyalist Rebellion in New Brunswick*, 74.
72 Bell, "The Republican Craft," 13–14.
73 Bell, *Loyalist Rebellion in New Brunswick*, 151.
74 Ibid., 77 Also interesting is the revelation that the name of maligned Shelburne Freemason Philip Lenzi appears on the New York Loyalists' memorial. Roubalet's Tavern was the meeting place of the New York Grand Lodge. As a member of Lodge 210, it is probable that Lenzi would have had access to the petitions. See Loyalist Memorial Counter-Petition, in Bell, *Loyalist Rebellion in New Brunswick*, 166.
75 Jasanoff, *Liberty's Exiles*, 197.
76 Blackstock and O'Gorman, "Loyalism and the British World," 5.
77 Elizabeth Mancke, "Stewarding a Canadian Culture of Comity," *Borealia: A Group Blog on Early Canadian History*," https://earlycanadianhistory.ca/2016/12/06/stewarding-a-canadian-culture-of-comity/
78 Jasanoff, *Liberty's Exiles*, 186–7.
79 Bell, *Loyalist Rebellion in New Brunswick*, 122.
80 Jasanoff, *Liberty's Exiles*, 189.
81 Bell, "A Republican Craft," 6.
82 Tabbert, *American Freemasons*, 11–12, 29–30; and Jacob, *The Origins of Freemasonry*, 18, 70.
83 Jacob, *The Origins of Freemasonry*, 47.
84 Eamon, *Imprinting Britain*, 11, 189. Also see review by Keith Grant, "Being Part of Something Larger: A Review of Imprinting Britain," *Borealia: A Group Blog on Early Canadian History*, https://earlycanadianhistory.ca/2015/09/28/being-part-of-something-larger-a-review-of-imprinting-britain/

14 Of Bludgeons and Ballots: Political Violence, Municipal Enfranchisement, and Local Governance in Mid-Nineteenth-Century Montreal

COLIN GRITTNER[1]

This chapter explores how violence helped shape municipal enfranchisement and local governance in Montreal, British North America's largest city, during the middle decades of the nineteenth century. Following the Rebellions of 1837 and 1838, imperial authorities agreed that the bloodshed surrounding the city had stemmed largely from Canadians' lack of political education. Elective municipal institutions offered a solution and, following an earlier attempt, Montreal received its first permanent city charter in 1840. Through participation in municipal politics – specifically, through annual elections, as opposed to quadrennial ones – Montrealers would learn proper political behaviour within the bounds of British constitutional practice as members of a clearly defined local public sphere. A broad municipal franchise sought to ensure these lessons reached as many as possible. This imperial project soon clashed with locally held beliefs about the role of municipal governance. Elite Montrealers, building upon the idea that municipalities ought to work for their wealthy stakeholders, championed property qualifications as a means to keep the ignorant and vicious away from the polls. As municipal electoral violence emerged and persisted, and as the Legislative Assembly of the United Canadas became more involved, further changes to the city's franchise and electoral laws ensued. Widespread political violence had ushered Montreal's first permanent franchise into existence, and continued political violence helped justify its reform. Both projects sought to secure local governance free from unrestrained intimidation and assault, but each grew from different understandings of the purpose of elective institutions within a municipal public sphere.

Michèle Dagenais's exploratory essay on municipal governance and liberal governmentality in mid-nineteenth-century British North America serves as the historiographic inspiration for this chapter. While Donald Fyson has shed considerable light on early nineteenth-century local governance under older systems of rule, Dagenais sees "the formation of the municipal domain in Quebec and Canada" as "insufficiently documented and theorized."[2] For her, the rapid spread of municipal corporations by the 1840s spearheaded a new liberal drive to objectify territory and make it more governable. Through a new formal level of government, population might be better administered for the sake of political stability.[3] Municipal corporations and their institutions thus acted as technologies of power in the Foucauldian sense: as means of determining the conduct of individuals and submitting them to particular ends.[4] Colonial administrators attempted to design these technologies so that populations might internalize and freely reproduce the conducts espoused, thus transforming them into technologies of the self. This transformative project defines liberal governmentality as Dagenais sees it and its goal to "regularize the diverse aspects of municipal politics."[5] As part of this discussion of municipal governance, Dagenais singles out the question of municipal enfranchisement. Although British North America's provincial franchises have drawn the attention of several scholars, "the evolution of the norms defining who could vote [municipally] remains to be traced."[6] The following arguments address Dagenais's question through a sustained focus on Montreal.

By the 1830s, Montreal had not only outgrown British North America's other urban centres, it had also become one of its earliest municipal corporations. While this chapter does not hold Montreal as typical of the British North American municipal experience – Darren Ferry's essay in this collection speaks to the everyday realities of municipal life more precisely – it does view it as archetypal within a nineteenth-century colonial context. Montreal's experiments with municipal governance provided early and clear examples of how the municipal sphere might work on British North American soil and what it might accomplish within a liberal project of rule, including whether municipal franchises might really enhance civic culture and reduce political violence. As legislators created new municipal corporations throughout the mid-nineteenth century, Montreal's example offered them evidence to draw upon. Given the repeated political violence that shook the city, and the challenges that such violence posed to both local authority and individual freedom, Montreal provided stark lessons in this regard.

Elective municipal government arrived haltingly across British North America. Despite the growing size and importance of places like Montreal, day-to-day operations by the 1830s still fell under the jurisdiction of executively appointed magistrates. The Colonial Office in London had preferred to handle local governance this way since before the American Revolution, as town halls had served to organize anti-imperial sentiment.[7] Only Saint John, New Brunswick, had received a city charter by the second quarter of the nineteenth century, and only then because the province's governor had granted it without the Colonial Office's prior approval.[8] Yet, Montreal in particular needed what Saint John had. Underpowered and overburdened magistrates no longer proved responsive enough.[9] As the city grew into British North America's commercial and industrial metropolis, strong and competing ethnic, religious, and linguistic communities sought to carve out spaces of their own.[10] After a failed petition in 1828, Montreal received its first act of incorporation in 1832.[11] The provincial legislature allowed this temporary charter to expire in 1836, alongside the freeholders' franchise it therein contained.[12] Another four years had to pass before Montreal received its second act of incorporation and its first permanent franchise.

Montreal obtained its first set of permanent electoral and franchise laws within the Ordinance to Incorporate the City and Town of Montreal of 1840. As its title suggests, the charter was not so much granted as imposed by the Special Council of Lower Canada. Given the Special Council's dictatorial reputation, Montrealers may have expected punishing property qualifications for their new city franchise.[13] After all, the Montreal region had not exactly endeared itself to the colonial executive in recent years. The most reactionary imperialists were still demanding reprisals for the violence of 1837 and 1838, when habitants from the District of Montreal engaged in open and direct warfare with British and government forces.[14] Given this political context, Montreal's 1840 municipal franchise was surprisingly broad, especially when compared to the province's £5 freehold and £10 leasehold franchises for towns and cities.[15] Instead of imposing minimum property values, or even Montreal's former freeholders' franchise, the legislation merely required "persons" to possess street-facing dwellings for at least one year through either freehold or leasehold, but not as a boarder or a lodger. These "persons" also had to have paid all of their local taxes by election day.[16] Because the ordinance never defined the term "person," it technically included women, much like the Canadas' provincial franchise.[17] A comprehensive householders' and ratepayers' suffrage thus lay at the heart of Montreal's 1840 municipal franchise. Ideas of class, ethnicity, religion, and even gender did not matter from a legal standpoint when it came to local enfranchisement. These stipulations, according to Robert Sweeny, created a municipal franchise twice as inclusive as that of the province. If one in twelve Montrealers held the vote provincially, then one in six did the same at Montreal's early civic elections.[18]

Although the Special Council may have enacted Montreal's peculiar municipal franchise, it had had little say in its design. Governor Charles Poulett Thomson had received the ordinance from his predecessor, Lord Durham, who had essentially fashioned it himself. According to Durham's biographer, Chester

New, "Radical Jack" had championed radical franchise reform in England since at least 1818. For Durham, a franchise based on rate payment and household suffrage was most effective when it came to local governance. On the one hand, it was narrow enough to exclude the transient "rabble" (Durham's word) who would destroy social order through irresponsibility and degradedness.[19] On the other hand, it was inclusive enough to "rally as large a portion of the ... people as possible around the existing institutions of the country" and show "they were also invested with privileges most valuable to them [that] rested on the basis of national unity."[20] In fact, before Durham had ever reached Canada, he had convinced his fellow Whigs to implement such a franchise across England. The Municipal Corporations Act of 1835 (based on Durham's suggestions of December 1834) had not only established annual municipal elections for Englishmen, it had made householding and ratepayment the two standards for municipal electoral participation.[21] Durham's contemporaries called it the "Durham suffrage."[22] It formed the basis for English municipal enfranchisement for the rest of the nineteenth century.[23]

When Durham arrived in Canada in May 1838, he had brought his Durham suffrage with him. The violence around Montreal had convinced him that Montrealers especially needed lessons in national unity, political propriety, and British constitutional behaviour.[24] Municipal institutions offered such instruction. With this in mind, Durham formed a commission of inquiry into Lower Canada's municipal institutions in August 1838. "The mass of the people," according to Durham's assistant commissioners William Kennedy and Adam Thom, had "been allowed the exercise of the greater privilege of electing provincial representatives, while, with singular inconsistency, they [had] been denied the minor right ... of choosing municipal authorities." Such backwardness had seemingly filled the Lower Canadian Assembly with rebels and traitors. A well-constructed municipal sphere, they asserted, should act as a "school of practical citizenship."[25] Through direct engagement at municipal elections, the people would "gradually [acquire] a disciplined knowledge of their social duties," which included paying one's taxes and keeping the peace. This discipline, in turn, would act as "a wholesome preparatory for the discharge of the superior trust" of provincial enfranchisement.[26] Over the next two years, Durham, Poulett Thomson, and the colonial secretary, Lord John Russell, all expressed their fundamental (if not a priori) agreement with these arguments.[27] Montreal received the Durham suffrage in 1840 on the basis of such beliefs.

Montreal's 1840 municipal franchise lasted five years and spanned three elections. If the municipal sphere "represented a chosen field of experimentation for liberal governance" – as Michèle Dagenais phrases it – then Montreal's experiment with the Durham suffrage seems to have failed.[28] Or, at the very least, it failed in the eyes of Montreal's city council. While Montreal voters may not have faced property qualifications at election time, council candidates certainly did. The £500 property requirement for councillors meant that only affluent Montrealers ran for municipal office. The colossal £1,000 requirement for aldermen, who held six of the council's eighteen seats and chaired its various committees, served only to compound this concentration of wealth.[29] It comes as no surprise, then, that Montreal's first elected city councils consisted of the city's professional, business, and landholding elite. None of these men shared in Durham's or Thomson's aristocratic paternalism. These elite men, once in office, needed only slight nudges to turn against the city's householding and ratepayment franchise. Instead, Montreal's persistent electoral violence gave them a mighty shove.

In the British North American world of open elections – where polls attracted crowds, votes were cast publicly, and everyone knew how everyone else voted – the potential for violence remained high. Fists and clubs had the power to shape voting as readily as stump speeches and the party press. For candidates, violence – by way of hired muscle – helped to clear the way towards electoral victory both figuratively and literally. For the disenfranchised, violence offered an extra-legal means to make themselves heard politically, express moral economies, and sway elections without having votes themselves.[30] A group of "illiterate and unsophisticated men," according to one condescending Halifax newspaper, could prevent "hundreds of respectable electors from going near the polls."[31] Older electoral customs imported from Great Britain encouraged this rough participation not only to diffuse high political tensions but also to ensure that elections spoke for whole communities. Because of Montreal's burgeoning population – and its particular ethnic, religious, and linguistic composition – contests in the city had the potential for greater violence than elsewhere. This potential found itself fully realized as early as 1832, when commonplace aggression at election time devolved into maiming and murderous violence.

In May 1832, Montreal held provincial by-elections for both its East and West Wards. During the early evening of 21 May, stone throwing among partisans had resulted in British soldiers positioning themselves at the corner of St James and St François-Xavier Streets. William Robertson – Montreal's senior magistrate and leading member of its anglophone elite – called upon the troops to open fire. The single volley killed three men and wounded four more.[32] Many French-speaking Lower Canadians, including Patriote leader Louis-Joseph Papineau, painted Robertson as a murderer who had abused his powers. Montreal's Patriotes, as the republican champions of a sovereign Lower Canadian people, soon heralded those killed as martyrs to the Patriote cause.[33] Anglophone elites, in response, heaped blame on the Patriotes for inciting the violence in the first place.[34] As both camps staked their positions, their animosity towards each other intensified.

Montreal's first act of incorporation, which came into effect in 1833, did little to reel in this sectarian violence. For the province's 1834 general election, the Patriote-controlled city council had assigned the city watch to keep the peace. So long as British regulars remained in their barracks, the deadly extremes of 1832 had fewer ways to repeat themselves. As Donald Fyson reveals, however, Patriote city councilmen had also hoped to secure Montreal's polls for the city's Patriote candidates. To do so, "the council had quite illegally increased the number of watchmen by several hundred" and filled these positions with Patriote sympathizers. Montreal's Tory opposition responded by mustering a private army of its own. Over the course of the election, the two groups clashed repeatedly as they patrolled the city's streets.[35] Louis-Joseph Papineau called the contest "la farce la plus glorieusement dégradante qu'eussent jamais joué [*sic*] les gentilshommes bretons dans un pays où ils en ont si souvent joué [*sic*] dans le genre tragico-burlesque."[36] The 1834 general election would be Lower Canada's last. By the end of 1837, the Patriotes had taken up arms against the imperial state, and colonial authorities had suspended the provincial legislature.[37] Parliamentary rule would resume only in 1841 with the formal amalgamation of the Canadas, East and West.

By the Union period, alcohol, axe-handles, and firearms had become customary tools of persuasion within the "Montreal way of electioneering" (as Reform leader Robert Baldwin learned of it).[38] Brutal beatings, if not murders, were almost expected. Montreal's British garrison found itself repeatedly called out to restore order.[39] Although such violence had originated at the provincial level, it soon carried over to the newly re-established municipal sphere. Indeed, Montreal's municipal elections fed off the raw emotions of its provincial contests, as had happened across England after the passage of the Municipal Corporations Act.[40] This was especially true after the province made Montreal its capital in October 1843. Problems began in earnest the following February when Benjamin Holmes resigned his Montreal seat in the provincial assembly. The subsequent by-election, scheduled for 11 April, pitted bilingual Irish Reformer Lewis Drummond against William Molson, "a notorious Tory who needed an interpreter to speak to his French electors."[41] Drummond proved victorious, but not because of his "éloquent[s] discours plein[s] d'ardeur et de patriotisme" or his "adhésion pleine et entière ... à la doctrine du gouvernement responsable."[42] Drummond's backers had instead united French Canadian and Irish canal/dock workers against Molson, whom they depicted as anti-French and anti-Catholic. Between the end of March and mid-April, these forces (aided by "whisky and enthusiasm") waged an increasingly ferocious campaign against Molson's supporters and their properties.[43] The week of 11 April, in particular, saw electoral mobs swarming the city and taking polls by force. Blood ran through the streets, and one man died, as the two camps resorted to their pistols. When the smoke cleared on 17 April, Drummond's men had forced Molson's resignation from the election.[44] Sore feelings on both sides would not dissipate so quickly.[45]

An October general election followed April's by-election. Montreal's chief returning officer, John Young, requested "a large addition to the Police Force" to keep the peace. The city council did not have the funds to oblige, so the British army filled in.[46] Montrealers had not seen precautions like these since the rebellions. Soldiers were positioned on McGill Street, the Champ de Mars, and Custom House Square. The latter location boasted a field gun, just in case. Provincial cavalry patrolled the streets and round-the-clock armed guards defended the polls. Two additional detachments of troops arrived while the election was underway.[47] Despite these measures, Jacques Monet argues that the city's "usual preference for violence over votes" shaped the election.[48] The troops could not keep bullies, armed with "bowie knives and pistols," from entering the city.[49] These new arrivals included an army of canal workers from Lachine that apparently numbered in the hundreds.[50] McGill Street and the Hay Market (now part of Victoria Square) saw the worst of the fighting. Partisans skirmished not only among themselves but with the soldiers as well. In an official protest following the election, the two defeated Reform candidates (Lewis Drummond and Pierre Beaubien) accused the troops of actively and violently suppressing Reform supporters. Although the polls stayed open for only two days, "the city bore all the appearance of being in a state of siege."[51]

Just over a month later, Montreal readied itself for its third municipal election under the new city charter. Troops had patrolled the city in the meantime, and an uneasy peace generally prevailed.[52] Apprehensions increased as the 2 December election date approached. Three days before the polls opened, Alderman Benjamin Holmes (the same Benjamin Holmes who had resigned his provincial seat in February) gave notice "to enable the Corporation in the event of a riot and the destruction of Property, through the Agency of any mob, or riot, to assess the Citizens to such extent as will make good the loss sustained by Individual Citizens."[53] Holmes never got the chance to formally table his proposal. On 1 December, the day before the election, a brawl broke out at the Hay Market. It took three hundred soldiers and two field guns from the local garrison to suppress it. Without new regulations, Ludger Duvernay in *La Minerve* had expected the earlier violence to repeat itself. "L'impunité nourrit l'impudence et le crime," he insisted, "et on devait s'attendre à voir se renouveler à nos élections municipales, les mêmes scènes qui ont déshonoré notre ville, il y a à peine un mois."[54]

Fighting resumed the next day, despite the army's presence. The Queens Ward – just to the west of the commercial centre – saw the worst of the clashes. A group of Irish Catholics had bunkered down inside Patrick Brennan's public house. From there, they took potshots at the polls and defended themselves from their largely Anglo-Protestant opposition. John Johnson, formerly of Belfast, was shot and killed when he and his compatriots attempted to storm the tavern. Once again, it took the local garrison to lift the siege. Nineteen defenders were arrested; Brennan's establishment was wrecked.[55] Although "something like order was restored" in the Queens Ward, no one could describe the election itself as orderly. Armed men both on foot and horseback had "swept the polls from one side to the other."[56] Louis-Hippolyte LaFontaine's assessment appeared correct: Montreal's 1844 municipal contest "[was] carried by no other means than the bludgeon."[57]

Montreal's city council found easy targets to blame: the poor, the brutish, and the ignorant. If one believed Lord Durham, municipal elections taught the untutored how to rationally participate in the public sphere. Instead, the city's councillors came to the opposite conclusion: the Durham suffrage had only offered a broad education in the continued effectiveness of political violence and intimidation. Montreal's so-called "school of practical citizenship" needed far more rigorous entry standards. Individual councillors, of course, refused to acknowledge their own complicity in what had taken place. Dan Horner has identified a bourgeois discourse within mid-nineteenth-century Montreal that idealized a "restrained masculinity" and conceived of "public violence as the antithesis of respectable decorum."[58] Montreal's monied elites, according to Horner, adhered to this discourse as a way to legitimize their authority and marginalize the claims of those who embodied alternatives to elite rule. Any admission of guilt thus meant a disavowal of respectability. For Montreal's city councillors, the blame had to fall on those beneath them.

Mere days following the 1844 municipal election, the city council petitioned the legislature to amend Montreal's act of incorporation. Clément Sabrevois de Bleury, a francophone Tory who held seats in both the Legislative Assembly and the city council, championed the request.[59] A parliamentary investigation followed into the state of Montreal's municipal governance, chaired by de Bleury himself. Following two months of testimonies, the investigators made their suggestions to better curb Montreal's municipal electoral violence. Their list included fines for those who wore partisan badges and three-month prison sentences for those "impeding or disturbing" municipal contests.[60] Topping this list, however, was a recommendation for a new municipal franchise.[61] Over the course of the committee's inquiry, a number of Montreal councillors revealed their thoughts on the city's franchise law. All but Joseph Bourret urged monetary property qualifications to reduce the number of voters.[62] Councillor François Perrin, for instance, suggested £6 annual value.[63] Such a franchise still would have offered most working families a vote. François Trudeau, William Lunn, Benjamin Holmes, and Mayor James Ferrier instead preferred a £10 rental qualification.[64] This franchise would have disqualified most Montreal labourers.[65]

Ferrier made this recommendation despite testifying that he "would have every householder contributing to the revenue ... entitled to vote at the election of a Representative for the Ward."[66] According to Ferrier's logic, those who could not meet a £10 rental qualification contributed nothing of value to the city. Their participation in civic elections actually hindered the corporation's growth.

De Bleury's committee ultimately recommended an £8 property and rental qualification for the city's elections.[67] Such a franchise would have disqualified most working-class Montrealers alongside anyone without steady work. De Bleury maintained that it did not "[set] the labourer over the man of wealth and intelligence."[68] The Legislative Assembly eventually accepted the proposal.[69] An impassioned Lewis Drummond had "call[ed] on the House to pass the bill if they did not wish to bear the responsibility of more bloodshed. He alluded to the riots of December [1844]; he said there was no repelling force by force ... He appealed to the Christian feelings of members to prevent a repetition of the scenes of bloodshed which then took place, by amending the law."[70] To curtail Montreal's municipal electoral violence, the assembly agreed to keep what it saw as disreputable men away from the polls. The occupation of real property worth £8 annually, in this case, served as a benchmark for civic propriety and value. The lesson in Montreal had thus changed from that planned by Lord Durham: only those capable of orderly contributions to the city deserved municipal enfranchisement. Montreal's wealthier stakeholders apparently did so. Its poorer residents did not.

Montreal's municipal franchise of 1845 had sought, in large part, to curb violence at the city's municipal elections. Within a year, it had failed. The city's 1846 municipal election – the first under the new civic franchise – was by far the most disorderly yet. A special legislative committee that followed revealed all the sordid details. As before, "several Wards of this City" had been "carried ... by open and undisguised violence."[71] Lachine's Irish canal workers had once again marched into the city. In Jacques Monet's colourful words, "There were shots, sticks, stones, and blood staining the streets."[72] The assembly's subsequent investigation focused upon two wards in particular: the St James Ward (to the east of the commercial centre) and the St Lawrence Ward (to the north).

The St James Ward election most resembled the contests of 1844. Thirty minutes after the polls opened on 2 March, "a great number of persons came up, commenced creating a disturbance, and appeared all at once armed with axe-handles." After "they struck several, and wounded some severely," they surrounded the hustings to prevent the supporters of Jacques Grenier and Joseph Hogue from casting votes.[73] According to Hogue's agent, J.C.A. Poitras, "it was sufficient for one to have a [French] Canadian or an Irish face to be pushed back and turned out of the poll."[74] Anglophile candidates Daniel Gorrie and William Connolly had come for a fight, especially against the better-known Grenier.[75]

The army's arrival broke up the crowd. Some were arrested and "between 60 and 70 axe-handles and bludgeons and other weapons" were confiscated.[76] Most of the assailants, however, had managed to scatter into the surrounding streets. When the army pulled back in the early afternoon, the crowd reconvened. Pushing and shouting (which police superintendent William Ermatinger accepted as "usual upon all elections") again gave way to armed violence. Ermatinger himself "was received with a shower of stones." Once the soldiers returned, "few ... voters could get to the poll."[77] Gorrie and Connolly took the contest handily.[78]

Clearly, pervasive violence had beleaguered the St James Ward election. Even so, the contest appeared orderly when compared to that of the St Lawrence Ward. There, sitting mayor James Ferrier and his running mate, John Kelly, faced stiff competition from Alfred Larocque and Louis Comte. Things remained peaceful for the first hour and a half, despite a large crowd having formed around the hustings. Shots then rang out at 10:30 to signal the attack. "Two hundred or more men armed with axe-handles" rushed the poll from nearby yards and buildings.[79] Voters scattered, many of them robbed of their voters' certificates. Most astonishing of all, the mayor himself, James Ferrier, had apparently orchestrated the violence. Onlookers testified that Ferrier snuck away from the poll when the axe-handle men arrived and mounted a waiting horse. From there, he marshalled his supporters in the surrounding streets. Ferrier's coachman pushed on "the rioters, sometimes armed with an axe-handle, and at others with a heavy whip" while "mounted on a grey horse belonging to Mr. Ferrier."[80] Nelson Davis "observed a Mr. Lewis armed with an axe-handle, who is in the employ of Messrs. Bryson and Ferrier, leading the rioters, and exclaiming, 'keep them from the poll.'"[81] Through such tactics, Ferrier secured the hustings for himself and Kelly.

Larocque and Comte had no shortage of muscle of their own. A full two-thirds of the ward backed the French Canadians, according to one commentator. Once these supporters regrouped and better armed themselves, the poll could have easily changed hands. Understanding this, Ferrier had already taken precautions. As the sitting mayor, Ferrier had authority to call upon the local garrison in times of riot. The 52nd Regiment arrived on Ferrier's command soon after the axe-handle men appeared. Town Major Colin Macdonald could not explain why Ferrier had signed the requisition thirty minutes *before* the violence ever started.[82] Observers testified that "Mr. Ferrier himself was generally placed between the troops and the rioters." From there, he "took command of the Troops" alongside Major Mark Evans of the Royal Artillery. For the rest of the day, the garrison acted as Ferrier's elite guard. Soldiers took aim at anyone who approached.[83] Under these conditions, Ferrier and Kelly could not help but secure victory in the contest.[84]

Montreal's municipal franchise of 1845 had no defence against what occurred in 1846. The newly disenfranchised, although they had lost their votes, still had their bodies to affect electoral outcomes. Aside from an appeal to the army, the nascent corporation had little means to prevent their physical involvement. Montreal's new franchise, moreover, had equated aggression and ignorance with privation and poverty. It offered no recourse when wealthier Montrealers – in other words, the enfranchised themselves – resorted to electoral violence. James Ferrier, as one of the city's richest men, provides the most extreme example. His wealth and position not only allowed him to pursue violence without real consequence, they allowed him to command it as well. If bourgeois Montrealers found their manly ideal in a restrained masculinity, as Dan Horner has argued, then Ferrier certainly ignored it here. His role in the St Lawrence Ward ran completely against the spirit behind Montreal's new civic franchise.

Ferrier, however, did not stand alone. Countless Montreal voters had taken to the polls in 1846 with both their votes *and* their fists at the ready. Two officials described the same emblematic scene. After the violence had begun, an elector came forward to vote. In one hand, he held his voter's certificate outstretched for the returning officer. In the other, he grasped "a stick ... covered with blood." When the same officials complained about the "axe-handle stained with blood," the partisan returning officer merely told the voter to "keep your stick down."[85] The man cast his vote despite the protest. Even direct evidence of premeditated assault did not offer sufficient grounds for disenfranchisement. The stick and the vote continued to serve the same purpose at Montreal's elections, even with a new franchise in place. It thus surprised no one when violence shook subsequent municipal contests in 1847, 1850, and 1851, as well as the provincial election of 1848. More heads were broken by the enfranchised and disenfranchised alike.[86] The 1846 election had offered only one lasting lesson: Montrealers should use horse-drawn sleighs to outmanoeuvre the troops.[87]

The remarkable violence of Montreal's most recent municipal contest convinced many that the city needed new election laws once again. As Ludger Duvernay declared in *La Minerve*: "Ce système atroce et barbare doit avoir uue [*sic*] fin."[88] Higher property qualifications, although imposed only recently, had certainly not worked. Municipal contests seemed as bad, if not worse, than before. Provincial assemblyman James Leslie made the first formal proposal on 27 April 1846, less than two months after the contentious local election of that year. No British North American government had implemented what he suggested, whether at the provincial or municipal level. His proposal: "to establish the vote by ballot in the Election of Councillors ... for the city of *Montreal*."[89] In other words, Leslie sought to close Montreal's system of open voting by means of the secret ballot.

Canadians during the middle part of the nineteenth century tended to cringe when anyone mentioned the secret ballot. The majority still viewed voting by ballot as both un-British (i.e., French or American) and unmanly (i.e., indirect and opaque).[90] George Emery argues that, in a British North American context, open voting "suited societies that were organized around patron-client relationships of deference. An elector in a client relationship commonly desires that his vote be known to his patron in return for benefits received and favours expected."[91] Amid the cultural tensions of mid-nineteenth-century Montreal, such deferential relationships had devolved into something more exploitative. Not only did James Ferrier compel his employees to vote for him, he had expected them to fight for him as well.[92] Other elites running for municipal office surely demanded something similar. William Molson, for instance, had fired every brewery employee who had sided against him during the elections of 1844.[93] For many, the choice between flexing some muscle and losing one's job was really no choice at all. The secret ballot offered a means to weaken these clientalist structures of electoral violence. A shroud of voter anonymity would descend. After all, if no one knew how anyone voted, no one knew whom to beat up.

Leslie's ballot amendment struck a chord. During the subsequent investigation into Montreal's 1846 municipal election, witnesses all responded similarly: that "the vote by ballot would be the best remedy for this state of things." Police superintendent William Ermatinger offered the plainest explanation: "The vote by ballot ought to be resorted to in these elections, as the only means of preserving peace in a mixed population like that of this City."[94] Montreal's particularly volatile combination of ethnicity, religion, and class had pushed its inhabitants towards increasingly experimental measures. By July 1851, eleven of fourteen councillors had finally decided that franchise reform alone could not stop street violence during Montreal's municipal contests. The most restrictive qualifications meant nothing when the enfranchised themselves chose bloodshed over rational debate. Based upon this logic – a logic that had found recent credence in violence-stricken New Brunswick as well – the city council informed the legislature that "it would be expedient to establish ... the system of voting by ballot for the election of Councillors."[95] The council had found no alternative other than to request the secret ballot.

Montreal's new Incorporation Amendment Act passed into law a month later. The municipal franchise it contained followed a different wording. Instead of "persons," it now only referred to "male persons" as voters. While historians have yet to discover women voting at Montreal's previous municipal elections, such a change coincided with the province's franchise reform of 1849, which also statutorily disenfranchised women as part of a broader imperial project to codify politics as patriarchial. In terms of property requirements, renters still had to pay a minimum £8 annually in rent while property owners had to own real estate worth only forty shillings annually. To compensate, the legislation subsequently (and contradictorily) restricted the vote to those who had received assessments on their property to the minimum value of £8 per annum.[96] Anyone who did not pay their taxes for the year continued to face disenfranchisement at Montreal's municipal elections.

Because women had apparently found themselves excluded from previous municipal elections, the Incorporation Amendment Act of 1851 had thus made only a small change to Montreal's municipal franchise in terms of its operation. The greatest alterations came instead in the form of electoral procedures. Montreal's city council had asked for the secret ballot, and the Legislative Assembly had obliged. Voters' certificates doubled as electoral ballots. Each certificate had three blank lines stamped on it. Voters wrote their choice for mayor on the first, and their two choices for councillors on the second and third.[97] The legislation emphasized that no one had any obligation to reveal for whom they voted. Electors then dropped their certificates into one of nine ballot boxes, each corresponding to one of Montreal's nine wards. The legislation stipulated that each box had to have five locks – one for each member of the Board of Revisors – and that the locked boxes must always remain within city hall.[98] The Incorporation Amendment Act had thus internalized *and* centralized Montreal's municipal elections. Electoral decisions now played out privately and on paper, instead of openly and before one's peers. Public sites of political confrontation, in the words of Elaine Hadley, gave way to more subdued and less spectacular surroundings.[99] The corporation, moreover, only had one venue to police. Electoral officers had full control over who entered, who exited, and who participated. Potential troublemakers faced a gauntlet of armed constables who, for the first time, congregated at one location. Montreal had thus placed all of its electoral eggs in one central basket. Through concentrated and persistent surveillance, it hoped to sort out what it perceived as the rotten ones.

Montreal's 1851 municipal legislation governed the city's elections for the next nine years. Over that time, municipal electoral violence began to recede. The secret ballot and centralized polling had apparently served their purpose. This is not to say that violence disappeared altogether from Montreal's mid-nineteenth-century electoral landscape. Provincial contests that passed without "disturbances, riots and bloodshed" gave the city's grand jury reason to celebrate.[100] From time to time, aggression seeped back into Montreal's municipal sphere. In 1854, for instance, electoral officer and city councillor Joseph Papin suffered a "murderous attack" as he tried to clear a path to the ballot boxes. Despite a heightened police presence, the assailant escaped into the crowd.[101] The following year, the corporation felt compelled to make better "arrangements for ensuring an orderly and peaceable conduct of the civic Elections in February next."[102] Even in 1860, heated mayoral contests continued to demand special arrangements. For that year's municipal election, the corporation erected barriers to corral voters and provided separate spaces for rival candidates. It also demanded the presence of every policeman in the city.[103] Despite these precautions, violence still broke out. Montreal's lightly armed police

14.1 Local forces mustered in the city centre in preparation for the 1860 Montreal municipal election. Source: William Notman, *Notre Dame Street during a municipal election, Montreal, QC, 1860*, McCord Museum, N-0000.193.8.2 (detail).

force remained powerless against crowds that broke the peace. With the British garrison reduced following the Crimean War, it fell upon local militia to stop the fighting.[104] The corporation, for its part, received a hefty $2,625 militia bill for services rendered.[105] Yet the contentious behaviour exhibited in Montreal's 1860 municipal election paled in comparison with those of the 1840s. The police made their arrests and polling concluded satisfactorily.[106]

Montreal's 1860 municipal election had proven that, with the right precautions, the corporation could contain moderate electoral violence. It also confirmed that the city still had room for improvement. Municipal disorder of any kind disrupted local stability and prevented propertied individuals from getting heard. Further changes to Montreal's municipal franchise arrived mere months later. According to the new legislation, "every male person, being an inhabitant householder in the city, whose name shall be entered on the said last Assessment Roll, as the tenant or occupant of a dwelling house ... of the assessed value of three hundred dollars or upwards, or of the assessed yearly value of thirty dollars or upwards" received a vote at Montreal's annual municipal elections.[107] This $30 annual value qualification reduced the former £8 rental qualification by two dollars. As always, voters had to have paid their taxes before casting their votes.[108]

These new qualifications would have looked exceedingly familiar to informed citizens. Montreal's new municipal franchise borrowed its language almost verbatim from the Canadas' most recent provincial franchise. The Elective Franchise Act of 1858 had enfranchised male city-dwellers who owned or occupied property to "the assessed value of three hundred dollars or upwards or of the assessed yearly value of thirty dollars, or upwards."[109] In other words, legislators imposed the same franchise qualifications used for provincial elections on to Montreal's municipal elections as well. State officials across British North America and Canada complained that inhabitants either did not understand their franchise laws or readily mistook different franchise regimes.[110] Montrealers now had no way to claim confusion between different franchise legislation. Those who did not belong at the city's municipal elections needed to know, without question, that they did not belong. In the process, the province had placed an essential instrument of its wealth-based order onto the city of Montreal. Accumulated wealth ruled the city in the same way accumulated wealth ruled the province. A subsequent 1866 amendment to the city charter would perpetuate the same property assessment franchise. Owners of multiple properties now received votes in every district where they owned property.[111] Montreal's city council had apparently seen no reason to demand more extensive changes, and poorer Montrealers remained disenfranchised. Municipal violence continued to decline. Montreal as a corporation had confirmed its purpose: it worked both for and through its wealthier property holders.

Bruce Curtis has argued that colonial authorities, through to the Union period, attempted to rule Canadians by means of public schooling. A formal education, they believed, disciplined people to govern themselves and to participate responsibly within the bounds of British representative institutions.[112] By the early 1840s, that project had apparently failed in Lower Canada. Publicly funded schools never got the money they needed as Lower Canadians resisted new tax burdens and centralized control of local education.[113] "The people," according to Curtis, had "played truant from J.S. Mill's Great Normal School of representative government."[114] Imperial administrators such as Lord Durham and Charles Poulett Thomson had designed early municipal institutions and municipal franchises to achieve similar goals. If Canadians did not learn to act as good citizens at school, they might learn to do so through repetitive experience at annual municipal elections. Imperial authorities, in essence, advocated education through performance as well. The idea was that the individual colonist, while perhaps not yet the ideal political actor, could understudy the role within a controlled local setting. He could live what citizenship entailed and develop the muscle memory to repeat it. Behaviours of proper citizenship would transform into technologies of the self. With any luck, their lordships hoped, colonists might bring these new technologies into the weightier sphere of provincial politics.

Montreal, as British North America's most important urban centre, witnessed firsthand how this liberal project worked itself out. The violence of 1837 and 1838 had led to the city's first permanent municipal franchise in 1840. As public violence continued through the 1840s, franchise reforms followed suit. Although conceived by imperial authorities as a disciplinary tool, the municipal franchise soon became a site of contest over the city's purpose and for whom it should operate. Elite Montrealers never shared in the same educational faith as their imperial rulers. For them, the municipality ought to operate for those who held a tangible stake in it: namely, its wealthier property-holders. As these elite Montrealers found their way onto the city council, they set about altering the municipal franchise to realize their own wealth-based visions of the city. These views clashed with older forms of political participation, where community violence as much as public debate had the power to shape electoral outcomes. Fists and clubs still wielded considerable power within the old process of electioneering. Wealthier Montrealers understood this well; they even encouraged it when it suited their purposes, all the while laying the blame upon those less fortunate than themselves. Montreal's city council, in response, repeatedly tried to minimize community involvement within the city's annual elections and curtail violent participation. Franchise reforms sought to ensure that the municipality worked primarily for its wealthier property-holding classes. The Incorporation Amendment Act of 1845 had partially achieved this goal; the Incorporation Amendment Act of 1851, in essence, completed the task. Subsequent municipal franchises of 1860 and 1866 merely served to reify restrictive ideas of governance that revolved around the rational accumulation and possession of city property. Much like Curtis's district schools, Durham's school of practical citizenship had closed and locked its doors. Poorer Montrealers, once fully fledged members of their municipal public sphere, found themselves on the outside looking in.

NOTES

1 I wish to thank the University of British Columbia History Department's Canadian Caucus and my fellow participants at the Unrest, Violence, and Search for Social Order workshops for their helpful comments on earlier versions of this chapter. I also wish to acknowledge SSHRC and the Peter Cundill Fellowship in History for financially supporting the research upon which this chapter is based.

2 See Donald Fyson, "The Canadiens and British Institutions of Local Governance in Quebec, from the Conquest to the Rebellions," in *Transatlantic Subjects: Ideas, Institutions, and Social Experience in Post-Revolutionary British North America*, ed. Nancy Christie (Montreal and Kingston: McGill-Queen's University Press, 2008), 45–82; and Fyson, "Les dynamiques politiques locales et la justice au Québec entre la Conquête et les Rébellions," *Bulletin d'histoire politique* 16, no. 1 (Fall 2007): 337–46. Also see Michèle Dagenais, "The Municipal Territory: A Product of the Liberal Order?" in *Liberalism and Hegemony: Debating the Canadian Liberal Revolution*, ed. Jean-François Constant and Michel Ducharme (Toronto: University of Toronto Press, 2009), 203.

3 Dagenais, "The Municipal Territory," 203, 207.

4 Michel Foucault, "Technologies of the Self," in *Technologies of the Self: A Seminar with Michel Foucault*, ed. Luther H. Martin, Huck Gutman, and Patrick H. Hutton (Amherst: University of Massachusetts Press, 1988), 18–19; and Foucault, "Governmentality," in *The Foucault Effect: Studies in Governmentality*, ed. Graham Burchell, Colin Gordon, and Peter Miller (Chicago: University of Chicago Press, 1991), 102–3. For more on liberal governmentality in British North America, see Bruce Curtis, *Ruling by Schooling Quebec: Conquest to Liberal Governmentality, A Historical Sociology* (Toronto: University of Toronto Press, 2012), 16–19.

5 Dagenais, "The Municipal Territory," 211.

6 For Dagenais's quotation, see Dagenais, "The Municipal Territory," 219n34. Also see John Garner, *The Franchise and Politics in British North America, 1755–1867* (Toronto: University of Toronto Press, 1969); Chief Electoral Officer of Canada, *A History of the Vote in Canada* (Ottawa: Public Works and Government Services Canada, 1997), 1–38; and Colin Grittner, "Privilege at the Polls: Culture, Citizenship, and the Electoral Franchise in Mid-Nineteenth-Century British North America" (PhD diss., McGill University, 2015), 34–207.

7 Bruce Curtis, "Representation and State Formation in the Canadas, 1790–1850," *Studies in Political Economy* 28 (Spring 1989): 63; Engin F. Isin, *Cities without Citizens: Modernity of the City as a Corporation* (Montreal: Black Rose Books, 1992), 99–101; and Elizabeth Mancke, *The Fault Lines of Empire: Political Differentiation in Massachusetts and Nova Scotia, ca 1760–1830* (New York: Routledge, 2005), 26–7.

8 James Hannay, *History of New Brunswick*, vol. 1 (Saint John, NB: John A. Bowes, 1909), 151; Ged Martin, "Geography and Governance: The Problem of Saint John (New Brunswick), 1785–1927," *Gedmartin.net* (May 2016), http://www.gedmartin.net/martinalia-mainmenu-3/237-geography-and-governance-the-problem-of-saint-john-new-brunswick-1785-1927, fn388; and T.W. Acheson, *Saint John: The Making of a Colonial Urban Community* (Toronto: University of Toronto Press, 1985), 27–31.

9 See Donald Fyson, *Magistrates, Police, and People: Everyday Criminal Justice in Quebec and Lower Canada, 1764–1837* (Toronto: University of Toronto Press for the Osgoode Society, 2006).

10 Robert C.H. Sweeny, *Why Did We Choose to Industrialize? Montreal, 1819–1849* (Montreal and Kingston: McGill-Queen's University Press, 2015), 29. Sherry Olson and Patricia Thornton have identified the three most prominent of these groupings as of 1842: French Catholics (roughly one-half of Montreal's urban population), Anglo-Protestants (one-quarter of the same population), and Irish Catholics (the final quarter). As late as 1901, only 4 per cent of Montreal's total urban population fell outside of these three groupings. Census figures indicate that Montreal had surpassed Quebec City as British North America's largest city by 1831, with a population of 27,000 for the former and 26,000 for the latter. By the middle of the nineteenth century, Montreal would boast a population of nearly 58,000, while Quebec City fell further behind with 42,000. See Sherry Olson and Patricia Thornton, *Peopling the North American City: Montreal, 1840–1900* (Montreal and Kingston: McGill-Queen's University Press, 2011), 11–12. Also see Serge Courville, *Quebec: A Historical Geography*, trans. Richard Howard (Vancouver: UBC Press, 2008), 127–8; and Cole Harris, *The Reluctant Land: Society, Space, and Environment in Canada before Confederation* (Vancouver: UBC Press, 2008), 266.

11 Lower Canada, An Act to Incorporate the City of Montreal, 1 Will. IV, c. 54. Although the Lower Canadian legislature passed the act in 1831, the governor would not proclaim his assent until 5 June 1832.

12 See ibid., s. 2.

13 See Steven Watt, "State Trial by Legislature: The Special Council of Lower Canada, 1838–1841," in *Canadian State Trials II: Rebellion and Invasion in the Canadas, 1837–1839*, ed. F. Murray Greenwood and Barry Wright (Toronto:

University of Toronto Press for the Osgoode Society, 2002), 263; Michael S. Cross, *A Biography of Robert Baldwin: The Morning-Star of Memory* (Don Mills, ON: Oxford University Press, 2012), 42–54; and Maxime Dagenais, "'Le conseil spécial est mort, vive le conseil spécial!' The Special Councils of Lower Canada, 1838–1841" (PhD diss., University of Ottawa, 2011), 146–7, 350–4.

14 See Allan Greer, *The Patriots and the People: The Rebellion of 1837 in Rural Lower Canada* (Toronto: University of Toronto Press, 1993), 308–31, 344–53.

15 See Great Britain, An Act to repeal certain parts of an Act, passed in the fourteenth year of His Majesty's reign, entitled, *An Act for making more effectual provision for the Government of the Province of Quebec, in British North America*; and to make further provision for the government of the said province, 31 Geo. III, c. 31, s. 20; Great Britain, *An Act to Re-unite the Provinces of Upper and Lower Canada and the Government of Canada*, 3 & 4 Vic., c. 35, s. 1.

16 Special Council of Lower Canada, An Ordinance to Incorporate the City and Town of Montreal, 3 & 4 Vic., c. 36, s. 11.

17 That said, I have yet to find any evidence of women voting in Montreal's municipal elections. Robert Sweeny has revealed that Montreal's 1832 act of incorporation denied women proprietors the municipal vote. Perhaps this tradition carried over into the city's second incorporation. See Robert C.H. Sweeny, "Property and Gender: Lessons from a 19th-Century Town," *London Journal of Canadian Studies* 22 (2006/7): 18.

18 Sweeny, *Why Did We Choose to Industrialize?* 250–1.

19 Chester W. New, *Lord Durham: A Biography of John George Lambton, First Earl of Durham* (Oxford: Clarendon Press, 1929), 44.

20 Durham, cited in New, *Lord Durham*, 314–15.

21 John A. Phillips and Charles Wetherell, "Parliamentary Parties and Municipal Politics: 1835 and the Party System," *Parliamentary History* 13, no. 1 (February 1994): 57. Also see Great Britain, An Act to provide for the Regulation of Municipal Corporations in England and Wales, 5 & 6 Will. IV, c. 76.

22 Phillips and Wetherell, "Parliamentary Parties and Municipal Politics," 59.

23 England's Municipal Franchise Act of 1869 continued the Durham suffrage but in such a way that enfranchised ratepaying women as well. See Great Britain, The Municipal Franchise Act, 1869, 32 & 33 Vic., c. 59.

24 New, *Lord Durham*, 369.

25 See William Kennedy and Adam Thom, "General Report of the Assistant Commissioners of Municipal Inquiry," *Appendix C to Report on the Affairs of British North America, from the Earl of Durham, Her Majesty's High Commissioner* (London: House of Commons, 1839), 7.

26 Ibid., 6–7.

27 John George Lambton, 1st Earl of Durham, *Lord Durham's Report*, ed. G.M. Craig (Ottawa: Carleton University Press, 1982), 67; "Lord John Russell to the Right Hon. C. Poulett Thomson" (7 September 1839), in *Documents of the Canadian Constitution, 1759–1915*, ed. W.P.M. Kennedy (Toronto: Oxford University Press, 1918), 519; and "Poulett Thomson to Russell" (16 September 1840) in ibid., 552. Also see Michael Ernest McCulloch, "The Defeat of Imperial Urbanism in Québec City, 1840–1855," *Urban History Review* 22, no. 1 (October 1993): 19; and Grittner, "Privilege at the Polls," 216–20.

28 Dagenais, "The Municipal Territory," 202.

29 See Special Council of Lower Canada, 3 & 4 Vic., c. 36, ss. 9–10. Also see Dagenais, "The Special Councils of Lower Canada," 138–40.

30 Frank O'Gorman, *Voters, Patrons, and Parties: The Unreformed Electoral System of Hanoverian England, 1734–1832* (New York: Oxford University Press, 1989), 1–11; O'Gorman, "Campaign Rituals and Ceremonies: The Social Meaning of Elections in England, 1780–1860," *Past and Present* 135 (May 1992): 100; James Vernon, *Politics and the People: A Study in English Political Culture, c. 1815–1867* (Cambridge: Cambridge University Press, 1993), 99–102; Carol Wilton, *Popular Politics and Political Culture in Upper Canada, 1800–1850* (Montreal and Kingston: McGill-Queen's University Press, 2000), 144–67; Renaud Séguin, "Pour une nouvelle synthèse sur les processus électoraux du XIXe siècle québécois," *Journal of the Canadian Historical Association* 16 (2005): 83–100; and Dan Horner, "Taking to the Streets: Crowds, Politics, and Identity in Mid-Nineteenth-Century Montreal" (PhD diss., York University, 2010), 226.

31 "The Provocation Game," *Acadian Recorder* (Halifax), 19 February 1859, 3.

32 James Jackson, *The Riot That Never Was: The Military Shooting of Three Montrealers in 1832 and the Official Cover-up* (Montreal: Baraka Books, 2009), 330; and Elinor Kyte Senior, *British Regulars in Montreal: An Imperial Garrison, 1832–1854* (Montreal and Kingston: McGill-Queen's University Press, 1981), 16–20.

33 See Michel Ducharme, *Le concept de liberté au Canada à l'époque des Révolutions atlantiques, 1776–1838* (Montreal and Kingston: McGill-Queen's University Press, 2010), 117–61.

34 Ibid., 104–23, 331–2. Also see E.H. Bensley, "Robertson, William," *Dictionary of Canadian Biography*, vol. 7 (University of Toronto / Université Laval), 750–1. For other discussions, see Bettina Bradbury, "Women at the Hustings: Gender, Citizenship, and the Montreal By-Elections of 1832," in *Re-Thinking Canada: The Promise of Women's History*, 6th ed., ed. Mona Gleason and Adele Perry (Toronto: Oxford University Press, 2006), 73–94; France Galarneau, "L'élection partielle du quartier-ouest de Montréal en 1832: Analyse politico-sociale," *Revue d'histoire de l'Amérique française* 32, no. 4 (March 1979): 565–84; Senior, *British Regulars in Montreal*, 11–23; and Horner, "Taking to the Streets," 221.

35 Fyson, *Magistrates, Police, and People*, 173. Also see Fyson, "La gouvernance municipale avant la municipalité: Montréal, 1760–1840," in *La gouvernance montréalaise: De la ville frontière à la métropole*, ed. Léon Robichaud, Harold Bérubé, and Donald Fyson (Montreal: Éditions MultiMondes, 2014), 38.
36 Louis-Joseph Papineau, "Aux libres et indépendans [*sic*] électeurs du Quartier Ouest de Montréal," *La Minerve*, 8 December 1834, 1.
37 Greer, *The Patriots and the People*, 332. Also see Jean-Marie Fecteau, "'This Ultimate Resource': Martial Law and State Repression in Lower Canada, 1837–8," in *Canadian State Trials II: Rebellion and Invasion in the Canadas, 1837–1839*, ed. F. Murray Greenwood and Barry Wright (Toronto: University of Toronto Press for the Osgoode Society, 2002), 215–34.
38 Quoted in Michael S. Cross, "'The Laws Are Like Cobwebs': Popular Resistance to Authority in Mid-Nineteenth-Century British North America," in *Law in a Colonial Society: The Nova Scotia Experience*, ed. Peter Waite, Sandra Oxner, and Thomas Barnes (Toronto: Carswell, 1984), 122.
39 Senior, *British Regulars in Montreal*, 72.
40 Boyd Hilton, *A Mad, Bad, and Dangerous People? England, 1783–1846* (Oxford: Oxford University Press, 2006), 517.
41 Jacques Monet, "La Crise Metcalfe and the Montreal Election, 1843–1844," *Canadian Historical Review* 44, no. 1 (March 1963): 14.
42 "Élection," *La Minerve*, 26 February 1844, 2.
43 Monet, "La Crise Metcalfe," 16. Also see J.I. Little, "Drummond, Lewis Thomas," *Dictionary of Canadian Biography*, vol. 11 (University of Toronto / Université Laval), 281; Horner, "Taking to the Streets," 210–17; and Senior, *British Regulars in Montreal*, 61–6.
44 Senior, *British Regulars in Montreal*, 65. Also see Monet, "La Crise Metcalfe," 17–19; Monet, *The Last Cannon Shot: A Study of French-Canadian Nationalism* (Toronto: University of Toronto Press, 1969), 169–78.
45 For a more sterile account, see Sir Francis Hincks, *Reminiscences of His Public Life* (Montreal: William Drysdale, 1884), 123–31.
46 Archives de la Ville de Montréal (hereafter AVM), VM1 Fonds Conseil de Ville de Montréal, S10 Procès-Verbaux, D24, vol. 15, 9 October 1844, 18.
47 Senior, *British Regulars in Montreal*, 68, 70.
48 Monet, *The Last Cannon Shot*, 192.
49 Ibid., 69. Also see "Latest News," *Montreal Gazette*, 22 October 1844, 2.
50 Little, "Drummond, Lewis Thomas," 281; Monet, *The Last Cannon Shot*, 192; and Senior, *British Regulars in Montreal*, 70.
51 Senior, *British Regulars in Montreal*, 71.
52 Ibid.
53 AVM, VM1 S10 D24, vol, 15, 29 November 1844, 72–3.
54 "Élections municipales," *La Minerve*, 2 December 1844, 2.

55 AVM, VM1 S10 D25, vol. 16, 20 December 1844, 21–2; Senior, *British Regulars in* Montreal, 71–2.

56 Province of Canada, *Debates of the Legislative Assembly of United Canada*, vol. 4, part 1, 27 March 1845, 2498.

57 Ibid., 2496.

58 For the quotations used here, see Dan Horner, "Solemn Processions and Terrifying Violence: Spectacle, Authority, and Citizenship during the Lachine Canal Strike of 1843," *Urban History Review* 38, no. 2 (Spring 2010): 41. Also see Dan Horner, "'Shame upon you as men!' Contesting Authority in the Aftermath of Montreal's Gavazzi Riot," *Histoire sociale / Social History* 44, no. 87 (May 2011): 38–45, and Horner, "Taking to the Streets," 16.

59 Province of Canada, *Debates of the Legislative Assembly of United Canada*, vol. 4, part 1, 17 December 1844, 387, and 20 December 1844, 535.

60 Province of Canada, *Appendix to the Fourth Volume of the Journals of the Legislative Assembly*, appendix S.S., 1. Also see Province of Canada, *An Act to Amend and Consolidate the Provisions and Ordinance to Incorporate the City and Town of Montreal, and of a Certain Ordinance Amending the Ordinance, and to Vest Certain Other Powers in the Corporation Created by the Said First Mentioned Ordinance*, 8 Vic., c. 59, s. 25.

61 Province of Canada, *Appendix to the Fourth Volume of the Journals of the Legislative Assembly*, appendix S.S., 1 (11 March 1845).

62 Ibid., 7 (8 February 1845).

63 Ibid., 14 (26 February 1845).

64 Ibid., 5 (20 January 1845); 8 (10 February 1845); 11 (24 February 1845).

65 Sherry Olson, "Ethnic Partition of the Work Force in 1840s Montréal," *Labour/Le travail* 53 (Spring 2004): 81.

66 Province of Canada, *Appendix to the Fourth Volume of the Journals of the Legislative Assembly*, appendix S.S., 5 (20 January 1845).

67 Ibid., 1 (11 March 1845).

68 Province of Canada, *Debates of the Legislative Assembly of United Canada*, vol. 4, part 1, 27 March 1845, 2498. Much like Ferrier, de Bleury fails to explain how wealth and intelligence necessarily go together, or how labourers have neither.

69 Province of Canada, 8 Vic., c. 59, s. 10.

70 Province of Canada, *Debates of the Legislative Assembly of United Canada*, vol. 4, part 1, 27 March 1845, 2498.

71 Province of Canada, *Appendix to the Fifth Volume of the Journals of the Legislative Assembly*, appendix E.E.E., 1.

72 Monet, *The Last Cannon Shot*, 230.

73 Province of Canada, *Appendix to the Fifth Volume of the Journals of the Legislative Assembly*, appendix E.E.E., 4–5.

74 Ibid., 6.

75 Gerald Tulchinsky, *The River Barons: Montreal Businessmen and the Growth of Industry and Transportation, 1837–53* (Toronto: University of Toronto Press, 1977), 15.
76 Province of Canada, *Appendix to the Fifth Volume of the Journals of the Legislative Assembly*, appendix E.E.E., 5.
77 Ibid.
78 Ibid., appendix A.A., 10.
79 Ibid., appendix E.E.E., 1.
80 Ibid., 1–2, 4.
81 Ibid., 2.
82 Ibid., 3. John Collins also testified that "the polling went on briskly until about ten o'clock; at that time Mr. Ferrier sent Robert Cook to Town Major McDonald [*sic*] for the troops. There was no appearance of disturbance then, beyond a little loud talk." Ibid., 2.
83 Ibid., 1–4, 6.
84 Ibid., appendix A.A., 10.
85 Ibid., appendix E.E.E., 4, 6. The partisan returning officer was William Footner.
86 AVM, VM1 S10 D46, vol. 37, 1 May 1848, 4–6.
87 Senior, *British Regulars in* Montreal, 72.
88 "Les élections municipales," *La Minerve*, 5 March 1846, 2. In a subsequent edition, letter writer "Un Passant" agreed that "de tous côtés il est donc désirer que de pareils outrages cessent..." "Pour La Minerve," *La Minerve*, 9 March 1846, 2.
89 Province of Canada, *Journals of the Legislative Assembly of the Province of Canada*, vol. 5, 27 April 1846, 166 (emphasis in original).
90 Vernon, *Politics and the People*, 102. For more on the institution of vote by ballot in Great Britain, France, and the United States during the eighteenth and nineteenth centuries, see Malcolm Crook and Tom Crook, "Ballot Papers and the Practice of Elections: Britain, France, and the United States of America, c. 1500–2000," *Historical Research* 88, no. 241 (August 2015): 536–45.
91 George Emery, *Elections in Oxford County, 1837–1875: A Case Study in Democracy in Canada West and Early Ontario* (Toronto: University of Toronto Press, 2012), 167.
92 Elsewhere in mid nineteenth-century British North America, one witnesses similar kinds of exploitation where cultural tensions existed. See Scott W. See, "Polling Crowds and Patronage: New Brunswick's 'Fighting Elections' of 1842–3," *Canadian Historical Review* 72, no. 2 (June 1991): 128–9, 153–6.
93 The provincial government also did much the same thing with workers along the Lachine Canal. See Monet, *The Last Cannon Shot*, 177.
94 Province of Canada, *Appendix to the Fifth Volume of the Journals of the Legislative Assembly*, appendix E.E.E., 4–6.

95 AVM, VM1 S10 D55, vol. 46, 25 July 1851, 15. Also see New Brunswick, An Act to repeal the several Acts for incorporating the City of Fredericton, and to make other provisions in lieu thereof, 14 Vic., c. 15, s. 20; New Brunswick, An Act to provide for the establishment of Municipal authorities in this Province, 14 Vic., c. 38, s. 7. For a brief history of the violence itself, see Scott W. See, *Riots in New Brunswick: Orange Nativism and Social Violence in the 1840s* (Toronto: University of Toronto Press, 1993), 149–59, 191.

96 Province of Canada, An Act to amend and consolidate the provisions of the Ordinance to incorporate the City and Town of Montreal, and of a certain Ordinance and certain Acts amending the same, and to vest certain other powers in the Corporation of the said City of Montreal, 14 & 15 Vic., c. 128, s. 11.

97 Ibid., s. 19. Voters who were unable to write could have their certificates filled out in the presence of two witnesses.

98 Ibid., ss. 18 and 19.

99 Elaine Hadley, *Living Liberalism: Practical Citizenship in Mid-Victorian Britain* (Chicago: University of Chicago Press, 2010), 46.

100 AVM, VM1 S10 D56, vol. 47, 31 January 1852, 24 (from grand jury report dated 14 January 1852).

101 Ibid., VM1 S10 D63, vol. 54, 15 March 1854, 44; VM1 S10 D64, vol. 55, 21 June 1854, 10.

102 Ibid., VM1 S10 D65, vol. 56, 12 December 1854, 10.

103 Ibid., VM48 Fonds Board of Revisors, Book 1, 1846–1882, "Special Committee to Manage the Elections, 1860," 7 February 1860, 97; 18 February 1860, 98.

104 See Senior, *British Regulars in Montreal*, 10, 220.

105 AVM, VM1 S10 D76, vol. 67, n.d., 149.

106 Ibid., 10 April 1860, 139.

107 Province of Canada, An Act to amend the provisions of the several Acts of the Incorporation of the City of Montreal, 23 Vic., c. 72, s. 4(1).

108 Ibid., s. 4(4).

109 Province of Canada, An Act to define the Elective Franchise, to provide for the Registration of Voters, and for other purposes therein mentioned, 22 Vic., c. 82, s. 2(1).

110 For example, see Archives of Ontario, RG22-5874 York County Court Voters' List records 1867–1875, Stephen Radcliff of the Toronto City Clerk's Office to County Judge George Duggan, 15 September 1874.

111 Province of Canada, An Act to amend the provisions of several Acts relating to the City of Montreal, and for other purposes, 29 & 30 Vic., c. 56, s. 2.

112 Curtis, *Ruling by Schooling Quebec*, 3.

113 Wendie Nelson, "'Rage against the Dying of the Light': Interpreting the Guerre des Éteignoirs," *Canadian Historical Review* 81, no. 4 (December 2000): 556.

114 Curtis, *Ruling by Schooling Quebec*, 429.

15 Boys, Young Men, and Disorder in Mid-Victorian Toronto

IAN RADFORTH

Boys and young men figured significantly both in the disorder that occurred in mid-nineteenth-century urban British North America and in the concomitant search for social order. This chapter makes this case by examining Toronto, then a rapidly growing commercial centre in the early throes of industrialization.[1] From the 1840s through the 1870s, the considerable rowdiness in Toronto was fuelled by lads hanging about the streets eager for action and by their fierce ethno-religious and partisan differences. The city's largest riots usually pitted Orange (militant Protestants) against Green (Roman Catholic Irish), but even minor clashes of young men in the streets often derived from ethno-religious tensions, or at least that is how they were represented by newspapers.

Toronto's lively press, essential in this work as a historical source, reported and commented on street violence and attempts to prevent it. Newspapers, especially the mighty *Globe*, which could afford to hire roving reporters, covered all manner of social conflict in the streets and in the courts.[2] The press's intense gaze on crime and violence suggests the voyeuristic fascination of many newspaper readers who derived reassurance about their own respectability and social distance from street violence.[3] In addition, the press publicized the authorities' attempts to combat crime and disorder, as well as middle-class activists' campaigns to reform troublesome boys.

This chapter deals both with boys and young men because of the similarities in experience, behaviour, and treatment of them when they were in city streets, where they were most likely to engage in conflict or come within the purview of the law. Boys also learned about masculinity by watching males older than themselves. As Craig Heron argues about a later period, for young men, being "one of the boys" was about performing masculinity in ways learned first on the streets as young boys and then in ongoing ways that extended that childhood experience.[4] In the mid-Victorian city, too, the continuity from childhood through adolescence and into a bachelor life (if not beyond) also gave substance and meaning to the imprecise but frequently invoked expressions, "the lads" and "the boys." Playful behaviour in the streets sometimes led to trouble. Boys liked to throw stones, and sometimes those stones broke windows or hit people, behaviour that older fellows took up during riots. Boys sorted out differences by fighting, just as young men used their fists to establish their place in the pecking order, or to challenge men from rival fraternal orders. Indeed, much of the violence of the mid-Victorian city grew out of the recreational life of boys and young men, and critics of rowdiness and crime struggled to find ways to curb them.[5] At a time when calls for "peace, order, and good government" were gaining increasing traction on the national scene, urban reformers sought the same rather elusive goal.[6]

Youthful Violence during Riots

From time to time, the streets of mid-Victorian Toronto erupted with riots. Newspapers reported that young men and boys actively participated in these confrontations and sometimes instigated them. In 1849, the Toronto press characterized the perpetrators of serious social violence as reckless youths. In March of that year, the Reform government allowed William Lyon Mackenzie, the rebel leader of 1837, to return to Toronto for the first time since the rebellion. Some Conservatives held a demonstration to protest his reappearance. Rumours circulated that two thousand protesters would gather in the evening to march in procession to the house where he was staying and burn an effigy of him. Partisan tensions were running high at the time because of the rebellion losses bill controversy.[7] Tory activists had prepared for the March demonstration by marshalling Orange rowdies, who gathered stones, armed themselves with sticks, and lit torches. At its climax, the demonstrators torched the effigy and stoned the house where Mackenzie was staying, smashing all its windows. These activities were overlooked by municipal authorities and a police force with Orange and Tory sympathies. The Reform press disparaged the demonstrators, underscoring their youth. "Young lads, half grown," reported the *Globe*, "were observed in small groups of two and three, generally carrying sticks, moving about in the neighbourhood. They were joined by some men and the procession moved off." The *Examiner* described the "the squalid and vicious looking cortege" as being composed of "unshaven, dirty looking, half-intoxicated men, and aged boys." Instead of the 2,000 demonstrators promised by the Tories, the *Globe* maintained that "they numbered from 100 to 120, many of them lads, and mostly raggamuffians [*sic*]." They had been mustered, the *Globe* charged, by Tory aldermen who "have a few rowdies whom they can move or restrain at pleasure." Their numbers included "a few college boys, or the off-scourings of Orangeism." The point of the rhetoric was to defend the moderation and respectability of the city and to dismiss the significance of opposition to Mackenzie and the Reform government by representing the protestors as few in number, young, and lacking independence, respectability, and good judgment.[8]

In 1855, the "circus riot," one of mid-nineteenth-century Toronto's largest riots, involved youthful violence fuelled by nativism and Orangeism. The trouble began on the evening of 12 July, the "Glorious Twelfth," the Orangemen's most important annual celebration, when social tensions always ran high in Victorian Toronto.[9] This time trouble erupted in a bawdy house on King Street when a local man knocked the hat off a clown from a visiting American circus. A brawl ensued in which the circus visitors sent the local fellows running "like nine pins."[10] Revenge would be swift. The next evening, young locals set the circus's ticket wagon on fire and rolled it down to the bay. The fire bells were sounded, a signal that called out not only the volunteer firemen, who were Orangemen, but all their brethren too, including those dressed in the costume of the Orange Young Britons, the order's youth wing. A crowd of perhaps two thousand people gathered on the fair ground, where young local men tried to confront the circus personnel. When the circus men refused to venture out of the big tent, the crowd hurled stones at it, set it on fire, and attempted to axe its guy ropes. Local men roared that "they would have out the livers of the Circus men" and shouted "murder the d – n Yankee son of a b – s." The volunteer firemen refused to douse the circus's property, both because the firemen sympathized with the incendiaries and because an Orangemen, Joe Bird, had been badly injured by a circus worker. The constabulary similarly did little, even when the mayor, George William Allan, implored them to restore the peace. When news circulated that Bird was nearly dead, the local lads demanded the police arrest the circus men, adding, "Why should our fellow citizens be murdered by a parcel of Yankees?" The confrontation lasted for a few hours before burning out.[11]

Witnesses to the violence underscored the leading role young men played in the riot. A city councillor noted that – particularly in its early stages – "the crowd consisted chiefly of boys, and did not seem to be very serious." The mayor declared, "One thing that struck him that night was the vast number of vagabond boys between 16 and 20 years of age who were present," adding that "those ruffian boys ... were the pest and curse of Toronto."[12] The violence of the circus riot was thus exacerbated by young men eager for excitement, high on Orange festivities, and fired by nativism directed at the "Yankee" circus men visiting the city.

Processions of Irish Catholics on St Patrick's Day (17 March) and by Orangemen on the Glorious Twelfth could be well ordered and impressive in their size, but, as often noted, some years saw serious clashes between Orange and Green.[13] Tragedy struck during rioting on St Patrick's Day in 1858 when Matthew Sheedy, a twenty-two-year-old Catholic stableman, was fatally stabbed. According to the police magistrate's findings, the trouble began when a boy driving a butcher's wagon tried unsuccessfully to pass through the St Patrick's Day procession. Orangemen rushed to the scene and the riot began.[14] Apparently, a boy triggered rioting that led to the death of a young man mourned as a martyr by the Irish Catholic community after the acquittal of the Orangemen charged with the murder. Yet, most remarkable is the fact that, notwithstanding intense Orange-Green hostility, Sheedy's death was the only one to arise from years of rioting, suggesting some self-restraint on the part of demonstrators.

The biggest riots in Victorian Toronto were the Jubilee riots, when, in 1875, militant Protestants attacked Roman Catholic pilgrims who processed through city streets.[15] The pope had declared 1875 a jubilee year, and, in celebration, Toronto's Roman Catholic archbishop, John Joseph Lynch, invited Catholics to join processions, including on two Sundays in the autumn. Beforehand it became public knowledge that militant Protestants, especially Orange Young Britons, threatened to disrupt the processions, which they saw as a challenge to Protestant domination of the city and a desecration of the sabbath.

Images from the *Canadian Illustrated News* featuring the Jubilee riots convey both the youthfulness of participants at the heart of the combat and the event's proximity to play. Figure 15.1 shows young men throwing and dodging stones in what looks like a game. All is not fun, however. The boy in the foreground on the right has fallen or been knocked down and nurses a head wound. In an attempt to restore order, out-numbered policemen dash onto the scene. In Figure 15.2, a boy wields a stick in the bottom centre, next to a girl and a woman who cower amid the fighting. Women and girls, although not usually present during Toronto's riots, were in the streets on this occasion because, as faithful Catholics, they were walking in the religious procession. The artist has followed Victorian convention by sharply contrasting masculine aggression and feminine vulnerability. At the centre of the image, one of several constables wields a baton over the head of a rioter. Indeed, the bloody riots resulted in injuries to many participants, police, and onlookers. And yet, as these images show, it was also an exciting confrontation that drew demonstrators and spectators – thrill-seeking youths – into the streets however troubled, or not, they were by the issues at stake.[16] The exhilarating occasion offered respite from a Victorian

15.1 and 15.2 The Jubilee riots as pictured in *Canadian Illustrated News* 12, no. 16, 16 October 1875. Source: Early Canadiana Online.

Toronto Sunday, normally pinched into dullness and inactivity by evangelical sabbatarianism.

Two of Toronto's newspapers blamed the violence of the Jubilee riots on the Orange Young Britons, an organization of young men in their teens and early twenties that was loosely associated with the Orange Order but lacked its discipline and growing respectability. According to the *Globe*, these fools were a "thoughtless class of lads" who purported to stand up for Orange principles about which they knew nothing. As for "their affected zeal for God's truth or God's law, or the sanctity of the Lord's Day," that was "one of the most transparent frauds that ever was attempted to be palmed off upon a long-suffering and highly charitable community."[17] The *Irish Canadian*, the city's voice of Irish nationalism, also blamed the Orange Young Britons for the attacks on the Jubilee processionists, who included many women and children, and it objected when authorities looked the other way. "The Young Britons," surmised the *Irish Canadian*, "had made up their minds to break up the procession and slaughter the weak and defenceless – if that could be done with impunity." They were emboldened in the knowledge that their unlawful conduct was permitted by the civic authorities.[18] This analysis connected the events to ongoing political struggles as the Irish Catholic minority resisted Orange dominance at city hall.

Sectarian conflict persisted in part because of city authorities' toleration of Orange violence. The Orangemen consistently positioned themselves as staunch loyalists in a British colonial setting where loyalism carried weight.[19] And, like the Masons of Saint John, they professed their loyalty even as they challenged constituted authority.[20] The colonial state, similar to the imperial state, both deplored Orange violence and tolerated it when it served state and political purposes.[21] As fierce defenders of the Protestant Crown, which had long privileged the Protestant minority in Ireland, Toronto's Orangemen promoted grass-roots activism in the name of loyalty, campaigning successfully in municipal elections so as to dominate at city hall and gain access to jobs, including on the police force. In the 1840s and 1850s, the Orange Lodge created and defended not a liberal order but an Orangemen's order. Equality before the law and "peace, order, and good government" were not its goals; instead, Orange bullying ran free, and the mayor's office, police court, and the constabulary acted with a blunt and undisguised bias in favour of its brethren and Protestants more generally.

Sectarianism did not underlie every large confrontation in nineteenth-century Toronto, however. During two 1886 strikes by streetcar operators, class sympathies and active boys were evident in Toronto streets when demonstrators rioted to register their opposition both to the Toronto Street Railway Company's anti-union policy and to strike-breaking streetcar operators, and to show their support for the well-disciplined strikers, who themselves sought to avoid violence and its repercussions.[22] Boys played a key role in provoking members of the crowds to take threatening and sometimes violent action. The first to hurl handfuls of mud and snowballs at scab-run streetcars and their operators, boys appear to have triggered men in the crowd to do the same. Young lads had good fun taking potshots at their targets, enjoyment that resembled the mischievous activity many of them undoubtedly engaged in daily in the streets.[23] In this situation, the sympathetic crowds offered some protection from the usual police reprisals, and, in any case, police initially tolerated the public-supported unruliness. On the first day of the March strike, police apprehended only two lads, one aged thirteen and the other twelve. During that strike, boys gained attention when they assisted older males in hounding operators to abandon their streetcars. Once they were successful, youngsters jumped aboard the vacated streetcars to the cheers of the throng celebrating the victory. At certain points, however, the boys' behaviour became violent. During the second strike, they threw not just mud but stones at scab-operated streetcars, provoking men to do the same. A spokesman for the strikers' executive committee, who regretted the violence, maintained that "the trouble commenced by the boys throwing rocks at the cars. A few of the rowdy element, taking advantage of the large crowd and enthusiasm displayed, took a hand in and finished the work the boys had commenced."[24] His observation neatly characterizes the manner in which boys participated in riots.

Quotidian Violence

In addition to riots involving large numbers of people, mid-Victorian Toronto saw countless incidents of violence that involved fewer people and appeared spontaneous. Young men were accused of "rowdyism" when, for recreation, they congregated in groups and preyed upon respectable residents in the streets. "Gangs of rowdies collect about the corners," the *Globe* reported in October 1853, "and they make a fiendish delight in insulting and maltreating all whom they think unable to defend themselves." On Yonge Street, a man and "an aged lady" were not only hassled but knocked down, "apparently from no other motive but a diabolical delight in working mischief."[25] On another occasion, around midnight a witness watched some "very rough-looking characters," armed with sticks and stones, attack and knock down passersby indiscriminately.[26] In the newspapers, groups of rowdies were casually referred to as "gangs," but it appears they lacked the coherence of organized gangs.

Mid-century Toronto's most notorious organized gang, "the Brook's Bush Gang," was composed equally of men and women in their mid-twenties.

About a dozen men and an equal number of women in summer lived rough in Brook's Bush, a wooded area east of the Don River bridge, and in winter they took shelter in nearby abandoned buildings. Gang members, who often harassed pedestrians crossing the Don bridge, appeared before the police court many times in the 1850s and 1860s, usually on drunk and disorderly charges.[27] Members were involved in two murder cases. In 1856, Michael Barry, twenty-five, was convicted of manslaughter for killing a young black man, Isaiah Sewell, who lived out the Kingston Road and stopped to talk to one of the women gang members on the edge of Brook's Bush. Barry had been drinking heavily and impulsively used a bottle he had in hand to clobber Sewell from behind. As he attacked, he shouted "You black b – g – r, go away!"[28] Thus, whiskey and racism combined with tragic results. In December 1859, John Sheridan Hogan, an Assemblyman, stopped to talk with a woman gang member near the Don River bridge. This provided the opportunity for the gang to attack him, bind him up, and toss him into the river. His disappearance was a mystery until the body literally surfaced a year later, and the story came out during a sensational inquest and several trials.[29] Eventually one gang member, James Browne, was executed for the murder.[30]

A rare case of murder where the victim, Samuel Reid, was a young man of eighteen illustrates how things could escalate into violence and tragedy. It occurred in the working-class St John's Ward on the night of the municipal election in 1855. Election nights were routinely a time for carousing and disputes, and this was no exception. Although Reid was too young to vote, he was active in the election because as a carter he needed a city licence and thus had an interest in seeing his Orange brethren maintain their grip on power and patronage. James Spence, his uncle and a candidate in the election, while walking down Elizabeth Street with a friend shortly after the polls closed, encountered two swaggering men from the rival political camp who said "Clear the planks," demanding control of the sidewalk. The uncle and his friend refused, and in the ensuing fight Spence was knifed and cut badly. Young Reid and a companion watched his parents clean up the wound, and they volunteered to go to the druggist for a sticking plaster. On their way back, they encountered two men they mistakenly believed had perpetrated the dispute and set upon them. One of the men pulled out a bowie knife and stabbed Reid in the thigh, severing an artery. "Boys, I'm done," cried Reid, "They've stuck me." And, indeed, he bled to death. Eight men were arrested as suspects in the killing and testified at the week-long inquest, but eventually another man, John Irving, was charged after his initials were discerned faintly etched on the murder weapon. He confessed to the stabbing. Recoiling from the damage done in a street fight, the coroner's jury urged a law prohibiting the importation and sale of bowie knives. The jury observed that they were too readily available, being found for sale "not only in hardware stores but in nearly all clothing stores, to the great demoralization of our youth."[31]

Newspapers and the police sometimes pointed to violence involving young boys. Much of it was petty and connected to play, but authorities and middle-class commentators took it seriously, worried that as boys grew up their violence would become more serious. One day in March 1855, for instance, three cases involving youngsters came before the Toronto police court. First, three "little boys" appeared on a complaint from a resident who alleged that they had broken a window in his house. The police chief took the trouble to appear and speak against them, saying that the lads "were part of a gang of incorrigible boys who frequent the corner of Church and Richmond Streets for the purpose of indulging in obscene language, committing petty larcenies, and insulting passers-by." In response, the boys defended their behaviour by saying they were "only fooling." They were sentenced to forty-eight hours in solitary confinement. Also appearing that day was Michael Hardy, "a lad of not more than fifteen years of age" whom Police Constable Jones maintained had been "pummeling two urchins to the infinite amusement of a crowd of boys." Because it was Hardy's first offence, he was discharged with a warning. And lastly, Patrick Donovan, also not more than fifteen, was charged that day "with conducting himself in a very improper manner on Sunday evening." A policeman observed Donovan entertaining a crowd of "ragged urchins" by "flourishing a stick over his head in Donnybrook style." When the constable approached, the young showman whistled and everyone fled, but he tumbled into a snow bank and the officer nabbed him.[32] All these incidents appear to have closely connected to "fooling around."

Given that the Orange/Green celebrations and conflicts were so prevalent in Victorian Toronto, it's not surprising to find young boys involved in them. In 1858, on the evening of the Glorious Twelfth, a Catholic boy about thirteen triggered a riot by plucking an Orange lily from the chest of one Charles Manson who was walking in a poor Catholic neighbourhood. As Manson testified in court, he turned around "to punish the boy" and was attacked by a dozen men, who struck him and kicked him in the head. Manson's friend and fellow Orangeman came to his rescue, firing a shot at one of the assailants and wounding him in the cheek. A crowd of some 150 gathered, and various scuffles occurred. Eventually Manson's friend was convicted for shooting the assailant.[33] Almost a year later, on another Orange commemorative occasion, a boy playing Protestant tunes on a fife in Cuthbert's Saloon, Adelaide Street, provoked a gang of working-class Catholics to smash the tavern's windows. Retaliation followed, when "a number of lads" marching through the streets playing militant Protestant music entered Stanley Street and broke many windows of Catholics' homes.[34] Thus, small acts by young boys could lead to serious trouble in the highly charged sectarian atmosphere of mid-century Toronto.

Mid-Victorian statistical reports on Toronto crime reinforce the point that boys and young men were accused of crimes and often convicted, but boys' crimes were overwhelmingly non-violent. The annual reports of Toronto's police officials from 1860 to 1875 document the frequent appearances of boys and young men before the police magistrate and reveal some patterns.[35] Boys and men under thirty-one made up about two-fifths of the court appearances by males and about one-third of total appearances. The trend was towards more appearances before the court over time, including increased numbers of boys and young men, a development explained both by population growth and a more active constabulary. Within the population under thirty-one, criminal appearances increased with age. Male appearances greatly outnumbered female ones in the lower age groups.

The reports mention boys in the case of only two types of crime: drunk and disorderly, and larceny and suspicion of larceny. It was reported in 1861, for example, that thirty-two boys appeared for being drunk and disorderly, and fifty-three boys for larceny or suspicion of larceny. At the time, individuals licensed to sell liquor were prohibited from selling intoxicating drink to any child or apprentice without the consent of a parent, master, or legal protector.[36] Determined lads, of course, found ways to gain access to alcohol.[37] Sometimes the police court exposed evidence of organized, premeditated larceny by youngsters. In February 1854, one newspaper alleged that about fifteen lads had formed a gang to steal from stores and the market. "Some of the secrets of the gang have come to light recently," reported the *Globe*, "which show that the members have a regular system on which they work, such as changing coats whilst committing a robbery – passing the article stolen from hand to hand, etc."[38]

Authorities deplored the extent of youth crime. Judge James Hagarty, in his address to the grand jury at the winter assizes held in Toronto in December 1865, reviewed the provincial and city statistics on crime and declared that "the darkest item in this black catalogue is that relating to young prisoners." Noting that, in 1864, there were 130 children under sixteen held in the demoralizing Toronto jail, he called it "a most melancholy fact." When the number of prisoners ranging in age from sixteen to twenty was added, the total came to 300. "We have hardly to ask," Hagarty harrumphed, "what may be the probably [*sic*] after-life of those who begin the world under such degrading conditions."[39] The *Globe* took up the judge's concerns, calling the 130 children serving time "a disgrace."[40]

In the 1870s, the local conflicts most troubling to authorities involved groups of young men, both Orange and Green, whose recreational activities sometimes included street fighting. As commerce and industrialization increased in Toronto, more young men had fixed workdays and thus clearly defined leisure time in the evenings. Many of them joined either the Orange Young Britons or, on the Catholic side, the Young Irishmen's Benevolent Association, fraternal organizations where youthful, masculine conviviality could be enjoyed with like-minded fellows.[41] Newspapers reported favourably on the picnics and other outings the organizations arranged, and reporters admired the young men's appearance in colourful uniforms during processions. On the other hand, commentators disapproved of gatherings that involved heavy drinking, late-night carousing, and violence.

The *Globe* denounced street violence, whether initiated by the Young Britons or the Young Irishmen. In August 1877, the Young Irishmen held a dance at a hall, and several men thereafter visited nearby Sholes' Saloon. "Whiskey being indulged in large quantities," observed the *Globe* report, "the young men's wits got out, and the result was a free fight, and the smashing of the windows of the place." When a constable entered the tavern and used his revolver to stop the fight, "six or seven roughs" attacked him, disarmed him, and beat his face to a pulp.[42] In August 1876, the Young Britons' excursion to St Catharines aboard the crowded steamer *Picton* turned violent when fighting erupted on-board, and it continued in St Catharines, resulting in more than "a few broken heads and disfigured countenances."[43] Reports such as these shaped the public's negative view of the young men and besmirched their organizations.

Those negative impressions deepened when members of the two organizations clashed. Sometimes the confrontations were unplanned. In July 1871, two Young Britons wearing orange neckerchiefs and "some other youngsters of the opposite persuasion" got into a scuffle aboard the ferry boat *Princess of Wales*, and, according to one report, "imprecations, mingled with the screams of the females on board, filled the air."[44] Sometimes the clashes of the youths were more concerted. One incident was said to have grown out of regular fights between Young Britons and Young Irishmen who all frequented Bailey's Tavern on Front Street. Bested too many times, eighty members of the Young Britons marched on the tavern one evening, but on their way they encountered a band of two hundred Young Irishmen, "and a regular fight ensued." After police dispersed the men and cleared out Bailey's, the Young Britons – marching four deep and playing party tunes – first stoned a rival's house, shattering its shutters, and then proceeded to Dummer Street to fight Catholic youths.[45] Such activity occurred repeatedly during the first half of the 1870s.

Historian William Jenkins has explored the connection the daily press made between Toronto's Catholic Irish and poverty, indolence, and crime, particularly when it came to depicting, or rather caricaturing, residents of Stanley Street and Dummer Street.[46] Yet, young, militant Protestants were frequent targets of complaint and ridicule too, although similar caricaturing was not applied. For instance, in 1870 the *Globe* simply observed that "the name of 'Young Briton' has come to be very nearly synonymous with 'rowdy.'"[47]

Young Britons came in for opprobrium when, in June 1869, some of them smashed windows and the lamp over the door of Police Station No. 2 because police had detained raucous members and seized a drum used in nightly marches. The *Globe* observed that even if the police handled the Young Britons unwisely, the youths should not have attacked police and a public building, which they would have realized "if they were not foolish beyond all hope of remedy." The *Irish Canadian* objected when the men were released, charging that it showed the police were "pandering to the tastes and wishes of these young sprigs of Orangeism."[48] Even Protestant members of the public denounced Orange raucousness. Protestant residents of the middle-class suburb of Yorkville complained in court about the band practices of Young Britons, where the music was "loud, shrill, discordant, tremendous, and annoying," set the neighbourhood dogs barking, and prevented sleep.[49] Magistrates sometimes fined Young Britons heavily, indeed to the point where the district master advised cheering Young Britons that, if they were attacked, "never to mind taking their assailant to the Police Court, where, perhaps, he would get but scanty justice, but just to have satisfaction there and then." The *Globe* fumed at the remarks, saying it was "a deliberate inculcation of mob rule and violence, and an attempt to bring law and justice into contempt." The worry was that the district master's advice would be followed by "the reckless lads" and "peppery young simpletons."[50]

When the courts or newspapers criticized the Young Britons and the Young Irishmen for rowdiness, officials of the organizations sometimes responded by maintaining that their benevolent associations did not condone violence and by insisting that every sectarian scuffle did not involve the organizations. While it is true that neither organization formally condoned violence, their clashing word views and encouragement of recreational drinking and public strutting clearly fostered conflict.

The Search for Order

In mid-Victorian Toronto, reformers and commentators troubled by the violence of boys and young men proposed various means to discourage it and bring order to the city. In the 1840s, reformers in the Legislative Assembly introduced measures intended to suppress Orange violence. The 1842 Freedom of Elections Act, one of many mid-century alterations in election procedures, aimed at making intimidation and violence at the polls less likely.[51] The 1843 Act to Restrain Party Procession in Certain Cases banned processions, the target being Orange processions in particular.[52] Seething with a sense of injustice at being singled out, Orangemen defied the ban by walking in procession on many occasions. Because the law proved unenforceable, a Reform government repealed it in 1851. Thereafter, when violence related to processions occurred, voices demanded a ban, but opponents ensured that no legislative action succeeded by pointing to the failure of the 1843 act.

A changing culture within the Orange Order proved to be more effective in reducing Orange unruliness. Orange leaders, often higher up the class ladder than the majority of the brethren, worked to make Ontario Orangeism more respectable and self-disciplined. Lodges increasingly used their disciplinary powers to prohibit drunkenness and unruliness at lodge meetings, in effect joining in the popular mid-century temperance campaign. Increasingly to enhance the Orange Order's public face, lodges passed dress codes and standards of behaviour for Orangemen taking part in public processions. Members also touted the order's philanthropic activities. Orange leaders denounced violence, and, when the Young Britons persisted, the Orange Order in 1881 brought the Young Britons firmly within the order and its disciplines.[53] Squabbles in the streets became increasingly rare. Nevertheless, many young men of Orange propensities got an opportunity in 1885 to engage in violence – this time state-sanctioned violence – when, as young militiamen, they ventured to the North-West as part of the Canadian military's bid to suppress the Riel resistance. The lads could imagine themselves to be avenging the "murder" of Thomas Scott, the Ontario Orangeman executed by Riel's provisional government in 1870. In their 1885 military action, in contrast to their previous street violence, they had the complete support of the Toronto public.[54]

Another strategy for diffusing violence was to channel rivalries into organized sports. Both Protestant and Catholic groups formed clubs to engage in popular sports, such as lacrosse, football, and rowing, sometimes with teams competing across the ethno-religious divide. Increasingly regulated, the games never completely suppressed violence, but at least it was less threatening when it was represented as rugged, manly athleticism. In August 1859, a team of twelve Irish Catholics challenged players from the English-Protestant St George's Society to a game of football, to the delight of 3,500 spectators. In May 1873, 8,000 spectators watched the Montreal Shamrocks, the visiting Irish Catholic lacrosse team, beat the Orange-dominated Toronto Lacrosse Club, a victory hailed by Shamrock supporters as "a great day for Ireland." The Irish Catholic Benevolent

Union's tug-of-war squad competed with the Orange-dominated regimental and police teams. Sports historians Dennis Ryan and Kevin Wamsley argue that, for Toronto's Irish Catholics, "competitive sport provided legitimate venues for the celebration of physical forms of masculinity, demonstrations of strength through victory, and masculine honour because the contests were rule bound and sanctioned by the Protestant majority."[55]

Police reform offered another means to discourage violence in Toronto. Incidents such as the circus riot exposed the ineffectiveness and Orange bias of the force.[56] In 1858, a new Board of Police Commissioners gained control from corrupt municipal politicians. The following year, it fired the entire Toronto police force, including the chief, and created a new force. Using Boston's system of police patrols as a model, the sixty constables were put on regular patrols to deter law breaking and to model public behaviour.[57] The constables were to be detached from the local community, including the Orange Order, so that they could fairly apply the law. It is likely that the newly structured force did deter some street crime, given formal reports that such crimes declined in the 1860s. Certainly the new chief constable boasted that, thanks to improved policing, "street rows and wanton assaults, committed on respectable persons, by disorderly and turbulent people, commonly called rowdies, and which were formerly of frequent occurrence in Toronto, are now very rare."[58] Like all the city's municipal institutions, the police force continued to be overwhelmingly composed of Protestants, and charges of ethno-religious bias continued. The reforms marked a step towards a liberal order, but the Orangemen's definition of order had not vanished. Nevertheless, the reformed force was said to have been an effective deterrent to disorder on several occasions, including during some parades.[59]

In contrast to attempts to rein in young men as part of a strategy aimed at all adult males, reformers saw unruly boys as a distinct social category that required specialized responses. A few well-educated social reformers mounted a campaign to address "the boy problem," by which they meant the presence in the streets of destitute lads whose pathetic appearance and lack of Christian virtue both drew at the heartstrings of sentimental Victorians and demanded stern measures of social control. Reformers urged that orphaned, neglected, and vagrant boys be provided with a substitute for the home life and supervision they lacked. Confident that the lads were young enough to be malleable, reformers believed the children could be taught the requisite habits and Christian outlook, thus saving them from a life of sin and hardship and an afterlife of torment, and saving society from crime and its many costs.[60] The projects pursued by the reformers drew upon ideas circulating among reforming elites in the North Atlantic world, a public sphere that promoted liberal modernity.[61]

In Toronto, reformers adopted several institution-building strategies to address the boy problem, three of which focused on schooling. First, they supported free common schools for all, justifying them on numerous grounds, including the belief that everyone would benefit from a schooling regime that would reverse the descent of vagrant and neglected children into crime and unruliness.[62] Experience soon showed, however, that few such children attended the common schools, and, in any event, the parents and teachers of children who did attend regarded the urchins as an unpleasant and disruptive element that should be excluded. Second, reformers proposed building separate institutions, "ragged schools," specifically for the urchins, where philanthropists or churches would provide clothing and lodging. But when a bill was drafted in 1862 to establish them, the public objected to this diversion of funds from the common schools, thus providing the momentum to kill the measure.[63] Third, reformers advocated that the state open industrial schools so that authorities could compel the attendance of incorrigibles who would be schooled and taught practical trades. Such schools would provide a viable alternative for magistrates who maintained that sentencing boys to the jail and the reformatory only increased the likelihood of recidivism. Ontario's 1874 Industrial School Act enabled school boards to found such institutions, but parsimonious boards were slow to do so.[64]

Reformers also campaigned to create home-like institutions to substitute for the proper families that the urchins lacked. In the 1830s, Toronto's House of Industry began its decades-long assistance to orphaned boys and girls, mainly by apprenticing them on farms, where it was hoped they would be useful, learn skills, and benefit from the family setting.[65] In the 1850s, reformers proposed building a provincial reformatory but were divided over whether it should house only juveniles convicted of crimes or if authorities should compel neglected children – "incipient criminals" – to be incarcerated as well. When the state established a reformatory for Canada West at Penetanguishene in 1858, it housed a heterogeneous population: convicts and others, and small lads and young men up to twenty-one years of age.[66] It was not the specialized facility envisaged by reformers. The Toronto police magistrate hesitated to sentence boys to the reformatory because he "never knew of a boy being sent there without becoming worse."[67]

Finally, reformers also promoted and established "children's homes," philanthropically supported institutions intended to replicate an ideal middle-class family situation, where street children could be cared for, disciplined, and instructed in Christianity, morality, and the habits of industry. Part of a transnational response to neglected children, the so-called family plan had been developed in France and Britain and transferred to Massachusetts and Ohio shortly before it arrived in Ontario.[68] The metaphor of the family was both inclusive, giving troublesome children a proper place within the community, and hierarchical, justifying and reinforcing the authority supervisors had over them. In Toronto, a group of Protestant men and women, inspired by a similar institution in London, England, opened the non-denominational (but Protestant) Toronto Boys' Home in 1859. It soon became one of more than a dozen children's homes in the province.[69] Its purpose was to house destitute boys who had not been convicted of crime but who lacked families to care properly for them, and thus to aid in "the prevention of juvenile crime."[70] G.W. Allan, heir to a local fortune, headed a board of prominent men, but its driving force was "lady volunteers," women from establishment families.[71] The venture was financed from donations and a small grant from the city council, which endorsed the home but hesitated to be generous in an era when public funding for welfare was viewed with extreme scepticism.[72] At the home, a male superintendent and a matron assumed the role of stand-in parents for the boys, but how many boys embraced that viewpoint is unclear. The plan was to train boys and send them to paying jobs – preferably in family settings – and a large portion of the boys were sent out to work.[73] Many other boys stayed in the home for a while and then were released to a parent or relative, often to the distress of the home managers, who feared the lads were returning to exploitative or risky family settings.[74] After a long campaign, reformers in 1872 succeeded in securing the right of the home's managers to assume legal guardianship of neglected children and prevent "unworthy" parents from taking control.[75] For all their shortcomings, as Charlotte Neff persuasively argues, this home and similar ones provided destitute and desperate parents with appreciated services, gave the first official recognition to child neglect, and laid a foundation for child welfare work taken up later by the foster parent movement.[76]

A decade after the 1859 founding of the Boy's Home, Toronto had two examples (one Catholic, the other Protestant) of a more specialized type of home for boys who worked principally as newsboys but also as bootblacks and at other trades. The condition, habits, and reputation of these boys drew the attention of reformers. The opening of a home for newsboys in New York was widely publicized and provided inspiration for other cities, including Toronto.[77] In 1868, the Roman Catholic Church, as part of a vigorous period of institution building, opened St Nicholas Home.[78] Newsboys and bootblacks were expected to work at their jobs in the daytime and return in the evening.[79] Boys in the street trades were by no means all Irish Catholics; an 1868 count showed more than half of two hundred such boys reported being Protestants. In 1869, a discussion in the Toronto diocesan synod of the Anglican Church and the activism of Professor Daniel Wilson of University College led to the opening of the News-boys' Lodging Home with accommodations for fifty boys.[80] Hailed as an improvement over miserable lodging houses where the boys "squander their petty gains in gambling and dissipation," boys were encouraged to avoid pauperization by paying twelve cents a day for food and lodging from their earnings. In 1873, the News-boys' Home reported it had sheltered 628 boys since its opening, and had sent 246 boys to jobs in the country.[81] Despite these inroads, the home's record disappointed its advocates. The strict regime of the home led many of its targets to opt for the freedom and pleasures of the penny boardinghouse or to remain with their exploitative or lax parents.

None of the specialized institutions intended to address the boy problem fulfilled advocates' expectations. Inadequate philanthropy and state support left the institutions struggling to reach their goals. Moreover, their approach failed to address the underlying structural problems of poverty, unemployment, and inadequate incomes that contributed to the hardships these boys faced, nor could they counteract the appeal of independence and transgression so central to the subculture the street boys created for themselves.[82] Moreover, the unruliness of boys extended well beyond the underclass that preoccupied these reformers; it was part of a much broader boy culture, if not bred in the bone.

This chapter has demonstrated that, in mid-nineteenth-century Toronto, boys and young men played a significant role in social disorder, which in turn spurred the search for order. When riots erupted, young men and boys were usually there. The press often highlighted their role as a means to dismiss the seriousness of the disorder and defend the city's respectability. Boys and young men also engaged in minor confrontations that grew from many causes, including lads hanging about the streets looking for a diversion, playful but destructive stone-tossing, performances of masculinity that determined the pecking order on the street, and Orange/Green and other partisan tensions that led to fisticuffs. Such incidents meant that boys and young men also encountered authorities when police and the courts attempted to suppress law breaking and disorder. Evidence strongly suggests that the behaviour and encounters of Toronto boys and young men were not unusual, and this chapter is an invitation to scholars researching disorder in other localities or regions to look for the presence of boys and young men.

Moreover, boys and young men were prominent in mid-Victorian Toronto's search for order. Middle-class commentators and authorities scolded and shamed young men in ways more likely to antagonize than to quell young hotheads. Top-down attempts to contain young men's disorderly practices were subsumed within broader suppressive strategies aimed at males of all ages: the provincial state's discouragement of intimidation at the polls and its ill-fated ban on Orange processions, and the municipality's police reforms. Disorder was also brought under attack, and partly under control, by the Orangemen's campaign of self-discipline, which took special aim at the rowdiness of the Young Britons. Organized sport directed rivalries into less threatening pursuits. By contrast, authorities and reformers devised institutional responses tailored for youth reforms focused on the waifs and strays whose predicament, it was feared, made them criminals and "incipient criminals" and thus a threat to property and persons alike. Through common, ragged, and industrial schools, the provincial reformatory, and boys' homes, reformers hoped to provide the specialized institutions that would convert disorderly youths into industrious and moral contributors to the expanding city. In their approach to constructing and resolving "the boy problem," Toronto reformers explicitly drew upon and acted in concert with campaigns launched by reformers in many cities, especially London to New York.

NOTES

1 Toronto's population was about 12,000 in 1841; 30,000 in 1851; 45,000 in 1861; 56,000 in 1871; and 86,000 in 1881.
2 From its 1844 founding in Toronto, the *Globe* was the Canada West's leading voice of Reform. George Brown, its publisher and editor, was a prominent Reform politician. See, J.M.S. Careless, *Brown of the Globe*, 2 vols. (Toronto: Macmillan 1959–63).
3 Paul Craven, "Law and Ideology: The Toronto Police Court, 1850–80," in *Essays in the History of Canadian Law*, vol. 2, ed. David H. Flaherty (Toronto: Osgoode Society and the University of Toronto Press, 1983), 248–307; and William Jenkins, "Poverty and Place: Documenting and Representing Toronto's Catholic Irish, 1845–1890," in *At the Anvil: Essays in Honour of William J. Smyth*, ed. Patrick J. Duffy and William Nolan (Dublin: Geography Publications, 2014), 477–511.
4 Craig Heron, "The Boys and Their Booze: Masculinities and Public Drinking in Working-Class Hamilton, 1890–1946," *Canadian Historical Review* 86, no. 3 (September 2005): 416.
5 Women and girls in mid-Victorian Toronto behaved, and were represented, differently from men and boys. Girls and women were virtually missing from accounts of collective street violence, and girls figured much less frequently than boys in the city's crime statistics. For reformers, "girls embodied delinquency in a way boys

could not," observes Tamara Myers. "Their maturing sexuality and promise of maternity were read as harbingers of society's destiny." See Tamara Myers, *Caught: Montreal's Modern Girls and the Law, 1869–1945* (Toronto: University of Toronto Press, 2006), 7.

6 See Scott See's chapter in this volume.

7 The rebellion losses controversy pitted Conservatives against the Reform government's policy of compensating Lower Canadians whose property had been damaged (mostly by British troops) during the 1837–8 rebellions. See Ian Radforth, "Political Demonstrations and Spectacles during the Rebellion Losses Controversy in Upper Canada," *Canadian Historical Review* 92, no. 1 (March 2011): 1–41.

8 *Globe* (Toronto), 5 May 1849; *Examiner* (Toronto), 28 March 1849; *Globe*, 5 May 1849.

9 Cecil J. Houston and William J. Smyth, *The Sash Canada Wore: A Historical Geography of the Orange Order in Canada* (Toronto: University of Toronto Press 1980); and Gregory S. Kealey, "The Orange Order in Toronto: Religious Riot and the Working Class," in *Essays in Canadian Working-Class History*, ed. Gregory S. Kealey and Peter Warrian (Toronto: McClelland and Stewart 1976), 13–34.

10 *Leader* (Toronto), 16 July 1855.

11 Ibid., 18 July 1855; *Globe* (Toronto), 24 July 1855.

12 "The Circus Riot: The Investigation by the City Council," *Globe* (Toronto), 24 July 1855.

13 Gregory S. Kealey, "The Orangemen and the Corporation," in *Forging a Consensus: Historical Essays on Toronto*, ed. Victor L. Russell (Toronto: University of Toronto Press and the City of Toronto Sesquicentennial Board 1984), 42–86; Brian Clarke, "Religious Riot as Pastime: Orange Young Britons, Parades, and Public Life in Victorian Toronto," in *The Orange Order in Canada*, ed. David A. Wilson (Dublin: Four Courts Press 2007), 109–27; William J. Smyth, *Toronto, the Belfast of Canada: The Orange Order and the Shaping of Municipal Culture* (Toronto: University of Toronto Press 2015), 47–50; Michael Cottrell, "St Patrick's Day Parades in Nineteenth-Century Toronto: A Study of Immigrant Adjustment and Elite Control," *Histoire sociale / Social History* 25, no. 49 (1992): 57–73; and Rosalyn Trigger, "Irish Politics on Parade: The Clergy, National Societies, and St Patrick's Day Processions in Nineteenth-century Montreal and Toronto," *Histoire sociale / Social History* 37, no. 74 (2004): 59–99.

14 *Globe* (Toronto), 24 April 1858.

15 Ian Radforth, "Collective Rights, Liberal Discourse, and Public Order: The Clash over Catholic Processions in Mid-Victorian Toronto," *Canadian Historical Review* 95, no. 4 (December 2014): 511–44.

16 For a study of recent rioting that documents such motivations, see Laura Naegler, "The Ritual of Insurrection and the 'Thrill-Seeking Youth': An Instant Ethnography

of Inner-City Riots in Germany," in *Riot, Unrest, and Protest on the Global Stage*, ed. Paul Pritchard and Francis Pakes (Basingstoke, UK: Palgrave Macmillan, 2014), 151–69.

17 *Globe* (Toronto), 5 October 1875.

18 *Irish Canadian* (Toronto), 29 September 1875.

19 See Jerry Bannister's chapter in this volume.

20 See Bonnie Huskins's chapter in this volume.

21 Ian Radforth, "Orangemen and the Crown," in Wilson, *Orange Order in Canada*, 69–88.

22 Ian Radforth, "Playful Crowds and the 1886 Toronto Street Railway Strike," *Labour/ Le travail* 76 (Fall 2015): 133–64.

23 On play, see E. Anthony Rotundo, *American Manhood: Transformations in Masculinity from the Revolution to the Modern Era* (New York: Basic Books, 1993), 35–7; and David Nassau, *Children of the City: At Work and at Play* (Garden City, NY: Anchor Press, 1985).

24 *News* (Toronto), 27 May 1886.

25 *Globe* (Toronto), 11 October 1853.

26 Ibid., 29 May 1854.

27 Ibid., 6 February 1856; 7, 9 April and 15 June 1858; 16 November 1858; 24 May, 22 June, 15 August, and 19 September 1859; 27 April, 9 May, 18 June, and 2 October 1860; 1 April 1861.

28 Ibid., 1 August 1860 (police court charges), and 30 October 1856 (trial).

29 Ibid., 1, 2, 6, 8, 9, 12, 14, 15, 18, 19, 20, 22, 26, and 30 April 1861; 1 May 1861; 3, 4, and 9 October 1861; 2, 17, and 31 December 1861; 7, 9, and 11 January 1862.

30 Ibid., 11 March 1862.

31 *Leader* (Toronto), 3, 4, 6, 8, and 10 January 1855; Barrie Dyster, "Captain Bob and the Noble Ward: Neighbourhood and Provincial Politics in Nineteenth-Century Toronto," in Russell, *Forging a Consensus*, 98–100.

32 *Globe* (Toronto), 14 March 1855.

33 Ibid., 30 October 1858, testimony at the fall assizes.

34 Ibid., 2 July 1859, commemorating the Battle of Aughrim (1691), a significant Williamite victory in Ireland.

35 City of Toronto Archives, Reports of the Chief Constable to Toronto City Council, appended annually to City Council Minutes, 1862–75.

36 Ibid., City Council Minutes for 1860, App. XVI, p. 44, By-law No. 310.

37 Craig Heron maintains that males were not part of saloon life until their late teens; see his *Booze: A Distilled History* (Toronto: Between the Lines, 2003), 113–15.

38 *Globe* (Toronto) 27 February 1854; Jenkins discusses some similar evidence of children's gangs in "Poverty and Place," 493.

39 *Globe*, 21 December 1865.

40 Ibid., 27 December 1865.
41 Clarke, "Religious Riot as Pastime."
42 *Globe* (Toronto), 15 August 1877.
43 Ibid., 16 August 1876.
44 Ibid., 17 July 1871.
45 Ibid., 3 September 1870.
46 Jenkins, "Poverty and Place."
47 *Globe* (Toronto), 21 September 1870.
48 Ibid., 5 July 1869; *Irish Canadian* (Toronto), 7 July 1869.
49 *Globe* (Toronto), 1 January 1875.
50 Ibid., 21 September 1870.
51 See Colin Grittner's chapter in this volume.
52 George Emery, *Elections in Oxford County, 1837–1975: A Case Study of Democracy in Canada West and Early Ontario* (Toronto: University of Toronto Press 2012), 40; and Ian Radforth, "Motley Crowds and Splendid Assemblies: Press Depictions of Election Culture in Mid-Victorian Toronto," *Histoire sociale / Social History* 51, no. 103 (May 2018): 1–25.
53 Smyth, *Toronto, the Belfast of Canada*, 99.
54 Ian Radforth, "Celebrating the Suppression of the North-West Resistance of 1885: The Toronto Press and the Militia Volunteers," *Histoire sociale / Social History* 47, no. 95 (November 2014): 601–39.
55 Dennis Ryan and Kevin Wamsley, "A Grand Game of Hurling and Football: Sport and Irish Nationalism in Old Toronto," *Canadian Journal of Irish Studies* 30, no. 1 (Spring 2004): 21–31.
56 Nicholas Rogers, "Serving Toronto the Good: The Development of the City Police Force, 1834–84," in Russell, *Forging a Consensus*, 120–1.
57 http://www.petervronsky.org/crime/cph5.htm
58 City of Toronto Archives, Report of the Chief Constable for 1863, p. 9, App. to the Minutes of the Toronto City Council, 1864.
59 See, for example, *Globe* (Toronto), 14 July 1862, 18 March 1864.
60 Susan E. Houston, "The Victorian Origins of Juvenile Delinquency: A Canadian Experience," *History of Education Quarterly* 12, no. 2 (Autumn 1972): 245–80; and Bryan Hogeveen, "'The Evils with Which We Are Called to Grapple': Elite Reformers, Eugenicists, Environmental Psychologists, and the Construction of Toronto's Working-Class Boy Problem, 1860–1930," *Labour/Le travail* 55 (Spring 2005): 37–68.
61 See Dan Horner's chapter in this volume.
62 Alison Prentice, *The School Promoters: Education and Social Class in Mid-Nineteenth Century Upper Canada* (Toronto: McClelland and Stewart 1977), 133–4.

63 Susan E. Houston and Alison Prentice, *Schooling and Scholars in Nineteenth-Century Ontario* (Toronto: University of Toronto Press, 1998), 307.

64 Charlotte Neff, "The Ontario Industrial Schools Act of 1874," *Canadian Journal of Family Law* 12 (1994–5): 171–208. In 1887 the Victoria Industrial School was opened in nearby Mimico. See Paul W. Bennett, "Taming 'Bad Boys' of the 'Dangerous Class': Child Rescue and Restraint at the Victoria Industrial School, 1887–1935," *Histoire sociale / Social History* 21, no. 41 (May 1988): 71–96.

65 This work was undertaken from 1853 by the Toronto Protestant Orphans' Home. See Charlotte Neff, "The Role of Protestant Children's Homes in Nineteenth-Century Ontario: Child Rescue or Family Support?," *Journal of Family History* 34, no. 1 (January 2009): 62–5.

66 Houston, "Victorian Origins of Juvenile Delinquency."

67 *Globe* (Toronto), 20 January 1877, where Prof. Daniel Wilson paraphrases the police chief.

68 Robert M. Mennel, *Thorns and Thistles: Juvenile Delinquents in the United States, 1825–1940* (Hanover, NH: University Press of New England 1973), 53–5.

69 *Globe* (Toronto), 19 and 27 September 1859; Charlotte Neff, "Role of Protestant Children's Homes," 51. On the Toronto Girls' Home founded in 1859, and care provided earlier by the Public Nursery, see Neff, ibid. 65–8.

70 *Globe* (Toronto), 28 October 1862, Annual Meeting of the Toronto Boys' Home.

71 Province of Canada, Sessional Papers 1862, No. 19, Second Annual Report of the Board of Inspectors of Asylums, Prison, etc. 1861, Separate Report of Mr E.A. Meredeth, 17.

72 Susan Elizabeth Houston, "The Impetus to Reform: Urban Crime, Poverty, and Ignorance in Ontario, 1850–1875" (PhD diss., Ontario Institute for Studies in Education, 1974), 395–6.

73 Neff, "Role of the Protestant Children's Home," 72–4.

74 Ibid., 76; Houston, "Impetus to Reform," 298–9.

75 Houston, "Impetus to Reform," 299.

76 Neff, "Role of the Protestant Children's Homes"; and Charlotte Neff, "Government Approaches to Child Neglect and Mistreatment in Nineteenth-Century Ontario," *Histoire sociale / Social History* 41, no. 81 (2008): 165–214.

77 On the Newsboys Lodging House in New York established in 1854, see David E. Whisnant, "Selling the Gospel News, or: the Strange Career of Jimmy Brown the Newsboy," *Journal of Social History* 5, no. 3 (Spring 1972): 269–309.

78 Brian Clarke, *Piety and Nationalism: Lay Voluntary Associations and the Creation of an Irish Catholic Community in Toronto, 1850–1895* (Montreal and Kingston: McGill-Queen's University Press, 1993).

79 *Globe* (Toronto), 24 October 1868.

80 Elizabeth Hulse, "'A Long and Happy Life': Daniel Wilson with Family and Friends," in *Thinking with Both Hands: Sir Daniel Wilson in the Old World and the New*, ed. Marinell Ash (Toronto: University of Toronto Press 1999), 262–3.

81 *Globe* (Toronto), 18 April 1873, Report of Annual Meeting, News-Boys Home.

82 On the self-fashioning of street children, see Thomas J. Gilfoyle, "Street-Rats and Gutter-Snipes: Child Pickpockets and Street Culture in New York City, 1850–1900," *Journal of Social History* 37, no. 4 (Summer 2004): 853–62; and Heather Shore, "Cross Coves, Buzzers, and General Sorts of Prigs: Juvenile Crime and the Criminal 'Underworld' in the Early Nineteenth Century," *British Journal of Criminology* 39, no. 1 (1999): 10–24.

16 "To Muse within These Peaceful Portals": Urban Space, Public Order, and the Makings of Montreal's Viger Square, 1818–1870

DAN HORNER

On 14 July 1818, Périne-Charles Cherrier, the widow of artisan and politician Denis Viger, made her way to the Montreal office of notary Thomas Bedouin. The daughter of a prominent commercial family, Cherrier was tying together some loose ends of her family's estate. As a result of her connections to two of Lower Canada's elite Canadien families – the Cherriers and the Papineaus[1] – she held the title to a parcel of properties on the city's northeastern periphery. The seventy-two-year-old widow had decided to donate the land, which measured eighty feet by three hundred feet, to the city. She did so, however, with a very specific stipulation: that the land be used as a market and as a space set aside for the common good.[2] Cherrier's donation is intriguing on a number of levels. First, it anticipated the continued expansion of Montreal. In the muggy summer months of 1818, the property she was donating consisted largely of marshland. As one observer recalled later in the century, "Viger Gardens was a swamp, and from this swamp a sluggish creek or ditch ran south-westerly ... Over its banks was thrown all the filth and refuse of the city, to be washed away once a year by the spring freshets."[3] Her insistence that this parcel of land would one day serve as a bustling marketplace and community hub rested on the ultimately correct prediction that the acceleration of migratory patterns that had been fuelling a steady increase in the city's population since the end of the Napoleonic Wars would continue to push settlement in Montreal northwards.

The donation also offers a glimpse into Cherrier's social and cultural vision. It suggests an engagement in a larger project of creating an orderly urban landscape. This undertaking encompassed reforms on several levels. It consisted of the management of the urban environment: the construction of a bridge across the Petite-Rivière and the draining of the marshes that sat on the land. It was also about the organization of effective and orderly urban social relations.

Marketplaces were conceptualized by local elites as nodes of governance, where commercial exchanges and the distribution of provisions could be regulated and monitored.[4] Providing this sort of public space to the residents of a rapidly growing suburb ought to be interpreted as an effort to cultivate social order on what was then the urban periphery. Spaces like this were closely connected in the public imagination to the democratic experiment.[5] They were a place where citizens could gather on equal terms not only for the purpose of commercial exchange, but also for sharing news and participating in public events and celebrations. The square would, in other words, serve as a locus of community formation.

While Cherrier might have been anticipating the way that Montreal would grow in the coming decade or two, the more distant future existed beyond the realm of imagination. Unbeknownst to her, the land donated during the summer of 1818 would become central to the project of creating an orderly Montreal for centuries to come. Périne-Charles Cherrier's vision of a bustling marketplace on the urban periphery was just the first in a succession of ideas about how a few hundred square feet of land could be used to foster public order. This chapter traces the evolution of this space across the nineteenth century, as its physical form was reimagined, redesigned, and rebuilt. Doing so provides an opportunity to reflect on shifting approaches to the broader civic project of making an orderly city. It also helps trace the evolution of the public as a dynamic concept. While Cherrier might have connected public order to a carefully regulated marketplace, the elites governing the city in the second half of the nineteenth century reconsidered this space as something that could be designed to more explicitly cultivate the manners and behaviours of the city's burgeoning working class. This shifting strategy demonstrates that, in the half century that separated the donation of the land to the magistrates charged with governing Montreal and its redesign as a lush Victorian pleasure garden by the municipal government in the 1860s, the city's civic elites had rethought issues around public order, the urban landscape, and social relations in some meaningful ways. It was through modest civic projects such as the management of this land that civic elites were able to communicate their vision of a modern, orderly society. This overarching concern about public order did not form in a vacuum. It was cultivated by broader debates and discussions about civic governance and authority, which are addressed throughout this collection of essays. The spectre of resistance and unrest was never far removed from the imagination of the often-anonymous civic officials charged with the task of remaking this parcel of land over the course of the nineteenth century.

While on paper the donation of the land was treated as a routine transaction, it must be interpreted as a political act, made in the context of the emergence of an engaged Canadien political elite that was slowly coalescing around the Parti canadien, the faction that represented the interests of Lower Canada's French-speaking community in the Legislative Assembly.[6] Sectarian and linguistic tension loomed over public life in the city. While the movement for democratic reform that would play such a significant role in fuelling the outbreak of political insurrection in the 1830s remained in its infancy, the vigourous strain of British chauvinism that had been reinvigorated by the conclusion of the Napoleonic Wars was the cause of a growing tension between Montreal's two major ethnic communities by 1818.[7] It is worth speculating that Cherrier was being mindful of her family's standing in the city's social, cultural, and political elite. Although her late husband was an artisan who won a seat in Lower Canada's Legislative Assembly late in life, the Cherrier family had moved in elite circles since the French regime, and the success of the family's next generation – with son Denis-Benjamin Viger and nephew Jacques Viger each becoming prominent figures in colonial public life – suggests that they possessed an aspirational streak. In the documents pertaining to her donation and the subsequent meeting of local officials to discuss her terms, there is no mention of the decision to bestow the name of her husband's family on the property, but it was immediately acknowledged in official documents as Viger Square.[8] In a city where the growing number of parks and squares frequently bore the name of British colonial officials and members of the royal family, having this public space named in honour of a Canadien family must have felt like a coup for Cherrier and the entire Canadien community.

A desire to foster public order was not unique to Périne-Charles Cherrier. The connections that she was drawing between public order and the common good were shaped by ideas that had been circulating across the Atlantic world since the Enlightenment. These discussions connected a group of reform-oriented elites that stretched across the city's deeply contested partisan and sectarian divides. This reform impulse was also intergenerational. The project of creating an orderly urban landscape and public culture would consume politically engaged elite Montrealers for the first two thirds of the nineteenth century. It was a disparate project, and many were engaged in only a single manifestation of it. At its core, however, was the notion that the disorderly impact of the social change being fuelled by mass migration, urbanization, and, eventually, industrialization could be effectively and liberally managed to foster a genteel and orderly social order. This project encompassed institutional responses, such as the expansion of popular schooling and the reform of policing, social responses like the temperance movement, and innovative ideas in the realm of governing urban space. It connected urban elites from across the North Atlantic world who shared and debated ideas through the emergence of a dynamic public sphere of meetings, lecture tours, and newspapers and other print publications that constructed the physical and social landscape of the city as something that could be effectively reformed.[9] Ultimately, their vision was about harnessing the authority and power that they had at their disposal to foster their vision of how an orderly modern society ought to look and function. No matter the portal through which they engaged with this diffuse project, the unruly and violent crowd became the primary embodiment of everything that was out of step with this vision.

These reforming projects were, however, contentious. The popular classes and the kind of unruly behaviour that was associated with them were typically the target of these reforms. Montreal's poor frequently resisted these measures, occasionally in explicit ways but more often than not by quietly – or, as other chapters make clear, not so quietly – refusing to abandon the sorts of practices that they had long used to navigate the material and cultural challenges of urban life. These forms of resistance included alcohol-fuelled revelry, the raucous practices of street vendors and hucksters, and the employment of unruly and confrontational political practices on the city's streets. Tensions over the use of urban space were in keeping with broader conflicts between the popular classes and politically engaged elites.[10]

Cherrier donated her land before Montreal had a municipal government. In 1818, the city was governed by a group of justices of the peace charged with the task by the colonial authorities.[11] When presented with her donation, they quickly organized a special session to discuss the logistics of the transaction.[12] After all, the land had come with strings attached that entailed an outlay of public finances to improve the land and to establish a public market. A study revealed that meeting these conditions would cost the colonial government an estimated £350. Cherrier, her sister Rosalie, and her nephew Louis-Joseph Papineau, were in attendance when the inspector of roads presented the justices of the peace with the official plan to turn the land into a functioning market at a meeting held later that summer.[13]

There was little mention of the Viger donation in the public record for the next twenty years. The stream that flowed through the property was filled in by 1825, as a neighbourhood emerged in the area that had been orchards and marshland when the donation was made. The land became the property of the municipal government when it was established in 1832, with Cherrier's nephew Jacques Viger serving as the first mayor. After the municipal government was re-established in the aftermath of the rebellions, one of its first actions was to oversee the expansion and modernization of the market, which now stood at the heart of a bustling and largely Canadien suburb in the city's east end. A bylaw was tabled, debated, and passed by the municipal government at the end of 1840 that solidified plans for the construction of a pound and cattle market on what was now being referred to in official documents as Place Viger.[14] The law reconsidered the scope of activity taking place on the square. While it appears to have been used very broadly as a public market, with vendors selling a variety of wares to residents, the bylaw proposed converting it exclusively into a site for the exchange of hay and cattle. Funds were set aside for the construction of a pound "for the purpose of shutting up and impounding therein all horses, horned cattle, sheep, goats and hogs found straying on or damaging the property of any person or straying on the beaches, highways, or public grounds within the city limits." The bylaw also earmarked money to hire "a fit and proper person" appointed by council to oversee the operation of this pound.[15]

Twenty-two years after the land was donated to the city, it was clearly still being used to foster public order. The wording of the law suggests that stray animals remained a problem in this ramshackle neighbourhood on the urban fringe.[16] The construction of a pound was introduced as an orderly solution to this problem. Furthermore, section 8 of the bylaw implemented a ban on the sale of cattle in the city's markets, with Place Viger being the only exception to this rule.[17] This suggests an attempt on the part of the municipal government to consolidate the exchange of cattle into single location that would be made particularly well equipped to deal with the logistics of this trade. The rest of the bylaw laid out the costs of renting stands in the market and the penalties for disobeying a variety of other provisions for selling goods in Place Viger, again pointing to the role that markets played in rapidly growing cities like mid-nineteenth-century Montreal. This rethinking of Viger Square occurred at a moment when civic elites were harnessing the newly expanded powers available to them through municipal government to foster their vision of an orderly city.[18] Setting aside a space like Viger Square as a site where some of the messier and more disorderly aspects of urban life could be contained and managed demonstrates their strategies around this civic project. They were motivated by an audacious vision of the sort of city that their reforms could foster, where disorderly barriers to circulation and gentility could be subdued through effective legislation, thereby creating an urban landscape that reflected their idealized notions of modernity.[19] Public projects, even this relatively minor retooling of Place Viger, were part of a larger effort to streamline the way that commodities and people circulated through the city. They created a node of governance that would tame the elements of the urban landscape that struck civic elites as problematic and out of step with modernity.[20] Such actions need to be interpreted as part of the process in which local elites used the civil powers at their disposal to foster an orderly public culture, a process that can be seen in other essays throughout this collection.

The construction of a permanent structure to house the cattle market on Viger Square helped reinforce its status as a community hub. The Agricultural Society of Lower Canada began hosting exhibitions in the square in the mid-1840s. These events drew crowds into the square to observe the latest advancements being made in animal husbandry. "The show of stock was numerous," read one review of the 1848 exhibition, "and several fine animals were on the ground, though intermixed with very inferior ones ... Several good horses and brood mares were shown, but we regret to see that the stallions exhibited do not appear to be of pure Canadian breed."[21] Public events of this nature were fitting for the city's cattle market; they were infused with the language of improvement and national accomplishment that were very much in keeping with these larger discussions of public order.[22] They also marked a shift, however, in how spaces like Viger Square were used. On the one hand, they remained places of open sociability. On the other hand, these sorts of exhibitions were pushing people who frequented the square towards a particular kind of sociability. While we cannot gauge how people reacted to these exhibits, or behaved while in attendance, the public became an audience for discussions of improvement.

The hope that Place Viger could remain something of an oasis of effective governance and regulation in a tumultuous and rapidly growing neighbourhood began to fray at mid-century. The 1840s were a tumultuous period in the city, with repeated outbreaks of sectarian popular violence that cast a long shadow over public life.[23] The decade was marked by a series of high-profile election riots, as described in greater detail in Colin Grittner's contribution to this collection. Debates over the parameters of democratic reform provided the spark for this conflict, but it was rooted in deeper tensions between the city's Canadien community and the British Protestant community.[24] Both of the leading political factions employed violence as a political strategy, surreptitiously encouraging their brawniest supporters to take to the streets during elections for seats in the Legislative Assembly and municipal council to intimidate and harass voters attempting to make their way to the polling station to record their votes. Outbreaks of collective violence frequently ensued from these confrontations. These riots were not sporadic outbursts separated by periods of sustained public order. Rather, they occurred against the backdrop of a contentious urban popular culture where violence was interwoven into the fabric of daily life. They were only the most visible and newsworthy manifestations of a raucous popular culture that was rooted in the streets and other public spaces of the city. Pivotal works in the history of unruly urban crowds situate this boisterous popular culture on the streets, but open spaces like Viger Square, integrated into the quotidian rhythms of urban life, were equally vital sites of cultural formation.[25]

As an open and easily accessible public space where local residents were accustomed to gathering in order to socialize, it is not surprising that Viger Square became the site of some of these tumultuous confrontations.[26] In April 1844, for example, during a parliamentary election, supporters of Tory candidate William Molson and Reform candidate Lewis Drummond clashed at numerous locations across the city. While a confrontation near Haymarket Square attracted a great deal of attention after twenty-eight-year-old Julien Champeau was stabbed by a soldier's bayonet and later succumbed to his injuries, one of the most prolonged riots occurred in Viger Square.[27] The fighting between supporters of Molson and Drummond grew so bloody that troops were called in.[28] It took several hours for peace to be restored. The newspapers interpreted this violence through a decidedly partisan lens, with both sides accusing the other of engaging in unrestrained violence that threatened to end in the loss of life.[29] Popular violence played a pivotal role in the shaping of elite identities during this period. In both the Canadien and English-speaking communities, civic leaders began to define themselves, their political endeavours, and their public identities in contrast to the city's fractious popular political culture.[30] They conceptualized this definition as a fundamentally spatial issue and threw their support behind projects to police violent popular behaviour, which included everything from demanding greater regulations of taverns to lobbying for the adoption of election by secret ballot. Such measures demonstrated their determination to create a city where encounters with this raucous culture could be eliminated from their daily experience. The cultural formation of elites in Montreal, as was the case in other urban communities, was increasingly shaped by anxiety that they were at risk of losing control of the streets and institutions of their city.

Riots such as the one that broke out on Viger Square during the 1844 election were clearly not something that Périne-Charles Cherrier had anticipated when she donated her family's property. The generation of urban elites that succeeded her, and who were wielding the authority provided to them through the municipal government in the 1840s, grew increasingly preoccupied with the problems of violence and disorder, and increasingly anxious about efforts to foster public order with the powers at their disposal. A mere glance at newspapers of this period illuminates this point: both the French and English press frequently printed stories about collective violence, not just at home but in cities across the world.[31] Concerns about social disorder, violence, and unrest fuelled a dynamic public sphere, where elites from across the North Atlantic world shared and debated ideas about how they could most effectively address the threat posed by the popular classes. Local elites who were engaged in the cultural and political process of creating an orderly and prosperous city saw the persistence of various manifestations of the raucous popular culture as the greatest impediment to their aspirations. The increasing attention devoted to concerns about popular violence and unrest in the local press was more indicative of a diminishing tolerance for such practices than it was an actual increase in violent incidents, a tendency that we see in numerous different contexts throughout this collection of essays.

The behaviour that troubled the reform-oriented urban elites was, in their minds, rooted in a problematic landscape. Montreal, like many cities across the North Atlantic world during this period, was growing at an unprecedented rate. The process of urbanization, which is often associated with industrialization, but, in the case of Montreal, preceded it by more than a decade, had wreaked havoc on the city. Neighbourhoods like the Quebec suburb where Viger Square was located had grown in an unchecked and virtually unregulated fashion. The growth in population and density was increasingly linked to disease in both the popular imagination and medical research. The bustling urban landscape that Périne-Charles Cherrier had hoped to bring order to with her donation was, with its stubbornly high infant mortality rates and repeated outbreaks of epidemic disease, an exceptionally challenging space to govern.[32] Attempts to impose greater sanitary measures in the city, and to isolate people suffering from communicable diseases, despite being vigorously endorsed in the public sphere, met with both subtle and explicit forms of resistance.[33] Disease was also associated with the accelerated scale of migration into the city, particularly from Ireland and the British Isles.[34] This was a process where regulation had largely been left to private interests, with minimal state oversight. As thousands of migrants began passing through the docks in Montreal each summer, however, the public began demanding that authorities provide them with more protection. Contentious public meetings and scathing letters published in the local press demonstrate that a vocal and politically engaged segment of the community was profoundly dissatisfied with the apparent inability of the local authorities to respond to these crises in public health, despite overwhelming evidence in support of a forceful intervention.[35]

This precarious or diminishing confidence in the institutions that were meant to protect public order was pervasive. The police, who were meant to play a critical role in the maintenance of public order in the city, frequently struggled to accomplish this task, thus becoming another example of what many reform-oriented elites considered to be institutional incompetence in the city. When faced with brawls spilling out of taverns, grog shops, and brothels, in addition to the sorts of large-scale outbursts of collective violence that occurred during elections, police frequently found themselves outnumbered and forced to retreat. Even when the police did manage to arrest suspects for engaging in disorderly actions, the accused were often rescued from custody by their peers. The records of the lower courts and Montreal's Police Commission reveal regular occurrences of violent attacks on police officers.[36] Evidence clearly indicates that the police force suffered from its relatively modest size and its funding, which could rise and fall based on economic conditions and the public's demands for greater protection. During the most serious outbreaks of violence on the city's streets, local officials had the option of calling in the troops stationed at the garrison in the city's east end. Doing so posed a considerable risk, however. The troops, who were trained to deal with large-scale cases of political insurrection, and whose experience in such cases was rooted in past encounters in other outposts of the British Empire, were accustomed to dealing with violent crowds primarily by firing their muskets into them.[37] Military officials became increasingly adamant that their troops needed to be extricated from the tumultuous popular unrest of the urban environment. Thus, the assumption that restrained liberal urban governance could foster an orderly urban community seemed to be becoming less tenable with each passing year. The methods used by civic elites of Périne-Charles Cherrier's generation to foster public order appeared insufficient in the face of the crises of the mid-nineteenth century.

With these twin concerns over public health and sectarian conflict, the notion that the urban environment was inherently disorderly gained traction during the middle decades of the nineteenth century.[38] Popular unrest and disease became inextricably linked in the public discourse to the city's narrow and dark streets. The reform-oriented segment of the urban elite, whose politically engaged ranks crossed the city's linguistic and sectarian divides, became determined to remake the city by improving lighting, widening streets, and planting trees along sidewalks.[39] This agenda was not crafted on aesthetic grounds alone. Reformers believed that such measures would have a pedagogical impact. The popular classes that had crowded into cities across the North Atlantic world in increasing numbers would change their behaviours and cultural practices when placed in this uplifting and rational environment. Broad, well-lit streets would provide fewer opportunities for a wide range of disorderly activities that included petty theft, prostitution, and drunken revelry to elude the gaze of police officers. This effort to reform the urban landscape as a means of transforming the most troubling aspect of a raucous popular culture was an undertaking that was profoundly modern and liberal. It was built around the notion that individuals could be gently nudged towards improvement. It revealed a connection in the social imaginary of local elites between rationality and legitimate cultural and political authority. This perspective, which was rooted in the Enlightenment, would shape social relations along the lines of class, gender, and race deep into the twentieth century.

This notion that the city's popular classes could be disciplined and reformed through landscape architecture reflected an important shift in how the governing elites of Montreal conceptualized the public.[40] In 1818, the social vision of Périne-Charles Cherrier and her family appears to have been shaped by the notion that an orderly urban society could be produced with minimal intervention. It was, fundamentally, an expression of confidence in the processes of liberal urban governance. Challenges such as social conflict, migration, disorderly activity, and economic uncertainty could be effectively managed. While this elite social vision was deeply hierarchical, it assumed that, no matter their ethnic or class background, the residents of Montreal could be moulded into orderly citizens. Ensuing social crises, however, had diminished this confidence, and the generation of civic elites who were wielding authority in the second half of the nineteenth century began to explore more coercive means of shaping popular behaviour. The impact of this shift was keenly felt on Place Viger.

By the end of the 1850s, civic leaders had transformed Place Viger into Viger Gardens, a greenspace with sumptuous vegetation and winding pathways designed to encourage restrained sociability and quiet contemplation. It was not an exclusive space. The city's industrial working class from the surrounding neighbourhoods were welcomed to pass through its gates and spend their leisure hours there. Nonetheless, it marked a notable shift in the relationship between the city's elites and the popular classes. Viger Gardens reflected a new approach to urban design that was based on the audacious assumption that the rowdy culture of the urban popular classes could be reformed to more closely resemble the genteel ideals of urbane elites. Open, expansive spaces like what had taken root on the land donated by Périne-Charles Cherrier could simply be remade to suit the cultural practices of the popular classes for their own needs, whereas the gardens would gently but forcefully foster a new kind of sociability.[41] This idea was rooted in a broader concern about the disorderly way in which the popular classes used the streets, and reflected an increasing social segregation in the city defined by wealth and privilege.[42]

The redesign of Viger Square was sporadic. It began in the middle of the 1840s and unfolded over the following two decades. Its status as a public market was not immediately extinguished, but this role as a well-regulated community hub was figuratively and literally pushed to the periphery. The transformation began when a parcel of land was donated to the city by the Lacroix family on the eastern border of the square, which could then be extended beyond St Hubert Street. The Lacroix donation came with some stringent conditions. It could not be used simply to expand the existing market on Place Viger. Instead, it was to be set aside as a green space, the focal point of which would be a fountain commemorating the contributions the late Hubert-Joseph Lacroix had made to public life in Lower Canada.[43] Much as Cherrier had two and a half decades earlier, the Lacroix family was bequeathing their property to the public good as an opportunity to weave their family's story into the city's landscape. The land the Lacroix family donated, however, implicitly demanded a different sort of relationship between the public and the space. Unlike the bustling marketplace made possible by the Cherrier donation, the Lacroix land was intended as a place of quiet contemplation, where the attention of passersby would be drawn towards the commemoration of a wealthy local family and their contributions to civic and colonial life. This final parcel of land that expanded the perimeter of Viger Square helped transform the square from a boisterous community hub to a space geared towards the sort of recreation favoured by urban elites.

Other events helped nudge this transformation forward. In 1852, a devastating fire swept through the east end of Montreal. The ramshackle suburban neighbourhood that surrounded the square, where the majority of homes were wooden, was nearly flattened by the blaze.[44] The fire had long-term consequences.[45] The bustling popular suburb would not be rebuilt. Instead, property in the streets adjoining the square was snapped up by wealthier families, predominantly of Canadien descent.[46] They built solid stone townhomes in what became a suburban enclave a short distance away from Montreal's bustling commercial centre. In the second half of the nineteenth century, and for the first decades of the twentieth century, the streets adjoining Viger Square would be among the most respectable addresses in the city, with both Catholic and Anglican cathedrals being built in close proximity to it.[47] The transformation of the square from a bustling market to a serene garden thus reflected the changing demographics of the neighbourhood, though it is important to note that it remained within walking distance of predominately working-class districts.

The remaking of Viger Square accelerated at the end of the 1850s, when the market was removed to the square's periphery to make room for fountains and gardens. In 1863, city council approved plans to build a greenhouse modelled on London's Crystal Palace, the site of the Great Exhibition of 1851. In some ways, this was in keeping with the agricultural exhibitions that had been held on the square when it was exclusively a market. The events that were held in the greenhouses, however, appear to have been of a more genteel quality, such as exhibits of plant life from the southern hemisphere. Officially renamed Viger Gardens in 1867, the square was now a resolutely elite space in one of the city's finest neighbourhoods. The market was pushed to the southeastern corner of the square during these renovations and would gradually be dismantled before being shuttered for good in 1892.[48] Events held in the gardens suggest an effort to cultivate a bourgeois sensibility. Montrealers flocked to the gardens to hear the Rifle Brigade Fanfare perform twice weekly concerts, and special events were marked with dramatic illuminations conducted by a Mr M. Globbenski.[49]

16.1 Engraving of the St Jean Baptiste celebrations in Viger Gardens, 1874. Source: *L'Opinion publique*, 2 July 1874.

Evidence suggests that, even before the École des hautes études commerciale opened its doors at the north end of the square in 1910, the area had become particularly popular with young men and women from the city's dynamic Canadien bourgeoisie. *Le Perroquet*, a short-lived literary journal published in Montreal in the middle of the 1860s, made frequent mention in its editorials of pleasurable afternoons and evenings spent relaxing in Viger Gardens. The gardens were, for several years, the site where the annual St Jean Baptiste Day parade drew to a close, and spectators would gather to hear inspiring speeches about the state of the Canadien nation.[50]

Courtship appears to have been integral to the Viger Gardens experience. A story published in *Le Perroquet* spoke of being so besotted by the sight of young women promenading through the square that a young man had no choice but to leap into the cold waters of the fountain in order to steady his nerves.[51] Other acts of youthful frivolity took place in the gardens and were reported on in the local press. During the summer of 1868, a rambunctious crowd of boys picked up a seal that had been found aboard a ship docked in Montreal harbour. Placing the creature on a cart, the boys wheeled him "Diogenes-like" through the city until they reached the gardens, where he was dumped into the fountain "where an admiring crowd soon collected, while he condescended to float with his nose and the tip of his back just above the water."[52] This particular scene, and others like it, demonstrated that, in the face of a more carefully engineered style of urban public space, Montrealers continued to negotiate opportunities for the sorts of rambunctious social interaction that was outside the official vision of how people ought to behave in Viger Gardens. Nevertheless, evidence suggests that the redesign of the space was successful in removing violent confrontations from its midst.

The press portrayed Viger Gardens as a welcome retreat from the bustle of the city, especially during the summer months. "Fortunately," read a report in the *Canadian Illustrated News,* "there is a cool retreat in the east-end of the city whither one may repair ... to enjoy the air and escape from the heated flag stones and the close atmosphere of the streets ... The Viger Gardens ... are a great boon to the citizens, and one need only go there any evening when the band plays to see how they are appreciated."[53] A long-time observer of the city's urban landscape remarked on the square's dramatic transfromation. Noting that it had once been little more than a dirty, muddy swamp, it had become "un centre d'attraction et de plaisir, un veritable petit paradis terrestre ou la nature étale ce qu'elle a de plus joli, de plus agréeable."[54] The gardens even inspired at least one poet to take up his pen. George Martin's "Viger Square" was published in 1864. Martin celebrated the restorative and calming qualities of the space: "All these [odorous flowers], and more, with beauty clad / Invite the City's weary mortals / The Pale-Faced Maid, the widow sad / And sinking merchant, going mad / To muse within these peaceful portals."[55] The poem alludes to the way in which these sorts of spaces could elevate individuals, in this case from sadness and poverty, but also, presumably, from a wide array of disorderly and raucous pursuits.

The apparent subtext to these sorts of celebrations of Viger Gardens was that it demonstrated the mastery of the Montreal elite over their urban surroundings. First, they had mastered the physical environment, which they drained and landscaped to suit their aesthetics and needs. Second, they had, in this contained and manufactured setting, demonstrated their ability to subdue the disorderly popular culture that had, in the 1830s and 1840s, all but defined social relations in the city. When crowds of Montrealers poured into Viger Gardens, it was not to engage in rough political pageantry and collective violence, but to while away a summer's evening to the strains of orchestral music and the excitement of genteel flirtation. All of this was part of civil government's larger project of crafting public order.

When journalists and other observers wrote about Viger Gardens in the 1860s and 1870s, they focused their attention on its beauty and serenity, drawing an obvious contrast with the bustling city that surrounded the space. In Viger Gardens, elite notions about landscape and sociability could be presented to a city that had become a complicated industrial metropolis. This is not to say that civic leaders could permanently sweep away concerns about disorder and popular unrest simply by building a lush garden with winding paths. Evidence suggests that the gardens were stringently policed. Pickpockets were arrested, drunkards hauled into custody, and fistfights broken up. Indeed, we must acknowledge silences in the archival record that obscure how the gardens might have been co-opted and used in ways that would signal the explicit and subtle resistance of the popular classes.

Using parks and other green spaces to communicate an elite social vision was a global phenomenon in the second half of the nineteenth century. In the midst of the tensions that coursed through urban life, like ethnic strife, emerging conflicts between labour and capital, and the dangers of unchecked urban development, spaces designed by prominent landscape architects such as Frederick Law Olmstead were infused with a pastoral vision that afforded little room for the rough cultural pursuits of the popular classes.[56] These spaces must be read in the context of broader efforts to transform the popular culture of the city that also included improving access to education and a calendar filled with national celebrations and pageantry. These were responses shaped by the realization that the heterogeneous residents of tumultuous cities could not be moulded into orderly and loyal citizens by policing alone. Parks could play a pedagogical role. What Montreal's civic leaders attempted to achieve with this elaborate redesign of the square was to provide a space that would communicate a sense of order to residents of a challenging environment. The design of Viger Gardens, with its focus on rational leisure and self-improvement, spoke volumes about how public order as a civic project had changed since 1818. It reflected an approach to social relations on the part of the elite that was more conscious of the city's social hierarchies, and more coercive when it came to pushing the city's popular classes to adopt the cultural practices of the elite. While civic officials and public commentators did not frame the park's transformation in these terms, the impact of the crises that had challenged the project of urban governance in the intervening decades – epidemic disease, collective violence, and the discordant daily rhythms of an unruly popular culture – left an important footprint on the design of spaces like Viger Gardens.

16.2 Viger Square, about 1907. Source: MP-0000.840.6 | *Print* | *Neurdein Frères* | © McCord Museum.

Public spaces are, by their very nature, dynamic.[57] They are used, conceptualized, and transformed by a myriad of factors: economic restructuring, cultural and ideological shifts, and demographic realities. They are also inextricably linked to changes that occur in the communities where they are physically and socially implanted. For the better part of fifty years, Viger Gardens stood as the crown jewel of a largely Canadien bourgeois neighbourhood. The design and the culture of the space began yet another transformation in the first two decades of the twentieth century. The most obvious factor at play was the evolution of the city's transportation infrastructure. Improvements to the city's streetcar network allowed the bourgeois families who had once resided adjacent to Viger Square to move even farther afield from the city's commercial centre, taking up residence to the east and north, where they could afford new and larger homes in elite gardens suburbs like Outremont. This touched off a decline in the prosperity and reputation of the genteel streets surrounding the gardens. Many of the residences of departing elites were purchased by speculators and converted into boarding houses and apartments. By the 1920s, the streets surrounding Viger Gardens were no longer addresses that communicated stability, power, and comfort.[58]

The municipal government, meanwhile, made no effort to maintain the square in the midst of the neighbourhood's decline. In fairly short order, its defining landmarks, including the ornamental fountain financed by the Lacroix family and the greenhouses unveiled with such pomp in the 1860s, were dismantled and moved to parks in the newer suburban areas where the area's affluent families were migrating. The fountain was transplanted to Carré St Louis, a park farther north along Rue St Denis, and the greenhouses to Parc Lafontaine, a massive new green space that rolled northwards from Sherbrooke Street in the city's east end. Stripped of its main attractions and elite neighbours, Viger Gardens declined precipitously. By the second half of the twentieth century, the gardens and the surrounding streets had entered the crosshairs of audacious urban reformers. It was once identified as a possible location for a multi-story parking garage, though these plans never came to fruition. The gardens were torn up and tunnelled under as the city aimed to present a modern vision to the world with Expo 67. Suburban commuters now sped under the square on a newly constructed expressway. The site was turned over to internationally acclaimed artist Charles Daudelin, who designed a concrete agora that was meant to be a boldly modernist take on the Victorian pleasure garden.[59] In what had become a troubled neighbourhood marked by itinerancy and poverty, the descendants of the genteel Montrealers who had flocked to Viger Gardens steered clear of its latest incarnation. It soon gained a reputation as a refuge for some of the city's marginalized and vulnerable homeless community. No longer designed as a space that could foster public order, the square became the embodiment of the twentieth-century city's most pressing maladies.

The urban landscape, however, is always a work in progress. Recent years have seen a return of the city's elites to the area surrounding the square. A residential construction boom in Old Montreal began in the final decade of the twentieth century. The construction of a state-of-the-art teaching hospital directly to the west of the square in recent years has further accelerated this process. In 2016 the municipal government announced plans for the next remaking of Viger Square. The area's well-heeled residents demanded a more comfortable and fitting place to while away their lunch hours and summer evenings. The plans promise more green space and gently bypass questions of what will happen to the vulnerable people who have been using this space as their own for decades. The entire project resonates with both continuity and change. It is a reworking as significant as that which occurred in the nineteenth century, when a bustling market became a lush garden. Simultaneously, it demonstrates how public space and the urban landscape remain a powerful tool in the hands of civic elites who seek to impose their vision of order on the city.

Civic officials in the present day, however, appear to be grappling with the same questions that resounded in the middle of the nineteenth century. How do you design a public space that will simultaneously welcome urban elites and nudge people characterized as disorderly towards altering their cultural practices? The answers to this question are as numerous as they are complex; they defined the civic project for much of the nineteenth century.[60] They often involved legal and regulatory reforms and changes to the practice of policing. This examination of Viger Square demonstrates that the design of public spaces plays a crucial role in this civic project. Reflecting on the spatial aspects of the project also reveals its dynamism. Elites did not approach the issue of public order through the same lens in the 1820s as they did in the 1860s. Persistent challenges to the project of making orderly cities pushed them to rethink the parameters of urban governance. The transformation of Viger Square from a public market to a pleasure garden was indicative of the growing division of Montreal society along the lines of class, with elites growing more determined to forcefully communicate their vision of the social order to the work classes. While the design and regulation of public space was an integral part of how elites wielded authority in cities like Montreal, their approach to this project changed significantly. Recent debates over the upcoming redesign of Viger Square demonstrate how conflicts over public order and urban space continue to challenge civic officials in the twenty-first century. The project of fostering order through remaking public spaces like Viger Square has left an indelible mark on Montreal's urban landscape. Perhaps, in the near future, Montrealers will once again stroll through a public space that was conceived of and designed in a way that encourages people to engage in a specific set of activities that civic elites understand to be orderly. In doing so, they will be engaging in a process that has been unfolding since Périne-Charles Cherrier made her donation on that summer day in 1818.

NOTES

1 Périne-Charles Cherrier was born in 1746 at Longueil. She was the daughter of merchant François-Pierre Cherrier and Marie Dubuc. She married Denis Viger, with whom she had a son, Denis-Benjamin, in 1774. She was the aunt of Jacques Viger, and had a sibling who married into the Papineau family.
2 Archives de Montréal (hereafter AVM), VM3-1-05, Fonds Juges de Paix de Montréal, 8 August 1818.
3 John Borthwick, *History and Biographical Gazetteer of Montreal to the Year 1892* (Montreal: Lovell, 1897), 50. For more on what is referred to as the Petite Rivière, see Michèle Dagenais and Caroline Durand, "Cleansing, Draining, and Sanitizing the City: Conceptions and Uses of Water in the Montreal Region," *Canadian Historical Review* 87, no. 4 (December 2006): 621–51.

4 For more on the role of markets in nineteenth-century urban communities, see Jens Toftgaard, "Marketplaces and Central Spaces: Markets and the Rise of Competing Spacing Ideals in Danish City Centres, c. 1850–1900," *Urban History* 43, no. 3 (June 2015): 1–19, and Sean Kheraj, "Living and Working with Domestic Animals in Nineteenth-Century Toronto," in *Urban Explorations: Environmental Histories of the Toronto Region*, ed. Anders Sandberg, Stephen Bocking, Colin Coates, and Ken Cruikshank (Hamilton, ON: Wilson Institute for Canadian History, 2013), 120–40.

5 See Sara Evans and Henry Boyte, *Free Spaces: The Sources of Democratic Change in America* (Chicago: University of Chicago Press, 1986).

6 Yvan Lamonde, *Histoire sociale des idées au Québec* (Montreal: Fides, 2000), ch. 3.

7 Such sentiments had periodically bubbled to the surface of public life in Montreal since the Conquest. For more on this at the turn of the nineteenth century, see F. Murray Greenwood, *Legacies of Fear: Law and Politics in Quebec in the Era of the French Revolution* (Toronto: University of Toronto Press, 1993).

8 AVM, VM3-1-05, Fonds Juges de Paix de Montréal, 8 August 1818; 15 August 1818.

9 Craig Calhoun, "Civil Society and the Public Sphere," in *The Oxford Handbook of Civil Society*, ed. Michael Edwards (Oxford: Oxford University Press, 2011), 311–23.

10 For a synopsis of this conflict, see Craig Calhoun, *The Roots of Radicalism: Tradition, the Public Sphere, and Early Nineteenth-Century Social Movements* (Chicago: University of Chicago Press, 2012).

11 For more on this period, see Donald Fyson, "La gouvernance municipale avant la municipalité: Montréal, 1760-1840," in *La gouvernance montréalaise: De la ville-frontière à la metropole*, ed. Harold Bérubé, Donald Fyson, and Léon Robichaud (Quebec: Multimondes, 2014), 24–41.

12 AVM, VM3–1-05, Fonds Juges de Paix de Montréal, 8 August 1818.

13 Ibid., 15 août 1818.

14 VM001 S33 SS01 D01, *Réglements Municipaux*, 14 December 1840, 15 June 1841, 12 April 1843.

15 Ibid., 14 December 1840.

16 For more on animals and nineteenth-century urban governance, see Kheraj, "Living and Working with Domestic Animals," 120–40; and Bettina Bradbury, "Pigs, Cows, and Boarders: Non-Wage Forms of Survival among Montreal Families, 1861–1891," *Labour/Le travail* 14 (Autumn 1984): 9–46.

17 AVM, VM001 S33 SS01 D01, *Réglements Municipaux*, 14 December 1840.

18 For a discussion of municipal power in Montreal during this period, see Michèle Dagenais, "The Municipal Territory: A Product of the Liberal Order?" in *Liberalism and Hegemony: Debating the Canadian Liberal Revolution*, ed. Michel Ducharme and Jean-François Constant (Toronto: University of Toronto Press, 2009), 201–20.

19 For more on these values and the sorts of reforms embarked upon in an effort to bring them to fruition, see David Harvey, *Paris: Capital of Modernity* (New York: Routledge, 2004).

20 These sorts of reforms both large and small were being undertaken on a global scale. See Patrick Joyce, *The Rule of Freedom: Liberalism and the Modern City* (London: Verso, 2003).

21 *Agricultural Journal and Transactions of the Lower Canada Agricultural Society* 1, no. 10 (October 1848), 307.

22 For a discussion of the links between agricultural exhibitions and larger ideas about reform and improvement, see Elsbeth Heaman, *The Inglorious Arts of Peace: Exhibitions in Canadian Society during the Nineteenth Century* (Toronto: University of Toronto Press, 1999), ch. 5.

23 For more, see Dan Horner, "Taking to the Streets: Crowds, Public Life, and Identity in Mid-Nineteenth-Century Montreal" (PhD diss., York University, 2010).

24 The Irish community occupied something of a middle ground between the Canadien majority and the city's Anglo-Protestant community. The community grew significantly during the 1840s because of the famine migration, and was deeply implicated in outbreaks of collective violence during this period. Their association with collective violence played a significant role in their marginalization in the city's public discourse during this period. See Sherry Olson and Patricia Thornton, *Peopling the North American City: Montreal, 1840-1900* (Montreal: McGill-Queen's University Press, 2013).

25 See, for example, George Rudé, *The Crowd in The French Revolution* (Oxford: Clarendon Press, 1959); Mary Ryan, *Civic Wars: Democracy and Public Life in the American City during the Nineteenth Century* (Berkeley: University of California Press, 1997); and Mark Harrison, *Crowds and History: Mass Phenomena in English Towns, 1790–1835* (Cambridge: Cambridge University Press, 1998).

26 In his examination of the French Revolution, social historian George Rudé notes that, on a number of occasions, markets were crucial sites of community organization. While it is in the realm of speculation, it seems likely that similar endeavours of political organization took place in Viger Square. See Rudé, *The Crowd in the French Revolution.*

27 Jacalyn Duffin, "The Great Canadian Peritonitis Debate, 1844–1847," *Histoire social / Social History* 19, no. 38 (November 1986): 407–24.

28 For more on the tense relationship between civil power and military officials during this period, see Elinor Senior, *British Regulars in Montreal: An Imperial Garrison, 1832–1854* (Montreal: McGill-Queen's University Press, 1981), ch. 5.

29 See, for example, *The Church*, 26 April 1844; *La Minerve*, 25 April 1844.

30 This was a period during which political legitimacy was increasingly linked to physical and emotional restraint. See, for example, Cecilia Morgan, *Public Men*

and Virtuous Women: The Gendered Languages of Religion and Politics in Upper Canada, 1791–1850 (Toronto: University of Toronto Press, 1996); and Ian McKay, "The Liberal Order Framework: A Prospectus for a Reconnaissance of Canadian History," *Canadian Historical Review* 81, no. 4 (December 2000): 617–45.

31 Take, for example, the extensive coverage in both *La Minerve* and the *Gazette* of the Astor Place Riot, a bloody sectarian conflict in New York City where the militia fired into a rioting crowd in May 1849. This coverage, which occurred in the immediate aftermath of the Rebellion Losses Crisis in British North America, demonstrates how newspapers provided their readers with examples of how other jurisdictions were dealing with popular violence.

32 Cholera struck Montreal on a large scale in 1832 and again in 1849. The typhus epidemic of 1847 was largely confined to those who came in close contact with ill Irish migrants in the city's fever sheds. See Jean-Claude Robert, "The City of Wealth and Death: Urban Mortality in Montreal, 1821–1871," in *Essays in the History of Canadian Medicine*, ed. Wendy Mitchinson and Janice Dickin McGinnis (Toronto: McClelland and Stewart, 1988), 18–38; and Geoffrey Bilson, *In A Darkened House: Cholera in Nineteenth-Century Canada* (Toronto: University of Toronto Press, 1980).

33 For more discussion of this, see Benoît Gaumer, Georges Desrosiers, and Othmar Keel, *Histoire du service de santé de la ville de Montréal, 1865–1975* (Montreal: Éditions de l'IQRC, 2002).

34 See Dan Horner, "'The Public Has the Right to Be Protected from a Deadly Scourge': Debating Quarantine, Migration, and Liberal Governance during the 1847 Typhus Outbreak in Montreal," *Journal of the Canadian Historical Association* 23, no. 1 (2012): 65–100. See also the chapter by Jane Errington in this collection.

35 For an overview of how these sorts of discussions were unfolding across the world, see Mark Harrison, *Disease and the Modern World: 1500 to the Present Day* (Cambridge: Polity Press, 2004), esp. ch. 6; and Charles Rosenberg, *The Cholera Years: The United States in 1832, 1849, and 1866* (Chicago: University of Chicago Press, 1962).

36 For more on policing in early nineteenth-century Montreal, see Donald Fyson, *Magistrates, Police, and People: Everyday Criminal Justice in Quebec and Lower Canada, 1764–1837* (Toronto: University of Toronto Press, 2006), ch. 4.

37 For details on two such incidents, see Bettina Bradbury, "Widows at the Hustings: Gender, Citizenship, and the Montreal By-Elections of 1832," in *Interdisciplinary Perspectives on Being Single*, ed. Rudolph Bell and Virginia Yans (Newark, NJ: Rutgers University Press, 2008), 82–113; and Dan Horner, "'Shame upon you as men!' Contesting Authority in the Aftermath of Montreal's Gavazzi Riot," *Histoire sociale / Social History* 44, no. 87 (2011): 29–53.

38 For more discussion on this perspective, see Richard Bushman, *The Refinement of America: Persons, Houses, Cities* (New York: Vintage, 1993); David Schuyler, *The Apostle of Taste: Andrew Jackson Dowling, 1815–1852* (Baltimore, MD: Johns Hopkins University Press, 1996); and David Scobey, *Empire City: The Making and Meaning of the New York Landscape* (Philadelphia: Temple University Press, 2002), particularly ch. 5.

39 Jason Gilliland, "The Creative Destruction of Montreal: Street Widenings and Urban (Re)Development in the Nineteenth Century," *Urban History Review* 31, no. 1 (Fall 2002): 37–51.

40 My understanding of the dynamics of the public is shaped by Ryan, *Civic Wars*; Craig Calhoun, *The Roots of Radicalism: Tradition, the Public Sphere, and Early Nineteenth-Century Social Movements* (Chicago: University of Chicago Press, 2012); and Geoff Eley, "Nations, Publics and Political Cultures," in *Habermas and the Public Sphere*, ed. Craig Calhoun (Cambridge, MA: MIT Press, 1995), 289–339.

41 This approach to the urban landscape is closely associated with the work of Frederick Law Olmsted. See Roy Rosenzweig and Elizabeth Blackmar, *The People and the Park: A History of Central Park* (Ithaca, NY: Cornell University Press, 1992).

42 For more on how urban design was used in an effort to foster genteel sociability, see Peter Baldwin, *Domesticating the Street: The Reform of Public Space in Hartford, 1850–1930* (Akron: University of Ohio Press, 1999).

43 See W. Stanford Reid's entry on Hubert-Joseph Lacroix in the *Dictionary of Canadian Biography*, vol. 6 (Toronto: University of Toronto / Quebec: Université Laval, 2003).

44 Viger Square was called into action, with temporary buildings hastily constructed for the market.

45 For more on the fire and the reconstruction that ensued, see Sherry Olson and François Dufaux, "Reconstruire Montréal, rebâtir sa fortune," *Revue BANQ* (2009): 44–57.

46 There was also a scattering of English-speaking residents in the area, including, in the aftermath of the Civil War, the family of Confederate president Jefferson Davis, who lived in a new stone house "kept in good, neat style, though there is no luxury about it." *Public Ledger* (Memphis, TN), 15 October 1866.

47 *Canadian Illustrated News*, 13 May 1871.

48 AVM, VM001 33-02-D07-202, Fonds conseil de ville de Montréal, Réglement décrétant l'abolition du Marché Viger, passé le 21 mars 1892.

49 Sherry Olson, "A Profusion of Light' in Nineteenth-Century Montreal," in *Espace et culture / Space and Culture*, ed. Serge Courville and Normand Séguin (Sainte-Foy, QC: Les Presses de l'Université Laval, 1995), 253–63.

50 *Le Perroquet*, 1 July 1865.
51 Ibid., 21 January 1865.
52 *True Witness and Catholic Chronicle*, 21 August 1868.
53 *Canadian Illustrated News*, 13 August 1870.
54 *L'Opinion publique*, 18 August 1870.
55 George Martin, "Viger Square," in *Selections from Canadian Poets: With Occasional and Biographical Notes and an Introductory Essay on Canadian Poetry by Edward Hartley Dewar* (Montreal: Lovell, 1864).
56 Olmstead was known primarily for New York's Central Park, Montreal's Mount Royal, and Detroit's Belle Isle Park. For more, see Witold Rybczynski, *A Clearing in the Distance: Frederick Law Olmstead and America in the Nineteenth Century* (New York: Touchstone, 1999); and Alvara Sevilla-Buitrago, "Central Park against the Streets: The Enclosure of Public Space Cultures in Mid-Nineteenth Century New York," *Social and Cultural Geography* 15, no. 2 (2014): 151–71.
57 My thinking on public space has been shaped by many of the essays in Setha Low and Neil Smith, eds, *The Politics of Public Space* (New York: Routledge, 2006); and Don Mitchell, *The Right to the City: Social Justice and the Fight for Public Space* (New York: Guilford, 2003).
58 Marc Choko, *The Major Squares of Montreal*, trans. Kathe Roth (Montreal: Meridian Press, 1990), 128.
59 Recent press coverage of plans to rebuild Viger Square have contained interesting and yet ahistorical discussions of these issues. "City Announces Its Second Redesign Plan for Viger Square," *Montreal Gazette*, 25 September 2015; "Le square Viger comme vous ne l'avez jamais vu," *Radio-Canada*, 25 May 2015; "Square Viger: Le Daudelin sauvé en partie," *La Presse* (Montreal), 25 September 2015; "Il faut faire revivre le square Viger," *Le Devoir* (Montreal), 21 September 2015.
60 Lisa Keller, *The Triumph of Order: Democracy and Public Space in New York and London* (New York: Columbia University Press, 2009).

SECTION V

Tools of Social Order: The Law and the Press

This section explores the legal and cultural tools for creating and contesting social order in British North America. The chapters cover a range of related topics – from statute law, to the press, and to local government – in a variety of locations and cultural contexts. By juxtaposing case studies from the borderlands and the heartland of British North America, they trace how people engaged with the varieties of governance and deployed different components of shared cultural and political patterns, most particularly the press, the judicial system, and offices of municipal government. Whether on the eastern or western borders of British territory, the politics of order were tied firmly to the twinned notions of identity and constitutionalism. The vibrant public sphere, particularly the press, supported sharp debates over colonial and imperial policies, but those debates operated within relatively stable parameters of accepted definitions of British justice. Press opposition to specific colonial policies often served to reinforce the legitimacy of the underlying constitutional order. The public sphere was both closely attuned to local conditions yet acutely sensitive to the imperial connections and appeals to loyalty to the British Crown. Despite the important differences between the political climate of the 1830s and the 1860s, the essays in this section reveal powerful continuities in how the press and the law functioned in the parts of North America claimed by Britain.

The chapters offer an expansive perspective on the development of public spaces, colonial spheres, and print culture from the Conquest through to Confederation. By spanning British North America from Nova Scotia to the Canadas, they compare patterns and experiences in older colonies with those in disputed territories where state authority was tenuous. They employ diverse methodological approaches to understanding the different ways in which officials and settlers created, negotiated, and contested social order. Donald Fyson and Bradley Miller investigate how law and judicial institutions developed to foster authority in territories without a majority of Protestant settlers; in doing so, they capture both the spectacle and the ambivalence of the colonial state. Stephen Smith and Mathias Rodorff examine the role of the newspaper press in two critical moments – during the aftermath of the Rebellion of 1837 and around Confederation in the 1860s – and their analyses probe debates over radical, republican, and alternative visions of British North America. Darren Ferry shifts our focus to the local and municipal roots of social order, where grass-roots activism, far more than imperial edicts, shaped governance.

Taken together, the chapters demonstrate the powerfully regional and colonial dimensions of state formation in the territories that became parts of Canada. They complicate the common presumption that the metropole dominated print culture. Newspapers, colonial officials, and settlers followed imperial events and trends in Europe closely, but they saw British authority through North American lenses. Local interests and imperatives shaped and limited attempts to impose imperial order, while public spheres fostered political debates that could veer into treasonous territory. Despite the remarkable level of local independence and political opposition, the colonies remained loyal to Britain. The chapters in this section raise, therefore, fascinating questions about the boundaries of loyalty and identity in colonial societies. They demonstrate that challenges to the social order were, in fact, parts of a larger process through which colonial authority was negotiated and constituted. Like the spectacle of the scaffold, the spectacle of colonial authority depended on public manifestations of political legitimacy. The law and the press formed the primary vehicles both to promote and to contest assertions of authority.

17 The Spectacle of State Violence: Executions in Quebec, 1759–1872

DONALD FYSON

Introduction

On the morning of 11 November 1871, Johan Ingebretsen, alias John Lee, was hanged in the yard of the Pied-du-Courant prison at Montreal for the murder of Mary Maroney. Ingebretsen was the first prisoner executed in Montreal under the provisions of an 1869 federal act that put an end to fully public executions by decreeing that hangings be conducted within prison walls. The gallows was located entirely out of the public eye, and, although 200–300 people still witnessed the spectacle, this paled in comparison to the thousands who had thronged to watch previous executions in Montreal. James Mack had been executed in 1866 on the same gallows later used for Ingebretsen, but the platform had been raised above the prison walls so that all could see him drop and convulse. Nevertheless, despite its purportedly "private" nature, Ingebretsen's execution resonated as much in the public sphere as Mack's. Both hangings received extensive coverage in local newspapers, both French- and English-language. Ingebretsen's was also the subject of a thirty-two-page pamphlet in French. Furthermore, the city's Ultramontane Catholic hierarchy was intensively invested in both executions. Clergy and nuns had constantly attended the prisoners in their cells in the days and weeks preceding their deaths; Bishop Ignace Bourget made visits to both; he also gave explicit directives as to how the clergy and the faithful were to act, with prayers and masses in the city's churches and further prayers at home. Church bells tolled at the fateful hour, and both executed men received full Catholic funerals and burials, even though in Ingebretsen's case, this technically contravened provisions of the 1869 act. The religious zeal was all the more significant since both men, promised redemption if they repented and embraced Catholicism, had converted or re-converted to that faith during the final weeks of their lives. They thus represented something of a coup for the Catholic Church, especially since, in both cases, they had rejected the efforts of Protestant ministers. But the outpouring of faith also partially turned what were supposed to be spectacles of state vengeance into pageants of religious redemption.[1]

Regardless of their respective "public" and "private" natures, both of these spectacles were far more similar to each other than to the execution of Jean-Baptiste Dufour for murder, also in Montreal but exactly one century before Ingebretsen, in 1771. Dufour's hanging began with a classic execution procession: he was dragged in a sled from the district gaol in the city's former Jesuit convent to the gallows outside of the city walls, probably to the east. While a priest may have attended him, there is no indication of any particular concern about his case among the Catholic hierarchy: the correspondence at the time between Bishop Briand and his Montreal subordinates focused instead on the existence of Freemasons at Montreal and the imprisonment of a priest for debt (in the same prison where Dufour was held). After the hanging, Dufour's body may have been given over to the surgeons for dissection, under the provisions of the English Murder Act of 1752; certainly, he did not receive a Christian burial. And the whole affair merited no more than three lines in the *Quebec Gazette*.[2]

Two broad analytical issues arise from these stories. The first is the relevance and chronology of the now-classic thesis of the "civilizing process," derived from Norbert Elias and applied to violence studies by scholars such as Pieter Spierenburg.[3] Was there a decline in public acceptance of the legitimacy of public state violence accompanying the rise of more pervasive but less publicly brutal forms of social regulation such as the prison? If so, did the "privatization" of executions in 1869 mark the decisive moment in this shift in Quebec? The second is the adaptation of European, and specifically English, practices of legal state violence to a conquered colony. Did the transformation of executions in Quebec simply follow trends elsewhere in North America, western Europe, and the British Empire, as part of a transcolonial, imperial, or transatlantic culture of executions? Or were there Quebec specificities, based on ethnicity and religion, that set it apart from the broader trends? These issues also tie in to themes addressed more generally in this volume, such as the legitimacy of British colonial criminal justice or the relative absence of lethal violence in British North America. To address these issues, this chapter provides a survey of the public spectacle of executions in Quebec between 1759 and 1872.[4] The chapter begins with a brief overview of the phenomenon of executions in Quebec over the period. It then focuses on three specific issues related to the spectacle of the ultimate expression of state violence in Quebec: the venues of executions; execution spectators; and the sacralization of the hanging ceremony.

Executions in Quebec, 1759–1872: Numbers and Trends

In contrast to the wealth of studies on the history of capital punishment in England, continental Europe, and the United States, relatively little has been published about executions in pre-Confederation Canada.[5] Most attention has focused on the post-Confederation period, in part because of the easy access to sources.[6] There is even less on this ultimate form of state violence in colonial Quebec, apart from accounts of a few high-profile cases such as the hangings of Marie-Josephte Corriveau in 1763 and David McLane in 1797, and the execution of twelve Patriotes in 1838–9. The British regime in Quebec, from the Conquest to Confederation, is thus particularly ill served.[7] Thus, my current study of executions is almost entirely based on original research in a wide variety of sources.[8]

Between 1759 and 1872, at least 141 people were executed in Quebec for non-military crimes. All but one was hanged.[9] Resort to judicial hanging varied considerably across the period. Up until the 1780s there were regular executions, with at least one or two in most years. But for reasons as yet unexplained, judicial death was imposed quite a bit less frequently in the 1790s and first decade of the nineteenth century.[10] Executions started up again with more regularity in the second decade of the century, and remained relatively high in the 1820s and 1830s, culminating with the hangings of twelve Patriotes in late 1838 and early 1839. After this intense pulse of raw state violence, there were no executions at all in Quebec for the next fifteen years, until one in 1854. Then, from 1858, there was one or sometimes two per year again through to 1872, followed by another pause of six years. Before its resumption in 1854, the last "civil" execution was in 1836, meaning that no one in Quebec was executed for non-political crimes for almost two decades. As far as rates of execution are concerned, they were highest from the 1760s to the 1780s, at around 1.5 executions per 100,000 population per year (comparable to both pre-Conquest Canada and to the white population of the British American colonies and United States). Hangings in Quebec dropped to about 0.5 in the first third of the nineteenth century, again similar to the trend in the United States; however, if the hanged Patriotes are excluded, the rate in the 1830s was barely over 0.1. When executions were revived in the late 1850s, the rate dropped to under 0.1, which was significantly lower than that in the United States at the same time.[11]

Change also occurred in the reasons people were hanged. Up to the 1820s, execution was used largely for murder and property crimes, in roughly equal proportions (with less hanging for property crimes than in England, but about the same as in Nova Scotia at the same time). After 1829, however, at almost exactly the same time as in Upper Canada, and about a decade before England, executions in Quebec were limited to those convicted of murder, apart from the twelve Patriotes.[12] Also in line with other jurisdictions, all but three of those executed were men. More specific to the Quebec case, only 40 per cent of those executed throughout the period under consideration were Canadiens (French-speaking settlers). The proportion of Canadiens was even lower in the eighteenth century, at 20 per cent, when they made up 90 per cent or more of the population. As Jean-Marie Fecteau pointed out long ago, British judicial violence had far less of a direct impact on the conquered Canadien population than on their anglophone counterparts. However, this was also linked to the fact that many of those hanged were military or recent ex-military, a professional group from which Canadiens were largely excluded.[13] This ethnic bias changed gradually in the nineteenth century: Canadiens made up almost half of those executed in the colony from 1800 to 1836 (when they accounted for about 80 per cent of the population), and 60 per cent between 1854 and 1872. Most of the other hanged were British and white, although eight Germans were executed in the eighteenth century (mainly soldiers or former soldiers), as were a small handful of Indigenous (four) and black (three) condemned.

This brief overview suggests the relevance of an interpretation based on a gradual rise in intolerance for public state violence and for the use of the death penalty for anything other than murder. Although the exact chronology in Quebec remains to be definitively established, the 1790s seem to mark a turning point, as do the late 1820s, which is similar to the English case.[14] This chronology also fits with the more general argument in this volume as to the relatively low levels of lethal violence in British North America as a whole. But what did this mean for the spectacle of state violence itself?

The Venues of State Violence

One aspect of the spectacle of state violence that has attracted much attention is its venues before the "privatization" of executions. Pieter Spierenburg, for example, has associated the sixteenth- and seventeenth-century shift to holding executions in known, regular locations with the "routinizing of public punishment" that accompanied its "civilization," while, in England, the abolition of the Tyburn procession and its provincial counterparts has generated considerable debate.[15] Changes in the venues of executions in Quebec followed general trends elsewhere, but with some specificities. For one thing, after a brief flirt with crime-scene executions and gibbeting (the post-execution exposure of bodies in chains or cages) before the establishment of civil justice in 1764, executions in Quebec up to 1840 were almost entirely an urban phenomenon, reflecting the high level of centralization of the superior criminal courts in the colony.[16] Almost all of the roughly one hundred executions between 1764 and 1839 took place in or near the two main towns, Quebec City and Montreal, with only a half-dozen at Trois-Rivières and one at Lévis, directly across the river from Quebec City.[17] Unlike in England, where crime-scene executions continued into the 1820s, there was no such tradition in Quebec. When the idea was suggested in 1779 for three soldiers convicted of a triple murder near Trois-Rivières, it was rejected as being "attended with many difficulties" and also because the victims' relatives would have considered it "a new misfortune." Similarly, the Lévis hanging in 1827, also a crime-scene execution, proved extremely costly to carry out and resulted in a botched hanging.[18] The urban centralization of executions diminished, however, after their revival in the 1850s, when executions began to move out into the newly created rural judicial districts. Between 1858 and 1872, six of the sixteen executions took place in rural judicial districts, in places as remote as Aylmer and New Carlisle. However, unlike crime-scene executions, this widening geographical distribution of executions in Quebec was a byproduct of the modernization of the justice system, rather than a reflection of an explicit desire to bring executions closer to the rural population.

The specific public venue of the execution spectacle also changed significantly, though this time more in line with English developments. The first major change came with the Conquest itself. Under French rule, almost all executions and corporal punishments were carried out in the towns' public squares (mainly in Quebec City), just as in Paris and, increasingly from the sixteenth century, in many French provincial towns.[19] The Conquest brought a shift to English execution traditions: both Quebec City and Montreal adopted the Tyburn model, much as in many English provincial towns, in Ireland, and in the American colonies.[20] In Quebec City, most of those executed up until 1800 were hanged on the highest spot of the Plains of Abraham, the Buttes à Nepveu, part of the promontory from which Montcalm's troops had charged down to their doom in 1759.[21] The symbolism was no doubt not lost on the city's Canadien inhabitants, although since only two of the thirteen who were definitely hanged there were Canadiens, it should not be interpreted simplistically as the brutal stamp of colonial domination. The site was about a kilometre outside the Saint-Louis gate, to the southwest, and overall a kilometre and a half from the common gaol, a bit shorter than the distance from Newgate to Tyburn, but still far enough for a full execution procession. It was also eminently visible from both the town and the main road running west, the Grande Allée. In Montreal, executions also took place outside of the city walls, and, although the exact spot is unknown – possibly to the east, outside the Quebec

Gate – it was also at a fixed place ("the usual place of execution") and involved processions. The execution processions themselves appear to have followed both French and English traditions, with the condemned in a cart or a sleigh, moving at a "slow and doleful pace," guarded by a military escort and accompanied by a large crowd.[22]

In both cities, the gallows were left up at least semi-permanently, so as to mark the place of execution. The Quebec City gallows even appears on several contemporary maps, and the spot was known to some as Gallows Hill.[23] The relatively remote location of the scaffolds, however, left them open to instances of popular resistance. The gallows in Montreal was cut down at least twice, and the same may have happened in Quebec City. In 1799, the sheriff of Montreal asked for the authority to have a new gallows made, but he suggested that it be moved from its previous location outside the town, which was not only inconvenient but also "exposed [it] to similar accidents." He recommended instead that the gallows be erected on a platform inside the wall of the prison, which was in the centre of town, high enough so that it was "as much exposed to public view as in the former situation," but built so that it could be taken down between executions.[24] When a new prison was built in 1808–11, it included a semi-circular platform for executions in the rear, within the walls, although at least part of the apparatus was temporary.[25] This placement within the prison walls meant that in Montreal, from the second decade of the nineteenth century onwards, the crowd was already excluded from direct contact with the scaffold, sixty years before this was mandated by the 1869 law. The only exception was the hanging of the Patriotes in 1838–9, at the new prison at Pied-du-Courant, when, for greater effect, the scaffold was placed directly over the main gate in the prison wall.[26] After the revival of executions in the 1850s, the scaffold was once again moved within the prison walls, as was the case for Mack. In Quebec City, the gallows had also moved into town by 1808, in front of the existing prison. Soon after a new prison opened in 1812, executions were carried out from an iron balcony permanently affixed to the building. In yet another sign of the civilization of elite mores hypothesized by those who follow Elias, this permanent reminder of state violence was taken down in 1844 after city elites denounced it as "un objet répugnant aux sentimens de l'humanité, d'horreur au voisinage, aux passants et notamment aux Etrangers qui visitent cette ville."[27]

The move of executions from outside city walls to the prisons echoed the move from Tyburn to Newgate just two decades before, and put Quebec at the forefront of the abolition of the gallows procession, long before many English and American cities.[28] In theory, doing away with processions through public space allowed authorities far more control over the spectacle. Based on the Montreal sheriff's justifications, one might be tempted to attribute the change to practical responses to particular situations, as Simon Devereaux has suggested for Tyburn.[29] But colonial officials were also well aware of criminal law reform movements in Great Britain, and it seems more than likely that they were inspired by the relatively recent moves in London and in Ireland. Furthermore, coming as it did just before the erection of new purpose-built common gaols in Quebec City and Montreal and the expansion of the use of mass imprisonment as a means of disciplining the urban poor, the move also had the effect of concentrating most judicial violence and punishment in one building that embodied the coercive power of the state. This was a very concrete example of the state formation then underway in Quebec, just as it was elsewhere in British North America.[30] When executions spread out into the rural districts after mid-century, they too were carried out in close proximity to the gaols, which, along with the courthouses to which they were attached, became the most visible architectural symbols of state power in the countryside. As well, when executions moved to the gaols, they brought execution crowds along with them.

Execution Spectators

Public executions needed their spectators, and the relationship between the crowd and the spectacle of violence has long been at the heart of studies of ancien régime punishments, whether it be the degree of consent of the crowd to the ceremony of state violence, or the event's carnivalesque nature.[31] One basic issue is the size of the crowd present at hangings. Since Quebec executions were essentially urban phenomena, there was always a significant population available to witness the scene. All accounts suggest that they were popular spectacles. As Quebec City Royal Engineer James Thompson noted in his journal in 1782 regarding the joint execution of John Tool and Robert Wallace for murder, "It is astonishing what a crowd of People followed to the Tragic Scene, Even our people on the works pray'd Captn Twiss for leave to follow the hard hearted crowd."[32] Reports on the size of execution crowds in Quebec give no impression of declining public appetite for these rituals of state violence across the period addressed in this chapter; indeed, crowds increased in size even as the number of public executions decreased. Commenting on the execution of the second group of Patriotes in January 1839, *L'Aurore des Canadas* made a very clear link between the popularity of the execution spectacle and the civilization of mores:

> Qu'on doive en attribuer la cause à un adoucissement dans nos mœurs ou à toute autre circonstance, le nombre de personnes présentes à ce spectacle déchirant était bien petit. Il le fut aussi à l'exécution de Mrs. Cardinal et Duquet [the first two

> Patriotes hanged]. On nous dit qu'à cette dernière il n'y avait pas une cinquantaine [de] Canadiens, tous de la plus basse classe de la société. Il y avait plusieurs années que l'échafaud n'avait pas été ensanglanté en Canada; mais les amis de l'humanité voyaient avec peine le peuple, des femmes mêmes et des enfans [*sic*] courir repaître leurs yeux des dernières angoisses de l'infortune. Si la différence sensible qu'on remarque cette année dans le nombre de spectateurs est due à un adoucissement dans nos mœurs, nous ne pouvons qu'en féliciter nos concitoyens.[33]

L'Aurore was to be disappointed, however, because the next quintuple execution attracted large crowds, including many Canadiens and both men and women.[34] When executions started up again in the 1850s, each one attracted large crowds, even in the rural districts with overwhelmingly francophone populations. After executions were moved within prison walls after 1869, the number of people physically present declined dramatically, as in the case of Ingrebetsen, but still hundreds were present, having got permission to attend from the sheriffs. Moreover, just as elsewhere in post-Confederation Canada and in American jurisdictions that mandated the end of public executions, large crowds often continued to gather outside the prisons, hoping to catch a glimpse of the scene (as was possible relatively often, especially outside of the two main cities) or just to see the black flag raised.[35]

While the execution crowds might have been considerable, the participants were largely passive. Descriptions right through the period give the impression not so much of the raucous crowds of early eighteenth-century London, but rather of the curiosity seekers identified by Shoemaker in late eighteenth- and early nineteenth-century London, accompanied by what he calls "a kind of primitive fascination with witnessing the process of dying."[36] There are certainly examples of a lack of the solemnity that the state ideally sought to attach to the event: in 1823, at the execution of three men in Montreal, one newspaper reported that "the usual mirth and hilarity were current that marks all numerous collections of people. The boys were playing, and the men and women talking with the same indifference with which they would have demanded themselves at a cock fight or a Fair; except perhaps, at the moment when the sufferers were turned off."[37] Although these executions were British justice carried out within a conquered colony, they seem not to have provoked much if any active resistance from the crowds attending them, even when Canadiens or those apparently sympathetic to them were being executed. In part this was due to the constant presence of constables and troops. But we know from other instances, such as charivaris, elections, or strikes, that urban crowds could easily overwhelm the forces that the state had at its disposition.[38] The relatively passive behaviour of Quebec execution crowds echoes those elsewhere in North America.[39] Philippe

Aubert de Gaspé's childhood memories of attending David McLane's execution in 1797 give some sense of the complex attitude of Canadien "spectators," as he calls them. In the published version, he emphasized the execution as a rite meant to shock and subdue the potentially rebellious Canadien populace, yet in an unpublished version he also suggested that the crowd was disappointed when the full rigour of the disembowelling and quartering was carried out only after McLane had been hanged until he was dead.[40]

Such apparent passivity did not mean that there was an unquestioning acceptance of the legitimacy of the state's imposition of capital punishment. On at least three occasions, as we saw, gallows left up permanently in the eighteenth century were cut down by unknown persons, suggesting a less than complete acceptance of the execution scene. And at the last fully public hanging in Quebec City, that of John Meehan in 1864, a well-known Quebec City street poet, Grosperrin, circulated the "Complainte du condamné," a mournful account in verse of Meehan's fate, set to the tune of "Le quatorze de juillet." Conservative anglophone and francophone newspapers published the ditty, perhaps not realizing that "Le quatorze de juillet" was a song from the French Revolution that explicitly celebrated the radical reversal of the social order, with lines such as "Les calotins sont à bas / Robins et finance" that directly attacked the church, the magistracy, and financiers.[41] But none of this suggests a broad-scale popular refusal of this most violent manifestation of the rule of British criminal law and criminal justice, despite the abolitionist debates that were raging at the same time.

The last example also raises questions about the changing role of the press in publicizing executions. Nineteenth-century Quebec saw the gradual intrusion of executions into the public sphere created by the colonial press – not just discussions of the relative merits of capital punishment, though these did occur with increasing frequency, but descriptions of the executions themselves.[42] Again, as was the case elsewhere in North America, detailed descriptions of executions were non-existent in the eighteenth-century Quebec press, with at best the reproduction of a couple of dying speeches as broadsheets.[43] This began to change at the end of the century. The first Quebec execution to be described in any detail in print was that of David McLane for treason in 1797, which, because of its highly political nature, resulted in several detailed yet contradictory accounts.[44] Thereafter, newspapers printed increasingly elaborate descriptions of executions, so that, by the 1830s, a much broader public could relive the scene. Quebec was no different in this respect than other British colonies, such as Australia.[45] Press coverage intensified after the revival of execution in the 1850s, along with the publication of a greater number of execution pamphlets (for about half of the executions between 1854 and 1872). Not only did newspaper accounts of executions broaden their potential audience, they also allowed readers and listeners to experience what the attending crowd could not, as they were progressively shielded from the spectacle of violence. Thus, at Meehan's execution in 1864, the sheriff had followed what was by then the usual practice of fencing off an area below the drop in order to prevent ordinary spectators from seeing the death throes of the accused. This is another sign of the progressive civilization of execution mores.[46] However, journalists had a privileged view from inside the gaol, allowing the usually sober, conservative *Morning Chronicle* to publish an account the next day filled with pathos and sensationalism:

> The unfortunate condemned appeared to suffer fearfully in the last throes of death. As he fell, the cap slipped from his face, and the upturned countenance, working with the pangs of death, was visible to the persons looking from the front windows of the gaol above the scaffold. From the first deep red flush of strangulation, it turned purple, and from purple to the livid hue of death. There was a violent convulsive motion of the whole frame at first, and struggles continued for fully five minutes.[47]

Readers of this and other similar accounts could vicariously experience the horror of the execution while maintaining a safe distance from the actual horror of the corpse. But the mid-century execution accounts also contained another fundamental component, this one far more particular to Quebec society: the sacralization of the execution rite.

Sacralizing State Violence

In his sweeping overview of the changes in the modes of capital punishment, David Garland identified the nineteenth century as a period when "the Western death penalty lost much of its religious character and became predominantly secular in orientation and organization ... Clerics remained at the scene of modern executions and the traditional rites of the 'last meal' and the 'last words' continued to be administered. But these were less a mark of presiding religious authority than a private consolation to the condemned and a means of smoothing the execution process."[48] As the opening stories of Lee and Mack make clear, executions in mid-nineteenth-century Quebec were heavily sacralized ceremonies, particularly through investment by the Catholic Church. One might simply conclude that these were examples of Quebec practices reflecting and trailing behind those elsewhere. After all, in England, the British Empire, and the early American republic, executions up to the early nineteenth century at least were also heavily laden with religious symbolism and religious activity, whether it be the active (though often unsuccessful) role of the Newgate Ordinary, or the sermons of Anglican or Puritan ministers.[49] In New France, just as in pre-revolutionary France, the exercise of state violence was heavily shaped by Catholic rituals.[50]

As the description of Dufour's execution in 1771 suggests, however, the place and role of religion in executions in Quebec under British colonial rule was not so clear-cut. In the decades following the Conquest, the religious dimension of the execution ceremony seems to have been minimized, perhaps because of the problems inherent in fully integrating Catholics into a ceremony that, at least nominally, incarnated the vengeance of a Protestant sovereign.[51] The Catholic clergy was still likely present during the executions of Catholic condemned;[52] however, before the beginning of the nineteenth century, there was no indication that Catholic or Protestant priests did more than accompany the hanged to the place of execution. At the gallows, the condemned might address the crowd, often to admit their guilt or to exhort them not to follow their evil example. As elsewhere, these speeches would certainly have included a religious dimension, but there is no indication that clergy took a more active role than they did in other jurisdictions, such as the United States.[53] However, this began to change during the 1820s. Clergy, both Catholic and Protestant, began to mount the scaffold with the condemned, where they remained in prayer with them until the fateful moment. This change was made possible by the recent move from traditional free-standing gallows to platforms.[54] In 1834, a Presbyterian minister even substituted his voice for that of the condemned man, reading his confession.[55] But, despite the shift towards greater integration of religion in the execution ceremonies, religious concerns remained secondary to the vengeance of the state. Hence, unless there was more than one condemned man, reports never mentioned more than one member of the clergy as present. Moreover, the clergy were as often Protestant as Catholic, and the two sometimes had to share the scaffold, as was the case during the hanging of five Patriotes in February 1839.[56]

After the resumption of executions in 1854, however, as we saw with Mack and Ingebretsen, the Catholic Church invested the public ceremony of executions with much greater force. One might be tempted to see this as simply another example of how the Catholic hierarchy sought to demonstrate its ostentatious loyalty to the British colonial administration by bolstering the legitimacy of British colonial justice.[57] However, the execution spectacle became something more. The Catholic hierarchy, especially in Montreal, seems to have targeted executions as major public events that allowed it to demonstrate its influence, and even to assert its supremacy over matters that elsewhere might devolve to the state. If murderers could be brought back into the fold, persuaded to publicly confess their crimes, repent, beg God for forgiveness, and show on the scaffold that they accepted their punishment in return for the assurance of salvation, the effects on the Catholic population could only be beneficial. As inspiration for the ceremonies, Bishop Bourget, true to his ultramontane tendencies, drew explicitly on what he had seen in Rome. In a pastoral letter of 1858 concerning the first execution in Montreal following the moratorium, that of Marie-Anne Crispin and Jean-Baptiste Desforges, Bourget declared, "nous allons vous raconter, dans un style simple et familier, comment, à Rome, se font les exécutions publiques." His intentions were crystal clear: "faire de cette exécution une fête triste et lugubre, à la vérité, mais souverainement salutaire."[58] The execution of Crispin and Desforges was to become a salutary religious feast, a stance that went far beyond the usual efforts of prison chaplains in other jurisdictions to convert the condemned.[59]

The elaborate religious execution ceremonies instituted in particular by Bourget, as illustrated by the stories of Mack and Lee, but also echoed in other dioceses, can only be briefly addressed here. With the tacit agreement of state authorities, those condemned to death and awaiting their hanging were the subject of intense efforts on the part of the Catholic hierarchy, clergy, and nuns. This even included Protestants: at least three of those hanged in Montreal in the 1860s and 1870s, including Mack and Lee, were Protestants at the time of their incarceration. In Montreal, even the convict's cell, in a prison under the authority of a supposedly non-denominational state, was decorated with Catholic religious engravings. Another cell next to it was converted into a temporary chapel where priests and nuns could also spend their time in prayer. Going even further, both the clergy and the Catholic press regularly referred to the imagery of martyrology, drawing explicit parallels between the condemned and Christian martyrs or even Christ himself. Thus, for the execution of Alexander Burns in 1861, *L'Ordre* asserted that, in seeing the huge crowd assembled, "involontairement l'esprit se reportait aux premiers âges du christianisme, alors qu'un peuple sanguinaire repaissait ses yeux de l'horrible spectacle de l'amphithéâtre et de la fosse aux lions"; and when Jean-Baptiste Beauregard was being pinioned before his hanging in 1859, his confessor told him, "Mon enfant, souvenez-vous que votre Sauveur a souffert la même chose pour vous," although he added that, while Jesus was innocent, Beauregard was guilty.[60] The church also asserted its control by actively dissuading the condemned from addressing the crowd, thus doing away with scaffold confessions; instead, the public learned of the condemned's acceptance of guilt (or insistence on innocence) only through the press. Finally, the church expanded its role in the execution itself: the processions from the prison up to the scaffold seem to have been composed of as many priests and nuns as they were of representatives of the state. All of this was reported in approving detail by the press, even many of the English-language papers. In short, Quebec's public executions increasingly became religious (and more specifically Catholic) ceremonies as much as civic ones, a trend not seen to the same extent in other Canadian provinces.[61] Such was the importance of this ceremony to the church that Bishop Bourget appeared to publicly regret the abolition of public executions in 1869.[62] Yet, even afterwards, the sacralization of the execution ceremony continued, still amply reported in the newspapers; the faithful were now summoned to pray for the deceased in their houses or churches.

A further example of the sacralization of the execution rites, and especially the growing influence of the Catholic Church, is the treatment of the corpses of the hanged. In eighteenth-century England, under the provisions of the 1752 Murder Act, the corpses of those executed for murder were either hanged in chains or anatomized.[63] Those executed for other offences were often buried unceremoniously in graves near the places of execution or, later, within prison yards, although they might also be released to family members for hasty burial.[64] The general intent was to deprive those executed of a proper Christian burial, thus adding to the terror of state execution.

In Quebec, the disposal of the corpses of the hanged was a more complex mixture of terror and mercy that shifted considerably across the period. Until their abrogation in 1839, the provisions of the Murder Act regarding the gibbeting or dissection of the bodies of those executed for murder were theoretically in force in the colony. However, while gibbeting continued in England until the 1830s, and even later in other parts of the empire, in Quebec, in an early sign of the declining taste for the public spectacle of death, it was effectively discarded as a punishment right from the beginning of civil government in 1764.[65] The only cases of gibbeting in the colony occurred in the early 1760s, under the military regime. Thereafter, those hanged for murder were generally given over to surgeons for dissection. Even this was further mitigated in practice: until the 1780s, this part of the sentence was seemingly not imposed in all murder convictions, as one newspaper correspondent complained in the early 1790s.[66] Dissection itself, on the other hand, seems to have been practiced, as elsewhere, in venues that were at least semi-public, attended by medical students and even members of the public.[67] Those executed for crimes other than murder, while they were not anatomized, in the eighteenth century at least, also did not receive Christian burials. Unlike in ancien régime France or Italy up to the nineteenth century, there was no order of penitents in Quebec under the British regime to take care of the corpses of the executed and provide them with a Christian burial.[68] And while the 1703 rite of the diocese of Quebec, following French practice, stated that repentant hanged could receive Christian burial in consecrated ground, this does not seem to have been done.[69] Instead, sheriffs generally arranged for the burial of the hanged, often by the sextons of Protestant cemeteries, but again not as normal religious burials: up to 1799, with only one exception, none of the executed, Catholic or Protestant, were entered into the various church registers. In a sense, they were erased from both public and religious memory; the full weight of state vengeance overrode any religious considerations as to the disposal of corpses.[70]

This exclusion of the corpses of the executed from normal Christian burial rites began to change at the beginning of the nineteenth century, at about the same time as the more pronounced religious presence during performances. In Quebec City in particular, the burials of an increasing number of the hanged were recorded in church registers, including at least one person executed for murder. However, the registers generally do not tell us whether they were buried in consecrated ground.[71] The names of both Catholics and Protestants were recorded. Organized religion was beginning to give back to the hanged the dignity that the violence of the state had deprived them of. But this did not apply everywhere: in Montreal, almost all of those executed continued to receive unregistered burials, including the Patriotes executed in 1838–39, even though several were certainly buried in Catholic cemeteries.

After the resumption of executions in 1854, the Catholic Church manifested its influence through the disposition of the bodies of the hanged. The provisions of the Murder Act no longer applied, and judicially mandated anatomization was a thing of the past. However, autopsies continued to be performed, often in the presence of medical students. In Mack's case, for example, not only was his body autopsied, but his eyes were then given by the gaol physician to a McGill anatomy lecturer for experimentation.[72] Nevertheless, an autopsy was a far cry from the brutal anatomization previously practised. More importantly, those hanged in Quebec after mid-century almost all benefited from regular Christian burials in consecrated ground.[73] The strength of this tradition was such that even the state submitted to it. The 1869 act that brought executions inside the prison walls also provided that the bodies of the hanged be buried in the prison yard, following the earlier English practice, unless special circumstances dictated otherwise. Even in those cases, an order in council was required. In Quebec, such orders in council apparently became the norm. Families and Catholic clergy regularly petitioned successfully for exceptions, and most of those hanged continued to be buried in cemeteries as before. Of the sixteen men and one women executed in Quebec between 1869 and 1900, at least thirteen received proper religious burials, and only two were buried in the prison yard, a stark contrast to the practice elsewhere in Canada.[74] Religious concerns outweighed the vengeance of the state, allowing the Catholic Church once again to demonstrate its influence with regards to temporal authorities.

Ironically, in the early 1870s, the Montreal church was caught up in an explosive public controversy concerning burials, the Guibord affair. As part of their attack on liberal and secular values in Quebec, church authorities had refused Catholic burial to Joseph Guibord, a member of the liberal and secularist Institut canadien.[75] The church offered instead to bury Guibord in that part of Notre-Dame Cemetery reserved for unbaptized children and those who had died out of communion with the church. Those supporting Guibord's widow objected that this was an infamous part of the cemetery, known as the "cimetière des pendus." Church officials replied that this was not true, because, since the 1850s, all Catholics hanged in Montreal had been reconciled to the church and buried in the main part of the cemetery. This was quite different from the situation in France, where, even under republican government, the hanged were still buried in separate sections.[76] What the Quebec Catholic Church refused Guibord, it granted to those convicted of murder – as long as they played their part in an execution ceremony that solidified church influence.

In its overall features, the evolution of the spectacle of executions in pre-Confederation Quebec hews fairly closely to general trends observed in England, continental Europe, and the United States. As elsewhere, there was a declining official and public appetite for these public spectacles of state violence, and a desire to replace them with more "civilized" forms of execution. In this respect, the rites of execution in Quebec, a white settler society with a heavily European-origin population, were far closer to those employed in England than in other parts of the British Empire, where, among other things, bodily mutilation and the desecration of corpses persisted far longer. In regard to executions, Quebec thus experienced little of the "colonial difference" that was applied to non-European subject peoples.[77] Instead, Quebec executions echoed the relative absence of lethal violence in general in British North America. The Quebec chronology was also quite similar to that in other Western societies. Most notably, many of the most important changes in the execution ceremony occurred long before the 1869 act mandating "private" executions, which was only one step in the process, and not even the most important one. These changes predated the purported "modernization" and liberalization of the Quebec state in the 1840s. Just as in England, the ancien régime state in Quebec showed considerable capacity to change, and ancien régime punishments were far from an undifferentiated and unchanging mass of suffering and horror.[78] Indeed, several changes, such as the early abandoning of gibetting and of crime-scene hangings, suggest that the civilization of the execution spectacle in Quebec came earlier than in England. There is no indication, however, that this made Quebec a model for other British jurisdictions, nor did the absence of gibbeting provoke any particular comment from visitors, unlike, for example, the continued presence of the whipping post in Montreal, noted unfavourably by an American visitor in the second decade of the nineteenth century.[79]

On the other hand, the transformation of the Quebec execution spectacle was fundamentally at variance with the general Western trend in one key respect: the increase, rather than decrease, in its sacralization, through the involvement of the Catholic Church. Mirroring the involvement of clergymen in the United States in the last quarter of the eighteenth century, mid-nineteenth-century executions in Quebec provided the Catholic hierarchy with an opportunity to solidify its influence in the post-Rebellions period.[80] The state appears to have willingly facilitated this shift. The theatre played out on the scaffold stage in Quebec was increasingly religious rather than purely secular; and that religion was Catholicism. This aligns well with other arguments about the intensification of Catholic practices in mid-nineteenth-century Quebec, although the church was already expanding its role in executions in the pre-Rebellions period, much as René Hardy has argued for Catholicism more generally.[81] The extent to which all of this provided actual comfort to the hanged is less clear. Newspapers often reported that the condemned were soothed by the presence of priests and, in particular, by the promise of salvation. But when the hangman put the noose around the neck of François-Xavier Séguin dit Laderoute at Aylmer in 1863, he was so terrified that he burst into tears and cried out to the curé of Aylmer, who had accompanied him onto the scaffold, "Oh! Monsieur le curé, je vous en prie, dites-leur donc de me laisser. Oh! mon Dieu! mon Dieu!" The curé's only response was to point to heaven and exhort him to prayer and contrition.[82] Ultimately, the vengeance of the state would have its way.

NOTES

1 On Ingebretsen's execution, see *Minerve* 17 and 18 November 1871; *Montreal Gazette* 18 November 1871; *Montreal Herald* 16 and 18 November 1871; *Le condamné à mort John Lee exécuté le 17 novembre 1871: Sa vie, sa condamnation, sa mort* (Montreal: Plinguet et Laplante, 1871); Library and Archives Canada (hereafter LAC) RG13, vol. 1408, file 36A; Kenneth Leyton-Brown, *The Practice*

of Execution in Canada (Vancouver: UBC Press, 2010): 41–2, 74, 137. On Mack's, see *L'Ordre* 26 November 1866; *Montreal Herald*, 24 November 1866; *Minerve*, 24 November 1866; *Montreal Witness*, 28 November 1866; *True Witness and Catholic Chronicle*, 30 November 1866; LAC, RG4 C1 1866, no. 1991. The 1869 Act was 32 & 33 Victoria c. 29 (1869); see also *Sessional Papers of the Parliament of Canada* (1870), no. 48. On the ultramontanism of the Montreal Catholic hierarchy and Bourget in particular, see Nadia Fahmy-Eid, *Le clergé et le pouvoir politique au Québec: Une analyse de l'idéologie ultramontaine au milieu du XIXe siècle* (Montreal: Hurtubise HMH, 1978); Philippe Sylvain and Nive Voisine, *Histoire du catholicisme québécois*, vol. 2, *Les XVIIIe et XIXe siècles*, Tome 2, *Réveil et consolidation (1840–1898)* (Montreal: Boréal, 1991); and Roberto Perin, *Ignace de Montréal: Artisan d'une identité nationale* (Montreal: Boréal, 2008).

2 On Dufour's execution, see *Quebec Gazette*, 21 March 1771; LAC, MG19 A2 III, vol. 85. Since the full sentence of the court has not been preserved, there is no positive indication of his anatomization; as shown below, that was typical though not constant practice at the time. He does not appear in the essentially complete records of Catholic burials in Quebec of the period, the Registre de la population du Québec ancien, *Programme de recherche en démographie historique*, www.prdh.umontreal.ca; my thanks to the PRDH for providing me with full access to these records. For the ecclesiastical correspondence of the time, see "Inventaire de la correspondance de Mgr J.-O. Briand (1741-1794)," *Rapport de l'archiviste de la Province de Québec* 10 (1929–30), and "Correspondance de cinq vicaires généraux avec les éveques de Québec," *Rapport de l'archiviste de la Province de Québec* 28 (1947–8).

3 Pieter Spierenburg, *The Spectacle of Suffering: Executions and the Evolution of Repression: From a Preindustrial Metropolis to the European Experience* (Cambridge: Cambridge University Press, 1984); and *Violence and Punishment: Civilizing the Body through Time* (Cambridge: Polity, 2013).

4 This is part of a broader research project into the history of executions in Quebec from the Conquest to the 1960s. For preliminary reflections on other aspects of the subject, see Donald Fyson, "La peine capitale au Québec, 1759–1869: Modèle européen ou spécificité coloniale?" in *Adapter le droit et rendre la justice aux colonies (16e–19e siècles)*, ed. Eric Wenzel and Eric de Mari (Dijon: Éditions universitaires de Dijon, 2015), 229–40.

5 The literature on capital punishment in the eighteenth and nineteenth centuries is extensive. Recent studies include Stuart Banner, *The Death Penalty: An American History* (Cambridge, MA: Harvard University Press, 2002); Andrea McKenzie, *Tyburn's Martyrs: Execution in England, 1675–1775* (London: Hambledon Continuum, 2007); Pascal Bastien, *Histoire de la peine de mort: Bourreaux et supplices, Paris, Londres, 1500–1800* (Paris: Seuil, 2011); and Paul Friedland, *Seeing Justice*

Done: The Age of Spectacular Capital Punishment in France (Oxford: Oxford University Press, 2012). For brief overviews of the main debates, see Paul Griffiths, "Introduction: Punishing the English," in *Penal Practice and Culture, 1500–1900: Punishing the English*, ed. Simon Devereaux and Paul Griffiths (New York: Palgrave Macmillan, 2004), 2–9; and Richard Ward, "Introduction: A Global History of Execution and the Criminal Corpse," in *A Global History of Execution and the Criminal Corpse*, ed. Richard Ward (Houndmills, UK: Palgrave Macmillan, 2015), 2–21.

6 See, for example, Kenneth B. Leyton-Brown, *The Practice of Execution in Canada* (Vancouver: UBC Press, 2010) and Dale Brawn, *Last Moments: Sentenced to Death in Canada* (Edmonton: Quagmire Press, 2011). Leyton-Brown's analysis unfortunately does not take into account changes in pre-Confederation executions. There are also several popular histories of executions in post-Confederation Canada, of which the most recent is Lorna Poplak, *Drop Dead: A Horrible History of Hanging in Canada* (Toronto: Dundurn, 2017). On executions in pre-Confederation Canada, see F. Murray Greenwood and Beverley Boissery, *Uncertain Justice: Canadian Women and Capital Punishment, 1754–1953* (Toronto: Osgoode Society for Canadian Legal History and Dundurn, 2000); Robert Lanning, "'Launched into Eternity': Sympathetic Interaction as a Response to Public Executions in Canada West, 1847–1869," *Journal of Historical Sociology* 13, no. 3 (2000): 365–86; Jerry Bannister, *The Rule of the Admirals: Law, Custom, and Naval Government in Newfoundland, 1699–1832* (Toronto: University of Toronto Press, 2003), 212–15; and Patrick J. Connor, "'The Purest of Gifts': Royal Clemency, Patronage, and the Politics of Identity in Upper Canada, 1791–1841" (PhD diss., York University, 2012).

7 On "La Corriveau," the latest study is Catherine Ferland and Dave Corriveau, *La Corriveau: De l'histoire à la légende* (Quebec: Septentrion, 2014). On McLane, see F. Murray Greenwood, *Legacies of Fear: Law and Politics in Quebec in the Era of the French Revolution* (Toronto: University of Toronto Press, 1993), 139–70. The literature on the trial of the Patriotes is extensive, although with little recent scholarship on the executions themselves. See, for example, the various articles in F. Murray Greenwood and Barry Wright, eds, *Canadian State Trials*, vol. 2, *Rebellion and Invasion in the Canadas, 1837–1839* (Toronto: Osgoode Society for Canadian Legal History and University of Toronto Press, 2002); and Beverley Boissery, *A Deep Sense of Wrong: The Treason, Trials, and Transportation to New South Wales of Lower Canadian Rebels after the 1838 Rebellion* (Toronto: Osgoode Society for Canadian Legal History and Dundurn Press, 1995). For a brief analysis of one execution during the period, see Alex Gagnon, *La communauté du dehors. Imaginaire social et crimes célèbres au Québec (XIXe-XXe siècle)* (Montreal: Presses de l'Université de Montréal, 2016): 229–32. The French regime has received somewhat broader coverage. For example, see André Lachance, *La justice criminelle du roi au Canada au XVIIIe siècle: Tribunaux et officiers* (Quebec City: Presses de l'Université Laval, 1978); *Crimes et criminels en Nouvelle-France* (Montreal: Boréal Express, 1984); *Délinquants, juges,*

et bourreaux en Nouvelle-France (Montreal: Libre Expression, 2011); and Peter N. Moogk, "The Liturgy of Humiliation, Pain, and Death: The Execution of Criminals in New France," *Canadian Historical Review* 88, no. 1 (2007): 89–112.

8 Space considerations limit me to listing briefly only the most notable sources. At Library and Archives Canada (hereafter LAC): RG1 E15A / R10870-13-X (public accounts); RG4 A1, RG4 C1, RG4 C2, RG7 G15C / R178-93-5, RG7 G17C / R178-103-4 (civil and then provincial secretary's correspondence received and sent); RG4 B20 (pardons); RG4 B21 (gaol calendars and lists of convictions); RG13 B1 / R188-53-2 (Department of Justice, capital case files); RG68 / R1002-34-0 and R1002-51-0 (Registrar general, pardons); MG11 CO42 / R10976-10-7 ("Q" series, transcripts of correspondence with the Colonial Office); MG19 A2 / R7712-0-7 (Ermatinger estate, records of the sheriffs of Montreal); MG21 Add.MSS. 21661-21892 / R11231-0-1 (Haldimand Collection, transcripts). At Bibliothèque et Archives nationales du Québec, Centre d'archives de Québec (BAnQ-Q): TL18,S1 and TP9,S1 (King's Bench criminal records); E17 (Ministère de la justice, gaol registers and records). At Bibliothèque et Archives nationales du Québec, Centre d'archives de Montréal (BAnQ-M): TL19,S1 (King's Bench criminal records). Finally, I also consulted the main Quebec City and Montreal newspapers of the time, along with some local newspapers, and the relatively few instances of Quebec execution pamphlet literature. Unreferenced observations on executions in general are based on a detailed database compiled from the above and other sources.

9 One Indigenous man condemned to death, Charles Nichau Noite, was executed by firing squad in 1784, an example of the parallel justice often applied to the Crown's allies in the eighteenth century: Donald Fyson, "Minority Groups and the Law in Quebec, 1760–1867," in *Essays in the History of Canadian Law*, vol. 11, *Quebec and the Canadas*, ed. G. Blaine Baker and Donald Fyson (Toronto: Osgoode Society for Canadian Legal History and University of Toronto Press, 2013), 281–90.

10 Source problems for 1790–1810 mean that there may be a few executions during that period that I have yet to identify, although there are several indicators that the number of missing cases is small and that the drop in executions was real; it also closely parallels a similar drop in executions in London, though the meaning of this concordance remains to be elucidated. See Simon Devereaux, "England's 'Bloody Code' in Crisis and Transition: Executions at the Old Bailey, 1760–1837," *Journal of the Canadian Historical Association* 24, no. 2 (2013): 71–113. I also know of approximately thirty-five executions for military crimes after 1764, essentially for desertion, almost all by firing squad. By Quebec I mean Quebec, Lower Canada, and Canada East, within the colony's 1791 boundaries, thus excluding what became Upper Canada and the United States.

11 For a more detailed analysis, see Fyson, "La peine capitale au Québec." Since publication of that text, I have identified a small number of additional executions, but the overall trends hold. I have calculated the pre-Conquest rates based on the

raw numbers provided by Lachance. Moogk apparently does not distinguish between death sentences and executions, and thus inflates the actual execution rate. Compare Moogk, "The Liturgy of Humiliation," 89–90, citing André Lachance, *Le bourreau au Canada sous le régime français* (Quebec: Société historique de Québec, 1966), 48, with the number of actual executions given by Lachance at 44. On the British American colonies and the United States, see Howard W. Allen and Jerome M. Clubb, *Race, Class, and the Death Penalty: Capital Punishment in American History* (Albany: SUNY Press, 2008), 16–21.

12 On English executions statistics, see V.A.C. Gatrell, *The Hanging Tree: Execution and the English People, 1770–1868* (Oxford: Oxford University Press, 1996), 616–19. On Upper Canada, Connor, "'The Purest of Gifts,'" 282. On Nova Scotia, Jim Phillips, "The Operation of the Royal Pardon in Nova Scotia, 1749–1815," *University of Toronto Law Journal* 42, no. 4 (1992): 421–48.

13 Jean-Marie Fecteau, *Un nouvel ordre des choses: La pauvreté, le crime, l'État au Québec, de la fin du XVIIIe siècle à 1840* (Montreal: VLB, 1989), 128–9. At least 40 per cent of those hanged 1759–99 were military or ex-military.

14 See, for example, Gatrell, *The Hanging Tree*, 225–324; Greg T. Smith, "'Civilized People Do Not Want to See That Sort of Thing': The Decline of Physical Punishment in London, 1760–1840," in *Qualities of Mercy: Justice, Punishment, and Discretion*, ed. Carolyn Strange (Vancouver: UBC Press, 1996), 21–51; and Robert Shoemaker, *The London Mob: Violence and Disorder in Eighteenth-Century England* (London: Hambledon and London, 2004), 79–110.

15 Spierenburg, *The Spectacle of Suffering*, 44–5. On Tyburn, see Gatrell, *The Hanging Tree*, 602–4; Smith, "'Civilized People'"; McKenzie, *Tyburn's Martyrs*, 7–29; and Simon Devereaux, "Recasting the Theatre of Execution: The Abolition of the Tyburn Ritual," *Past and Present* 202, no. 1 (2009): 127–74. For England outside of London, see Peter King, *Crime, Justice, and Discretion in England, 1740–1820* (Oxford: Oxford University Press, 2000): 340–52; and Steve Poole, "'For the Benefit of Example': Crime-Scene Executions in England, 1720–1830," in Ward, ed., *A Global History of Execution*, 72–8.

16 Between 1760 and 1763, one man was hanged at Saint-Charles-de-Bellechasse and another at Laprairie; furthermore, the bodies of two others of the hanged were then exposed near the scene of their crimes, including Marie-Josephte Corriveau, hanged at Quebec but then gibbeted at Lévis.

17 Executions in Quebec were even more centralized than in Nova Scotia, for example, where, between 1749 and 1815, there were thirty-nine executions in Halifax and eleven elsewhere (Jim Phillips, personal communication, 24 February 2017).

18 Mabane to Haldimand, 1779-11-19, LAC MG21 Add.MSS. 21661-21892 / R11231-0-1, vol. 204, p. 43; *Quebec Mercury*, 24 February 1827; LAC, RG1 E15A, vol. 60, file 1827 – Sheriff – Quebec. On England, Poole, "'For the Benefit of Example.'"

19 Lachance, *Le bourreau au Canada*, 44; Moogk, "The Liturgy of Humiliation," 95; Friedland, *Seeing Justice Done*, 102; and Bastien, *Histoire de la peine de mort*, 52–62.

20 On Ireland, James Kelly, "Punishing the Dead: Execution and the Executed Body in Eighteenth-Century Ireland," in Ward, ed., *A Global History of Execution*, 37–70. On the American colonies, Banner, *The Death Penalty*, 11, 24–7.

21 The place of execution is unknown for a few men hanged in 1759–60 and between 1794 and 1800. Three men were hanged in 1771 on the Place d'Armes; Charles Nishonoit was shot in 1784 on a different part of the Plains of Abraham; and David McLane was executed for treason in 1797 just to the northwest of the fortifications.

22 The only descriptions I have found of the processions concern Quebec City and are in the journals of James Thompson, BAnQ-Q, P450, notably 18 November 1782. There are also indications for both cities in the sheriffs' accounts in LAC, RG1 E15A, such as expenditures for cart hire.

23 Maps of Quebec City that indicate the gallows include LAC, H3/350/Quebec/[1762] (NMC2311); LAC (R)H1/340/Quebec/1785 (NMC 17048); and National Archives CO 700/CANADA55 (1791). The site was described as "the Gallows Hill" in 1776 by Hugh Finlay, "Journal of the Siege and Blockade of Quebec by American Rebels in Autumn 1775 and Winter 1776," Literary and Historical Society of Quebec, *Historical Documents*, Series 4, no. 4 (Quebec: Dawson, 1875): 15. That name was also applied to a different spot, the Côte à Coton, where McLane was executed: J.M Le Moine, *Picturesque Quebec: A Sequel to Quebec Past and Present* (Montreal: Dawson, 1882), 227.

24 Gray to Gale, 1 April 1799, LAC, MG23 GII3 / R3233-0-5, vol. 6.

25 *Journals of the House of Assembly of Lower Canada* 19 (1810–11): 42; Amédée Papineau, *Souvenirs de jeunesse (1822–1837)* (Quebec: Septentrion, 1998), 54; sheriffs' accounts in LAC, RG1 E15A.

26 *Quebec Mercury*, 26 December 1838; J. Douglas Borthwick, *History of the Montreal Prison from A.D. 1784 to A.D. 1886* (Montreal: A. Périard, 1886), 45, 86–7 (though Borthwick gets the details of the hangings wrong).

27 Donald Fyson, "Prison Reform and Prison Society: The Quebec Gaol, 1812–1867," in *From Iron Bars to Bookshelves: A History of the Morrin Centre*, ed. Louisa Blair, Patrick Donovan, and Donald Fyson (Montreal: Baraka Books, 2016), 60–1; LAC, RG4 C1 1844 no. 875.

28 On Tyburn, see n. 15. On elsewhere in England, Poole, "'For the Benefit of Example.'" In the United States, there were still lengthy gallows processions in Philadelphia and New York in the mid-1820s: see Michael Meranze, *Laboratories of Virtue: Punishment, Revolution, and Authority in Philadelphia, 1760–1835* (Chapel Hill: University of North Carolina Press, 1996), 24–5; and Michael Madow, "Forbidden Spectacle: Executions, the Public, and the Press in Nineteenth-Century New York," *Buffalo Law Review* 43, no. 2 (1995): 470–1.

29 Devereaux, "Recasting the Theatre of Execution."

30 Donald Fyson, "Between the Ancien Régime and Liberal Modernity: Law, Justice, and State Formation in Colonial Quebec, 1760–1867," *History Compass* 12, no. 5 (2014): 412–32.

31 The nature and role of the London execution crowd has been particularly debated. Apart from works cited above, see also Thomas Laqueur, "Crowds, Carnival, and the State in English Executions, 1604–1868," in *The First Modern Society: Essays in English History in Honour of Lawrence Stone*, ed. A.L. Beier, David Canadine, and James Rosenheim (New York: Cambridge University Press, 1989), 305–55; Robert Shoemaker, "Streets of Shame? The Crowd and Public Punishments in London, 1700–1820," in *Penal Practice and Culture, 1500–1900: Punishing the English*, ed. Simon Devereaux and Paul Griffiths (New York: Palgrave Macmillan, 2004), 232–57; and Matthew White, "'Rogues of the Meaner Sort'? Old Bailey Executions and the Crowd in the Early Nineteenth Century," *London Journal* 33, no. 2 (2008): 135–53.

32 BAnQ-Q P450, 18 November 1782.

33 *L'Aurore des Canadas*, 22 January 1839.

34 Space precludes discussion here of the composition of execution crowds, including their gendered nature; the theme will be addressed in much greater detail in my book-length study, which is currently underway.

35 Louis P. Masur, *Rites of Execution: Capital Punishment and the Transformation of American Culture, 1776–1865* (New York: Oxford University Press, 1989), 113–14; and Leyton-Brown, *The Practice of Execution*, 99–100, 104–17.

36 Shoemaker, *The London Mob*, 108.

37 *Canadian Times*, 28 October 1823.

38 René Hardy, *Charivari et justice populaire au Québec* (Quebec: Septentrion, 2015); Donald Fyson, "The Trials and Tribulations of Riot Prosecutions: Collective Violence, State Authority, and Criminal Justice in Quebec, 1841–1892," in *Canadian State Trials*, vol. 3, *Political Trials and Security Measures, 1840–1914*, ed. Susan Binnie and Barry Wright (Toronto: Osgoode Society for Canadian Legal History and University of Toronto Press, 2009), 161–203; and Dan Horner, "Solemn Processions and Terrifying Violence: Spectacle, Authority, and Citizenship during the Lachine Canal Strike of 1843," *Urban History Review / Revue d'histoire urbaine* 38, no. 2 (2010): 36–47.

39 Masur, *Rites of Execution*, 46.

40 Philippe Aubert de Gaspé, *Les Anciens Canadiens* (Quebec: Desbarats et Derbishire, 1863), 359–60; LAC, MG18 H44 / R7949-0-0, series 2, vol. 6, file 1.

41 *Morning Chronicle*, 23 March 1864; *Journal de Québec*, 23 March 1864; *Poésies révolutionnaires et contre-révolutionnaires* (Paris: Librairie historique, 1821), 1: 111–12.

42 Claude Desaulniers, "La peine de mort dans la législation criminelle de 1760 à 1892," *Revue générale de droit* 8, no. 1(1977): 151–64, 178–81; and Fecteau, *Un nouvel ordre des choses*, 166–70.

43 Masur, *Rites of Execution,* 114–16. Leyton-Brown incorrectly assumes that newspapers had always played this role; see *The Practice of Execution*, 11. In seventeenth- and eighteenth-century New England, it was execution sermons that took pride of place: Scott D. Seay, *Hanging between Heaven and Earth: Capital Crime, Execution Preaching, and Theology in Early New England* (DeKalb: Northern Illinois University Press, 2009).

44 Greenwood, *Legacies of Fear*, 139–70.

45 Tim Castle, "Constructing Death: Newspaper Reports of Executions in Colonial New South Wales, 1826–1837," *Journal of Australian Colonial History* 9 (2007): 51–68.

46 The first instance of this practice in Quebec was the 1823 hanging of William Pounden in Quebec City, long before the 1868 Toronto example provided in Leyton-Brown, *The Practice of Execution*, 107.

47 *Morning Chronicle*, 23 March 1864.

48 David Garland, "Modes of Capital Punishment: The Death Penalty in Historical Perspective," in *America's Death Penalty: Between Past and Present*, ed. David Garland, Randall McGowen, and Paul Merantz (New York: New York University Press, 2010), 53.

49 McKenzie, *Tyburn's Martyrs*; Harry Potter, *Hanging in Judgment: Religion and the Death Penalty in England from the Bloody Code to Abolition* (London: SCM Press, 1993), 17–29; Seay, *Hanging between Heaven and Earth*; Karen Halttunen, "Early American Murder Narratives: The Birth of Horror," in *The Power of Culture: Critical Essays in American History*, ed. Richard Wightman Fox and T.J. Jackson Lears (Chicago: University of Chicago Press, 1993), 67–101; and Castle, "Constructing Death," 57–60.

50 Moogk, "The Liturgy of Humiliation"; Michel Bée, "Le spectacle de l'exécution dans la France d'ancien régime," *Annales: Economies, Societes, Civilisations* 38, no. 4 (1983): 843–62; Bastien, *Histoire de la peine de mort*, 145–82; and Friedland, *Seeing Justice Done,* 101–6.

51 Irish Catholic priests were also seen as problematic in eighteenth-century London executions, as they were considered a threat by the Ordinaries: Barbara White, "'The Inferior Sort of the Kingdom of Ireland': Irishmen and Tyburn Tree," *Irish Studies Review* 6, no. 1 (1998): 22–4.

52 This was explicitly noted for the 1786 execution at Montreal of Cornelius Landraskin: *Montreal Gazette*, 19 October 1786.

53 Banner, *The Death Penalty*, 24, 32–6; Madow, "Forbidden Spectacle," 471–2.

54 The first explicit report of priests mounting the scaffold with the condemned is in Montreal in 1823.

55 *Quebec Gazette*, 4 April 1834.

56 Ibid., 18 Februrary 1839.

57 On Catholic loyalty in Quebec and elsewhere in British North America, see the chapters by Damien-Claude Bélanger and Denis McKim in this volume.

58 *Précis historique de l'exécution de Jean-Bapt. Desforges et de Marie-Anne Crispin, veuve Jean-Baptiste Gobier dit Belisle meurtriers de Catherine Prévost, femme d'Antoine Desforges, 25 juin 1858*, 2nd ed. (Montreal: L. Perrault, 1859), 35–45.

59 For example, in early Victorian England, see Potter, *Hanging in Judgment*, 46–54.

60 *L'Ordre*, 9 September 1861; *La Minerve*, 17 December 1859.

61 Leyton-Brown, *The Practice of Execution*, 38–48, 73–4.

62 *Le condamné à mort John Lee*, 31.

63 Elizabeth T. Hurren, *Dissecting the Criminal Corpse: Staging Post-Execution Punishment in Early Modern England* (Houndmills, UK: Palgrave Macmillan, 2016); and Peter King, *Punishing the Criminal Corpse, 1700–1840: Aggravated Forms of the Death Penalty in England* (Houndmills, UK: Palgrave Macmillan, 2017).

64 McKenzie, *Tyburn's Martyrs*, 20.

65 On England, see Sarah Tarlow, *The Golden and Ghoulish Age of the Gibbet in Britain* (Houndmills, UK: Palgrave Macmillan, 2017); and Clare Anderson, "Execution and Its Aftermath in the Nineteenth-Century British Empire," in Ward, ed., *A Global History of Execution and the Criminal Corpse*, 172–86.

66 The more rigourous imposition of anatomization from the late 1780s reflected not a decline in the civilization of state violence but rather the greater attention paid to the letter of the law by Quebec's increasingly professional high court judges.

67 Hurren, *Dissecting the Criminal Corpse*; Steven Robert Wilf, "Anatomy and Punishment in Late Eighteenth-Century New York," *Journal of Social History* 22, no. 3 (1989): 507–30.

68 On penitent orders and executions, see Régis Bertrand, "Que faire des restes des exécutés?" in *L'exécution capitale: Une mort donnée en spectacle, XVIe–XXe* siècle, ed. Anne Carol and Régis Bertrand (Aix-en-Provence: Publications de l'Université de Provence, 2003), 49–53; Friedland, *Seeing Justice Done*, 105; and Annamaria Monti, "From Prison to Scaffold: Confraternities of Comforters in Early Modern Italy," Bocconi Legal Studies Research Paper No. 2549551, http://dx.doi.org/10.2139/ssrn.2549551.

69 *Rituel du Diocèse de Québec publié par l'ordre de Monseigneur l'évêque de Québec* (Paris: Simon Langlois, 1703), 291; and Friedland, *Seeing Justice Done*, 91, 99.

70 This was also the case in Newfoundland: Bannister, *The Rule of the Admirals*, 214. The one exception was Charles Nichau Noite.

71 According to Quebec priest Thomas Maguire, all burials in church cemeteries, even of those not in communion with the church, were meant to be recorded in the registers: *Recueil de notes diverses sur le gouvernement d'une paroisse, l'administration des sacremens, etc. adressées à un jeune curé de campagne* (Paris: Décourchant, 1830), 251.

72 *Morning Chronicle*, 26 November 1866; and George E. Fenwick, "Fracture of the Lens: Does It Occur in Death from Violent Hanging," *Canadian Medical Journal* 3, no. 5 (1866): 195–6.

73 Between 1854 and 1868, ten of the fourteen Quebec hanged received a Catholic burial.

74 Leyton-Brown, *The Practice of Execution*, 133–44.

75 On the political and legal ramifications of the Guibord affair, see Rainer Knopff, "Quebec's 'Holy War' as 'Regime' Politics: Reflections on the Guibord Case," *Canadian Journal of Political Science* 12, no. 2 (1979): 315–31; and David Gilles, "Confronter les normes aux revendications religieuses: les débats judiciaires à Montréal (1764–1900)," *Revue de droit de l'Université Sherbrooke* 43 (hors-série) (2013): 67–74. Despite its being discussed in numerous publications, no rigorous full-length scholarly treatment of the affair exists.

76 *Affaire Guibord: question de refus de sépulture* (Montreal: La Minerve, 1870); "Court of Queen's Bench (Appeal Side): Dame Henriette Brown, Appelant, and Les curé et marguilliers de l'oeuvre et de la fabrique de la paroisse de Montréal, Respondents," *Lower Canada Jurist* 17 (1873): 119, 135; and Bertrand, "Que faire des restes," 53–7.

77 Anderson, "Execution and Its Aftermath," 171.

78 Fyson, "Between the Ancien Régime and Liberal Modernity."

79 Joseph Sansom, *Sketches of Lower Canada, Historical and Descriptive* (New York: Kirk and Mercein, 1817), 233. The question of the continued use of non-lethal corporal punishment in Quebec remains to be fully explored, but the practice essentially disappeared in the 1830s; see Donald Fyson, *Magistrates, Police, and People: Everyday Criminal Justice in Quebec and Lower Canada, 1764–1837* (Toronto: Osgoode Society for Canadian Legal History and University of Toronto Press, 2006), 258–9.

80 On the United States, see Seay, *Hanging between Heaven and Earth*, esp. ch. 5, as well as Masur, *Rites of Execution*, 42–3.

81 René Hardy, *Contrôle social et mutation de la culture religieuse au Québec, 1830–1930* (Montreal: Boréal, 1999); and "Regards sur la construction de la culture catholique québécoise au XIXe siècle," *Canadian Historical Review* 88, no. 1 (2007): 7–40.

82 *Courrier d'Ottawa*, 18 October 1863.

18 Making a Patriot Order: Violence, Respectability, and the Patriot Press in Exile, 1838–1847

STEPHEN R.I. SMITH

In November 1838, William Lyon Mackenzie, leader of the rebellion in Upper Canada and by then exiled in the United States, organized a meeting in New York City, with paid admission, of patriots – those who desired a republic in the Canadas. Mackenzie invited radical American social reformer Frances Wright to address the gathering. As she began to speak, however, there was suddenly an "uproar and confusion" and the meeting "became very disorderly."[1] This chapter considers various aspects of the invitation and reaction to Wright. Why did Mackenzie invite Frances Wright to speak at a patriot meeting? What does that choice suggest about his assumptions of the gathering's social boundaries? What are the implications of admission-paying attendees revolting with such disorder against Wright's presence? What does this disorder reveal about the assumptions of both Mackenzie and the attendees about the boundaries of the patriot movement?

Mediating these different values and assumptions was the challenge of the patriot press in exile. *Patriot press* refers to those newspapers founded in support of or uniquely devoted to republicanism, anti-monarchism, and immediate independence for the Canadas from British control. The patriot press in the United States strove to build a coherent press community of readers and printers made up of Canadian refugees and their American sympathizers. Patriot newspapers also had to define the boundaries of this community in the public sphere to translate a Canadian movement to an American milieu.

This chapter investigates two strategies by which the patriot press formed a new press community: first, members explicitly defined which papers and individuals did or did not form part of this community; second, members of this press community defined themselves as united by "suffering." I will then examine two instances where ideas of order diverged between the Canadas and the

United States. These involved the challenges of placing the patriots within the US partisan landscape as well as conforming to American ideas about women's participation in the public sphere.

Scholars have identified the importance of the press in the development of civil society. Significantly, the press could play just as important a role in the formation of a patriot order in the aftermath of defeat and exile.[2] The patriot press community in the United States attempted to clearly define, in the public sphere, the boundaries of the patriot movement. Analysing the creation of a patriot order in the United States intervenes in two historiographical understandings, both of which reflect important themes that underpin this collection of essays. The first relates to order and disorder and their relationship to the rebellion of 1837–8 in Upper and Lower Canada. The second understanding also revolves around notions of order, disorder, and violence but focuses on differences in this area between the Canadas and the United States in the early nineteenth century.

Much scholarly work on the period has continued to view the rebellion's significance as, ultimately, an episode of disorder. Order reappears in the failure of the rebellions: after this episode, order in the Canadas had to be "reconstituted."[3] Historians view the significance of the rebellion in its failure to secure an alternative to the existing order, whether that alternative was civic humanism, continued seigneurialism, radical politics, Quebec's "anticolonial spring," or a republican conception of liberty.[4] The story then becomes how, after this defeat, the forces of order reconstituted themselves to create a "modern" Canada in such forms as a Foucauldian bureaucratic state or as a liberal order.[5] What might be missed with such a focus is that the rebellion was *also* an exercise in order, and not only an instance of disorder. This chapter examines continuing attempts by patriots to "reconstitute legitimate rule on new foundations" after the initial military defeats of late 1837 and exile to the United States.[6]

The fact that the patriots had to translate their movement from being situated in the Canadas to one based in the United States allows a comparison of notions of order, disorder, and violence between the United States and the Canadas in the early nineteenth century. In the past, scholarship has contrasted the "order" in the colonization of Canada with the disorder in the United States.[7] The patriot movement in exile also faced the challenge of how to fashion a patriot press community. This community of newspapers and readers in turn faced the challenge of fitting into an American partisan landscape and American understandings of female participation in the public sphere. The particular methods that the patriot community in exile employed to cope with these challenges, such as how they deployed race and gender tropes in discourse, reflect changes in Canadian and American understandings of unrest, violence, and disorder that had occurred by the 1830s.

The Formation of a Patriot Press Community

The patriot press in the United States comprised approximately twenty-one papers in fifteen separate towns and cities.[8] Begun between 1837 and 1841, these papers were clustered around the Vermont-Lower Canada border, the Erie Canal corridor, the Western Reserve region of Ohio, Detroit, southeastern Michigan, and New York City. Canadian political refugees as well as American sympathizers ran these papers to promote republicanism and carry news from the Canadas. Beyond the numerous locations of these papers, a number had an expansive geography of agents extending even to New Orleans. Patriot papers could also have an extensive reach, with Mackenzie having a peak circulation of four thousand for his *Gazette*, which was first based in New York and later in Rochester.[9] Nonetheless, patriot papers in the United States were short lived: even successful papers lasted for only about three years; others produced just their initial issue.[10] In addition, a number moved, merged, or switched editors. Because of this instability, defining the patriot press community was particularly important.

The patriot press in the United States formed a tight-knit community that continually corresponded with one another, forwarded copies of their newspapers to each other, and republished one another's articles.[11] Patriot newspapers in exile policed members of the pro-patriot press by publishing lists of fellow "journals friendly to Canadian emancipation" as well as singling out papers that were defined as "unfriendly."[12]

As constituents of a press community in constant flux as papers started or folded, patriot newspapers warmly welcomed new additions and marked when one of their own ceased publication.[13] Previously editing the patriot *Constitution* in Toronto, Mackenzie escaped to Buffalo after the failure of the rebellion in December 1837. He began his patriot newspaper the following spring in New York City.[14] The patriot *Lewiston Telegraph* announced to its readers that it had received copies of the prospectus of *Mackenzie's Gazette*, noting that "his paper will be of great service to the Canadian Patriots."[15] In his *Gazette*, Mackenzie in turn discussed the prospectus of the *Patriote canadien* of Burlington, Vermont, as well as the *Canadian* of Jackson, Michigan. Mackenzie wished the former success, and, as evidence of a sense of common cause, he titled his article on the latter "Another Fellow Laborer in the Vineyard."[16] The *Freeman's Advocate* of Lockport, New York, and Edward Alexander Theller's *Spirit of '76* of Detroit also noted the coming arrival of the *Patriote canadien*.[17] The *Bald Eagle* of Cleveland copied a notice for establishment of the *North American* of Swanton, Vermont, and one of the editors of the latter paper, Jackson Vail, placed an advertisement for his services as a lawyer in the *Canadian Patriot* of Derby Line, Vermont.[18] Mackenzie provided readers of his *Volunteer* with a description of a new paper located in New York City: Theller's second paper, the *Truth*. Mackenzie spoke of it in positive terms and noted that Benjamin Kingsbury Jr, who had previously edited the patriot *Detroit Morning Post*, would be assisting with the *Truth*.[19]

The patriot press also noted when a fellow journal moved or closed. Thomas Nichols advised readers of his *Weekly Mercury and Buffalonian* that *Mackenzie's Gazette* had moved to Rochester.[20] In an April 1839 issue of his *Gazette*, Mackenzie copied a report of the public dinner given in honour of Kingsbury's retirement from the *Detroit Morning Post*, and both Mackenzie and Samuel Hart of the *Lewiston Telegraph* mourned that the *Buffalonian* had ceased operation.[21]

As well as welcoming papers, the community could shun others.[22] Theller's *Spirit of '76* advised readers that the *Mt. Clement Patriot* was not a patriot but rather a Democrat newspaper.[23] Through his *Bald Eagle*, editor Samuel Underhill attacked a number of papers for being "tory," and the *Lewiston Telegraph* rebuked a compliment from the *Niagara Falls Recorder*.[24] Such definitions of who was and who was not part of the community would have mattered to Underhill and his readers, as they sought to maintain legitimacy for and support of the movement for severing the monarch's control of the Canadas.

United as Victims

The second way in which the patriot press worked to create a community of refugees and sympathizers in the United States and to delineate the boundaries of the movement was to define patriots in the public sphere as victims of mistreatment in the form of violence, abuse, or injustice that had been directed at them. Ample historical evidence demonstrates heart-wrenching stories of personal vendettas, assault, harassment, arbitrary arrest, property destruction, and long imprisonment without trial in the reaction to the rebellion.[25] Refugee patriots continued to emphasize their victimhood even though, in the United States, they were safe from British arrest or imprisonment.[26] In publications, resolutions, and meetings, authors, editors, and meeting attendees often referred to the "suffering" patriots.[27]

This trauma was not limited to past exposure to violence during the rebellion itself, but included ongoing hardship experienced after exile to the United States. The patriot press in exile complained of verbal abuse and threats of violence that they or patriots in general received because of their beliefs. Samuel Underhill complained of a Cleveland grocery store having individuals "who make it their business to abuse every Patriot who comes within hearing distance of their Tory slang."[28] In a similar vein, Mackenzie proposed in a letter to Edmund Bailey O'Callaghan that the title page for his forthcoming *Lives of Remarkable Irishmen* would note how "monarchy proscribed and democracy imprisoned

[Mackenzie] for endeavouring with others in 1837–8 to carry into effect the views of congress in 1775 and 1812, relative to Canadian independence."[29] This would be an explicit link between Mackenzie's torment in the Canadas and his continued victimization in the United States.

Perhaps the best example of this sense of shared victimhood that defined the exiles was an 1839 letter in the *Canadian* addressed "to our friends & brethren – the refugees from Canada" from "a refugee." Following the salutation "Dear brethren in affliction," the letter described "the dragon[']s wrath" suffered by Canadians who had sought refuge in the United States. The letter then reminded its readers to be thankful for assistance from American inhabitants because, even in exile, they confronted "cold misanthropes, who scoff and sneer at the idea of Canadians having any rights and cast a contemptuous jeer at the unfortunate Refugee." The letter's valediction read "Yours affectionately, In Bonds of affliction."[30] The open letter clearly demonstrates the collective sense of victimization, propagated in the patriot press, which defined the community as one of suffering exiles and recognized US nationals who were attuned to the exiles' undue suffering. Such notions of shared suffering fostered a distinctive identity among patriots and a common commitment to advocacy.

The use of suffering as a community marker for the patriot press in the United States harkened back to the way in which Loyalists had portrayed themselves as beleaguered exiles from a successful republican revolution.[31] As was the case with the Loyalists, not only did such language help define the community, it could also evoke aid from sympathizers. Even though patriots made heavy use of American revolutionary imagery, it is possible that those exiled from the Canadas could have absorbed the loyalist framing of victimhood, which was reinforced in Upper Canada by the invasions of the War of 1812.[32]

A significant aspect of this self-definition as victims was the racialization of people who perpetrated the abuses suffered by patriots, including many that escaped to the United States. Such language not only set boundaries around the patriot movement as victims of mistreatment but also coded the patriot movement as white and disparaged opponents using common racial tropes of the day.[33] The patriot press highlighted the victimization suffered by the movement from "black guards" and "Indian Savages." Such language spoke to patriot umbrage at the added insult of mistreatment by those of perceived inferior status.[34] The epithetic nature of "black guard" was not lost on contemporary readers, as *blackguard* referenced a scoundrel or someone who was rude or used foul and abusive language. *Mackenzie's Gazette* accused the British of encouraging the formation of "Royal Black Guards" who harassed the Upper Canadian population. This double use of the term *black guard* was always racialized in the patriot press community. The *Lewiston Advocate* accused "Her Majesty's Negroes at

Chippewa" of perpetrating violence.[35] By associating monarchy and "negroes," the patriot press community in the United States reinforced the conception of monarchy as contrary to deliberation, independent manhood (coded as white), and citizenship. Black attendance at events could be cast in the wider press in this period in a manner to discredit a public meeting, the presence of blacks pointing to a "fringe cause."[36]

The patriot press also highlighted examples of victimization against the patriot movement by "Indian Savages" in a manner that evoked images from the American Revolution and the War of 1812.[37] Rumours and accusations swirled in patriot circles about killings by Indigenous warriors sent by Upper Canadian authorities to suppress the December 1837 rising in western Upper Canada.[38] In one specific instance, an exile living in Ypsilanti, Michigan, sent a letter to *Mackenzie's Gazette* outlining his escape from Upper Canada after being charged with planning a conspiracy. He related how the local militia hired "Indians" to pursue him, plied them with liquor, and promised them money for his scalp.[39]

In another example, the editor of the *Buffalonian* commented on a gathering in 1838 of local Seneca at Perry's Coffee House in Buffalo. The editor linked such a gathering to reports that a chief had admitted that the Seneca were bribed by the British "to cross to Canada, and help the Queen's Troops hunt down the Patriots – a large sum having been offered them for every scalp!" Evoking images of past conflicts with the British, the editor intoned, "This is British to the back bone – so were our fathers hunted down by savages, hired by British gold." He also noted that "hiring our Indians to do the brutal and bloody work they [the British] have not the courage to accomplish is perfectly characteristic."[40]

Both the editor of the *Buffalonian* and Mackenzie made direct links between the role of First Nations in the rebellion and accusations of Indigenous violence reflected in the Declaration of Independence. Their rhetorical strategy cast the monarchy as supported by violence inflicted by non-white "dependents." The patriots' struggle was thus linked to the American Revolution. Drawing a direct connection between the 1838 Battle of the Windmill and American images of Indigenous people's involvement in the revolution, Mackenzie transcribed for his readers a grievance contained in the Declaration of Independence accusing George III of endeavouring "to bring on the inhabitants of our frontiers, the merciless Indian Savages, whose known rule of warfare, is an undistinguished destruction of all ages, sexes and conditions." Mackenzie followed this with a report on the battle by the constitutionalist Upper Canadian *Kingston Chronicle*, which stated that "a party of Indian Warriors" had arrived at the Windmill "anxious" to attack the patriots.[41] Through Mackenzie's editorial handiwork, the "merciless Indian Savages" of 1776 were transposed to 1838. The *Buffalonian* quoted a similar grievance from the Declaration of Independence in its discussion of the aforementioned rumours of Seneca-British cooperation.[42] These accounts of racialized violence and abuse served to help define the patriot press and its readers as victims. Importantly, it also publicly coded the community as white.

The patriots were correct that persons of colour constituted some of the strongest opposition during the rebellion. Mary Fryer notes how "Blacks were among the most reliable troops for service on the frontiers because they viewed Americans as implacable enemies for tolerating slavery."[43] Josiah Henson, an escaped slave and local notable in the Upper Canadian black community, recounted his experience helping to lead the 2nd Essex Coloured Volunteers during the rebellion. He clearly explained the motives for members of the black community: "The coloured men were willing to help defend the government that had given them a home when they had fled from slavery."[44] Several historians have chronicled black participation in the rebellion on the side of the colonial administration, and Gerald Horne has noted the long history of perceived and actual support for Britain among African Americans in the United States.[45]

The patriot press contributed to the formation of a community in the United States by explicitly naming "fellow laborers," friendly papers, and those opposing them. They reinforced their commonality by casting themselves as "brethren in affliction," facing hardships, including at the hands of racialized people, because of their beliefs.

A Place in a Partisan Press Landscape

There is a great deal of scholarly literature about the partisan nature of the US press in this period.[46] Patriot papers openly disclaimed interest in American party politics, instead promising Canadian news and a republican stance.[47] The *Canadian* of Jackson, Michigan, is a good example. The newspaper proclaimed in bold type below its title: "The Canadian is edited by a refugee – published by a Democrat – printed by a Whig, and read by all the world."[48] In his prospectus for the *North American*, Jackson Vail proscribed any "meddling with party politics of the United States."[49] Edward Theller, in the pages of his *Spirit of '76*, went further and spoke adamantly against party politics, declaring party discipline "a curse to social intercourse; and a disgraceful barrier to the promotion of the public good." Outlining the position taken by his *Spirit of '76*, Theller explained that "we have always been, and ever will continue to be, a genuine democratic republican in the strictest sense."[50] The aversion among patriot papers to party dynamics could have been imported. The development of political parties, especially in Upper Canada, was ongoing and the press in the Canadas, while political, typically disclaimed interest in "factions" or parties.[51] This is not to say that patriot papers were never partisan; for example, from its inception, the patriot *Morning Post* promoted Democratic agendas.[52]

Members of the patriot press community in the United States had to determine their relationship with the American partisan press. Letter writers to patriot newspapers debated the patriot credentials of federal officeholders, such as President Martin Van Buren, and of the two major political parties, the Democrats and Whigs.[53] Individual patriot papers varied in their responses to these pressures. The *North American* did not engage in partisan politics. For example, it refused to print most of the proceedings of a Democratic meeting because it had "no desire to commit ourselves with any political party in the States."[54] Theller vacillated in such matters. When pressed on who he would endorse in the election for Michigan governor, Theller picked the Whig politician John Biddle.[55] Theller, however, switched to supporting the Democrats at the federal level, endorsing the Van Buren-Johnson ticket in the presidential election the next year.[56] Mackenzie drifted into the Democratic Party orbit in Rochester, possibly because of his close association and increasing reliance on Henry O'Reilly, Rochester postmaster, editor, and Democratic Party activist.[57] However, as a sign of the cross-party nature of the patriot press, Mackenzie's move to endorse the Democrats cost him a sizeable number of Whig subscribers.[58]

Patriot papers cast themselves as "republican" in contrast to opponents, whom they labelled as "tories." When attacked by the *Detroit Free Press* as a Whig, Theller responded that he would not be bothered by how others cast him but that, if he were indeed a Whig, he was "a Whig – of '76!"[59] In a following issue, Theller noted how Democratic papers branded his editorial line as follows: in "principle '*Patriot*' – in politics, neutral."[60]

The patriot press perceived those newspapers that attacked them not as of a different party but rather as opponents of republicanism. If papers were republican and patriot rather than partisan, then those in opposition to the patriots were "tory." Such attacks resulted in the destruction of two patriot papers. Dr Samuel Underhill, editor of the *Bald Eagle*, embroiled himself in an argument and eventually a violent conflict with A.H. Curtis, a fellow Cleveland editor with whom he had previously clashed.[61] Underhill accused "Mr. C." of having "Toryish" principles and of reading and sometimes taking the *Bald Eagle*, *Herald*, and *Intelligencer* from a store on Cleveland's Bank Street. The short article proclaimed that "the spunging of newspapers is a leading trait of the tories. We hope Mr. C., will step out of this bad habit. Mr. C. has said that if the Eagle fellows call him a Tory he would call up and give 'em a licking. You are a Tory Mr. C. NOW COME ON."[62] Curtis did come on. One of his friends recounted in a letter his participation in the expedition to trash the *Bald Eagle* office. According to the friend, Underhill had attacked "the private character" of Curtis "in a most foul and libelous manner"; Curtis, the friend, and others "decided that the whole establishment was a nuisance and ought to be demolished." The group attacked the *Bald Eagle* office and pounded the press "as fine as the type" with a sledgehammer.[63] Underhill had brought a republican/anti-republican dichotomy to an existing conflict with a local political figure, and violence was one of the consequences.

Thomas Low Nichols of the *Mercury and Buffalonian* had a similar experience. Nichols, a frequent critic of local Whig politician Hiram Pratt, wrote in March 1839 that "none but a deep dyed tory [would] vote for Hiram Pratt."[64] A few weeks later, after Nichols was threatened and refused to back down, Pratt's supporters destroyed the office of the *Mercury and Buffalonian*.[65] Nichols kept up his attacks on Pratt, eventually being imprisoned for libel, after which he published a book on his suffering at the hands of Pratt.[66]

As the patriot press community coalesced in the United States, the editors of these papers sought to find their place in the existing US political landscape. Returning to the case of Francis Wright described in the opening of this chapter, the commotion as she began speaking could have been a product of the patriot press still finding its place in this landscape: Wright was, after all, a controversial radical reformer and not all in attendance would have been interested in or agreed with her views.[67] But did the "uproar" greeting her speech result from her views or from her gender and patriots' views about the place of women in the patriot movement in exile?

The Patriot Press Addresses the Place of Women in the Movement

A possibility regarding the controversy with Frances Wright is that Mackenzie may have transgressed respectable gender boundaries in the patriot movement by having a woman speak to a group of men. The patriot press used the language of respectability to set boundaries of female participation in the movement. It was faced with the challenge of determining boundaries of participation based on contemporary understandings of women's participation in the public sphere.

In patriot public writings, women were relegated to "traditional" roles as spectators or as "auxiliaries" that is, doing "women's work" such as food preparation and sewing. When patriot women did form patriot voluntary associations – which were covered in the patriot press – they stayed within appropriate female spheres. However, patriot women in the United States did evince a more activist "republican motherhood" role in public than was the case in the

Canadas, and that more proactive stance was supported as acceptable participation by the patriot press, if not by constitutionalist editors in the Canadas.[68]

There were clear gendered divisions – social and spatial – in the patriot press community, as was the case in popular politics and voluntary associations more generally. The patriot press made use of the ritualized female gaze, common for other public political displays, to define what it perceived as the proper place of women. One of the ways the patriots publicly acknowledged women's participation in the movement was by strategically placing women as a conspicuously visible audience for male ceremony, in a manner similar to women's roles in other public gatherings.[69]

A story by patriot Daniel Heustis is relevant to this discussion. In his 1847 memoir, Heustis provides an account of events following his arrest by authorities on charges of breaching American neutrality laws.[70] Heustis was indicted and ordered to travel to the trial site, accompanied by the US marshal who had charged him. The marshal, reputedly wanting to inflate his reputation by "capturing a big fish," asked Heustis to impersonate William Lyon Mackenzie when they stopped at a local tavern.[71] Heustis wrote of the interest of those who had gathered at the tavern. He recounted how one tavern goer had "sent his horse and sleigh the distance of a mile and a half, after his beloved wife, that she might see the distinguished stranger."[72] The man was going to great lengths to have his wife participate in supporting the patriot movement, for her, female participation was limited to gazing at a "distinguished" patriot. Heustis, after having a meal, ventured to the sitting room to find it full of women of all ages. The women circled then around him two to three deep. Writing on this event, Heustis reasoned that "such manifestations of interest in the fate of those who have risked fortune and life in a struggle for liberty, are not uncommon. In all such contests the heart of WOMAN instinctively entwines its sympathies around the oppressed and unfortunate."[73] The language of sentiment, evident in the characterizations of patriot victimhood, extended to women to bind them to the cause, albeit it in a limited role. Heustis was keen to use this story as an opportunity to publicly identify women in his memoir as supporters of the patriots and to mark their participation through their gaze. Such language spoke to contemporary gendered constructs around women as providing emotional support and a caring role in the home and in public.[74]

Theller played a role in defining female participation in the public sphere as spectators. Patriots in Cleveland and Detroit participated in the civic welcome of Vice President Richard Johnson during a tour of the region. In his *Spirit of '76*, Theller noted that "Patriot Artillery" had been lent to the "Johnson Committee" formed to welcome the vice president to Detroit.[75] He wrote with a female audience in mind as, according to him, "our paper has become popular, and much read by the Ladies."[76] In an announcement in his paper that followed the headline "LADIES!" Theller gave advice on where to "find arrangements for review of [the] formation of [the] procession" for those women interested in witnessing the demonstration for Johnson. These locations included "City Hall, National Hotel, and adjoining buildings, and gentlemen have been designated to pay you proper attention."[77] The last phrase points to Theller's desire to direct women in a manner that reflected their role in other public demonstrations, where they were seated so that they could see and be seen by the male participants in the event.[78]

As was the case outside of the patriot movement, gender constructs also directed patriot women's organizing into "auxiliary roles" based on certain domestic talents coded as female, namely cooking and sewing. In the *Bald Eagle*, a "True Patriot" asked if a benefit ball for the distressed patriots could be organized by the citizens of the city where the "Ladies furnish the refreshments (as has been the case in Buffalo) and the gentlemen the room and music." This short letter was accompanied by an approbatory statement by Underhill that similar events had taken place in Rochester and Watertown.[79] Speaking at the celebration to honour Vice President Johnson's visit to Detroit, Theller declared that "we always knew the ladies were Patriots ... just witness their handy work at the Barbacue [*sic*] tables today."[80] Thus the extent to which women were regarded as patriots in the press was dependent on the quality of their female-coded labour. Women were positioned by the press into "auxiliary" roles, albeit ones that still allowed for a political subjectivity on their part.

The patriot press also celebrated women's contribution of sewn articles to the cause. In his memoir, Heustis recounts how the Patriot Hunters at the Battle of the Windmill unfurled a flag that had been created by the "Patriotic ladies of Onondaga County."[81] In British North America, both cooking and sewing were coded as the main acceptable forms of female public participation.[82] Patriots, in their endeavours to define their movement in exile, borrowed and reinforced those boundaries of respectability.

When women did organize for the patriot cause, it was likely in avenues seen as acceptable to female participation: boycotts and benevolence. In conformity with sewing as women's work, during the non-importation campaign in Lower Canada, women had taken an active part in the creation, consumption, and promotion of homemade goods beyond what would normally have been the practice.[83] Similar boycotts emerged after the exile of the patriot movement to the United States. A patriot association in Rochester in December 1838 passed a pledge that those in attendance would boycott British goods and would work to spread this ban to the surrounding county. Directly referencing the boycotts of the American Revolution, the association requested, "Let the pledge be conscientiously observed, as our ancestors observed their pledge against the use of Tea, and let us persevere till the end is accomplished."[84] While the names of those undertaking this pledge are not known, women could join such pledges in other boycotts. As historian Timothy Breen found during the American Revolution, while such initiatives were developed by male politicians, women could – and often did – take part in boycotts and non-importation campaigns.[85]

Patriot women also formed their own voluntary associations, although this work was restricted to the role of traditional female benevolence. An example reported in the patriot press involved a group of women who met in the ladies' parlour of the United States Hotel in Buffalo on the first anniversary of the burning of the *Caroline*, an American ship set afire by the British for supplying patriots in Upper Canada.[86] The meeting resulted in the formation of the Buffalo Ladies Benevolent Society. Made up of an executive of women who occupied the roles of president, vice-president, secretary, treasurer, and a "committee of seven," the society resolved to meet monthly.[87] The proceedings of their meetings were originally published in one of that city's patriot papers, the *Buffalonian*. The story was copied and commented on by other patriot papers based in Rochester and Cleveland.[88] Moreover, a contributor named J. Van Kleeve published a letter thanking the "ladies" for their patriotism.[89]

This benevolent society resolved to dedicate itself to "relieving the sufferings of such Canadian Patriots of their families as may be thrown destitute among us, and to aid them in their laudable efforts to break the galling chains of the oppressor."[90] This sentence seems to inch beyond benevolence for the needy and points to a different understanding of the possibilities of political engagement for women in public. Here patriot women were speaking the same communal bounding language of victimization, with references to "galling chains" and "sufferings." Patriots appear to have accepted this form of organizing by women. It is possible that this statement – more political than what was common in the press in the Canadas – is representative of what historians have termed "republican motherhood."[91] Mary Kelley argues that the involvement of women in literary societies and reform organizations helped lay the groundwork for women's increasing involvement in civil society. This could also be the case when women engaged with the patriot cause and were recognized in the press for their contributions.[92]

The coverage of the Buffalo Ladies Benevolent Society was also taken up across the border in Upper Canada. While not publishing its proceedings, the constitutionalist *Cobourg Star* published a long article ridiculing the organization. Its editor, R.D. Chatterton, wrote: "The working of flags and making of shirts and stockings for runaways and rebels, may be a very lady-like and interesting occupation; but a public meeting of petticoat sympathisers is a farce so ridiculous – an exhibition so unwonted and uncalled for." Chatterton initially believed the story to be fictitious until he enquired and "found that the names were real, and the women (we beg pardon, 'ladies') were well known to several persons here."[93]

Chatterton's report on the Buffalo Ladies Benevolent Society meeting across the lake in turn provoked a public discussion in Cobourg, Upper Canada. A writer named "Quiz" sent a letter to the editor on the subject of the Buffalo ladies group, which Chatterton declined to print because it "would shock 'the delicacy' of those advocates of rebellion."[94] Gendered understandings of respectability proved a firmer boundary than did Lake Ontario. As an opponent of the patriots, Chatterton would have looked upon a patriot meeting negatively. However, his response also indicates different understandings by patriots in the United States and constitutionalists in Upper Canada regarding the boundaries of respectable female participation in the public sphere. As Chatterton stated, "We say it with pride, we have never yet known British or Canadian Women go quite so far as a public political meeting." Notably, Chatterton withheld markers of respectability from the women in Buffalo as the way to belittle the appropriateness of their organizing. He selectively used the term "lady" – the "lady-like" auxiliary work of producing socks and flags – in contrast to the "farce" of "women" holding a public meeting supporting the patriots.[95]

In a similar manner, the patriot press itself policed firm boundaries around women's public participation in the patriot movement, raising the criterion of "respectability" when these boundaries were transgressed. One such transgression involved efforts in Detroit to secure William Lyon Mackenzie's release from imprisonment in Rochester after his conviction in June 1839 for violating American neutrality laws. A number of patriots in Detroit circulated a petition for his release. In his *Spirit of '76*, Theller reported that "nearly fifteen hundred of our most respectable citizens signed it." However, Theller was incensed that the petition was left out at a bar, resulting in the collection of certain "irreputable" signatures including "Peggy Welsh and the inmates of her BROTHEL." Theller explained to his readers that such signatures were the result of a scheme to leave the petition in a compromising location by a lawyer and other "members of the aristocracy."[96] Here, issues of class and morality joined that of gender. The discrediting of a petition by noting its inclusion of disreputable signatures, such as those of women, boys, or men of low social standing, was a common tactic in British North America.[97] In Theller's view, clear boundaries of gendered respectability were prerequisites to protecting the reputation of the patriot community and to claim political standing. One of the political venues open to women in the nineteenth century was petitioning. In this case, however, the women in question were publicly rejected by a patriot organizer for not meeting societal norms of respectability around social class, family, and chastity.

Canadian refugees and their American sympathizers worked to re-establish a patriot press once in exile in the United States after November 1837. That press worked to build a community and to accommodate what had been a Canadian movement now in a different political and social environment. The patriot press created a community by explicitly defining which newspapers belonged and which did not. Through its writings, the press helped defined the community as one united by "suffering," including at the hands of those whom patriots deemed racially inferior. As was made clear by the uproar in response to Frances Wright, members of the patriot press community encountered difficulties in placing themselves within the American partisan milieu and in discerning "proper" understandings of women's participation in the public sphere.

This study of unrest, violence, and social order parallels the work of other contributors to this volume. The difficulties faced by the patriots in exile as a result of divergent notions of order in Canada and the United States echo Bradley Miller's contribution on the difficulties of establishing order on a borderland. In addition, the ways in which patriots in exile worked towards the goals of binding together a community in exile and maintaining order in patriot circles without a state apparatus speaks to the importance of language, community formation, and the public sphere in the formation of social order, in ways that echo the chapters by Scott See, Darren Ferry, and M. Max Hamon.

NOTES

1 See Eugene P. Link, "Vermont Physicians and the Canadian Rebellion of 1837," *Vermont History* 37 (1969): 182; and Albert B. Corey, *The Crisis of 1830–1842 in Canadian-American Relations* (New Haven, CT: Yale University Press, 1941), 84.

2 For British North America, see Jeffrey L. McNairn, *The Capacity to Judge: Public Opinion and Deliberative Democracy in Upper Canada, 1791–1854* (Toronto: University of Toronto Press, 2000); Michael Eamon, *Imprinting Britain: Newspapers, Sociability, and the Shaping of British North America* (Montreal and Kingston: McGill-Queen's University Press, 2015); and Duncan Koerber, "Faction and Its

Alternative: Representing Political Organizing in the Print Public Sphere in Early Canada," *Journalism History* 40, no. 1 (2014): 51–8.

3 Allan Greer, "1837–38: Rebellion Reconsidered," *Canadian Historical Review* 76, no. 1 (1995): 16.

4 Ian McKay, "The Liberal Order Framework: A Prospectus for a Reconnaissance of Canadian History," *Canadian Historical Review* 81, no. 4 (2000): 635; Allan Greer, *The Patriots and the People: The Rebellion of 1837 in Rural Lower Canada* (Toronto: University of Toronto Press, 1993), 362–3; Stanley Bréhaut Ryerson, *Unequal Union: The Roots of the Crisis in the Canadas, 1815–1873* (Toronto: Progress Books, 1973); Louis-Georges Harvey, *Le printemps de l'Amérique française: Américanité, anticolonialisme, et républicanisme dans le discours politique québécois, 1805–1837* (Montreal: Les Éditions du Boréal, 2005); and Michel Ducharme, *Le concept de liberté au Canada à l'époque des Révolutions atlantiques, 1776–1838* (Montreal and Kingston: McGill-Queen's University Press, 2010).

5 For a Foucauldian bureaucratic state, see some of the contributions in Allan Greer and Ian Radforth, eds, *Colonial Leviathan: State Formation in Mid-Nineteenth Century Canada* (Toronto: University of Toronto Press, 1992); and Jean-Marie Fecteau, *Un nouvel ordre des choses: La pauvreté, le crime, l'État au Québec, de la fin du XVIIIe siècle à 1840* (Outremont, QC: VLB éditeur, 1989). For a liberal order, see McKay, "Liberal Order Framework," 617–51. Others take care to not imbue the rebellion with too much significance; they stress continuity over the rebellion period. For example, see Donald Fyson, *Magistrates, Police, and People: Everyday Criminal Justice in Quebec and Lower Canada, 1764–1837* (Toronto: University of Toronto Press, 2006).

6 I take this phrase from Greer, *The Patriots and the People*, 6. Greer is referencing events in the district of Montreal.

7 Elizabeth Jameson and Jeremy Mouat, "Telling Differences: The Forty-Ninth Parallel and Historiographies of the West and Nation," *Pacific Historical Review* 75, no. 2 (2006): 183–230.

8 The 1837 *Frontier Sentinel* of Lewiston, New York, constitutes a probable patriot paper that I cannot verify as no known issues remain extant. Early newspaper chroniclers, the earliest being Follett, noted that Thomas P. Scovill established the paper in connection to the "Patriot War." Frederick Follett, *History of the Press of Western New York* (Rochester: Jerome and Brother, 1847), 65. In addition to this noted connection, Scovill was an agent for *Mackenzie's Gazette* in Lewistown. *Mackenzie's Gazette*, 23 March 1839, 9 March 1839, 2 March 1839.

9 Julien Mauduit, "'Vrais républicains' d'Amérique: Les patriotes canadiens en exil aux États-Unis (1837–1842)" (PhD diss., Université du Québec à Montréal, 2016), 252; and Lillian F. Gates, *After the Rebellion: The Later Years of William Lyon Mackenzie* (Toronto: Dundurn Press, 1988), 36, 41.

10 Because of the limited number of surviving issues, determining an average lifespan is difficult and any calculation would be somewhat artificial.
11 *Bald Eagle* (Cleveland), 8 January 1839.
12 For example, see *Mackenzie's Gazette* (New York City/Rochester), 10 November 1838; *Bald Eagle*, 21 December 1838 and 8 January 1839; *Spirit of '76* (Detroit), 26 March 1840.
13 *Mackenzie's Gazette,* 29 December 1838.
14 The paper would move to Rochester at the beginning of 1839. Frederick H. Armstrong and Ronald J. Stagg, "William Lyon Mackenzie," *Dictionary of Canadian Biography* (hereafter cited as *DCB*), vol. ix.
15 *Lewiston Telegraph*, 25 April 1838.
16 *Mackenzie's Gazette*, 29 December 1838.
17 *Freeman's Advocate* (Lockport, NY), 11 January 1839; *Spirit of '76*, 5 September 1839.
18 *Canadian Patriot* (Derby Line, VT), 2 February 1838; *Bald Eagle*, 15 January 1839.
19 *Volunteer* (Rochester), 15 May 1841.
20 *Weekly Mercury and Buffalonian*, 2 February 1839. See also *Freeman's Advocate*, 11 January 1839.
21 *Mackenzie's Gazette*, 27 April 1839; *Lewiston Telegraph*, 26 April 1839.
22 *Lewiston Telegraph*, 26 April 1839.
23 *Spirit of '76*, 26 March 1840.
24 *Bald Eagle*, 21 December 1838; *Lewiston Telegraph*, 26 April 1839.
25 For Upper Canada, Wilton notes that the period "was sometimes referred to as a 'Reign of Terror.'" Carol Wilton, *Popular Politics and Political Culture in Upper Canada, 1800–1850* (Montreal and Kingston: McGill Queen's University Press, 2000), 190. For Lower Canada, see Greer, *Patriots and the People*, 327–37, 351–6. This language of suffering was also used by prisoners in Lower Canada. See Jarett Henderson, "Banishment to Bermuda: Gender, Race, Empire, Independence, and the Struggle to Abolish Irresponsible Government in Lower Canada," *Histoire sociale / Social History* 46, no. 92 (2013): 321–48.
26 They were, however, not safe from US imprisonment. While there was much enthusiasm for the driving of Britain from North America, the US government, aware that assistance to the patriots meant war with Britain, adhered to a policy of neutrality and actually enacted a stronger neutrality act in 1838. Some patriots, such a Mackenzie, were imprisoned for violations of the act. However, sympathetic juries acquitted a number of others such as Robert Nelson. See Kenneth R. Stevens, *Border Diplomacy: The* Caroline *and McLeod Affairs in Anglo-American-Canadian Relations, 1837–1842* (Tuscaloosa: University of Alabama Press, 1989); Matthew Karp, *This Vast Southern Empire: Slaveholders at the Helm of American Foreign Policy* (Cambridge, MA: Harvard University Press, 2016), 19–20; and Richard Chabot, Jacques Monet, and Yves Roby, "Robert Nelson," *DCB*, vol. x.

27 See, for example, *Mackenzie's Gazette*, Prospectus, 17 April 1838. Circular of the Monroe County Convention "The Cause of Freedom," box 4, Papers of Henry O'Reilly, Rochester Historical Society, Rochester, New York (hereafter PHOR). Resolution from a meeting in Cayuga County, New York, *Bald Eagle* (Cleveland), 11 January 1839; resolution from a meeting in Conneaut, Ohio, the *Budget* (Conneaut), 1 February 1838; resolution from the Buffalo Ladies Benevolent Society, *Bald Eagle*, 8 January 1839. "Sufferings" is even in the title of one of the more well-known patriot memoirs: Daniel D. Heustis, *A Narrative of the Adventures and Sufferings of Captain Daniel D. Heustis and His Companions in Canada and Van Dieman's land* ... (Boston: Silas W. Wilder, 1847).

28 *Bald Eagle*, 21 December 1838.

29 Mackenzie to O'Callaghan, 16 January 1844, vol. 1, O'Callaghan Papers, Library and Archives Canada, MG 24 B 50. The book was published as *Sons of the Emerald Isle* and does not contain a biography of the author on the title page.

30 *Canadian* (Jackson, MI), 1 January 1838. From the content of the paper and its reception by other patriot papers, it is clear that the issue is from 1 January 1839 and the date on the paper is a major typographical error.

31 D.G. Bell, *Early Loyalist Saint John: The Origin of New Brunswick Politics, 1783–1786* (Fredericton: New Ireland Press, 1983); and Maya Jassanoff, *Liberty's Exiles: American Loyalists in the Revolutionary World* (New York: Alfred A. Knopf, 2011). Re petitioning, see Janice Potter-MacKinnon, *While the Women Only Wept: Loyalist Refugee Women in Eastern Ontario* (Montreal and Kingston: McGill-Queen's University Press, 1993), esp. 50–100. For an example of similar self-depictions as suffering on the patriot side of the American Revolution see Linda Kerber, "'I Have Don ... much to Carrey on the Warr': Women and the Shaping of Ideology after the American Revolution," in *Women and Politics in the Age of Democratic Revolution*, ed. H.B. Applewhite and D.G. Levy (Ann Arbor: University of Michigan Press, 1990). In the United States, this transitioned into republican motherhood.

32 See Alan Taylor, *The Civil War of 1812: American Citizens, British Subjects, Irish Rebels, and Indian Allies* (New York: Alfred A. Knopf, 2010), 443–5.

33 This is not to say that there were no people of colour who were interested in or participating in the patriot movement. There is a record of people of colour attending a patriot meeting in Washington, according to the *American* quoted in the *Brockville Recorder*, 29 November 1838. Patriots Donald McLeod and Henry S. Handy wrote in 1839 of many First Nation warriors willing to serve in patriot forces. While their claims seem too vague and grandiose to be credible, it does suggest openness on the part of certain patriots to working with First Nations as allies. See Charles Lindsey, *The Life and Times of William Lyon Mackenzie* (Toronto: P.R. Randall, 1862), 236–7.

34 McNairn, *The Capacity to Judge*, 104.
35 *Mackenzie's Gazette*, 16 and 9 June 1838.
36 The *Liberal* had used this same tactic in the Canadas. See *Liberal* quoted in the *Brockville Recorder*, 9 November 1837.
37 See, for instance, the *Buffalonian* (copied in *Mackenzie's Gazette*, 30 June 1838) and *Mackenzie's Gazette*, 24 November 1838.
38 These rumours were finally put to rest by historian Colin Read, a century and a half later, in *The Rising in Western Upper Canada 1837–38: The Duncombe Revolt and After* (Toronto: University of Toronto Press, 1982).
39 *Mackenzie's Gazette*, 15 September 1838.
40 *Buffalonian* extra, 25 June 1838, extras from various papers, box 4, PHOR. See also the partial copy in *Mackenzie's Gazette*, 30 June 1838.
41 *Mackenzie's Gazette*, 24 November 1838.
42 *Buffalonian* extra, 25 June 1838, PHOR.
43 Mary Beacock Fryer, *Volunteers and Redcoats, Raiders and Rebels: A Military History of the Rebellion of Upper Canada* (Toronto: Dundurn Press, 1987), 67.
44 Josiah Henson, *Autobiography of the Rev. Josiah Henson*, ed. John Lobb. (London: Office of the *Christian Age*, 1878), 176.
45 Melody Brown, "Blacks in the Rebellion of 1837," in *1837 Rebellion Remembered* (Willowdale: Ontario Historical Society, 1988), 113–16; Fred Landon, "Canadian Negroes and the Rebellion of 1837," *Journal of Negro History* 7, no. 4 (1922): 377–9; and Gerald Horne, *Negro Comrades of the Crown: African Americans and the British Empire Fight in the US before Emancipation* (New York: New York University Press, 2012).
46 Jeffrey L. Pasley, *The Tyranny of the Printers: Newspaper Politics in the Early American Republic* (Charlottesville: University of Virginia Press, 2002); and Thomas C. Leonard, *News for All: America's Coming-of-Age with the Press* (New York: Oxford University Press, 1995).
47 *Bald Eagle*, 21 December 1838. Thomas Richards Jr has argued that patriots were non-partisan because Americans interested in independence for the Canadas envisioned creating in Upper Canada "the ideal – nonpartisan – republic." I posit that, rather than an American desire for a new and better republic, the non-partisan nature of the patriot press was a combination of a number of factors, one being that it was a holdover from the patriot press's origins in the Canadas. It is of note that, for example, Richards cites those with a connection to the Canadas, namely Mackenzie and his son James. Richards's argument rather could have been why Americans were attracted to these papers (i.e., why we have a ready American readership for non-partisan patriot papers, not why we have non-partisan patriot papers). Thomas Richards Jr, "The Texas Moment: Breakaway Republics and Contested Sovereignty in North America, 1836–46" (PhD diss., Temple University, 2016), 172–5.

48 *Canadian*, 1 January 1839.
49 *Bald Eagle*, 15 January 1839.
50 *Spirit of '76*, 23 December 1839.
51 Jane Errington, *The Lion, the Eagle, and Upper Canada: A Developing Ideology*, 2nd ed. (Montreal and Kingston: McGill-Queen's University Press, 2012), 188; McNairn, *The Capacity to Judge*, 107, 136–8; Duncan Koerber, "The Role of Agents in Partisan Communication Networks of Upper Canadian Newspapers" *Journal of Canadian Studies* 45, no. 3 (2011): 137–65; and Koerber, "Faction and Its Alternative."
52 Detroit Institute of Arts, *American Paintings in the Detroit Institute of Arts*, vol. 2 (New York: Hudson Hills, 1997), 38.
53 *Mackenzie's Gazette*, 15 September 1838; *Spirit of '76*, 26 August 1839.
54 *North American* (Swanton, VT), 19 June 1839.
55 *Spirit of '76*, 26 August 1839.
56 Ibid., 8 October 1840.
57 Gates, *After the Rebellion*, 81; and Mauduit, "'Vrais républicains' d'Amérique," 262.
58 Gates, *After the Rebellion*, 84; Richards, "The Texas Moment," 173–4; and *Mackenzie's Gazette,* 18 August 1838 and 25 August 1838.
59 *Spirit of '76*, 21 August 1839.
60 Ibid., 26 August 1839.
61 A.H. Curtis also held minor political offices during the period. He was acting city clerk for two days in April 1837 and appears as street commissioner in the 1838 list of officers of the city of Cleveland. See *Historical Record of Public Officeholders in Cuyahoga County* (Cleveland: Library Service Project, Work Projects Administration in Ohio, 1942), 125; and Crisfield Johnson, *History of Cuyahoga County, Ohio* (Cleveland: D.W. Ensign, 1879), 323. Curtis was involved with the *Cleveland Advertiser* and the *Green Thistle*. See David Van Tassel and John Grabowski, *The Cleveland Encyclopedia* (Bloomington: Indiana University Press, 1987), 197; and *Bald Eagle*, 28 December 28.
62 *Bald Eagle*, 21 December 1838. "Spunging" in this case referred to taking or reading newspapers from a location without paying for them. For the norms and practices around copying and exchanging news among American editors of the period, see Laura J. Murray, "Exchange Practices among Nineteenth-Century US Newspaper Editors: Cooperation in Competition," in *Putting Intellectual Property in Its Place: Rights Discourses, Creative Labor, and the Everyday*, ed. Laura J. Murray, S. Tina Piper, and Kirsty Robertson (New York: Oxford University Press, 2014), 86–109.
63 Duncan to E. Ned Morgan, 22 January 1839, "Cleveland Riots," Ohio Historical Society, Columbus. VFM 407; and D.W. Cross, "The Log Book I.: The Death of the Bald Eagle" *Magazine of Western History* 7, no. 1 (1887): 617–19.

64 *Semi Weekly Mercury and Buffalonian*, 5 March 1839; *Daily Mercury and Buffalonian*, 14 March 1839; and Michael F. Rizzo, *Through the Mayors' Eyes: Buffalo, New York 1832–2005* (Morrisville, NC: LuLu Enterprises, 2005), 20–2.

65 *Daily Mercury and Buffalonian*, 13 March 1839; *Mackenzie's Gazette*, 30 March 1839.

66 Thomas L. Nichols, *Journal in Jail* ... (Buffalo: A. Dinsmore, 1840).

67 Such politics were not foreign to the patriot movement. A number of patriot editors held or propagated similar radical views and were involved in causes such as Owenism, Fourierism, Locofocoism, abolitionism, and freethought. On Underhill and H.D. Robinson, see Albert Post, *Popular Freethought in America, 1825–1850* (New York: Octagon Books, 1974), 42–4, 62–3, 91, 116, 141, 181, 214; Andrew Bonthius, "The Patriot War of 1837–1838: Locofocoism with a Gun?" *Labour/Le travail* 52 (2003): 9–43; Colin Read, "Edward Alexander Theller, the 'Supreme Vagabond': 'Courageous, Honest' and True'?" *Ontario History* 84, no. 1 (1992): 1–14; and Mauduit, ""Vrais républicains" d'Amérique," esp. chs. 5 and 6.

68 Cecilia Morgan, "'When Bad Men Conspire, Good Men Must Unite!' Gender and Political Discourses in Upper Canada, 1820s–1830s," in *Gendered Pasts: Historical Essays in Femininity and Masculinity in Canada*, ed. Kathleen McPherson, Cecilia Morgan, and Nancy M. Forestell (Toronto: Oxford University Press, 1999). To be sure, participation of women in the patriot cause did expand to slightly more active roles beyond what was publicly defined in the press. The most notable examples are two women who were engaged in ferrying messages for the patriots: Eunice Whiting and Anna Burch. See Charles Dickens, *American Notes* (Harmondsworth, UK: Penguin, 1972), 80; Dennis Curtis and Cecilia Blanchfield, *Kingston Penitentiary: The First Hundred and Fifty Years, 1835–1985* (Ottawa: Correctional Service of Canada, 1985), 86; and Lewis Adelbert Norton, *Life and Adventures of Col. L.A. Norton* (Oakland, CA: Pacific Press Publishing House, 1887), 58–9. Marguerite-Julie Cornelier, administered the oath for membership in the Chasseurs, as her husband was illiterate, and continued to do so even when other literate Chasseurs were present. Beverley Boissery and Carla Paterson, "'Women's Work': Women and Rebellion in Lower Canada, 1833–9," in *Canadian State Trials*, vol. 2, *Rebellion and Invasion in the Canadas, 1837–1839*, ed. F. Murray Greenwood and Barry Wright (Toronto: University of Toronto Press, 2002), 362; and Mary Kelley, *Learning to Stand and Speak: Women, Education, and Public Life in America's Republic* (Chapel Hill: University of North Carolina Press, 2006).

69 Bruce Curtis and Mark Francis discuss the importance of this in the "display of social virtues." See Mark Francis, *Governors and Settlers: Images of Authority in the British Colonies, 1820–1860* (Houndmills, UK: Macmillan, 1992), 49–50; and Bruce Curtis, "The 'Most Splendid Pageant Ever Seen:' Grandeur, the Domestic, and

Condescension in Lord Durham's Political Theatre," *Canadian Historical Review* 89, no. 1 (2008): 55–88.

70 Heustis had played an active role in the abortive patriot raid on Hickory Island, Upper Canada, on 22 February 1838.

71 Heustis, *A Narrative*, 35.

72 Ibid.

73 Ibid., 36–7.

74 Cecilia Morgan, *Public Men and Virtuous Women: The Gendered Languages of Religion and Politics in Upper Canada, 1791–1850* (Toronto: University of Toronto Press, 1996).

75 See the Papers of Henry O'Reilly for patriots organizing an address to Johnson in Cleveland and Johnson's reply dated from Detroit: Draft Address to VP Richard M. Johnson upon his visit to Cleveland, 26 September 1840; Reply to the Address, dated Detroit, 30 September 1840, box 4, PHOR. *Spirit of '76*, 28 September 1840.

76 *Spirit of '76*, 22 November 1839.

77 Ibid., 28 September 1840.

78 The trend of placing women in highly visible, if not ceremonial, positions can be seen in the arrival of Governor-General Sydenham in Kingston in May 1841, the funeral after his death on 19 September 1841, an 1839 military demonstration for Durham in Montreal, and the 1860 visit of the Prince of Wales. For Sydenham, see *Kingston Chronicle and Gazette*, 29 May 1841 and 25 September 1841. For the military demonstration, see Curtis, "The 'Most Splendid Pageant Ever Seen,'" 59. For the 1860 visit of the Prince of Wales, see an engraving from the *Illustrated Times* in Ian Radforth, *Royal Spectacle: The 1860 Visit of the Prince of Wales to Canada and the United States* (Toronto: University of Toronto Press, 2004), 117.

79 *The Bald Eagle*, 1 January 1839.

80 *Spirit of '76*, 28 September 1840.

81 Heustis, *A Narrative*, 44. Graves reports that Isabel Mackenzie used her sewing talents for a somewhat non-traditional purpose – sewing cartridges for muskets. Donald E. Graves, *Guns across the River: The Battle of the Windmill* (Prescott, ON: Friends of Windmill Point, 2001), 35. Perhaps the reference by Heustis invoked in the minds of his American readers the memory of Betsy Ross and the "flag of '76."

82 Morgan, *Public Men and Virtuous Women*, 48; and Bonnie Huskins: "From Haute Cuisine to Ox Roasts: Public Feasting and the Negotiation of Class in Mid-19th-Century Saint John and Halifax," *Labour/Le travail* 37 (1996): 9–36. In Kingston, Harriet Dobbs Cartwright was limited to organizing lunches for her husband's electoral campaign. Cartwright Family Letterbook, 226, Harriet Dobbs Cartwright Fonds, Queen's University Archives. The role of women in sewing articles has arguably much more significance, as banners were an important display, the

physical presentation of which created a highly visible gendered ritual of public participation. Women created banners and flags that they presented to male fraternities, voluntary associations, and militia units in the Canadas. See David Sutherland, "Voluntary Societies and the Process of Middle Class Formation in Early Victorian Halifax," *Journal of the Canadian Historical Association* 5, no. 1 (1994): 252. During the rebellion, women had sewn flags for *patriote* forces that would be involved in the Battle of Ste Eustache. Boissery and Paterson, "'Women's Work,'" 359. The *Western Herald* (Sandwich, UC) on 31 January 1838 recounted the ceremony of new colours being presented by the ladies of Sandwich to the local militia. Such gendered ceremonies, however, did not rely exclusively on sewn articles. A group of women presented a mace to a voluntary militia battalion, the Queen's Own Rifles, in the early 1860s. See Ernest Chambers, *History of the Queen's Own Rifles: History of a Splendid Regiment's Origin, 1862–1925* (Toronto: Ruddy, 1901), 49.

83 Boissery and Paterson, "'Women's Work,'" 359–60.

84 Patriot Association, *At the Last Meeting of Our Association, a Pledge in the Following Words Was Presented for the Consideration of the Members* (Rochester, NY: n.p., 1838), Baldwin Room Ephemera, Toronto Reference Library, CIHM Microfiche.

85 For non-importation, see T.H. Breen, *The Marketplace of Revolution: How Consumer Politics Shaped American Independence* (New York: Oxford University Press, 2004).

86 In mid-December 1837, a patriot force from Buffalo crossed the border and occupied the Upper Canadian Navy Island in the Niagara River downstream from the town. A stalemate developed, with British forces on the Upper Canadian mainland and patriots on the island. The patriots were being resupplied from the American shore by the *Caroline*. By 29 December, the British had had enough and led an expedition to destroy the boat. They attacked and burned the boat at night while it was docked on the American mainland, causing a popular uproar and a serious diplomatic incident. For a diplomatic perspective see Stevens, *Border Diplomacy*. For its impact on American popular feeling, see Arthur L. Johnson, "The New York State Press and the Canadian Rebellions," *American Review of Canadian Studies* 14, no. 3 (1984): 279–90.

87 *Bald Eagle*, 8 January 1839.

88 Ibid., 8 January 1839; and *Mackenzie's Gazette*, 12 January 1839.

89 *Mackenzie's Gazette*, 9 March 1839. He referred to the ladies group as "The Buffalo Patriotic Association."

90 *Bald Eagle*, 8 January 1839.

91 For Upper Canada, see Morgan, *Public Men and Virtuous Women*. For the United States, see Linda Kerber, "'I Have Don ... much to Carrey on the Warr.'"

92 Kelley, *Learning to Stand and Speak*.

93 *Cobourg Star*, 9 January 1839. The knowledge of some in Cobourg of a number of patriot women in Buffalo speaks to the tight-knit nature of a rebellion-era borderlands community.

94 Ibid., 23 January 1839.

95 Ibid., 9 January 1839.

96 *Spirit of '76*, 17 August 1839.

97 For petitioning, see Gail G. Campbell, "Disenfranchised but Not Quiescent: Women Petitioners in New Brunswick in the Mid-19th Century," *Acadiensis* 18, no. 2 (1989): 22–54. These included political petitions on subjects such as temperance (36–9). See Lex Heerma van Voss, ed., *Petitions in Social History* (Cambridge: Cambridge University Press, 2002); and Wilton, *Popular Politics and Political Culture in Upper Canada*, 7, 43.

19 The Ambivalence of Order: Jurisdiction in the Disputed Northeast

BRADLEY MILLER

During his 1828 sedition trial in New Brunswick, John Baker rose to deny the legitimacy of the legal process in which he was enmeshed: "I am a citizen of the United States, and owe allegiance to that country ... I live in American Territory, and hold myself only liable to the Courts of that place," he said. "I enter on no defence, and call no evidence. I do decline the jurisdiction of this Court."[1] What Baker meant in his brief remarks was that the settlement of Madawaska in which he lived, and in which he was alleged to have criminally disturbed the peace and undermined the Crown and colonial government, was disputed between New Brunswick and the state of Maine. He considered the United States and not the British Empire to be the rightful sovereign, and Maine and not New Brunswick to have the legitimate jurisdiction over the community. In other words, Baker invoked the territorial limitations on law. Since he asserted that Maine law and not English law governed Madawaska, when Baker hoisted an American flag and pledged to block the operation of English law and the delivery of the Royal Mail in the area, he was doing nothing more than deferring to the only legitimate authority.[2]

His legal strategy was not successful. Both the Crown and the court used the same logic of exclusive and territorially bounded jurisdiction, but both declared that this authority resided with New Brunswick alone. Attorney General Robert Parker stressed the gravity of challenges to jurisdiction, telling the court that Baker's actions had "struck at the root of all society; for if individuals could be permitted to unite for the purpose of subverting the Jurisdiction, putting down the Laws, and bringing the Government into contempt ... all protection for life and property was taken away." He then proceeded to call a long series of witnesses that testified not simply to Baker's crimes but also to the history of New Brunswick's exercise of jurisdiction in Madawaska.[3] Likewise, when Justice Ward Chipman, Jr charged the jury he told them that, if they found that New Brunswick had exercised jurisdiction there in the past, they were bound to uphold its right to do so in this case. They were not deciding the larger question of full sovereignty – what he called "the national right to this Territory" – but rather the much narrower question of jurisdiction, and in this neither Baker's citizenship nor the broader boundary dispute created any exemptions in domestic criminal law.[4] After the jury quickly returned a guilty verdict, the attorney general again emphasized New Brunswick's jurisdiction in the disputed territory, telling the court that Baker should be "taught subjection to the Laws ... so long as he remains within their reach." Moreover, he hoped that the decision would reassure settlers in Madawaska that they would enjoy the protections of colonial law "so long as His Majesty acknowledges them as subjects resident within his dominions."[5]

Baker's case exemplifies much about the nature and power of territorialized ideas of jurisdiction and sovereignty in nineteenth-century North America. Madawaska, together with the Indian Stream territory on the border of Lower Canada and New Hampshire, was at the epicentre of a decades-long dispute between Britain and the United States over the location of the boundary in northeastern North America. For over half a century, imperial and federal governments clashed over the meaning of the boundaries' provision in the 1783 Treaty of Paris, first attempting to settle the matter by surveyors and commissioners and then by an arbitration before the king of the Netherlands before turning to bilateral diplomatic negotiations to settle the question with the 1842 Webster-Ashburton Treaty.[6] As historians such as Albert Corey have long noted, the fifteen years before that treaty was a crisis period in Anglo-American relations, and the location of the boundary was one of the key issues that brought the two countries to the brink of war and that enflamed domestic political divides; in the United States it was enmeshed dramatically in deep and heated debates over the interplay of state and federal government power and clashes between the governments of Maine and Massachusetts, while in Canada it ultimately became an emblem, for some, of Britain's purported inability to represent Canadian interests effectively on the world stage.[7]

Yet the boundary dispute and its many flashpoints like the Baker trial also transcended domestic politics and the different dynamics of governance on both sides of the border. Rather, as they grappled for territorial sovereignty, Britain and the United States expressed the importance of that concept as a core pillar of statehood. As recent scholars have shown, from the seventeenth century onwards, sovereign power was increasingly expressed in territorial terms, with the limits of that power demarcated by linear, inviolable, and mappable borders within which a power had universal or near-universal jurisdiction and claimed exclusive rights to the lawful use of force, an orthodoxy scholars have varyingly called modern, settler, or settler-state sovereignty, depending in part on the context of its application.[8] As Charles Maier has written, "bordering state space established the domain of law and control. It determined the transactions between subjects within and peoples outside: their trade, their coexistence, their right to cross or transport in each direction, the tribute that might be collected."[9] In other words, while physically at the edge of the state, boundaries were increasingly at the conceptual centre of state authority.[10] As a result, the ways in which governments in northeastern North America wielded and defended their jurisdiction in the boundary dispute period highlights much about core early nineteenth-century conceptualization of that power.

Sovereignty, however, was not the crucial issue in the Baker case in 1828 or in the long series of other criminal cases and outbreaks of state and settler violence in the disputed territories of Madawaska and Indian Stream.[11] As Justice Chipman argued in the Baker case, until Britain and the United States agreed to a final settlement, the issue being contested was jurisdictional authority, the right of immediate rule, which was at once a more confined but in practice more meaningful notion than sovereignty. Recent scholars such as Lisa Ford have shown how the nineteenth-century crystallization of territorial sovereignty rested "on the conflation of sovereignty, territory, and jurisdiction"; this chapter attempts to disentangle those three elements.[12] It explores the conception and exercise of jurisdiction in territories where the larger right of sovereignty was fundamentally uncertain. In doing so, it makes a different point from much recent historiography on jurisdiction and sovereignty in the nineteenth-century imperial world. In particular, as P.G. McHugh argues, elsewhere in many parts of the British Empire in this same period, imperial officials were still willing to explore what he calls "jurisdictional options short of full sovereignty," illustrating the continuing fluidity and even pluralism of imperial legalism, especially, though not exclusively, apparent in respect of authority over Indigenous peoples.[13] Even in North America, Britain and the United States were enacting concurrent and pluralistic jurisdiction by treaty in the Oregon Territory.[14] But in the Northeast, jurisdictional notions were more orthodox, modern, and settler-state oriented. To borrow McHugh's metaphor, officials may have reached into "the tool ... box of jurisdictional possibilities," but they retrieved only one instrument.[15]

While the choices that governments made in the boundary dispute to invoke exclusive and territorialized ideas of jurisdiction were often political in nature – that is, they often flowed from imperatives of maintaining legitimacy and popularity among publics and of out-manoeuvring partisan opponents and other levels of government – politics did not define the legal content of jurisdiction. In fact, as this chapter shows, this version of jurisdiction was one of the most divisive concepts at play in the boundary dispute. Almost all of those affected by the boundary dispute, from settlers to colonial and state governments to more distant authorities in London and Washington, considered jurisdiction vital to some form of desirable order along the boundary. Yet this chapter argues that jurisdiction had ambivalent meanings in the disputed territories: it was at once key to order but conversely an incitement to disorder and violence. This ambivalence was particularly evident in the realm of criminal jurisdiction, which involved blunt displays of state power over the bodies of citizens and subjects. The version understood by key settlers and most officials echoed the territorial exclusivity applied in the Baker case, a notion that proved difficult to adapt to the border zone. While most officials agreed on what jurisdiction meant and how it could be achieved, they sharply disagreed on who held it in these contested areas. That cleavage made it a potentially disastrous doctrine in the early nineteenth-century Northeast.

Constructing Jurisdiction in the Border Zone

In August 1836, a Baptist elder from Stewardstown, New Hampshire, named David Kent swore in a deposition that "I never knew or heard of any other Government, except the State of New Hampshire, exercising or claiming to exercise any jurisdiction over said territory," meaning Indian Stream.[16] Other settlers from New Hampshire, Vermont, and Indian Stream itself echoed him in starkly similar phrasing: all of them swore that Lower Canada had never exercised or proclaimed jurisdiction in the territory until the previous summer. These similar phrasings were not an accident. Rather, the depositions of Kent and other settlers were among more than thirty assembled by New Hampshire state officials in the wake of an incident the previous October. Narratives of the incident varied, depending in part on the allegiance of the witness. In Canadian versions, compiled after a similar investigation by colonial officials, a Lower Canadian magistrate named Alexander Rea had issued an arrest warrant for a suspected criminal in Indian Stream, as was commonly done in that area. As the alleged criminal was being conveyed to the magistrate's house, a group of New Hampshire and rogue Indian Stream settlers kidnapped him from custody and then attacked the magistrate violently, severely wounding him before forcing him across the border into US territory as a prisoner, during which they nearly murdered him when he tried to escape.[17] American descriptions of the events varied. One version came directly from the arrested prisoner, who stressed that he was stunned by the unprecedented use of extra-territorial authority by a foreign judge, and that, after the other Americans confronted the constable, "I was at length released, without any force being used on either side."[18]

The rival investigations and the evidence that they generated both documented and justified each side's jurisdiction in Indian Stream. As each government sought to legitimize the actions of its officers or citizens in each new controversy, they also tried to bolster their own claims to authority by charting the continuing exercise of that power – that they, unlike the other side, were and had been the single and exclusive de facto authority in the disputed territory. But this de facto authority had implications in law; each side used the rival histories of jurisdiction it compiled to legitimate the continuation of its jurisdiction until the final location of the boundary was settled by Britain and the United States. This contest over de facto jurisdiction highlights much about the broader meaning of that concept in the border zone, especially the way in which it was entangled with a crystallized idea of territorial sovereignty but was also distinct from that idea.

The key distinction between sovereignty and jurisdiction in the Northeast was the temporary nature of the latter and its disconnection from the permanent settlement of the boundary. That is, jurisdiction continued to exist even as sovereignty remained contested; the two were severable. As Foreign Secretary Lord Aberdeen told a US diplomat during the controversy following Baker's arrest and conviction by New Brunswick authorities, the question of sovereignty was being dealt with by other means. "It is the question of actual jurisdiction alone which can now be discussed ... and between these questions, of Sovereignty, and the actual exercise of jurisdiction," he wrote, "there is a broad and clear distinction."[19] This version of jurisdiction was what US secretary of state Henry Clay called a few weeks later "intermediate possession."[20] Officials on all sides agreed that the exercise of criminal jurisdiction and other aspects of state power would not play a role in the final determination of sovereign rights. In October 1827, New Brunswick lieutenant governor Sir Howard Douglas dismissed the international importance of Baker's arrest in Madawaska by saying that nothing his government was doing or could do would shape the final disposition of the border.[21] Likewise, when Governor General Lord Aylmer complained about the arrest of Indian Stream settler Enos Rowell by New Hampshire officials in April 1835, he depicted the assertion of New Hampshire's authority as pointlessly aggressive, since it could not establish any broader support for the state's permanent claim to the disputed territory.[22] Although American officials agreed with the technical and legal distinction of sovereignty and jurisdiction, they resisted the British and colonial argument for the purported retention of British jurisdiction until a final settlement. "Without imputing to [Britain] a disposition to procrastination," Clay wrote, "she would, in such a state of things, be in the substantial enjoyment of all the advantages of a decision of the controversy in her favor."[23] With the exercise of jurisdiction assured, Britain would have little motivation to seek a final settlement.

As part of this contest for "intermediate possession," each side sought to make a different case, generating rival histories to demonstrate that their government had actually exercised power, as both Lower Canada and New Hampshire tried to do after the attack on Alexander Rea. Throughout the 1820s and 1830s, both state and provincial governments sent officials into Indian Stream and Madawaska to collect information on questions such as which settlers held land grants from which government and whether or how often settlers were held amenable in provincial or state court. After New Brunswick arrested more pro-American settlers in Madawaska in 1831, the Maine government sought to show that the use of colonial authority there was intermittent at best until the past few years – that is, that New Brunswick's provincial jurisdiction was not continuous.[24] The New Brunswick attorney general used this same tactic in the Baker case in 1828. Parker called an array of witnesses that testified both against Baker in respect of the sedition charges but also that New Brunswick had exercised continuous and regular jurisdiction in Madawaska. Witnesses testified that Madawaskans were enrolled in the colonial militia, that settlers there – including Baker – had received the colonial grain bounty, voted in colonial elections, and been subject to the orders of colonial courts.[25] "I live under this Government, and have always lived under it. All the Madawaska settlers live under the same government," said one settler.[26] As a result, when the lieutenant governor defended the prosecution against American criticism, he specified that not only had Baker's criminality been proven but also New Brunswick had been shown to have exercised "an actual practical Sovereignty" in the region for decades.[27]

While Governor Douglas and many other officials understood that this "actual practical sovereignty" was temporary in nature, most officials did not see it as a flexible, permeable, or discretionary concept, or as one limited in law by the uncertainty surrounding the final location of the border. Instead, governments advocated treating the territories as simply parts of the internally homogeneous polities over which they presided – the boundaries claimed by the imperial and federal governments were the boundaries within which local officials claimed unimpaired jurisdiction. In 1835, New Hampshire attorney general George Sullivan told the governor that state jurisdiction in Indian Stream was absolute. According to Sullivan, Indian Stream settlers "can have no more right to resist officers, than the inhabitants of any other part of the State."[28] Two weeks later, a New Hampshire sheriff from Coos County informed the local government in Indian Stream that he was going to discharge his duty as an officer of the county, as he put it, "fearlessly," and that he hoped the community would "quietly and peaceably submit to the laws & authority of the State of New Hampshire."[29] Colonial officials took a similar view of the homogeneity of colonial authority, with Douglas writing that he was bound to consider Madawaska as part of New Brunswick and that he could not suspend what he called the "ordinary operation" of colonial law there.[30]

Besides being unfettered by the boundary dispute, officials also treated their jurisdiction as exclusive, just as in territories for which sovereignty was undisputed. In the late 1820s, the US federal government periodically protested what it called New Brunswick's exercise of "exclusive jurisdiction," and sometimes suggested a cooperative or concurrent exercise of authority, resembling that which the two countries had negotiated for the Oregon Territory, but Britain and the colonies rejected that idea uniformly.[31] In his sentencing submissions in the Baker case, Attorney General Parker openly ridiculed the idea of non-exclusive jurisdiction. "The idea of two distinct sovereignties, one Monarchical, the other Republican: two sets of laws, one administered at Fredericton, the other at Penobscot; peaceably binding the same place at the same time, is too preposterous to be seriously maintained."[32] While the imperial government did seek legal advice from international law advisers at the time of the Baker trial, the response was similarly clear: criminal jurisdiction was exclusively vested in the Crown, and all people of whatever citizenship inside the king's territories owed allegiance to English and colonial law.[33]

However, colonial, state, imperial, and federal governments were not the only ones to espouse this kind of exclusive territorial jurisdiction. In early 1835, the Indian Stream council, which had declared the territory to be a self-governing jurisdiction independent of Canada and the United States until the boundary dispute was resolved, wrote to Lord Aylmer to protest the incursions of a New Hampshire sheriff into the community. They told Aylmer that the settlers in the territory had been allowed "to enjoy ourselves, as a neutral nation, or people, and govern ourselves by our own laws."[34] According to the settlers, the sheriff's assumption of jurisdiction was "without any lawful authority, and a violation upon our right."[35] Likewise, in Madawaska the core of the case against John Baker rested on his insistence not on some kind of legal pluralism or shared jurisdiction but instead on the idea that Maine, and not colonial, law was in force. As witnesses asserted, Baker and his supporters pledged not to allow English law to have any force in Madawaska and declared that the colony had no right to deliver the Royal Mail through the district.[36] According to the information filed by the attorney general, Baker told a crowd in Madawaska that the British and colonial governments "had no right to exercise any authority over the inhabitants of the said settlement."[37] Territoriality, in other words, was no more flexible for many of the settlers in Madawaska and Indian Stream than it was for the officials outside of the disputed areas who contemplated the exercise of colonial and state power within them.

That invocation of inflexible territoriality is telling. In one sense, the jurisdiction envisioned in the disputed territories in the two decades before 1842 by imperial, federal, colonial, and state governments was different from the increasingly orthodox version articulated throughout the imperial world: it was impermanent and ultimately detachable from the broader concept of sovereign rights. But jurisdiction in the border zone was in crucial ways not adapted to the underlying territorial uncertainty in the region. As in the case of Alexander Rea, both settlers and officials drew on a repertoire of jurisdictional orthodoxies at the core of modern sovereignty: they envisioned the disputed areas as normal parts of their homogeneous polities, bounded as anywhere else by inviolable borders within which their authority was unimpaired and fundamentally exclusive of other national and sub-national governments.

Managing Disorder: The Imperatives of Jurisdiction

In June 1837, New Brunswick attorney general Charles Peters recommended prosecuting a Mainer named Ebenezer Greely, who had been arrested in Madawaska for conducting a census under the authority of the state. Peters told Lieutenant Governor Sir John Harvey that Greely's offence was a serious one, on which the government should take action. According to Peters, Greely had either "voluntarily put himself forward to create disturbance and produce dissatisfaction among the peaceable inhabitants of Madawaska, in which case he personally and most justly deserves punishment, or he is the covert agent of the Government of the State of Maine."[38] Either way, he told the governor, the colony should bring the case to court and discredit Greely's activities or Maine's assertions of authority with the force of law.

For Peters, as for the other officials on the front lines of the boundary dispute, exercising jurisdiction in Madawaska and Indian Stream was an imperative duty. For them, the actual exercise of their authority was the only assurance of order in the settlements – without the enforcement of law, there could be no property rights or personal safety for those whom they considered to be fellow subjects and citizens. But jurisdiction was also an openly acknowledged tactical imperative in the boundary dispute period: asserting anything less than unimpaired and unqualified authority would not simply compromise general notions of order or the security of life and property along the border but would also weaken a government's claim to assert lawful power in the future. In other words, having claimed authority in Madawaska and Indian Stream, governments were obliged to continually risk the diplomatic chaos of actually using it.

Many officials maintained that anything short of full jurisdiction exercised actively by their governments would have disastrous consequences for the settlements, leaving the communities without any social or legal order. In some versions of the argument, officials drew a basic link between the administration of the law and general order. After Baker's arrest, Sir Howard Douglas wrote that what he called the "long established British settlements" in Madawaska "must necessarily remain under the jurisdiction of this Government, or be abandoned to anarchy in the absence of all rule."[39] Attorney General Thomas Wetmore, who initiated Baker's arrest and prosecution, agreed, telling an investigator sent into Madawaska by the Maine government that the colony was doing "no more ... than was absolutely necessary to preserve the supremacy of the laws, without which there would be an end of liberty and all personal security."[40]

Officials often cast jurisdiction as especially essential in the territories, manifesting a belief that these border zone areas were particularly unruly or prone to criminality, in part because of the larger uncertainty about permanent sovereign rights. This conception of border areas was common throughout the nineteenth century, as I have argued elsewhere: officials often saw them as less loyal and less amenable to the rule of state-derived law than were territories closer to the metropolitan heart.[41] In the aftermath of the attack on Alexander Rea, the British minister in Washington reported back to London that Indian Stream had become chaotic. "The territory on the disputed line of frontier has become the asylum of vagabonds and outlaws from both sides," he wrote, "who profess allegiance to one country or the other, or to either, according as it may suit their own lawless purposes."[42]

For some colonial officials, jurisdiction was especially imperative in Madawaska because most of its inhabitants were Acadians, whom they deemed more susceptible to American ideas of governance. The New Brunswick magistrate George Morehouse, who issued the arrest warrant for Baker and witnessed his proclamation that Madawaska was under the control of Maine, personally urged the attorney general to take action against him, in part for this reason. Shortly after returning from the settlement, where he met with Baker, he wrote to Wetmore, "I trust his Majesty's Government will speedily take such measures as will convince the French settlers of Madawaska that the Americans have no right to act as they do, and crush this banditti, for I feel convinced that, unless [Baker's declaration of American jurisdiction, and his pledge to block colonial law and the Royal Mail] is promptly followed by some other to suppress them, the French will shortly consider us the intruders."[43]

Jurisdiction was not simply a tactic between governments and settlers, however. It was also an openly acknowledged tactical imperative in the broader boundary dispute. That is, because of the legitimating focus on the historical exercise of jurisdiction by colonial and state authorities, governments were obliged to continue asserting their own power and protesting the other side's allegations. In 1835, Governor General Lord Gosford used this imperative to explain why he could not end the prosecution of a pro-American Indian Stream settler. As Gosford wrote, he could not take "any steps which may be considered as compromising the right claimed by Great Britain to exercise jurisdiction over the territory now in dispute."[44] In this case, he noted, the law must be left to take its course. Likewise, in 1837 New Brunswick lieutenant governor Sir John Harvey remarkably took the time to meet with Ebenezer Greely and, according to a witness to the conversation, explained to the prisoner that he regretted having to arrest and detain him. Harvey reportedly said "that necessity was imposed on him for the assertion of the principle, which it was his duty to maintain, of the right of jurisdiction."[45] But according to Harvey, "enough had been done for that purpose," and he was pleased to order Greely's release.[46]

This imperative of jurisdiction served in many ways as an agent of both order and disorder, prompting each side to resist the other's power. In 1831, after the lieutenant governor of New Brunswick led a force into Madawaska to arrest a group of Americans for attempting to form a municipal government there, Maine governor Samuel Smith launched a heated and protracted protest. Maine was obliged to both actively oppose New Brunswick's jurisdiction and to assert its own, he said, or else imperial and colonial governments would use this restraint as evidence to support increasing their hold on the territory.[47] This exercise of authority ensured that jurisdiction, considered by officials and policymakers on both sides of the border to be the essence of order, was also an agent of continued, decades-long confrontation and aggression. Bringing order to the territories, in other words, was in crucial ways an enduringly self-defeating project.

Jurisdiction and Violence

After the 1831 arrests in Madawaska, a group of settlers who fled their homes just before the arrival of the colonial authorities described in a petition how they eluded arrest. "We have now slept in the woods three nights, without fire or covering, and by stratagem have obtained potatoes from the fields for subsistence," they wrote, claiming that New Brunswick was now keeping a garrison in the area in order to, as they put it, "starve us to compliance."[48] John Baker, who also escaped arrest and made his way to Portland, emphasized in an affidavit how the colony was attempting to punish his community criminally for exercising the right of local democracy and echoed his friends by saying that the new Madawaska garrison was intended to "force me into a compliance to the British authorities."[49] Governor Samuel Smith used these narratives of suffering and oppression, alongside those from prisoners whom the colonial government did manage to capture, in his protests and demands for American federal action against Britain and New Brunswick. As he told the federal government, "our peaceful and defenceless citizens [are] imprisoned in a British jail for obeying the laws and constitution of the State which claims their allegiance," which imprisonment, he said, was perpetrated "by a foreign power, in violation of the sovereignty of this State."[50] Clearly, incursions into the territories and exertions of authority there took on intense symbolic and rhetorical value, as officials depicted them as striking at the heart of territorial rights and citizenship. Since neither side regarded the other's jurisdiction as legitimate, each characterized the other's exercise of it as nothing more than illegitimate and unjust violence.

Each side in the dispute invariably described the other's exercise of authority as fundamentally unlawful. The American chargé d'affaires in London pointed out this ambivalence in the wake of Baker's arrest in 1828, reminding the Foreign Office that, if the American view of the larger and unresolved question of sovereign rights were correct, Baker's trial had been before a court that was "wholly without Jurisdiction in the case," meaning that, rather than being part of a legal process, Baker had been subjected to simple, state-organized violence.[51] The same dichotomized perspectives were apparent in Indian Stream. In January 1836, after New Hampshire moved sheriffs and militia into the community, a team of Canadian officials travelled there to investigate. They subsequently reported what they saw as a tyrannical military occupation that defied all Canadian authority. The group described being stopped "at the point of a bayonet" by a militiaman who would not permit them to travel further, although they informed him that they were working under the authority of the Canadian government. The group told Gosford that pro-British settlers had been driven from their homes and had their property destroyed by the militia, and that several had been, as they wrote, "carried prisoners" into New Hampshire for what they called "rebellion against the laws of that State."[52]

New Hampshire's move into Indian Stream was a stark echo of the efforts of New Brunswick in Madawaska in 1831.[53] In this case, it was repackaged by colonial officials as an abjectly unjust invasion. The gravity of this assertion of authority was affirmed by Foreign Secretary Lord Palmerston, who told the British minister in Washington to deliver a simple but ominous message to the federal government about what would happen in the event of a recurrence: "Her Majesty's Government will feel it their duty to use all means in their power to protect from aggression the Subjects of Her Majesty, and the territories of Her Majesty's crown; that force will be repelled by force; and that the responsibility of all the evils which may ensue from such collisions must rest on the heads of those who become the aggressors."[54]

In many of these incidents, a key to official outrage and the rhetoric of violated sovereignty was the claim that the perpetrators were not civilians, as John Baker had been in 1828, but rather agents of government. When the Lower Canadian investigators reported on circumstances in Indian Stream, they denounced what they called "acts of violence and oppression committed on the inhabitants by persons professing to act under authority from the State of New Hampshire."[55] President John Quincy Adams used almost identical language when he relayed papers on the Baker case to the Senate, which he called "alleged aggression on the rights of citizens of the United States by persons claiming authority under the Government of the province of New Brunswick."[56] The involvement of government agents, and especially of commissioned military officers, transformed border zone disorder into a violation of international law, as Governor Smith illustrated in his 1831 protests.

But while government agents were continually the perpetrators of these assertions of jurisdiction, they were also often the targets of reprisals, political prosecutions, and local resistance to the authority that they represented. When a York County constable attempted to serve an arrest warrant on an American settler in Madawaska in 1827, he was surrounded by John Baker and others for whom he was an embodiment of the English law that they wished to usurp. The constable reported that the prisoner was rescued from his custody, that the settlers surrounded him, and that Baker stepped forward and "addressed himself to this deponent in most violent language, threatening to take his life for attempting to serve that writ."[57] On the Lower Canada border, the attack on Magistrate Alexander Rea went well beyond threats in 1835. After he and his constable tried to take an Indian Stream settler into custody, the constable was shot, and he himself was cut by a sabre before being hauled across the border into Vermont.[58]

Governments keenly understood these inherent threats in exercising jurisdiction, even as they felt the imperative of doing so. In fact, on both sides of the border, officials tried to mitigate the exercise of their authority – or sometimes avoid it altogether while not sacrificing the principle of maintaining jurisdiction. During the Greely case, for example, New Brunswick authorities actively tried not to have to make the arrest or to keep Greely in custody. Nonetheless, he was arrested in Madawaska in June 1837 by the New Brunswick magistrate J.A. Maclauchlan, who confronted him while Greely was conducting the census. In his report to Harvey, Maclauchlan described how he first argued with Greely, telling him that, if he would desist from taking the census, he would not be arrested and would face no charges. When Greely refused to stop his work, Maclauchlan claimed that he was left with no option but to make the arrest and return to Fredericton with him in custody.[59] After his release on those charges, Greely announced his return to Madawaska and his resumption of the census, at which point the colonial solicitor general travelled there, met with him, and warned him that, in espousing the jurisdiction of Maine and the American citizenship of the settlers, he was breaking colonial law and would be arrested.

After Greely said that he was willing to be arrested in the performance of his mandate, the solicitor general offered to write him a certificate showing that he was prevented by colonial authorities from carrying out those duties; the solicitor general hoped that this would induce Greely to return to the United States without being embarrassed by his lack of success on the census project. Only after Greely rejected this proposition did authorities arrest him and again transport him to Fredericton.[60]

Even when officials set out to enforce their government's law by making arrests, they often understood the delicate nature of exercising criminal jurisdiction in the disputed territories. Thus, in an effort not to leave their government vulnerable to charges of invasion, military occupation, or tyranny, officials often deliberately sought to minimize the use of force. In 1827, after the colonial government decided to arrest John Baker, Attorney General Thomas Wetmore instructed the magistrate in charge that Baker should be offered bail immediately on being taken into custody.[61] He also wrote directly to the sheriff tasked with entering Madawaska to make the arrest, telling him that, while he had to act with "firmness," he had to be careful to use no unnecessary force. In fact, Wetmore specified that the sheriff should take no more than two or three people with him. "It is very desirable that the service should be performed quietly, and with the least possible parade," wrote Wetmore.[62] A few days later, however, when Wetmore learned that the sheriff had left for Madawaska with what he described as a posse, he sent his son riding after the party with an order for the sheriff to abide by his original command, writing that, "if you make any parade of force until after you meet with opposition and resistance, you will incur his excellency's great displeasure."[63] When the sheriff refused to proceed into Madawaska without his large group, Wetmore cancelled the arrest.[64] This tactical restraint did not prevent Baker's ultimate arrest, trial, and conviction from becoming a flashpoint between the governments. Nevertheless, it likely minimized the rhetoric about violence, tyranny, and invasion that was deployed by both sides in the jurisdictional contests of the 1820s and 1830s.

In 1957, the renowned international law writer Charles de Visscher observed that, "It is because the State is a territorial organization that violation of its frontiers is inseparable from the idea of aggression against the state itself."[65] This aggregation of statehood and borders has not always been true, and, in the early nineteenth century, other models of authority still operated in North America and around the world. But along the northeastern boundary of British North

America and the United States, the modern notions of territorial sovereignty and exclusive jurisdiction implicit in de Visscher's conception of the state were present, powerful, and potentially disastrous. Doctrines that were so central to order, and that were meant to safeguard life and property by ensuring the rule of law, instead subjected the border zone, its occupants, and the governments that claimed authority there to decades of jurisdictional competition, aggression, and uncertainty. Depending on the actor and the observer, the exertions of governments that adhered to these doctrines were orderly or disorderly, necessary for the rule of law or simply violent. Along the border, then, order and disorder sprang from the same conceptual source.

NOTES

1 "Report of the Trial of John Baker," in *Remarks upon the Disputed Points of Boundary under the Fifth Article of the Treaty of Ghent*, 2nd ed. (Saint John, NB: D.A. Cameron, 1839), xii.
2 On Baker and his role in the boundary dispute, see Roger Paradis, "John Baker and the Republic of Madawaska," *Dalhousie Review* 52, no. 1 (1972): 78–95.
3 "Report of the Trial of John Baker," vii–xii; the quote is on vii.
4 Ibid., xii–xiv; the quote is on xii.
5 Ibid., xiv.
6 See Francis M. Carroll, *A Good and Wise Measure: The Search for the Canadian-American Boundary, 1783–1842* (Toronto: University of Toronto Press, 2001); and P.E. Corbett, *The Settlement of Canadian-American Disputes: A Critical Study of Methods and Results* (New Haven, CT: Yale University Press, 1937), 7–23.
7 See Albert Corey, *The Crisis of 1830–1842 in Canadian-American Relations* (New Haven, CT: Yale University Press, 1941); Carroll, *A Good and Wise Measure*, 195–219; Kenneth R. Stevens, *Border Diplomacy: The* Caroline *and McLeod Affairs in Anglo-American Relations, 1837–1842* (Tuscaloosa: University of Alabama Press, 1989); Howard Jones, *To the Webster-Ashburton Treaty: A Study in Anglo-American Relations* (Chapel Hill: University of North Carolina Press, 1977); and Wilbur Devereux Jones, *The American Problem in British Diplomacy* (London: Macmillan, 1974).
8 The literature on the history of sovereignty is large. For recent contributions that inform this study see Jordan Branch, *The Cartographic State: Maps, Territory, and the Origins of Sovereignty* (Cambridge: Cambridge University Press, 2014); Lisa Ford, *Settler Sovereignty: Jurisdiction and Indigenous People in America and Australia, 1788–1836* (Cambridge, MA: Harvard University Press, 2010); P.G. McHugh, "'A Pretty Gov[ernment]!' The 'Confederation of United Tribes' and Britain's Quest for Imperial Order in the New Zealand Islands during the

1830s," *Legal Pluralism and Empires, 1500–1850*, ed. Lauren Benton and Richard Ross (New York: New York University Press, 2013), 233–60; and P.G. McHugh, *Aboriginal Societies and the Common Law: A History of Sovereignty, Status, and Self-Determination* (Oxford: Oxford University Press, 2004).

9 Charles S. Maier, *Once within Borders: Territories of Power, Wealth, and Belonging since 1500* (Cambridge, MA: Belknap Press of Harvard University Press, 2016), 9.

10 Bradley Miller, *Borderline Crime: Fugitive Criminals and the Challenge of the Border, 1819–1914* (Toronto: University of Toronto Press and the Osgoode Society, 2016).

11 On the disputed territories in particular, see Robert Tsai, *America's Forgotten Constitutions: Defiant Visions of Power and Community* (Cambridge, MA: Harvard University Press, 2014), 18–48; Daniel Doan, *Indian Stream Republic: Settling a New England Frontier, 1785–1842* (Hanover, NH: University Press of New England, 1997); Paradis, "John Baker and the Republic of Madawaska"; and W.E. Campbell, *The Aroostock War of 1839* (Fredericton, NB: Goose Lane Editions, 2013).

12 Ford, *Settler Sovereignty*, 2.

13 McHugh, "'A Pretty Gov[ernment],'" 234–5.

14 Frederick Merk, *The Oregon Question: Essays in Anglo-American Diplomacy and Politics* (Cambridge, MA: Harvard University Press, 1967).

15 McHugh, "'A Pretty Gov[ernment],'" 234.

16 Deposition of David Kent, 5 August 1836, "North American boundary. B," Part 10, *Parliamentary Papers* (London: J. Harrison, 1838), no. 146, 1837–8, 122.

17 See Lord Gosford to Charles Bankhead, 6 February 1836, ibid., 94–5; Report of Edward Short, J. McKenzie, and Benjamin Pomroy, 1 January 1836, ibid., 96–7.

18 Deposition of Richard J. Blanchard, 11 August 1836, ibid., 129–30.

19 Lord Aberdeen to W.B. Lawrence, 14 August 1828, *Diplomatic Correspondence of the United States* (hereafter *DCUS*), vol. 2, ed. William Ray Manning (Washington, DC: Carnegie Endowment, 1942), 747.

20 Henry Clay to Sir Charles Vaughan, 17 March 1828, Correspondence relative to the arrest and imprisonment of John Baker by the British authorities of New Brunswick (hereafter Baker 1828), *American State Papers*, no. 498, 22 May 1828, 1018.

21 Sir Howard Douglas to Vaughan, 4 October 1827, "Presidential message on arrest of John Baker in New Brunswick, and boundary of Maine" (hereafter Baker 1829), *House and Senate Documents*, vol. 186, no. 90, 21 January 1829, 26.

22 Lord Aylmer to Vaughan, 6 April 1835, *DCUS*, vol. 2, 974.

23 Clay to Vaughan, 17 March 1828, Baker 1828, 1019.

24 See John G. Deane to Gov. Samuel E. Smith, 2 November 1831, Message from the President of the United States, with documents relating to the capture, abduction, and imprisonment of American citizens by the provincial authorities of New Brunswick, and the measures adopted in consequence thereof by the Government

(hereafter Capture of American Citizens), *House and Senate Documents,* vol. 212, no. 3, 13 December 1831, 17–20.

25 Report of the Trial of John Baker, ix–xi.

26 Ibid., xi.

27 Douglas to Vaughan, 12 May 1828, *DCUS*, vol. 2, 715.

28 Sullivan to Gov. William Badger, 3 January 1835, ibid., 975.

29 John H. White to the Councillors of Indian Stream, 17 January 1835, ibid., 975–6.

30 Douglas to Vaughan, 4 October 1827, Baker 1829, 26.

31 For American views, see Clay to Vaughan, 20 February 1828, *DCUS*, vol. 2, 148; Clay to Lawrence, 31 March 1828, *DCUS*, vol. 2, 172–3; Clay to Vaughan, 17 March 1828, Baker 1828, 1019. For the British rejection, see Vaughan to Clay, 25 March 1828, Baker 1828, 1020.

32 Report of the Trial of John Baker, xv.

33 Sir Herbert Jenner to Aberdeen, 3 June 1828, *Law Officers' Opinions to the Foreign Office, 1793–1860*, vol. 3, ed. Clive Parry (Westmead, UK: Gregg International, 1970), 291–304. See also Vaughan to Clay, February 1828, Baker 1828, 1017.

34 John Haynes and Reuben Sawyer to Aylmer, n.d. [ca January 1835], *DCUS*, vol. 2, 977.

35 Ibid.

36 George Morehouse to Thomas Wetmore, 22 August 1827, Aggressions on John Baker and other citizens of the United States by the authorities of Great Britain in New Brunswick. (hereafter Aggressions on John Baker), *American State Papers,* no. 473, 3 March 1828, 847; Affidavit of Joseph Sanfacon, 9 November 1827, Aggressions on John Baker.

37 Information against John Baker, 13 October 1827, ibid., 846.

38 Charles Peters to Sir John Harvey, 5 June 1837, "North American boundary. B," Part 7, 57.

39 Douglas to Vaughan, 4 October 1827, Baker 1829, 26.

40 Thomas Wetmore to S.B. Barrell, 23 December 1827, Aggressions on John Baker, 844.

41 See Miller, *Borderline Crime*, 19–48.

42 H.S. Fox to Lord Palmerston, 25 January 1837, "North American boundary. B," Part 10, 118.

43 Morehouse to Wetmore, 11 August 1827, Aggressions on John Baker, 853.

44 Gosford to Vaughan, 5 September 1835, "North American boundary. B," Part 9, 91.

45 Deposition of W.H. Robinson, August 1837, ibid., Part 7, 65.

46 Ibid.

47 Smith to Livingston, 10 November 1831, Capture of American Citizens, 16.

48 Petition of John Harford, Amos Maddocks, Nathaniel Bartlett, Walter Powers, Joseph Miles, Augustin Webster, and Charles M'Pherson to Smith, 29 September 1831, ibid., 15.

49 Affidavit of John Baker, 12 October 1831, ibid., 13.
50 Smith to Livingston, 10 November 1831, ibid., 16, 15.
51 Lawrence to Aberdeen, 22 August 1828, *DCUS*, vol. 2, 754.
52 Report of Edward Short, J. McKenzie, and Benjamin Pomroy, 1 January 1836, "North American boundary. B," Part 10, 96–7.
53 Tsai, *America's Forgotten Constitutions*, 33–48.
54 Lord Palmerston to Fox, 22 July 1837, ibid., 142.
55 Report of Short, McKenzie, and Pomroy, 1 January 1836, 96.
56 John Quincy Adams to the Senate of the United States, 3 March 1828, Aggressions on John Baker, 838.
57 Deposition of Joseph Sanfacon, 9 November 1827, Aggressions on John Baker, 847.
58 Deposition of Alexander Rea, 29 December 1835, "North American boundary. B," Part 10, 98–102.
59 J.A. Maclauchlan to Harvey, 10 June 1837, ibid., Part 7, 58.
60 Solicitor General of New Brunswick to Harvey, 5 September 1837, ibid., Part 8, 67–8.
61 Thomas Wetmore to Morehouse, 7 September 1827, Aggressions on John Baker, 854–5.
62 Wetmore to Edward Miller, 7 September 1827, ibid., 855.
63 Wetmore to Miller, 13 September 1827, ibid., 850.
64 Ibid., 851; T.R. Wetmore to Wetmore, 13 September 1827, ibid., 851.
65 Charles de Visscher, *Theory and Reality in Public International Law*, trans. P.E. Corbett (Princeton, NJ: Princeton University Press, 1957), 198.

20 For the Better Administration of the Town's Affairs: Civic Engagement, Local Governance, and Grass-Roots Activism in Canada West / Ontario, 1849–1870

DARREN FERRY

Although imperial and legal provisions for local or municipal governance emerged in Upper Canada as early as 1791 as a result of the Constitutional Act, the notion of *elected* town governments evolved throughout the region only after the political turbulence of the 1830s. After the granting of responsible government in 1849, the passage of the Municipal Corporations Act incorporated a number of townships, which had grown to nearly four hundred in Canada West by 1850. Combining these parliamentary reforms with an embryonic, yet vibrant, local political culture of community self-management, politicians in Upper Canada / Canada West during this period fostered a polity that endeavoured to enhance and defend local autonomy from the encroachments of outside influences.[1] As a result of this nascent "democratic" culture, one of the key negotiations surrounding local governance emerged as various town councils considered the kind of services the town or village could offer. Often these discussions touched on the nature of governance itself, as town/village councils deliberated which services were within the public sphere of the community and which constituted the private domain of the individual citizen.

One particularly instructive example of these debates occurred in the council meetings of Niagara Township in 1857. In January of that year, a Mr Zimmerman was encouraged by the town council to repair the dock found on his property, for "although the same is private property, yet it is such a nature that all the inhabitants of the town are deeply interested in the same being placed in an efficient state." Notwithstanding the Niagara council's appeal to Mr Zimmerman's sense of "civic duty" and good citizenship in encouraging him to obey town bylaws, a very dissimilar attitude would arise within the town council regarding the poorer inhabitants of the community. While the Niagara council established an indigent committee to deal with the poor of the region, clearly the council wrestled with what *its own* civic responsibility was to poverty-stricken residents of the town. In September 1857, when the number of impoverished citizens appearing before the town council rose sharply in Niagara, the overworked indigent committee brought forward a motion that "the whole of the indigent be struck off the list and left to the support of the respective denomination they adhere to." While this motion ultimately did not pass, the committee's frustration with what they considered a "private matter of poverty" between religious denominations and their congregations, rather than the civic responsibility of town leaders, illustrates the nature and negotiations of power at the local level during the 1850s and 1860s.[2] Municipal governance, and the extension of a local social order in Canada West / Ontario, would constantly involve a complex weave of negotiations between the local governing authorities and the citizens of the town or village.

The rising importance of local governance after the period of rebellion has mirrored significant historical interest in the process of nascent state formation within the colonies. Explanations for the emergence of municipal government during this period centre on advocates of responsible government and their desire to extend institutional reform, the decentralization of administrative power to the municipal level in the united Canadas after the 1840s, and, particularly in the context of this volume of essays, the real and perceived threats to the social order in the pre-Confederation period.[3] The publication of Ian McKay's seminal article on the emergence of a "liberal order" in Canada after the rebellions assisted historians in connecting the rise of local governance with a liberalizing reform impulse.[4] Still other scholars argue that debates over the nature of governance itself emerged from a complicated negotiation between conservative and liberal elements. Examining colonial politics from a cultural lens, such studies illustrate how political culture in the Canadas entailed a complex series of negotiations and interplay between governors and governed, through various methods such as the legal system, petitions, patronage, political violence, and other forms of political expression.[5] While this chapter aims to further examinations of an emerging "democratic" political culture during the post-rebellion period, it also recognizes that the agents of local governance in Canada West / Ontario focused largely on local concerns and the maintenance of a "township" social order, rather than solely concerning themselves with the maintenance of empire or the larger machinations of the nascent "Canadian" nation-state.[6] Therefore, even though the aim of various town councils in the region was to provide their citizens with "democracy" on a limited scale, most of their crucial decision-making would take into account complicated local circumstances and the collective and individual idiosyncrasies at play between the governors and the governed. As a result, while, ultimately, the authority of local governing structures and regulatory bodies rested with township councils, individual citizens could and did exert their agency, while fostering a sense of a grass-roots "active citizenry" by supporting petitions, developing negotiating tactics, applying frequent use of the legal system, or advocating general non-compliance of town bylaws and ordinances. Far from providing an overarching synthesis of "deliberative democracy," municipal governing structures during this period reflected the rather intricate and *human* interactions of the local community.

With the passage of the Municipal Corporations Act in 1849 came the foundation and the blueprint for local/municipal governance throughout Canada West. The act not only created new territorial units of districts and counties within Canada West, but it also established procedures regarding the elections of town councils, as well as regulating their financial and administrative responsibilities, and setting the rules for public accountability.[7] While scholarly examinations of the political culture of the liberal order during this period have focused largely on political ideologies and democratic principles only recently, in comparison to nineteenth-century British historiography, have Canadian historians interacted with the Foucauldian concept of liberal "governmentality." The concept of "governing through" various liberal institutions of the emerging nation-state, such as the legal apparatus, the educational system, the postal system, public health, and even the census, is a hallmark of this scholarship, highlighted by the work of Jean-Marie Fecteau, Bruce Curtis, and, most recently, Elsbeth Heaman.[8] The elected township council system in Canada West / Ontario after 1849 provides a fascinating glimpse into the workings of liberal governmentality and the negotiations surrounding the "rule of freedom," or the construction of an active citizenship through the patterns of "proper" socio-political behaviour, within the localized context of township governajnce. This chapter therefore undertakes a comparative look at local township/village governance in the post-rebellion political landscape, illustrating the negotiated nature of power, governance, and political culture in this period. It reveals the civic engagement of township citizens with local governance and an embryonic form of grass-roots activism, as residents could vigorously negotiate their relationship with the municipality and with local township officers and political leaders.[9]

The rise of the elected town council municipal system mirrors the emergence of prominent middle-class families throughout the towns and villages of Canada West / Ontario, as these "prominent citizens" often took the reins of local governance.[10] Jacob Hespeler, for example, was, not unsurprisingly, made the reeve of the township of Hespeler in 1859, and the entire eight-man town council of Cornwall during the early 1850s came from the Dixon and MacDonald clans.[11] A bourgeois "sense of decorum" and respectable political discourse was also in evidence during township council meetings in this period. Most of the first township or village bylaws outlined the need for "orderly" meetings of the town council to ensure that the rules and regulations of public discourse were respected during its sessions. The Mariposa town council went so far in its regulation of political discourse that it proclaimed that "no councillor shall speak disrespectfully of the Queen or any of the Royal Family or persons administering the Government of this Province, nor shall he use insolent or unmannerly language against the proceedings of the council or against any individual councillor." Niagara Township echoed these sentiments in its rules and regulations for discourse in council meetings, even adding a fine of one shilling for any councillor who was over ten minutes late to the meeting, "unless a reasonable excuse be given."[12]

Despite the regulations and protocols for political discourse in these town councils, even the expectations of procedural decorum became a difficult issue to grapple with for some townships. The executive of the Dereham town council pled with fellow members to tone down the "angry feelings" they expressed with conflicting petitioners asking for funds before the council, as they tended to amplify the emotions of greed and division. When the Bowmanville town council debated the merits of prohibition and how such legislation would affect the granting of licences for saloons and public houses, the debate became so heated that the members of the council voted to take a five-minute recess. When they returned from their break, the reeve, James Milne, was so incensed with this breach of protocol that he tendered his resignation.[13] Often disagreements between council members involved the dispensing of township funds, and this process could lead to conflict-of-interest allegations as well as accusations of embezzlement and other financial chicanery. The township of Cornwall had the unfortunate circumstance of having a former township treasurer abscond with town funds, and it determined to hire a lawyer to retrieve the four pounds stolen. Citizens of a town could also collude with officials in fraudulent activity, such as in a conspiracy to siphon township funds and funnel them into their own pockets. Lewis Durocher of Cornwall provided a fraudulent claim for a road through his property to the town's land commissioners, who overrode the council's decision and paid Durocher's claim. Not only did the Cornwall town council charge Durocher with "duplicity" in providing a fraudulent claim, it also censured the town's land commissioners for paying it.[14]

Another important order of business for many early township councils in Canada West after the passage of the Municipal Act was the establishment of town services as a foundation of local governance. As these public works required funding, town council business often concerned devising more efficient means to collect taxes from local citizens. Often town councils were forced to resort to legal methods to enforce the collection of taxes or to employ the services of a tax collector. The township of Alfred added a financial incentive for the town tax collector and treasurer when they offered these officials a 7 per cent and 4 per cent fee, respectively, on their collection of taxes within the town's boundaries. Retrenchment clearly was the watchword for the Alfred town council, as it also auctioned out repairs for the Lake Road "to the lowest bidder, and if there is money in the treasury the contractor to be paid and if not for him to wait until there are funds on hand to pay him with."[15] Despite these manifestations of authority from local town officials, the collection of taxes, tolls, and assessments could also be negotiated with a town's inhabitants. The township of Caledon, for example, refunded Thomas Furley fourteen dollars when, upon petition, it was found that his taxes were paid twice; similarly, Anthony Ferguson had part of his taxes repealed because he had not lived in the township of Hespeler for a full year. The citizens of Niagara appeared to have been so negligent in their payment of taxes to the collector that the town council passed a motion in 1869 that "immediate steps be taken by the collector, to enforce the payment of arrears of taxes and ground rents due." After forty-three citizens of the township of Bowmanville successfully petitioned their town council to remove a tollgate from the road immediately in front of their dwellings, the various religious ministers of the town won their petition five months later to allow them access to the town's roads free of charge.[16]

Of even more significance to the negotiation of power in local governments was the awarding of town offices, such as postmaster, pound keeper, fence viewers, and statute labour overseers. On the surface, most of this power/authority rested with local officials. Indeed, the townships of Caledon and Alfred forced local officials to sign oaths of office, signing their pledges in the town minute book that "we sincerely promise and declare that we will faithfully and diligently perform the duty of town warden for the present year."[17] The township of Alfred is a highly illustrative example of negotiated power relations when it came to township offices and the payment of labour performed by town officers. In December 1856, Robert Watson and "other contractors" in Alfred Township fruitlessly demanded higher wages for their roadwork in the town, as "they considered they have bid it too low and by so doing hindered other competitors of taking the work at a fair value." Some four years later, Watson was again forced to petition the town council to pay him for the ditch he built during the summer. A contentious debate in council over these issues boiled over when the town treasurer, John Bault, moved to pay the road commissioners with the first funds available to the town. The reeve, Thomas Brady, declared that the only "moneys" available to the commissioners would be the town's funding for building roads, which had been exhausted.[18]

As the above example illustrates, citizens could negotiate with the town over the money paid to them or even have recourse in the courts when council decided against them. Instructive in this regard was the case of James Lewis in Caledon, who demanded fifty dollars for damages to his horse while he was travelling. The town council agreed that it should compensate Lewis, given that he was travelling on town business, and offered him the sum of thirty dollars. James Lewis summarily turned down this offer and sued the council for forty dollars; the judgment was returned in his favour. The Caledon town council was positively magnanimous in comparison to the township of Niagara, which offered only five dollars in compensation to a man who fell into the town's main drain with his entire team of horses.[19]

One of the more neglected areas of study related to local governance is the significance of statute labour in enhancing the transportation infrastructure of a city, town, or village. The advantage of the statute labour system was that it required only a local labour force armed with existing farming technologies while limiting bureaucratic input in an essentially cashless method of constructing roads and highways. In order to connect pre-industrial agricultural settlements to burgeoning markets, the vast majority of townships in Canada West and early Ontario adopted the statute labour system to construct their transportation infrastructure.[20] Once again, the most significant aspect of statute labour was the negotiation of local power, more than the roads, bridges, or economic development that such labour would bring to the township. Many early township bylaws attempted to regulate the performance of statute labour in the town. For example, the Streetsville town council decreed that statute labourers needed to be between twenty-one and sixty years of age, and that they would work two days a year – a full eight-hour day, "not counting the time to arrive" – for seventy-five cents a day. The township of Bromley effectively organized its statute labour, dividing the township into twenty-one separate sections and recording the exact amount of statute labour required by its citizens.[21] On the surface, the authority of township officials to ensure the completion of statute labour tended to be all-encompassing. The penalties for non-compliance often ranged from small fines to a few days' confinement in the county jail; the Albion town council went so far as to authorize the reeve to send a constable to William Longhead's residence to "seize [his] goods for costs on him for nonperformance of statute labour." Statute labour could extend past the usual construction of roads and highways, as the Caledon town council required its statute labourers to "destroy weeds and thistles that may be hurtful to good husbandry."[22]

Yet many petitions before various township councils illustrate that even statute labour could be a negotiated commodity, and residents often petitioned the town council to shift the burden of their roadwork labour. Various citizens in the townships of Townsend, Moulton, Walsingham, and Manvers petitioned their town council to allow them to perform statute labour in the immediate vicinity of their houses rather than having to travel to the location of the road or highway to be built. The citizens of Mariposa Township employed this device so successfully over a period of several years that the town council flexed its regulatory muscles and commanded that the statute labour overseers "shall have entire control over the performance of statute labour in their respective beats, and shall determine where the work is to be performed, and [for] any person refusing to perform the work in accordance with the instruction of the overseer, such refusal shall be deemed a violation of this bylaw."[23] Town councils could also allow citizens to perform their statute labour at another point in time, if their claims were deemed to be legitimate. John Hayes of Albion Township successfully petitioned his town council for a month-long extension to perform his statute labour, while six citizens from Dereham Township were also successful in receiving six extra months to work on the town's roads. Even more significantly, the township of Cornwall exempted three citizens from statute labour when a petition revealed their difficulty in arriving at the work location. One statute labourer in the township of Caledon, who paid a fine rather than engage in his obligated roadwork, was overcharged by two dollars, and the township sheepishly requested the overseer to return the money to the erstwhile labourer.[24]

A particularly difficult challenge for municipal authorities came in dealing with the poor and indigent either residing in or just passing through a township. Whether members of the various town councils in Canada West / Ontario were ardent Tory paternalists or "liberal-minded" reformers, the lack of Poor Law legislation and the basic philosophy of poverty as a moral failing ensured rather haphazard policies regarding the poor throughout all levels of government in British North America.[25] And town councils throughout Canada West / Ontario in the 1850s and 1860s were no different, as they attempted to understand their role in relieving the distress of the poor and indigent within their community. Initially, many town councils would deny any responsibility on their part to deal with the challenges of poverty, distress, and indigence within their town or village. Most town councils were unsure at the beginning of their tenure whether or not poor relief was a task required of them as town officials. The Caledon town council refused one of the first petitions of this nature from a certain James Dawson, claiming that "the present law does not authorize the council to grant any assistance to persons in a state of poverty."

When Dunnville town councillors found themselves overwhelmed with petitions for relief, they initially established a poor committee to deal with the workload. However, the funds dispensed for the relief of the poor became so "extravagant" that some councillors objected to the use of town funds for these purposes, claiming "that as it is necessary to do something for the poor and destitute among us, it should be done by voluntary subscription of the people generally, or those who feel disposed to do so."[26] Both the Streetsville and Saltfleet town councils sent the township reeve to visit the poor, sick, and the indigent in order to determine the level of assistance that should be provided. While the Saltfleet reeve generally proposed that indigents be denied aid or sent to the local House of Refuge, the Streetsville town council proposed an alternate solution. When James Madigan applied for financial assistance to the Streetsville council in early 1863, his petition was denied, as the council felt it was "not legally justified in diverting public funds for that object, unless on the petition of a large majority of ratepayers of the Corporation." When James Fletcher was awarded eight dollars because eight ratepayers supported his petition a few months later, the town council became concerned. In October 1863, the Streetsville town council denied Sarah Bennett any aid, claiming that it was "not warranted by law to make such grants."[27]

Relief of the destitute in each township was therefore established on an ad hoc or case-by-case basis, as each town council attempted to deal with the poorer citizens and the indigents of the vicinity as it saw fit. These practices were diametrically opposite to the care of the poor in Britain, where the Poor Laws provided municipal funding and infrastructure, however limited, for the relief of the impoverished and indigent in British parishes.[28] In Canada West, the Townsend town council often gave cash donations from the town funds for poor, destitute, and "indigent" persons in their township, but drew the line for a Mrs Higgins and James Bodfish, as the former was not "a resident of this Township for any length of time" and the latter had three children who could work and "should not be supported in idleness." The Caledonia town council decided to reduce the Widow Shea's taxes "in consideration of her large family and extreme poverty," but declined to do so for a Mrs Malcolm, as she was "not taxed out of proportion with other property of equal value, and [council] can see no good reason for releasing that amount of property from taxation." The township of Caledon supported an infirm James Stewart for nearly four years, but when petitioners demanded that Stewart receive a yearly or half-yearly sum from township funds, the council balked at setting such "an injurious precedent," stating that, "if as represented in the petition that James Stewart has been of such great advantage to private individuals as a moral and religious instructor, those parties should contribute something towards his support."[29]

Townships also adopted a hybrid system of dealing with the indigent and distressed – they would utilize public funds while working closely with other voluntary organizations to assist with the poor and needy. The Bowmanville town council attempted to provide cash donations for "indigent" persons in the township, and, when this list grew too large, council created a "standing relief committee." Then, when this committee began to drain town funds, the council turned to the local Dorcas Society for assistance, providing this organization with grants from the municipality to keep their operation going. The Belleville town council began its relief of the poor and distressed by providing large grants to the Belleville Ladies' Benevolent Society, to "honour the charitable feeling that distinguishes their sex." Unfortunately, the local Benevolent Society simply could not keep up with the numbers of "indigent cases" arising in the town, and a "committee for the relief of the poor" was struck.[30]

The relative poverty of British emigrants settling in Canada West / Ontario from the 1830s would prove to be the greatest challenge of those desiring to maintain a "British" identity and those who recognized just how these emigrants would affect local conditions. Arriving emigrants possessed a "shared identity of Britishness" and socio-cultural expectations, and a transatlantic network of both kin and community which existed between those in the colonies and those left behind. Nonetheless, pauper immigrants could also engender a sense of anxiety in a town's citizenry, given perceptions regarding "unruly" poor immigrants from Great Britain, as evidenced in Jane Errington's contribution in this volume.[31] Given these circumstances, it was not surprising that the Dunnville town council provided lodging for two emigrant families in the vicinity, or that the Moulton town council wrote to the Canada West Bureau of Agriculture in 1857 "inquiring information how many, or if any emigrants might find employment as servants in this municipality." The Albion and Niagara town councils took their concern for the poor and needy of British extraction even further, when they established a working fund for the orphans and widows of the Crimean War and called upon neighbouring municipalities to establish their own charities for that purpose.[32] The advent of the American Civil War in 1861 provided a new challenge for those with working-class relatives back in Great Britain. The resulting "cotton famine" caused widespread suffering, particularly among workers in the Lancashire region's textile mills.[33] In 1862, both the Belleville and Caledon town councils held a special town meeting to raise funds for the "distressed operatives in Lancashire owing to the difficulties between the Northern and Southern States" and called on other municipalities to do the same. That same year, the Cayuga town council called on the county council to provide a thousand-dollar grant to "the oppressed operatives of Great Britain." However, not all town councils were eager to assist those afflicted in Great Britain. Not surprisingly, this was particularly true in those townships with relatively few British settlers. For example, the township of Hespeler, originally settled by Pennsylvania Mennonites of German descent, and its town council declined to assist the Lancashire operatives during the American Civil War, as "nothing could be sent as there were poor people to be provided for within the municipality."[34]

Another important component of local or municipal governance was the regulation of the community at large, and bylaws central to that purpose were enacted all over Canada West / Ontario during the 1850s and 1860s. These township bylaws tended to govern the socio-economic and cultural behaviour of town residents, from the regulation of morality, crime, and vice, to economic control over local markets and development.[35] The governing philosophies of community regulation varied across townships. The Bowmanville town council published its bylaws with a local printer, to ensure the "welfare and good government" of its citizens. The Mariposa town council claimed that its bylaws would regulate the destruction of private property and protect the "personal safety" of town residents, while the Oshawa town council charged its bylaws committee to enact bylaws "for the better administration of the affairs of this village."[36] Most town bylaws therefore attempted to regulate community behaviour and to protect the property and person of town inhabitants. Among the more frequent bylaws enacted to protect *both* property and persons within the community were those aimed at controlling errant livestock and dogs from running wild in the streets, with pound keepers frequently employed to control roaming animals. Similar bylaws were legislated to protect roads, streets, and bridges from wanton destruction and vandalism from town inhabitants. One bylaw emanating from the Cornwall town council in the early 1850s promised to prosecute anyone who "maliciously, willfully or neglectfully" destroyed township roads, while the Caledon town council passed a bylaw that anyone neglecting to remove obstacles in the road near their domicile was liable to be fined. Still other locales attempted to pass bylaws regulating the economic life of the town; the Bowmanville town council enacted several bylaws to establish a town market and tolls on various roads, while one of the earliest bylaws passed by the Niagara town council regulated the price of bread in the township.[37]

Town councils passed other bylaws to regulate, if not control, a community's socio-cultural behaviour, such as the licensing of exhibitions, games of chance, and other "criminal or immoral" activities. The Caledonia and Ramsay councils were dismayed that ball alleys for the "low" Irish sport of handball had infiltrated their townships, and consoled themselves with licensing such activities, while the Cayuga and Cornwall town councils ensured that they licensed all the billiard tables within the town boundaries. Given the history of rather unsavoury activities in the Niagara region resulting from the tourism industry, the Niagara town council took great pains to regulate "theatres, menageries, exhibitions, common showmen, mountebanks, circus riders, jugglers and other persons exhibiting any idle arts or feats for gain or profit."[38] The Bowmanville town council attempted to set strict community boundaries for the socio-cultural behaviour of its citizens, passing bylaws to limit noise by restricting the setting off of church bells or discharging of firearms, setting limits to bathing naked from before sunrise to after eight in the evening, and fining citizens for swearing and blasphemy and for "drawing indecent words, figures or pictures on any building or public place." The fine for such activities in Bowmanville was set at five pounds or twenty days in the county jail. Another important facet of regulating a town's socio-cultural behaviour was to ensure that rambunctiousness did not turn into criminal activity. The Bowmanville town council was particularly strict with its citizens on a number of fronts, and it is unclear whether the area's citizens required such regulation or merely rebelled against town authority on an ongoing basis. In the early 1860s, town officials not only offered a fifty-dollar reward for the "apprehension of the incendiaries who have been lately at work in this town," they also offered a ten-dollar reward for information leading to the conviction of window breakers. A few years later, the council offered a fifty-dollar reward to find the "evil disposed person or persons who did break open the door of the Roman Catholic Church" and vandalized the interior.[39]

One of the most severe challenges to the authority of town councils in Canada West / Ontario during the 1850s and 1860s came in the licensing of taverns and the control over "spirituous liquors." This was particularly true in the mid-nineteenth century, as tavern keepers, distillers, and temperance advocates competed to capture the minds of citizens within the region.[40] Most townships viewed the tavern, inn, or "houses of entertainment" as a necessary evil from a business perspective, but one that needed to be regulated or constrained. Thus, the vast majority of township bylaws, in most of the townships themselves, attempted to regulate and negotiate the sale, consumption, and production of "intoxicating beverages" in various towns and villages. Most such bylaws involved the hiring of more town officials, from tavern inspectors to those overseeing the entire licensing process, a process that, in turn, generated more revenue for the township. Alfred Township also provided an incentive for citizen whistle blowers, by offering to share with the complainant half the fine for those selling liquor without a licence. Still other bylaws attempted to regulate the behaviour of town citizens frequenting taverns, inns, and other places where spirituous liquors were sold. These rules included prohibiting the sale of liquor on the Sabbath day and selling alcohol to minors or "intoxicated persons." According to one Oshawa town council bylaw, houses of entertainment could have "no gambling with cards or dice, no quarrelling, fighting, profane swearing, obscene, immodest or indecent language, disloyal songs or tales, slight of hand, tumbling, rope dancing or other exhibitions."[41] Other townships wrestled with the issue of prohibition and temperance, often within a town council itself. The interest of many a town council in calling for prohibition of the sale of alcohol in their township was almost in direct proportion to the social and political influence of temperance advocates such as the Sons of Temperance. The Mariposa Sons of Temperance successfully applied to hold their meetings in the town hall in 1858; it was no coincidence that two town councillors would successfully petition the provincial legislature to pass a prohibition bill, or that they were instrumental in denying a licence to a notorious innkeeper within the township.[42]

The wielding of power and authority within the townships of Canada West / Ontario during the 1850s and 1860s was a fiercely negotiated process between town councils and citizens, generally played out within a particular locality, but occasionally rising to the provincial level. While ultimately authority would rest within local governing structures and regulatory bodies, individual citizens could and did exert their agency through the use of petitions, recourse to the legal system, and general non-compliance with town ordinances and bylaws. The authority divide was marked, on one side, by appeals to "civic responsibility" by those exercising the powers of liberal governmentality and, on the other, by appeals to the "larger community," from ordinary citizens who were contesting that authority. The "quest for order and democracy" in townships throughout Canada West / Ontario during the post-rebellion period would remain contested terrain for all levels of government well past Confederation.

For town councils and those involved in municipal governance, local circumstances and individual idiosyncrasies would play a much larger role in the municipal governance of township communities than did overarching debates on the nature of deliberative democracy or possessive individualism. Without a doubt, for most township councils and active citizens in Canada West / Ontario in the 1850s and 1860s, the "better administration of the town's affairs" truly became the guiding principle for local governance.

NOTES

1 Allan Greer argued that this emerging democratic culture attempted to instil in its citizenry a "glowing vision of a community where the people rule, where independent and equal citizens deliberate on the good of the whole, free from the overbearing influence of wealth and privilege." See Allan Greer, "Historical Roots of Canadian Democracy," *Journal of Canadian Studies* 34, no. 1 (Spring 1999): 7–26. Similar themes are explored in the work of Albert Schrauwers, *Union Is Strength:*

W.L. Mackenzie, the Children of Peace, and the Emergence of Joint Stock Democracy in Upper Canada (Toronto: University of Toronto Press, 2009). For a rudimentary history of local governance in the region during the nineteenth century, see C.P. de T. Glazebrook, "The Origins of Local Government," and C.F.J. Whebell, "Robert Baldwin and Decentralization, 1841–9," in *Aspects of Nineteenth-Century Ontario*, ed. F.H. Armstrong et al., (Toronto: University of Toronto Press, 1974), 36–64.

2 See the Niagara Township records in the Archives of Ontario (hereafter AO), F 1805-11, MS 178, reel 1, council minute book, 27 January 1857 and 3 September 1857.

3 For an argument emphasizing localized powers as a decentralization impulse, see Whebell, "Robert Baldwin and Decentralization," 48–64. On the embryonic nature of state formation in the Canadas, see Allan Greer and Ian Radforth, eds, *Colonial Leviathan: State Formation in Mid-Nineteenth-Century Canada* (Toronto: University of Toronto Press, 1992). See also J.I. Little, *State and Society in Transition: The Politics of Institutional Reform in the Eastern Townships, 1838–1852* (Montreal and Kingston: McGill-Queen's University Press, 1997); Bruce Curtis, *The Politics of Population: State Formation, Statistics, and the Census of Canada, 1840–1875* (Toronto: University of Toronto Press, 2002); Bruce Curtis, *Ruling by Schooling Quebec: Conquest to Liberal Governmentality. A Historical Sociology* (Toronto: University of Toronto Press, 2012); and Donald Fyson, "Between the *Ancien Regime* and Liberal Modernity: Law, Justice, and State Formation in Colonial Quebec, 1760–1869," *History Compass* 12, no. 5 (2014): 412–32. The vast majority of essays in this volume catalogue the responses of local authorities to both real and perceived threats to their authority and to the collective social order in the British North American colonies.

4 Ian McKay, "The Liberal Order Framework: A Prospectus for a Reconnaissance of Canadian History," *Canadian Historical Review* 81, no. 4 (December 2000): 616–45; Daniel Samson, *The Spirit of Industry and Improvement: Liberal Government and Rural-Industrial Society, Nova Scotia, 1790–1862* (Montreal and Kingston: McGill-Queen's University Press, 2008); Darren Ferry, *Uniting in Measures of Common Good: The Construction of Liberal Identities in Central Canada* (Montreal and Kingston: McGill-Queen's University Press, 2008); and Jean-François Constant and Michel Ducharme, eds, *Liberalism and Hegemony: Debating the Canadian Liberal Revolution* (Toronto: University of Toronto Press, 2009).

5 The two most important works examining emerging "democratic" political cultures in Upper Canada are Jeffrey McNairn, *The Capacity to Judge: Public Opinion and Deliberative Democracy in Upper Canada, 1791–1854* (Toronto: University of Toronto Press, 2000); and Carol Wilton, *Popular Politics and Political Culture in Upper Canada, 1800–1850* (Montreal and Kingston: McGill-Queen's University Press, 2000). See also S.J.D. Noel, *Patrons, Clients, Brokers: Ontario Society and*

Politics, 1791–1896 (Toronto: University of Toronto Press, 1990); and George Emery, *Elections in Oxford County, 1837–1875: A Case Study in Democracy in Canada West and Early Ontario* (Toronto: University of Toronto Press, 2012). A comparison of emerging "democratic" ideologies in Upper/Lower Canada and Australia can be found in Michel Ducharme, *Le concept de liberté au Canada à l'époque des Révolutions atlantiques, 1776–1838* (Montreal and Kingston: McGill-Queen's University Press, 2010); and Benjamin Jones, *Republicanism and Responsible Government: The Shaping of Democracy in Australia and Canada* (Montreal and Kingston: McGill-Queen's University Press, 2014).

6 A more recent phenomenon in nineteenth-century Canadian historiography is the rediscovery of the role of empire in Canadian institutions, cultural practices, ideologies, and political ideas. For some key examples, see Nancy Christie, ed., *Transatlantic Subjects: Ideas, Institutions, and Social Experience in Post-Revolutionary British North America* (Montreal: McGill-Queen's University Press, 2008); Philip Buckner, ed., *Canada and the British Empire* (Toronto: Oxford University Press, 2010); and Michael Eamon, *Imprinting Britain: Newspapers, Sociability, and the Shaping of British North America* (Montreal and Kingston: McGill-Queen's University Press, 2015). While this imperial scholarship is a welcome corollary to the navel-gazing nature of early colonial historiography, this study will attempt to provide a more balanced and nuanced view of the adaptation of British political culture for colonial needs.

7 See Whebell, "Robert Baldwin," 48–64; and Mary McAllister, *Governing Ourselves? The Politics of Canadian Communities* (Vancouver: UBC Press, 2004), 82–90.

8 Patrick Joyce has focused on the centrality of liberal governmentality within political structures in Great Britain and the larger empire: see *The Rule of Freedom: Liberalism and the Modern City* (London: Verso Press, 2003); and *The State of Freedom: A Social History of the British State after 1800* (Cambridge: Cambridge University Press, 2013). See also Chris Otter, *The Victorian Eye: A Political History of Light and Vision in Britain, 1800–1910* (Chicago: University of Chicago Press, 2008); and Tom Crook, *Governing Systems: Modernity and the Making of Public Health in Britain, 1830–1910* (Berkeley: University of California Press, 2016). Tentative examinations into these concepts were first introduced in Canadian historiography by Jean-Marie Fecteau in *Un nouvel ordre des choses: La pauvreté, la crime, l'État au Québec, de la fin du XVIIIe siècle à 1840* (Montreal: VLB, 1989) and *La liberté du pauvre: crime et pauvreté au XIXe siècle québécois* (Montreal: VLB, 2004), as well as in the essays found in *Colonial Leviathan*. Bruce Curtis and Elsbeth Heaman are the champions of liberal governmentality in more recent Canadian political scholarship, particularly with Curtis's hallmark works *The Politics of Population* and *Ruling by Schooling Quebec*, and Heaman's *A Short History of the State in Canada* (Toronto: University of Toronto Press, 2015).

9 There are over 120 township council records housed in the Archives of Ontario of townships that were created in 1849 or earlier, and they are found largely in Record Group (RG) 21. The database for this study is based on over eighty of these records. In creating this database, I made a conscious effort to choose at least one township from each of the twenty-four counties created by the Municipal Corporations Act of 1849.

10 On the critical role played by middle-class families in local governing structures, see J.K. Johnson, *Becoming Prominent: Regional Leadership in Upper Canada, 1791–1841* (Montreal and Kingston: McGill-Queen's University Press, 1989); Little, *State and Society in Transition*; Andrew Holman, *A Sense of Their Duty: Middle-Class Formation in Victorian Ontario Towns* (Montreal and Kingston: McGill-Queen's University Press, 2000); and Marguerite Van Die, *Religion, Family, and Community in Victorian Canada: The Colbys of Carrollcroft* (Montreal and Kingston: McGill-Queen's University Press, 2007).

11 For Jacob Hespeler, see the Hespeler records, AO, MS 368, reel 1, council minute book, 17 January 1859; for Cornwall, see AO, F 1621-1, MS 749, reel 1, council minute book, 21 January 1850. In the township of Alfred, Thomas Brady, Baptiste Morin, John Bault, and William Legan served on the same town council in various positions from its inception in 1854 to the 1860s, while the Carpenter, Springstead, and Williamson families dominated the Saltfleet town council from 1850 to 1870. See the records of Alfred in AO, F 1521-, MS 724, reel 1, council minute book, 1854–65, and the Saltfleet records in AO, F 1901-1/2, MS 468 reel 1, council minute book, 1850–70.

12 See the records of Niagara in AO, F 1805-1, MS 178, reel 1, council minute book, 11 September 1850, and the Mariposa records in AO, F 1761-1, MS 678, reel 1, council minute book, 3 March 1850. Similar rules of conduct and order were established for the Athol and Townsend town councils; see the records of Athol in AO, F 1522-1, MS 679, reel 1, council minute book, 4 February 1850, and the records of Townsend in AO, F 1964-1, MS 306, reel 1, council minute book, 13 February 1850.

13 The township of Dereham, AO, F 1613-1, MS 381, reel 1, council minute book, 21 April 1851; the Bowmanville records, AO, F 1451-1, MS 451, reel 1, council minute book, 15 May 1859.

14 Cornwall town records, AO, F 1621-1, MS 749, reel 1, council minute book, 10 January 1853 and 17 February 1854. Some town councils had very distinct rules regarding potential conflicts of interest, such as the Halton town council, which told its representatives that if they were "personally interested in the question" up for a vote, they were to abstain from judging the petition; Halton town records, AO, F 1965-1, MS 614, council minute book, 3 July 1855.

15 Niagara records, AO, F 1805-1, MS 178, reel 1, council minute book, 3 August 1869. For Alfred Township, see AO, F 1510-1, MS 724, reel 1, council minute book, 7 March 1854 and 1 January 1855.

16 Caledon records, AO, MS 378, reel 1, council minute book, 2 December 1865; Hespeler Township, AO, F 1701-1, MS 368, reel 1, council minute book, 2 March 1863; Niagara records, AO, F 1805-1, MS 178, reel 1, council minute book, 3 August 1869. After the debacle with the ministers, the town council cut off any further petitions citizens presented to bypass the toll roads. See the records of Bowmanville, AO, F-1459-1, MS 457, reel 1, council minute book, 19 October 1857, 15 February 1858, 17 March 1858, and 18 October 1858.

17 Caledon records, AO, MS 378, reel 1, council minute book, 19 September 1846; Alfred Township, AO, F 1510-1, MS 724, reel 1, council minute book, 16 January 1860.

18 Alfred Township, AO, F 1510-1, MS 724, reel 1, council minute book, 1 September 1856, 27 December 1856, and 1 October 1860.

19 Caledon records, AO, MS 378, reel 1, council minute book, 1 and 15 December 1860 and 30 November 1861; Niagara Township, AO, F 1805-1, MS 178, reel 1, council minute book, 3 November 1856.

20 There are very few scholarly examinations regarding statute labour in Canada West / Ontario; see Robert Summerby-Murray, "Statute Labour on Ontario Roads, 1849–1948: Responding to a Changing Space Economy," *Canadian Geographer* 43, no. 1 (March 1999): 36–52; and Derek Murray, "Equitable Claims and Future Considerations: Road Building and Colonization in Early Ontario, 1850–1890," *Journal of the Canadian Historical Association* 24, no. 2 (2013): 156–88.

21 Streetsville records, AO, F 1946-1, MS 304, reel 8, bylaws, no. 54; Bromley records, AO, F 1559-1, MS 6809, reel 1, council minute book, 2 April 1860. The town councils of Ramsay and Caledon kept extensive records of statute labour performed in their township; Caledon records, AO, MS 378, reel 1, council minute book, 19 September 1846 to 11 April 1868, and Ramsay records, AO, F 1887-1, reel 1, council minute book, 21 April 1849 to 9 April 1864.

22 Caledon records, AO, MS 378, reel 1, council minute book, 25 June 1854; Albion township, AO, MS 388, reel 1, council minute book, 2 October 1865. For fines and threats of confinement in jail for non-compliance of statute labour, see Cornwall records, AO, F 1621-1, MS 749, council minute book, 28 March 1850.

23 Mariposa records, AO, F 1671-1, MS 678, reel 1, council minute book, 7 March 1851 and 22 March 1864, and MS 678, reel 3, Bylaw 96, 3 July 1867. See also Manvers records, AO, MS 677, reel 1, council minute book, 25 February 1857; Walsingham township, AO, F 1983-1, MS 215, reel 1, council minute book, 16 October 1852; Moulton records, AO, F 1791-1, MS 592, reel 1, council minute book, 3 April 1851; and Townsend Township, AO, F 1964-1, MS 306, reel 1, council minute book, 4 May 1858.

24 Albion records, AO, MS 388, reel 1, council minute book, 12 April 1856; Dereham Township, AO, F 1613-1, MS 381, reel 1, council minute book, 18 June 1866;

Caledon records, AO, MS 378, reel 1, council minute book, 16 November 1867; and Cornwall Township, see AO, F 1621-1, MS 749, reel 1, council minute book, 11 June 1855.

25 On the lack of Poor Law legislation in Upper Canada, see Judith Fingard, "The Winter's Tale: The Seasonal Contours of Pre-industrial Poverty in British North America, 1815–1860," Canadian Historical Association *Historical Papers* 9, no. 1 (1974): 65–94, and Rainer Bahere, "Paupers and Poor Relief in Upper Canada," Canadian Historical Association *Historical Papers* (1981): 57–80. That the challenges of poverty were not met by either Tory paternalism *or* reform liberalism in British North America, compare the approaches of Tory paternalism found in Wendy Cameron and Mary Maude, *Assisting Emigration to Upper Canada: The Petworth Project, 1832–1837* (Montreal and Kingston: McGill-Queen's University Press, 2000) and a more "liberal" approach to the challenge of poverty found in Jean-Marie Fecteau, *La liberté du pauvre.*

26 Caledon records, AO, MS 378, reel 1, council minute book, 9 April 1858; Dunnville Township, AO, F 1621-1, MS 616, reel 1, council minute book, 22 February 1865.

27 Streetsville records, AO, F 1946-1, RG 21, MS 304, reel 1, council minute book, 27 March 1863, 24 June 1863, and 9 October 1863; Saltfleet Township, AO, F 1901-1/2, MS 468, reel 1, council minute book, 7 November 1863, 16 January 1865, and 1 December 1866.

28 The seminal description of how the British Poor Law operated during this period in Britain can be found in David Green, *Pauper Capital: London and the Poor Law, 1790–1870* (Farnham, UK: Ashgate, 2010). For comparisons on how poor relief worked in British North America as opposed to Great Britain, see "British North America and the Poor Law," in Alvin Finkel, *Social Policy and Practice in Canada: A History* (Waterloo, ON: Wilfrid Laurier University Press, 2006), 39–61; and Kevin Siena, "Hospitals for the Excluded or Convalescent Homes? Workhouses, Medicalization, and the Poor Law in Long-Eighteenth-Century London and Pre-Confederation Toronto," *Canadian Bulletin of Medical History* 27, no. 1 (2010): 5–25.

29 Caledon records, AO, MS 378, reel 1, council minute book, 23 February 1863, 2 May 1863, 23 July 1863, 26 November 1864, and 6 January 1866; Townsend records, AO, F 1964-1, MS 306, reel 1, council minute book, 25 April 1860 and 20 November 1865; and Caledonia Township, AO, F 1572-1, MS 765, reel 1, council minute book, 26 November 1853 and 6 December 1853. Leeds Township also chose to waive the taxes of widows in the town as a means of welfare. See Leeds records, AO, F 1668-1, MS 614, reel 1, council minute book, 1 May 1854.

30 Belleville records, AO, F 1535-1, MS 889, reel 2, council minute book, 18 February 1852 and 23 February 1859; Bowmanville township, AO, F 1459-1, MS 457, reel 1, council minute book, 1 February 1858, 17 January 1859, and 5 May 1862. The

importance of female benevolent societies providing necessary "welfare" services is examined in Charlotte Neff, "The Role of Protestant Children's Homes in Nineteenth-Century Ontario: Child Rescue or Family Support?" *Journal of Family History* 34, no. 1 (January 2009): 48–88; and Carmen Nielson, *Private Women and the Public Good: Charity and State Formation in Hamilton, Ontario, 1846–93* (Vancouver: UBC Press, 2014).

31 On the challenges of British emigration to the colony, see Rainier Baehre, "Pauper Emigration to Upper Canada in the 1830s," *Histoire sociale / Social History* 14, no. 28 (November 1981): 349–67; and Cameron and Maude, *Assisting Emigration to Upper Canada*; and especially Jane Errington, *Emigrant Worlds and Transatlantic Communities: Migration to Upper Canada in the First Half of the Nineteenth Century* (Montreal and Kingston: McGill-Queen's University Press, 2007). On the perceived threat of poor British immigrants to the social order in this period, consult the excellent essay by Jane Errington in the present volume.

32 Albion records, AO, MS 388, reel 1, council minute book, 10 February 1855; Niagara Township, AO, F 1805-1, MS 178, reel 1, council minute book, 11 February 1855; Moulton records, AO, F 1791-1, MS 592, reel 1, council minute book, 9 February 1857; and Dunnville town records, AO, F 1621-1, MS 616, reel 1, council minute book, 22 December 1864.

33 On the many socio-economic trials of Lancashire textile workers during the cotton famine, see George Boyer, "Poor Relief, Informal Assistance, and Short Time during the Lancashire Cotton Famine," *Explorations in Economic History* 34 (1997): 56–76; and Peter Shapely, "Urban Charity, Class Relations, and Social Cohesion: Charitable Responses to the Cotton Famine," *Urban History* 28, no. 1 (2001): 45–64.

34 Belleville Township, AO, F 1535-1, MS 889, reel 2, council minute book, 23 July 1862; Caledon records, AO, MS 378, reel 1, council minute book, 22 February 1863; Cayuga Township, AO, F 1581-1, reel 1, council minute book, 1 December 1862; and Hespeler records, AO, MS 368, reel 1, council minute book, 18 December 1862. On the settlement of Hespeler by German Mennonites, see Angelika Sauer, "German-Canadian Immigration Agents in the Second Half of the Nineteenth Century," in *Transnational Networks: German Migrants in the British Empire, 1670–1914*, ed. John R. Davis, Stefan Manz, and Margrit Schulte Beerbühl (Leiden, NL: Brill Publishing, 2012), 117–40.

35 Historians studying community "regulation" in mid-nineteenth-century Canada East / Quebec are far ahead of those examining the societies of Canada West / Ontario. See Jean-Marie Fecteau, *Un nouvel ordre des choses* and *La liberté du pauvre*; Little, *State and Society in Transition*, 83–118; and Mary Anne Poutanen, *Beyond Brutal Passions: Prostitution in Early Nineteenth-Century Montreal* (Montreal and Kingston: McGill-Queen's University Press, 2015). For examples of community regulation in Canada West / Ontario, see Katherine McKenna,

"Women's Agency in Upper Canada: Prescott's Board of Police Record, 1834–1850," *Histoire sociale / Social History* 36, no. 72 (November 2003): 347–70; and Raphaël Fischler, "Development Controls in Toronto in the Nineteenth Century," *Urban History Review* 36, no. 1 (Fall 2007): 16–31.

36 Bowmanville records, AO, F 1459-2, MS 457, reel 4, bylaws, 1 February 1853; Mariposa records, AO, F 1671-2, MS 678, reel 3, bylaws, Bylaw 9; and Oshawa Township, AO, F 1844-1, MS 671, reel 1, council minute book, 1 February 1858.

37 For Cornwall records, see AO, F 1621-1, MS 749, reel 1, Bylaw 13, 18 June 1850; Caledon records, AO, MS 378, reel 1, council minute book, Town Bylaw 2, 11 February 1850; Bowmanville Township, AO, F 1459-2, MS 457, reel 4, bylaws, 1 February 1853; and Niagara records, AO, F 1805-1, MS 178, reel 1, council minute book, 19 May 1845.

38 Niagara Township, AO, F 1805-1, MS 178, reel 1, council minute book, Town Bylaw 3, 3 May 1845; Caledonia records, AO, F 1572-1, MS 765, reel 1, council minute book, 23 February 1854; Ramsay Township, AO, F 1887-1, reel 1, council minute book, 25 October 1867; Cayuga records, AO, F 1581-1, reel 1, council minute book, 5 February 1867; and Cornwall records, AO, F 1621-1, MS 749, reel 1, Bylaw 70, 17 February 1854. On the "moral" challenges of early Niagara tourism, see Karen Dubinsky, *The Second Great Disappointment: Honeymooning and Tourism at Niagara Falls* (Toronto: Between the Lines Press, 1999), 19–54.

39 Bowmanville records, AO, F 1459-2, MS 457, reel 1, council minute book, 16 December 1861 and 19 March 1866 and reel 4, bylaws, 1 February 1853.

40 On the challenges inherent to tavern licensing and the production of alcohol, see Craig Heron, *Booze: A Distilled History* (Toronto: Between the Lines Press, 2003), 51–130; Ferry, *Uniting in Measures of Common Good*, 95–135; and Julia Roberts, *In Mixed Company: Taverns and Public Life in Upper Canada* (Vancouver: UBC Press, 2009).

41 Oshawa records, AO, F 1844-2, MS 671, reel 7, bylaws, no. 106, 24 February 1864; and Alfred Township, AO, F 1521-1, MS 724, reel 1, council minute book, 6 March 1856.

42 Mariposa records, AO, F 1671-1, MS 678, reel 1, council minute book, 13 February 1858, 21 February 1859, and 21 January 1860; Bowmanville records, AO, F 1459-2, MS 457, reel 1, council minute book, 12 June 1859, 8 April 1861, and 21 November 1865; and Dereham Township, AO, F 1613-1, MS 381, reel 1, council minute book, 7 February 1859. The Sons of Temperance also influenced prohibition sentiment and tougher regulations for inns and taverns in Bowmanville and Dereham.

21 The Role of Halifax Newspapers during the Confederate and the Repeal Movements, 1865–1869

MATHIAS RODORFF

The Dominion of Canada, supported by the leading representatives of the United Province of Canada, New Brunswick, and Nova Scotia, was born on 1 July 1867. However, the advocates of Confederation faced stiff resistance, and supporters of the movements against Confederation prevailed in the provincial elections in New Brunswick in 1865 and Nova Scotia in 1867. The resistance in Nova Scotia, first apparent in the Confederate movement and then ascendant in the repeal movement, offers an opportunity to reflect on the significance of the public sphere – in this case, how the press and elections shaped how Nova Scotians responded to Confederation. The debates lasted for almost three years, from the publication of the Quebec Resolutions in December 1864 to the provincial and federal elections in September 1867. The Confederation debates were intensified by related debates over the constitutional practices of responsible government – most specifically, whether the citizenry had a right to vote on a change as momentous as Confederation.[1]

The Quebec Resolutions, the terms negotiated for federal union, had to be approved by the legislatures of each of the three provinces – Nova Scotia, New Brunswick, and the United Province of Canada. Following approval, each provincial government was entitled to send delegates to the Imperial Parliament in London, which was developing the legislation authorizing Confederation, long known as the British North America Act and, since 1982, as the Constitution Act. The debates about the merits and demerits of Confederation, however, could not be contained within the legislature. Newspapers reported legislative proceedings within the public sphere, disseminating any debate or speech it deemed meaningful, and journals published pamphlets and editorials expressing the different views of opponents and supporters of Confederation. In response, both political parties in Nova Scotia – Conservatives and

Liberals – mobilized significant numbers of Nova Scotian readers, with the ruling Conservatives, led by Premier Charles Tupper, advocating Confederation, and the Liberals, led by William Annand, opposed. Tupper's government prevailed, gaining legislative approval of the Quebec Resolutions. The Imperial Parliament passed the British North America Act in March 1867. But Tupper had alienated the electorate and lost the provincial and federal elections of September 1867, both of which were dominated by the Confederation issue. These defeats had been caused, above all, by the unwillingness of the government to approve any measures for the direct participation of the voters at the polls on the Confederation issue before the union was enacted. In hundreds of petitions presented to the House of Assembly, supported by several members of the assembly and by editorials in anti-confederate newspapers and journals, the citizenry had repeatedly requested an opportunity to debate Confederation. Yet the government remained unwavering in its dismissal of these requests, contending that legislators alone had the constitutional power to "have the final word on Confederation."[2]

The Liberals achieved an overwhelming majority in the legislature in September 1867 and activated a repeal movement. The movement sought to nullify the agreements made by the Tupper government, as well as those with the imperial government. Annand's Liberal government sought to achieve this goal through cooperation and negotiation rather than through unrest; indeed, it suspended any forms of unlawful or violent measures that opponents might see as acts of secession, such as those that had triggered the American Civil War (1861–5). The British imperial government, however, rejected Nova Scotia's overtures, and in June 1869 the Nova Scotian government, with great dismay, accepted "better terms" and remained in the Dominion of Canada.

An analysis of the repeal movement offers two compelling perspectives on the relationship between the "public sphere" and "social order." First, the ambition to repeal was a form of unrest against the agreed terms of the British North America Act, which proponents justified with the argument that the Nova Scotia government had refused voters a say on the issue. A tension developed between proclaimed loyalty to the authority of British institutions – provincial assemblies and the Imperial Parliament – and the aim to withdraw from Confederation. This tension first emerged in December 1864, when the Quebec Resolutions were released. During the subsequent debates over the merits or flaws of Confederation, the disagreements on this constitutional issue shifted from theoretical questions about loyalty to British institutions to the real consequences of actions. Second, in the 1867 election, the Conservatives lost all but two seats in the assembly, and, therefore, any form of critical debate shifted from the assembly to the public sphere and the press.

Earlier scholars, most particularly J. Murray Beck, D.C. Harvey, John Heisler, and P.B. Waite, have researched the press and the Confederation debates in Nova Scotia, but they used a primarily biographical approach to analyse them.[3] They used newspapers to explain the actions of leading Nova Scotian politicians, such as Joseph Howe, Jonathan McCully, and Charles Tupper. But scholarship over the past three decades on the public sphere suggests that the character of the newspapers and journals themselves and the environments in which they were published and circulated offer possibilities for new studies. If we want to understand public sentiments towards Confederation (and political polls were not conducted in the 1860s), newspapers offer important insights into the opinions of Nova Scotians because they were the dominant arena for distributing news, expressing views, and debating issues. As well, an examination of the debates in the context of the public sphere draws into question an older historiography that argued that Confederation was largely consensual, that the differences turned on economic and regional tensions, or were significantly shaped by prominent men.[4]

Moreover, the Confederate movement accentuated a crucial divide between the elected and the electors because the Tupper government asserted that approval of the Quebec Resolutions was solely the decision of elected members of the Legislative Assembly, and not within the rights of the electors. Newspapers and journals moved into that breach and offered venues for debating Confederation. Thus, understanding the reception of Confederation in Nova Scotia means considering the editorial policies of diverse Halifax newspapers and journals. While they initially operated passively, as a vehicle to convey the debates and speeches in the legislature or at public meetings, over time they actively influenced the course of debates in the public sphere, as editors made decisions about which pamphlets, counter-pamphlets, editorials, and counter-editorials would be published. These actions made newspapers, as Michael Eamon argues, an "important forum of social interaction that both formed and informed."[5]

This fluid, at times ambiguous, role of the media in conveying and shaping public debates explains the need to understand the place of Halifax papers in the debates around Confederation and the Repeal Movement. This role merits re-examination for several reasons. First, during the debates and votes in the assembly and in the general elections of 1867, the number of published editorials on the subject reached a peak. Moreover, editors targeted specific audiences, and eligible voters were mobilized to influence the results. Second, some politicians leading the debates in the legislature were at the same time the owners or editors of the newspapers facilitating these debates in the public sphere. William Annand, the premier of the anti-confederate government elected in 1867, was the owner and chief editor of the *Morning Chronicle*, the most widely read newspaper in Nova Scotia. Joseph Howe, who had lost his premiership to Charles Tupper in 1863, became the most prominent orator of the anti-confederates. His pamphlets and speeches, exclusively published in the *Chronicle*, made the paper the backbone of the anti-confederate movement. Jonathan McCully, head of the Legislative Council and a delegate to the Charlottetown and Quebec conferences, was the editor of the *Unionist and Halifax Journal*, the *Chronicle*'s main competitor.

Third, in the 1860s, many publishers in Halifax and Halifax County increased the publication rates of their journal from weeklies to tri-weeklies or dailies, responding to public demand for news and attempting to shape the debates. The newspapers of Halifax dominated the distribution of news in Nova Scotia. Several of the less populated cities and counties had one to two "County newspapers." Yarmouth had two journals, the *Herald* and the *Tribune*; Pictou County had the *Colonial Standard* (Pictou) and the *Eastern Chronicle* (New Glasgow). Each followed its own editorial policy and focused on local news and politics.[6] Given their local networks and limited financial capabilities, these newspapers did not directly report news from the legislature in Halifax or the British Parliament; rather, they tended to reprint news and editorials from Halifax papers, thereby amplifying those papers' impact. Denominational newspapers like the Protestant *Burning Bush*, the Baptist *Christian Messenger*, and the *Presbyterian Witness* occasionally engaged in the debates about Confederation, but not at a significant level.

Another visible component of the vibrant Halifax press was short-lived papers and journals like the anti-confederate *Bullfrog* and the *Gunboat*. Although neither was widely circulated or influential, they distinguished themselves in their use of satirical language and in fostering debates about Nova Scotia and Confederation. In his survey of Nova Scotia's mid-nineteenth-century newspapers, D.C. Harvey concluded that the *Bullfrog* was a valuable example of "contemporary criticism of Nova Scotian journalism," criticism that was more and more characterized by the "tendency to deal in their [newspapers'] personalities, and in their intense local patriotism."[7] The *Bullfrog* and the *Gunboat* represent a common problem that scholars face with short-lived newspapers: the available information is not sufficient to verify the papers' relevance.[8] Nevertheless, Harvey declared the *Bullfrog* to have been a crucial anti-confederate mouthpiece, in addition to the well-established *Acadian Recorder*, the *Chronicle*, and the Halifax *Citizen*. Editorials in the Halifax *Unionist* and *British Colonist* indicate that the *Bullfrog* had an impact, but probably a less crucial one than Harvey contended.[9] In short, the contributions and perspectives of denominational and short-lived newspapers are not irrelevant, but their impact was often derivative of the Halifax media.

The most widespread and loyal readership was enjoyed by newspapers that politicians either owned or edited and that focused on publishing political debates; theses papers engaged in competitive publishing of debates and offered valuable reports and editorials about Nova Scotia and Confederation.[10] In Halifax eight newspapers shared these elements. The oldest was the *Acadian Recorder* (1813–1930), founded by Anthony Holland. Since the publication of the Quebec Resolutions, it remained an adamant agitator against the pro-Confederation policy of the government and its supporters.[11] The *British Colonist* (1848–74), founded by A. Grant, was, besides the *Unionist*, the platform of the Confederate movement.[12] The *Evening Express* (1858–73), owned and edited by William Compton, was the only newspaper in Halifax County that published articles on Roman Catholic matters, but it focused primarily on Nova Scotian trade and economic matters.[13] It was a chief advocate of Confederation because of the economic opportunities anticipated by the construction of the Intercolonial Railway. The *Evening Reporter* and the *Citizen* were relatively new newspapers. The *Reporter* (1860–78) was owned and edited by Joseph C. Croskill and George John Bourinot, who represented Cape Breton County in the House of Assembly (1859–67).[14] In 1866 the *Reporter* published Bourinot's three pamphlet letters, "Confederation of the Provinces of British North America," and thus accentuated the paper's clear support of Confederation. The *Citizen* (1863–present) was owned and edited by William Garvie and Edmund Mortimer McDonald. Garvie became famous for his satirical letters, "Barney Rooney's Letters on Confederation," that targeted the arguments of Charles Tupper and Jonathan McCully.[15]

The *Novascotian* (1824–present), founded by George Young and bought by Joseph Howe in 1827, had long been one of the leading weekly newspapers in British North America.[16] In late 1843, William Annand purchased both the *Novascotian* and the *Chronicle*, which had been founded by James Barnes in 1842. Thereafter, the editorials in the former were reduced to a weekly summary of the editorials of the *Chronicle*.[17] With the support of his two popular editors, Joseph Howe (1844–6) and Jonathan McCully (1854–65), Annand managed to establish the *Chronicle* as the most circulated newspaper of Nova Scotia in 1868.[18] Furthermore, in August 1864 this journal expanded from a tri-weekly to the first provincial daily and maintained that position until 1869, when the *British Colonist* and the *Acadian Recorder* also expanded into daily circulation. With his two papers, William Annand possessed the greatest media presence in Nova Scotia, owning the only daily newspaper as well as the most influential weekly.[19] At first, the *Chronicle*, under the editorship of Jonathan McCully, showed substantial support for the Quebec Resolutions and emphasized the economic opportunities that Confederation would bring.[20] McCully's editorial position caused tensions with William Annand, and on 10 January 1865 the *Chronicle* announced that "the proprietor re-assumes the control of the paper."[21] Annand dismissed McCully, took over editorial management, and instructed Joseph Howe to turn the *Chronicle* into the voice of the anti-confederate movement.

Immediately upon leaving the *Chronicle*, McCully was hired by William A. Penney, who, since 1850, had been the proprietor and editor of the *Morning Journal and Commercial Advertiser* (1781–1869).[22] On 16 January 1865, a mere six days after the *Chronicle* made a public display of shifting its editorial position on Confederation, Penney made an equally bold statement. He began publishing his newspaper under the new name, the *Unionist and Halifax Journal* (1865–9), an unmistakable endorsement of Confederation, with McCully as the new editor. Until then, the paper's editorial focus had been on supporting the war efforts of the American Confederacy, and initially Penney avoided taking a position in the Confederation debates. Indeed, he announced on 23 November 1864 that, although he was "an advocate of a Union of the British North American Colonies," he welcomed "opposition to the Quebec Resolutions because nothing tends so much to success of any political movement as healthy opposition."[23] But with his January decision to hire McCully and to begin publishing his paper under its new name, Penney shifted his editorial position to advocating for the Quebec Resolutions and countering any criticism of that agreement, especially from the *Chronicle*.[24]

At the Quebec Conference (10–27 October 1864), the vision for the future federal union was embodied in seventy-two resolutions, known as the Quebec Resolutions.[25] The reorganization of Halifax's newspapers roughly coincided with public debate on these resolutions. The press had been excluded from the conference, and, as a result, reports about the deliberations and decisions were scarce. Consequently, Halifax newspapers and journals were unable to launch any immediate substantive debates about the resolutions. Hints about them had leaked out during the conference's social events and through hearsay, but details tended to be inconsistent, and so theoretical discussions about the benefits of legislative versus federal union characterized early news coverage. This lack of information was also the reason why news on the American Civil War and the re-election of Abraham Lincoln continued to have greater prominence in the media than did events in Quebec. This media landscape quickly changed after the first public meetings in December 1864, when the Quebec Resolutions were discussed in Halifax in front of a broad audience.

The Confederate movement in the Maritimes commenced on 9 December 1864, when three of the five Nova Scotia delegates to the Quebec Conference – Charles Tupper, Jonathan McCully, and Adams G. Archibald – presented their views at the first public meeting at Temperance Hall in Halifax. They structured their presentation to persuade people and the press of the virtues of Confederation, and thereby to eradicate any serious opposition among legislators. These three prominent men were using the public sphere tactically to influence how legislators would vote in the assembly. In all three provinces, the legislatures normally met for a few months, usually from February to April. At the Quebec Conference, Nova Scotia's delegates agreed that the legislature would discuss and approve the resolutions in the session starting on 9 February 1865. Premier Charles Tupper foresaw no reasons for any difficulties or delays because his government enjoyed a clear majority in the assembly, with forty seats to the Liberals' fourteen.[26] Moreover, Tupper believed he had created a "great coalition" because he had recruited the leaders of the opposition benches, especially Jonathan McCully (Liberal leader in the Legislative Council and editor of the *Chronicle*) and Adams G. Archibald (Liberal leader in the assembly). Both men were at Charlottetown and Quebec and supported the Quebec Resolutions. Although newspapers like the *Acadian Recorder* and the *Citizen* demanded that the "people ought to know that changes ... are bound up in the scheme for Confederation," the lack of information coming out of the Quebec Conference meant that their criticism was not pointed enough to reach any broad audience.[27] Throughout November 1864, the *British Colonist* celebrated the achievements of the Quebec Conference as reflecting the strength of unity. On 30 November 1864, McCully, as editor of the *Chronicle*, officially announced that "the conductors of this journal propose henceforth to advocate" for Confederation.[28] With McCully as an ally, Tupper could count on the assistance of the most-read journal of the province. Given these circumstances, Christopher Moore's assessment that Tupper was "full of [his] usual confident bluster" and "expected to have the Quebec Resolutions quickly ratified," is legitimate.[29]

Tupper and his supporters, focused as they were on winning the support of members of the Legislative Assembly, had undervalued the relevance of the public sphere to the process of ratifying the resolutions and had underestimated the potential for opposition in public meetings or among Halifax newspapers and their readers. After the first public meeting on 9 December, the Halifax newspapers and journals began examining the possible consequences of Confederation for Nova Scotians. Two more meetings at Temperance Hall, on 19 and 23 December, that featured the critical opinions of leading merchants and financiers, such as James Cochran, Alfred G. Jones, Patrick Power, and William Stairs, generated close attention. The focus turned to the commercial terms that the delegates had accepted at Quebec. No "great enthusiasm" was expressed during the debate, proclaimed the *British Colonist*; instead, participants focused their anxiety on the possible impact of new federal tariffs or taxes.[30] At three meetings in Windsor (28 December) and in Halifax (30–1 December), Tupper and McCully failed to calm these economic concerns and lost the initiative in determining the topics to be debated at the public meetings and in the press.[31]

In short, the public meetings provided the necessary platform for the delegates and for their critics to name their arguments and their objections in lively debates in front of a thousand or more listeners.[32] Until then, the press had not played an active role because no general public debate had been possible. During these joint meetings, the editors began to decide whom to endorse, and both sides gained needed attention. The meetings decisively disturbed the premier's schedule to get Confederation approved by the legislature and changed the balance of power in favour of the anti-confederates.

The major turning point in this ordering and contesting came when William Annand dismissed Jonathan McCully as editor of the *Chronicle* because his editorials "do not reflect the calm deliberations of a Delegate charged to give his countrymen a fair and dispassionate view of the arguments for and against."[33] At the joint public meetings in December 1864, the publisher and editor of the *Chronicle* had found themselves debating each other: Annand spoke for anti-confederates, whereas McCully thought he could consolidate the *Chronicle* to become the leading mouthpiece of the pro-confederate lobby. This led to growing dispute, and, in the 11 January 1865 issue of the *Chronicle*, Annand announced that he himself would be the new editor. He immediately began to publish the "Botheration Scheme" series, which Joseph Howe anonymously wrote.

McCully, on the other hand, "purchased" the *Journal*.[34] That paper, as noted above, was already in favour of a union of the British North American colonies, but it welcomed dissenting perspectives, noting the importance of a "healthy opposition."[35] On 16 January 1865, in the first edition published by McCully, Penney announced that, under its new name and new editor, the "*Unionist* and *Halifax Journal* [would] be devoted to the advocacy of a Union of the British Provinces."[36]

The shift in the editorial policies of the *Chronicle* and the *Unionist* had two crucial effects on the Confederation debates. First, as James Murray Beck has correctly argued, in the winter of 1864 the most articulate speakers, influential politicians, and newspapers supported Confederation, and the opposition was nothing more than a nascent "grass-roots movement."[37] However, he underestimated both the effect that the letters in the Botheration Scheme series would have. Their publication resulted in growing efforts of the new editor of the *Unionist* to counter these letters and to expose the anonymous author. Moreover, the dismissal of Jonathan McCully from the *Chronicle* led to a personal and political journalistic feud with William Annand that both shaped the rhetoric of any discussion between the *Unionist* and the *Chronicle* and gave prominence to articles of the *Unionist* by the other pro-confederate papers.[38] This feud, with all its personal accusations, took place in public; both sides used their journals to undermine the reputation and integrity of their opponents. The Quebec Resolutions thus gained greater attention among the readership than might otherwise have happened. These shake-ups also hindered efforts to facilitate any productive debates because other influential newspapers, such as the *British Colonist*, the *Citizen*, and the *Express*, joined in the rhetoric of these two rivals.[39]

Second, during the public meetings of December 1864, opponents of the Quebec Resolutions lacked any powerful platform to present their arguments to a broad citizenry in Halifax and Nova Scotia more broadly. This changed after the *Chronicle* shifted its editorial policy, giving the scattered anti-confederates a decisive institution for the distribution of their future agitation. Further, the fame of Joseph Howe, and the direct confession of his authorship of the Botheration letters by the editor of the *Chronicle* on 7 March 1865, guaranteed a considerable interest among the readership. The *Chronicle*, strong in circulation and finances, and Howe, prominent and eloquent, gave the movement a platform that the other anti-confederate mouthpieces, the *Acadian Recorder*, the *Bullfrog*, and the *Citizen*, could neither match nor maintain. The ongoing vociferous debates in the Halifax journals sparked by the Botheration letters determined the news coverage and debates throughout Nova Scotia. The county newspapers reprinted the Botheration Scheme or communicated the debates about them and pursued a strategy similar to the main Halifax journals. The pro-confederate *Colonial Standard* in Pictou County criticized the sudden turn of the *Chronicle*.[40] On the other hand, the anti-confederate *Tribune* in Yarmouth reprinted all the letters of the Botheration Scheme series.[41] Yet James Murray Beck argues that Joseph Howe's contribution to "the emergence of anti-confederate sentiment" during the first months of 1865 was "a modest one."[42] Beck supported this conclusion with the fact that Howe had lost his seat in the assembly during the 1863 election and, as the appointed imperial fishery commissioner sent to negotiate with the Americans, he was absent from Nova Scotia from May 1865 until March 1866 and could not actively intervene in the debates.[43] Concentrating on Howe's biographical details, Beck neglected the public sphere and, with that, the combined effects caused both by the feud between Annand and McCully and the publication of Howe's Botheration letters, which did not require him to be in Halifax.

Howe's series switched the agenda from the economic and political terms discussed at the Quebec Conference to the "participation of the people." The issue about constitutional authority connected the diverse interests of the anti-confederates and became the backbone of their mobilization efforts. The strategy was outlined in the first letter of the Botheration Scheme, published on 11 January:

> I resist the Quebec scheme of government because I do not like the plan for sweeping away the institutions of my country, without the consent of the people because

> it is an atrocious violation of legal rights. Who then will manage Nova Scotia? Some wily Canadian, who will have his own correspondents and servile creatures here ... men that no Novascotian likes that no man trusts ... Now, is this the country for Novascotians to unite with, and to whose entire control we should hand over the management of our affairs?[44]

The advocates of Confederation failed to dispose of such accusations; they first ignored them and then challenged them with their concepts of economic progress and prosperity. Furthermore, the Botheration letters also revealed that the opposition against the "Quebec Scheme" was not automatically against Confederation. The letters highlighted the financial and judicial disadvantages of Confederation as well as the government's strategy to debate and adopt the resolutions within the legislatures and ignore the sentiment for public input.

From 11 January to 2 March 1865, twelve anonymous Botheration letters were published. In reply, the *Unionist* published, from 25 January to 29 March 1865, twelve letters "To the Young Men of Nova Scotia." McCully personally addressed the voters ("the young men") "whom I can more appropriately address, than you, my young friends."[45] He appealed to their conscience, especially to those "who oppose the scheme of Confederation," to consider the way "to address your reason and understanding" because then "there would be less personal abuse of the advocates, fewer 'Botheration' articles."[46] McCully called for support "to defend my public reputation" against the "old compeers of the Liberal Party that are now forsaking their principles" and "the Editors of the *Chronicle* and the *Citizen*."[47] McCully's letters had the sole purpose of retaliating against the Botheration letters and to undermine the integrity of the anti-confederate editors and politicians.

During the Confederate period, sentiments about whether to consult the people offer a crucial insight into the relationship between social order and the public sphere. This insight is not offered just by the anti-confederate newspapers. The 317 petitions against the federal union presented to the Nova Scotia House of Assembly in 1865 and 1866 clearly show the relevance of this sentiment as well. Petitions signed by committed voters expressing their opinion on regional issues like taxes, infrastructures, or laws were a common feature in House of Assembly debates. Petitions were generally read by the member who represented the petitioner's county of origin.[48] Petitions that addressed provincial matters rather than local ones were relatively uncommon. Before the Confederation debates, the key issue that engendered provincial-wide attention was the Free School Act of 1864. During the session held in 1865 (9 February to 2 May), 183 petitions concerning Confederation were presented asking the government "to afford the people an opportunity of passing on the measure at the polls."[49] Most petitions contained the same prefabricated opening text that "your Petitioners earnestly pray that before finally passing upon the measure, your honorable House will afford the people at large an opportunity of giving expression to their wishes, at the Polls."[50] During the 1866 legislative session, 134 more such petitions were presented. Significantly, in both years, not one petition was presented on behalf of the Confederation movement.[51]

The report of the "repeal delegation" sent to the Imperial Parliament in 1868 stated that the petitions of 1865 and 1866 had 23,500 signatures.[52] These numbers and the associated relevance of the petitions require a few remarks. First, only a fraction of the signed petitions are extant. Second, numerous petitions were presented from the same counties: Antigonish (51), Inverness (28), Lunenburg (27), and Halifax (24).[53] Third, these petitions did not oppose Confederation but rather requested the assembly "not to adopt Confederation without consulting the people at the polls."[54] Fourth, the members who presented these petitions to the assembly did not automatically support them. Hiram Blanchard from Inverness presented seven petitions and was, besides Henry Gesner Pineo Jr, the only pro-confederate candidate who was elected in 1867. Despite these caveats, these petitions demonstrate that a considerable number of members and voters objected to the adoption of Confederation "without consulting the people" and that the opposition led by *Chronicle* cannot be reduced to the agitation of "loud minority." As a result, on 24 April 1865, the House of Assembly postponed any vote for an immediate union and instead resumed negotiations on the possibility of Maritime union.[55]

In April 1866, Lieutenant Governor Sir William Fenwick Williams moved a resolution in the House of Assembly to appoint delegates to be sent to the British Parliament. Their mission was to further negotiate how the Quebec Resolutions would be implemented through the pending British North America Act. In preparation for the vote, the anti-confederates in the assembly, led by William Annand and Stewart Campbell, tried to dominate the debates with the question, "Who should have the final word on Confederation," the voters or the legislators?[56] They understood the constitution as built upon British principles that required that the voters be consulted because "Confederation would destroy the current provincial constitution and would create a new one with reduced legislative powers."[57] The *Chronicle* endorsed Campbell's motion to consult the people. In the assembly, Annand directly addressed Charles Tupper: "You must carry with you the sentiment of the people."[58] In the *Chronicle*, Annand stated that "the members of the House of the Assembly have no right to vote away the Constitution. It is not theirs to give."[59]

The *Unionist* and the government had a different statutory interpretation of parliamentary sovereignty. Their strategy concentrated on securing a majority among the legislators and not among the voters. As a result, the debate whether to consult the voters, opened by the anti-confederates, was avoided. Instead the *Unionist*, hoping to weaken the movement he represented, declared the agitation of Joseph Howe absurd: "Hear him, the impotency of his wrath, in his bitter disappointment."[60] In the assembly, Tupper accused the leader of the anti-confederate opposition, William Annand, of conducting disloyal actions: "I hold in my hand the *Morning Chronicle* of April 6: As it is well known, a few designing politicians doing the work of conspirators, traitorously contemplate the destruction of our constitution."[61] In the public sphere the *Unionist* supported this position by quoting and commenting on the letters of Howe "To the people of Nova Scotia": "Every Nova Scotian has the right, nay, it is his duty, to stand up and defend the institutions of his country."[62] The strategy of Howe and the *Chronicle* to mobilize readers against the policy of the government was countered by the *Unionist*, which accused him of conducting unlawful and disloyal measures: "How dare Mr. Howe, or any other man, venture thus to utter and publish these words of treason."[63]

In the assembly Tupper rebutted Campbell's contention about the need to consult the people by asserting that "the representatives of the people, had the power to deal with all such matters" because "the people are assumed to be present in the persons of those whom they have elected to represent them."[64] Campbell challenged that argument, pointing out that "this house was elected entirely independent of that question – it was not before the people when we were elected."[65] Moreover, he referred to the public sentiments echoed in the anti-confederate press and in the petitions – "Now we are asked to deliberately ignore the expressed sentiments of this people: we are told that these petitions are to be disregarded."[66] On 17 April 1866, Campbell's bill was denied and the act to appoint the delegates to London was passed by thirty-one to nineteen. In reporting on the vote, the *Unionist* praised the loyalty of the representatives: "We have been rescued from that ignominy, thanks to the loyalty, the constituency, the determination of that brave majority, who stood to their country, and their Queen."[67]

The anti-confederate movement became the repeal movement when the *Chronicle* and anti-confederates members failed to stop the approval of the Quebec Resolutions in the assembly. About two weeks after this vote, the League of the Maritime Provinces was founded to fight the repeal battle, with Joseph Howe as its president. The league was financed by the leading merchants of the province: Patrick Power, William Stairs, and Alfred Jones.[68] Its purpose was to send Annand, Howe, and Hugh McDonald to the Imperial Parliament "to assert the right of the people to be consulted" before Confederation was formally approved. Since the league delegates were not part of the officially selected delegation, their aim was to "cultivate support amongst the leading politicians and editors of the London press." Before the official delegates left in July, the repeal forces, to strengthen their arguments, collected more signed petitions, often at public meetings where Howe was speaking.These added to the total number of anti-Confederation petitions already submitted to the assembly. Although the league attracted some attention in the London press, it failed to gain any appreciable support in the House of Commons or in the Colonial Office.

After Nova Scotia's entry into Confederation, the *Chronicle*'s strategy shifted to winning the coming elections, to bring "defeat and punishment" to the "minority rule," and then to repeal Confederation.[69] The position of the *Chronicle*, the *Acadian Recorder*, and the *Citizen* remained that Confederation was "forced on Nova Scotians in the most insulting way."[70] In its editorials, the *Chronicle* not only tried to form the opinion of its readers but declared itself to be the representative of the "outraging public feeling" in the province.[71] The newspaper also addressed the readers as voters: "Come up to the polls Nova Scotians, and vote for the People's candidates"; or "Nova Scotians remember [election day] Wednesday, 18th September. No terms with the traitors."[72]

The *Colonist*, the *Evening Express*, and the *Unionist* maintained their focus on the constitutional correctness of all the acts passed by the government and commented with contempt on any agitation by the *Chronicle*. For example, the *Express* noted, "Let us put our heel upon this demon, and stamp the life out of him. Within less than twelve months we will have a flourishing commerce with every part of the continent of North America."[73] The themes were "pride" in the current achievements (Confederation), "confidence" in economic prosperity (i.e., through the Intercolonial Railway), and "anxiety," which was used to challenge the anti-confederate agitation. Confederates linked anxiety with loyalty to the mother country, announcing the 1867 election as a crossroads whether the choices were "Union or Disunion" and "British Connection or Annexation" to the United States.[74] The *Unionist* also directly addressed voters, urging them to support the Canada Party: "Upon each elector will rest the individual responsibility of deciding whether to uphold British institutions or to aim an assassin thrust at British rule in Nova Scotia."[75] The *Chronicle*, in contrast, continued to focus on the failure to consult the people. Since the eligible voter was a man with property, the *Colonist* focused on creating anxiety through the spectre of economic downturn: "Is it for your interests, Citizens of Halifax, to send men to parliament to repeal that Union? To repeal a measure which secures for your city the means of becoming the chief commercial emporium."[76]

The pro-confederates were organized in the Canada Party, and the anti-confederates formed the Nova Scotia Party, which emerged from the League of the Maritime Provinces.[77] The Nova Scotia Party won thirty-six of thirty-eight seats in the provincial assembly and eighteen of the nineteen seats for representatives sent to the House of Commons in Ottawa. These numbers, however, did not fully reflect the electorate results. Regarding the popular vote, the Nova Scotia Party had about 20 per cent more votes than the Canada Party; however, in some counties the results were close.[78] Nevertheless the objective to punish "the traitors who sold us"[79] was achieved, and the *Chronicle* credited its contribution to this victory: "The 'people rights' we have sought to sustain, and we have sustained them. Shoulder to shoulder with Nova Scotians, our own fellow-citizens, we have marched; shoulder to shoulder we win; shoulder to shoulder in all our policy, in all our striving for good, we march with our own people – the true men of Nova Scotia. We have won."[80]

By focusing on the "people rights," the *Chronicle* and the anti-confederates had succeeded at the ballot box in replacing Charles Tupper with William Annand as premier of Nova Scotia. Yet, as Kenneth Pryke argued, with respect to the future security of Nova Scotia in the dominion, "the victory itself changed little."[81] Aware of that dilemma, the *Chronicle* pensively asked, "What, now, will the Parliament of England do? Our abhorrence to the Union is plain – will the Imperial authority force us into it?"[82] For the *Unionist*, this defeat was the result of disloyal promises: "The Antis corrupt[ed] every constituency ... and expended foreign [American] capital to buy-up the loyalty of the people"[83] Pro-confederate papers largely did not discuss the possibility that the electors might have misconceptions about the meaning of Confederation, and the *Unionist* ignored the idea that the agenda of the anti-confederates could have contributed to this defeat. On the contrary, the *Unionist* expressed unshakeable confidence in the inability of the anti-confederates to achieve their goal to repeal: "THE UNION IS AN ACCOMPLISHED FACT. They cannot disturb that!"[84] The dilemma that the new government faced amused this paper: "Mr. Howe hold out no prospect whatever to the Repealers to hope for success"[85]

Nonetheless, the idea "that the people of Nova Scotia were systematically prevented from expressing their will on the subject of Confederation" was not just a mobilization strategy to win the elections.[86] It became the main argument of the elected government to justify its decision to seek repeal in the British Parliament. On 25 February 1868, the province sent a delegation to Britain with the order not to accept any alteration of their repeal instructions. Besides the familiar argument that the "scheme of confederating Canada was never submitted to the polls ... in defiance of petitions, signed by many thousands of the electors of the province," the delegation also contended "that at the recent election the question of confederation exclusively occupied the attention of the people, and the result has proved that the province does not desire to be annexed to Canada."[87]

The decision to send this delegation, led by Howe and Annand, was a form of unrest, although the provincial government assured its citizens that they intended to negotiate and in the end to accept the outcome. The British Parliament informed the delegates that it had the absolute power to bind Nova Scotia to Confederation, with or without precedent legislation. As a result, the only hope was to convince Parliament to approve repeal.[88] On 18 June 1868, when the news reached Nova Scotia that repeal had been dismissed by Parliament, the editorials in the *Chronicle* were filled with disappointment and confidence that the "Repeal agitation has not ended yet." Not surprisingly, the *Unionist* concluded that the repeal movement was lost and predicted that "the Antis will see the folly of pursuing their fruitless policy."[89] Even though the government had failed, its allegiance to Great Britain was not seriously questioned. Such persistent loyalty, both within the provincial government and at the *Chronicle*, counterbalaced pleas for annexation to the United States, uttered especially by the local merchants of Yarmouth. But Premier Annand, through the *Chronicle*, publicly broke with Howe, and Howe became a scapegoat because he was the initiator of the "better terms" that lowered Nova Scotia's financial duties.

During the Confederate movement, the newspapers of Halifax were in control of contesting and ordering the public sphere. The political debate about Nova Scotia and Confederation was, above all, a contest between the *Chronicle* and the *Unionist* for the leading role in influencing the public sphere. Anti- and pro-confederates needed the *Chronicle* and the *Unionist* to inform readers about their goals and thereby mobilize them as voters. With the agenda of "consulting the people" introduced by the *Chronicle*, the anti-confederates won the elections of 1867 because the *Unionist* did not offer persuasive arguments for denying such participation of the voters. However, as Nova Scotia's repeal movement clearly shows, proclaiming the voters' interests and fomenting unrest in relation to political institutions was sufficient to win elections but not necessarily enough to repeal acts brokered by these institutions.

NOTES

1 Janet Ajzenstat, Paul Romny, Ian Gentels, and William D. Gairdner, eds, *Canada's Founding Debates* (Toronto: University of Toronto Press, 1999), 22f.

2 Ibid., 357.

3 J. Murray Beck, *Joseph Howe*, vol. 2, *The Briton Becomes Canadian, 1848–1873* (Montreal and Kingston: McGill-Queen's University Press, 1983); D.C. Harvey, "Newspapers of Nova Scotia, 1840–1867," *Canadian Historical Review* 26, no. 3 (1945): 279–301; John Heisler, "The Halifax Press and B.N.A. Union, 1856–1864," *Dalhousie Review* 30, no. 2 (1950): 188–95; and Peter B. Waite, "Halifax Newspapers and the Federal Principle, 1864–1865," *Dalhousie Review* 37, no. 1 (1957): 72–84.

4 Important studies of the consensual approach are Donald Creighton, *The Road to Confederation: The Emergence of Canada, 1863–1867* (1964; Don Mills, ON: Oxford University Press, 2012); William L. Morton, *The Critical Years: The Union of British North America, 1857–1873* (Toronto: McClelland and Stewart, 1964); and Peter B. Waite: *The Life and Times of Confederation, 1864–1867: Politics, Newspapers, and the Union of British North America* (Toronto: Robin Brass Studio, 2001), 209–47. For more information on the consensus approach, see Phillip Buckner, "The Maritimes and Confederation: A Reassessment," in *The Causes of Confederation*, ed. Ged Martin (Fredericton: Acadiensis Press, 1990), 86–129; and Phillip Buckner, "Beware the Canadian Wolf: The Maritimes and Confederation," *Acadiensis* 46, no. 2 (Summer/Autumn 2017), 177–95. On regional and economic tensions, see D.A. Muise, "The 1860s: Forging the Bonds of Union," in *The Atlantic Provinces in Confederation*, ed. Ernest R. Forbes and D.A. Muise (Toronto: University of Toronto Press, 1993), 13–47. For a differentiated overview of the scholarly approaches and school of thoughts, see Buckner, "The Maritimes and Confederation" and "Beware the Canadian Wolf." On prominent men, see Christopher Moore, *1867: How the Fathers Made a Deal* (Toronto: McClelland and Stewart, 1997), 36–59, 168–98; and Beck, *Joseph Howe*, vol. 2.

5 Michael Eamon, *Imprinting Britain: Newspapers, Sociability, and the Shaping of British North America* (Montreal and Kingston: McGill-Queen's University Press, 2015), xiii.

6 In 1871, Yarmouth County had 18,500 inhabitants, Pictou County 32,200, and Halifax County over 57,000. Canada Dominion Bureau of Statistics, *Eighth Census of Canada 1941*, vol. 2 (Ottawa, 1944), 56–63.

7 Harvey, "Newspapers of Nova Scotia," 283.

8 According to the front page of the *Bullfrog*, the first edition appeared on 3 September 1864. At the Nova Scotia Archives, only three issues are available: no. 9, 29 October 1864; no. 20, 14 January 1865; and no. 1 (new series), 4 February 1865. Only four

issues of the *Gunboat*, from 29 May 1867 until 19 June 1867, were distributed under the supervision of the *Acadian Recorder* and are available at the Nova Scotia Archives.

9 Harvey, "Newspapers of Nova Scotia," 283; and "The *Bullfrog* and the *Chronicle*," *Unionist*, 19 April 1865.

10 The *Acadian Recorder*, the *British Colonist*, the *Morning Chronicle*, the *Citizen*, the *Evening Express*, the *Evening Reporter*, the *Novascotian*, and the *Unionist* were all published in Halifax and are accessible on microfilm at the Nova Scotia Archives. I collected most of the information through my archival research and through Gertrude Tratt, *A Survey and Listing of Nova Scotia Newspapers, 1762–1957* (Halifax: 1979).

11 From 1813 to 1864, the *Acadian Recorder* was as a weekly, published on Saturday. In January 1865, it became a tri-weekly (Monday, Wednesday, Friday), and in January 1869 daily issues were added. From July 1857 until his death in June 1863, Hugh William Blackadar was the publisher, then there was a short partnership between the Blackadar brothers, Hugh and Henry D., and John English. From November 1864, his son Hugh Blackadar Jr was the owner and publisher, with his brother, Henry D. Blackadar, as editor. Tratt, *A Survey*, 42ff.

12 A. Grant, the founder, owner, and editor of the *British Colonist*, published weekly (Wednesday), and then tri-weekly (Tuesday, Thursday, Saturday). In 1870 the *British Colonist* became a daily, though the tri-weekly editions continued as summarized versions of the daily issues. In December 1874, the paper ceased. "Discontinuance of the *British Colonist*," *British Colonist*, 31 December 1874.

13 The full name was *Evening Express and Commercial Record*. It was the only paper that remained a tri-weekly, published on Monday, Wednesday, and Friday. Tratt, *A Survey*, 55.

14 From 1861 to 1867 the tri-weekly *Evening Reporter* (Tuesday, Thursday, Saturday) published the Debates and Proceeding of the House of Assembly. After the 1867 electoral victory of the Liberals, these were published by the *Chronicle* instead. Bourinot left the *Reporter* in May 1867. "Notice of Dissolution," *Evening Reporter*, 9 May 1867.

15 The *Citizen* started as a tri-weekly, and from 1864 until 1870 added a weekly edition published on Saturdays. In 1877, the *Chronicle* purchased the paper. Renamed the *Citizen and Evening Chronicle*, it became a daily. In August 1866, Garvie quit and McDonald became editor and proprietor. "Dissolution of Partnership," *Citizen*, 28 August 1866. For the satirical letters, see Josephine Shannon, "Two Forgotten Patriots," *Dalhousie Review* 14, no. 1 (1934): 85–90.

16 Harvey, "Newspapers of Nova Scotia," 285.

17 Ibid., 293.

18 Kenneth Pryke, *Nova Scotia and Confederation, 1864–1874* (Toronto: University of Toronto Press, 1979), 230.

19 Although Annand was one of the most influential newspaper magnates of Nova Scotia and was premier from 1867 to 1874, there is as yet no comprehensive biography. David A. Sutherland, "Annand, William," in *Dictionary of Canadian Biography*, vol. 11, University of Toronto / Université Laval, 2003–, http://www.biographi.ca/en/bio/annand_william_11E.html, accessed 9 November 2018.

20 Phyllis R. Blakely, "Jonathan McCully: Father of Confederation," *Collections of the Nova Scotia Historical Society* 36 (1968): 165.

21 For business purposes, William Annand had moved to England in July 1864. He was the proprietor and his son, Charles Annand, was the publisher. This temporary office was handed back in January 1865. "The Editorial Management," *Chronicle*, 10 January 1865, and "The Botheration Editor," *Chronicle*, 16 January 1865.

22 The *Journal* was founded by John Howe in 1781 and published on Monday, Wednesday, and Friday. On 2 July 1869, it was announced that "the proprietor of this Journal is desirous of retiring from the printing and publishing business," and no further issues were published. "Notice," *Unionist*, 2 July 1869.

23 "The Union Question," *Morning Journal*, 23 November 1864.

24 Blakely, "Jonathan McCully," 165f.

25 For all seventy-two resolutions, see Philip Buckner, "Québec Conference," http://www.thecanadianencyclopedia.ca/en/article/quebec-conference/, accessed 9 November 2018.

26 "The Confederation Question," *Reporter*, 10 December 1864; Shirley B. Elliott, *The Legislative Assembly of Nova Scotia, 1758–1983: A Biographical Directory* (Halifax: Province of Nova Scotia, 1984), 293f.

27 "Popular Interest in Federation," *Acadian Recorder*, 10 December 1864.

28 *Chronicle*, 1 December 1864.

29 Moore, *1867*, 178.

30 "The Confederation Question," *Colonist*, 13 December 1864.

31 "Confederation Meeting," *Chronicle*, 2 January 1865.

32 Ibid.

33 Annand's letter to McCully, quoted in the first edition of the *Unionist* under the new management. "Correspondence," *Unionist*, 18 January 1865.

34 Most studies note that McCully purchased the *Journal*, yet Penney was still named as proprietor. Blakely, "Jonathan McCully," 166; and "The Unionist," *Unionist*, 16 January 1865.

35 "The Union Question," *Morning Journal*, 23 November 1864.

36 "The Unionist," *Unionist*, 16 January 1865.

37 James M. Beck, "Joseph Howe, Anti-Confederate," in *Canadian Historical Association* 17 (1965): 10; and Beck, *Joseph Howe*, 2: 183.

38 "Correspondence," *Chronicle*, 16 January 1865, and "The Botheration Editor," *Chronicle*, 16 January 1865.

39 "Misrepresentation," *Colonist*, 26 January 1865.
40 "Confederation," *Colonial Standard*, 17 January 1865; and "The Archbishop of Halifax on Confederation" (to the Editor of the *Morning Chronicle*), *Colonial Standard*, 24 January 1865.
41 From the *Morning Chronicle Halifax*, "The Botheration Scheme," *Yarmouth Tribune*, 18 January 1865. See also the issues of 25 January, 1, 8, 15, and 23 February 1865 for the reprinted Botheration Letters.
42 Beck, *Joseph Howe*, 2: 186.
43 Ibid., 188–97.
44 Beck, "Howe: Anti-Confederate," 10.
45 "To the Young Men of Nova Scotia (no. 1)," *Unionist*, 25 January 1865.
46 "To the Young Men of Nova Scotia (no. 10)," *Unionist*, 13 March 1865.
47 "To the Young Men of Nova Scotia (no. 2)," *Unionist*, 27 January 1865.
48 Nova Scotia House of Assembly (hereafter NSHA), *Journal and Proceedings of the House of Assembly, 1865*, Compton & Co., Printers to the Assembly, xxv.
49 Ibid., index, xxv–xxvii.
50 Ibid.
51 NSHA, *Journal and Proceedings, 1866*, index, xxiv.
52 NSHA, *Journal and Proceedings, 1868*, Appendix 10, 22f.
53 This collection has about 110 of the 183 petitions sent to the House of Assembly in 1865. Nova Scotia Archives, Petitions against Federal Union in 1865, RG 5, series P, vol. 19, no. 3-135.
54 NSHA, *Journal and Proceedings, 1868*, App. 10, 22f.
55 NSHA, *Journal and Proceedings, 1865*, 114.
56 Ajzenstat et al., *Founding Debates*, 357.
57 Ibid., 360.
58 NSHA, *Debates and Proceedings of the House of Assembly*, Crosskill and Bourinot, "Evening Reporter" Office, 1866, 206.
59 "The Situation," *Chronicle*, 9 April 1866.
60 "Hear Him!" *Unionist*, 13 April 1866.
61 NSHA, *Debates and Proceedings 1866*, 212.
62 "To the People of Nova Scotia," *Chronicle*, 12 April 1866.
63 "Hear Him!" *Unionist*, 13 April 1866.
64 NSHA, *Debates and Proceedings 1866*, 217.
65 Ibid., 259.
66 Ibid.
67 "Confederation Safe," *Unionist*, 20 April 1866.
68 G. Patterson, "Joseph Howe and the Anti-Confederation League," *Dalhousie Review* 10, no. 3 (1930), 397–9.
69 "Nova Scotia and the 'Birthday,'" *Chronicle*, 12 July 1867.

70 "Ill-Timed Rejoicing," *Chronicle*, 1 July 1867.
71 "The Candidates Admit the Sacrifice of Nova Scotia," *Acadian Recorder*, 3 July 1867; and "The Union Orators and Their Newspapers ...," *Citizen* (Weekly Edition), 27 July 1867.
72 "Nova Scotians Remember Wednesday," *Chronicle*, 17 September 1867.
73 "The Coming Fruits," *Evening Express*, 16 September 1867.
74 "Number Four," *Unionist*, 18 September 1867; "Correspondence Number One," *Unionist*, 6 September 1867.
75 "Number Four," *Unionist*, 18 September 1867.
76 "Truly the Anti-Unionists Have [...]," *Colonist*, 17 September 1867.
77 Delphin A. Muise, "The Federal Election of 1867 in Nova Scotia: An Economic Interpretation," *Collections of the Nova Scotia Historical Society* 36 (1968): 332.
78 The result of the provincial election was that the Nova Scotia Party garnered 44,339 votes (60 per cent) and the Canada Party 29,095 (40 per cent). See James M. Beck, *The Government of Nova Scotia* (Toronto: University of Toronto Press, 1957), 351.
79 "We Need Not to Tell," *Chronicle*, 20 September 1867.
80 "The Battle Is Won," *Chronicle*, 19 September 1867.
81 Pryke, *Nova Scotia*, 60.
82 "Retrospective," *Chronicle*, 26 September 1867.
83 "The Elections," *Unionist*, 20 September 1867.
84 Ibid.
85 "Happy New Year," *Unionist*, 1 January 1868.
86 NSHA, *Journal and Proceedings, 1868*, Appendix 10, 46.
87 Ibid., 9.
88 R.H. Campbell, "The Repeal Agitation in Nova Scotia, 1867–69," *Collections of the Nova Scotia Historical Society* 25 (1942): 113.
89 "It Has Been Constant," *Chronicle*, 29 June 1868; "The Answer," *Unionist*, 24 June 1868; and Patterson, "Joseph Howe," 397–402.

Epilogue

ELIZABETH MANCKE, JERRY BANNISTER, DENIS McKIM, AND SCOTT W. SEE

As countless commentaries on the sesquicentennial of Confederation demonstrated, the idea that the United States' northern neighbour is a "peaceable kingdom" defined by a widespread commitment to "peace, order, and good government" is alive and well.[1] This long-standing interpretation is not without validity. Unlike the United States, the nation with which the "Dominion of the North" is most often compared, Canada lacks a blood-drenched history replete with revolutionary tumult, chronic "frontier" warfare, vast slave societies, and fratricidal civil war.[2] Yet many Canadians have offered robust challenges to these perceptions. For example, on 28 May 2015, Beverley McLachlin, then chief justice of the Supreme Court of Canada, stated in a lecture to the Global Centre for Pluralism that "the most glaring blemish on the Canadian historic record" was the wilful policy of "cultural genocide," long pursued and justified as a necessary, if not benevolent, policy of assimilation targeting the nation's Indigenous peoples and their cultures. As Justice McLachlin acknowledged, Canada has a violent past with painful and damaging repercussions that continue to reverberate in the present day.[3] These sentiments dovetailed with critical arguments that historians had been making for decades vis-à-vis Canada's mistreatment of First Nations, Inuit, and Metis communities.[4] Such accounts lay bare the fact that the peaceable kingdom myth and "peace, order, and good government" ideal obscure at least as much as they reveal.

Many of the essays in this collection provide historical analysis of the kinds of violent phenomena that played a crucial role in shaping Canadian history. Sporadic and overtly violent episodes – the deportation of the Acadians, the suppression of the Lower Canadian Rebellion, the quashing of the Red River resistance, the Cypress Hills massacre, among others – placed significant imprints on the Canadian experience. Equally, if not more, important were the insidious and less overt forms of violence that contributed to the consolidation of British rule in northern North America beginning in the mid-eighteenth century and then undergirded the transcontinental dominion that coalesced a century later. For profound evidence of these forms of violence, one need look no further than the treaties by which Indigenous peoples were displaced, the legal regimes that stifled radical dissent, and the assimilative pressures that bore down with seemingly relentless force on ethnic and linguistic minorities.

Depictions of Canada as a benign alternative to the United States therefore mask the centrality of subtly violent phenomena in Canadian history. Indeed, such factors went a considerable distance in allowing Canada (which was by no means immune to the ideological ferment of the so-called Age of Revolution) to chart an alternate course to modernity, one that differed in fundamental ways from that of the raucous American republic. Furthermore, an ingrained emphasis on Canada's remarkably – perhaps uniquely – placid development ignores the complex, critically important ways in which the peaceful circumstances enjoyed by empowered groups – privileged white settlers, for example – were often realized through the violent suppression of their disempowered counterparts, including Indigenous communities, black slaves, and *habitants*. In the British North American context, peace and violence were not antithetical to one another, but rather were inseparably entwined. Their intrinsic interconnectedness was fundamental to the colonies' political, social, economic, and environmental development.

Our approach shares with historical studies elsewhere a common concern for two fundamental problems. First, it deals directly with the powerful and enduring legacies of colonialism and imperialism, and contributes to a scholarly discussion about the impact of settler colonialism on Indigenous peoples around the world. In part, it is a critique of modernity and some of its central tenets, such as the myth of the "vanishing Indian." Nineteenth- and twentieth-century settler societies justified their policies of "cultural genocide" because "science" held that the cultures of Indigenous peoples in places like North America and Australia were inferior, and naturally destined to disappear; government policies to assist and speed that outcome were thereby justified.

While the concept of settler colonialism encompasses many of these legacies, we believe that additional perspectives are necessary to understand the complex social transitions of modernity that the essays in this volume address. Many of the chapters do engage themes in settler colonialism, such as the transition from eighteenth-century relations between Indigenous peoples and relatively weak colonial states to the nineteenth-century formation of a sophisticated federal state governing a settler society that instituted profoundly new ways of reordering social relations. But other essays address relations between social elites and people of lesser means, how governments expanded or contracted access to the public sphere, and how the press engaged in political debates. These themes are not exclusive to settler societies but rather occurred in various permutations across Europe.

Thus, Canada is, in large part, the product of settler colonialism, but it is also the successor to political cultures and social dynamics that were both firmly planted in the eighteenth century and in a transatlantic agenda to shape modern societies. The national order that emerged after Confederation can be understood only in the contexts of the eighteenth- and nineteenth-century disorders – including Indigenous resistance to colonization, struggles for imperial dominance, the expansion of political participation, and rebellious insurgencies – that shaped how people thought about questions of governance in 1867.[5]

Second, the ongoing struggles against colonialism in Canada are part of a global phenomenon. The dispossession of Indigenous peoples of their lands and access to resources in Canada followed patterns of settler colonialism established in other countries, such as Australia, but it also reflected distinctive characteristics that depended on regional patterns of language, ethnicity, religion, labour, and the physical environment.[6] The role of staple economies and resource extraction in Canada is similar to patterns in South Africa and large parts of South America, where the nuclear family was neither the dominant social unit nor the agent for agricultural development. As in other northern countries, nationalist dreams of northward expansion faced environmental realities that limited the scope of settlers' activities. And, as in other Commonwealth countries, efforts to establish a powerful national state confronted the continued cultural and constitutional powers of the imperial state via the royal prerogative and appeals to the Crown.

The monarchical polities that emerged in the mid-nineteenth-century British Empire, beginning with the Dominion of Canada, were products of transimperialism – that is, of forces transforming imperial relations globally – as much as transnationalism. Canada shares, for example, many elements of New Zealand's imperial legacy; however, Canada's transnational relationship with the United States differs in important ways from New Zealand's relationship with Australia. More than any other country touched by settler colonialism, Canada's experience as a continental borderland, in the shadow of a mighty republic, has entailed powerful waves of violent revolution and administrative evolution. Like other countries with large linguistic and ethnic minorities, Canada was built on multifaceted colonial polities on which the federal state could not impose a single national identity.[7]

In grappling with both the forces of colonialism and imperialism, the chapters in this volume place British North America in continental, imperial, and global contexts. Canada is the product of forces that are at once shared with other nations yet distinctive to northern North America. Its development in the twentieth and twenty-first centuries follows patterns established before 1867, including those of ethnic pluralism, cultural conflict, and the inescapable necessity of accommodation. The legacy of the eighteenth and nineteenth centuries is still with us – from the negotiation of treaty rights to the rhetoric of social order – and concerns over the surge in violent extremism today have echoes that can be heard in political disputes that raged centuries ago.

NOTES

1 For recent examples of the currency of these ideas, see Andrew Potter, "Canadians Can Celebrate the Fact That We've Never Had to Fight for Our Survival," *National Post*, 23 June 2017; Adam Gopnik, "We Could Have Been Canada: Was the American Revolution Such a Good Idea?" *New Yorker*, 15 May 2017; and John Ibbitson, "In a World of Closing Doors, Canada Is Embracing Inclusion," *Globe and Mail*, 1 July 2016.

2 On America's violent tradition, see Carroll Smith-Rosenberg, *This Violent Empire: The Birth of an American National Identity* (Chapel Hill: Omohundro Institute of Early American History and Culture, University of North Carolina Press, 2010); and Richard Slotkin, *Regeneration through Violence: The Mythology of the American Frontier, 1600–1860* (Middletown, CT: Wesleyan University Press, 1973).

3 Beverley McLachlin, "Reconciling Unity and Diversity in the Modern Era: Tolerance and Intolerance," 2015 Annual Lecture to the Global Centre for Pluralism, https://www.pluralism.ca/event/annual-lecture-4/

4 See, for example, Sarah Carter, *Aboriginal People and Colonizers of Western Canada to 1900* (Toronto: University of Toronto Press, 1999); John Milloy, *"A National Crime": The Canadian Government and the Residential School System, 1879–1986* (Winnipeg: University of Manitoba Press, 1999); and J.R. Miller, *Compact, Contract, Covenant: Aboriginal Treaty-Making in Canada* (Toronto: University of Toronto Press, 2009).

5 Jerry Bannister, "Canada as Counter-Revolution: The Loyalist Order Framework in Canadian History, 1750–1840," in *Liberalism and Hegemony: Debating the Canadian Liberal Revolution*, ed. Jean-François Constant and Michel Ducharme (Toronto: University of Toronto Press, 2009), 98–146.

6 On dispossession in North America, see Allan Greer, *Property and Dispossession: Natives, Empires, and Land in Early Modern North America* (Cambridge: Cambridge University Press, 2018).

7 James Belich, *Replenishing the Earth: The Settler Revolution and the Rise of the Anglo-World, 1789–1939* (New York: Oxford University Press, 2009); and E.A. Heaman, *A Short History of the State in Canada* (Toronto: University of Toronto Press, 2015), 1.

Notes on Contributors

Jerry Bannister teaches history and Canadian studies at Dalhousie University. He is co-editor with Liam Riordan of *The Loyal Atlantic: Remaking the British Atlantic in the Revolutionary Era* (2012).

D.C. Bélanger is an associate professor of Canadian history at the University of Ottawa and the co-founder of *Mens: Revue d'histoire intellectuelle et culturelle*. His research interests include French-Canadian intellectual history and Canadian-American relations. He is the author of two monographs, *Prejudice and Pride: Canadian Intellectuals Confront the United States, 1891–1945* (2011) and *Thomas Chapais, historien* (2018), and is currently working on a history of loyalism in French Canada.

Jane Errington is a member of the Department of History at Queen's University and former dean of arts at the Royal Military College of Canada. In addition to numerous articles and edited collections, she has written three award winning books: *The Lion, the Eagle, and Upper Canada: A Developing Colonial Ideology* (1987), *Wives and Mothers, School Mistresses and Scullery Maids: Women and Work in Upper Canada* (1995), and *Emigrant Worlds and Transatlantic Communities* (2007). Her current research interests focus on how understandings of gender, class, and race shaped colonial societies and cultures, particularly in Upper Canada.

Darren Ferry has taught history for over a decade at McMaster University and at Nipissing University. His research interests lay in studying radical transatlantic political cultures and the complicated rise of local governance in the nineteenth century. He has published several articles on the connection of liberal ideologies and voluntary associations, culminating in his first book, *Uniting* *in Measures of Common Good: The Construction of Liberal Identities in Central Canada, 1830–1900* (2008).

Donald Fyson, a specialist in Quebec history, is a professor at the Département des sciences historiques at Université Laval. His work focuses on the relationship between state, law, and society, especially as seen through the criminal and civil justice systems, the police, prisons, and local administration. He is currently working on a book on capital punishment in Quebec between 1760 and 1960.

Colin Grittner is a postdoctoral fellow in history at the University of New Brunswick. He is presently completing a monograph on civic participation and the electoral franchise across nineteenth-century British North America.

Max Hamon defended his dissertation, "The Many Worlds of Louis Riel: A Political Odyssey from Red River to Montreal and Back, 1840–1875," at McGill University in 2017. The work offers a new interpretation of the life of Louis Riel in the context of Montreal, the British Empire, and the Canadian-US borderlands. He is interested in questions of state legitimacy, the history of colonization, and the resistance of Indigenous peoples in French and British North America. He is currently a course lecturer at McGill University and is working on turning his dissertation into a book manuscript.

E.A. Heaman teaches history at McGill University. She has published several monographs on the political, economic, and social history of Britain and Canada, including, most recently, *A Short History of the State in Canada* (2015) and *Tax, Order, and Good Government: A New Political History of Canada 1867–1917* (2017). She is beginning new work on violence, poverty, and the writing of history in nineteenth-century Canada.

Dan Horner is an assistant professor in the Department of Criminology at Ryerson University. He has published numerous articles on popular violence and public life in nineteenth-century Montreal. He is currently at work on a project that examines the translocal circulation of ideas about urban public order in the first two-thirds of the nineteenth century.

Bonnie Huskins teaches colonial American and Atlantic world history at St Thomas University and at the University of New Brunswick, where she is also Loyalist studies coordinator. Her research interests include eighteenth-century sociability, freemasonry, and the diaspora created by American Revolutionary War Loyalists.

She has two ongoing monograph projects: one on late eighteenth-century military engineer William Booth, and the other on Loyalist freemasonry in the Maritimes.

Jeffers Lennox is an assistant professor of history at Wesleyan University and author of *Homelands and Empires: Indigenous Spaces, Imperial Fictions, and Competition for Territory in Northeastern North America, 1690–1763* (2017). His current project, *North of America: Revolution, British Provinces, and Creating the United States, 1774–1815* (forthcoming), explores how the colonies that became Canada influenced Patriot actions during the revolutionary era.

Denis McKim teaches in the History Department at Douglas College. He is the author of *Boundless Dominion: Providence, Politics, and the Early Canadian Presbyterian Worldview* (2017), and is at work on an intellectual biography of George Brown.

Elizabeth Mancke is a professor of history and Canada Research Chair at the University of New Brunswick. Her research and writing address issues of political change in the British Empire, ca 1500–1830, with a special interest in pre-Confederation Canada.

Bradley Miller is an assistant professor of history at the University of British Columbia, where he holds the Keenleyside Chair in Canada and the World. He is the author of *Borderline Crime: Fugitive Criminals and the Challenge of the Border, 1819–1914* (2016).

Thomas Peace is an assistant professor of Canadian history at Huron University College. His research focuses on the histories of Indigenous schooling and literacies within the context of emerging settler colonial normalcy. With Kathryn Magee Labelle, he is the co-editor of *From Huronia to Wendakes: Adversity, Migrations and Resilience, 1650–1900* (2016); with Alison Norman, he is the co-editor of the special issue of *Historical Studies in Education*: "Revisiting the Histories of Indigenous Schooling and Literacies." He is also an editor at ActiveHistory.ca.

Émilie Pigeon is the research coordinator at the Métis Family and Community Research Lab and a part-time professor at the Institute of Canadian and Aboriginal Studies, both of which are housed at the University of Ottawa. She is a digital/social historian and consultant specializing in the study of Roman Catholicism among Metis polities. She is presently transforming her doctoral dissertation into a monograph, tentatively titled *A Distinct Faith: Métis Lived Catholicism from the Great Lakes to the Northern Plains, 1750–1937.*

Carolyn Podruchny is an associate professor of history at York University. Her research focuses on the relationships forged between Indigenous peoples and French newcomers in northern North America. Her first monograph is *Making the Voyageur World: Travelers and Traders in the North American Fur Trade* (2006). She co-edited, with Laura Peers, *Gathering Places: Aboriginal and Fur Trade Histories* (2010), and co-edited, with Nicole St-Onge and Brenda Macdougall, *Contours of a People: Metis Family, Mobility and History* (2012). She is currently writing a book about the meeting of stories in the fur trade.

Ian Radforth, professor emeritus in the Department of History, University of Toronto, is the author of *Royal Spectacle: The 1860 Visit of the Prince of Wales to Canada and the United States* (2004). He has published a series of articles on celebrations, demonstrations, and conflict in the streets of mid-Victorian Toronto. Currently he is researching murder cases in late-Victorian Ontario.

John G. Reid is a member of the Department of History at Saint Mary's University in Halifax, and senior research fellow of the Gorsebrook Research Institute. A former co-editor of *Acadiensis: Journal of the History of the Atlantic Region*, his research fields include imperial-Indigenous relations in early modern northeastern North America and the history of sport in a settler colonial context.

Mathias Rodorff is a doctoral candidate at the Ludwig-Maximilians University of Munich. His dissertation examines how transatlantic processes interacted with local spaces and how the public sphere was created in Great Britain and Canada from the 1850s to the 1870s. He recently participated in the "Slavery and Its Legacy" series for the Gilder Lehrman Center at Yale University.

Scott W. See is Libra professor emeritus at the University of Maine. The author of *Riots in New Brunswick: Orange Nativism and Social Violence in the 1840s* (1993) and *The History of Canada* (2001), he is currently working on a book that explores collective disturbances in British North America and early Confederation Canada.

Stephen Smith is a historian based in Halifax. His recently completed dissertation focused on the relationship between violence, voluntary associations, and the press, using as case studies the newspapers and voluntary organizations that emerged around the 1837–8 Rebellions in Lower Canada, Upper Canada, and the United States. He has taught history at Queen's University and worked in heritage interpretation at a number of museums and historic sites.

Harvey Amani Whitfield is a professor of history at the University of Vermont. He is the author of *Blacks on the Border: The Black Refugees in British North America, 1815–1860* (2006), *North to Bondage: Loyalist Slavery in the Maritimes* (2016), and *Black Slavery in the Maritimes: A History in Documents* (2018).

Index

www.ingramcontent.com/pod-product-compliance
Lightning Source LLC
LaVergne TN
LVHW090757070826
844660LV00022B/1007

* 9 7 8 1 4 8 7 5 2 3 7 0 1 *